A Conversation with
Dr. Ezra Sadan

A Conversation with
Dr. Ezra Sadan

Combating Inflation in Israel

Held on March 18, 1981
at the American Enterprise Institute for Public Policy Research
Washington, D.C.

ISBN 0–8447–3465–9

Library of Congress Catalog Card No. 81–68887

AEI Studies 339

Printed in the United States of America

Introductory Remarks

HERBERT STEIN

American Enterprise Institute

By looking to the economic experience of Israel we hope to see what we can learn from a country that has a rate of inflation of 135 or 140 percent per annum. What can we learn about the causes of such a rate of inflation? How does one live with high inflation? What can be done to reduce it? I think that we in the United States are interested in Israel not only as a kind of test tube of economic experience carried to an extreme but also as a friend and an ally. We are interested in her economic performance as people who wish her success. From this standpoint we are also greatly concerned about economic conditions in Israel, and about economic relations between Israel and the United States, as reflected in our aid program, credit programs, and so on.

We are very fortunate to have here this afternoon Dr. Ezra Sadan, the top civil servant in the treasury department of Israel. He is well informed about the economic policy of Israel and will explain to us the new anti-inflationary economic policy of Israel, which consists of stimulating an enormous boom for durable consumer goods.

Many of us have a special interest in the fact that Dr. Sadan holds a Ph.D. from the University of Chicago. I think that among all the University of Chicago economists, he probably holds the record for presiding over the highest rate of inflation. We are also very pleased that we have here Dan Halperin, the economic minister of the Israeli embassy. I hope he will participate in the discussion, particularly with reference to the question of U.S. aid and credit relations with Israel.

A Conversation with
Dr. Ezra Sadan

I am presiding today over a highly inflationary system, but I must confess that I have inherited it. I am new to that system. I am a university professor and the director of a consulting firm that specializes in South America; so I have experienced, personally, an inflation much worse than the one that we have now in Israel. Also I know what the consequences of an uncontrolled inflation would be should that occur in Israel.

I suppose the best thing to do is to ask some questions and then propose answers for them; but, with your permission, I will make a personal statement first. I must explain the position of a person such as myself. It is not easy. In Israel we are expecting general elections on June 30. For civil servants—particularly for the general directors of the ministries, who play a role equivalent to that of a deputy secretary here—this is the worst time to address a meeting because we are not permitted to make political remarks. It would be quite impossible, however, for me to explain the root causes of inflation in Israel unless I first say something about the political framework. I will try to be as objective as I can.

Let me start with two questions: How does one live with an inflation of 130 percent? (This is what we have experienced until recently in Israel.) Also, how did we get to this point?

The answer will satisfy both questions. If someone can live with 130 percent inflation and if there is nothing in the political framework to pressure him politically to fight inflation, then somehow he is going to get there and stay there.

First, let me explain how someone can live with 130–150 percent inflation. Then I shall speculate as to what may happen if he lives with it too long. Next, I shall deal with the question of how such a high rate of inflation came about. Finally, I shall try to say something about reducing the 130 percent inflation.

The real issue is inflation under indexation. Many years ago we established a system that was quite innocent; it did not have anything to do with high rates of inflation. We had inflation of 5 or 10 percent a year or even lower. Quite innocently, wages were indexed—that is, a cost-of-living compensation was calculated every six months. It did not do any harm at the time. On the contrary, instead of having labor negotiations every six months, some of the negotiations were made unnecessary by adding this compensation periodically.

We also had a law, inherited from the British, that placed a ceiling on interest rates. Instead of just writing the law off the books and allowing financial institutions to charge whatever interest they wished, we led them in a different direction. We said, "You can charge up to 10 percent, which is the upper limit, but you may also charge an inflation premium." These were the beginnings of a system that has become completely indexed.

Today bonds are indexed, savings accounts and loans are indexed, wages are indexed—even fines are indexed. If you do not pay your income tax on time, the residual and fines are indexed. Similarly, agreements or contracts for new investments and other purposes are indexed. So far this indexation has permitted the economy to function without major disruption.

Indexation is not without cost—it brings significant costs with it. The banking system, for example, must be large enough to allow customers to hedge against inflation. Accounting becomes a headache; so many additional employees are needed in the accounting firms. In other words, hedging against inflation in a system like ours is expensive in real terms. Yet, I repeat, we do not have major disruptions. Most important, we have industrial peace, so to speak, without major labor disruptions.

We came that far innocently. We did not know that inflation was going to develop this way. Can we live with it for a long period of time? The answer, in my opinion, is no! Not for the real cost of hedging; that cost is significant but not prohibitive. This is not to say that there is some sort of a process of deterioration. There is none. The risk is that there may be a total collapse of the whole system if there is an increase in the rate of inflation. Instant collapse could be occasioned by a sudden acceleration in the inflation rate, say, from 125 or 150 percent to 250 or 300 percent.

The survival or collapse of the system depends upon the time intervals of indexation. Consider, for instance, an individual living in Israel at present. That person receives his indexed wages once a month; his savings accounts are indexed once a month. To hedge against inflation with regard to his savings and current accounts he visits his bank two or three times a month. At the bank he buys or sells indexed instruments such as bonds or foreign exchange against

4

unindexed Israeli shekels. Finally, to spend his shekel balances he goes to the supermarket once a week or so.

We can live with this. If we speed up inflation, however, the indexation intervals will become shorter and, eventually, prohibitive. Indexation and the payment of weekly rather than monthly wages are more expensive but feasible. Daily or hourly indexation, however, is prohibitive, as are daily visits to the bank or hourly shopping trips to the supermarket to hedge against inflation.

In other words, there is a danger that the whole system of indexation will stop working. This would mean that the banks could no longer help people hedge against inflation. Employers would no longer be able to index wages, and so forth. This is a dangerous situation that may occur in a very short period of time. At present the effect of inflation under indexation at a rate of 100–150 percent per year is comparable to that resulting from an inflation of 10–25 percent without indexation. Should the system of indexation collapse at a rate of 250 percent, for example, the outcome would be comparable to an instant acceleration of an unindexed inflation of 10–25 percent to the rate of 250 percent. Our government, in view of this risk, rather than the current cost of an indexed inflation, should not permit high rates of inflation. Yet, once we have such high rates, it is difficult to decelerate. In fact, because of indexation there is no political incentive to reduce inflation: as long as it functions, indexation protects people from inflation. Inflation, however, is protected by people using the same device, indexation.

How did such high rates of inflation come about? In my opinion there are several mechanisms involved. Rarely is the mechanism "purely economic." In 1978, for instance, as part of a policy to "liberalize" transactions in foreign exchange, our government and the central bank permitted the free inflow of short-term credit from abroad. For a while the country was flooded with foreign exchange and the government lost control over the quantity of money. Finally, the government caught up with it, but in the meanwhile we had a burst of inflation. "Purely" monetary or economic errors are rare, and the causes of our continuing inflationary pressures are systematic and political-economic or socioeconomic in nature.

A major factor is the mechanism associated with the determination of—really, I don't have any new message—the government budget. There is a permanent attempt on behalf of the government to implement a nominal budget that is inconsistent with the capacity of the real economy to support. One of the difficulties of our parliamentary system is this: we do not have a president, and the government is a coalition government. I do not mean a coalition of political parties but a coalition of ministries and ministers. In this coalition there is a prime minister—let's leave him aside for now—and there is a minister of finance, who is the only person not receiving political support from any organized group in the society. In contrast, the minister of education has regiments behind him—the teachers' associations, the PTAs, and so on. The minister of defense has the military; the minister of public works is supported by large contracting firms, and so on. They all have the organized backing of particular pressure groups in the society. They all exert these pressures upon the treasury. The minister who should possess the power necessary to face and fight all the rest is the minister of finance.

This system is balanced and functions well under the right circumstances. Israel did enjoy two such balanced periods: one under Finance Minister Levi Eshkol, who later became the prime minister; and the other under Minister Pinchas Sapir, who was offered the post of prime minister and declined it for personal reasons. The important fact is that both Eshkol and Sapir had the power of their political parties behind them. They were the "bosses" of their parties, and this was a sufficient counterweight to the pressures exerted by the other ministries.

In the past few years, we have not had a proper balance of power in this respect. The outcome is very simple. We arrive at a budget prescribed by the government and voted on by the parliament. Because there is no way to implement the budget, the government starts inflating in order to live with that budget. It creates a deficit in order to finance part of its expenditures. Worse still, certain parts of the budget, under the system of indexation, are autonomous. Whoever determines the number of employees in education, health, and so on, for example, also determines the wage bill. Because the wage bill is indexed, the government may be forced to spend more than the amount prescribed by the budget. Contracts signed by the government in the past few years are indexed. Hence expenditures on these contracts may exceed the budgeted amount.

Indexation of government expenditures is nearly perfect. Revenues, however, particularly income taxes, are imperfectly indexed. As a result, the initial deficit is being multiplied by the inherently imbalanced arrangements of budget indexation.

Within this framework there is another mechanism that can affect the inflationary processes. It is referred to as the "psychological" factor. In practice, people's expectations of future inflationary developments affect price levels. This would be a temporary effect were it not for indexation and the imperfectly indexed government budget. Once a rise in price levels is recorded, the autonomous part of government expenditures must rise. As the corresponding increase in revenues is lacking, the result is a larger deficit and accelerated inflation. Finally, the government's response to union pressures reflects yet another social-political mechanism that maintains inflationary pressures.

I must add something about Israel's budget. Close to 50 percent of current expenditures is devoted to defense, and this makes life in the treasury rather difficult. If you try to play games with defense expenditures (as I did in the past ten months), you run against general public opinion and the defense-oriented establishment. Public concern reflects risk aversion which is quite often insurmountable.

Now, what do I think about reducing the rate of inflation. First, let me cite a case. In the mid-1970s Israel experienced a substantial decrease in the rate of inflation. In other words, indexation does not prevent a reversal of inflation. In my opinion it may even be useful in this way.

A reduction in the government's real expenditures is the necessary condition for recovering from high rates of inflation. Although an increase in expenditures is a sufficient condition for accelerating inflation, a decrease will not suffice for reducing inflation. Acceleration is relatively simple because it is instantaneous and spontaneous—we do not have to worry about it. The only thing we have to do is create the necessary conditions, and inflation will materialize. I do not think that an instantaneous and spontaneous response is to be expected in the opposite case, at least not in a reasonably short period of time. Of course if we had all the time in the world, we could wait and perhaps the reverse process would materialize. The trouble is that we do not have the time—I am not talking about "economics" now but about the political economy of it. If a government tries to reduce the budget, it does not have a long enough period of time (politically) to wait without having some results.

So, I think that what is needed as a *basis* is a reduced budget. I'll be even more explicit. In the case of Israel, it is not the budget that must be reduced but the government payroll, the number of people employed in the public sector. In addition we need a series of government or government-influenced actions that will affect people's expectations more quickly. This is particularly important under the system of indexation, and it can be accomplished by indexing futures rather than compensating according to past rates. We may arrive at an agreement with the labor unions, for instance (and such an agreement—known in Israel as a "package deal"—can be arrived at shortly after an election). Then instead of paying compensation for the earlier inflation, employers and employees are going to bet on the inflation to come. We should make similar arrangements in various other fields, but labor is the major field. In view of people's expectations and their potential effects, we have to create the impression that prices will stop rising as rapidly as they did before. We have to do this even at the cost of spending money on subsidies for a short period of time, for six months or so, or at the expense of permitting a more liberal inflow of imports and of exposing our industry to competition faster than we had intended under our trade agreements. People's expectations, or the so-called psychological effect, should contribute to decelerating inflation just as they contribute to accelerating inflation—under indexation.

Since I have not tried my prescription so far, I cannot report any progress along these lines. I doubt that I or anyone else will be able to attempt that before, say, January 1982, after the general elections and after we have a new government. Therefore I cannot prove my plan to be valid, but I think that this composite approach can work.

Questions and Answers

ARTHUR F. BURNS, American Enterprise Institute: You spoke of each of the ministers having his own constituency. In this country we do not have a parliamentary system, but we understand that. But my question is this: Doesn't the very fact that individual ministers find themselves responding to their constituency, fighting for their constituency, reflect a certain weakness, perhaps an unavoidable weakness in the political leadership of the country? In the abstract at least, it is conceivable that you could appoint individuals to head up ministries so that they would be immune to that kind of pressure, and instead of responding to their normal constituency of the ministry, they would be responding, to the best of their ability, to the national interests, with each minister doing the kind of job within his limited sphere that the minister of finance has tried to do.

DR. SADAN: The answer is very simple. I can give you an example of ministers' acting this way, and that is in defense. As the strongest politicians or the strongest figures in government, they can afford to pursue such a policy. It definitely reflects the weakness of the other politicians, but I think it reflects a weakness of the system in the following sense. In a parliamentary system every minister has a vote, and decisions are made by a committee—not by an individual or a small committee but by a very large committee. The minister of defense has one vote, and the minister of religious affairs also has one vote. One controls half of the economy, and the other does not actually control anything. The system calls for weak personalities. I am being frank with you. This is the same system that did not work in France and elsewhere. Maybe the solution is in the system itself, in having a cabinet within the cabinet.

Another solution is of course to switch to some sort of presidential system. That would eliminate decision making by a committee. I believe it is opportunity that causes weakness—weak personalities become unimportant ministers, but they have their votes.

DAN HALPERIN, economic minister of the Israeli embassy: May I say something on this? If I may give an example from another field, it is like an institution that has a publication. Everybody wants the publication to be prestigious, but it is the editor who takes pride in the quality of the publication. Each scholar will look first at his own article to see that it is published in the best publication. He is all for having a very prestigious periodical produced by this institution, but there is a limit to what he will sacrifice for that. It is very simple. The minister of finance is the editor, and as for the others, each one is writing his own article and trying to publish it in the best place.

JUDITH KIPPER, American Enterprise Institute: To follow up on Dr. Burns's question, there is a lot of speculation now in terms of the elections. How much of an impact would you estimate the majority government will have in terms of dealing with this political problem? To what extent has Israel been successful in selling its products and exporting to Europe, in particular markets that I think Israel has been eager to tap for some time?

DR. SADAN: There is something that I did that seems wrong. I avoided the bright side of Israel's economy, but I did it on purpose as I expected a question like yours. In real terms, we are doing quite nicely. That is, we are now exporting about $11 billion worth of goods and services.

MS. KIPPER: What percentage is that?

DR. SADAN: It is one-fourth of the gross national product (GNP) in value added, and, to put it in even nicer terms, if we take our current civilian balance-of-payments deficit as a percentage of our exports, then it is about 22 percent today. In the 1970s it was one-third, 33 percent, and it was 50 percent in the 1960s. Exports are growing nicely. We are selling something like $1 billion worth of goods to the United States. To the world as a whole we are selling $4 1/2 billion worth of industrial goods and a wide assortment of other things.

Ms. KIPPER: Agriculture?

DR. SADAN: Agriculture is small, very small. Agriculture is the pride of the country, but agricultural exports amount to about half a billion dollars. In 1950, that was the only thing we exported, and at that time the exports amounted to one-fifth of the deficit in the balance of payments. So we were quite successful in selling to Europe, and actually we have increased our exports to Europe and elsewhere. The real increase last year is something close to 8 percent, despite the recession in Europe. This is a privilege of being a small country, of being unimportant, or the importance of being unimportant. We are concentrating, as I said, on a wide assortment of goods and services, but in general I would say that these are quality goods and tailor-made goods and services.

Our main services are transportation and tourism. Note that because the economy was not disrupted by inflation, the economy grew in 1980 quite nicely as far as the balance of payments was concerned. In 1980 we paid $2 1/2 billion for oil, which is more or less our deficit, but in 1979 we paid less than half of that. So what we did was to use exports to absorb the blow and keep the deficit below that of 1979. I could have told you about the good things we did, and forgotten about inflation. But as I was asked to speak about inflation, I spoke about inflation.

As for the question concerning a majority government after June 30, I am sure that we will have one and that it will be composed of responsible political parties. The political system in Israel is quite stable. I do not know who is going to take over in July. I have watched the polls like most other people in Israel, and they are the most confusing polls I have ever seen. They look very much like the polls in the United States in normal years. No one really knows. Too many people have not yet made a decision, and so no one knows what the outcome will be. But whatever the outcome, I do not foresee any difficulty in forming a government. Any combination works. You must understand one thing. There are 120 members in the parliament in Israel, of which 110 or 115, more or less, are eligible for membership in the coalition. There are five Communists—they are out. There are, say, three or four radicals on the right and on the left who will not join—so 110 can form a coalition, whatever coalition you can think of.

DR. BURNS: Form a stable coalition?

DR. SADAN: Yes, it will be stable. We have a stable coalition now. There are two different questions. The political stability is there. Stability in itself is not a virtue. Labor may join with the Likud. We have already had a government under what the Germans call the "red and black" coalition. We can have that again. If you ask me, the red and black is the best combination under present conditions. That, in my opinion, is what we need right now. It may very well happen because we may be reaching an equally divided Knesset. This Knesset could produce the best government.

WILLIAM FELLNER, American Enterprise Institute: Is there some spreading of the realization that these burdens—say, the defense burden—whatever they are, are borne by someone, so that the difference between taxation and inflation is not that the burden disappears? The difference between those two is that the burden is articulated in some fashion in one case and is haphazard or differently distributed in the other. Economists have an easy way of understanding each other on the subject, but is there some spreading of the realization of this among the public? That would make people very much more receptive to anti-inflationary measures. The second question—in the deceleration phase, wouldn't indexation be quite helpful?

DR. SADAN: Let me answer the first question. Yes, I think that "realization" is the key word, but I must explain the background. I did not respond to the question about the new economics, raised at the outset of this discussion. There is no new economics in Israel. There is an attempt by the government to increase savings. So we have permitted the banks to have savings programs that were as short as two years, back to back with government bonds, which are, naturally, indexed. We did not permit that before. We permitted it for two months, and we are going to absorb something like $500 million worth of money from the public. This is a simple device to take money off the market. It is a clean device politically. Supply economics is not involved—it is purely and simply the Chicago approach. You take the money from the people and put it away; or if you cannot put it away, at least you do not spend the money you print, but the money that you took from the public.

There is another device that, economically speaking, is as legitimate as the first. We taxed cars and television sets at rates above 100 percent, so that people paid over 200 percent for these items, which are mainly imported from Europe. As economists, we proposed about nine or ten months ago to reduce the tax rate by 10 to 15 percent. We said that demand was so elastic that the government would lose some foreign exchange but would gain in taxes at least an equivalent amount, and this is exactly what happened. Economically speaking, we sold the public foreign exchange for over twice the price, and the public bought an extra $100 million or so. Now we hear from around the world about the $100 million, but no one talks about the $500 million that we have absorbed. This is because it seems to involve politics too. The opposition parties say that the government took this step to pamper the public before elections. This is a question I cannot address, but I must say that it looks that way, and, if it looks like that way, you can read about it in the Israeli press, and the foreign press copies that.

I did not answer your question right away because I do not think we have a new message for our people. We are not really proposing a new set of ideas. This is a one-time thing. We can do this once, but we cannot do it forever. Had we absorbed all this money along with a cut in the budget and a "package deal," we would have started a deceleration. Unfortunately, we did this as an emergency device, and with the growing imports of consumer goods we have created an atmosphere of spending.

Now, to the second question. Despite the atmosphere, the public is aware that the government must do something about inflation. The public still believes in the government, not in this government necessarily but in government as an institution. The public understands that the government cannot really keep up a 100–150 percent inflation. It is willing to take the "punishment." It is waiting for a government that will pressure inflation down, even at the cost of deferring consumption or reducing consumption.

DR. FELLNER: And it is being reduced anyway, isn't it?

DR. SADAN: It was reduced considerably last year. Consumption per capita went down last year 6 percent, and it has not been rising for three years (this takes into account the technological changes that took place at the same time at least in part of the economy). This is quite a punishment. The public is willing to take it; the public expects the government to do something about inflation. Indexation can help. I will repeat the example I used earlier. Suppose there is a new program that will eventually cut prices, and it succeeds. If we are going to pay cost-of-living compensation, we will be paying for what happened five to six months ago before the program was introduced. We should therefore come to an agreement to bet on the future, not to compensate for the past. That is, instead of *backward indexation*, there should be *forward indexation* for at least a certain period of time. And trade unions, as I said, are willing to accept this, should the government show its determination. We are not dealing with ignorant people. The heads of the unions know about Chicago economics and about other schools of thought; they understand the relationship between inflation and the budget. With their experts they have figured out what rate of inflation one can expect from a budget like the present one. If the government undertakes to cut the budget, it will find a partner in our federation of trade unions, which holds the power over the individual unions and can force them into line. If the government comes to an agreement with the federation on forward indexation for a while at least, we can use indexation in our favor.

WILLIAM SAUNDERS, consultant: You talked about expectations in broad terms—that is, at the national level. Would there be a problem in that individual segments of the economy have different goals and different pressures? If you found, for example, that bus drivers are being paid exceptionally well or have unusually good work rules or that employees of El Al perhaps have special arrangements, then dealing with the national-global rates of indexation does not get at the distortions within the economy. How do you deal with this when you really face the political pressures of special groups?

DR. SADAN: That is one question I left open. I was not sure you were interested in it because in this respect Israel resembles other countries. There is nothing unique except for one thing: Israel has a federation of labor, and it affects the political economy of labor relations.

I will explain what happened last year. In principle it was the worst year for labor relations in Israel. There was a government controlled not by Labor but by the right-wing Likud. Labor unions traditionally support the Labor party. The labor federation is controlled by the Labor party. Nevertheless, in April of last year, because of the fear of what inflation may do to the country, we signed an agreement with the labor federation prohibiting any change in real (and relative) wages for two years. We accepted wage distribution in the public sector as it was in March 1980. We have agreed upon the very question you raised. We will not have the bus drivers or El Al employees receive an increase in real pay and then let somebody else in the economy demand compensation on account of a change in relative position.

We are now experiencing a teachers' strike in Israel because of that April agreement, which prohibits special treatment. The teachers want a raise. Unfortunately, there was a public commission to determine the status of teachers in the society, with an ex–supreme court judge as chairman. The judge and the commission believe that teachers are underpaid. That may be so, but if we pay the teachers, the unions have already declared that they will consider this to be an infringement of the April agreement. The last minister of finance, Mr. Horwitz, lost his job because he insisted on upholding the April agreement. To an extent, his predecessor, Mr. Erlich, also lost his job because he could not live up to a similar agreement he had with labor. The agreement was broken by paying a certain group more than their initial (relative) real income.

It was agreed that the only raises in the public sector would be cost-of-living compensation. In the private sector extras were permitted within limits. In the private sector, however, there have been no real problems so far. Real problems arise in the public sector when the minister of finance gives in. If next year is a year of a Labor government, it should be easier to have an agreement that freezes for another year the relative wage differentials as they stand today.

DR. BURNS: To what extent do you have under-the-table payments?

DR. SADAN: To an extent, the question arises with respect to government-owned industries such as Israel Chemicals and the electric company. Israel Chemicals is under the agreement between the private employers, not the government, and the federation of trade unions. It is a clear-cut case, and extra payments within limits are legitimate. So we do not have under-the-table payments there. The trouble starts with government-owned public utilities. What does one do with the public utilities? Although they are formally organized as government-owned industries, they are in a sense part of the public sector. Thus this is the dividing line: there are no problems with profit-earning corporations within the government setup. Trouble arises in that gray area, which includes the electric company, where naturally the labor union is very powerful. This is where under-the-table payments are more common.

WALTER BERNS, American Enterprise Institute: This is a question that perhaps Mr. Halperin will also answer. Is the Israeli economy expanding at a rate to accommodate what I would assume to be the increased cost of rapidly more sophisticated weaponry?

DR. SADAN: The question is whether we can export enough to cover the foreign exchange bill of purchasing new arms, in increased quantities and of higher quality, and whether we can raise enough money in other forms to carry manpower and maintenance costs. Another question is whether we can pay back the debt we have already accumulated (the outstanding debt), accumulate new debt, and manage the debt service, should we face another phase in the arms race in the Middle East. There are two answers to this (I will let Mr. Halperin give you the figures). If the arms race should stop tomorrow, we can manage. If it continues, we may run into trouble unless we do something very radical about our exports, and/or we do not borrow more to accumulate the new weaponry. That means taking a heavier risk.

MR. HALPERIN: I just want to add some historical background. I think that we had two phases in the arms race in the area. Immediately after 1973, we jumped into a new phase with a massive Russian supply of arms, especially to countries like Syria and Iraq. This is when the aid package from the United States to Israel grew dramatically. It grew from several hundred million dollars a year—it was about $500 million before the Yom Kippur War, the 1973 war—to about $2 billion a year afterward, in most of the years though not all of them. I think that you rightly pointed out that we might be facing a new phase in which American quality joins with Russian quantity in the arms race in our area. This will no doubt cause some difficulties for Israel in its attempt to face the new situation.

In terms of foreign aid, Israel has received from the United States almost the same nominal sum for several years, from 1976 on, as I said, approximately $2 billion a year. The money is given in several ways. Part is economic aid, or what used to be called, and I think properly so, security-supporting assistance, which is mostly grants, or all very soft loans with perhaps a grant component of 95 percent; this amounts to about $800 million in round figures. We receive money for military aid or military support, which finances directly the purchase of arms in the United States. That has been $1 billion per year in the past five years. In 1981, it was raised to $1.4 billion, but—there is a great "but" here—half a billion of this sum is in the form of a grant. The other part—whether it was $500 million in most of the years or $900 million last year—came in the form of a guarantee. It is a Federal Financing Bank (FFB) loan on which we pay the same rate of interest that the U.S. Treasury pays on Treasury notes. The concession is that it is long term and that in the first ten years we will pay back only the interest; the principal is to be paid back in the following twenty years. The interest burden is heavy. As you probably know, it cannot be refinanced, even if the rate of interest goes down, so this makes us partners with Mr. Stockman. I mean that we both have a vested interest against the FFB, from different points of view, and at the same time we are paying back about $700 million this year to the U.S. government, mostly in interest, not yet principal, and we will go up to a billion dollars in no time.

In the wake of the peace agreement, we are also financing the huge redeployment project in the Negev for which we received specific assistance from the United States, mostly once again in the form of an FFB loan, which adds to the interest, the debt service. Actually, we spread out the redeployment because of many difficulties, such as inflationary pressures stemming from the work itself. We spread out the form of financing over more years than we had anticipated doing in the past. We will not accomplish all this in three years. We might have the air bases but not the other installations. Let's not forget that we are talking about the redeployment that is taking place to replace our deployment in the Sinai, which is three times as large as all of Israel, let alone the Negev itself, in which we invested huge sums of money for eleven years.

What we are trying to do now is to convince the administration and our friends on Capitol Hill that this situation will lead us nowhere, that we are aggregating the debt service in a way that overburdens us and forces us to curtail defense expenditures at the same time that we are facing some difficulties, especially on our eastern border, that is, the border shared with Syria, Jordan, Iraq, and Saudi Arabia. We hope to see some changes made, not so much in the level of payments, but rather in the terms of payment, which really amounts to the same thing. From a public-relations point of view perhaps it is better to get not more money but better money.

Just to point out one additional issue, there is talk now about what is happening with the F-15s for Saudia Arabia. There was talk of offering us a loan to offset the damage, or the danger to Israel, caused by having additional arms in the hands of neighboring unfriendly countries. Economically speaking, if we are going to get permission to obtain loans here to purchase additional arms, we really get very little if anything. It will mean increasing the debt service to the point where we cannot carry it, and we will have to think twice about whether we can buy additional arms in spite of the additional dangers. A country that fears that it is weakening is jumpy.

Finally, if what I hear from administration people is true—namely, that they want to have a strong and modern Israeli army not only for Israel's purposes but also for the purpose of stabilizing the Middle Eastern region—this is not the right way to go about it. We do hope that there will be some rethinking about the whole idea of supplying Saudi Arabia with modern arms. If this happens, however, we do hope that the ideas of offsetting the dangers will also be in the shape of an economic package with which we can deal—otherwise, it is not meaningful at all.

DR. SADAN: It is said that the administration is considering a loan to us that will permit us a purchase of F-15s. Someone mentioned the figure of $600 million. What Mr. Halperin is saying is, that if this is the way we are being compensated for what happens in Saudi Arabia, then we will have to say no, perhaps, and take the risk. It does not sound reasonable, I know, that we would decline the hardware, but if it implies a new FFB loan of the said magnitude, I do not see how we can take it. To give you an idea of the burden involved, $600 million amounts to 3 percent of Israel's GNP. The new phase may be a very dangerous phase unless we find some other way to face it.

MARVIN KOSTERS, American Enterprise Institute: I have a short question. What are the dimensions of the fiscal problem that you describe? What fraction of the GNP would be required in terms of either tax increases or spending decline?

DR. SADAN: Before answering your question, I should say that tax collection in Israel is close to one-half of the national income. We collect as much as we can in all forms, mainly as income taxes and a value-added tax. What determines the deficit is the level of government expenditures.

Let me say that in an economy that produces $20 billion worth of GNP, the government deficit we are concerned with is about $1 billion, or 5 percent of the GNP. If we can get rid of half of it, we will have the kind of a budget I was talking about with regard to anti-inflationary policies. Although that reduction will help solve

Israel's inflationary problem, it will not solve the problem of our balance of payments.

MR. HALPERIN: I would like to add one figure. The allocation for defense from our GNP is about 18 percent, and this is after taking into account U.S. aid to Israel and deducting it. This is one figure to be remembered about the Israeli economy. It's what makes it different from other economies.

DR. SADAN: It makes our lives more complicated.

DR. STEIN: Thank you very much Dr. Sadan and Mr. Halperin. It has been very instructive.

Selected AEI Publications

The AEI Economist, Herbert Stein, ed., published monthly (one year, $10; single copy, $1)

Experiences with Stopping Inflation, Leland B. Yeager (184 pp., paper $6.25, cloth $14.25)

The Congressional Budget after Five Years, Rudolph G. Penner, ed. (199 pp., paper $7.25, cloth $15.25)

Contemporary Economic Problems: Demand, Productivity, and Population, William Fellner, project director (350 pp., paper $9.25, cloth $17.25)

Health and Air Quality: Evaluating the Effects of Policy, Philip E. Graves and Ronald J. Krumm (156 pp., paper $6.25, cloth $14.25)

The Consumer Price Index: Issues and Alternatives, Phillip Cagan and Geoffrey H. Moore (69 pp., $4.25)

The Economy: Is This a Change in Direction? John Charles Daly, mod. (31 pp., $3.75)

Reforming the Income Tax System, William E. Simon (53 pp., $4.25)

The Economics of Legal Minimum Wages, Simon Rottenberg, ed. (534 pp., paper $10.25, cloth $18.25)

Minimum Wages and On-the-Job Training, Masanori Hashimoto (72 pp., $4.25)

Prices subject to change without notice.

AEI Associates Program

The American Enterprise Institute invites your participation in the competition of ideas through its AEI Associates Program. This program has two objectives:

The first is to broaden the distribution of AEI studies, conferences, forums, and reviews, and thereby to extend public familiarity with the issues. AEI Associates receive regular information on AEI research and programs, and they can order publications and cassettes at a savings.

The second objective is to increase the research activity of the American Enterprise Institute and the dissemination of its published materials to policy makers, the academic community, journalists, and others who help shape public attitudes. Your contribution, which in most cases is partly tax deductible, will help ensure that decision makers have the benefit of scholarly research on the practical options to be considered before programs are formulated. The issues studied by AEI include:

- Defense Policy
- Economic Policy
- Energy Policy
- Foreign Policy
- Government Regulation
- Health Policy
- Legal Policy
- Political and Social Processes
- Social Security and Retirement Policy
- Tax Policy

For more information, write to: American Enterprise Institute
1150 Seventeenth Street, N.W.
Washington, D.C. 20036

**A Conversation with Dr. Ezra Sadan: Combating Inflation in th[e]
Israeli Economy** is an edited transcript of a discussion with the t[op]
civil servant in the treasury department of Israel. How does Isra[el]
live with an inflation rate of 130 percent? How did such a high ra[te]
of inflation come about? What is being done to reduce it? Dr. Sad[an]
addresses these and other questions in his remarks to scholars a[nd]
guests of the American Enterprise Institute. Some of Dr. Sadan['s]
comments:

*"There is a danger that the whole system of indexation will stop workin[g].
This would mean that the banks could no longer help people hedge again[st]
inflation. Employers would no longer be able to index wages, and so fort[h].
This is a dangerous situation that may occur in a very short period of time[."]*

*"Because of indexation there is no political incentive to reduce inflation: [as]
long as it functions, indexation protects people from inflation. Inflatio[n]
however, is protected by people using the same device, indexation."*

*"In the case of Israel, it is not the budget that must be reduced but t[he]
government payroll, the number of people employed in the public sector. [In]
addition we need a series of government or government-influenced actio[n]
that will affect people's expectations more quickly."*

*"If the government undertakes to cut the budget, it will find a partner [in]
our federation of trade unions, which holds the power over the individu[al]
unions and can force them into line. If the government comes to an agreeme[nt]
with the federation on forward indexation for a while at least, we can u[se]
indexation in our favor."*

ISBN 0–8447–3465–9

American Enterprise Institute for Public Policy Research
1150 Seventeenth Street, N.W., Washington, D.C. 20036

Tribology

University of Southampton, United Kingdom

2–4 April 2012

FARADAY DISCUSSIONS

Volume 156, 2012

RSCPublishing

The Faraday Division of the Royal Society of Chemistry, previously the Faraday Society, founded in 1903 to promote the study of sciences lying between Chemistry, Physics and Biology.

EDITORIAL STAFF

Editor
Philip Earis

Deputy editor
Jane Hordern

Development editor
Heather Montgomery

Senior publishing editor
Anna Watson

Publishing editors
Erica Mills, Tamsin Phillips

Publishing assistants
Aliya Anwar, Ella Mitchell, Claire Sissen

Publisher
Niamh O'Connor

Faraday Discussions (Print ISSN 1359-6640, Electronic ISSN 1364-5498) is published 6 times a year by the Royal Society of Chemistry, Thomas Graham House, Science Park, Milton Road, Cambridge, UK CB4 0WF. Volume 156 ISBN-13: 978 1 84973 447 9

2012 annual subscription price: print+electronic £709, US $1,322; electronic only £673, US $1,256. Customers in Canada will be subject to a surcharge to cover GST. Customers in the EU subscribing to the electronic version only will be charged VAT. All orders, with cheques made payable to the Royal Society of Chemistry, should be sent to RSC Distribution Services, c/o Portland Customer Services, Commerce Way, Colchester, Essex, UK CO2 8HP.
Tel +44 (0) 1206 226050;
E-mail sales@rscdistribution.org

If you take an institutional subscription to any RSC journal you are entitled to free, site-wide web access to that journal. You can arrange access *via* Internet Protocol (IP) address at www.rsc.org/ip. Customers should make payments by cheque in sterling payable on a UK clearing bank or in US dollars payable on a US clearing bank.

US Postmaster: send address changes to *Faraday Discussions*, c/o Mercury Airfreight International Ltd., 365 Blair Road, Avenel, NJ 07001. All despatches outside the UK by Consolidated Airfreight.
PRINTED IN THE UK

Faraday Discussions documents a long-established series of *Faraday Discussion* meetings which provide a unique international forum for the exchange of views and newly acquired results in developing areas of physical chemistry, biophysical chemistry and chemical physics.

Tribology

Faraday Discussions

www.rsc.org/faraday_d

A General Discussion on Tribology was held at the University of Southampton, United Kingdom on the 2nd, 3rd and 4th of April 2012.

CONTENTS

ISSN 1359-6640; ISBN 978-1-84973-447-9

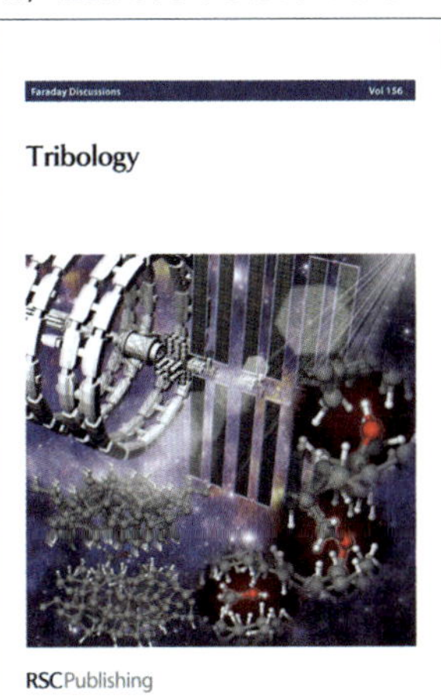

Cover
See Kubo *et al.*, *Faraday Discuss.*, 2012, **156**, 137–146.

Diamond-like carbon (DLC) is one of the most promising solid lubricants for aerospace instruments. Our tight-binding quantum chemical molecular dynamics simulations reveal that the chemical reactions of a methanol molecule sandwiched between DLC films lead to OH-termination of the DLC surface, leading to good low friction properties.

Image reproduced by permission of Dr Momoji Kubo, from *Faraday Discuss.*, 2012, **156**, 137.

INTRODUCTORY LECTURE

PAPERS AND DISCUSSIONS

CONCLUDING REMARKS

ADDITIONAL INFORMATION

Bio-tribology

Duncan Dowson*

Received 8th May 2012, Accepted 11th May 2012
DOI: 10.1039/c2fd20103h

It is now forty six years since the separate topics of friction, lubrication, wear and bearing design were integrated under the title 'Tribology' [Department of Education and Science, *Lubrication (Tribology) Education and Research. A Report on the Present Position and Industry's Needs*, HMSO, London, 1966]. Significant developments have been reported in many established and new aspects of tribology during this period. The subject has contributed to improved performance of much familiar equipment, such as reciprocating engines, where there have been vast improvements in engine reliability and efficiency. Nano-tribology has been central to remarkable advances in information processing and digital equipment. Shortly after widespread introduction of the term tribology, integration with biology and medicine prompted rapid and extensive interest in the fascinating sub-field now known as Bio-tribology [D. Dowson and V. Wright, *Bio-tribology*, in *The Rheology of Lubricants*, ed. T. C. Davenport, Applied Science Publishers, Barking, 1973, pp. 81–88]. An outline will be given of some of the developments in the latter field.

1. Introduction

Bio-tribology is an immense field of study, embracing basic concepts in physics, chemistry, biology, materials science and engineering. The subject of tribology itself, with applications related to engineering equipment and systems, emerged slowly and it is helpful to identify a few established concepts essential to the understanding of progress in bio-tribology.

Two distinct modes of lubrication, '*Fluid film*' and '*Boundary*', were revealed late in the nineteenth (Tower;[1] Reynolds[2]) and early in the twentieth (Hardy and Double-day[3,4]) centuries. Craftsmen and engineers had grappled for hundreds of years with challenging bearing problems encountered in the manufacture and operation of both fixed and moving machinery, often developing remarkable empirical solutions.

1.1. Early 20th century concepts of lubrication

An interesting summary of the state of knowledge of lubrication early in the 20th century emerged in a '*Review of existing knowledge of lubrication*'[5] prepared by a Special Committee of the Department of Scientific and Industrial Research (DSIR). A clear distinction was drawn between three modes of lubrication as outlined in Table 1.

1.2. Fluid-film lubrication

Tower's exciting observation of pressure rises in loaded journal bearings in the 1880s prompted Osborne Reynolds to develop his theoretical analysis of '*fluid-film lubrica-tion*'. His differential equation relating hydrodynamic pressure to bearing geometry

School of Mechanical Engineering, The University of Leeds, Leeds, LS2 9JT, UK. E-mail: D.Dowson@leeds.ac.uk

Table 1 Three stages of lubrication (1920)

Stages of lubrication	Laws	Coefficient of friction
1. Unlubricated surfaces	Dry friction	0.10–0.40
2. Partially lubricated surfaces	Greasy friction	0.01–0.10
3. Completely lubricated surfaces	Viscous friction	0.001–0.01

and independent variables such as the applied load, speed and lubricant viscosity, became one of the best known and extensively used equations in tribology. Reynolds addressed the problem of lubrication of bearings used on the railways and in machinery. Exciting experimental and theoretical revelations, supported by clear scientific explanations of the impressive load carrying potential of films of viscous lubricants, were reported with great clarity. It nevertheless took twenty years before the new knowledge of fluid-film lubrication had a major influence upon bearing design (Mitchell;[6] Kingsbury[7]). This remarkable form of load support became known as the ideal mode of lubrication, since wear was theoretically zero and remarkably low coefficients of friction (10^{-3}–10^{-2}) were achievable. The replacement of plain thrust collars by tilting pad bearings early in the 20th century increased the load carrying capacity by a factor of about 10 and reduced the friction coefficient from about 0.04 to the range 0.002–0.005. Fitting such fluid-film lubricated bearings to naval ships saved the British Government about £0.5m in the price of coal in 1918.

Confidence in the merits and efficacy of fluid-film bearings resulted in many valuable design procedures by the mid-20th century. Design data emerged from numerical solutions to the Reynolds equation, moderated by practical experience. Numerical analysis of lubrication problems, particularly through application of the recently developed 'relaxation methods', contributed to the databases upon which design charts were based. Procedures involved hand calculations, mechanical calculating machines and in due course digital computers. Confidence abounded in the basic assumption that lubricated plain bearings behaved according to hydrodynamic expectations, although I still remember the reluctance of a coalmine engineer to accept that the carefully aligned journal bearings in his winding gear could ever run eccentrically! It was soon possible to analyse dynamically loaded bearings, although the development of numerical procedures for time dependent loadings and speeds became ever more complex. The mobility method (Booker[8]) was particularly valuable for engine bearing analysis.

One problem remained in relation to the understanding of fluid-film lubrication in highly stressed machine components such as gears and rolling element bearings. Machining marks were still evident on gears after long service, while balls and rollers in bearings retained their excellent finish. Furthermore, film thicknesses in piston-ring/cylinder liner conjunctions, calculated from solutions to the Reynolds equation, failed to predict separations in excess of the surface finish.

In due course the incorporation of elastic deformations and lubricant pressure–viscosity characteristics in the calculations gave birth to the subject of '*elastohydrodynamic lubrication*' (Grubin and Vinogradova;[9] Dowson and Higginson[10]). This promoted a clearer understanding of the physics of effective fluid-film lubrication in both highly stressed metallic machine elements and in low elastic modulus components such as seals. The subject has dominated the lubrication literature for the past half century.

1.3. Boundary lubrication

Sir William Bate Hardy introduced us to the concept of '*boundary lubrication*'. Hardy was a zoologist and physiologist who worked on colloids and surface tension. From 1915–1925 he was the biological secretary to the Royal Society. In 1919 and 1920 he published papers in the Philosophical Magazine on static friction in which he drew attention to the relationship between the molecular structure of substances and their effectiveness as lubricants. Hardy introduced the term '*boundary lubrication*' for this mode of lubrication, governed by chemical rather than viscous properties of lubricants. He studied the orientation of mono-molecular films on surfaces and concluded that their influence extended well beyond the range of single molecular layers. Classical papers by Hardy and Miss Ida Doubleday in 1922 firmly established the concept of boundary lubrication. The role of chemistry in lubrication was clearly established and for paraffins, alcohols and acids, the coefficients of static friction decreased with increasing molecular weight.

For severe operating conditions, boundary lubricants greatly enhance the ability of engineers and chemists to design reliable and efficient lubricants and bearings. Additives became essential features of the armoury of lubrication engineers. It nevertheless took many decades for this last line of defence of lubricated bearing surfaces to become established. Friction coefficients for boundary lubrication in engineering are generally of order $1–5 \times 10^{-1}$, which is one or two orders of magnitude greater than those achieved in many fluid-film lubricated bearings.

Representations of late 20th century concepts of the basic features of fluid-film and boundary lubrication are shown in Fig. 1. In fluid-film lubrication, the bearing surfaces are separated by a coherent film of lubricant of variable film thickness (h). Entrainment of the lubricant into a film of gradually diminishing thickness in the direction of sliding generates a pressure which balances the applied load. Under increasing load, the separation of the surfaces reduces until the molecules of the boundary lubricant adsorbed on the surfaces, or protective surface films formed by chemical reaction, protect them from excessive wear and friction.

1.4. Mixed lubrication

The basics of *fluid-film* and *boundary* lubrication were deemed to be simple. Most engineering bearings were designed and manufactured to enjoy fluid-film lubrication, but if the operating conditions were too severe for this '*ideal*' mode of lubrication, additives to the lubricant would develop protective boundary lubricating films at the bearing surfaces. However, it became clear that the friction characteristics of the two regimes of lubrication were quite different, as indicated in Table 1. The coefficients of friction in boundary lubrication were relatively high, but little affected by load, speed or viscosity, while in fluid-film bearings the coefficients were much lower but functions of these variables.

The well defined regimes of 'fluid-film' and 'boundary' lubrication were thus joined by a transition region in which the friction rose quite rapidly from relatively low values associated with viscous shearing to the much higher levels of boundary lubrication. This connecting region was labelled '*mixed*' lubrication, to indicate that the load was supported partly by hydrodynamic action and partly by asperity interactions or the protective, adhering, surface films of boundary lubrication.

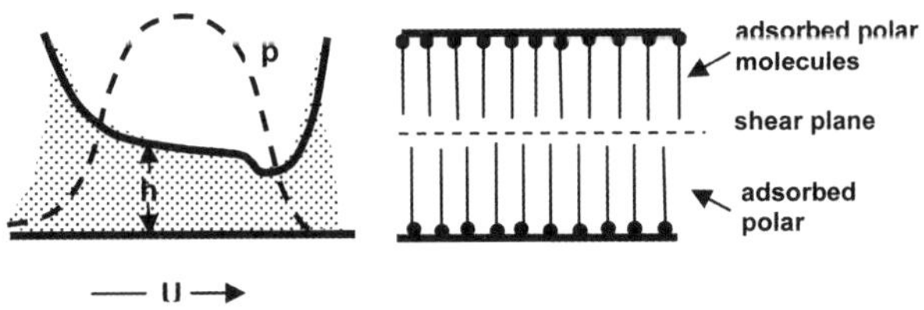

Fig. 1 Principal lubrication concepts (late 19th and early 20th centuries): lubricant adsorbed on the surfaces, or protective surface films formed by chemical reaction, protect them from excessive wear and friction.

With two distinctive principal lubrication regimes presenting relatively high and low coefficients of friction, it was inevitable that there would be a transition zone between them. Thurston,[11] whose father manufactured steam engines and who became the first President of the American Society of Mechanical Engineers, appears to have been the first to report a minimum in the friction trace as the speed and/or the load on a bearing were varied.

...*"there must always be ultimately reached a point at which, with increasing pressures, the limit of bearing power is attained or approached, and the friction must experience a change of law, the coefficient increasing, beyond that limit, as the intensity of pressure is augmented."*

Stribeck[12] subsequently reported an impressive experimental study of the friction of journal bearings used on the rapidly expanding railways. The operating conditions for several bearings were varied over a wide range of loads and speeds and clear minima were noted in the friction traces as the speed decreased or the load increased.

Sommerfeld[13] provided an elegant analysis of infinitely wide journal bearings considered by Reynolds and revealed that, if the lubricant did not cavitate, the application of load would cause the shaft to move at right angles to the load vector. The marine engineer Gümbel[14] found that the various friction traces to the right of the heel in the Stribeck curves could be condensed onto a single trace, if the coefficient of friction was plotted against the parameter $\eta\omega/p$, where η represents the lubricant viscosity, ω the shaft rotational speed and p the mean pressure on the bearing. Such traces became known as 'Stribeck curves' (Fig. 2) and the parameter on the abscissa in Fig. 1 variously known as the Sommerfeld or Gümbel number. It is evident from Fig. 2 that the coefficient of friction can change rapidly over about two orders of magnitude in the mixed lubrication regime.

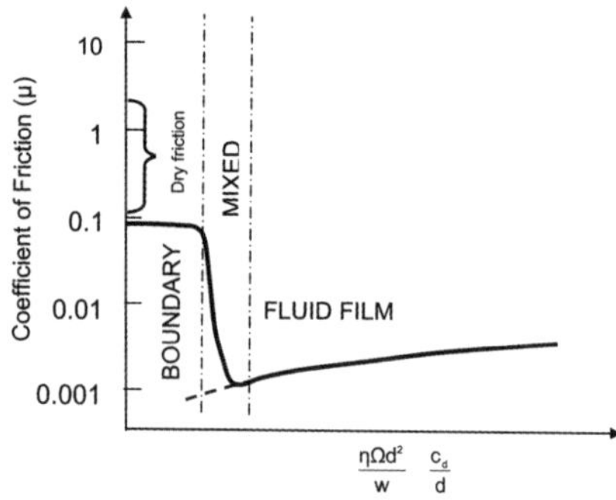

Fig. 2 Stribeck curve.

2.   Bio-tribology

The list of subjects considered under the title of Bio-tribology has grown enormously since the term was introduced in the 1970s. A brief selection is shown in Table 2.

2.1.   Biological attachment and detachment

Biologists and zoologists have explored extensively the different and remarkable systems of attachment to horizontal, inclined and vertical surfaces adopted by creatures ranging from beetles and flies to snails and geckos. The principal approaches adopted by nature range from intimate proximity between fine hairs or pads and the surfaces being traversed, suction pads, capillarity, or mechanical claws and hooks (Scherge and Gorb[15]). Many exhibit vast numbers of terminal structures on very fine, flexible hairs which enable impressive van der Waals forces to achieve

Table 2 Some topics in Bio-tribology

Some aspects of Bio-tribology	
Biological attachment and detachment	Soft tissue tribology
Tribology in the animal world	Skin
Natural synovial joints	Hair and textile fibres
Total joint replacements	Oral tribology
Synthetic cartilage and lubricants	Ocular tribology
Tribology of footwear	Micro-circulation

attachment to surfaces. In the presence of liquids, surface tension around the periphery of the nominal contact region can ensure substantial adhesion. If contacts occur only between asperities, capillary bridges can form to produce similar effects.

In recent times, attention has focussed more upon the mechanism of release rather than attachment. If creatures attached to horizontal or vertical walls are to retain mobility, they must be able to release the strong attachment system rapidly and effectively. Peeling mechanisms have attracted considerable attention.

2.2. Tribology in the animal world

Extensive studies of animal mechanics and skeletons have been reported (Alexander;[16] Currey[17,18]). Allometry indicated that synovial joints in vertebrates operate at very similar stress levels, irrespective of animal size; from frogs to elephants and even the extinct dinosaurs.

Attention has been drawn to the remarkable features of flagella motors in bacteria such as *Escherichia coli* and *Salmonella typhimurium* (Berg;[19] Berry;[20] Hutchings[21]). The helical flagella are rotated at speeds up to about 1 700 Hz by the flow of ions down an electro-chemical gradient. The bearings in the cell walls are only about 45–50 nm in diameter, with a stepping motor operating at about 400 steps per revolution. The flagella motors are immersed in water or lipid. Molecular forces play a major role in determining friction between solids in micro and nano-tribology and it is now clear that similar considerations apply to lubrication at the scale of flagella motors.

Studies of gastropod locomotion have revealed that net forward movement is achieved by muscle action, with a *pedal* wave passing along the foot. This repeatedly relaxes 'contact' with the surface locally and facilitates forward motion. The pedal wave traverses the foot at roughly twice the forward speed of the gastropod. The mucus layer separating the foot of a snail from the floor has been studied by Kobayashi *et al.*[22] The anterior and posterior film thicknesses ranged from 2–6 µm and 8–16 µm respectively. It is interesting to compare the rheology of the snail traction fluid (mucus) with that of the lubricant (synovial fluid) utilised in human joints (Fig. 3).

2.3. Natural synovial joints

Studies of many topics now embraced by the title 'Bio-tribology' have a long history, whereas others are of recent origin. However, all present novel tribological features and full understanding of most is still awaited. One of the subjects with a long history is the tribology of synovial joints. Well functioning bearings, particularly in the lower limb, are essential for the health and mobility of humans and animals.

Synovial joints have long been considered as bearings, as illustrated over a quarter of a millennium ago by the writings of the famous Scottish anatomist, physician and surgeon William Hunter.[23]

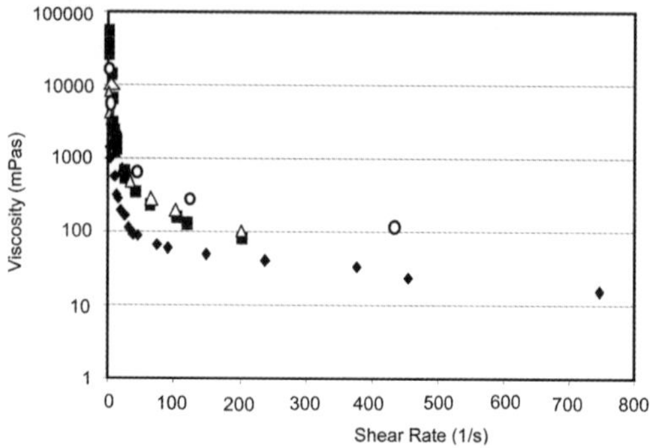

Fig. 3 Comparison of viscosity–shear rate characteristics for snail mucus and synovial fluid. Snail mucus: ■ high viscosity, ◆ low viscosity. Synovial fluid: ○ high viscosity, △ low viscosity. (To be published in the book 'Biotribology' by John Wiley & Sons Ltd., 2013).

"Where-ever the Motion of one Bone upon another is requifite, there we find an excellent Apparatus for rendering that Motion fafe and free: We Fee, for Inftance, the Extremity of one bone moulded into an orbicular Cavity, to receive the head of another, in order to afford it extenfive Play. Both are covered by a fmooth elaftic Cruft, to prevent mutual Abrafion; connected with ftrong Ligaments, to prevent Diflocation; and inclofed in a Bag that contains a proper Fluid depofited there, for lubricating the Two contiguous Surfaces"

It is evident that Osborne Reynolds also considered the lubrication of natural synovial joints when he prepared his classical paper on fluid-film lubrication, for he wrote:

"The only other self-acting system of lubrication is that of reciprocating joints with alternate Pressure on and separation (drawing the oil back or a fresh supply) of the surfaces. This plays an important part in certain machines, as in the steam engine, and is as fundamental to animal mechanics as the lubricating action of the journal is to mechanical contrivences."

It appears that Reynolds considered that synovial joints relied upon fluid-film lubrication, although he did not use his famous equation to analyse them and to assess their ability to develop film thicknesses capable of separating the cartilage surfaces.

The essential features of a synovial joint are shown in Fig. 4. All the requirements of a plain bearing are evident, but while they present many similarities to engineering bearings, they also exhibit a number of novel features. The nominal contact region accommodates loads of varying magnitude acting in various directions. The bearing material, articular cartilage, having a thickness ranging from about 1 mm to 5 mm, is attached to bone which acts as the hard backing material.

The bearing surfaces are lubricated by synovial fluid, contained within a synovial membrane lining a fibrous capsule. The bearing space at the edges of the loaded cartilage contacts may contain wedge shaped menisci, acting as seals but capable of transmitting substantial proportions of the load applied to the joint (Seedhom[24]). Discussion of the lubrication mechanisms in synovial joints began in earnest in the 1930s (MacConaill[25]); the central question being to ascertain whether or not the lubricant, synovial fluid, could separate the cartilage surfaces by hydrodynamic action. Jones[26] carried out simple pendulum tests on the proximal interphalangeal joint of an amputated finger. The logarithmic decay in amplitude supported the concept of viscous friction. Dintenfass[27] and Dowson[28] applied elastohydrodynamic analysis to synovial joints, but Charnley[29] favoured boundary lubrication.

Some felt that the relatively rough surfaces of articular cartilage, the severity of loading and the demands of complex linear and rotational motion would preclude fluid-film lubrication. A simple hydrodynamic lubrication calculation supported

     This journal is © The Royal Society of Chemistry 2012

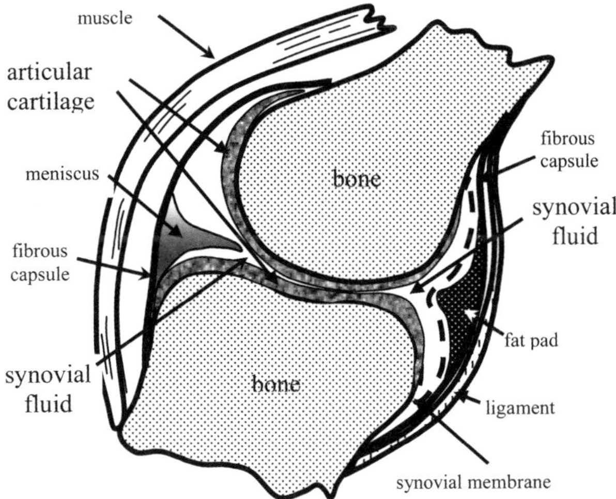

Fig. 4 Diagrammatic representation of a synovial joint. (To be published in the book 'Biotribology' by John Wiley & Sons Ltd., 2013).

this view (Dowson[28]), since the predicted film thicknesses were about 0.1 μm, while the measured surface roughnesses (Davies *et al.*[30]) were in the range 1–10 μm.

The debate intensified in the 1960s, with supporters declaring themselves for fluid-film or boundary lubrication, with little mention of mixed lubrication. The views swung to and fro like the bob of a pendulum, as new results emerged! Bio-chemical and bio-tribological tests were performed to try to identify the constituents of synovial fluid capable of effective boundary lubrication, while rheological studies were carried out to refine the fluid-film lubrication concept. When elastohydrodynamic action was taken into account, the possibility of fluid-film lubrication in synovial joints re-emerged, as indicated by the 1967 data shown in Table 3.

Several concepts of synovial joint lubrication emerged, or were developed, in the second half of the twentieth century, including *boundary* (Swann and Radin;[31] Hills and Butler;[32] Hills;[33] Ateshian;[34] Pickard *et al.*[35]); *hydrodynamic* (Dowson;[28] Unsworth[36]); *elastohydrodynamic* Dintenfass;[27] Dowson[28]) and *micro-elasto-hydrodynamic* (Dowson and Jin[37]); *weeping* (McCutchen[38]); *squeeze film* (Fein;[39] Higginson and Unsworth[40]); *gells/boosted* (Maroudos;[41] Walker *et al.*[42]); *biphasic/triphasic* (Mow and Lai[43]); *mixed* and *multi-mode* (Dowson;[28] Murakami *et al.*[44]).

Further advances resulted when the potential modes of lubrication outlined above were combined with in depth studies of the porous, elastic, frictional properties of articular cartilage. It had long been recognised from simple laboratory experiments that time dependent friction of loaded articular cartilage could be explained by initial interstitial fluid pressurisation followed by a gradual transfer of load to the

Table 3 Predicted film thicknesses in the knee and hip

		Film thickness (μm)	
		Hydrodynamic	Elasto-hydrodynamic
Knee	$P = 49$ kN m^{-1}; $u = 0.025$ m s^{-1}; $E' = 10^6$ N m^{-2}; $\eta = 0.001$ Pa s; $R = 50$ mm	0.125 μm	1–2 μm
Hip	$P = 4.5$ kN; $u = 0.075$ m s^{-1}; $E' = 10^7$ N m^{-2}; $\eta = 0.001$ Pa s; $R = 1$ m	—	2–4 μm

solid matrix of the cartilage (Edwards;[45] McCutchen;[46] Kempson;[47] Ateshian;[34,48] Forster and Fisher;[49,50] Huang *et al.*[51] It was an exciting and productive period, yet many of the concepts are still the subject of further research.

A few significant findings contributed to the development of an overall view of synovial joint lubrication. These include a recognition of the powerful fluid-film lubrication concepts of *micro-elastohydrodynamic* lubrication and *squeeze-film* action; the *biphasic/triphasic* properties of porous-elastic articular cartilage, with time dependent sharing of load by the fluid and solid constituents and the effective *boundary lubrication by certain proteins* in synovial fluid, *surfactants* and *polymer brushes.*

Spikes[52] demonstrated that engineering lubricants could develop elastohydrodynamic films which followed extraordinarily well the theoretical film thickness equations down to separations of only a few nm. The situation is more complicated for relatively rough biological tissues and synovial fluid. It nevertheless suggests that micro-elasto-hydrodynamic action should be carefully assessed in soft tissue lubrication investigations.

Attention has been drawn to the presence of surface active phospholipids at various sites in the body, such as the pericardium; pleural mesothelium; peritoneal cavity; eustachian tube and synovial joints (Hills[32,33]). It was observed that the oligolamellar structures exhibited thicknesses of about 0.2 μm, built up from interlamellar layers with spacings of about 45 Å. It was suggested that these phospholipids provided boundary lubrication whenever fluid-film lubrication was inadequate at the relatively low velocities encountered in biological systems.

The characteristics of synovial joint lubrication are truly remarkable. Nature's bearings do not rely upon a single mode of lubrication, but on several, some of which are unique to biological situations. As in engineering bearings, particular forms of fluid-film, mixed and boundary lubrication can be encountered, depending upon the properties of the cartilage and synovial fluid and the imposed operating conditions.

More recently Briscoe *et al.*[53] have drawn attention to the robustness of polymer brushes and their potential to act as very effective boundary lubricants for biological tissues.

2.4. Total joint replacements

The replacement of worn, damaged or diseased human joints probably represents the greatest advance in orthopaedic surgery during the past century. The subject has a long history, as outlined in relation to the hip by Scales.[54] In the early years, interposition procedures used a wide range of materials, including ivory, oak, gold foil and glass. Current implants are based mainly upon CrCoMo stainless steels, polymers and ceramics.

Major developments took place in the mid 20th century. The metal-on-metal McKee–Farrar[55] (Fig. 5(b)) and the Charnley[56] metal-on polymer (Fig. 5(a)) total hip replacements were launched and both were to make major contributions to the subject. Most of the McKee–Farrar joints functioned well, albeit only for a few years, yet intriguingly, some served their hosts well for over twenty years. The major problems were excessive friction and loosening. Assessment of the first fifty cases in the 1960s looked promising, but in due course the Charnley joint was seen to offer lower friction, a reduced tendency to loosen, and better survival rates. Charnley was convinced that excessive frictional torque was the main problem with previous hip replacements. He therefore turned to the low friction polymer poly-tetra-fluoroethylene (PTFE) for the acetabular cups. He also applied sound principles of mechanics to minimise the frictional torque by reducing the femoral head diameter to only 7/8 in ($\approx$ 22 mm). The PTFE was disastrous due to excessive wear; a timely reminder that low friction does not necessarily equate to low wear. After about three hundred operations, acetabular cups were made from the much

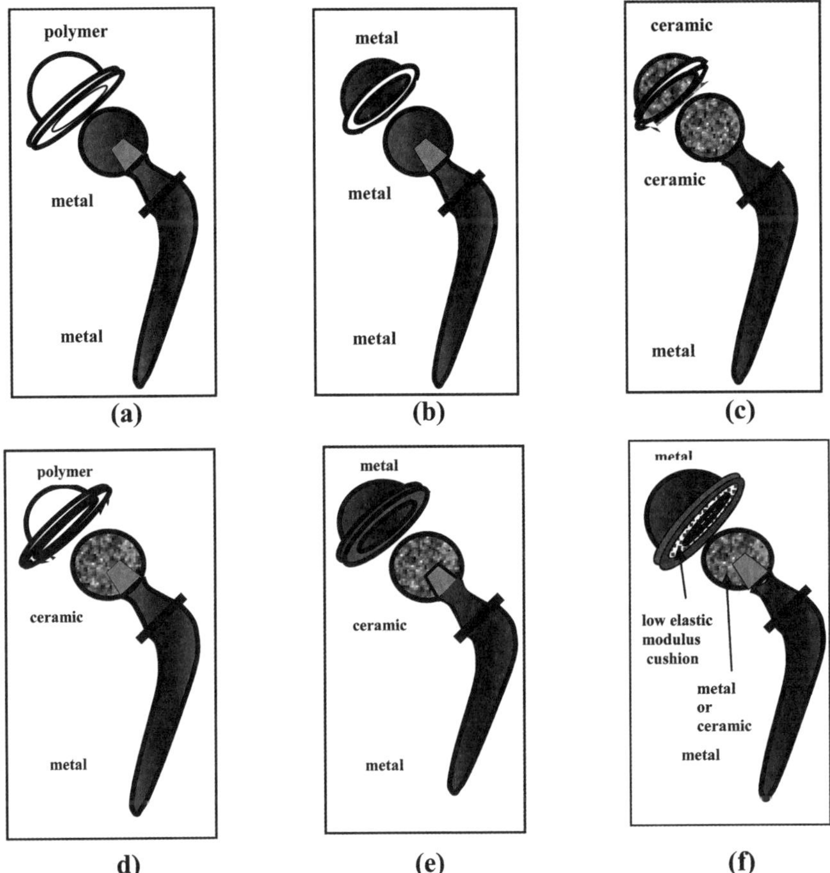

Fig. 5 Potential material pairs in hip joints. (To be published in the book 'Biotribology' by John Wiley & Sons Ltd., 2013).

more wear resistant ultra-high-molecular-weight polyethylene (UHMWPE). The metal-on-UHMWPE combination (Fig. 5(a) represented the major form of total hip replacement after the 1960s.

Hard-on-hard joint replacements experienced a renaissance later in the 20th and early in the 21st centuries. Progress in materials science, design, manufacture and the development of understanding of tribological principles of hip replacements offered opportunities for the development of longer lasting hip replacements. This provided the opportunity for orthopaedic surgeons to offer hip replacement operations to much younger patients, with greatly reduced likelihood of revisions in later life. New forms of metal-on-metal joints were devised, polyethylene wear resistance was improved by processing, particularly cross-linking, while toughened ceramics offered even longer survival times due to outstanding wear resistance and enhanced strength (Fig. 5(c,d,e)). While surgical and tribological skills are stretched by some of these developments, total hip replacement remains an outstanding development in orthopaedics. Millions of patients have benefitted from total joint replacement, not only of the hip, but also of the knee, ankle, shoulder, elbow, wrist and finger joints.

While many tribological studies of hip and knee replacement performance have been reported, the need for further studies is clear. Boundary, mixed and elasto-hydrodynamic modes of operation have all been supported. It seems clear that, in overall terms, mixed lubrication is most likely, for most of the time, in most implants. A persistent problem for analysts and experimentalists alike is that it is extremely difficult to model, or represent in simulators, the full range of conditions experienced by joint replacements in the body. This is a view shared by John Charnley.

There remains a puzzling feature of these impressive developments (Dowson[57]). Materials of manufacture for joint replacements have presented ever increasing moduli of elasticity, particularly over the past half century. Yet nature does not adopt this solution in her remarkable load bearing synovial joints, where articular cartilage presents a relatively soft bearing material. This has promoted a number of investigations into the possibility of using low modulus, porous bearing materials which more closely mimic the behaviour of cartilage (Fig. 5(f)). Durability is a challenge, but wear is minimal in a mildly mixed lubrication regime. In the long run, optimum solutions may arise from stem cell research and attempts to develop suitable scaffolds for cartilage growth.

2.5. Synthetic cartilage and lubricant

Clear indications that cartilage lesions and/or synovial fluid deterioration are often associated with arthritic conditions prompted considerable interest in both cartilage repair/replacement and synovial fluid supplementation. Replacement cartilage plugs have been developed and inserted into regions of damaged or diseased cartilage. Integration with existing cartilage and bone presents difficulties, but lower friction has been noted. The possibility of enhancing the lubricant in afflicted joints has promoted further studies of the modes of lubrication in joints and the contributions of various constituents of synovial fluid to the lubrication process.

Various low modulus, compliant, materials such as silicone rubbers, hydrogels and polyurethane have all been considered as cartilage repair materials (Unsworth et al.;[58] Corkhill;[59] Auger et al.;[60] Murakami[61]). Their tribological significance depends primarily upon their durability and ability to encourage satisfactory lubrication and minimum wear under biological conditions. Comparisons of friction in replacement hip joints fitted with either UHMWPE or polyurethane acetabular cups demonstrated a marked advantage of the latter in a hip joint simulator.

The selection of suitable lubricants to improve friction and wear in arthritic joints has proved to be a difficult process. It is difficult to formulate suitable lubricants if there is a lack of understanding of the mechanism of synovial joint lubrication. However, now that it is widely recognised that there is no unique mode of lubrication in natural bearings, and that alternative or additional lubricants must promote elasto-hydrodynamic lubrication whilst offering effective protection under mixed and boundary lubrication conditions, the position is improving. It is known that hyaluron enhances lubricant viscosity and that this increases fluid film thickness, while boundary lubricating constituents of synovial fluid have been identified (Radin et al.;[62] Swann and Radin;[63] Swann et al.;[64] Hills and Butler;[32] Higarki and Murakami[65]). Hyaluron is present in the vitreous humour and skin as well as cartilage. Visco-supplementation, effected orally or by injections is an ongoing subject of investigation and has attracted considerable attention for about forty years. Higaki and Murakami have revealed important contributions of γ-globulin and phospholipid to the preservation of low friction in films prepared on glass by the Langmuir–Blodgett process.

2.6. Tribology of footwear

Protection of the feet of both horses and humans has attracted attention for centuries and certainly since Roman times. Leather was the main material of construction until the mid 20th century, but synthetic materials such as rubber, PVC and polyurethane now dominate the scene.

Tribological aspects of footwear have focussed upon wear and friction, although the contribution to slipping and accidents of water and other liquids on pavements and floors is particularly important. Force platform studies have shown that normal reaction forces between shoes and the ground generally range from $(0.8–1.2) \times$ body weight. Tangential forces are about 15% of body weight, while contact pressures range from 0.5–6 MPa.

The wear coefficients of leather soles in dry and wet conditions respectively have been found to range from about $10^{-4}–10^{-3}$ mm^3 N^{-1} m^{-1}. Precision measurements need to be made in clean environments and footwear can present difficult problems. It has been estimated that about 10^4 wear particles are generated by every step taken with unprotected leather shoes.

2.7. Soft tribology

Bio-tribology has contributed substantially to the rapid growth of interest in the friction, wear and lubrication of '*soft*' or low elastic modulus materials. The field covers many applications ranging from seals, flexible materials such as paper, textiles, porous polymers and foodstuffs to biological tissues such as menisci, tendons, contact lenses, eyelids, synovial membranes and articular cartilage.

Low modulus materials readily deform under modest pressure, whether developed by solid-to-solid contact or pressure in adjacent fluids. The behaviour of lubricated, soft bearing materials differs in certain important details from that of many engineering materials. In particular, the pressures are often so low that their influence upon the lubricant viscosity is negligible. The elastic deformations of the materials and the film thicknesses are also relatively large. The viscosity–pressure coefficient and the materials term (G) thus vanish from the elastohydrodynamic film thickness equations. The similarities and differences between minimum film thickness expressions for steady-state elastohydrodynamic conditions are evident in eqn (1) and (2).

Piezo-viscous, elastic:

$$H_{\min} = 3.63\,U^{0.68}G^{0.49}W^{-0.073}(1 - e^{-0.68k}) \tag{1}$$

Iso-viscous, elastic:

$$H_{\min} = 7.43\,U^{0.65}W^{-0.21}(1 - 0.85e^{-0.31k}) \tag{2}$$

The latter equation is particularly useful for the interpretation of friction data for '*soft*' materials operating in the fluid-film lubrication regime.

2.8. Skin

Skin and articular cartilage are two of the most widely studied tissues in bio-tribology. The nerve rich skin forms our interface with the outside world, and is important in relation to tactile response, locomotion, temperature control, grasping and holding objects. Skin tribology is complex, calling for close collaboration between clinicians, materials scientists, engineers, physicists and chemists.

Skin consists of three distinct layers, the lower connective tissue (*hypodermis*) supports a thick middle layer (*dermis*) which is in turn surmounted by a thinner outer layer (*epidermis*). The thickness varies from one site to another, being thicker and harder than elsewhere on the soles of the feet and on the palms of the hands.

The outer layer, epidermis or epithelium, is cellular and avascular, having a total thickness of some 60–100 µm. The epithelial cells in the *stratum corneum* develop a flattened appearance due to evaporation. Polygonal regions known as *corneocytes* can be seen on the free surface. Furrows and wrinkles contribute to the extensibility of the skin membrane and are usually quite clear and well defined, with depths in the range 20–100 µm. Peak to valley depths (R_t) range from about 120 µm to 160 µm, with mean slopes of about 25° to 40°.

The *dermis* is much thicker, 2–4 mm, than the *epidermis*. The *hypodermis*, consists of a layer of connective tissue and both the dermis and hypodermis are well supplied with blood. Cells formed on the basal layer divide and move through the superficial layer towards the surface where they are flattened into dead cells, rich in *keratin*. *Keratinization* leads to the formation of the dead cells known as the *stratum corneum*. It takes some two to four weeks for the cells to migrate from the basal layer to the surface. The surface of the skin is an inert, flexible, water resistant membrane consisting of closely packed cells in *sebum*—a waxy material formed in sebaceous glands. The limiting shear stress that can be sustained on the surface of these cells results in coefficients of friction in the range 0.1–1.0.

Many measurements have been made of friction at various sites on the body, resulting in a few well recognised features of the friction of skin (Adams *et al.*;[66] Johnson *et al.*[67]). Hydration has a significant effect. The lowest coefficients are found when the skin is dry or when it is very wet and well lubricated. When hydrated the friction is highest and erratic, with stick–slip characteristics. Typical values of steady, dry friction are about 0.1–0.3, while a mean value of about unity is typical of fully hydrated conditions.

The coefficient of friction also varies with the body site. A collation of data published by different authors has been prepared and mean values are shown in Fig. 6. The mean coefficient of kinetic friction is just under 0.5 (0.46–0.49), but the six-to-one range of 0.2–1.2 for different sites is considerable. It should be noted, however, that different measuring devices were used in the experiments, individual test procedures were adopted, the skin preparations were not necessarily the same, although all applied to 'normal skin', and the measurements involved different subjects and different times. When the analysis was repeated to take account of the different number of readings for each site, the pattern remained quite similar, but the value for the forearm dropped from 0.51 to 0.41 and for the tibia from 0.66 to 0.54. The rankings for these two sites changed from eleventh to ninth and fifteenth to twelfth respectively. There is clearly a case for caution when talking of a single value for the coefficient of kinetic friction of skin.

Adhesion is the major mechanism determining the friction of skin, with smaller contributions coming from a ploughing or deformation process, hysteresis losses and, under some conditions, viscous dissipation losses.

2.9. Hair and textile fibres

While man-made fibres have a reasonably uniform diameter, natural hair and wool have outer layers of cells some 0.5–1.0 μm thick and 40–100 μm long, arranged like

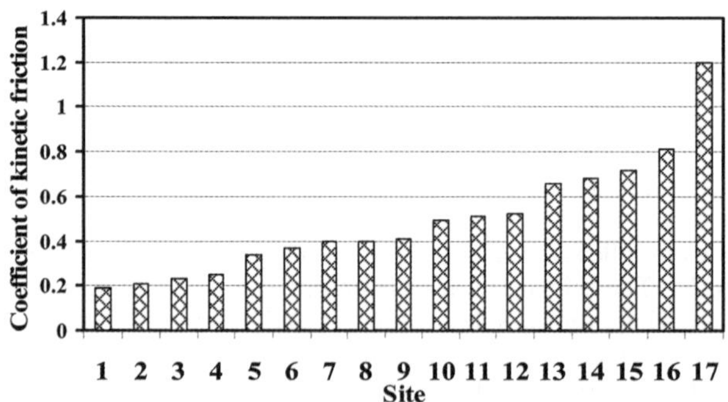

Fig. 6 Skin coefficient of kinetic friction at various sites. (To be published in the book 'Biotribology' by John Wiley & Sons Ltd., 2013). 1: back (lower); 2: ankle; 3: arm (upper); 4: back (upper); 5: postauricular; 6: abdomen; 7: leg (anterior); 8: leg (posterior); 9: hand (dorsum); 10: forehead; 11: forearm; 12 hand (all); 13: vulvar; 14: hand (palm); 15: tibia; 16: finger; 17: foot (sole).

tiles on a roof. This structure bestows interesting tribological characteristics upon natural fibres. The recorded diameters of hair range from 15 μm to 220 μm, with most being in the range 50–100 μm. The mean value of 70 μm is slightly less than one tenth of a millimetre. There are distinct effects of racial origin upon ovality. Its density is about 1.32 kg m^{-3}. As the hair grows in the follicle it undergoes keratinisation, in which cells harden and die.

Friction tests along the length of fibres show that values for hair differ, depending upon the direction of sliding, whereas values for man made fibres are essentially constant. Individuals and hairdressers readily recognise this directional or differential friction effect, with back-combing towards the scalp being harder than towards the tip.

Friction is the most important feature of hair and wool, engaging the attention of the textile and pharmaceutical industries. The differential friction effect (D.F.E.) has been the subject of much research and debate, since it is important in fibre processing and the performance of textile products. Its values, defined as the difference in coefficients of friction in each direction, span a full order of magnitude ($\mu = 0.05$ to 0.5). Representative values of hair coefficients of friction, with (μ_w) and against (μ_a) the cuticles, straddle the mean value of 0.49 associated with skin, but at 0.41, the root to tip values are much closer to the mean value for skin. High humidity generally increases hair friction, particularly for untreated specimens, whereas temperature has little effect for either treated or untreated hair.

2.10. Oral tribology

Initially, studies of oral tribology were concerned with teeth, but the subject now embraces the mastication and transport of chewed food to the back of the mouth, ready for swallowing, and temporomandibular joints.

Saliva is the lubricant which protects the unique structures of the tongue surface and other soft tissues from excessive wear. The temporomandibular joint permits rotation and translation of the jaw and teeth, while hard enamel allows the teeth to cut and grind food.

Coefficients of friction for the tongue against other biological tissues range from about 0.1 to 0.3. Food scientists have suggested that there may be links between the friction of oral tissues and our perception of different foodstuffs (Valentová and Pokorný[68]), and the possibility of interaction between friction and sensory perception (de Wijk and Prinz[69]) has attracted attention in recent years. Foodstuffs such as chocolate (Luengo et al.;[70] Lee et al.[71,72]), vanilla custard (de Wijk and Prinz[69]), milk, cream, butter, ice-cream, cheese, whipped cream, desserts, sauces and mayonnaise (Giasson et al.[73]) were studied. As a result of these investigations the complex rheology and tribology of soft foodstuffs, like chocolate, have been well established. These basic characteristics may interact with sensual perspectives during mastication and food transport over the tongue.

Temporomandibular joints (TMJs) permit movement of the jaw and load transmission for activities such as biting, chewing and talking (Fig. 7). Van Loon et al.[74] prepared a historical review of TMJ prostheses covering the period 1946 1994, while Johnson[75] has outlined their biomechanics.

Temporomandibular joints are slider bearings with translations of 10–15 mm which experience small but important rotations. The mandibles rotate as the mouth opens or closes, while the axis of rotation, parallel to the coronal plane, also moves forwards and backwards. Joint loads usually range up to 100–600 N and coefficients of friction from about 0.015 to 0.025. While direct evidence of the mode of lubrication is difficult to obtain, a theoretical estimate can be made of the likely film thicknesses and compared to the surface roughness of the bearing materials (Table 4).

The estimated film thicknesses for total replacement temporomandibular joints clearly suggest that fluid-film lubrication is unlikely. For natural joints and those with replacement condyles, mixed lubrication seems to be the likely mode of

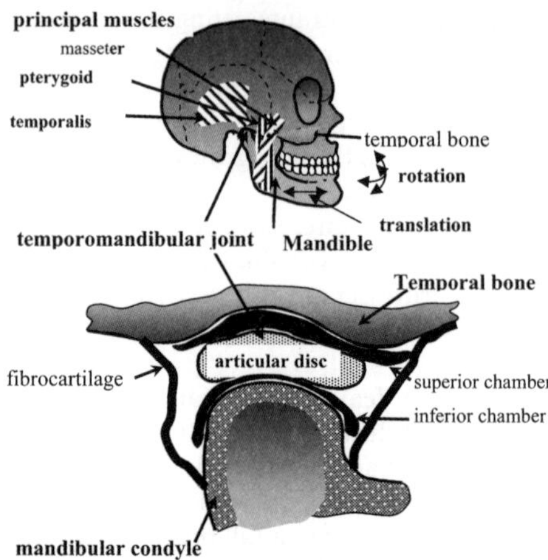

Fig. 7 Temporomandibular joint. (To be published in the book 'Biotribology' by John Wiley & Sons Ltd., 2013).

lubrication. Temporomandibular joints are versatile natural joints and generally most successful bearings.

Laboratory studies of teeth have been directed mainly towards wear. The literature is voluminous, with attention focussing upon the wear of natural tissues (enamel and dentine) and restorative materials. A collection of eight papers on oral and dental tribology has been published on this topic (Zhong-Rong and Dwyer-Joyce[76]). Dental equipment has also been considered, particularly the development of high speed drills, toothbrushes and dentifrice.

Saliva is the lubricant in the mouth, while enamel is the hardest tissue in the body. Bite forces between teeth are usually in the range 30–850 N. Measured coefficients of friction for enamel-on-enamel range from 0.2–0.6 when dry and 0.03–0.6 in saliva. Wear is mainly abrasive and corrosive and takes place at rates of 10–50 μm year^{-1}. This equates to dimensionless wear factors (K) in the range 10^{-4}–10^{-3}. Restorative materials achieve wear factors covering a wide range of 10^{-4}–10^{-1}.

2.11. Ocular tribology

Motion of the eyelid over the cornea, some 5–30 times a minute in blinking, presents a fine example of soft tissue tribology. If contact lenses are worn, the tear film between eyelid and lens and the lens–cornea present two separate tribological regions. In all three cases effective lubrication not only ensures low friction (Dowson;[77] Rennie et al.;[78] Jones et al.[79]), but protects the cells on the natural tissue and flushes minute particles away from the eyelid and the surfaces of the cornea and

Table 4 Elastohydrodynamic film thickness predictions for temporomandibular joints. (To be published in the book 'Biotribology' by John Wiley & Sons Ltd., 2013)

Material pairs	Predicted iso-viscous-elastic film thickness (nm)
Natural condyle and natural disc	11–18
UHMWPE or CoCrMo condyles and natural disc	8–13
CoCrMo condyle and UHMWPE disc	0.5–1.2
CoCrMo condyle and CoCrMo condyle	0.07–0.1

contact lens. It is more than a century since interest developed in glass contact lenses. Acrylics were then introduced, followed in the 1960s by hydrogels.

Most investigators have estimated the speed of the eyelid over the cornea, or contact lens, to be about 0.15 m s^{-1} and the shear rate to be about 10^{-4} s^{-1}. The viscosity of the tear will thus be about 30% greater than that of water. This results in calculated elasto-hydrodynamic film thicknesses as high as 8–10 µm. There is, however, a protective layered structure of mucin, some 30 µm thick, on the corneal epithelium, followed by a thin lipid rich layer about 0.1 µm thick. The central aqueous layer appears to be capable of establishing protective fluid films in blinking, but other lower speed movements, such as those involved in glancing sideways, may depend upon boundary films for protection of the eye surface.

2.12. Micro-circulation

The final example, from many aspects of bio-tribology, is the flow of red blood cells (erythrocytes) in narrow capillaries. The dished form of a red cell is shown in Fig. 8. Typical diameters are about 5–8 µm and un-stressed widths 2 µm.

Lighthill[80] recognized at an early stage that the passage of deformable erythrocytes along a close fitting tube would present an opportunity for elasto-hydrodynamic lubrication between the cell and capillary walls. He quantified the film thicknesses and revealed the typical elastohydrodynamic film profiles twixt cell and wall. Fitz-Gerald[81] quickly followed Lighthill's pioneering work and predicted that distortion of the cell under normal pressures and viscous tractions would result in a '*bullet*' or '*parachute form*' as depicted in Fig. 9.

It was also observed that the erythrocytes travelled along narrow capillaries like stacked coins. This configuration, and the associated streamlines, became the subject of considerable analysis. It was further recognised that the diameter of capillaries varied along their lengths. It was, however, a recognition of the glycocalyx on the inner wall of capillaries that prompted development of present day understanding of the subject (Secomb *et al.*[82]).

The glycocalyx consists of carbohydrate rich, long polysaccharide chains bound to a protein core with a layer thickness of 0.2–1.5 µm. This is shown in Fig. 10, alongside Hardy's 1932 concept of boundary lubrication. The distinctive features of both boundary and elasto-hydrodynamic lubrication are thus evident in the flow of red blood cells through narrow capillaries.

3.   Key issues in bio-tribology

3.1.   The importance of mixed lubrication

Two major events in tribology were undoubtedly the recognition of '*fluid-film*' and '*boundary lubrication*'. These concepts so dominated 20th and early 21st century thinking that the intermediate '*mixed*' regime attracted less than its fair share of

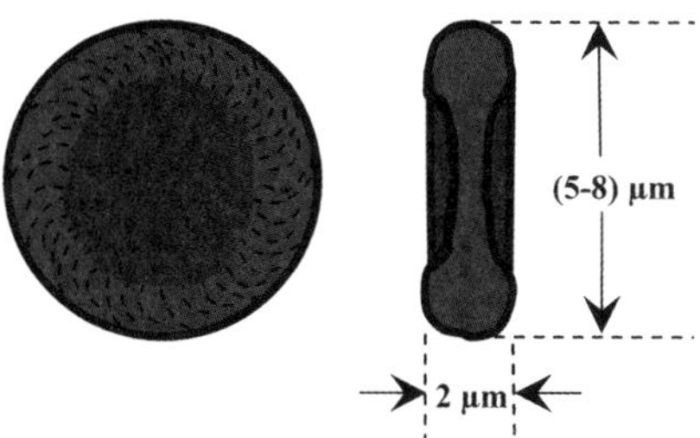

Fig. 8 Representation of dished erythrocyte. (To be published in the book 'Biotribology' by John Wiley & Sons Ltd., 2013).

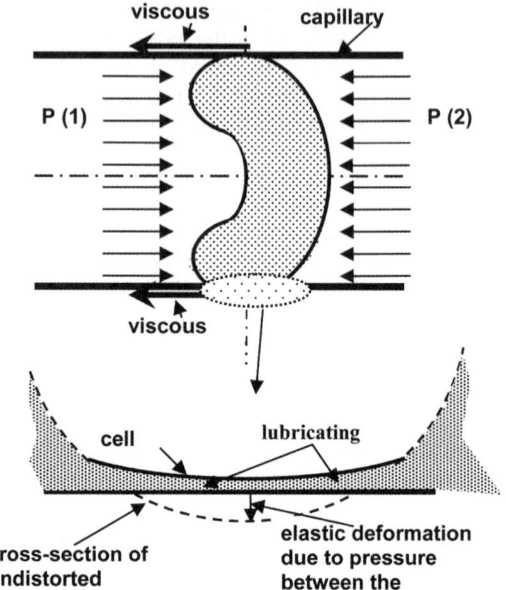

Fig. 9 'Parachute' form of flowing erythrocyte in a narrow capillary (after J. M. Fitz-Gerald, 1969). (To be published in the book 'Biotribology' by John Wiley & Sons Ltd., 2013).

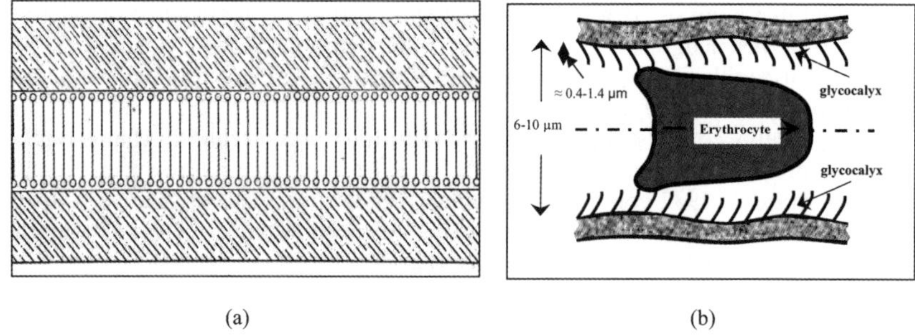

(a) (b)

Fig. 10 (a) Hardy's concept of boundary lubrication. (b) Concept of combined boundary and elasto-hydrodynamic lubrication of red blood cells. (To be published in the book 'Biotribology' by John Wiley & Sons Ltd., 2013).

attention. There is still much work to be done on this major, central lubrication regime, both in engineering tribology and bio-tribology. Load bearing is gradually transferred from *solid/boundary* to *hydrodynamic/ elastohydrodynamic* lubrication in this important zone.

It is interesting to note that different expertise and experience of investigators has often polarised views on the mode of lubrication in both *man-made* and *biological* bearings. Firm convictions about the universality of one or other of the well recognised main regimes of lubrication is unfortunately evident in the literature and debate, but this situation is by no means restricted to tribology. It would seem to be timely to encourage the adoption of a more *holistic* view if genuine progress is to be made in the field of tribology.

Most lubricated tribological components encounter, and may well be dominated by, '*mixed*' lubrication. Starting and stopping of lubricated bearings requires passage through the mixed regime, while it is often impossible to separate completely the opposing surfaces by fluid films, particularly during running-in. Likewise, designers usually try to avoid boundary lubrication as much as possible, to reduce friction and power loss and to minimise surface damage and wear. In short, the majority of bearings run under conditions of mixed lubrication for much of their operating life. This was increasingly recognised at the end of the 20th century and it is encouraging that theoretical and experimental studies of mixed lubrication in both engineering and bio-tribology are now gathering pace.

3.2. Transition

If a lubricant can develop separations of the bearing surfaces such that asperity contacts are avoided, fluid film lubrication will be achieved. A full numerical analysis of lubricated, rough surfaces is complicated and expensive, particularly if there are cyclic variations in load, speed and viscosity. It is therefore interesting to observe the development of useful empirical guide lines to assist design and manufacture.

3.2.1 Lambda ratio.
In the 1960s, Dawson[83,84] investigated the phenomenon of pitting at very high stresses. He reported that the fatigue limit was related to the dimensionless ratio (D) defined as:

$$D = \frac{\text{total initial roughness (c.l.a.)}}{\text{oil film thickness}} \tag{3}$$

a larger value of D giving rise to earlier pitting.

Wellauer[85] extended the concept to gear failure, his findings being embedded in the American Gear Manufacturers Design Guides. It was evident that the ratio of film thickness to a mean composite surface roughness (rms) in excess of 3 or 4 should avoid tooth distress. Tallian[86] confirmed the vital role of elastohydrodynamic lubrication in determining the performance and life of rolling element bearings. He studied load sharing between the elasto-hydrodynamic films (thickness h) and composite (rms) roughness. He found it helpful to determine load sharing as a function of the ratio of mean elastohydrodynamic film thickness (h) to rms roughness, now widely known as the lambda ratio (Λ). At $\Lambda = 0.3989$, the asperity contact area fraction was calculated to be 0.50, while at $\Lambda = 4.5$ it was 0.0000034, but still falling. Practical considerations generally make it very difficult to exceed lambda ratios in excess of 3 or 4.

3.3. Low elastic modulus (*soft*) tribology

Studies of elasto-hydrodynamic lubrication were originally developed in an attempt to explain the remarkable ability of very highly stressed engineering components, such as gears and rolling element bearings, to perform in the fluid film regime. Most biological tissues do not come into this category since pressures are relatively low and have a negligible effect upon viscosity, while the tissues also exhibit a relatively low elastic modulus. There have, however, been a number of analyses of the relevant iso-viscous elastic mode of lubrication which can be adopted to interpret experimental friction data and to give an insight into the film behaviour in such conjunctions.

A striking difference in both film shapes and pressure distributions is evident for the high and low modulus materials. In the former case a near parallel film is followed by a '*nip*' with a local reduction of film thickness of about 10–20%. A sudden and narrow pressure '*spike*' is often associated with this distinctive film shape. In the case of low elastic modulus materials, the lubricant film thickness decreases from inlet to outlet, sometimes almost linearly, and there is no pressure spike.

3.3.1 Lubrication regimes for *in vitro* friction experiments on '*soft*' biological tissue.
A number of laboratory tests on biological tissue, such as the synovial

membrane, menisci, fat pads and tendons, have revealed that fluid film lubrication can be established under some conditions.

A number of solutions to the low elastic modulus problem (Dowson and Yao[87]) have shown that the pressure distribution is remarkably symmetrical about the midpoint of the deformed region. The central film thickness, (H_{cen}) where the pressure is a maximum, can be written as

$$H_{cen} = \frac{h_{cen}}{R} \propto \frac{U^{0.54}}{W^{0.18}}$$

(4)

where

$$U = \frac{(\eta u)}{(E'R)}$$

and

$$W = \frac{(w)}{(E'R^2)}.$$

In most friction experiments one member is held stationary while the other slides past it with velocity (u_1) and if the effective modulus of elasticity (E') and radius in the entraining direction (R) remain constant, the coefficient of friction for a viscous fluid in Couette flow over a sheared area (A) can be written as

$$\mu = \frac{(\eta u_1)}{(h)} \cdot \frac{(A)}{(w)} \propto \frac{(\eta u_1)^{0.46}}{(w)^{0.82}} (A)$$

(5)

Rheological experiments have indicated that the viscosity of synovial fluid falls with increasing shear rate until it is sensibly constant and very similar to that of water at shear rates in excess of about 10^4–10^5 s^{-1}. If it is further assumed that the area (A) is given approximately by the Hertzian relationship, $A \propto (w)^{2/3}$, the coefficient of friction should follow the relationship

$$\mu \propto \frac{(u_1)^{0.46}}{(w)^{0.15}}$$

(6)

If experimental data for the coefficient of friction follows this relationship, it is a good indication that the iso-viscous elastic lubrication regime was operative.

3.4. Pre-clinical simulation

The widespread adoption of total joint replacement in orthopaedics has made it desirable, and indeed essential, to subject new materials and joints to laboratory testing prior to implantation in the body. In the majority of cases, the implants are subjected to internationally agreed representations of the loading and motion encountered in steady walking. Repetitive cycles are applied over several weeks or months to enable predictions to be made of implant performance over the initial years. Material loss from the implant components is recorded and comparisons made of wear, and increasingly of friction and corrosion. Current indications are that a considerable proportion of the material loss previously attributed to mechanical wear is associated with tribo-corrosion.

In all simulation work in tribology it is essential that the service conditions should be replicated as accurately as possible in the laboratory tests. The difficulties encountered when simulating tribological characteristics of engineering components can be difficult enough, but when some other significant factor or environment is involved, such as scale in nano-tribology, space, high temperature or biological, the problems can be even more acute. Joint simulators have become ever more sophisticated since their introduction in the 1930s. The test conditions may nevertheless fall short of the clinical environment and functioning. For example, the test fluid may not replicate significant features of synovial fluid, while the repetitive load cycle for walking hardly represents the nature or magnitude of daily activity. A vivid recognition of the latter was presented by Bowsher *et al.*[88] When the repetitive loading cycle represented fast jogging, rather than steady walking, the wear in metal-on-metal hip replacements increased by a factor of seven, there was a significant increase in the number of wear particles and a thirty three percent increase in mean wear particle diameter.

Recommendations for simulator comparisons of the tribological performance of total replacement joints to be based upon more realistic daily cycles of activity, kinematics and loading, with lubrication conditions as close as possible to those in the biological environment are attracting increasing attention.

References

1 B. Tower, First report on friction experiments (friction of lubricated bearings), *Proceedings of the Institution of Mechanical Engineers*, November 1883, pp. 632–659.
2 O. Reynolds, On the theory of lubrication and its application to Mr. Beauchamp Tower's experiments, including an experimental determination of the viscosity of olive oil, *Philos. Trans. R. Soc. London*, 1886, **177**, 157–234.
3 W. B. Hardy and I. Doubleday, Boundary lubrication-the paraffin series, *Proc. R. Soc. London, Ser. A*, 1922, **100**, 550–574.
4 W. B. Hardy and I. Doubleday, Boundary lubrication-the temperature coefficient, *Proc. R. Soc. London, Ser. A*, 1922, **101**, 487–492.
5 DSIR, Report of the lubricants and lubrication inquiry committee, *Advisory Council of the Department of Scientific and Industrial Research*, HMSO, London, 1920.
6 A. G. M. Mitchell, Improvements in thrust and like bearings, *Br. Pat.*, 875, 1905.
7 A. Kingsbury, Thrust bearings, *U.S. Pat.*, 947242, 1910.
8 J. F. Booker, Dynamically loaded journal bearings-mobility method of solution, *Trans. Am. Soc. Mech. Eng.*, 1971, **D187**, 537.
9 A. N. Grubin and I. E. Vinogradova, *Investigation of the contact of machine components*, ed. Kh. F. Ketova, Central Scientific Research Institute for Technology and Mechanical Engineering, Moscow, Book 30, DSIR Translation No. 337, 1949.
10 D. Dowson and G. R. Higginson, *Elasto-hydrodynamic lubrication–The fundamentals of roller and gear lubrication*, Pergamon Press, Oxford, 1966, pp. 1 235.
11 R. H. Thurston, *A treatise on friction and lost work in machinery and millwork*, Wiley, New York, 7th edn, 1885, p. 1903.
12 R. Stribeck, Die Wesentlichen Eigenschaften der Gleit und Rollenlager, *Z. Ver. Dt. Ing.*, 1902, **46**, No. 38, 1341–8; 1432–8; No. 39, 1463–70.
13 A. Sommerfeld, Zur hydrodynamischen theorie der schmiermittehreibung, *Z. Math. Phys.*, 1904, **50**, 97–155.
14 L. Gümbel, Das problem der lagerreibung, Mbl. Berl. BezVer. Dt. Ing. (VDI), 1914, 1 Apr. and No. 5, May, 6 June, 87–104 and 109–20 July 1916.
15 M. Scherge and S. N. Gorb, *Biological micro-and nanotribology*, Springer-Verlag, Berlin, 2001, pp. 1–304.
16 R. McN Alexander, *Animal Mechanics*, Sidgwick & Jackson, London, 1968.
17 J. D. Currey, *Animal Skeletons, The institute of biology's studies in biology no. 22*, Edward Arnold (Publishers) Ltd, 1970, pp. 1–52.
18 J. D. Currey, Properties of bone, cartilage, and synovial fluid; (A. Bone), in *Introduction to the biomechanics of joints and joint replacement*, ed. D. Dowson and V. Wright, Mechanical Engineering Publications Ltd., London, 1981, ch. 12, pp. 103–119.
19 H. C. Berg, Constraints on models for the flagellar rotary motor, *Philos. Trans. R. Soc. London, Ser. B*, 2000, **355**, 491–501.
20 R. M. Berry, Theories of rotary motors, *Philos. Trans. R. Soc. London, Ser. B*, 2000, **355**, 503–509.
21 *Friction, lubrication and wear of artificial joints*, ed. I. M. Hutchings, Professional Engineering Publishing, Bury St. Edmunds, U.K., 2003, pp. 1–134.
22 A. Kobayashi, I. Yamamoto and T. Aoyama, Tribology of a snail (terrestrial gastropod), *Proceedings of the 29th. Leeds-Lyon Symposium on Tribology, 'Tribological Research and Design for Engineering Systems'*, Elsevier B.V., Tribology Series 41, 2003, pp. 429–436.

23 W. Hunter, Of the structure and diseases of articulating cartilages, *Philos. Trans. R. Soc.*, 1743, **42**, 514–521.

24 B. B. Seedhom, Bio-mechanics of the lower limb; The knee, in *An introduction to the bio-mechanics of joints and joint replacement*, ed. D. Dowson and V. Wright, Mechanical Engineering Publications Ltd, London, 1981, pp. 73–81.

25 M. A. MacConaill, The function of intra-articular fibrocartilages, *J. Anat.*, 1932, **66**, 210–267.

26 E. S. Jones, Joint lubrication, *Lancet*, 1936, **227**, 1043–1045.

27 L. Dintenfass, Lubrication in synovial joints: A theoretical analysis, *J. Bone Joint Surg.*, 1963, **45A**(6), 1241–1256.

28 D. Dowson, Modes of lubrication in human joints, *Proceedings of the Institution of Mechanical Engineers, 1966-1967, part 3J*, 1967, **181**, 45–54.

29 J. Charnley, The lubrication of animal joints in relation to surgical reconstruction by arthroplasty, *Ann. Rheum. Dis.*, 1960, **19**, 10–19.

30 D. V. Davies, C. H. Barnett, W. Cochrane and A. J. Palfrey, Electron microscopy of articular cartilage in the young adult rabbit, *Ann. Rheum. Dis.*, 1962, **21**, 11.

31 D. A. Swann and E. L. Radin, The molecular basis of articular lubrication:1, Purification and properties of a lubricating fraction from bovine synovial fluid, *J. Biol. Chem.*, 1972, **247**, 8069–8073.

32 B. A. Hills and B. D. Butler, Surfactants identified in synovial fluid and their ability to act as boundary lubricants, *Ann. Rheum. Dis.*, 1984, **43**, 641–648.

33 B. A. Hills, Boundary lubrication in vivo, *Proc. Inst. Mech. Eng., Part H*, 2000, **214**, 83–94.

34 G. A. Ateshian, A theoretical model for boundary friction in articular cartilage, in *Proceedings of the 4th. China-Japan-USA-Singapore Conference on Biomechanics*, ed. K. Yang, K. Hayashi, SL.-Y. Woo *et al.*, 1995, pp. 142–145.

35 J. E. Pickard, J. Fisher, E. Ingham and J. Egan, Investigation into the effects of proteins and lipids on the frictional properties of articular cartilage, *Biomaterials*, 1998, **19**, 1807–1812.

36 A. Unsworth, Tribology of human and artificial joints, *Proc. Inst. Mech. Eng., Part H*, 1991, **205**, 163–172.

37 D. Dowson and Z.-M. Jin, 'Micro-Elastohydrodynamic Lubrication of Synovial Joints', *Eng. Med.*, 1986, **15**(2), 63–65.

38 C. W. McCutchen, The frictional properties of animal joints, *Wear*, 1962, **5**(1), 1–17.

39 R. S. Fein, Are synovial joints squeeze-film lubricated?, *Proceedings of the Institution of Mechanical Engineers, 1966-1967, part 3J*, 1967, **181**, 125–128.

40 G. R. Higginson and A. Unsworth, The lubrication of natural joints, in *Tribology of natural and artificial joints*, ed. Dumbleton, Elsevier, 1981, ch. 3, pp. 47–72.

41 A. Maroudas, Hyaluronic acid films, *Proceedings of the Institution of Mechanical Engineers, 1966–1967, part 3J*, 1967, **181**, 122–124.

42 P. S. Walker, D. Dowson, M. D. Longfield and V. Wright, *'Boosted Lubrication'* in Synovial Joints by Fluid Entrapment and Enrichment, *Ann. Rheum. Dis.*, 1968, **27**(6), 512–520.

43 V. C. Mow and W. M. Lai, Recent developments in synovial joint biomechanics, *SIAM Rev.*, 1980, **22**, 275–317.

44 T. Murakami, N. Ohtsuki and H. Higaki, The adaptive multimode lubrication in biotribological systems, *Proceedings of the International Tribology Conference*, Yokohama, 1995, pp. 1–6.

45 J. Edwards, Physical characteristics of articular cartilage, *Proceedings of the Institution of Mechanical Engineers, 1966–1967, part 3J*, 1967, **181**, 16–24.

46 C. W. McCutchen, Physiological lubrication, *Proceedings of the Institution of Mechanical Engineers, 1966–1967, part 3J*, 1967, **181**, 55–62.

47 G. E. Kempson, Mechanical properties of articular cartilage, in *Adult Articular Cartilage*, ed. M. A. R. Freeman, Pitman Medical, 1973, pp. 171–227.

48 G. A. Ateshian, A theoretical formulation for boundary friction in articular cartilage, *J. Biomech. Eng.*, 1997, **119**, 81–86.

49 H. Forster and J. Fisher, The influence of loading time and lubricant on the friction of articular cartilage, *Proc. Inst. Mech. Eng., Part H*, 1996, **210**, 109–119.

50 H. Forster and J. Fisher, The influence of continuous sliding and subsequent surface wear on the friction of articular cartilage, *Proc. Inst. Mech. Eng., Part H*, 1999, **213**, 329–345.

51 C.-Y. Huang, V. C. Mow and G. A. Ateshian, The role of flow-independent viscoelasticity in the biphasic tensile and compressive responses of articular cartilage, *J. Biomech. Eng.*, 2001, **123**, 410–417.

52 H. Spikes, The borderline of elastohydrodynamic and boundary lubrication, *Proceedings of the Institution of Mechanical Engineers*, 2000, **214**, 23–37.

53 W. H. Briscoe, S. Titmuss, F. Tiberg, R. K. Thomas, D. J. McGillivray and J. Klein, Boundary lubrication under water, *Nature*, 2006, **444**, 191–194.

54 J. T. Scales, Arthroplasty of the hip using foreign materials: a history, *Proceedings of the Institution of Mechanical Engineers, 1966–1967, part 3J*, 1967, **181**, 63–84.

55 G. K. McKee, Developments in total hip joint replacement, *Proceedings of the Institution of Mechanical Engineers, 1966–1967, part 3J*, 1967, **181**, 85–89.

56 J. Charnley, *Low friction arthroplasty of the hip; theory and practice*, Springer-Verlag, Berlin, Heidelberg, New York, 1979, pp. 1–376.

57 D. Dowson, Are our joint materials adequate, Proceedings of the Institution of Mechanical Engineers, *Journal of Engineering in Medicine, part H*, 1991, **205**, 1–10.

58 A. Unsworth, M. J. Pearcy, E. F. T. White and G. White, Soft layer lubrication of artificial hip joints, *I.Mech.E. Conference on Tribology-Friction, Lubrication and wear, 50 years on, Paper C219/87*, Mechanical Engineering Publications, 1987, pp. 715–724.

59 P. H. Corkhill, A. S. Trevett and B. J. Tighe, Potential of hydrogels as synthetic articular cartilage, *Proc. Inst. Mech. Eng., Part H*, 1990, **204**, 147–155.

60 D. D. Auger, D. Dowson and J. Fisher, Cushion form bearings for total knee joint replacement, *Proceedings of the Institution of Mechanical Engineers*, 1995, volume 209, part 1: Design, friction and lubrication, pp. 73–81, Part 2: Wear and durability, pp. 83–91, in medicine, volume 204, pp. 147–155.

61 T. Murakami, Y. Sawae, K. Nakashima and J. Fisher, Tribological behaviour of artificial cartilage in thin film lubrication, in *Thinning films and Tribological Interfaces, Interface Engineering Series 38*, ed. D. Dowson *et al.*, Elsevier Sciences, 2000, pp. 312–327.

62 E. L. Radin, D. A. Swann and P. A. Weisser, Separation of a hyaluronate-free lubricating fraction from synovial fluid, *Nature*, 1970, **228**, 377–378.

63 D. A. Swann and E. L. Radin, The molecular basis of articular lubrication: Purification and properties of a lubricating fraction from bovine synovial fluid, *J. Biol. Chem.*, 1972, **247**, 8069–8073.

64 D. A. Swann, F. H. Silver and H. S. Slater, The molecular structure and lubricating activity of lubricin from bovine and human synovial fluids, *J. Biochem.*, 1985, **225**, 195–201.

65 H. Higaki and T. Murakami, Role of constituents in synovial fluid and surface layer of the articular cartilage in joint lubrication (Part 1): Experimental study in application of enzyme digestion, *Jpn. J. Tribol.*, 1994, **39**(7), 859–869.

66 M. J. Adams, B. J. Briscoe and S. A. Johnson, Friction and lubrication of human skin, *Tribol. Lett.*, 2007, **26**(3), 239–253.

67 S. A. Johnson, D. M. Gorman, M. J. Adams and B. J. Briscoe, The friction and lubrication of human stratum corneum, in *Thin Films in Tribology*, ed. D. Dowson *et al.*, Proceedings of the 19th. Leeds-Lyon Symposium on Tribology, Elsevier Science Publishers, B.V., 1993, pp. 663–672.

68 H. Valentová and J. Pokorný, Effects of edible oils and oil emulsions on the perception of basic tastes, *Nahrung*, 1998, **42**, 406–408.

69 R. A. de Wijk and J. F. Prinz, The role of friction in perceived oral texture, *Food Qual. Preference*, 2005, **16**, 121–129.

70 G. Luengo, M. Tsuchiya, M. Heuberger and J. Israelachvili, Thin film rheology and tribology of chocolate, *J. Food Sci.*, 1997, **62**(4), 767–772.

71 S. Lee, M. Heuberger, P. Rousset and N. D. Spencer, Chocolate at a sliding interface, *J. Food Sci.*, 2002, **67**(7), 2712–2717.

72 S. Lee, M. Heuberger, P. Rousset and N. D. Spencer, A tribological model for chocolate in the mouth: General implications for slurry-lubricated hard/soft sliding counterfaces, *Tribol. Lett.*, 2004, **16**(3), 239–249, April.

73 S. Giasson, J. Israelachvili and H. Yoshizawa, Thin film morphology and tribology study of mayonnaise, *J. Food Sci.*, 1997, **62**(4), 640–645.

74 J.-P. van Loon, L. G. M. de Bont and G. Boering, Evaluation of temporomandibular joint prostheses, Review of the literature from 1946–1994 and implications for future prosthesis designs, *J. Oral Maxillofacial Surg.*, 1995, **53**, 984–996.

75 G. R. Johnson, Biomechanics of joints, in *Joint Replacement technology*, ed. P. A. Revell, Woodhead Publishing Limited, Cambridge, England and CRC Press, Boca Raton, USA, 2008, ch. 1, pp. 26–27.

76 Zhou Zhong-Rong and R. S. Dwyer-Joyce, Special issue on oral and dental tribology, Proceedings of the Institution of Mechanical Engineers, *Journal of Engineering Tribology, Part J*, 2010, **224**(6), 519–594.

77 D. Dowson, A tribological day, *Proceedings of the Institution of Mechanical Engineers, Journal of Engineering Tribology, Part J*, 2009, **223**, 261–273.

78 A. C. Rennie, P. L. Dickrell and W. G. Sawyer, Friction coefficient of soft contact lenses: measurement and modelling, *Tribol. Lett.*, 2005, **18**(4), 499–504.

79 M. B. Jones, G. R. Fulford, C. P. Please, D. L. S. McElwain and M. J. Collins, Elastohydrodynamics of the eyelid wiper, *Bull. Math. Biol.*, 2008, **70**, 323–343.

80 M. J. Lighthill, Pressure-forcing of tightly fitting pellets along fluid-filled elastic tubes, *J. Fluid Mech.*, 1968, **34**(01), 113–143.

81 J. M. Fitz-Gerald, Mechanics of red-cell motion through very narrow capillaries, *Proc. R. Soc. London, Ser. B*, 1969, **174**, 193–227.

82 T. W. Secomb, R. Hsu and A. R. Pries, Tribology of capillary blood flow, Proceedings of the Institution of Mechanical Engineers, *Proc Inst. Mech. Eng., Part J*, 2006, **220**(8), 767–774.

83 P. H. Dawson, Effect of metallic contact on the pitting of lubricated rolling surfaces, *J. Mech. Eng. Sci.*, 1962, **4**(1), 16–21.

84 P. H. Dawson, The effect of metallic contact and sliding on the shape of the S-N curve for pitting fatigue, *Institution of Mechanical Engineers, Proceedings of the Symposium on Fatigue in Rolling Contact*, 1964, pp. 41–45.

85 E. J. Wellauer, AGMA experience in establishing coordinated gear rating standards, invited paper presented to the Semi-International Symposium, *Japan Society of Mechanical Engineers*, 1967.

86 T. E. Tallian, The theory of partial elastohydrodynamic contacts, *Wear*, 1972, **21**, 49–101.

87 D. Dowson and J. Q. Yao, Elastohydrodynamic lubrication of soft-layered solids at elliptical contacts, Part 2: film thickness analysis, *Proc. Inst. Mech. Eng., Part J*, 1994, **208**, 43–52.

88 J. G. Bowsher, A. Hussain, P. A. Williams and J. C. Shelton, Metal-on-metal hip simulator study of increased wear particle surface area due to 'severe' patient activity, *Proc. Inst. Mech. Eng., Part H*, 2006, **220**(2), 279–287.

Cell friction

T. E. Angelini,[a] A. C. Dunn,[a] J. M. Urueña,[a] D. J. Dickrell, III,[a] D. L. Burris[b] and W. G. Sawyer[a]

Received 14th December 2011, Accepted 1st February 2012
DOI: 10.1039/c2fd00130f

Cells sense and respond to their environment. Mechanotransduction is the process by which mechanical forces, stress, and strains are converted into biochemical signals that control cell behavior. In recent decades it has been shown that appropriate mechanical signals are essential to tissue health, but the role of friction and direct contact shearing across cell surfaces has been essentially unexplored. This, despite the obvious existence of numerous biological tissues whose express function depends on sliding contacts. In our studies on frictional interactions of corneal cells we find that the friction coefficients are on the order of $\mu = 0.03$–0.06 for *in vitro* and *in vivo* experiments. Additionally, we observe cell death after single cycles of sliding at contact pressures estimated to be $\sim$12 kPa. These experimental results suggest that frictional contact forces produce mechanical stresses and strains that are in the cellular mechanosensing ranges.

1. Introduction

The human body is an extremely complex moving mechanical assembly of living tissue, with a myriad of contacting interfaces. In tissues, the cell's ability to sense and respond to static and dynamic mechanical cues is essential to physiological processes in development, health and disease;[1,2] mechanical sensing by the cell is implicated in wound healing, angiogenesis, stem cell differentiation, cancer metastasis, and tissue homeostasis.[1–6] Cells sense mechanical signals through mechanotransduction, the process by which physical strains are converted into intracellular biochemical signals, analogous to the conversion of mechanical strain into electrical current in piezoelectric transducers.[7] Mechanotransduction elicits many types of active cellular responses. A cell senses the stiffness of its surroundings and generates increased contractile forces when adhered to increasingly stiff materials.[8] The higher level of contractility results in higher levels of tensile stress within the cell, stiffening the cell itself.[9] Moreover, at higher levels of contraction, the cell increases the strength of its adhesions to remain attached to its surroundings, which modulates cell shape, surface spreading, and migration rate.[8,10] Thus, the material properties of a tissue feed back to cell mechanical behaviors through mechanotransduction to influence tissue function or malfunction.

Just as cells are sensitive to their static extracellular mechanical environment, dynamic forces and stresses will also elicit cellular responses. The complexity of tissues and organs within living organisms allow for many types of forces to be generated within tissues and between contacting tissues. Great progress has been made in understanding mechanotransduction in cell–ECM interactions and cell–cell interactions, in which forces are transmitted directly through adhesions. However, forces can be transmitted through sliding contacts, from cell to cell,

[a]Dept. of Mechanical and Aerospace Engineering, University of Florida, Gainesville, FL, 32611, USA
[b]Dept. of Mechanical Engineering, University of Delaware, Newark, DE, 19716, USA

from ECM to cell, or from tissue to tissue. Although sliding contacts are tremendously numerous in living organisms, the role of friction forces in mechanotransduction has been almost entirely unexplored.[11] Here we report on our *in vitro* and *in vivo* effort to measure friction coefficients under direct contact stimulation.

2.   Mechanotransduction: a biochemical stress–strain sensor

Cells in tissues are anchored to an extracellular matrix (ECM) or to other cells by membrane-bound adhesion proteins. When a cell is strained, the membrane-bound proteins are physically forced to undergo conformational changes, exposing otherwise hidden domains to the intracellular cytoplasm, or to the extracellular space. These exposed domains bind signaling molecules, setting off a cascade of shifts in biochemical equilibria which, ultimately, results in changes in gene expression. By this mechano-chemical process, physical forces can mediate the expression levels and the activity of cytoskeletal filaments, motor proteins, adhesion proteins, and adenosine tri-phosphate (ATP). In turn, the expression levels and activities of these cytoskeletal components create a mechanical feedback, mediating cell-generated forces and the elasticity of the cell itself.

When a single cell probes its surroundings, mechanotransduction occurs by the action of the cell and the response of the environment. The cytoskeleton of a cell in isolation, anchored to a solid surface through membrane proteins, contracts to sense the stiffness of the substrate. If the substrate is very compliant, the elastic restoring forces are low, and the cell must generate high levels of strain to unfold the mechanotransductive proteins. By contrast, if the substrate is very rigid, the mechanotransductive proteins will unfold at low levels of average cell-generated strain. Through this mechanosensitive mechanism, the cell actively responds to the stiffness of its substrate. The cell responds to a stiffer substrate by exerting higher levels of stress, increasing its adhesion to the surface, and stiffening its cytoskeleton.[8–10] Remarkably, the same correspondence between substrate stiffness, stress generation, and intracellular cell stiffness occurs in tissues; compliant neural tissue, less-compliant soft tissue, and rigid bone tissue follow this trend.[1] Moreover, substrate stiffness and mechanosensing is essential for most cell types to proliferate in culture.

Cells sense externally imposed forces through mechanotransduction. Spatially separated cells can sense one another by straining a shared substrate,[12] and confluent layers of cells transmit forces over long distances through cell–cell junctions and cell–substrate adhesions, resulting in a macroscopic tug-of-war among hundreds of thousands of cells.[13,14] Individual cells can sense shear flows; leukocyte activation is triggered by the mechanotransduction of fluid shear stresses at the blood vessel wall.[15] Individual cells held between microcantilevers or held in optical cell stretchers exhibit active responses to externally applied forces.[16] These responses suggest that tissue cells at interfaces sense contact and friction through the same mechanotransductive mechanisms.

3.   Friction in living tissues

Exciting advances over the past decade have moved the traditional engineering field of tribology to the point of considering macroscopic interfaces in atomic and molecular terms. These developments have entailed ultra-low force measurements sensitive to the rupture of single chemical bonds and friction measurements spatially resolved to the level of individual atoms. The opportunity now exists to address the role of tribological action within biological systems, seeking to characterize, understand, and exploit, cellular interfaces and interactions on a molecular scale.

The most frequently discussed biological bearing surface is articular cartilage; unfortunately, cartilage's remarkable ability to provide low friction and pain free motion is most obviously appreciated when it is lost (*e.g.* various forms of arthritis). The body also contains a number of other visible tribological systems such as the eye, skin, and teeth (Fig. 1 and 2). In the case of eyes and knees, the lubrication mechanisms rely on the maintenance of the aqueous environment and the health of the cell surfaces.

Cartilage lubrication: the role of fluid pressurization

Articular cartilage is the tribological material in diarthrodial joints and consists of approximately 75% water and 25% cells and extracellular matrix (chondrocytes, collagen, and proteoglycans). Cartilage possesses a time-dependent mechanical response that serves critical roles during joint loading and sliding, controlled by the permeability and the bulk or aggregate modulus of the tissue.[17,18] *In vivo* contact stresses in joints of humans, sheep, dogs, and cats lie in the range from 0.5–5 MPa,[19] which is surprising considering the aggregate modulus of cartilage is in the same range (0.5–1 MPa).[17,20,21] These joint contact pressures are in part supported by fluid pressure, where the interstitial fluid supports more than 90% of the normal stress. This fluid pressurization increases load capacity while reducing matrix stresses and friction.[22] Interstitial fluid pressure is maintained between moving contacts, but is not maintained under the typical cartilage mechanics and stationary contact friction studies.[23] Interstitial lubrication is sustained through motion *in vivo*[24] and friction coefficients are maintained in the range from $\mu = 0.02$–0.03.[23,25,26]

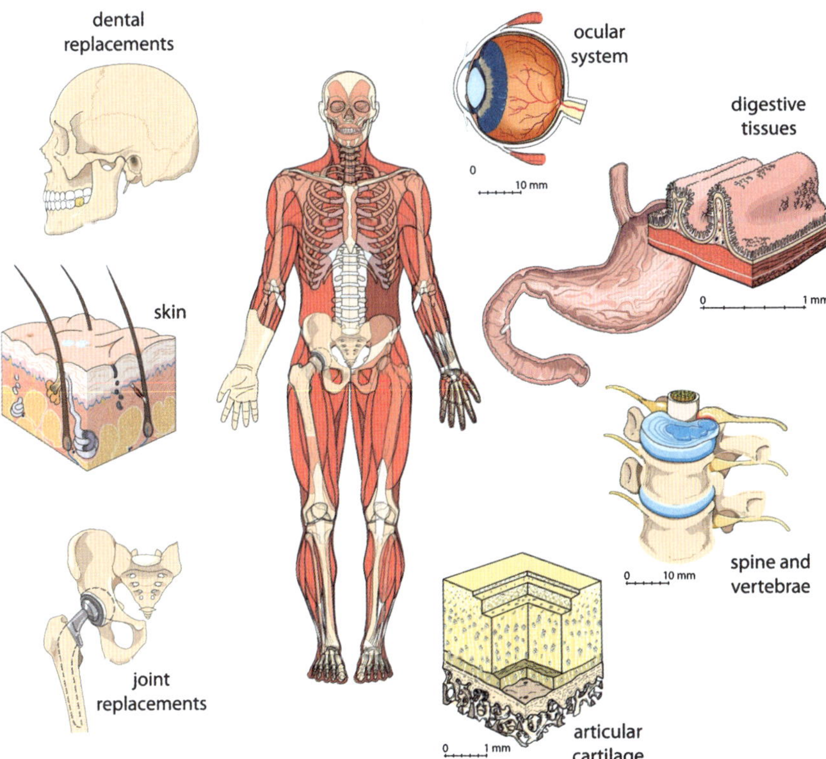

Fig. 1 The human body has a wide variety of contacting surfaces, and for most natural tribological systems from joints to eyes these contacts could be accurately described as soft. However, the pressure demands on these surfaces vary widely, from MPa in joints to single kPa in the eye. The cells that make up the intimate areas of contact have unique adaptations to enable low friction and provide durability. To date, upon failure of the systems engineering has provided materials systems to restore some degree of function (joint replacements, hernia repairs, bone fusion, crowns, stents, *etc.*). The future holds opportunities for regenerative medicine and tissue engineering to radically change the treatment strategies.

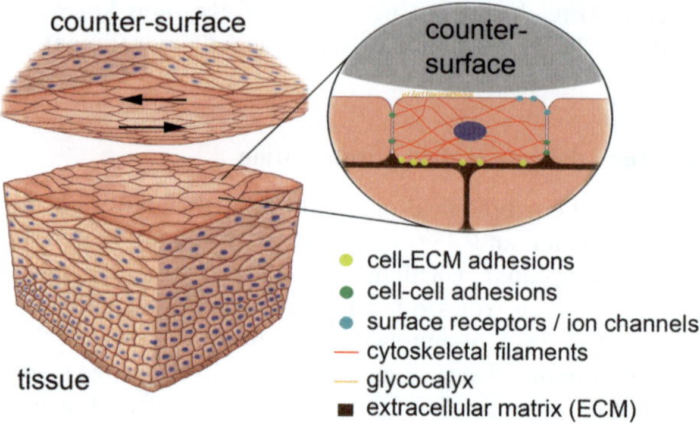

Fig. 2 Sliding interfaces in the body experience frictional forces. These contacts exist between the surfaces of tissues and counter surfaces, including adjacent tissues or foreign bodies. Friction forces can elicit mechanotransductive responses in interfacial cells by deforming cell–ECM adhesions (focal adhesion complexes), cell–cell adherens junctions, the extracellular glycocalyx layer, or surface receptors and mechanosensitive ion channels.

Interstitial pressurization effectively shields the matrix from the applied contact stress.[27,28] While the apparent contact pressure in a joint can reach 5 MPa,[19] it can be shown that the time constant for depressurization is on the order of 10 hours.[17,29] Motion serves to continuously replenish interstitial pressure, and thus reduces matrix stresses, friction and wear by more than an order of magnitude.

Cornea lubrication: boundary and hydrodynamic lubrication

The cornea, which is the optical portal to the visual system, is also a tribological system. The cornea forms a dense, transparent connective tissue barrier that protects the eye. Most tribological studies of friction and lubricity in the eye focus on the hydrodynamic lubrication that occurs during the blink; however, recent work with contact lenses points to boundary lubrication being the key to providing comfort and maintaining lubricity during extended wear.[30–33] Microtribological friction measurements on confluent layers of corneal epithelial cells gives friction coefficients on the order of $\mu = 0.03$.

Maintenance of the proper cellular and extracellular matrix composition of the cornea is also essential to its function. The external surface of the cornea is lined with a thin epithelium composed of 5–6 layers of fibroblastic cells that form a protective layer over the corneal stroma. These cells rapidly regenerate the epithelium following injury. Trauma, inflammation or infection can have profound influences on the cells and extracellular matrix of the cornea, and in turn directly impact visual acuity. For example, damage to the corneal stroma can induce the local keratocytes to differentiate into mitotic fibroblastic cells that secrete altered extracellular matrix components, resulting in stromal scar formation and reduced transparency (cornea).

Bone, teeth, skin: cell generated structural materials

Bone, teeth and skin are also important tribological materials, but unlike cartilage and the cornea, the contacting surfaces are not cellular. The cells that generate and maintain these structures are sensitive to mechanical extracellular stimulation. However, these cells are not themselves the primary interface in direct contact and tribology.

4.   Corneal tribology *in vitro* and *in vivo*

The stratified epithelial cells of the cornea form the protective barrier for the eye, and work together with the eyelid and tear film to provide low friction and low stress lubrication during ocular activity. Similar stratified epithelial cells can be found in the lung and mouth, and interestingly as linings of blood vessels and pericardium.

In vitro experiments with human corneal epithelial cells

Tribological experiments on corneal epithelial cells were performed using a micro-tribometer, which consist of a flexure based biaxial load transducer on a series of piezo-positioning stages. This apparatus can simultaneously apply the normal force while measuring the friction force response. The displacement of the flexure was measured *via* capacitive sensors. These tribometers and the associated uncertainties have been previously reported in the literature.[34,35] In these experiments with cells the goal is to perform direct contact friction measurements on living cells, which require very fine load control with low contact pressures and relatively low sliding speeds to eliminate hydrodynamic effects.

The cells used in this study were immortalized human corneal epithelial cells and the cell culture process is more completely described in prior publications;[36–38] briefly, they were cultured in a 1 : 1 blend of Dulbecco's Modified Eagle's Medium and Ham's F12 media (DMEM/F12) containing 200 U ml^{-1} each of penicillin and streptomycin, 5% (v/v) fetal bovine serum (FBS), 0.1 µg cholera toxin ml^{-1}, 0.5% (v/v) dimethyl sulfoxide, 5 µg insulin ml^{-1}, and 10 ng human epidermal growth factor ml^{-1}. When the single cell layers reached confluence they were rinsed in Hank's Balanced Salt Solution and detached with 0.25% (w/v) trypsin-EDTA, and then subsequently seeded into the specialized cell holders at a density between 5×10^4 and 1×10^5 cells cm^{-2}. The cells were then subcultured within the holder for approximately 24 h so that 100% confluency was reached before frictional testing was performed. The cultured cell density as measured optically was 2 750 cells mm^{-2}. Before and after testing, cells were submerged in 10% trypan blue staining in order to evaluate damage before and after tribological testing.

In order to perform friction experiments on a single layer of cells a special pin sample made from a hydrogel was prepared. The hydrogel material was taken from a commercially available contact lens, and had a bulk modulus of approximately 250 kPa. As a contacting probe, the hydrogel was bent around a spherical pin giving a radius of curvature of approximately 1 mm. Experiments were performed under a contacting load of 500 µN, and 2–20 cycles of reciprocation were performed (see schematic in Fig. 3a). The contact pressure was estimated to be on the order of 12 kPa (based on the imaging of cell disturbances and elastic contact models). Fig. 3b shows the surface of the cells after 5 cycles of sliding. There are clearly a number of dead cells (dark stained) within the contacting zone. The friction loop (friction coefficient *vs.* track position) for a representative cycle of testing is also shown. Based on all of our experiments the friction coefficient between a hydrated hydrogel and the living epithelial cells is $\mu = 0.03$. After cell death and detachment the friction coefficients rise approaching $\mu = 0.06$ (Fig. 3c), which is the value that we have seen for hydrogels in aqueous environments containing proteins when run against highly polished glass surfaces.

In vivo experiments with murine corneas

A portable microtribometer was designed and constructed with the express purpose of performing friction experiments on animals. In this configuration, the flexures and the probe move on a multi-axis piezoelectric stage and the animal is held stationary under the frictional probe. The same experimental uncertainties regarding the measurements of forces apply ($\sim$20 µN), and the dynamic effects are negligible at the 250 µm s^{-1} sliding speeds.

The mouse used in this study was a C57 black 6, widely used for models of human disease. The mouse was first anesthetized using isoflurane 2–5% mixed with air, then the head was immobilized in a three-point stereotactic restrainer that provided

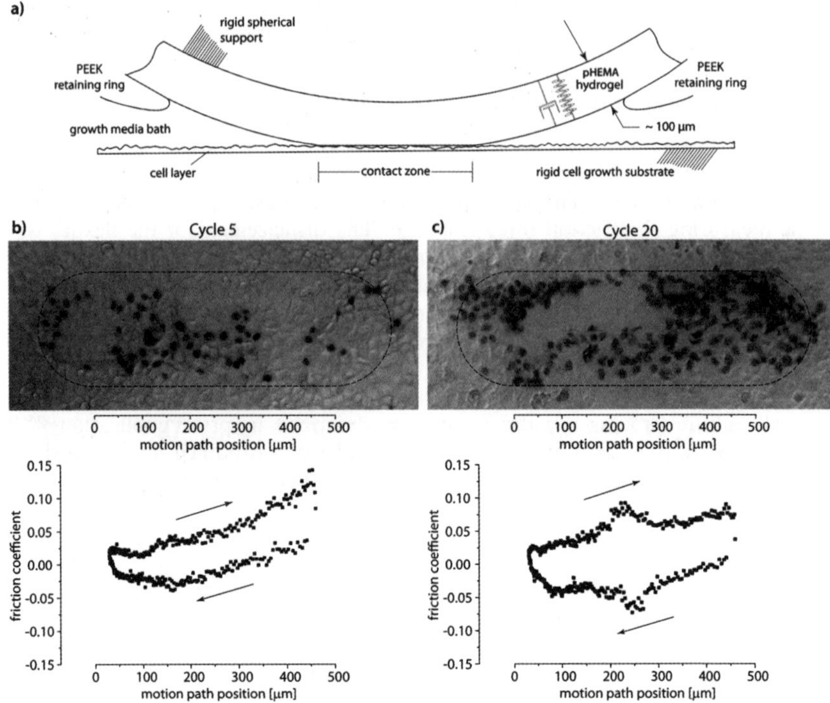

Fig. 3 Direct contact experiments under a 500 μN load on a confluent layer of epithelial cells. a) shows a schematic of the contact geometry, where there is only a single layer of cells trapped between the pHEMA hydrogel and the plastic growth plate. b) and c) show a bright field microscope image of the cell surfaces after experimentation. The dark spots are cells that have died during testing. Below each image is a friction loop for the corresponding cycle (5 or 20) respectively. The estimated contact zone is illustrated on the optical microscope images. The micrographs clearly reveal that gross cell damage increases monotonically with the number of sliding cycles, the average contact pressure is estimated to be approximately 12 kPa in these experiments.

continuous inhalational anesthetic during all friction testing and imaging. This fixture was mounted onto a coarse vertical positioning stage that was located directly below the microtribometer. Before and after friction testing, the mouse left eye was rinsed for 2 min in a fluorescein saline solution, saline rinsed, and imaged under blue light to reveal any scratches or physical damage that was on the cornea. The same process was performed after tribological experiments. No measurable damage was observed on any of the corneas that were tested using this protocol. Post-testing, the mouse was removed from anesthesia and observed until normal activity resumed. The animal was housed in specific pathogen-free conditions in a micro-isolator cage and was treated in accordance with the guidelines provided in the ARVO Statement for the Use of Animals in Ophthalmic and Vision Research.

For these *in vivo* studies motion was provided by a 250 μm piezoelectric stage. At a sliding speed of 250 μm s⁻¹ the reciprocating frequency is 0.5 Hz. The pin was made by melting the end of a capillary tube to form a very smooth 0.5 mm radius spherical probe on the end of an 8 mm standoff. The entire probe assembly was adhesively mounted onto the flexure assembly. Fig. 4a shows a schematic of the mouse eye and probe assembly.

The experiments were performed by gently (but quickly) loading the 1 mm diameter glass probe into contact with the exposed cornea. The measured loads were between 3–5 mN and varied from experiment to experiment and spatially varied during an experiment due to the relatively small curvature of the mouse eye.

   This journal is © The Royal Society of Chemistry 2012

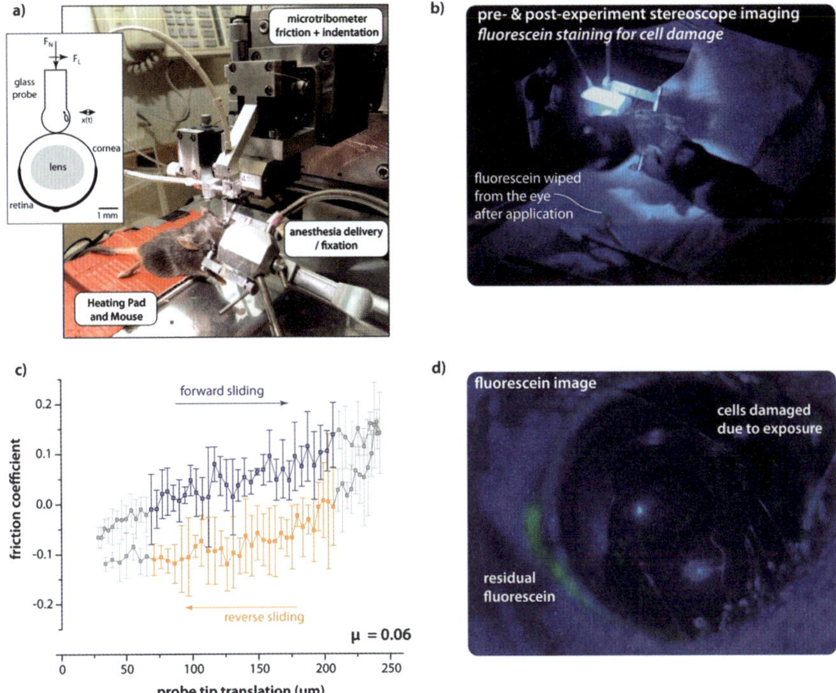

Fig. 4 Direct contact experiments under a 3–5 mN load on an anesthetized mouse cornea. a) shows the contact geometry and the experimental setup. b) Prior to each experiment the eye is gently wiped with a fluorescein stain and imaged using a stereoscope. The fluorescein will stain any damaged epithelial cells and they will appear green under the higher energy illumination. c) Friction experiments repeatedly give a friction coefficient of $\mu = 0.06$, and (d) no damage could be distinguished after testing with these smooth glass probes under these conditions.

Fig. 4c shows a friction loop that was measured during an experiment. The average friction coefficient was found to be $\mu = 0.06$. Post experimental analysis of the cornea showed no measureable damage after fluorescein staining (Fig. 4d).

5. Closing discussion

The transduction of sliding contact forces into biochemical signals has not been extensively studied *in vitro*. However, the great depth of knowledge in the areas of cartilage tribology and cornea tribology can be used to make baseline predictions about the cell's potential response to friction forces both in the laboratory and in the body. Oscillatory rheological measurements on a wide range of cell types in culture have been employed to explore the cell's response to mechanical forces. In frequency response measurements *in vitro*, cells exhibit active and passive stress stiffening, as well as dramatic cytoskeletal re-organization, when strained at frequencies within the approximate range of 0.1 to 1 Hz.[16,39,40] In the body, reciprocation frequencies of sliding contacts are within this range; the average time between blinks in the eye is on the order of 5 s, and the average joint reciprocation period is approximately 1 s.

In stress response measurements *in vitro*, cells also exhibit a wide range of sensitivity; shear stresses as low as 1 Pa can activate leukocytes and, by contrast, shear stresses as high as 20 kPa are required to elicit a mechanosensitive response of chondrocytes in cartilage.[15,41] Threshold stresses required for mechanosensitive responses in most fibroblast-type cells lie in the middle of this range at approximately 0.01–1 kPa. In the body, shear stresses at reciprocating contacts can be estimated in multiple ways. Assuming hydrodynamic lubrication with sliding speeds of 1–100 mm s^{-1} and film thicknesses from 0.1–1 mm, the shear stresses would be on the order of tens to hundreds of Pascals. Alternatively, assuming boundary lubrication conditions, the shear stress at the tissue surfaces is given by $\sigma_s = \mu\sigma_N$, where μ is the friction coefficient and σ_N is the normal stress. In Fig. 3 and Fig. 4 we show that typical friction coefficients lie within the range of 0.03 to 0.06. Normal stresses vary from 6 kPa in the eye to 1 MPa in cartilage; we therefore estimate that shear stresses in these sliding contacts are within the range of 0.18 to 60 kPa, directly within the mechanosensitive range found *in vitro*.

Taken together, these comparisons suggest that typical sliding contact forces within the body occur within the range of shear stresses and frequencies necessary to generate a mechanotransductive response of interfacial cells. Recently it has become clear that mechanical signals have a major impact on cell fate and function, and we propose that frictional contact forces can generate these mechanical signals at the molecular level within interfacial cells. We have found in our studies of epithelial monolayers *in vitro*, and of stratified epithelial cells *in vivo*, that the friction coefficients in protein containing aqueous environments is $\mu = 0.03$–0.06. Based on models and estimates of contact area, this corresponds to shear stresses on the order of 0.3–0.5 kPa. Such low values of surface shear stresses are consistent with brush type aqueous lubrication, and we suggest that the cell surfaces are maintaining low friction interfaces through similar mechanisms. To control the cellular mechanotransductive response in new engineering strategies for replacing biological tissues with synthetic materials like metal, ceramics, and plastics, these lubricating properties at the surfaces of living tissues must be employed. In general, the mechanical microcellular environment significantly impacts many kinds of cell behavior, including contractility, migration, proliferation, apoptosis, and stem cell differentiation; cell friction may be a key contributor to these mechanosensitive behaviors at interfaces.

References

1 D. E. Discher, P. Janmey and Y.-l. Wang, Tissue Cells Feel and Respond to the Stiffness of Their Substrate, *Science*, 2005, **310**(5751), 1139–1143.
2 D. E. Jaalouk and J. Lammerding, Mechanotransduction gone awry, *Nat. Rev. Mol. Cell Biol.*, 2009, **10**(1), 63–73.
3 A. Mammoto, *et al.*, A mechanosensitive transcriptional mechanism that controls angiogenesis, *Nature*, 2009, **457**(7233), 1103–1108.
4 A. J. Engler, *et al.*, Myotubes differentiate optimally on substrates with tissue-like stiffness: pathological implications for soft or stiff microenvironments, *J. Cell Biol.*, 2004, **166**(6), 877–887.
5 P. Friedl, Y. Hegerfeldt and M. Tusch, Collective cell migration in morphogenesis and cancer, *Int. J. Dev. Biol.*, 2004, **48**(5–6), 441–9.
6 T. Omelchenko, *et al.*, Rho-dependent formation of epithelial "leader" cells during wound healing, *Proc. Natl. Acad. Sci. U. S. A.*, 2003, **100**(19), 10788–10793.
7 P. A. Janmey and D. A. Weitz, Dealing with mechanics: mechanisms of force transduction in cells, *Trends Biochem. Sci.*, 2004, **29**(7), 364–370.
8 C. M. Lo, *et al.*, Cell movement is guided by the rigidity of the substrate, *Biophys. J.*, 2000, **79**(1), 144–152.
9 N. Wang, *et al.*, Cell prestress. I. Stiffness and prestress are closely associated in adherent contractile cells, *Am. J. Physiol.-Cell Physiol.*, 2002, **282**(3), C606–C616.
10 R. J. Pelham and Y.-l. Wang, Cell locomotion and focal adhesions are regulated by substrate flexibility, *Proc. Natl. Acad. Sci. U. S. A.*, 1997, **94**(25), 13661–13665.
11 T. Pompe, *et al.*, Friction-Controlled Traction Force in Cell Adhesion, *Biophys. J.*, 2011, **101**(8), 1863–1870.
12 C. A. Reinhart-King, M. Dembo and D. A. Hammer, Cell-Cell Mechanical Communication through Compliant Substrates, *Biophys. J.*, 2008, **95**(12), 6044–6051.
13 X. Trepat, *et al.*, Physical forces during collective cell migration, *Nat. Phys.*, 2009, **5**(6), 426–430.
14 T. E. Angelini, *et al.*, Cell Migration Driven by Cooperative Substrate Deformation Patterns, *Phys. Rev. Lett.*, 2010, **104**(16), 168104.
15 S. Fukuda and G. W. Schmid-Schönbein, Regulation of CD18 expression on neutrophils in response to fluid shear stress, *Proc. Natl. Acad. Sci. U. S. A.*, 2003, **100**(23), 13152–13157.

16 P. Fernandez, P. A. Pullarkat and A. Ott, A master relation defines the nonlinear viscoelasticity of single fibroblasts, *Biophys. J.*, 2006, **90**(10), 3796–3805.

17 V. C. Mow, *et al.*, Biphasic Creep and Stress Relaxation of Articular Cartilage in Compression: Theory and Experiments, *J. Biomech. Eng.*, 1980, **102**(1), 73–84.

18 C. W. McCutchen, The frictional properties of animal joints, *Wear*, 1962, **5**(1), 1–17.

19 R. Brand, Joint Contact Stresses: A reasonable Surrogate for Biological Processes?, *Iowa Orthop. J.*, 2005, **25**, 82–94.

20 K. A. Athanasiou, *et al.*, Interspecies comparisons of *in situ* intrinsic mechanical properties of distal femoral cartilage, *J. Orthop. Res.*, 1991, **9**(3), 330–340.

21 L. A. Setton, *et al.*, Mechanical Properties of Canine Articular Cartilage Are Significantly Altered Following Transection of the Anterior Cruciate Ligament, *J. Orthop. Res.*, 1994, **12**(4), 451–463.

22 S. Park, *et al.*, Cartilage interstitial fluid load support in unconfined compression, *J. Biomech.*, 2003, **36**(12), 1785–1796.

23 M. Caligaris and G. A. Ateshian, Effects of sustained interstitial fluid pressurization under migrating contact area, and boundary lubrication by synovial fluid, on cartilage friction, *Osteoarthritis Cartilage*, 2008, **16**(10), 1220–1227.

24 A, A. Gerard, The role of interstitial fluid pressurization in articular cartilage lubrication, *J. Biomech.*, 2009, **42**(9), 1163–1176.

25 C. J. Bell, E. Ingham and J. Fisher, Influence of hyaluronic acid onthe time-dependent friction response of articular cartilage under different conditions, *Proc. Inst. Mech. Eng., Part H*, 2006, **220**(1), 23–31.

26 E. Bonnevie, *et al.*, *In Situ* Studies of Cartilage Microtribology: Roles of Speed and Contact Area, *Tribol. Lett.*, 2011, **41**(1), 83–95.

27 G. A. Ateshian, *et al.*, An asymptotic solution for the contact of two biphasic cartilage layers, *J. Biomech.*, 1994, **27**(11), 1347–1360.

28 R. L. Spilker, J.-K. Suh and V. C. Mow, A Finite Element Analysis of the Indentation Stress-Relaxation Response of Linear Biphasic Articular Cartilage, *J. Biomech. Eng.*, 1992, **114**(2), 191–201.

29 C. G. Armstrong, W. M. Lai and V. C. Mow, An Analysis of the Unconfined Compression of Articular Cartilage, *J. Biomech. Eng.*, 1984, **106**(2), 165–173.

30 H. D. Conway and M. W. Richman, The Effects of Contact Lens Deformation on Tear Film Pressure and Thickness During Motion of the Lens Towards the Eye, *J. Biomech. Eng.*, 1983, **105**(1), 47–50

31 S. Kamiyama and M. M. Khonsari, Hydrodynamics of a Soft Contact Lens During Sliding Motion, *J. Tribol.*, 2000, **122**(3), 573–577.

32 A. Chauhan and C. J. Radke, Modeling the vertical motion of a soft contact lens, *Curr. Eye Res.*, 2001, **22**(2), 102–108.

33 M. Jones, *et al.*, Elastohydrodynamics of the Eyelid Wiper, *Bull. Math. Biol.*, 2008, **70**(2), 323–343.

34 P. L. Dickrell, *et al.*, Temperature and Water Vapor Pressure Effects on the Friction Coefficient of Hydrogenated Diamondlike Carbon Films, *J. Tribol.*, 2009, **131**(3), 032102–5.

35 A. C. Rennie, P. L. Dickrell and W. G. Sawyer, Friction coefficient of soft contact lenses: measurements and modeling, *Tribol. Lett.*, 2005, **18**(4), 499–504.

36 A. Dunn, *et al.*, Friction Coefficient Measurement of Hydrogel Materials on Living Epithelial Cells, *Tribol. Lett.*, 2008, **30**(1), 13–19.

37 J. Cobb, *et al.*, A novel method for low load friction testing on living cells, *Biotechnol. Lett.*, 2008, **30**(5), 801–806.

38 A. C. Dunn, *et al.*, *Mechanical Response of Living Cells to Contacting Shear Forces Cellular and Biomolecular Mechanics and Mechanobiology*, A. Gefen, Editor 2011, Springer Berlin Heidelberg. p. 125–141.

39 R. Kaunas, *et al.*, Cooperative effects of Rho and mechanical stretch on stress fiber organization, *Proc. Natl. Acad. Sci. U. S. A.*, 2005, **102**(44), 15895–15900.

40 P. Bursac, *et al.*, Cytoskeletal remodelling and slow dynamics in the living cell, *Nat. Mater.*, 2005, **4**(7), 557–561.

41 A. J. Grodzinsky, *et al.*, Cartilage tissue remodeling in response to mechanical forces, *Annu. Rev. Biomed. Eng.*, 2000, **2**, 691–713.

Dynamic surface microstructural changes during tribological contact that determine the wear behaviour of hip prostheses: metals and ceramics

W. Mark Rainforth,[a] Peng Zeng,[a] Le Ma,[a] Akemi Nogiwa Valdez[a] and Todd Stewart[b]

Received 4th January 2012, Accepted 23rd January 2012
DOI: 10.1039/c2fd00002d

It is often the dynamic microstructural changes induced by tribological contact that determine whether or not a material exhibits good wear resistance. It is well known that the mechanical properties of a surface are significantly different from the bulk, an effect amplified by wear induced plastic deformation and electrochemical effects. Despite the importance of these dynamic microstructural changes, there remains little quantitative understanding of how the surface microstructure changes during tribo-contact, and how this modifies the surface mechanical properties and chemical activity. This contribution will focus on key total hip arthroplasty materials, specifically CoCrMo alloys, third and fourth generation alumina/zirconia toughened alumina. High resolution techniques have been used to characterise the wear induced microstructural changes for both *in vivo* and *in vitro* samples, which has provided new insight into the wear mechanisms. The results are discussed in detail, in particular, how they inform future materials development for this important application.

1   Introduction

The market for hip and knee replacements is significantly increasing world-wide (*e.g.* 166 000 hip and knee replacements in England and Wales in 2010, corresponding to a rise of ~50 000 on the previous year). The life span of total hip arthroplasty (THA) has greatly improved over the years (current average ~15 years), but challenges remain from the increasing number of younger and more active patients and the need for new THA materials that are more damage tolerant in order to extend the life of the hip replacement.

Metals, ceramics, and polymers are all extensively used in THAs, each with significantly different material properties. While the choice is largely the personal clinical preferences of the surgeon, there remain significant concerns about the performance of each material type. The market for metal on metal (MoM) hip arthroplasty grew up to 2007 when it accounted for around 35% of the USA market.[1] However, there has been a recent history of problems with MoM joints. For example, in 2007, DePuy International issued a warning notice to all medical professionals who used a particular system (Ultima TPS and Ultima MoM made from CoCrMo alloys) as a result of an unusually high rate of extensive periprosthetic soft tissue necrosis of 6.1%.[2] High soft tissue necrosis was attributed to wear debris produced in MoM

[a]Department of Materials Science and Engineering, The University of Sheffield, Mappin Street, Sheffield, S1 3JD, UK. E-mail: m.rainforth@shef.ac.uk; Fax: +44 114 2225943; Tel: +44 114 2225469
[b]School of Mechanical Engineering, University of Leeds, Leeds, LS2 9JT, UK. E-mail: t.d. stewart@leeds.ac.uk; Fax: +44 113 242611; Tel: +44 113 3432133

articulations.[3] However, subsequent investigations have failed to identify the specific reason for the high corrosion rates. There have been several other alerts released by the Medicines and Healthcare products Regulatory Agency (MHRA) since this case, and in April 2010, an alert was released advising all medical professionals concerned to closely monitor the chromium and cobalt levels in the patient's blood. In the notice, the high soft tissue necrosis was attributed to wear debris produced in MoM articulations.[3] Most recently, an alert was issued on the 7th of September 2010 by the MHRA regarding the DePuy ASR™ hip replacement system after the release of an urgent field safety notice by DePuy. DePuy had found that their ASR™ system was producing revision rates of 12% at 5 years,[4] thus causing them to issue a voluntary recall of all of their ASR™ range and they advised clinicians to stop implanting this device. Again, this higher revision rate was attributed to wear debris causing soft tissue necrosis and aseptic loosening. Interestingly, despite these alerts, the market share for MoM in Europe has continued to increase, from ~6% in 2004 to 9% in 2010, while the market for metal on polyethylene has fallen from ~41% to ~30% in the same period.[5]

A popular alternative to MoM articulation is ceramic on ceramic (CoC) hip replacements, which currently occupies ~26% of the European cementless THA market.[5] Alumina has now been extensively used for hip replacement since its introduction in the 1970s due to its high wear resistance and consequently the reduced number of wear particles liberated into the body. However, concerns have remained about the fracture strength of alumina, which has led to the introduction of the 4th generation ceramic, Biolox® *delta*, developed by CeramTec AG, a zirconia toughened alumina based ceramic composite. This material has been successfully implanted and has offered outstanding performance in the last 8 years. The wear mechanisms in ceramic-on-ceramic joints are unique to this material combination, and depend strongly on a number of factors. Explanted THAs often show a distinctive localized region of severe wear (often referred to as stripe wear). While the mechanisms associated with such wear is not entirely clear, laboratory studies have shown that it is a direct result of microseparation.[6] While the zirconia toughened alumina joints appear to offer the best performance, concerns remain about the hydrothermal degradation of the zirconia (which led to the withdrawal of zirconia hip joints throughout much of the world following the events of Prozyr® zirconia heads 2001).[7]

Irrespective of whether the joint is metal, ceramic or polymer, the performance appears to depend strongly on two factors. Firstly, the size, chemical activity and number of wear debris particles that are liberated by wear, which migrate into the body and are known to be the origin of joint failure, *e.g.* through aseptic loosening. Secondly, the chemical activity of the material is important, particularly for metal on metal joints. It is well known that the wear performance of a material is not just a function of the starting microstructure, but more specifically a result of the microstructure that dynamically evolves as a result of contact stresses and the chemical interactions with the counterface and local environment. There have been a number of studies of the worn surface microstructure in metals and ceramics,[8,9] but there remains a lack of clear understanding as to how the microstructure evolves and whether it is beneficial or not. In this paper, both metal and ceramic THA worn surfaces are examined in detail with a particular focus on the high "stripe" wear regions, and some interesting comparisons drawn between the very different material types. Samples were derived from a number of different sources, including explanted hips, *in vitro* testing on a hip simulator and standard ball on flat testing to see whether the characteristics of the high wear region depended on the test technique or whether the mechanisms are similar.

2 Experimental procedure

Explanted metal on metal hips were obtained from a number of different sources. The particular hip reported here was a Durom™ resurfacing system (forged high carbon CoCrMo alloy manufactured by Zimmer Inc. Germany), which had been implanted in a female patient for approximately 600 days.

In vitro testing of full hip joints was undertaken in a Leeds Mk II hip joint simulator at Leeds University, UK. For this work, alumina ceramics used in this work were hot isostatic pressed (HIPed) commercially available Biolox® *forte* alumina (CeramTec AG, Plochingen, Germany), the 3rd generation of medical-grade alumina. Surface proliferometry (Taylor Hobson, Surtronic 3+, UK) of the alumina femoral head before testing was undertaken giving a starting roughness of 37 ± 5 nm. Prostheses were placed in the anatomical position and lubricated in a bath of 25% bovine serum. Under micro-separation conditions a small lateral to medial load was applied with a spring, which provided 500 µm of medio-lateral motion during the swing phase of the gait cycle. Tests were conducted up to 5 million cycles at a frequency of 1 Hz. The nominal diameter of the prosthesis was 28 mm. Results are presented here from one of the 18 tests.

Further *in vitro* testing was undertaken on Biolox® *delta* samples (CeramTec AG, Plochingen, Germany). While these materials were compositionally identical to the material used for hip prosthetics, the sintering route used differed as a result of the differing geometries between a small flat disc and the hip prosthetic. The as-received surfaces were metallographically polished to produce a high quality surface finish ($R_\mathrm{a} \approx 5$ nm). Sliding wear tests were performed on a reciprocating ball-on-flat UMT tribometer (Center for Tribology, Inc., USA). A high purity 4 mm diameter alumina ball (Oakwade Ltd, UK) was used as the counter body, with roughness 5–8 nm. The tests were lubricated using 25 vol% new-born calf serum solution (First Link Ltd, UK) with phosphate buffered saline (PBS) $1 \times$ (0.01 M), with 0.1 wt% sodium azide (Fisher Scientific, UK) added to avoid bacterial growth and problems with protein degradation of the serum. This serum solution had a viscosity of 0.0012 Pa s. The normal load in the wear test was 0.5, 1, 2, and 4 N, yielding an initial Hertzian contact stress of $\sim$3156 MPa, which fell rapidly during running-in. Such a value is in-line with rim-contact stresses for ceramic-on-ceramic articulation.[10] The reciprocating motion was set at 500 rpm, 600 rpm and 700 rpm, which corresponded to frequencies of 8.333 Hz, 10 Hz and 11.667 Hz, respectively.

The worn surfaces for all materials were investigated using a JEOL 6500F FEG-SEM, a JEOL 6400 SEM (JEOL, Japan) and an FEI Inspect F. Atomic force microscopy (AFM) was performed using a Digital Instruments Dimension 3000 Scanning Probe Microscopy (Veeco Instruments, US) operating in the contact mode. The area scanned by AFM is sufficiently small that the curvature on the prosthesis is not a problem. Standard silicon cantilevers with a pyramidal silicon tip were used to acquire images [20]. The sub-surface microstructures of the worn surfaces were investigated by either taking cross-sections by focused ion beam (FIB) milling (on both normal or longitudinal sections), or back-thinning. FIB was undertaken using either a JEOL F*abrika*, (JEOL, Japan), which comprises a JEOL 6500F FEGSEM with Orsay Physics Ion Column FIB, or an FEI Quanta 200 3D. A thin layer of gold was first deposited to label the original worn surface and prevent charging during FIB processing. This was followed by a layer of sputtered carbon to protect the worn surface. Either tungsten deposition or carbon deposition was then applied on the region of interest to prevent Ga^+ implantation and sputter erosion of the top portion of the surface. A 700 pA Ga^+ ion beam was used for coarse milling, and a 50 pA Ga^+ ion beam was used to polish the sub-surface cross-sections. For back thinned samples, following grinding and polishing of material from below the worn surface, standard ion beam milling was used (Gatan PIPS, USA), with thinning taking place below the surface. TEM was performed on various microscopes. Routine bright field imaging was performed on a Philips 430 operating at 300 kV, while high resolution TEM was undertaken on a JEOL 2010F operating at 200 kV.

3 Results

3.1 *In vivo* and *in vitro* metal on metal

Fig. 1 gives an optical micrograph of the explanted Durom™ resurfaced femoral head. There is a region of high wear, approximately 0.5 mm wide running around about three quarters of the circumference at ~1.5 mm from the pole of the head. The regions adjacent to the high wear stripe exhibited relatively little damage and showed mild abrasion, some of which was locally aligned, but much of which was random in orientation.

Site-specific focused ion beam sections were removed from the region shown in Fig. 1, from within the high wear stripe and adjacent from the low wear region which locally exhibited minimal damage. Fig. 2 shows a FIB cross-section from the low wear region and gives a montage of TEM bright field images taken from the surface to the maximum depth at which deformation was observed at ~4.5 μm. The first evidence of deformation (*i.e.* that observed furthest from the surface) was in the form of stacking faults and fine mechanical twins. At ~150 nm closer to the surface, ε-martensite plates were observed, initially with one orientation, but within a short distance with two and then three orientations. In between the ε-martensite plates, fine twins were present, with an increase in twin density as the surface was approached. At ~1.8 μm below the worn surface there was a small cluster of carbides, but these do not appear to have particularly affected the local deformation structure. The grains that comprised the contacting surface contained a high density of ε-martensite plates, with three orientations, typically ~300 nm apart, interspersed with a high dislocation and twin density. The contacting surface is shown in Fig. 3. The surface exhibited undulations consistent with the grooving observed in optical and SEM images. The contacting surface comprised a thin (70–115 nm) layer which exhibited darker contrast in bright field images. Tilting studies in the TEM failed to reveal the true structure of this layer, but there was some evidence that it contained fine subgrain boundaries, *i.e.* it appeared to be a nanocrystalline layer. Chemical analysis in the TEM indicated that the layer was metallic with no difference in chemical composition to the underlying metal.

Fig. 4 shows a similar section to Fig. 2, but taken inside the high wear stripe region. The depth to which deformation could be measured was ~4 μm, but varied from grain to grain. The general change in deformation structure with depth below the worn surface was essentially the same as for the section taken outside the high

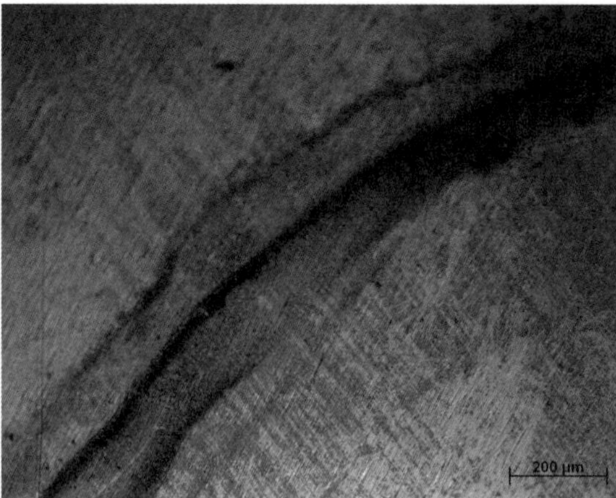

Fig. 1 Optical micrograph showing the region of high wear (stripe running bottom left to top right) on the explanted femoral head.

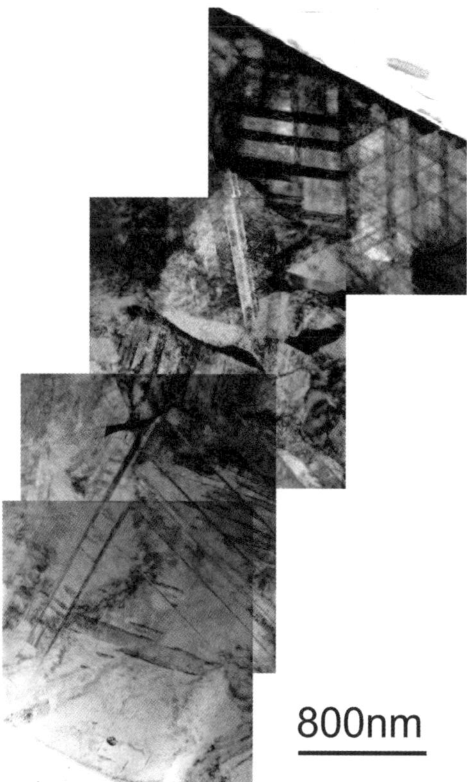

Fig. 2 Montage of bright field TEM micrographs from a cross section taken outside the high wear region of the femoral head shown in Fig. 1. Section was transverse to the direction of the scratch.

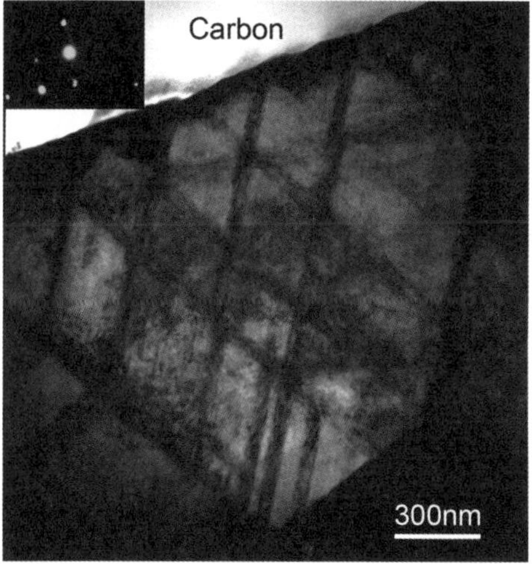

Fig. 3 Bright field TEM micrograph showing the extreme worn surface. Note the ε-martensite plates with three orientations. The dark surface region is believed to have a nanocrystalline structure. Note the fine surface undulations.

Fig. 4 Bright field TEM micrograph of a surface cross-section, taken from inside the high wear region of the femoral head in Fig. 1.

wear stripe, namely, stacking faults and twins rapidly giving way to ε-martensite plates which formed at three orientations and became more densely populated as the surface was approached. The outer region is shown in Fig. 5, which indicates two distinctive features. Firstly, a thin (30 nm maximum) nanocrystalline layer was present in places (*e.g.* left hand side of Fig. 5), but completely absent in other locations (*e.g.* right hand side of Fig. 5). Secondly, a thin (~10 nm) amorphous carbonaceous layer was present on the surface, just visible in the centre of Fig. 5.

A similar region of high wear was observed on a CoCrMo acetabular cup which had been tested *in vitro* on a hip simulator. Fig. 6 gives an SEM micrograph taken from a high wear region that locally exhibited pitting. A FIB section was taken from the contacting surface into the pit, along the line in Fig. 6, also including the particle of what appears to be loose wear debris at the bottom of the pit. A bright field TEM image from the FIB section is given in Fig. 7, which shows the region from the edge of the pit (left hand side) to the debris particle at the base of the pit. The outer surface was labelled with gold prior to FIB sectioning (labelled Au on Fig. 7

Fig. 5 Montage of bright field TEM micrographs showing the outer worn surface from Fig. 4. Note the ε-martensite plates with three orientations. The outer surface region, which is just ~10 nm thick has a nanocrystalline structure. A thin layer of carbonaceous material is also present.

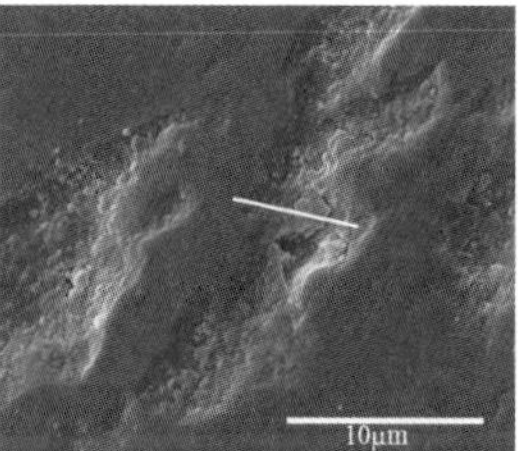

Fig. 6   SEM micrograph showing a pitted region on the MoM acetabulum.

Fig. 7   Bright field TEM micrograph taken from a FIB cross-section on the line shown in Fig. 6. The surface was coated with gold prior to milling to label the true surface. There is a carbide at the upper left region, which was the contacting surface. The upper right region shows a nanocrystalline layer (3) and material that corresponds to the particle that looks as though it is about to detach in Fig. 6.

and 8) to ensure that the protecting deposited layer was differentiated from the worn surface features. Below the gold layer is a region of amorphous material, shown enlarged in Fig. 8 (labelled 1) and which EDS indicated was predominantly carbon, but also containing Ca, Cl, Fe and Si. Below this there was a layer with an elongated structure that appeared to be a mixture of ultra fine crystallites (1–5 nm) embedded in an amorphous structure (labelled 2). This region had a chemical composition the same as the substrate metal. The substrate metal below this had a nanocrystalline structure, Fig. 8 (region 3). The average crystallite size was 35 ± 8 nm, with some equiaxed grains but many elongated, but with no evidence of any preferred crystallographic orientation. The depth of the nanocrystalline layer was substantial at about $\sim$1 µm. There was a large carbide at the left of the pit (left of Fig. 7). Below the carbide the deformation extended to $\sim$8 µm.

3.2   Biolox® *forte* on Biolox® *forte*

In vitro testing with microseperation generally led to the formation of stripe wear regions on both the acetabular cup and the femoral head. In some cases numerous stripes were formed. In the majority of cases the stripe wear was characterised by predominantly intergranular fracture, with occasional transgranular fracture and

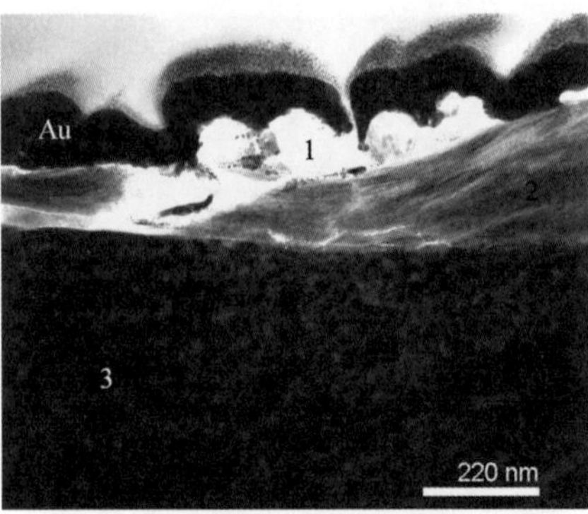

Fig. 8 High magnification bright field TEM image from the nanocrystalline layer (3), and the wear debris particle (1, 2). The upper dark contrast film is the gold (Au) label of the original surface.

partially filling of the pits by fragmented wear debris. However, in some cases the stripe wear region exhibited clear evidence of significant plastic deformation, as shown by the development of grooving, Fig. 9. Locally the plastically deformed material had been lost through subsurface fracture, Fig. 9 right, with most of the cracking being intergranular, but with some regions of distinct transgranular fracture. Fig. 10 shows a bright field TEM image of a FIB cross-section from the groove region, taken in the transverse orientation to the long axis of the groove. The material comprised a nanocrystalline structure, with average crystallite size ~15 nm. The inset diffraction pattern from this region showed that there was a crystallographic texture, with a strong distribution of the diffraction spots varying over ~12°.

Back-thinned TEM samples were also removed from regions local to the stripe wear, but not within the stripe wear region itself. Fig. 11 gives one example that was representative of all the regions examined (over several mm). The alumina grains all contained dislocations, but the dislocation density varied significantly from grain to grain. Most of the dislocations were associated with grooves such as the two grooves running through the centre of Fig. 11b. Interestingly, the groove width and orientation tended to change abruptly at a grain boundary (*e.g.* at the centre of Fig. 11b). In addition, the worn surface contained randomly oriented acicular shaped wear debris particles (darker contrast in Fig. 11a and b, some examples of which are shown by arrows). A diffraction pattern from one such particle is

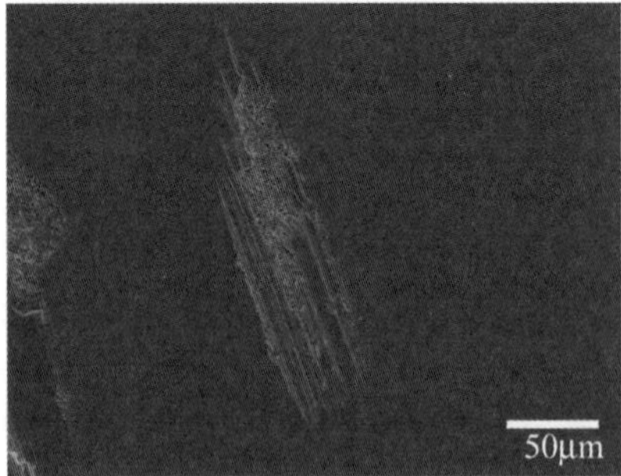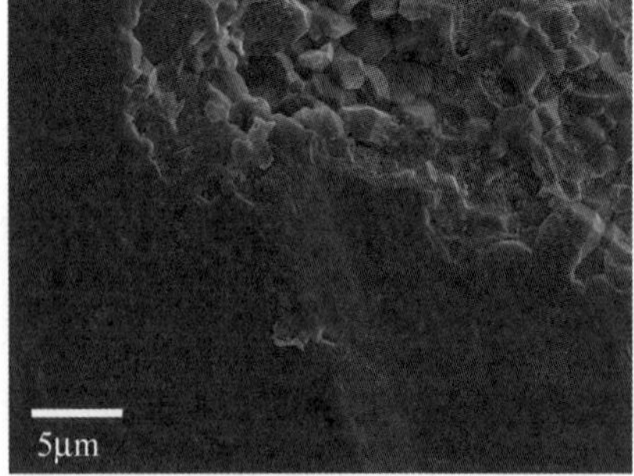

Fig. 9 Secondary electron SEM images of a Biolox® *forte* femoral head tested *in vitro* against Biolox® *forte* acetabular cup, showing a groove associated with cracking and intergranular fracture.

   This journal is © The Royal Society of Chemistry 2012

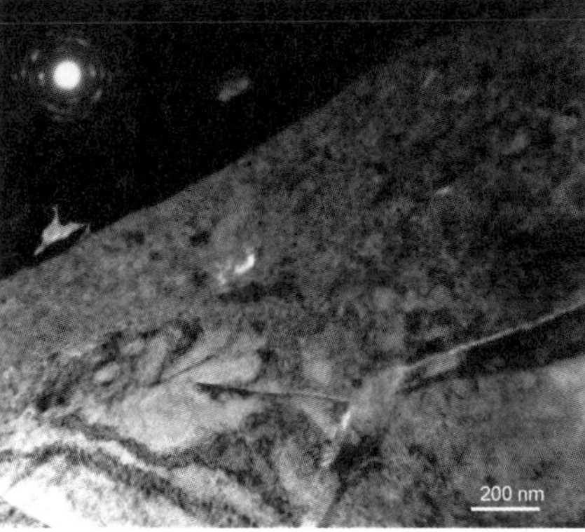

Fig. 10 Bright field TEM image taken from a cross section through the region of plastic deformation shown in Fig. 9, showing a nanocrystalline structure. Section taken normal to the long axis of the groove.

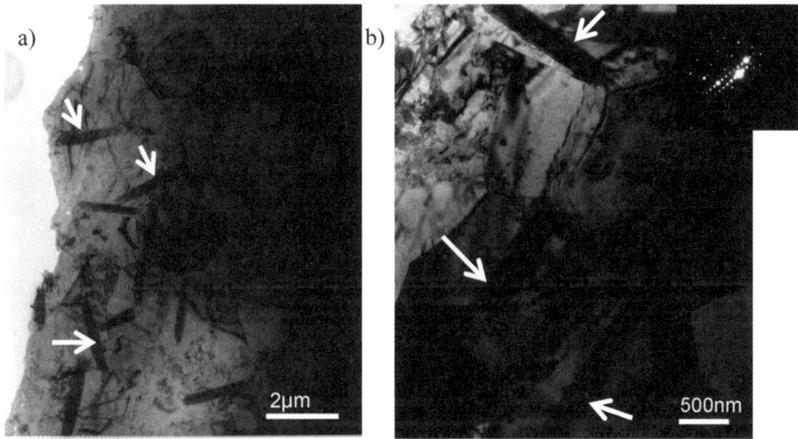

Fig. 11 TEM bright field images taken from a back-thinned sample in a region close to that shown in Fig. 9. a) Evidence of needle-like wear debris (arrowed) on the surface of the sample, in a region that shows a significant dislocation density. b) Detail showing micro abrasive grooves that change direction at a grain boundary, which are also associated with a high dislocation density. Wear debris in (b) is shown by the white arrows.

shown in Fig. 11b, which confirms that the debris was alumina, with the long axis of the particle parallel to the trace of the (0001) plane.

Similar back-thinned samples were removed from a region adjacent to the stripe wear on the acetabular cup. Generally, the features were similar to those observed for the femoral head in Fig. 11, with the exception that no wear debris was observed. While relatively rare, transgranular fracture was observed, Fig. 12a, constrained within a single grain. The fracture direction was parallel with the trace of the (0001) plane suggesting basal cleavage. As with the femoral head, extensive dislocation activity was observed which varied from one grain to another, Fig. 12b. Intergranular fracture was evident and tended to occur adjacent to a grain that exhibited a particularly high dislocation density, such as the grain in the lower part of Fig. 12b.

3.3 *In vitro* testing of Biolox® *delta*

Biolox® *delta* is the 4th generation of ceramic hip joint material, and differs from the 3rd generation alumina ceramic in that it contains ~17% zirconia that imparts

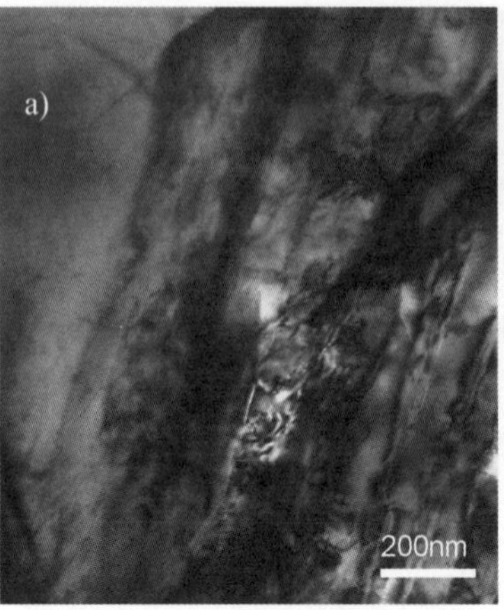
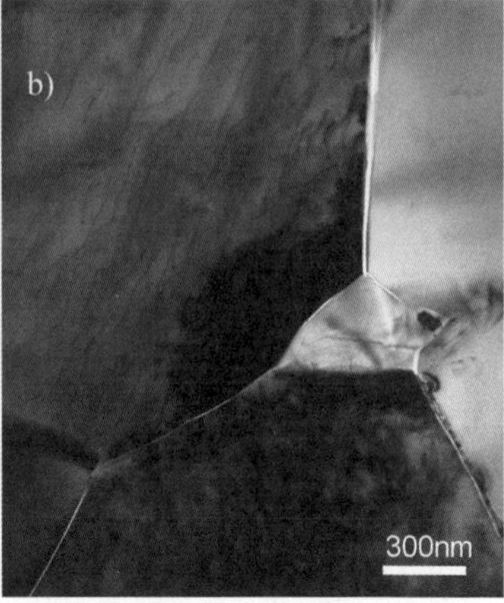

Fig. 12 Bright field TEM micrographs taken from a back-thinned sample of the Biolox® *forte* acetabular cup. Panel a) shows transgranular fracture that occurs along twin boundaries; b) intergranular cracking in a region showing a locally high dislocation density, particularly in the lower grain in the micrograph.

transformation toughening and also reduces the grain size. A wide matrix of tests were performed on this material yielding a range of lubrication regimes (boundary lubrication through to full fluid film, as suggested by the relationship between friction and Sommerfeld number). Testing was undertaken to the point at which extensive pitting covered the worn surface, indicating the on-set of stripe wear. Fig. 13 gives an AFM image which shows local pitting, but a remarkably smooth surface in between the pits. There was some evidence that the pits initially formed from loss of zirconia grains, as shown by the size, but since the particle was lost on formation of the pit, this would be impossible to prove.

Site specific FIB cross sections were taken from the sample shown in Fig. 13 to include the smooth contacting worn surface and local pitting. A bright field image from one such section is given in Fig. 14. The alumina grain in the centre contains a high dislocation density, but the dislocations are located in the surface region and do not extend to the bottom of the grain. The zirconia grains (exhibiting the darker contrast in Fig. 14) exhibited monoclinic crystal symmetry and contained the characteristic twinned structure.

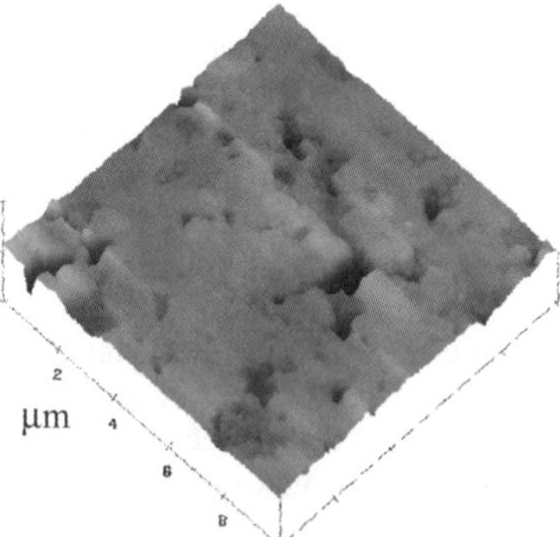

Fig. 13 AFM image from a Biolox® *delta* sample tested in bovine serum at 4 N. Note the pitting, with some pits containing wear debris, but otherwise the surface is quite smooth in between the pits.

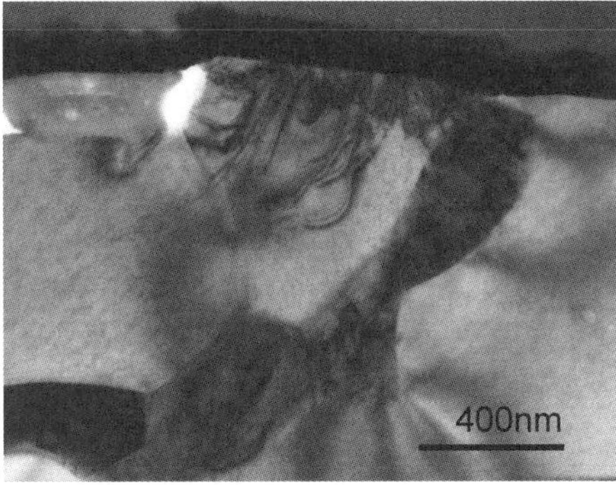

Fig. 14 Bright field TEM image taken from a longitudinal FIB section from a region similar to that shown in Fig. 13. The surface was labelled with gold prior to sectioning (upper dark layer). The outer alumina grain contains a significant dislocation density. The zirconia grains (darker contrast) have transformed to monoclinic symmetry. There is a pore on the left hand side of the worn surface that has been filled with wear debris.

The pits on the worn surface generally contained wear debris (*e.g.* the pit on the left hand side of Fig. 14). Some of the wear debris was identified as crystalline alumina, as shown in the bright and dark field TEM images in Fig. 15a,b. However,

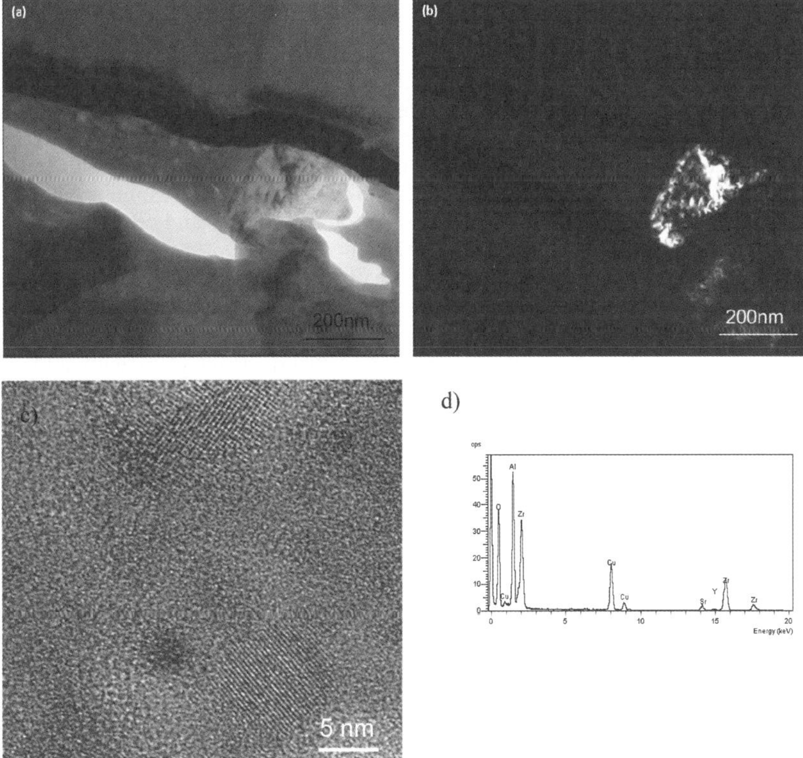

Fig. 15 TEM images taken from a region adjacent to that in Fig. 13. a) Bright field TEM image showing a pit that contains wear debris. b) Dark field TEM images from the same region as (a) showing a particle of alumina wear debris. c) High resolution TEM image from the left hand side of the wear debris in (a), showing fine (5–10 nm) alumina crystallites, in diameter, in an amorphous matrix. (d) EDS spectrum from the amorphous region showing that the alumina, zirconia and bovine serum appear to be intimately mixed.

the majority of the wear debris was a mixed structure comprising nanocrystals in an amorphous matrix (*e.g.* left hand side of Fig. 15a). High resolution TEM of such wear debris was undertaken and confirmed the amorphous structure of the majority of the wear debris, Fig. 15c. In addition, the nanocrystals, 3–15 nm in size, were found to be alumina as suggested by the plane spacing observed in the lattice fringe contrast. EDX analysis (using a nominal 4 nm beam) of the amorphous region indicated that it contained both Al and Zr, as well as O and C. This composition did not vary appreciably from region to region.

4   Discussion

It has been recognised for some time that the dynamic changes at a worn surface are critical in determining the wear performance of a material.[8,9] There has been extensive work on model metal systems under dry sliding conditions, for example copper, aluminium and stainless steel. Under conditions dominated by adhesion, the surface region exhibits extremely high plastic strains, well in excess of strains achieved in any normal metal working process.[8] In general, the wear resistance scales with the stacking fault energy of the material, which determines the work hardening rate, and therefore the increase in hardness of the surface as a result of the wear process. For example, for austenitic stainless steel that has a comparatively low stacking fault energy, substantial hardening occurs as a result of a refinement in grain size to around 10 nm at the worn surface.[11] However, the number of studies that have examined the surface changes during lubricated wear are comparatively few, despite the obvious point that the majority of materials are used in lubricated conditions. In addition to the reduction in the contact stresses at the surface and the substantial reduction in the adhesive component of the wear mechanism, the lubricant significantly changes the material's chemical interaction with the environment. The chemical aspects of wear are particularly topical in relation to metal on metal THAs and are believed to contribute 20–30% of the material loss for CoCrMo alloys.[12] In this paper the high wear regions (usually referred to as stripe wear) are examined in detail and some interesting common themes emerge for both metals and ceramics and are observed for both *in vitro* and *in vivo* operation.

There has been considerable interest in the observations by Fischer, Wimmer and co-workers[13–18] who have observed major microstructural changes at the surface of CoCrMo THAs that fall into two categories: the formation of a nanocrystalline surface layer on explanted and *in vitro* tested metal on metal systems and the mechanical mixing of the metal with the proteins in the synovial fluid to form a metal–organic composite. Surface nanocrystalline layers have also observed on CoCrMo alloys subject to abrasion.[19] Pourzal *et al.*[15] and Wimmer *et al.*[17] suggest that this layer enables the alloy to adjust to the applied load and promotes low wear rates. Indeed, recent work by Liao *et al.* has identified graphitic carbon on explanted worn metal on metal hip joints which would suggest a dynamical change that yields a solid lubricant that should improve wear resistance.[20]

While there have been several observations of nanocrystalline layers on the surface of CoCrMo alloys, the method of TEM sample preparation has not been site specific and therefore it has been difficult to correlate the nanocrystalline layer with regions of high wear or otherwise. Pourzal *et al.*[15] compared the surface microstructure for the stripe wear region on a simulator test and a retrieved joint. The retrieved joint showed a thin (~250–400 nm) nanocrystalline layer, while the simulator tested region did not exhibit a clear nanocrystalline layer. In the present work there appeared to be a nanocrystalline layer in both the low wear region and the high stripe wear region. However, the layer was much thinner than observed by Fischer and co-workers,[13–18] and importantly, the layer was thinner in the high wear region compared to the low wear region. This is clearly inconsistent with the view that it is the wear process that is responsible for forming the nanocrystalline layer.

The stripe wear region appeared to have extensive plastic deformation, as shown by the surface morphology in SEM images. Given that the nanocrystalline layer can only form by severe plastic deformation (discussed further below), its absence in a region of high wear implies that this layer was removed by the wear process. Given that the majority of wear originated from the stripe wear region, most of the wear debris that will have been liberated into the body will have had a nanocrystalline structure. While the nanocrystalline layer would be expected to have a higher mechanical strength than the starting CoCrMo material, the fine grain size leads to a high grain boundary area, which will have made the material chemically much more active. This must be important in considering the mechanisms by which metal wear debris leads to soft tissue necrosis and ultimately aseptic loosening.

The mechanisms by which the nanocrystalline structure forms is not entirely clear. It has been suggested that the fine grain size forms through a recrystallisation mechanism.[14] Equally, it has been suggested that the nanocrystals are in fact a result of the sub-division of the microstructure by the repeated formation of ε-martensite with three orientations that ends up producing a fine microstructure.[14] However, the current results are inconsistent with these proposals. In Fig. 3 and 5 the interface between the material deformed by twinning/ε-martensite formation and the nanocrystalline layer is very sharp, which could not have been formed by a sub-division of the structure by the formation of ε-martensite. Moreover, the spacing of the ε-martensite plates close to this interface is substantially larger than the substructural unit size in the nanocrystalline layer. A much more likely mechanism for the formation of a nanocrystalline layer is by shear banding. It is well known that in low stacking fault energy metals (and CoCrMo alloys have particularly low stacking fault energy) deformation at low strains initially occurs by dislocation glide, but because cross-slip is so difficult rapid work hardening ensues and the imposed strain cannot be accommodated by dislocation flow alone. As a result, deformation then occurs by mechanical twinning. In CoCrMo alloys, the twinning cannot accommodate the imposed strain and this leads to the transformation of the fcc structure to produce ε-martensite. However, the strain produced by the combined effect of twinning and ε-martensite formation is moderately small and some other form of deformation must take place. This occurs the formation of shear bands. Shear bands have been observed in the deformation of many low stacking fault energy metals, including brass, austenitic stainless steel and silver.[11] The shear bands are local regions of high strain (estimates up to true strains of 10) associated with an "avalanche" of dislocation flow that cuts through the twinned structure and results in a fine nanocrystalline layer. Shear banding has been observed at the worn surface of an austenitic stainless steel, with the same progression of deformation structure with strain as that observed in cold rolling the same material.[8,11] Rainforth *et al.* have demonstrated that the wear debris is derived from the nanocrystalline surface layer during sliding of a 316 stainless steel, with wear debris particles probably liberated during the formation of a shear band itself.[11]

The nanocrystalline layer observed on the stripe wear region of the acetabular cup is consistent in appearance with that observed in the literature. However, surprisingly, the nanocrystalline layer was observed in a pit, some distance below the contacting surface. This is difficult to explain, particularly given the suggestion that the nanocrystalline layer forms as a result of high shear stresses. It is also not clear how the pits were formed. Pitting has often been observed on CoCrMo alloys associated with the fracture of carbides.[21] In the current work, carbides were observed at the edge of the pits, suggesting that the pits were formed in an area locally rich in carbide. It may be that the nanocrystalline layer formed through 3rd body abrasion during break-up of a load supporting carbide.

Another interesting observation in the base of the pit on the acetabular cup is the wear debris particle in Fig. 8 that appears to be detaching from the surface. This particle has the same composition as the substrate, but has a much finer structure than the nanocrystalline layer and appears to be partly amorphous and must have formed through extremely high strain deformation. This material would appear to be part way through the process of forming the metal–organic composite layer reported by Wimmer *et al.*,[17] particularly as it was associated with some amorphous material likely to have come from the bovine serum lubricant.

Stripe wear on alumina CoC THAs has been extensively characterised by SEM, which has repeatedly shown the intergranular nature of the surface fracture.[22–24] The stripe wear region is known to form early in the life of the THA,[25] with other regions of the articulating surface experiencing more gradual build up of surface damage. While it is now well established that stripe wear is associated with microseparation,[24] there remains significant uncertainty as to the micro-mechanisms of formation and how a region of high wear can develop with a sharp interface to adjacent regions of comparatively low wear. Fig. 9 showed a region of stripe wear, clearly associated with locally severe plastic deformation, with local delamination yielding the characteristic intergranular fracture. The structure of the heavily deformed region, Fig. 10, is remarkable in that it shows similar characteristics to severe plastic deformation in metals, namely, a fine nanocrystalline structure that exhibits a strong crystallographic texture. It is interesting to compare the metallic nanostructure Fig. 8 with the ceramic nanostructure, Fig. 10, which are very similar. While it is generally believed that plastic deformation cannot occur in brittle ceramics, there are several observations of dislocation flow at a worn ceramic surface.[26,27] For example, high strain deformation has been observed at the surface of a zirconia ceramic, but this was believed to have been associated with high surface temperatures.[28,29] Dislocation flow has often been observed at the worn surface of alumina, but this has been associated with plastic strains that are too small to measure. Thus, this is the first time that such a fine nanocrystalline layer has been observed on the surface of alumina.

The worn surface away from the stripe wear region, Fig. 11, showed similar features to those observed for standard pin on disc laboratory testing of alumina.[26] The alumina grains generally contained an appreciable dislocation density, the extent of which varied from grain to grain. Barceinas and Rainforth[26] investigated the slip systems in detail for a pin on disc geometry and water lubrication and found that slip occurred preferentially on the pyramidal slip system and where the slip planes were at ~6–33° to the worn surface. Consistent with the current observations, dislocation slip was most frequently associated with 3rd body abrasive grooves. The current work also shows that the depth and orientation of these abrasive grooves depends on the local crystal orientation, such that the groove often abruptly changes direction, depth and extent of damage from one grain to the next (for example, at the centre of Fig. 11). The observation of dislocation slip at the worn surface is quite significant. Although the extent of dislocation flow is relatively limited, there is compelling evidence that it is the dislocation flow that is responsible for initiating grain boundary cracking, providing the time dependent component for the well known transition from mild to severe wear in alumina. For example, intergranular cracking was particularly observed adjacent to grains exhibiting a high dislocation density, such as that in Fig. 12b. The time to this wear transition is known to be grain size dependent, which is a result of a reduction in dislocation density with a reduction in grain size. This is one reason for the reduction in grain size in going from the 1st to 3rd generation medical grade alumina, as well as the associated increase in fracture strength.

The observation of acicular shaped wear debris in Fig. 11 is unusual, and specific to the femoral head. Diffraction patterns confirmed that the wear debris was alumina and that the long axis of the particles was parallel to the trace of the basal planes, implying that they formed as a result of transgranular fracture. Transgranular fracture is often observed in the stripe wear region, although it is the minority fracture mechanism. Fig. 12a shows local transgranular fracture occurring in a single alumina grain, with the cracks propagating preferentially along the basal planes and with spacing between the cracks consistent with the size of the wear debris observed.

It is therefore suggested that the acicular wear debris was a result of local transgranular fracture in some of the alumina grains.

The 4th generation medical grade ceramic, based on an alumina toughened zirconia, was developed to offer higher fracture strength and is now the material of choice over 3rd generation alumina ceramics. While the short time that this material has been in service limits the knowledge of the *in vivo* wear mechanisms, it is known that they also exhibit stripe wear. In the present study, *in vitro* testing was undertaken using a simplified geometry using load, speed and test duration that gave a worn surface with significant pitting, suggesting the onset of the wear transition, *i.e.* stripe wear. FIB sections, Fig. 14, showed that the dislocation activity was confined to the region close to the surface and rarely extended to the grain boundary below the worn surface. However, in common with the *in vitro* tested Biolox® *forte* surface intergranular cracking was present and adjacent grains tended to exhibit a high dislocation density, Fig. 14, suggesting that the same basic mechanisms of pit formation occurred in both materials. A similar result has been shown by serial FIB sectioning and 3D reconstruction of worn (sliding and abrasion) Biolox® *delta*.[30,31]

One important issue with the zirconia toughened alumina is the stability of the tetragonal zirconia particles. Hydrothermal degradation, the uncontrolled transformation of tetragonal to monoclinic zirconia in the presence of water, has been shown to occur in explanted zirconia THAs, and can result in the total disintegration of the component.[7,32] In the present work, all zirconia particles at the worn surface were shown to have monoclinic symmetry, indicating stress assisted transformation, possibly accelerated by the presence of water. However, there was no evidence of microcracking in most of the transformed particles, which is usually observed in monolithic zirconia, and could obviously enhance the ease with which particles are pulled out during sliding contact. The absence of cracking may well be a result of the residual thermal mismatch stresses in the composite material. Another important observation is that the transformation of the zirconia only extended a few tens of microns below the worn surface, indicating that there was no uncontrolled transformation propagating into the material that is a standard characteristic of hydrothermal degradation in zirconia ceramics.

Fig. 14 and 15 give interesting observations of wear debris that has a composite amorphous nanocrystalline structure. The amorphous component was shown to contain aluminium, zirconium, carbon and oxygen, with some traces of calcium. This demonstrates that all components of the tribosystem, the zirconia, the alumina and the bovine serum, have become intimately mixed together by the attrition of wear debris between the two articulating surfaces. Such material shows many similarities to the metal–organic composite observed by Pourzal *et al.*[15] and Wimmer *et al.*[17] and also found in the current study as shown in Fig. 8. This demonstrates the importance of the interaction of the bearing material with the lubricant in THA operation. It also shows that such films can form even in the absence of electrochemical effects given that they should not be present for ceramic on ceramic articulation.

Stripe wear is known to be associated with microseparation. This locally raises the contact stresses to the point that plastic deformation is induced in the material. This work has clearly demonstrated the importance of plastic deformation in ceramics leading to grain boundary cracking that induces intergranular fracture and consequently the characteristic locally high wear in ceramics. The situation in metals remains less clear and further controlled *in vitro* studies of the formation of stripe wear are required and specifically, on the formation of nanocrystalline layers on the surface. It remains unclear whether nanocrystalline layers are beneficial or detrimental; on the one hand the fine structure will impact a higher mechanical strength that should be more wear resistant, but counteracting this, such a structure would have low ductility and would be expected to be chemically much more active.

5   Summary

This paper focused on the high wear regions of metal on metal and ceramic on ceramic total hip arthroplasties. Despite the major differences in material properties, similarities have also been observed, in particular the observation of localised high strain plastic deformation at the surface, the formation of a nanocrystalline structure and the interaction with the lubricant to form a metal–organic composite or a ceramic–organic composite which is largely amorphous and exhibits intimate mixing of the articulating surfaces with the lubricant.

For the metal on metal explanted resurfaced CoCrMo alloy, site-specific sections were removed from a region of high wear and compared to a region that exhibited relatively little damage. Surprisingly little difference was seen between the two, with a thin (30–100 nm) nanocrystalline layer seen on both, suggesting that wear in the stripe wear region led to the removal of the nanocrystalline layer. The mechanism of formation of the nanocrystalline layer is suggested to be by the formation of shear bands and not by the gradual sub-division of the structure through the formation of the ε-martensite. In contrast, a thick ($\sim$1 μm) nanocrystalline layer was found in a pitted region on an *in vitro* tested acetabular cup. Formation of this layer was tentatively believed to be associated with fragmentation and ejection of a previously load bearing carbide, which had induced microstructural change when previously loaded.

Dislocation generation and glide was shown to be important in the wear of Biolox® *forte*. Locally high strain deformation was observed, which generated a nanocrystalline structure with similar characteristics to that observed or the CoCrMo alloy.

For the Biolox® *delta* tested *in vitro* in bovine serum, pitting was also associated with intergranular fracture and appeared to be located next to grains that contained a high dislocation density. The zirconia near the worn surface had all undergone stress induced transformation to monoclinic crystal symmetry, but there was no evidence of uncontrolled hydrothermal degradation. Wear debris was observed that was a ceramic–organic composite, exhibiting an intimate mixture of all components of the tribosystem. This had many similarities to the metal–organic composite films that have been observed in this study and reported in the literature.

Acknowledgements

The authors are grateful to EPSRC for funding part of this work. They are also grateful to Prof. A. Fischer and Dr R. Pourzal for the supply of the CoCrMo samples.

References

1 J. J. Jacobs, A. K. Skipor, L. M. Patterson, N. J. Hallab, W. G. Paprosky, J. Black and J. O. Galante, *J. Bone Joint Surg. Am.*, 1998, **80**, 1447–1458.
2 Medicines and Healthcare products Regulatory Agency; Total hip replacement: DePuy Ultima TPS femoral stem used in combination with Ultima metal-on-metal articulation; MDA/2007/054; http://www.mhra.gov.uk/Publications/Safetywarnings/ MedicalDeviceAlerts/CON2031467.
3 Medicines and Healthcare products Regulatory Agency; All metal-on-metal (MoM) hip replacements; MDA/2010/033; http://www.mhra.gov.uk/Publications/Safetywarnings/ MedicalDeviceAlerts/CON079157 (accessed on 26/10/2010).
4 Medicines and Healthcare products Regulatory Agency; Joint Prosthesis - DePuy International Limited - A Johnson & Johnson Company - Recall; Metal-on-Metal; NJR; National Joint Registry; Resurfacing; DPYOUS2, updated; August 2010; http:// www.mhra.gov.uk/Safetyinformation/Safetywarningsalertsandrecalls/ FieldSafetyNoticesformedicaldevices/CON076186.
5 Avicenne Market Research and Consulting, Implants 2011, www.avicenne.com.

6 J. Nevelos, E. Ingham, C. Doyle, R. Streicher, A. Nevelos, W. Walter and J. Fisher, *J. Arthroplasty*, 2000, **15**, 793–795.
7 J. Chevalier and L. Gremillard, *J. Eur. Ceram. Soc.*, 2009, **29**, 1245–1255.
8 W. M. Rainforth, *Wear*, 2000, **245**, 162–177.
9 D. A. Rigney, *Wear*, 2000, **245**, 1–9.
10 M. Mak, Z. Jin, J. Fisher and T. D. Stewart, *J. Arthroplasty*, 2011, **26**, 131–6.
11 W. M. Rainforth, J. Nutting and R. Stevens, *Philos. Mag. A*, 1992, **66**, 621–641.
12 Y. Yan, A. Neville and D. Dowson, *Tribol. Int.*, 2007, **40**, 1492–1499.
13 M. A. Wimmer, C. Sprecher, R. Hauert, G. Täger and A. Fischer, *Wear*, 2003, **255**, 1007–1014.
14 R. Buscher and A. Fischer, *Wear*, 2005, **259**, 887–897.
15 R. Pourzal, R. Theissmann, M. Morlock and A. Fischer, *Wear*, 2009, **267**, 689–694.
16 R. Pourzal, R. Theissmann, S. Williams, B. Gleising, J. Fisher and A. Fischer, *J. Mech. Behav. Biomed. Mater.*, 2009, **2**, 186–191.
17 M. A. Wimmer, A. Fischer, R. Buscher, R. Pourzal, C. Sprecher, R. Hauert and J. J. Jacobs, *J. Orthop. Res.*, 2010, **28**, 436–443.
18 R. Pourzal, I. Catelas, R. Theissman, C. Kaddick and A. Fischer, *Wear*, 2011, **271**, 1658–1666.
19 D. Sun, J. A. Wharton, R. J. K. Wood, L. Ma and W. M. Rainforth, *Tribol. Int.*, 2009, **42**, 99–110.
20 Y. Liao, R. Pourzal, M. A. Wimmer, J. J. Jacobs, A. Fischer and L. D. Marks, *Science*, 2011, **334**, 1687–1690.
21 A. Wang, S. Yue, J. D. Bobyn, F. W. Chan and J. B. Medley, *Wear*, 1999, **225–229**, 708–715.
22 A. Nevelos, P. A. Evans, P. Harrison and W. M. Rainforth, *Proc. Inst. Mech. Eng., Part H*, 1993, **207**, 155–162.
23 J. E. Nevelos, E. Ingham, C. Doyle, J. Fisher and A. B. Nevelos, *Biomaterials*, 1999, **20**, 1833–1840.
24 J. E. Nevelos, E. Ingham, C. Doyle, R. Streicher, A. B. Nevelos, W. Walter and J. Fisher, *J. Arthroplasty*, 2000, **15**, 793–795.
25 P. Zeng, W. M. Rainforth, B. Inkson and T. D. Stewart, *J. Biomed. Mater. Res., Part B*, 2012, **100B**, 121–132.
26 O. Barceinas and W. M. Rainforth, *Acta Mater.*, 1998, **46**(18), 6475–6483.
27 P. Zeng, B. Inkson and W. M. Rainforth, *Acta Mater.*, 2012, **60**, 2061–2072.
28 W. M. Rainforth and R. Stevens, *J. Mater. Res.*, 1998, **13**, 396–405.
29 O. Barceinas and W. M. Rainforth, *J. Am. Ceram. Soc.*, 1999, **82**, 1483–1491.
30 L. Ma, W. M. Rainforth, D. Sun and R. J. K. Wood, *Wear*, 2009, **267**, 2122–2131.
31 L. Ma and W. M. Rainforth, *Tribol. Int.*, 2010, **43**, 1872–1881.
32 A. Nogiwa Valdez, W. M. Rainforth and T. Stewart, submitted to *J. Mech. Behav. Biomed. Mater*

A stratified approach to pre-clinical tribological evaluation of joint replacements representing a wider range of clinical conditions advancing beyond the current standard

John Fisher†*

Received 4th January 2012, Accepted 10th January 2012
DOI: 10.1039/c2fd00001f

A new stratified approach to pre-clinical tribological simulation of joint replacements is presented, which extends beyond present standard conditions used. It includes variations in surgical delivery, variations in kinematics, variations in the patient population and degradation of the biomaterials technology. Examples of the new methods are presented, which have been validated against clinical experience of existing devices. The stratified approach has differentiated the performance of joint replacements, which had previously been shown to have similar tribological performance under standard conditions. The stratified approach to pre-clinical tribological simulation of joint replacements has the potential to support the development of robust designs and improve safety and reliability of joint replacements in the future.

1.   Introduction

Joint replacement is one of the most successful surgical interventions, with over 50 years clinical use. Joint replacements have to transmit biomechanical forces and enable movements for the whole of the patient's lifetime. They are increasingly used in younger more active patients with higher demand, with "50 active years after 50®" and with higher levels of expectations of function, reliability and survivorship. Pre-clinical tribological simulation and evaluation systems allow the performance of the implant system to be evaluated under simulated *in vivo* biomechanical and kinematic conditions, allowing the contact mechanics, friction, wear, wear debris and biological reactivity to be assessed.[1–3] Increasing demands and expectations of patients and surgeons now require improved pre-clinical simulation systems and evaluations.

During the period 1960 to 1990, there was limited pre-clinical tribological evaluation of whole joint prostheses. Recognition of the importance of wear and wear debris induced osteolysis as a major failure mode of hip prostheses during the 1990s[1–3] led to extensive development of hip simulation systems and knee simulation systems. Typically they have applied a simulation of the standard walking cycle, for pre-clinical evaluation of hip prostheses[4–6] and knee prostheses.[7–9] Wear rates, wear mechanisms and wear debris from simulators were compared to clinical retrievals for conventional polyethylene to validate the simulation systems.[10] The average wear

Institute of Medical & Biological Engineering, School of Mechanical Engineering, University of Leeds, Leeds, LS2 9JT, UK. E-mail: J.Fisher@leeds.ac.uk

† Statement of potential conflicts of interest: JF is a paid consultant to DePuy, JF and the University of Leeds receive royalty income from DePuy, JF is a share holder and paid adviser to Tissue Regenix.

rates and debris size and morphologies were found to be similar in the simulator to those found from retrievals for conventional polyethylene. However, there was greater variation in the wear rates and mechanisms found *in vivo*. Some of this variation was attributed to degradation of the prosthetic biomaterials *in vivo* due to damage to the metallic femoral head and/or oxidative degradation of the polyethylene material.[1–3,10,11]

The simulation methods using the standard walking cycle, which involve using correctly positioned, concentric and aligned components, have been widely adopted by companies and international standards bodies. These standard simulations have been primarily adopted over the last decade and were validated against clinical studies and retrievals based on the average wear rates.[4–6,10] They do not replicate or represent the variation in performance found in the patient under a much wider set of clinical conditions.

The standard walking cycle conditions have been applied to demonstrate a reduction in average wear under standard walking cycle conditions with new biomaterials and designs such as cross linked polyethylene, which have subsequently been verified upon introduction of the technology clinically.[12]

Simulation methods using a standard walking cycle and ISO and ASTM recommended standard conditions have also been applied extensively to other alternative bearing materials such as metal on metal and ceramic on ceramic for the hip. Under the standard walking cycle conditions, the wear rate of these bearings is extremely low.[13,14] While these pre-clinical simulations under standard conditions replicate some of the lower wear rates and wear mechanisms found *in vivo* for these alternative bearings, they fail to simulate the variation found clinically and in particular fail to replicate some of the higher wear rates and more severe wear mechanism found in some patients and some retrieved components.[15]

The majority of current joint replacement prostheses perform well with low wear under standard walking conditions and indeed are predicted to meet the needs of many patients. However, while an acceptable clinical performance is assessed by NICE as greater than 90% survivorship at ten years in the average population, there is significant interest in reducing failure rates further, producing more reliable and robust solutions that have low wear under increased demand and accommodate the wide variation in clinical conditions.

It is therefore critically important to be able to pre-clinically evaluate performance under a wider set of clinically relevant conditions, in order to assess the variation and increases in wear rates associated with the different conditions found clinically. In particular it is essential to identify pre-clinically designs that not only have acceptably low wear rates under the standard conditions, but also have low wear rates under a wider set of clinical conditions, a more robust design, and which avoid high wear rates under adverse clinical conditions that can cause failure.

In this paper we present a new systematic and stratified approach to pre-clinical simulation and evaluation of joint prostheses under a wide set of clinical conditions, which advance well beyond the current standard and practice. By analysis of our bank of over 5 billion cycles of pre-clinical data, we have established a baseline reference of acceptable wear performance under standard conditions for different material combinations and provide examples of how our new stratified approach can be used to assess the increase in wear of the different types of prostheses under the wider set of clinical conditions. This allows the magnitude of the risk associated with an increased wear rate to be determined, which can be combined with the frequency of occurrence of the condition to determine the total risk of increased wear.

2. Methods and the stratified approach

The current standards for pre-clinical tribological evaluation of joint prostheses define:

   This journal is © The Royal Society of Chemistry 2012

- A correctly positioned prosthesis, with correct rotational and translational positions

- A single standard walking cycle
- An average standard patient, in terms of anatomy and physiology
- A perfect prostheses without degradation

These standard conditions have been used to determine average wear rates for different prosthetic devices from our existing data set, which have been compared to average clinical wear rates.[4–14]

We have defined a new stratified approach to systematically address the wider set of conditions found clinically and have developed and validated examples for the set of new simulation methods for pre-clinical evaluation. The stratified approach includes:

- Conditions associated with variation in the surgical delivery of the device such as rotational and translational mal-position.[15–27] In particular these relate to the rotational position of the cup and the intersection of the tribological contact patch on the head with the edge of the cup and in the translational positions of the centres of the head and cup, the alignment of their centres to each other and to the natural centre of the hip. Mal-positioning can occur during surgery, but also as a result of impingement, offset deficiency and stem subsidence.

- Conditions associated with different types of patient activities, joint kinematics in the hip,[5,27] levels of activities, levels of loading, jogging, stop-start motion, levels of swing phase load,[28,29] different input kinematics[30,31] and influence of lift off in the knee.[32]

- Conditions associated with different types of patients and stratifications of the population, such as variations in the natural lubricant,[33] inflammatory response,[34] metal ion sensitivity, variation in anatomy and physiology and disease state.

- Conditions associated with degradation of the device technology, such as femoral head damage[6] and oxidative degradation of polyethylene.[35,36]

As the overall tribological performance of the hip prosthesis is dependent on the full set of conditions found clinically, interactions within each and across each set of conditions also need to be considered, but extend beyond scope of current studies. Applying the standard walking conditions simulation and through comparison with average clinical wear rates a normal range for acceptable average wear rates for different materials has been established, which can be associated with clinical success. Using the new stratified approach to pre-clinical testing and selecting particular sets of conditions, examples of the effect of variation in specific conditions on wear rate and mechanism have been determined. The pre-clinical predicted wear results are presented in the context of the normal range of wear rates under standard conditions.

In consideration of the biological response to the wear and wear debris which cause failure, it is also necessary to consider the relative reactivity of different types of wear debris in terms of its type of reaction, inflammation and osteolysis or toxicity and necrosis, as well as severity of response to volumetric doses.[2,3] Laboratory studies have shown metal debris to have a higher level of toxicity at lower doses than ceramic or polyethylene debris, while ceramic debris has been shown to produce similar or lower levels of inflammatory cytokines to polyethylene debris. This is considered when interpreting relative wear rates under different conditions.

3. Results

Results for standard condition wear simulation

The normal range for average wear rates under standard conditions from pre-clinical simulation studies derived from a single laboratory is given in Table 1. Standard condition simulation studies showed the highest level of wear rate with conventional polyethylene, reducing with cross linked polyethylene, then metal on metal, to the

Table 1 Results of average wear rates for standard condition simulation studies

Type of bearing	Material combination	Head size (range in mm)	Wear rate (mm³ per million cycles)	Source references	Comments
Hip	Metal on conventional polyethylene	28	25 to 40	4–6	Validated clinical study[10,11]
Hip	Metal on cross linked polyethylene (7.5–10 MRad)	28–36	5 to 10	12	
Hip	Metal on metal	28	0.1 to 1	14,21	Clinical studies higher
Hip	Metal on metal	36	0.4 to 0.8	36	Clinical studies higher
Hip	Metal on metal	39–55	0.1 to 0.4	37	Clinical studies higher
Hip	Ceramic on metal	28 to 36	0.02 to 0.1	36	
Hip	Alumina ceramic on ceramic	28	0.02 to 0.1	13	Clinical studies stripe head wear[15]
Hip	Delta ceramic on ceramic	28	0.02 to 0.1	18,25	Clinical studies stripe head wear
Knee	Conventional polyethylene	Medium	6 to 12	8,9,30	Standard kinematics
Knee	Cross linked polyethylene (5 MRad)	Medium	3 to 6		Standard kinematics

lowest with ceramic on metal and ceramic on ceramic. Clinical studies have validated the reduction in average wear with cross linked compared to conventional polyethylene. For conventional polyethylene a wear rate of 40 mm³ per million cycles has been shown to exceed the critical volume of 500 mm³ needed to cause osteolysis at ten years in an active patient. The reduction in wear rate with cross linked polyethylene indicates this risk is substantially reduced. A wear rate of less than 10 mm³ per million cycles was indicative of acceptable wear performance for cross linked polyethylene under standard conditions in a low or medium demand patient.

In metal on metal the different devices showed similar wear rates under standard walking cycle conditions of 0.1 to 1 mm³ per million cycles. There is clinical evidence that this low level of debris may be tolerated from the bearing surfaces, and clinical and retrieval studies show a much greater variation and substantially higher wear rates in individual patients.[26] Wear rates above 1 mm³ per million cycles were consistent with metal ion levels above 10 ppm, which may produce adverse reactions clinically.[26]

In ceramic on ceramic bearings the lowest wear rate was found under standard conditions, less than 0.1 mm³ per million cycles and accurate measurement of wear below this level is difficult *in vitro*. However the standard wear simulation did not replicate the stripe wear and higher wear rate found on retrieved prostheses.[15–17] As with metal on metal the standard simulation did not predict the variation or higher levels of wear found clinically. However, the clinical wear rates of the order of 1 mm³ per million cycles for ceramic do not appear to produce adverse reactions.

In the knee with polyethylene bearings the wear rate was reduced with cross linked polyethylene under standard condition testing, showing similar effects to that found in the hip. The wear rate for conventional polyethylene in the knee was less than in the hip, which reflects the lower incidence of osteolysis in the knee under normal conditions. Again, as with the hip, a wear rate of less than 10 mm^3 per million cycles may be considered an acceptable performance for polyethylene in the knee.

Results for examples of stratified approach for different simulation conditions

Conditions associated with variation in the surgical delivery of the device. In this section examples of wear under conditions associated with variation in the position of the hip prosthesis are presented, in particular variation in the rotational position of the cup with an increased inclination angle of 60°, variation in the translational position of the head and cup with a microseparation of the centres by 0.5 mm and a combination of both conditions.

Table 2 shows the results for adverse variation in position. The response to surgical mal-position was dependent on bearing type and design. The Delta ceramic wear rate remained less than 1 mm^3 per million cycles, as did the ceramic on metal bearing, which could be considered an acceptable level of wear. In contrast the metal on metal bearings all give wear rates above 1 mm^3 per million cycles. The increase was less with the smaller diameter metal on metal total joint replacements, and was greatest with the larger diameter sub hemispherical surface replacement under translational and rotational mal-position. The pre-clinical evaluations which considered the variation in component position were able to differentiate the wear performance of different materials and designs, and provide a potential explanation for variation in clinical performance and outcomes with different designs of metal on metal bearings. Further evidence of the value of this type of pre-clinical testing has been demonstrated in the development of surface engineered bearings for hips, where simulation of mal-positioning and rim loading was able to demonstrate failure of surface coating prior to the device entering clinical trials.[38]

Conditions associated with variations in kinematics. In this section variations in wear rate associated with changes in kinematics inputs in the knee are presented. In particular the effect of higher kinematic inputs, increased anterior posterior translation and also introduction of abduction/adduction lift off and medial lateral translation were studied (Table 3). The wear under high kinematic input conditions for conventional polyethylene increased above 10 mm^3 per million cycles with both increased anterior posterior (AP) translation and with the introduction of lift off, abduction/adduction rotation and medial lateral translation. These higher kinematic

Table 2 Wear rates corresponding to adverse variation in position of prostheses

Prosthesis type	Material	Size (mm)	Adverse condition	Wear rate (mm^3 per million cycles)	Source reference
Hip	Alumina ceramic	28	Translational mal-position	0.5 to 1.8	15,18
Hip	Delta ceramic	28	Translational mal-position	0.5 to 0.25	25
Hip	Metal on metal	39	Rotational mal-position	1 to 10	24
Hip	Metal on metal	39	Translational rotational mal-position	8 to 14	24
Hip	Metal on metal	28	Translational mal-position	0.5 to 3	36
Hip	Ceramic on metal	28	Translational mal-position	0.1 to 0.5	36

Table 3 Variation in kinematic conditions in the knee

Type	Size	Material	Condition	Wear rate mm³/ million cycles	Reference
Knee	Medium fixed bearing	Conventional polyethylene	Increased anterior posterior translation	9 to 15	30,31
Knee	Medium fixed bearing	Cross linked polyethylene (5 MRad)	Increased anterior posterior translation	4.5 to 8.5	
Knee	Medium fixed bearing	Conventional polyethylene	Lift off	12 to 19	32

demands demonstrated the potential for wear debris induced osteolysis in the knee with conventional polyethylene. With cross linked polyethylene and high kinematic inputs of increased AP translation, the wear rate increased compared to the standard conditions, but remained below 10 mm³ per million cycles, demonstrating the potential advantage of cross linked polyethylene in high demand kinematic conditions.

Conditions associated with degradation of prostheses. In this section variations in the wear rate associated with degradation of the prostheses and in particular deterioration of the femoral head roughness were considered (Table 4), which is particularly relevant as the prosthesis enters the second decade of its life *in vivo*. Clinically, damage to smooth metallic femoral heads has been observed in retrievals[10] and this has been replicated in the simulator with discrete scratches on the femoral head which produced an increase in polyethylene wear.

Damage to the femoral head produced a three-fold increase in wear with conventional polyethylene, compared to standard condition testing, substantially increasing the risk of osteolysis. While hip simulator studies have not been undertaken on highly cross linked polyethylene on scratched femoral heads, pin on plate studies of highly cross linked polyethylene also show a three-fold increase in wear rate[39] on scratched counter-faces. If this was replicated with scratched heads in the simulator pre-clinically and in the patient, this would lead to wear rates in the range 15 to 30 mm³ per million cycles and potential for osteolysis.

4. Discussion

Patients, clinicians, regulators and healthcare providers expect greater than 90% success rate after ten years implantation for joint replacements. Wear and adverse reactions to wear debris remain the major cause of failure in joint replacements.[1–3] Pre-clinical tribological simulation and evaluation, aligned to developments of

Table 4 Deterioration of femoral head roughness

Prosthesis	Material	Size (mm)	Condition	Wear rate (mm³ per million cycles)	Reference
Hip	Conventional polyethylene	28	Scratched head	100 to 140	6

improved prosthetic solutions, can contribute to improved wear performance, reliability, safety and efficacy and meeting the expectations of users and patients. However, current standard pre-clinical tests, which focus on a single set of conditions are not adequate to evaluate performance across a much wider set of conditions found clinically. Indeed current ISO standard pre-clinical tests have indicated the adequate wear performance for the majority of current prostheses and have not been able to predict wear related failure or wear mechanisms found clinically in some current devices. Many clinical failures from high wear currently occur under conditions outside the standard walking cycle condition described in the standard pre-clinical test.

A new stratified approach to pre-clinical evaluation has been defined and proposed, which provides a frame work to systematically assess the wider range of clinical conditions and variables found in the patient population in order to more rigorously evaluate the tribology of joint replacements. The key to the success of this approach is to define conditions that are realistic and representative of the clinical environment, which can differentiate current devices and which can be validated against current clinical experience. Equally important is the ability to assess the level and change in wear rate with respect to that obtained under standard walking conditions, under which the majority of current prostheses perform adequately, and to compare to wear rates of current materials to clinical performance.

In first part of this paper we have established the baseline tribological performance under the current standard walking cycle test for different bearing materials for historical and current prostheses from our existing data set of over 5 billion test cycles. When combined with clinical experience, we have defined indicative levels of acceptable performance in terms of wear rates for different materials. This indicates a clinical tolerance of a greater wear rate for polyethylene than for metal, due to their differing bio-reactivity and cellular response.

The new stratified approach to pre-clinical testing has been demonstrated in the second part of the paper, with examples of how the different types of clinical conditions influence the wear rate of different prostheses. The amount and rate of increase in wear rate, as well as absolute level of the wear rate compared to the indicative level of acceptable performance is important in determining the clinical significance of the increased wear. Different types of prostheses have been found to respond differently to the different clinical conditions.

In the hip, the intersection of the wear contact patch of the head with the edge of the cup, which results in distinctive stripe wear on the femoral head, was produced by both translational or rotational mal-position of the prosthetic components.[26] The effect of component mal-positioning and edge loading in the hip can lead to a tenfold increase in wear rate for some metal on metal bearings for both types of mal-position and some ceramic on ceramic bearings under translational mal-position only. However the absolute level of wear rate is much higher in metal on metal bearing and the debris more reactive, and therefore more damaging clinically.

This new approach to pre-clinical testing also has allowed us to differentiate between different designs of metal on metal prostheses and different types of ceramic materials, which were not differentiated by the standard test cycle.

In the polyethylene hip, cross linking has been demonstrated to reduce wear under standard conditions, but concerns remain around deterioration of the metallic femoral head with the potential of causing increased wear in the longer term. The scratch resistant ceramic femoral head may mitigate this risk.[40,41]

In the knee an increase in polyethylene wear has been demonstrated with increased kinematic demand, through both an increase anterior posterior translation and femoral lift off. Moderately cross linked polyethylene can reduce the wear under these high demand conditions as well as under standard conditions. Given the wide variations in kinematics seen in knee replacement patients it is essential to study performance of current knee designs under a wider set of kinematic conditions, beyond the single set defined by the standard, rather than try to refine or define the single standard condition to match the ideal patient.

Conditions associated with every single movement or all activities are likely to have more clinical impact than conditions associated with specific activities which occur less frequently. For example a mal-positioned prosthesis will affect every step and result in elevation of wear on every step, as will offset deficiency and leg length discrepancy, which can also cause rim loading in the hip. Similarly in the knee joint laxity and instability, increased AP displacement, or femoral condylar lift off can cause high kinematic demand and increased wear on every step. In contrast raising from a chair, or stair climbing may only impact on less than ten percent of the tribological cycles. Additionally deterioration of prosthetic material or design over time will also impact on the wear on every single movement.

Clearly only a few examples of the application of specific conditions in the stratified framework for pre-clinical testing have been presented in this paper and to date we have not addressed the variation intrinsic in the populations receiving prostheses. Examples of immediate gaps in the knowledge base include, in the hip, the effect of component position on polyethylene wear, particularly the effect of edge loading in thinner polyethylene liners, the influence of cup version on edge contact and wear, the potential for degradation of both cross linked polyethylene and ceramic matrix composites and the role of variations in individual patient reactivity and their tolerance to debris of different types. In the knee surgical alignment and positioning as well as further studies of different kinematic inputs are required. These are just a few examples of different clinical conditions requiring further investigation.

From an academic perspective accurate prediction of wear rates is required. However from a clinical, patient and user perspective, it is more important to define the envelope of conditions in which different prostheses can operate effectively with acceptably low wear rates, and to identify combinations of prosthesis technology and clinical conditions where wear rates exceed the acceptable levels or start to increase rapidly, recognising that each material has a different safe acceptable level of wear rate. Additionally given that the prostheses operate in a complex set of clinical conditions it will be important in the future to address interactions between the different conditions within the groups of conditions and across the groups of conditions.

Bioengineers, tribologists and implant designers have successfully reduced the average wear rates in current prosthetic designs under standard conditions to acceptable low levels for each material type. It is now necessary to focus on producing acceptable tribological performance in the much wider set of conditions found clinically. The stratified approach presented in this paper provides a frame work in which to address this future challenge.

Acknowledgements

JF is an NIHR senior investigator. His research is funded by the EPSRC, by the NIHR LMBRU Leeds Musculoskeletal Biomedical Research Unit, by the centre of excellence in Medical Engineering funded by Wellcome Trust and EPSRC WT 088908/z/09/z, by the Innovation and Knowledge Centre in medical technologies, regenerative therapies and devices, funded by EPSRC, BBSRC and TSB and by ORUK, ARUK, NIH and EU-ERC.

References

1 J. Fisher, Tribology of artificial joints, *Proc. Inst. Mech. Eng., Part H*, 1991, **205**, 73–79.
2 E. Ingham and J. Fisher, Biological reactions to wear debris in total joint replacement, *Proc. Inst. Mech. Eng., Part H*, 2000, **214**, 21–37.
3 E. Ingham and J. Fisher, The role of macrophages in osteolysis of total joint replacement, *Biomaterials*, 2005, **26**, 1271–1286.

4 R. J. A. Bigsby, C. S. Hardaker and J. Fisher, Wear of ultra-high molecular weight polyethylene acetabular cups in a physiological hip joint simulator in the anatomical position using bovine serum as a lubricant, *Proc. Inst. Mech. Eng., Part H*, 1997, **211**, 265–269.

5 P. S. M. Barbour, M. H. Stone and J. Fisher, A hip joint simulator study using simplified loading and motion cycles generating physiological wear paths and rates, *Proc. Inst. Mech. Eng., Part H*, 1999, **212**, 455–467.

6 P. S. M. Barbour, M. H. Stone and J. Fisher, A hip joint simulator study using new and physiologically scratched femoral heads with ultra-high molecular weight polyethylene acetabular cups, *Proc. Inst. Mech. Eng., Part H*, 2000, **214**, 569–576.

7 J. Fisher, H. M. J. McEwen, P. I. Barnett, C. J. Bell, T. D. Stewart, M. H. Stone and E. Ingham, Total knee replacement - practical considerations (i) Wear of polyethylene in artificial knee joints, *Curr. Orthop.*, 2001, **15**, 399–405.

8 P. I. Barnett, H. M. J. McEwen, D. D. Auger, M. H. Stone, E. Ingham and J. Fisher, Investigation of wear of knee prostheses in a new displacement/force-controlled simulator, *Proc. Inst. Mech. Eng., Part H*, 2002, **216**, 51–61.

9 H. M. J. McEwen, J. Fisher, A. A. J. Goldsmith, D. D. Auger, C. Hardaker and M. H. Stone, Wear of fixed bearing and rotating platform mobile bearing knees subjected to high levels of internal and external tibial rotation, *J. Mater. Sci.: Mater. Med.*, 2001, **12**, 1049–1052.

10 J. L. Tipper, E. Ingham, J. L. Hailey, A. A. Besong, J. Fisher, B. M. Wroblewski and M. H. Stone, Quantitative analysis of polyethylene wear debris, wear rate and head damage in retrieved Charnley hip prostheses. Materials Science, *J. Mater. Sci.: Mater. Med.*, 2000, **11**, 117–124.

11 E. Ingham, J. Fisher and M. H. Stone, Wear of historical polyethylene in hip prostheses. Biomechanical success and a biological failure, *Hip Int.*, 2003, **13**, S17–S27.

12 A. L. Galvin, J. L. Tipper, L. M. Jennings, M. H. Stone, Z. M. Jin, E. Ingham and J. Fisher, Wear and biological activity of highly crosslinked polyethylene in the hip under low serum protein concentrations, *Proc. Inst. Mech. Eng., Part H*, 2007, **221**, 1–10.

13 J. E. Nevelos, E. Ingham, C. Doyle, A. B. Nevelos and J. Fisher, The influence of acetabular cup angle on the wear of "BIOLOX Forte" alumina ceramic bearing couples in a hip joint simulator, *J. Mater. Sci.: Mater. Med.*, 2001, **12**, 141–144.

14 P. J. Firkins, J. L. Tipper, M. R. Saadatzadeh, E. Ingham, M. H. Stone, R. Farrar and J. Fisher, Quantitative analysis of wear and wear debris from metal-on-metal hip prostheses tested in a physiological hip joint simulator, *Bio-Med. Mater. Eng.*, 2001, **11**, 143–157.

15 J. Nevelos, E. Ingham, C. Doyle, R. Streicher, A. Nevelos, W. Walter and J. Fisher, Microseparation of the centers of alumina-alumna artificial hip joints during simulator testing produces clinically relevant wear and patterns, *J. Arthroplasty*, 2000, **15**, 793–795.

16 J. E. Nevelos, E. Ingham, C. Doyle, A. B. Nevelos and J. Fisher, Analysis of retrieved alumina ceramic components for Mittelmeier total hip prostheses, *Biomaterials*, 1999, **20**, 1833–1840.

17 J. E. Nevelos, Prudhommeaux, M. Hamadouche, C. Doyle, E. Ingham, A. Meunier, A. B. Nevelos, L. Sedel and J. Fisher, Comparative analysis of two different types of alumina-alumina hip prosthesis retrieved for aseptic loosening, *J. Bone Jt. Surg., Br. Vol.*, 2001, **83**, 598–603.

18 T. Stewart, J. L. Tipper, R. Streicher, E. Ingham and J. Fisher, Long-term wear or HIPed alumina on alumina bearings for THR under microseparation conditions. Journal of Materials Science, *J. Mater. Sci.: Mater. Med.*, 2001, **12**, 1053–1056.

19 A. Hatton, J. E. Nevelos, A. A. Nevelos, R. E. Banks, J. Fisher and E. Ingham, Alumina-alumina artificial hip joints. Part I: A histological analysis and characterisation of wear debris by laser capture micro-dissection of tissues retrieved at revision, *Biomaterials*, 2002, **23**, 3429–3440.

20 S. Williams, M. Butterfield, T. Stewart, E. Ingham, M. H. Stone and J. Fisher, Wear and deformation of ceramic-on-polyethylene total hip replacements with joint laxity and swing phase microseparation, *Proc. Inst. Mech. Eng., Part H*, 2003, **217**, 147–153.

21 S. Williams, T. D. Stewart, E. Ingham, M. H. Stone and J. Fisher, Metal-on-Metal bearing wear with different swing phase loads, *J. Biomed. Mater. Res.*, 2004, **70B**(2), 233–239.

22 J. Fisher, Z. Jin, J. Tipper, M. Stone and E. Ingham, Tribology of Alternative Bearings, *Clin. Orthop. Relat. Res.*, 2006, **453**, 25–34.

23 S. Williams, I. Leslie, G. Isaac, Z. Jin, E. Ingham and J. Fisher, Tribology and wear of metal-on-metal hip prostheses: influence of cup angle and head position, *J. Bone Jt. Surg.*, 2008, **90**(Supplement 3), 111–117.

24 I. J. Leslie, S. Williams, G. Isaac, E. Ingham and J. Fisher, High Cup Angle and Microseparation Increase the Wear of Hip Surface Replacements, *Clin. Orthop. Relat. Res.*, 2009, **467**, 2259–2265.

25 M. Al-Hajjar, I. J. Leslie, J. Tipper, S. Williams, J. Fisher and L. M. Jennings, Effect of cup inclination angle during microseparation and rim loading on the wear of BIOLOX® delta ceramic-on-ceramic total hip replacement, *J. Biomed. Mater. Res. B*, 2010, **95**, 263–268.

26 J. Fisher, Bioengineering reasons for failure of metal on metal hip prostheses, a bioengineers perspective, *J. Bone Jt. Surg., Br. Vol.*, 2011, **93**, 1001–1004.

27 P. J. Firkins, J. L. Tipper, E. Ingham, M. H. Stone, R. Farrar and J. Fisher, Influence of simulator kinematics on the wear of metal-on-metal hip prostheses, *Proc. Inst. Mech. Eng., Part H*, 2001, **215**, 119–121.

28 C. Brockett, S. Williams, Z. M. Jin, G. Isaac and J. Fisher, Friction of total hip replacements with different bearings and loading conditions, *J. Biomed. Mater. Res. B*, 2007, **81**(13), 508–515.

29 S. Williams, D. Jalai-Vahid, C. L. Brockett, Z. Jin, M. H. Stone, E. Ingham and J. Fisher, Effect of swing phase load on metal-on-metal hip lubrication, friction and wear, *J. Biomech.*, 2006, **39**, 2274–2281.

30 H. M. J. McEwen, P. I. Barnett, C. J. Bell, R. Farrar, D. D. Auger, M. H. Stone and J. Fisher, The influence of design, materials and kinematics on the in vitro wear of total knee replacements, *J. Biomech.*, 2005, **38**, 357–365.

31 J. Fisher, L. M. Jennings, A. L. Galvin, Z. M. Jin, M. H. Stone and E. Ingham, 2009 Knee Society Presidential Guest Lecture: Polyethylene Wear in Total Knees, *Clin. Orthop. Relat. Res.*, 2010, **468**, 12–18.

32 L. M. Jennings, C. J. Bell, E. Ingham, R. D. Komistek, M. H. Stone and J. Fisher, The influence of femoral condylar lift-off on the wear of artificial knee joints. Journal of Engineering in Medicine, *Proc. Inst. Mech. Eng., Part H*, 2007, **221**(3), 305–314.

33 J. Bell, J. L. Tipper, E. Ingham, M. H. Stone and J. Fisher, The influence of phospholipid concentration in protein-containing lubricants on the wear of ultra-high molecular weight polyethylene in artificial hip joints, *Proc. Inst. Mech. Eng., Part H*, 2001, **215**, 259–263.

34 J. B. Matthews, A. A. Besong, T. R. Green, M. H. Stone, B. M. Wroblewski, J. Fisher and E. Ingham, Evaluation of the response of primary human peripheral blood mononuclear phagocyted to challenge with *in vitro* generated clinically relevant UHMWPE particles of known size and dose, *J. Biomed. Mater. Res.*, 2000, **52**, 296–307.

35 A. A. Besong, J. L. Tipper, E. Ingham, M. H. Stone, B. M. Wroblewski and J. Fisher, Quantitative comparison of wear debris from UHMWPE that has and has not been sterilised by gamma irradiation, *J. Bone Jt. Surg., Br. Vol.*, 1998, **80**, 340–344.

36 S. Williams, A. Schepers, G. Isaac, C. Hardaker, E. Ingham, D. van der Jagt, A. Breckon and J. Fisher, THE 2007 OTTO AUFRANC AWARD: Ceramic-on-Metal Hip Arthroplasties A Comparative *In Vitro* and *In Vivo* Study, *Clin. Orthop. Relat. Res.*, 2007, **465**, 23–32.

37 I. Leslie, S. Williams, C. Brown, G. Isaac, Z. Jin, E. Ingham and J. Fisher, Effect of bearing size on the long-term wear, wear debris, and ion levels of large diameter metal-on-metal hip replacements-An in vitro study, *J. Biomed. Mater. Res., Part B*, 2008, **87B**, 163–172.

38 I Leslie, Surface engineered hip prostheses, PhD thesis, University of Leeds, 2008.

39 A. L. Galvin, L. Kang, J. L. Tipper, M. H. Stone, E. Ingham, Z. Jin and J. Fisher, Wear of crosslinked polyethylene under different tribological conditions, *J. Mater. Sci.: Mater. Med.*, 2006, **17**(3), 235–243.

40 H. Minakawa, M. H. Stone, B. M. Wroblewski, J. G. Lancaster, E. Ingham and J. Fisher, Quantification of third-body damage and its effect on UHMWPE wear with different types of femoral head, *J. Bone Jt. Surg., Br. Vol.*, 1998, **80**, 894–9.

41 A. L. Galvin, L. M. Jennings, J. L. Tipper, E. Ingham and J. Fisher, Wear and creep of highly cross linked polyethylene against cobalt chrome and ceramic femoral heads, *Proc. Inst. Mech. Eng., Part H*, 2010, **224**, 1175–1183.

Synovial fluid lubrication of artificial joints: protein film formation and composition

Jingyun Fan, Connor Myant, Richard Underwood and Philippa Cann*

Received 12th December 2011, Accepted 6th February 2012
DOI: 10.1039/c2fd00129b

Despite design improvements, wear of artificial implants remains a serious health issue particularly for Metal-on-Metal (MoM) hips where the formation of metallic wear debris has been linked to adverse tissue response. Clearly it is important to understand the fundamental lubrication mechanisms which control the wear process. It is usually assumed that MoM hips operate in the ElastoHydrodynamic Lubrication (EHL) regime where film formation is governed by the bulk fluid viscosity; however there is little experimental evidence of this. The current paper critically examines synovial fluid lubrication mechanisms and the effect of synovial fluid chemistry. Two composition parameters were chosen; protein content and pH, both of which are known to change in diseased or post-operative synovial fluid. Film thickness and wear tests were carried out for a series of model synovial fluid solutions. Two distinct film formation mechanisms were identified; an adsorbed surface film and a high-viscosity gel. The entrainment of this gel controls film formation particularly at low speeds. However wear of the femoral head still occurs and this is thought to be due primarily to a tribo-corrosion mechanisms. The implications of this new lubrication mechanism and the effect of different synovial fluid chemistries are examined. One important conclusion is that patient synovial fluid chemistry plays an important role in determining implant wear and the likelihood of failure.

1. Introduction: synovial fluid lubrication

Recent research in our group has focused on studies of fundamental lubrication mechanisms in MoM hip joints and the effect of synovial fluid composition on film formation and CoCrMo wear.[1,2] This work was prompted in part by the current problems of early failure of some designs of MoM hips[3] which has been related to the effects of metallic wear or corrosion products and the resulting adverse tissue reactions.[4] Wear of prosthetic joints is controlled by the properties and mechanism of formation of the synovial lubricating film and the nature of the articulating surface. The interfacial film thickness is the most important parameter determining wear and this will be influenced by the operating conditions (contact pressure, speed), implant design, manufacture and materials and properties of the lubricant (rheology, chemical composition). Two lubrication mechanisms are normally associated with artificial implants; these are Boundary (BL) and Elastohydrodynamic (EHL). When comparing these regimes it is important to understand that the fundamental mechanisms of generating the lubricating film are different as is the response to changing operating conditions (load, speed, temperature, materials) of the contact.

Tribology Group, Department of Mechanical Engineering, Imperial College London, SW7 2AZ. E-mail: p.cann@imperial.ac.uk

Boundary lubrication (BL) is usually described as the formation of a thin (~1–10 nm), adherent layer on the contacting surfaces which maintains surface separation and prevents adherence under load.[5] Boundary lubricants are typically polar molecules which preferentially react or adsorb at the solid surfaces; they are usually dispersed as a minor component (additive) in a carrier fluid (base oil). As the mechanism relies on a chemical interaction at the surfaces the film thickness is usually independent of speed, however BL film formation is very sensitive to the surface material properties.

Elastohydrodynamic lubrication (EHL) relies on the relative movement of the surfaces to entrain lubricant into the contact zone[6] where the combined effect of hydrodynamic action and surface elastic deformation provides the separating film. Thus film thickness is determined by the operating conditions (kinematics, contact pressure and contact geometry) of the contact and the bulk properties (high shear rate viscosity, pressure-viscosity coefficient) of the lubricant. Thus EHL films increase with increasing speed and are relatively insensitive to pressure. The nature of the contacting surfaces plays a lesser role in EHL.

It is commonly assumed that MoM joint lubrication is determined by EHL "rules" and operates in the "fluid film" regime,[6] thus many of the new generation MoM hips have been designed to optimise this mechanism.[7] This theory is based on the assumption that synovial fluid acts as a single-phase, isoviscous fluid[6] and thus has a predictable response to the changing loads and speeds occurring during the gait cycle. Synovial fluid has a complex rheology; it is rheopectic at low shear rates[8] but shear-thinning at high shear rates,[9] thus it is normally assumed that synovial fluid is essentially Newtonian at physiological shear rates with an effective viscosity of 0.0009 Pa s.[6]

Synovial fluid is a complex mixture of large and surface-active molecules;[10] these include proteins, phospholipids, hyaluronic acid, cholesterol and glycoproteins. The component concentration, particularly for the proteins, can vary greatly.[10] Diseased and periprosthetic synovial fluid undergoes changes including decreased effective viscosity, increased protein content and increased pH.[10] It is possible that variations in synovial fluid chemistry affect implant wear, however these effects are not predicted by the "fluid film" model. One key question in the current work is the effect of patient synovial fluid chemistry on implant wear, the formation of corrosive products and the likelihood of revision. Many papers[11–14] have studied the effect of protein concentration and test fluid chemistry on implant wear. However this work is mainly confined to polymer (UHMWPE) wear and the results are often contradictory as it is very difficult to interpret lubrication mechanisms from implant simulator tests.

An alternative mechanism is that the joints operate in the boundary lubrication regime where adsorbed or reacted chemical films are formed on the sliding surfaces. There are a number of components in synovial fluid that could fulfil this role including, proteins[15,16] phospholipids[17] and glycoproteins.[18] Evidence of protein[15,16] and phospholipid[17] species at the surface or in the near-surface fluid has been reported for *in vitro* and *in vivo* test implants. Wang *et al.*[15] suggested the surface film formed by "insoluble" proteins acted to reduce adhesion and protect rubbing surfaces from wear.

Although the fluid film and boundary lubrication mechanisms have been presented separately it is more likely that both mechanisms occur over the gait cycle. One of the problems however when considering implant lubrication mechanisms is these theories were developed for high-contact pressures and hydrocarbon lubricants and might not be applicable to the very different conditions for implants. In well-positioned hip joints the contact pressures and sliding speeds are low compared to engineering contacts. The aim of our research therefore has been to examine synovial fluid lubrication mechanisms without "high-pressure" preconceptions.

Previous papers[1,2] in this study reported film thickness measurements for bovine serum and protein-containing fluids; evidence of boundary and high-viscous film formation with proteins was presented. The objective of the current paper was to summarise film thickness and wear results already published in the research programme, to present new work on the nature of surface films and to explore in more depth the mechanisms of synovial fluid film formation and wear. Specifically we examine the effect of different SF chemistry representative of changes due to OA; this includes increased protein content and pH, on film formation and wear.

2. Experimental programme

2.1 Film thickness and wear measurements

Film thickness and wear measurements were carried out with a thin film optical interferometric test device using a femoral head/glass disc contact. The test device was supplied by PCS Instruments London. The measurement technique was reported in earlier papers[2,19,20] and only a brief description will be given here. Optical interferometry was used to measure central film thickness over a range of 1–1000 nm. The measured Ra surface roughnesses (Ra: centre line average of the surface roughness) of the glass disc and CoCrMo surface were 15 and 20 nm respectively. Film thickness was measured either at constant speed (0, 10, 20 mm s^{-1}) as a function of time (or sliding distance) or for changing speed over a range of 5–50 mm s^{-1}. A load of 5 N was used; this corresponds to a mean Hertzian contact pressure of 130 MPa at the start of the test.

It is also possible to observe film formation directly using a thin film imaging method (SLIM).[19] A diagram of the test method is shown in Fig. 1. In a recent development wear scar measurements on the CrCoMo head were also made during the film thickness tests.[20] This allows simultaneous measurement of film thickness, wear and contact pressure (estimated from the effective contact area).[20]

Film formation and femoral head wear was measured for a range of model synovial fluids, the effect of composition (protein content and pH) and sliding condition (load, speed) was studied. One of the aims of the work was to simulate changes occurring in synovial fluid chemistry due to disease (OA) or post-implant.[10] Thus increases in pH (7.4 to 8.5) and protein content (10 mg ml^{-1}–30 mg ml^{-1} albumin) were investigated. Tris buffer solution (modified with the addition of HCl) was used to prepare the pH samples. The measured high shear rate (1000 s^{-1}) viscosity

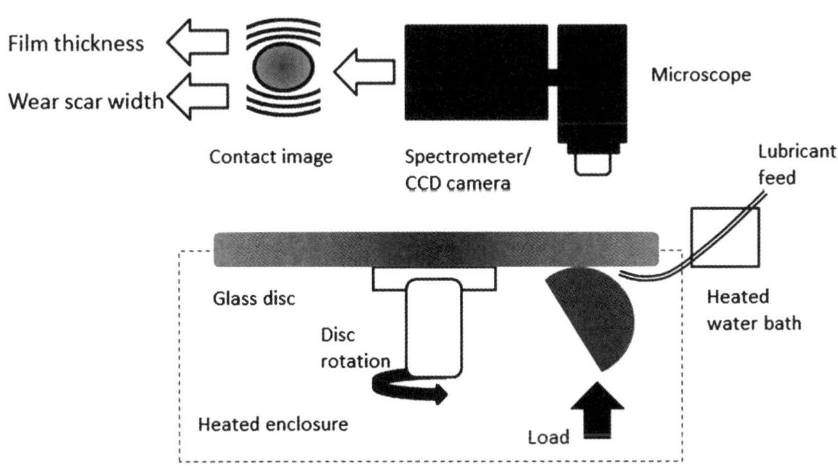

Fig. 1 Schematic diagram of film thickness and wear measurement.

Table 1 Model synovial fluid solutions[a]

Test fluid	Composition	pH @ 23 °C
AGW	10 mg ml⁻¹ albumin and 2 mg ml⁻¹ γ-globulin	7.2
BCS25	25% BCS in deionised water	7.34
pH 7.4	25% BCS in Tris-HCl	7.37
pH 8.0	25% BCS in Tris-HCl	7.95
pH 8.5	25% BCS in Tris-HCl	8.48
Alb10	10 mg ml⁻¹ albumin in saline	—
Alb30	30 mg ml⁻¹ albumin in saline	—
Gb6	6 mg ml⁻¹ γ-globulin in saline	—

[a] Albumin: bovine serum albumin Sigma Aldrich A7906. γ-globulin: bovine γ-globulin Sigma Aldrich 4030. Bovine serum: Sigma Aldrich 12133C protein concentration 72 mg ml⁻¹. Tris: tr solution pH modified by addition of HCl. Saline solution: 0.0154 M sodium chloride in distilled water.

Table 2 Test conditions

Test condition	Value
Load	5 N (130 MPa mean Hertz pressure)
Speed sweep range (mean)	5–50 mm s⁻¹
Constant speed (mean)	0, 10, 20 mm s⁻¹
Test temperature	35–37 °C
Upper specimen	Glass disc, chromium/silica coating
Lower specimen	CrCoMo femoral head 38 mm diameter
Number of tests	2 per condition

of 25% bovine serum fluids were in the range 0.002–0.003 Pa s. The lubricants and test conditions are summarised in Tables 1 and 2.

2.2 Examination of femoral head surfaces

The femoral head surface was examined before and after testing using an optical microscope and optical interferometric surface profilometer (Wyko NT1100). The femoral head was rinsed with deionised water to remove the bulk fluid prior to examination.

3. Results and discussion

3.1 Film thickness measurements

An example of film thickness formed under constant speed conditions is shown for 25% BCS in Fig. 2. Film thickness gradually increases with time over a period of 720 s. The film thickness at 10 mm s⁻¹ (~35 nm) was significantly greater than at 0 mm s⁻¹ (~10 nm). These results are summarised in Fig. 3 for a range of albumin and globulin solutions, similar results were reported in ref. 20. In all tests the globulin-containing fluids formed the thickest films. Images taken of the loaded contact at the start and after 10 min and 20 min are shown in Fig. 4 for a mixed albumin/globulin solution formed at 0 mm s⁻¹. The images show the Hertzian contact in the centre of the picture. The formation of a boundary film is initially seen as discrete yellow regions within the Hertzian contact. As the test proceeds these spots coalesce and turn dark brown/red indicating a local increase in film thickness. The film is not

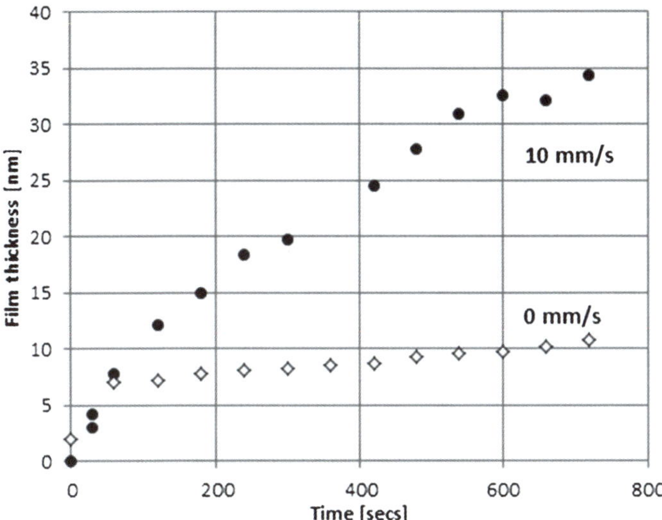

Fig. 2 Summary of film thickness measurements, 0 and 10 mm s^{-1} BCS25.

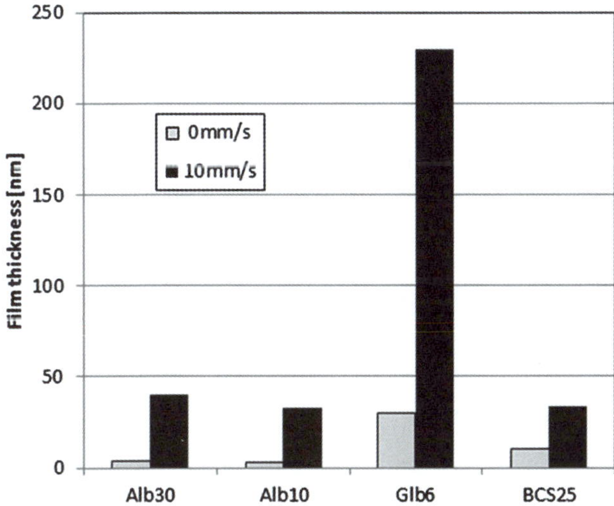

Fig. 3 Summary of film thickness measurements after 10 min for different speeds.

uniform over the contact region and this probably reflects the topography and composition of the CrCoMo alloy surface. A photograph of the femoral head surface is shown in Fig. 5. The femoral head is "as cast" (no heat treatment) and the photograph shows the characteristic "blocky carbide" structures associated with this manufacturing process.[21]

Film formation at different speeds is shown in Fig. 6, these measurements were taken at the end of the constant speed (10 mm s^{-1}) test. In this case significant wear of the surface had occurred and the corresponding contact pressures were low, typically <50 MPa. The film thickness speed response is very different for the low and high protein concentration fluids. For the low-protein solutions film thickness increased with sliding speed; the high protein solutions showed the opposite

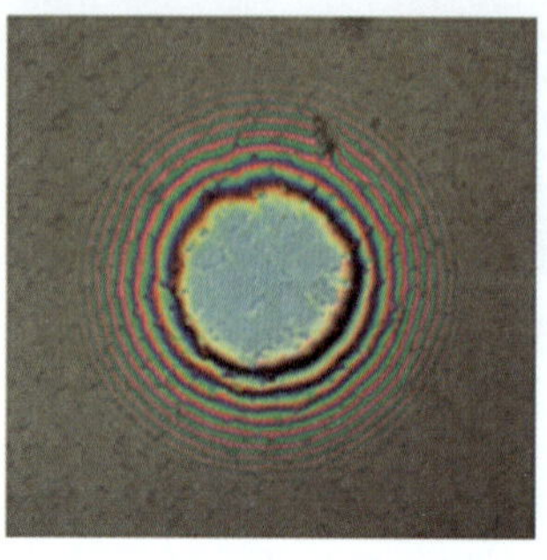
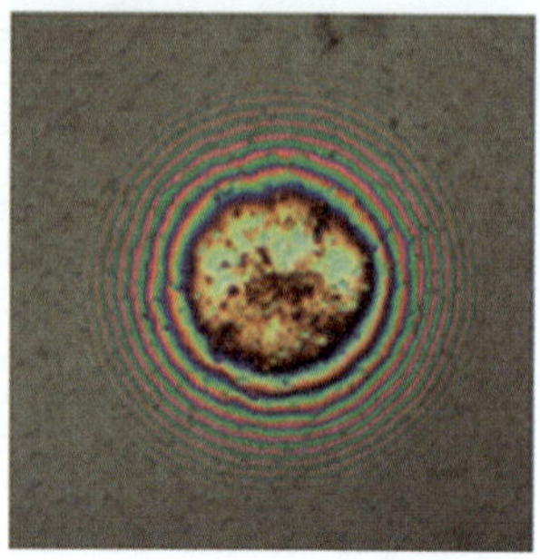

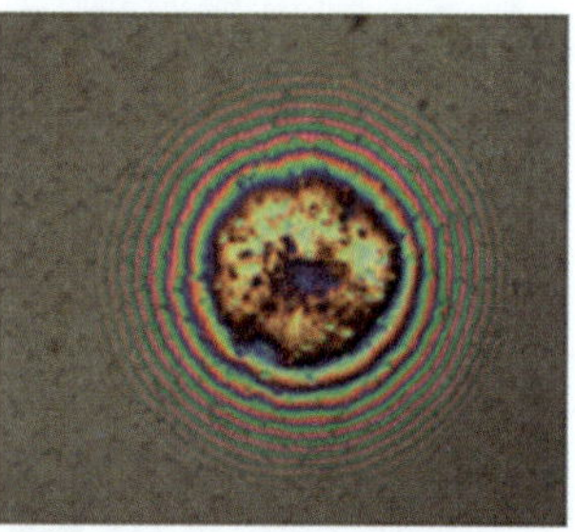

Fig. 4 SLIM images from a static, loaded contact with an albumin/globulin fluid present. The initial blue colour is due to the silica spacer layer. The formation of a separating film is seen initially as yellow regions and then brown/red areas.

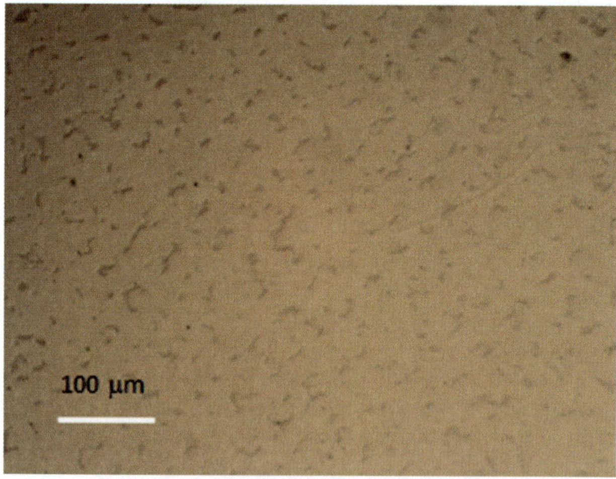

Fig. 5 Photograph of femoral head surface.

effect. Significantly, for 25% bovine serum the response corresponded to the "high" concentration model. Our (albeit limited) results suggest this is observed for total protein concentrations of >20 mg ml^{-1}. 25% bovine serum typically contains

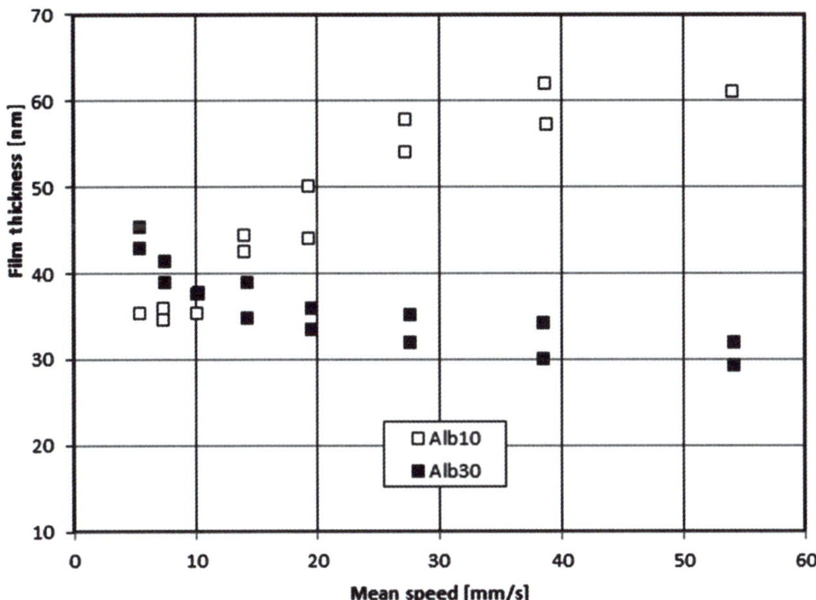

Fig. 6 Film thickness as a function of speed: low and high albumin concentrations. Two tests for each concentration.

18–20 mg ml⁻¹ but this includes significant globulin content. The presence of globulin has been shown to promote the formation of very thick films at low speeds.[2,20]

An in-contact image for 25% BCS fluid is shown in Fig. 7 where the colours in the Hertzian region correspond to different film thicknesses. At low speeds the BCS solution forms very thick lubricant films and this behaviour is usually associated with the development of a new gel-phase in the inlet region. At higher speeds this new phase disappears and the film thickness decreases. This behaviour is not seen for simple fluids where the film thickness increases with speed. This unusual lubricating behaviour is discussed in Section 3.4.

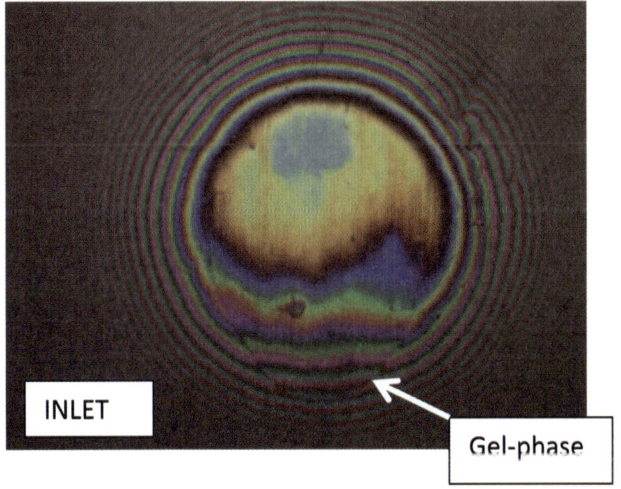

Fig. 7 In-contact image for low speed sliding with BCS25 solution.

In a separate series of tests the effect of solution pH on film formation was examined. Representative film thickness results are presented in Fig. 8 for pH 7.4, pH 8.0 and pH 8.4 as a function of time for 0 (repeat loading) and 20 mm s^{-1}. In these

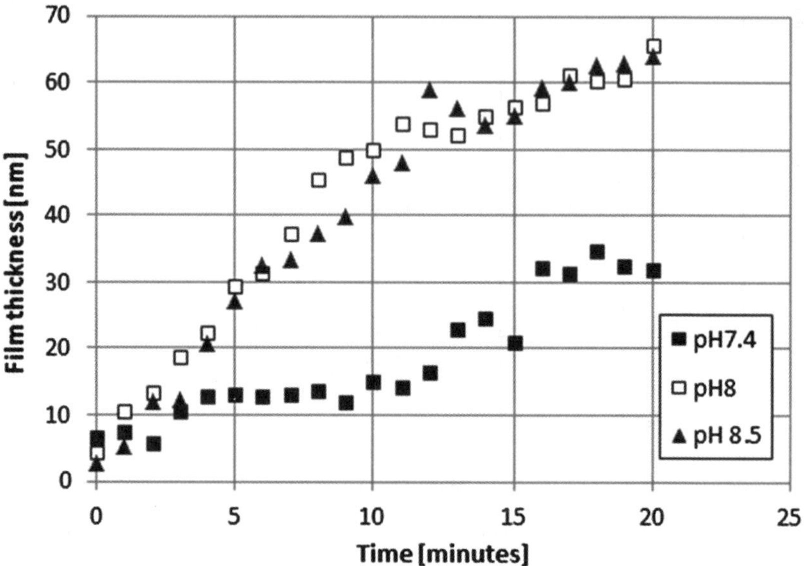

(a) 0 mm/s static loading

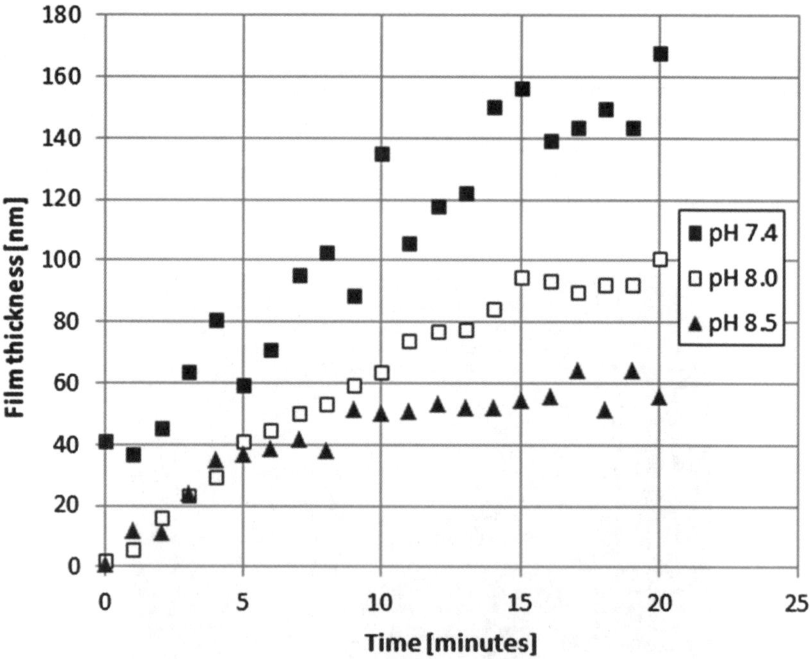

(b) 20 mm/s

Fig. 8   Film thickness results at constant mean speed (0, 20 mm s^{-1}) for Tris solutions: pH 7.4, pH 8.0 and pH 8.5.

graphs film thickness is plotted against time over 20 min. Clear differences are measured in the film thickness at the end of the test as follows:

$$0 \text{ mm s}^{-1} \quad \text{pH } 8.0, \text{ pH } 8.5 \gg \text{pH } 7.4$$

$$20 \text{ mm s}^{-1} \quad \text{pH } 7.4 > \text{pH } 8.0 > \text{pH } 8.5$$

3.2 Wear measurements

The optical test method allows the simultaneous measurement of film thickness and wear scar width. In an earlier paper the effect of protein content on wear was investigated.[20] The current study examines the effect of BS solution pH on wear scar width. The development of the wear scar is plotted against sliding distance in Fig. 9 for 25% BCS at pH 7.4 and 8.5 (the pH 8.0 results were similar to pH 8.5). Two speeds are plotted for each pH level and quite clearly for both speed levels the wear scar width pH7.4 < pH 8.5. The results for pH 7.4, pH 8.0 and pH 8.5 solutions (after 12 m sliding) are summarised in Fig. 10. The wear results are plotted as normalised effective Hertzian width ((measured contact width (a_i)/contact width at start (a_0)) $-$ 1). Significant differences were obtained in wear scar diameter for the different solutions the wear ranking was as follows:

$$\text{pH } 7.4 < \text{pH } 8.0 \sim \text{BCS25} < \text{pH } 8.5$$

$$\text{Least} \qquad\qquad \text{Highest}$$

3.3 Surface analysis

Images of the wear scars formed on the femoral head are shown in Fig. 11. These were taken after light rinsing with distilled water. The wear scar is seen in

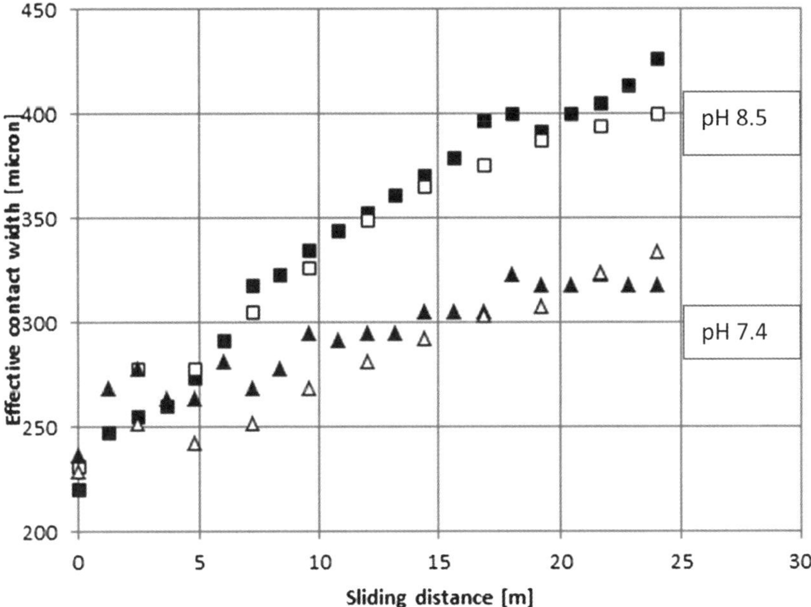

Fig. 9 Examples of effective contact width growth for pH 7.4 and pH 8.5 BCS solutions plotted as a function of sliding distance. Closed symbols 10 mm s^{-1}, open symbols 20 mm s^{-1} mean sliding speed.

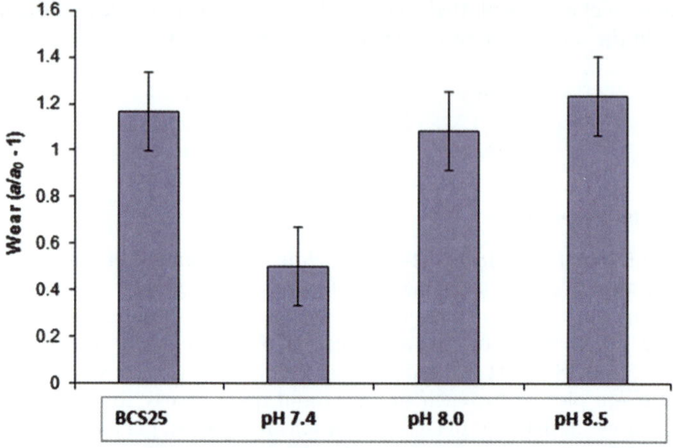

Fig. 10   Summary of wear scar measurements (12 m sliding distance) for different solutions.

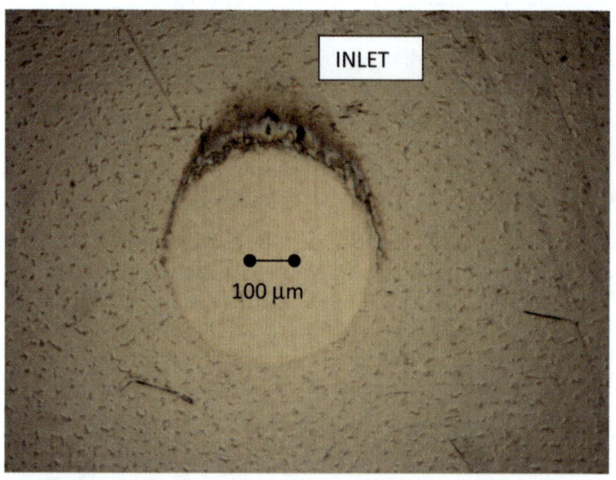

(a) ALB20 after rinsing

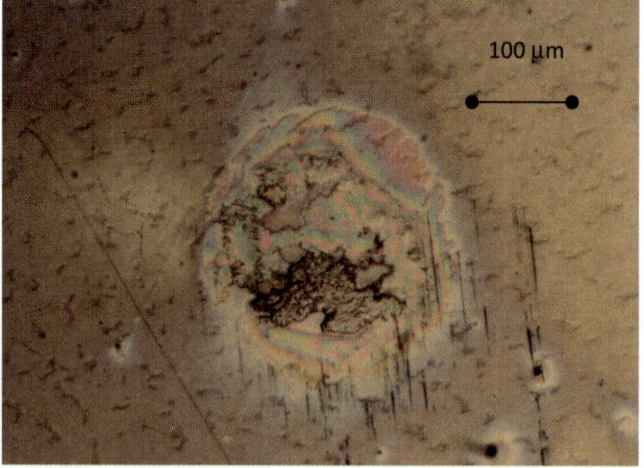

(b) GLB6 after rinsing

Fig. 11   Images of wear scars after testing (note different magnifications).

the centre of the Alb20 image, the surface appears polished with almost complete loss of the carbide structures. On the inlet side of the scar there is a halo of deposited material. For the Glb6 image there is considerable material in and around the contact area. With repeated washing this material was removed and a small, wear scar with the typical polished surface was revealed. One general observation from this work is that once removed from the fluid environment and allowed to dry the protein deposits were very difficult to remove.

Surface topography images are shown in Fig. 12 for areas outside and within the wear scar. The block structures on the fresh surface are typically 80–100 nm high with typical surface dimensions of 40 μm × 15 μm. This compares to a Hertzian width of 250 μm at the start of the test. Within the wear scar substantial loss of the carbide surface structures occurs, in-contact imaging indicates these were lost within a few minutes of the start of sliding.

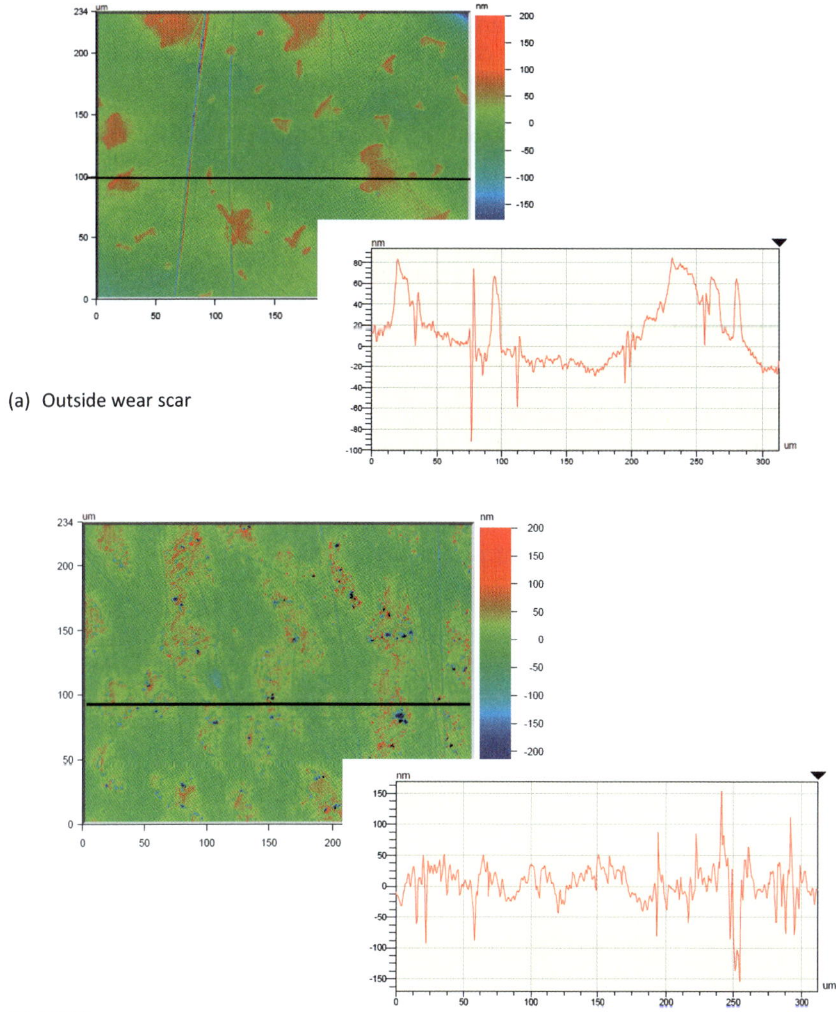

(a) Outside wear scar

(b) Within wear scar

Fig. 12   Surface topography of femoral head within and outside wear scar.

3.4 Discussion: film formation and wear mechanisms

3.4.1 Lubrication mechanisms. The film thickness measurements have shown very different behaviour depending on the protein content and solution pH. Two distinct mechanisms of film formation were observed:

Boundary film formation. Protein "boundary" films deposited on static surfaces; this was observed for both unloaded and repeat loaded surfaces. Film formation is discontinuous over the surface and probably related to local composition. The film thickness results for the albumin solutions agree with published results from AFM measurements on static surfaces.[22] When γ-globulin was present much thicker films were measured (Fig. 4). These films support the load in static contacts which suggest they resist sliding or are replenished during rubbing. The results from this and earlier papers[1,2] indicate two different levels of film formation:

1. Thin residual film which is formed by mono or multilayer adsorbed protein molecules; this is adherent and is typically less than 10 nm thick.

2. In static, repeated loaded contacts additional loosely-bound layers (20–60 nm) are formed possibly due to denaturing and deposition of proteins within the contact zone under load. This material can be removed from the contact zone by relative movement of the disc and head surface.

Inlet agglomeration. In rubbing contacts a second film formation mechanism has been observed; this is driven by the formation of a local reservoir of high viscosity gel in the inlet region and is essentially hydrodynamic in origin. This behaviour has been reported in earlier papers[1,2,20] and only a summary is given here. The mechanism predominates at low speeds where a new-phase is observed in the inlet (Fig. 7). High-viscosity material collects in the convergent region at the entrance to the contact and appears to be associated with the static (femoral head) surface. Period-ically this material is entrained into the contact, locally increasing the film thickness. The measured film thickness is much greater than predicted from EHL calculations using the bulk fluid viscosity,[2] suggesting a highly-concentrated protein solution. The EHL model uses a simple isoviscous, incompressible formulation which clearly does not predict the behaviour seen in the film thickness tests. Globular proteins form gel-networks at low shear rates and this is the origin of the rheopectic behav-iour of SF.[8] The formation of precipitates during hip simulator tests with BCS is also attributed to this mechanism rather than thermal denaturing.[23] The protein gel forms in the inlet region and is often still present on the surface after rinsing (Fig. 11) and this was very evident for γ-globulin-containing fluids which formed very thick deposited layers. One important observation from this work is that in the fluid environment these protein deposits are mobile and easily removed by surface scratches or sharp protuberances. The carbide structures measured on the as-cast surfaces are typically 100 nm high,[21] as well as producing high local contact pressures, these artefacts tend to sweep away the gel layers which are then reformed with continued sliding. Once these films are removed from the fluid environment and allowed to dry they become highly-adherent and very difficult to remove. The forma-tion of adherent organic deposits has been reported by many workers[15,16] but only for the dried films. Thus *in vivo* these organic layers have gel rather than solid properties.

The film thickness distribution observed with this mechanism is very different from a classical fluid EHL film (Fig. 7b) which is fairly constant over the central region. Film thickness decreases rapidly towards the centre of the contact and this is thought to be due to combined effects of shear and pressure. This material is retained within the contact as an "entrapment" if the contact is stopped under load. Static tests with these protein films showed the film thickness was very sensitive to increasing load but they elastically recovered once the load was removed.[20] The sensitivity to load is demonstrated in Fig. 13 which plots film thickness for a BCS25, Alb30 and Glb6 films. The film reduction with increasing load is thought to be due to extrusion of water from the porous protein-gel; this recovers almost

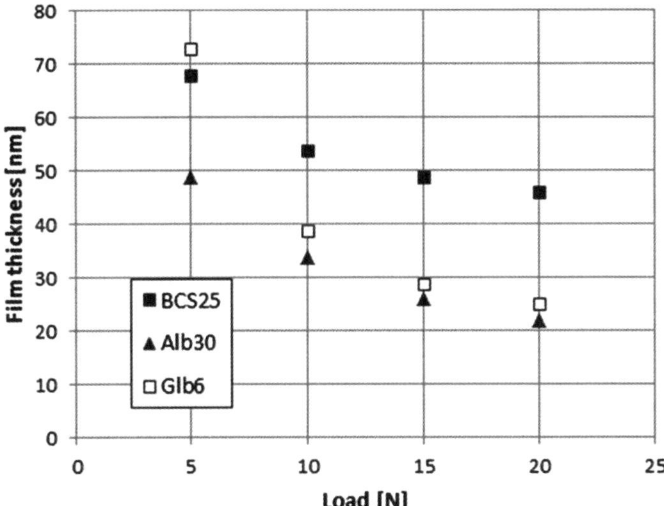

Fig. 13 Effect of load on film thickness in a static contact.

completely once the load is reduced. The ability of this gel-material to form an elastic separating film under static loading has important implications for lubrication of implants and surface protection at during stance and at start-up.

3.4.2 Wear mechanisms. One surprising aspect of this work was the rapid formation of a wear scar on the femoral head. In earlier work using conventional hydrocarbon lubricants, where damage has occurred to the metal surface there has been matching loss of the silica spacer layer. In the current study very little damage to the spacer layer occurred although in some cases scratches were observed. This lack of damage suggested the predominant wear mechanism was due to corrosion rather than abrasion. In an earlier paper[20] wear measurements were made for a series of protein solutions; the most important parameter was the presence of globulin which significantly decreased the size of the wear scar.

Observation of the contact during sliding showed the 'blocky' surface structures were rapidly lost within the first few minutes of sliding. In some cases this material appeared to embed in the glass disc and caused scratches in the contact zone (Fig. 11) during successive revolutions of the disc. As-cast CoCrMo alloys have a bi-phasic surface structure which is characterised by the formation of carbides with locally increased chromium, molybdenum and carbon contents.[21] Once these surface structures were lost the effective contact width increased rapidly; this is clearly seen in Fig. 9 and in the results at 12 m sliding (Fig. 10). Increasing effective contact width corresponds to the formation of a flat wear scar on the femoral head. One consequence of this is that the effective contact pressure drops significantly and it is possible to esti mate this change. In these tests the mean contact pressure ranges from $\sim$120 MPa at the start of the test to <50 MPa for an effective contact width of 400 μm. In earlier work[20] we reported that film thickness appeared to be highly sensitive to contact pressure and similar results have been obtained in the current study.

The loss of the carbide structures occurs very rapidly at the start this is followed by the development of a smooth wear scar as the test continues. The very rapid formation of a smooth wear scar with very little accompanying damage to the silica layer strongly suggests that the wear process is dominated by chemical-corrosion rather than a physical abrasion process. This conclusion is supported by the current results which show a correlation of wear with pH of the BCS solution. It is well known that tribocorrosion plays an important role in metal implant wear and debris formation.[24–26] Yan, Neville and Dowson[24] reported that 20–30% of wear in the steady-state regime is corrosion related. Lewis *et al.*[26] suggested that protein films play a dual role in controlling surface reactions; firstly, by forming a negatively-charged protective layer, they prevent attack at the CrCoMo interface by corrosive anions. However the protein layer also contributes through ligand-induced dissolution at the interface which increases the chromium concentration in the SF.[26] Thus the role of synovial fluid components in film formation is only part of the story. Although such films will protect against mechanical wear (adhesion/abrasion) they play a more ambiguous role when chemical or corrosive damage mechanisms are considered.

3.5 Implications for artificial implant tribology: patient and design factors

One objective of the research programme was to explore factors that are likely to influence implant performance particularly the effect of patient SF chemistry and implant design. In this and a previous paper[20] we report the effects of protein content and test fluid pH on film formation and femoral head wear. A number of studies have reported changes in the protein content and composition of diseased (OA) and periprosthetic SF.[10,11,27] The overall protein content is reported to increase from 18–20 mg ml^{-1} to 30–32 mg ml^{-1} for OA and >30 mg ml^{-1} for periprosthetic SF.[10,11,27] In addition the albumin/γ-globulin ratio decreases. The pH of healthy SF is in the range 7.3–7.43 but for OA or periprosthetic patients this can increase to pH 8.6.

The current results indicate that increasing protein content and particularly γ-globulin (Fig. 3) increases film thickness and there was a direct correlation with femoral head wear.[20] The protein concentration range used in this study covers the healthy/diseased range. The measured wear ranking[20] was as follows:

$$GLb6 \ll BCS25 < Alb30 < Alb10$$

Least wear   Highest wear

However these results were measured at a constant speed of 10 mm s^{-1} where the high protein content would be expected to provide thicker films and this might not necessarily be true for other speed conditions. The results plotted in Fig. 6 show more complex speed dependence where the high protein content film thickness reduces with increasing speed. These results, if translated to the more complex kinematics of real hip joints, suggest that implant wear will depend on SF protein content and implant design. Increasing head size (for example from 28 to 60 mm diameter) associated with the new generation resurfacing and LHMoM designs results in higher sliding speeds and would favour patients with low protein content SF. Patient SF with high protein/globulin content would provide increased surface protection at low speeds and at stance however this advantage is lost at higher speeds. However this hypothesis represents a significant leap from the model test results presented in this paper and much further work is needed to verify these tentative conclusions. The other patient SF factor studied was test fluid pH and wear scar width increased significantly with increasing pH.

Recent trends in MoM design have been towards increasing head diameters (up to 60 mm) and decreasing clearance.[6] The increased head size results in higher sliding speeds, from simple EHL calculations this should result in thicker fluid films[6,7] (typically film thickness $\sim$ mean speed$^{0.7}$) and thus greater surface protection. However the more complex speed behaviour observed in this work suggest this relationship cannot be assumed. The combined effect of increasing head size and decreasing clearance is to decrease the contact pressure (typically from 80 MPa to 40 MPa). The protein-gel film have been shown to be extremely sensitive to pressures in this range and this might be one reason improved MoM wear results were obtained for the new designs in hip simulator tests.

One significant criticism of the current work is that the rubbing test is a poor simulation of gait kinematics and loading in real life. In-hip simulators and *in vitro* implants experience complex multidirectional sliding patterns. In our tests the sliding is simple and unidirectional; the speed and load are fairly constant. Thus the observed pattern of inlet gel formation might not be applicable to highly transient (speed, load, cross-shear) operation. In reality neither surface is stationary so that inlet build-up is unlikely to occur over a significant time-scale. However the entrainment speeds and contact pressures are typical of hip implant walking gait. Therefore we suggest this mechanism is responsible for localised aggregation of proteins that pass into the contact zone and contributes to increased film formation.

A second criticism of the experimental approach is the material combination. In the current tests a glass counterface was used as the moving surface. The presence of the galls was not thought to influence gel formation as this was the result of shear flow through a converging gap. The protein gel build-up occurred on the static surface which was the CoCrMo alloy. However movement of the gel through the contact was due to adherence to the glass surface and this will be influenced by wetting characteristics of the surfaces. With this in mind we are currently expanding our experimental capability to address these issues.

The very simple results reported in this and earlier papers[20] indicate that patient SF chemistry will play a significant role in determining wear and this could be design-specific. At present the function of SF properties in determining implant performance is implicitly ignored in all the lubrication models. Our work suggests that patient SF chemistry should be considered as a factor in determining the choice of implant.

4. Conclusions

The paper examines lubrication and wear mechanism for protein-containing solutions in a model test device. Our conclusions are as follows:

1. Two distinct film formation mechanisms: boundary and "gel" hydrodynamic:

a. Boundary lubrication mechanism: proteins adsorb at the CrCoMo surface to form thin, discontinuous deposited films. These appear to survive rubbing.

b. High-concentration protein fluids form an inlet reservoir of viscous material that is entrained into the contact forming a separating film.

c. The organic deposits reported in the literature on implant surfaces are formed by agglomerated-proteins. In the fluid environment these deposits are viscous and can be easily removed by surface scratches. Once removed from the fluid they dry to form highly-adherent, solid films.

2. Wear mechanisms are primarily driven by tribocorrosion processes:

a. Increasing pH increases CoCrMo wear.

3. Patient synovial fluid chemistry plays an important role in determining implant wear and the likelihood of failure. This factor should be included in the choice of implant.

List of abbreviations

BCS	Bovine calf serum
BL	Boundary lubrication
CoCrMo	Cobalt chromium molybdenum alloy
EHL	Elastohydrodynamic lubrication
HA	Hyaluronic acid
MoM	Metal-on-Metal
SF	Synovial fluid
TRIS	Tris(hydroxymethyl)aminomethane

Acknowledgements

The authors wish to thank the UK EPSRC for funding this research: "In Contact Analysis of Synovial Fluid Lubricating Film Properties" (EP/H020837/1) and Platform Grant "Nanotribology: Measurement and Modelling across the Rubbing Interface" (EP/G026114/1).

References

1 A. Mavraki and P. M. Cann, Lubricating Film Thickness measurements with Bovine Serum, *Tribol. Int.*, 2011, **44**, 550–556.
2 J. Fan, C. Myant, R. Underwood, P. M. Cann and A. Hart, Inlet Protein Aggregation: A New Mechanism for Lubricating Film Formation with Model Synovial Fluids, *Proc. Inst. Mech. Eng., Part H*, 2011, **225**, 696–709.
3 National Joint Registry 7th Annual Report 2010.
4 P. A. Revell, N. Al-Saffar and Kobayashi, Biological reaction to debris in relation to joint prostheses, *Proc. Inst. Mech. Eng., Part H*, 1997, **211**, 187–197.
5 F. P. Bowden, and D. Tabor, *The Friction and Lubrication of Solids, Part I*, Oxford Press, 1950.
6 D. Dowson, Tribological principles in metal-on-metal hip joint design, *Proc. Inst. Mech. Eng., Part H*, 2006, **220**, 161–171.
7 W.-Z. Wang, Z. M. Jin, D. Dowson and Y. Z. Hu, A study of the effect of model geometry and lubricant rheology upon the elastohydrodynamic lubrication performance of metal-on-metal hip joints, *Proc Inst. Mech. Eng., Part J*, 2008, **222**, 493–500.
8 K. Oates, W. E. Krause, R. L. Jones and R. H. Colby, Rheopexy of synovial fluid and protein aggregation, *J. R. Soc. Interface*, 2006, **3**, 167–174.
9 A. F. Cooke, D. Dowson and V. Wright, The rheology of synovial fluid and some potential synthetic lubricants for degenerate synovial joints, *ARCHIVE: Engineering in Medicine 1971-1988 (vols 1-17)*, 1978, **7**, 66–72.
10 T. Kitano, G. A. Ateshian, V. C. Mow, Y. Kadoya and Y. Yamano, Constituents and pH changes in protein rich hyaluronan solution affect the biotribological properties of artificial articular joints, *J. Biomech.*, 2001, **34**, 1031–1037.
11 A. Wang, A. Essner and G. Schmidig, The Effects of Lubricant Composition on *in vitro* Wear Testing of Polymeric Acetabular Components, *J. Biomed. Mater. Res.*, 2003, **68B**, 45–52.
12 Y.-S. Liao, P. D. Benya and H. A. McKellop, Effect of Protein Lubrication on the Wear Properties of Materials for Prosthetic Joints, *J. Biomed. Mater. Res.*, 1999, **48**, 465–473.
13 Y. Sawae, A. Yamamoto and T. Murakami, Influence of protein and lipid concentration of the test lubricant on the wear of ultra-high molecular weight polyethylene, *Tribol. Int.*, 2008, **41**, 648–656.
14 V. Saikko, Effect of lubricant protein concentration on the wear of ultra-high molecular weight polyethylene sliding against a CoCr counterface, *J. Tribol.*, 2003, **125**, 638–642.
15 A. Wang, A. Essner, V. K. Polineni, C. Stark and J. H. Dumbleton, Lubrication and wear of ultra-high molecular weight polyethylene in total joint replacements, *Tribol. Int.*, 1998, **31**, 17–33.
16 M. A. Wimmer, C. Sprecher, R. Hauert, G. Täger and A. Fischer, Tribochemical reaction on metal-on-metal hip joint bearings. A comparison between in vitro and in vivo results, *Wear*, 2003, **255**, 1007–1014.
17 B. Purbach, B. A. Hills and B. M. Wroblewski, Surface-active phospholipid in total hip arthroplasty, *J. Orthop. Res.*, 2002, **396**, 115–118.
18 M. Roba, M. Naka, E. Gautier, N. D. Spencer and R. Crockett, The adsorption and lubrication behaviour of synovial fluid proteins and glycoproteins on the bearing-surface material of hip replacements, *Biomaterials*, 2008, **30**, 2072–2078.
19 P. M. Cann, Hutchinson and H. A. Spikes, The Development of a Spacer Layer Imaging Method (SLIM), *Tribol. Trans.*, 1996, **39**, 915–921.
20 C. Myant, R. J Underwood, J. Fan and P. M Cann, Lubrication of Metal-on-Metal Hip Joints: The Effect of Protein Content and Load on Film Formation and Wear, *J. Mech. Behav. Biomed. Mater.*, 2012, **6**, 30–40.
21 Modern Hip Resurfacing Ed. McMinn, D. Springer, 2009, ISBN 978-1-84800-087-2.
22 C. M. Pradier, F. Karman, J. Telegdi, E. Kalman and P. Marcus, Adsorption of Bovine Serum Albumin on Chromium and Molybdenum Surfaces Investigated by Fourier-Transform Infrared Reflection-Absorption Spectroscopy (FT-IRRAS) and X-ray Photoelectron Spectroscopy, *J. Phys. Chem. B*, 2003, **107**, 6766–6773.

23 V. K. Maskiewicz, P. A. Williams, S. J. Prates, J. G. Bowsher and I. C. Clarke, Characterization of protein degradation in serum-based lubricants during simulation wear testing of metal-on-metal hip prostheses, *J. of Biomedical Mat. Res - Part B Applied Biomaterials*, 2010, **94**, 429–440.

24 Y. Yan, A. Neville and D. Dowson, Biotribocorrosion—an appraisal of the time dependence of wear and corrosion interactions: I. The role of corrosion, *J. Phys. D: Appl. Phys.*, 2006, **39**, 3200–3205.

25 Y. Yan, A. Neville and D. Dowson, Biotribocorrosion of CoCrMo orthopaedic implant materials - Assessing the formation and effect of the biofilm, *Tribol. Int.*, 2007, **40**, 1492–1499.

26 A. C. Lewis, M. R. Kilburn, I. Papageorgiou, G. C. Allen and C. P. Case, The effect of synovial fluid, phosphate buffered saline solution and water on the dissolution and corrosion properties of CoCrMo alloys as used in orthopaedic implants., *J. Biomed. Mater. Res., Part A*, 2005, **73A**, 456–467.

27 J. Delecrin, M. Oka, S. Takahashi, T. Yamamuro and T. Nakamura, Changes in joint fluid after total arthoplasty, *Clin. Orthop. Rel. Res.*, 1994, **307**, 240–249.

General discussion

Professor Klein opened the discussion of the paper by Professor Dr Sawyer: The issue of friction at cell surfaces and cellular response to shear stress, which your talk emphasizes, is intriguing. I have two comments, related to friction at articular cartilage surfaces, possibly the most highly mechanically-stressed environments in the body. You mention in your paper that *in vivo* pressures in human articular cartilage reach up to 1–5 MPa. Presumably you meant mean pressures across the joint as a whole. Detailed studies using a femoral head hip implant fitted with pressure sensors indicate that the distribution of pressures across the articular cartilage surface is highly non-uniform, reaching up to 18 MPa at some points.[1] This is important since presumably wear of the cartilage would tend to commence at such high-pressure 'hotspots', and any synovial lubrication mechanism needs to be efficient up to at least such pressures in order to ensure wear-free articulation.

My second point concerns the surface of the articular cartilage, which in your paper is implied to be cellular. Ultrastructural studies suggest the uppermost layer of articular cartilage (to a depth of *ca.* 1 μm) is acellular and is composed of a thin filamentous network pervaded by the cartilage macromolecular components and water (*e.g.* Jurvelin *et al.*[2] and Klein[3]). In that case the frictional mechanism during articulation would not directly involve the cellular surfaces but rather the outermost surface of the cartilage itself, which is likely to expose some of these different components. It is also of interest that the chondrocyte cells within the cartilage actually require the high stresses within the joints in order to operate optimally (see *e.g.* J. Urban[4]).

1 W. A. Hodge, R. S. Fijan, K. L. Carlson, R. G. Burgess, W. H. Harris and R. W. Mann, *Proc. Natl Acad. Sci. U. S. A.*, 1986, **83**, 2879.
2 J. S. Jurvelin, D. J. Müller, M. Wong, D. Studer, A. Engel and E. B. Hunziker, *J. Struct. Biol.*, 1996, **117**, 45.
3 J. Klein, *Proc. Inst. Mech. Eng. Part J: J. Eng. Tribol.*, 2006, **220**, 691–710.
4 J. P. G. Urban, *Br. J. Rheumatol.*, 1994, **33**, 901–908.

Professor Dr Sawyer responded: Agreed, let us assert that the instrumented metal components that Hodge *et al.* installed onto healthy cartilage represent an upper bound for the contact pressure in joints. The broader point we make in the paper is that shear stresses in many different contexts within the body are large enough and persist over the right timescales to elicit a mechanotransductive response in cells at sliding interfaces. If contact stresses at articular cartilage surfaces reach 18 MPa and shear stresses are a few hundred kPa, then it is even more likely that cells near the interface will sense friction forces through mechanosensing pathways.

Contact pressures in the megapascal range will certainly generate shear stresses on the order of tens or, as you pointed out, potentially hundreds of kilopascals. Such shear stresses at the surface of soft polymeric materials like the acellular surface layer of cartilage will certainly generate strain fields that penetrate deep into the tissue below. Thus, the friction forces at the sliding contact may, in part, provide the stresses required by chondrocytes to operate optimally.

Professor Spencer commented: The statements made by you and Duncan Dowson support the idea that the distinction between boundary and fluid-film lubrication becomes extremely blurred in the case of biological, or indeed brush lubrication. The viscosity gradient you showed on the surface of the eye clearly demonstrates that the situation will not vary in a simple "Stribeck-Curve" manner, and recent measurements in our lab with oil-compatible polymer brushes show that the viscosity of the lubricant plays a role in what would normally be considered as the boundary regime. This is presumably due to squeezing out of the lubricant from the brush, which will be a time- and therefore velocity-dependent phenomenon. Such a squeezing mechanism would be expected also in the glycocalyx or high-mucin-concentration region on the surface of the eye at slow speeds.

Professor Dr Sawyer replied: Exactly! For high water content gels and biological materials (which are generally soft and permeable), aqueous lubrication at such interfaces must be time dependent. In our lab we have made many permeability measurements of acellular dermis, muscle, and bone. In all of these materials, it takes about 1 s to achieve a compressive strain of 0.1 at an applied pressure of ~10 kPa. In the case of hydrogels, even at moderate strain rates, viscous forces dominate the compression of these gels, and the 1 s timescale is typical of poroelasticity in hydrogels. If the glycocalyx or mucin at the apical surface of the corneal epithelium is similar to other high water content gels, then stresses from the blink are too short in duration to significantly separate any water from the surface. Moreover, hydrodynamic pressures must cause the lid to lift off of the eye, given the speed of the blink. However, slower and more persistent forces can easily squeeze fluid from the polymeric material at the cornea surface. The interaction between the back of a contact lens and the cornea may involve squeezing out solvent and compressing the mucin and glycocalyx, for example.

Dr Myant remarked: This is in relation to comments about defining lubrication regimes for biological interfaces; boundary or EHL, and the lack of real engineering contacts for comparison. The use of polymer additives in base oils for lubricated point contacts was investigated by Smeeth *et al.*[1] They posed a similar question when very thick boundary films were observed. In their concluding remarks the coined the phrase 'Boundary Elastohydrodynamics'.

1 M. Smeeth, H. A. Spikes and S. Gunsel, The Formation of Viscous Surface Films by Polymer Solutions: Boundary or Elastohydrodynamic Lubrication, *Tribol. Trans.*, 1996, **39**, 720.

Professor Dr Sawyer said: Thank you for raising this point. It is evident that adsorbed polymer layers can behave as a viscous boundary layer, providing fluid-film support even at slow speeds. Certainly under physiological conditions, it is safe to assert that the biological liquid lubricants such as synovial fluids and tears are substantially different than simply water.

Professor Dowson noted: Your observation that nature has adopted both *fluid-film* and *boundary* modes of lubrication in the eye is most interesting. Bio-tribology seems to be contributing to a better understanding of the transitions that occur between lubrication regimes. A more comprehensive range of lubrication conditions should normally be assessed when undertaking bio-tribological investigations. It seems likely that transition from one lubrication regime to another may take place during normal functioning of some biological systems. If it is established that the system operates in fluid-film, mixed or boundary lubrication alone, the appropriate tribological conditions can more readily be examined.

I am anxious to encourage a more holistic approach to bio-tribology and to avoid a commitment to a single mode of lubrication without adequate support for the dominance of a particular behaviour. We often seem to be tied to the defence of a single mode of lubrication in bio-tribology! Some of these issues are addressed in my Introductory lecture.

The flow of erythrocytes in narrow capillaries appears to offer an interesting insight into the interaction of various modes of lubrication. I wonder if your work on the eye has shed any light on these intriguing, but apparently more highly stressed conjunctions?

Professor Dr Sawyer responded: What a great perspective; biology is not forced into specific modes of lubrication! The softness of cells, their ability to respond to stresses, proliferate, build extracellular matrix, and even create surface gels with mucins does not limit their lubrication to a passive response to slip velocities. One curious set of measurements and calculations that we have done for lubrication in the eye shows that the hydrodynamic shear stresses are the same as the shear stresses that we measure under boundary lubrication and mixed lubrication; perhaps this is only a curious measurement to the scientist—why would nature have any other way? Regarding your comments and work on the mixed reports on erythrocyte interactions in narrow capillary walls, since erythrocytes deform dramatically to fit through capillaries of $\sim$2–3 μm diameter it was long believed that they must remain separated from the walls by flowing at high speeds (analogous to elastohydrodynamic lubrication). However, recent observations have shown that even at low speeds ($\sim$0.1 mm s^{-1}) the cells appear to remain separate from capillary walls. The cause of this low friction in a low-speed lubrication regime is likely related to many of the questions we have been discussing: is the underlying mechanism molecular in nature? Is it the mechanics of very soft polymer networks at these interfaces? Is it that the cell surfaces themselves are incredibly compliant 2D fluid membranes? We expect these questions to be explored in future cell friction work. We also appreciate the importance of understanding the transitions between lubrication regimes, or even properly defining them in this new scientific territory.

Dr Polcar enquired: The friction coefficient measured *in vitro* on un-damaged cells is lower than that of damaged (*i.e.* dead) cells. However, the friction of damaged cells is still very low and similar to the results obtained *in vivo*. Could we thus use the friction measurement for diagnostics?

Professor Dr Sawyer replied: We are at the very beginning stages of exploring cell friction. It will be important to correlate changes in friction coefficient with variations in the cell surface. Different cell types and cells from different organisms have very different apical surfaces. Lung epithelial cells have cilia that beat in a coordinated manner to move mucus; corneal epithelial cells maintain a mucin network bound to their microvilli; endothelial vascular cells present a layer of short carbohydrate ligands to bind white blood cells. Each of these cell types may have different frictional properties and cells with deficiencies may differ from healthy cells in their frictional properties. If such differences in cell friction are large enough to be detected, then friction measurements could be used as a diagnostic tool *in vitro*. In cases where cells are accessible to tribometers, friction measurements could be used as a clinical diagnostic tool. One possibility is the diagnosis of dry eye, dry mouth, and other dryness syndromes through friction measurements.

Dr Mischler commented: We are now discussing the performance of biological lubricants in terms of viscosity only. This is a valid approach for traditional oil lubricated steel contacts where good adhesion between the oil and the metal surface is established. In bio tribological contacts (water/protein lubricated) as well as engineering contacts involving polymeric materials this condition is not necessarily achieved. I am wondering if we should not more systematically consider surface energy properties such as wettability or capillarity to appraise the hydrodynamic and boundary efficiency of biological fluids. Could you comment on this?

Professor Dr Sawyer responded: This is an excellent point. The forces associated with cell friction can be very low, and may be comparable to capillary forces. An understanding of lubrication conditions would be improved by understanding the interfacial energy of the three phase tissue–fluid–tissue contact line. Contact angle measurements or simultaneous friction measurement and visualization of the contact would be of great value in answering this question.

Professor Williams queried: Is it feasible to estimate the shape of the velocity profile across the film? Does this follow a linear Couette relation or are there layers of enhanced resistance—or enhanced slip—close to the boundaries?

Professor Dr Sawyer replied: If we look at the blink, the sliding velocities are on the order of 100 mm s^{-1} and the eyelid and corneal epithelia are only separated by a few micrometers of tear film. The epithelium and nerves are protected by the glycocalyx and mucins, which constitute a significant fraction of the fluid layer (see Fig. 1 here). These complex gel-like layers are significantly more viscous than the aqueous portion of the tear film and should enhance the resistance to slip at the boundaries.

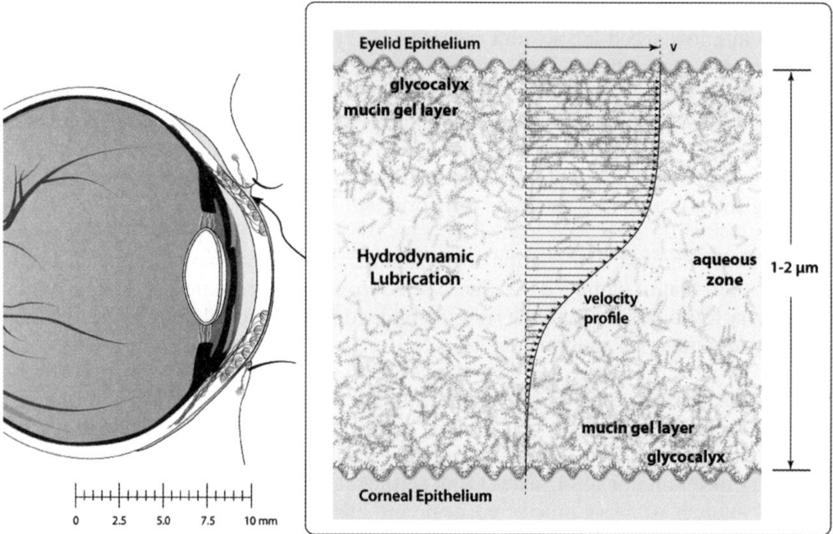

Fig. 1 A speculative view of the velocity profile through the film thickness during a blink. The epithelium of both the cornea and the eyelid are protected through a complex gel layer that is made up of glycoproteins and mucins. These gel layers protect the delicate surfaces of the cells, prevent direct contact during static loading, and reduce the shear deformation of the surfaces during a blink. Effectively, these gel layers are responsible for a graded viscosity across the tear film.

Dr Taylor asked: Sliding seems to lead to high friction coefficients (0.03 to 0.06) and in some circumstances to cell death. In engineering, when sliding contacts get difficult, we move to rolling contacts. Are there examples in the animal world where rolling contacts occur rather than sliding contacts?

Professor Dr Sawyer answered: Not for low friction—rolling contacts do appear to be used in the animal world for locomotion and ambulatory functions. For example, certain snakes roll rather than slide, and the heal-strike/toe-off gait patterns are a type of rolling contact that tries to minimize slip and thus maximize traction. In the case of cells, one well known example of a rolling contact is that of rolling leukocytes (white blood cells). Leukocytes adhere to the surfaces of blood vessels and roll along with the flow of blood fluid. The rolling contact is generally interpreted from a signaling perspective: the location of inflammation is identified by a leukocyte through ligands bound to the blood vessel surface. Given the high flow rates in blood vessels, if leukocytes were not adhered to the endothelial cells, they would rarely make contact with the blood vessel walls.

   This journal is © The Royal Society of Chemistry 2012

Professor Wood enquired: How does the eye lid/eye contact deal with entrainment of dust particles which are always present in the atmosphere and with dusty environments? Is friction of the contact influenced?

Professor Dr Sawyer replied: We suspect that this is one of the hidden mechanisms of the lipid layer. In addition to limiting evaporation of the tear film, the lipid layer reduces tear film break-up and acts as a cleaner/filter. On the one side it acts to clean denatured proteins and mucins from within the tear film, and on the other it sequesters fine dust, debris, and airborne particles into the waxy lipid layer surface. The lipid layer is gradually, but continuously, being renewed and restored during blinks.

Professor Dowson asked: I wonder if your fascinating investigations of cell friction have involved consideration of the elastohydrodynamic mode of lubrication? The Stribeck curve emerged from studies of plain bearings on the railways. For more highly stressed components, where elastohydrodynamic conditions may occur, the Stribeck curve in the fluid-film regime has to be adopted with care. The friction coefficient is not such a simple function of speed, load and viscosity. It is necessary to take account of the effect of load, temperature, speed and lubricant rheology (particularly the effect of shear rate on viscosity) upon film thickness and hence the viscous shear stress. Full consideration of these factors helps to ascertain the mode of lubrication and is particularly relevant to *soft*, *biological* systems.

Professor Dr Sawyer responded: Recently we have been plotting the Stribeck curve as a functional relationship between the shear stress and the slip velocity. As demonstrated earlier in Fig. 1, we suspect that the biological systems frequently involve dramatically graded viscosities within the liquid lubricants. We hypothesize that under high enough slip conditions the hydrodynamic pressure separates the surfaces and allows for shearing to be concentrated within a low viscosity region of the fluid film, but if there is insufficient fluid pressurization then the surfaces touch and shear across these viscous polymeric gels and brush-like surfaces. Because of the low modulus of these cell, we expect elastic deformations under almost all contact conditions; effectively, elasto-fluid lubrication throughout the entire lubrication regime from boundary to hydrodynamic. I completely agree with your views and comments on biology not being tied to a single mode of lubrication.

Mr Gustavsson communicated: Do you think it would be possible to change the coefficient of friction between the cells inside the body, perhaps with some drugs or injections? If so, what effect do you think it would have for the cells and the body?

Professor Dr Sawyer communicated in response: If we focus on cells at sliding contacts, we can speculate about the biological origins of the friction coefficient. Generally, sliding contacts will occur between groups of epithelial cells in adjacent tissues, or between epithelial cells and connective tissue. At the apical surface of the epithelium, many cells are covered with glycoprotein-coated microvilli or cilia. These cells can excrete mucin, a branched glycoprotein polyclectrolye. Cilia have been observed to actively drive mucus layers around the apical side of lung epithelial cells in culture. Some fraction of mucins are membrane bound, attached to microvilli. We believe that mucin is one of the primary lubricants in sliding cell contacts. Several different approaches could be taken to change the coefficient of friction at mucin-lubricated contacts. Proteases could be added to degrade the chains, though this approach could degrade other extracellular proteins. The ionic strength could be tuned to change the conformational stiffness of the mucin chains, or multivalent ions could be used to condense mucin. In cases where mucin concentrations are too low to sufficiently lubricate a contact, an exogenous polymer could be added in its place. However, long chain polymers at high concentrations are known to exert large osmotic stresses on cell layers, altering cell behavior.

Professor Spencer opened the discussion of the paper by Professor Rainforth: Can you comment on the recent publication in Science, referred to in your paper, in which graphite has been identified by TEM to be present in explanted metal-on-metal hip joints, and a suggestion which was made that it may be a widespread contributor to the tribological properties of such joints?

Professor Rainforth replied: The contribution from Liao *et al.*[1] is very interesting. There have been previous observations of graphite formation from frictional contact (*e.g.* Zhou *et al.*[2]), but such observations have only been found for dry sliding conditions where the frictional heating is essential to drive the transformation of amorphous carbon to graphite. It is very difficult to envisage how such a transformation could occur at the temperatures observed in a hip joint (maximum 50 °C). In the main paper by Liao *et al.* some elegant electron microscopy provides persuasive evidence for the presence of graphite, through both high resolution imaging and electron energy loss spectroscopy. However, I would be concerned that the process of removing the sample for TEM, namely scraping with a sharp tungsten tool, had the potential for changing the film structure. In the supporting material to the paper, high resolution images are shown from a focused ion beam section through the film while still attached to the explanted metal surface, which should give more direct evidence. The authors claim the presence of onion-like graphite in one location in a high resolution TEM image. However, the image is dominated by strong Fresnel fringe contrast and I do not believe that it can be concluded that graphite is present. Thus, this image gives evidence for amorphous material, not graphite and even if graphite was present, it was a very small fraction of the total. Accompanying EELS spectra have been taken from a region where the sample is comparatively thick and so the quality of the carbon K edge is not good enough to conclude the presence of graphite or not. However, far more persuasive evidence for the presence of graphite comes from the strong D and G bands in Raman spectra taken from the surface of the retrieved hip joint, obtained without the need for any specimen preparation. On the basis of this, graphite is present. This raises the question as to why in our current work we have never observed graphite on the surface of explanted hip joints, rather we only see amorphous material, often present as an organo–metal composite. Indeed, our results are very much in line with the work published by Wimmer and Fisher and co-workers over the last 10 years.

I am concerned that there is a large jump in faith to suggest that the presence of graphite will lead to self lubricating properties. The graphite, if present, is one component of a complex structure and it is the friction of that structure as a whole that is important. In our laboratory tests where we observed graphite formation, the friction actually increased. The frictional heating that led to the transformation to graphite gave additional structural changes that were detrimental to friction, even with graphitic carbon present.

1 Y. Liao, R. Pourzal, M. A. Wimmer, J. J. Jacobs, A. Fischer and L. D. Marks, *Science*, 2011, **334**, 1687–1690.
2 Z. Zhou, I. M. Ross, L. Ma, W. M. Rainforth, A. P. Ehiasarian and P. Hovsepian, *Wear*, 2011, **271**, 2150–2156.

Professor Spencer asked: Are locally elevated temperatures during implant use going to have an influence on the processes that you observe?

Professor Rainforth answered: Prichett[1] placed probes inside hip joints in patients who had had one or both joints resurfaced, and measured temperature rises up to 8 °C for metal-on-metal after the patient had been walking for 60 min. A similar study of instrumented hip joints *in vivo* by the Julius Wolff Institut for Biomechanics and Musculoskeletal Regeneration showed a maximum temperature of 43 °C, which is somewhat lower than that predicted by modelling of 51 °C. Such temperature rises will have no effect on the metal surface mechanical properties. However, it would be expected that frictional heating will not only alter the viscosity of the synovial fluid, but will also will induce chemical changes. Perhaps the frictional heating is an important component in the potential formation of graphite on the surface of retrieved hip joints as reported by Liao *et al.*[2]?

1 J. Pritchett, *J. Long-Term Eff. Med. Implants*, 2011, **21**(1), 55–62.
2 Y. Liao, R. Pourzal, M. A. Wimmer, J. J. Jacobs, A. Fischer and L. D. Marks, *Science*, 2011, **334**, 1687–1690.

Dr Mischler enquired: On CoCrMo alloys, could you observe a thin oxide film situated in between the carbonaceous surface layer and the nanocrystalline zone? If not, this could indicate that direct contact of proteins with bare metal is a prerequisite for their denaturation.

Professor Rainforth responded: This is an important question. We failed to observe the thin oxide film between the carbonaceous surface layer and the nanocrystalline zone. We would expect such a film to be around 5 nm thick and so it should be easily resolvable given that the 5–10 nm carbonaceous film was clearly visible. It is generally assumed that such a thin oxide film is present on the surface, but it was not obvious in our studies. The image in Fig. 5 of our paper shows direct metal contact with the carbonaceous material, giving evidence that direct contact of the proteins with bare metal is important for the denaturation, and indeed may well be a prerequisite.

Professor Klein remarked: Adding up the European market shares of metal-on-metal (9%), ceramic-on-ceramic (26%) and metal-on-polyethylene implants (30%) leaves quite a bit unaccounted for. What types of implant surfaces would these involve?

Professor Rainforth answered: The remainder, just under 35%, is ceramic-on-polyethylene.

Professor Klein queried: I am just slightly puzzled by the high initial Hertzian contact stress (> 3 GPa) in your CoC measurements, which is some 1000-fold higher than the mean stress in the major joints. Even given that this compares with rim-contact stresses in CoC implants, would not the mean pressure across the contact be very much lower, and more appropriate to use in the wear study? Also, you mention that this initial pressure falls rapidly during running in; does this happen as a result of increasing contact area? It would also be interesting to have the lower values to which the stress falls.

Professor Rainforth responded: Thank you for raising this important issue. The initial contact stresses are high, and these are in line with the rim-contact stresses, as shown by Mak *et al.*[1] It was a specific objective of the work to investigate the high wear regions, which are normally associated with locally high contact stresses, for example, from rim contact. We also found that the damage mechanisms we observed are similar to those found on hip simulators.[2,3] You are quite right that mean contact pressures across the contact are much lower, and indeed this is crucial to the successful operation of hip joints. In respect of your specific question on a falling contact pressure, yes, this is a result of increased contact area, which is also the case for most initially non-conformal contacts. Nevertheless, this is a clear drawback of such laboratory investigations that the apparent contact area changes with time. Investigations of wear processes at lower contact pressures are important and indeed we have published these widely (*e.g.* Ma and Rainforth[4]). The reduction in contact pressure depends on the extent of wear (and therefore the apparent contact area), but values of $\sim$100 MPa would be typical.

1 M. Mak, Z. Jin, J. Fisher and T. D. Stewart , *J. Arthroplasty*, 2011, **26**, 131–136.
2 P. Zeng, W. M. Rainforth, B. J. Inkson, and T. D. Stewart, Characterization of worn alumina hip replacement prostheses, *J. Biomed. Mater. Res. Part B*, 2012, **100B**(1) 121–132.
3 P. Zeng, W. M. Rainforth, B. J. Inkson and T. D. Stewart, *Acta Mater.*, 2012, **60**, 2061–2072.
4 L. Ma and W. M. Rainforth, *Acta Biomater.*, 2012, **8**, 2348–2359.

Dr Cook commented: Your paper presents evidence of microstructural changes in regions of high wear (edge wear) and lower wear areas for a CoCrMo hip resurfacing. The explanation of the microstructural development in the low wear region and the formation mechanism of the 70–115 nm thick nanocrystalline layer are excellent. However, your paper talks about the microstructural changes in a higher wear region where edge wear (stripe wear) has occurred. Edge wear is undesirable and occurs due to poor implant alignment and is not the normal situation for the bearing surface *in vivo*, in a well performing implant. It is recognised that when edge loading occurs, the lubrication is disrupted, the contact stresses are considerably higher and that adhesive wear results. This adhesive wear process results in much larger wear particle release (100–500 nm) than the 20–30 nm sized particles released from the nanocrystalline layer during normal wear. This difference in size suggests that these larger particles have not been generated from a nanocrystalline layer. In recognition of the change of wear mechanism in this edge worn region, the inconsistency and thinness of the nanocrystalline layer within the edge wear region in this paper, would you be willing to pass comment on your findings?

Professor Rainforth replied: Your description of the process and specifically edge wear is insightful. The results we have presented, where the same structure is observed in the high wear region and outside it, is not what we expected to find and is difficult to explain. The nanocrystalline structure is formed by a shear banding process, as has been observed many years ago for low stacking fault energy materials (ref. 8, 9 and 11 in the paper). The same metal can exhibit different deformation structures depending on the stress system, and shear banding is only observed where there is a combination of compressive stress and a local constraint (*e.g.* in rolling) which promotes localised shear stresses. Thus, for a nanocrystalline layer to form, shear stresses must dominate the surface region. This what we would expect for adhesive wear, and indeed nanocrystalline layers are formed at the surface of low stacking fault energy stainless steel under adhesive wear.[1] Thus the absence of a nanocrystalline layer presumably means that the local shear stresses were insufficient to give shear banding, suggesting adhesive wear was not dominant. This in itself may be an important observation.

The one point on which I disagree is that you suggest that wear particles from a nanocrystalline layer are 20–30 nm. Shear banding is a high strain process that takes the material to its ductility limit. Shear banding during the wear of stainless steels leads to the formation of large (>100 nm) wear particles because the surface material has exceeded its ductility limit. While I do not believe that this was the case in the current results, the presence of a nanocrystalline layer does not necessarily lead to fine wear debris.

1 W. M. Rainforth, R. Stevens and J. Nutting, *Philos. Mag. A*, 1992, **66**(4), 621–641.

Dr Oesterle said: Since you have not observed any chromium oxide at the worn surface I would assume that the native oxide layer of the Co–Cr–Mo-alloy has been removed by wear before the protecting amorphous film has formed. It would be interesting to look for oxide particles in the wear debris. Have there been attempts made to reveal the structure of wear particles by TEM?

   This journal is © The Royal Society of Chemistry 2012

Professor Rainforth answered: The observation of no oxide film on the surface is an important one and has important implications in the denaturing of proteins since proteins will be in direct metal contact rather than metal oxide contact. The topic of the structure of metal wear debris particles is of considerable current interest. However, there is little agreement on the state of the wear debris. Williams *et al.*[1] observed numerous fine wear debris from *in vitro* tests, but did not identify their state. Huber *et al.*[2] observed Cr phosphate, while Catelas *et al.*[3] observed Cr based oxide. In a more detailed study, Hart *et al.*, found $Cr(\text{III})PO_4$, with Co in the metallic state and some oxidised form of Mo. Therefore, the situation is complicated and the suggestion of a simple CoCrMo oxide forming is clearly not the entire story. There is much need for further work in this area.

1 S. Williams, T. D. Stewart, E. Ingham, M. H. Stone and J. Fisher, *J. Biomed. Mater. Res. Part B*, 2004, **70B**, 233.
2 M. Huber, G. Reinisch, G. Trettenhahn, K. Zweymüller and F. Lintner, *Acta Biomater.*, 2009, **5**, 172.
3 I. Catelas, P. A. Campbell, J. D. Bobyn, J. B. Medley and O. L. Huk, *Proc. Inst. Mech. Eng. Part H: J. Eng. Med.*, 2006, **220**, 195.

Professor Beake enquired: Has anybody done micromapping of heavily worn regions of explants? Is the nanocrystalline layer detectable by nanoindentation, either in lab worn samples or explants?

Professor Rainforth responded: By micromapping, I assume you mean mapping the hardness by nanoindentation. To the best of my knowledge, no one has attempted this. One problem is that the surface roughness makes such micromapping difficult and prone to large errors. However, there is little evidence that the nanocrystalline layer can be detected by nanoindentation. For example, Perret *et al.*[1] failed to find that such nanocrystalline layers are harder. It is particularly difficult in CoCrMo alloys where indentation will induce the formation of η-martensite, which in itself will give a high hardness value. Nevertheless, it is clear that more work needs to be undertaken on this.

1 J. Perret, E. Boehm-Courjault, M. Cantoni, S. Mischler, A. Beaudouin, W. Chitty and J.-P. Vernot, *Wear*, 2010, **269**, 383–393.

Dr Mischler noted: Carrying out nano-indentation measurements to characterise the mechanical properties of nanocrystalline surface layers is certainly reasonable. However, we have to consider that the stress conditions (in particular shear rate) are very different in real contacts. Therefore care should be taken when extrapolating nano-indentation response to tribological behaviour.

Professor Rainforth replied: I agree. There is no doubt that nanocrystalline layers would be expected to have higher hardness. Similar layers with very fine structures have been observed on the worn surface of other metals, for example, stainless steels.[1,2] However, measuring hardness at a surface is difficult given the free surface effects give errors in hardness measurements. However, I am not sure that measuring hardness is entirely relevant. The nanocrystalline surface layer forms by a shear banding process. The observed structure is the static structure that forms after the deformation event. It is believed that the dynamic structure present during shear band formation is quite different and would therefore have quite different mechanical properties. Measurement of the post-process mechanical properties is unlikely to give an accurate indication of the dynamic surface properties.

1 W. M. Rainforth, R. Stevens and J. Nutting, *Philos. Mag. A*, 1992, **66**(4), 621–641.
2 J. Perret, E. Boehm-Courjault, M. Cantoni, S. Mischler, A. Beaudouin, W. Chitty and J.-P. Vernot, *Wear*, 2010, **269**, 383–393.

Dr Myant asked: You showed evidence of nanocrystalline structure in and outside of the worn areas. Does this suggest that a critical set of contact conditions can be determined at which wear occurs, and, therefore advice to manufacturers, surgeons or patients be offered so that these conditions might be avoided?

Professor Rainforth answered: That is an interesting question. One problem with making a definitive statement about the effect of the nanocrystalline layer is that such layers can be formed during surface preparation prior to implantation making it very difficult to tell what role they have had during articulation in the body. The nanocrystalline structure is formed by a shear banding process, as has been observed in most low stacking fault energy metals (ref. 8, 9 and 11 in the paper). Thus, for a nanocrystalline layer to form, shear stresses must dominate the surface region and must exceed the yield strength of a heavily work hardened material. This implies adhesive wear and therefore the local loss of lubricating body fluids. This situation is only likely to arise when there is a problem, such as misalignment leading to edge loading.

Dr Walker queried: With respect to the nanocrystalline layer observed below the worn surface, at the base of the pit in Fig. 7, is it possible that the presence of nearby surface carbide particles acts to transfer the contact stress to the sub-surface matrix and is this beneficial or detrimental to the wear resistance of this system?

Professor Rainforth responded: Yes, I think it is both possible and the only realistic explanation for the observation of a nanocrystalline region at the base of a pit. Sections around the pit generally showed carbides, strongly suggesting that the pit had been formed through loss and break up of the carbides. Load transfer through the carbides has been shown to lead to high strain deformation in the matrix below a reinforcement (*e.g.* see Walker *et al.*[1]). Moreover, the TEM image in Fig. 7 shows the nanocrystalline layer extends below the retained carbide, giving further evidence that this mechanism occurs. As to whether this is beneficial or not, if high strain occurs in the matrix adjacent to a particle in which there is no strain, then the strain discontinuity must result in cracking and therefore loss of the carbide. Therefore, I would suggest that it is detrimental.

1 J. C. Walker, I. M. Ross, W. M. Rainforth and M. Lieblich, *Wear*, 2007, **263**, 707–718.

Dr Oesterle commented: The superficial layers of the worn alumina surfaces show a partly amorphous surface film and a zone of plastically deformed alumina grains, but no transition layer between the two zones. Do you have any idea why such a structure has formed?

Professor Rainforth replied: The majority of this structure is formed through the mechanical attrition of wear debris. Fig. 15 shows a ~200 nm alumina particle that was liberated most probably through intergranular fracture. Such particles cannot easily escape from the interface given the small gap between the articulating surfaces. The consequence is that such particles are broken up, and become mechanically mixed with the organic components of body fluids, leading to the amorphous–nanocrystalline composite observed in Fig. 15d. While there is little evidence for a transition in structure between the ceramic and this composite structure as part of the wear process itself, work carried out after the acceptance of the current paper, and presented in my talk, does show a worn surface with a gradual change from the crystalline to amorphous state. This observation requires further investigation, the results of which will be published in the future.

Professor Fisher asked: Are nanometre wear particles mixing with proteins in the contact zone and playing a role in forming the nano boundary layer on the bearing?

Professor Rainforth answered: Thank you for the question. The observation of an organo–metallic composite surely indicates that the nanometre wear particles are mixing with the proteins in the contact zone, and must therefore play a role in the nano boundary layer. However, I think that one should be careful in extrapolating a local observation to suggest that this is pervasive across the whole surface. For example, in Fig. 5, there is a thin organic film that does not contain any metallic wear debris. There has been much interest in the paper by Liao *et al.*[1] which suggests that graphite may also be present. However, these authors also showed that the graphite was present as part of a complex structure which includes metallic wear debris components. However, it is clear that, as you suggest, the interaction of fine wear particles with the proteins in the contacting zone is an important aspect of the contact conditions.

1 Y. Liao, R. Pourzal, M. A. Wimmer, J. J. Jacobs, A. Fischer and L. D. Marks, *Science*, 2011, **334**, 1687–1690.

Professor Klein opened the discussion of the paper by Professor Fisher: Your Tables 1 and 2 showing wear rates for different material combinations are most instructive. It was not clear whether they include polyethylenes (PEs) that have undergone surface treatments, which could dramatically change the wear rate. For example, in 1994 it was shown[1] that polymer brushes acting as boundary lubricants could massively reduce sliding and also static friction, while in 2003 this was extended to the case of hydrated (charged) polymer brushes.[2] Just over a year later, Moro *et al.*[3] grafted hydrated polymer brushes to the PE acetabular of a hip implant, and showed using a hip-simulator that wear was massively reduced, to some 0.1 mm^3 per million cycles after about 2 million cycles of articulation. This low wear value makes this modified polyethylene/metal pair better than MoM implants, and even comparable with CoC implants from the point of view of wear (your Table 1). So my question is, do you know why such surface modifications are not more common, and would such wear values likely lead to a change in trend to increasing use of metal-on-PE implants?

1 J. Klein, E. Kumacheva, D. Mahalu, D. Perahia and L. J. Fetters, *Nature*, 1994, **370**, 634–636.
2 U. Raviv, S. Giasson, N. Kampf, J.-F. Gohy, R. Jérôme and J. Klein, *Nature*, 2003, **425**, 163–165.
3 T. Moro, Y. Takatori, K. Ishihara, T. Konno, Y. Takigawa, T. Matsushita, U. Chung, K. Nakamura and H. Kawaguchi, *Nat. Mater.*, 2004, **3**, 829.

Professor Fisher replied: The research on grafted hydrated polymer surfaces is an interesting approach to reducing wear in polyethylene. Today cross linked polyethylene is most commonly used which reduces the wear rate compared to conventional polyethylene. I am aware of research that is now grafting hydrated polymers onto the surface of cross linked polyethylene. I do not know if this has yet been used in patients.

One concern I have with modifying the surface of the polyethylene relates to the depth of penetration of the surface treatment. Even in low wearing hips the linear wear may be up to 10 μm per million cycles. So the question remains as to whether the surface modification will prove to be effective in reducing wear in the medium to long term.

Dr Cook commented: Your paper states that it is presenting a new stratified approach to pre-clinical tribological simulation of joint replacements. This new stratified approach is not clearly defined in the paper. Could you please outline what tests should be included in all future pre-clinical tribological simulations?

Professor Fisher responded: The new stratified approach consists of systematically considering variables that occur in clinical practice including variations in surgical approach and positioning, different patient activities, variations that occur in individual patient populations and sub populations, and changes and degradation in the biomaterials over time. It is important to consider all of these in designing a portfolio of pre-clinical tests for a new device, within the context of a risk analysis, failure modes and effects analysis and overall design portfolio.

In systematically selecting a portfolio of pre-clinical tests it is important to consider clinical experience with previous prostheses of similar type and also existing pre-clinical test data determined under different conditions. Our laboratory has a data bank of over 5 billion pre-clinical test results using this stratified approach. Specific examples of the stratified approach are provided in the paper.

It would be helpful for international standards to start to move beyond the current position of recommending a set of test conditions for standard walking with a standard patient with a perfectly positioned prosthesis.

Dr Cook asked: In light of the recent spate of failures of large diameter heads for hip replacements related to the taper/trunnion connection in modular joints, do you believe that pre-clinical testing should test intact implant systems and incorporate factors such as frictional torque measurement?

Professor Fisher replied: My paper reports a stratified approach to pre-clinical testing of the tribology of the articulating bearings. It does not consider non articulating fixation of taper junctions, or trunnions in modular joints, or stem or cup fixation to bone. Separate pre-clinical tests and standards are required to assess trunnions and taper fixation as well as stem and cup fixation to bone.

It is worth noting that taper/trunnion junctions on modular joints were originally designed for smaller size femoral heads, and in general they worked effectively for over two decades in these systems with smaller size heads. The same tapers have recently been used for large diameter femoral heads, where the forces and torques are greater. In some cases additional spacers and interfaces have also been introduced.

In most other engineering systems, the mechanical engineering design of taper or trunnion fixation systems would be geometrically scaled in relation to the loads and torques to be transmitted through the system. Apparently this has not been done in the case of large diameter metal-on-metal heads in total joint replacements. The torques associated with both the loading and friction in large diameter joints have been measured. I do not know if these have been used in the pre-clinical evaluation of the taper junctions, trunnions or fixation interfaces in large diameter prostheses.

Dr Oesterle noted: The origin of the micrometre-sized and nanometre-sized wear particles of the ceramic joints seems to be revealed quite clearly by Professor Rainforth's paper: intergranular cracks will produce the micrometre-sized alumina particles and the nanometre-sized alumina particles are released from the partly amorphous surface films. Will there be a difference of these two types of particles in terms of toxicity?

Professor Fisher responded: Yes, I agree. In 2001 we first reported the stripe wear on the ceramic femoral head and the intergranular cracks and intergranular fracture on both clinical retrievals and from *in vitro* simulations with microseparation and head loading on the rim of the cup. In the laboratory studies, stripe wear and intergranular cracks were required to generate micron size wear particles *in vitro*. Micron size particles were found in retrieved tissues from explants with stripe wear.

I do not believe we have seen any difference in toxicity with the nanometre and micron size ceramic particles. *In vivo* the nano size particles are readily transported away from the prosthesis, while we believe the micron size particles remain in the periprosthetic tissues and can cause local inflammatory reactions.

Dr Taylor asked: You mention in your paper that standard tests simulate a patient walking. Are actual leg motions measured in patients, and are there more severe test cycles that can be used to screen potential hip and knee joint materials?

Professor Fisher answered: Actual motions and loads are measured in patients in gait laboratories, these have been used to define a wider set of conditions representing a wider range of patient activities and more severe test cycles in our laboratory simulators using our stratified approach. For example in the knee we have varied the amount of flexion from 65° up to 100°, the amount of internal–external rotation from 5° to 10°, and the amount of AP translation from 5 mm to 10 mm. Such changes in kinematics can change the wear rate in the knee by a factor of four.

In the hip we have simulated different swing phase loads, small medial lateral translation, and also variations in component positioning, which we have shown can increase the wear rates by a factor of between 10 and 50 times in some bearing materials.

We now undertake pre-clinical testing under a wider set of conditions (including adverse). Our stratified approach for enhanced reliability (SAFER) simulation methods are now being used to pre-clinically test new designs and materials and we have demonstrated that they can screen out inferior designs and materials and prevent them reaching the patient, as well as providing additional pre-clinical evidence to support the introduction of robust designs which produce low wear under a wider set of clinical conditions.

Professor Williams remarked: I have heard Professor John O'Connor who played a large part in the development of the 'Oxford' knee prosthesis stress the importance of the correct alignment of the artificial joint in relation to the geometry of the patient's skeletal structure, and how this can be achieved by providing what we would think of as an appropriate jig or fixture in which the long bones can be located during surgery. In view of your comments about the importance of various forms of misalignment of hip prostheses influencing their subsequent performance, are similar techniques commonly used? As a follow up, we often hear today about personalised therapies designed to suit individual patient needs—can a time be foreseen when personalised prostheses could be produced with geometries optimised to suit individual patient needs?

Professor Fisher replied: Personalised femoral stems and custom prostheses have been tried in the past. Personalised or custom prostheses are available as a service for special individual patient cases today. The health economics of the widespread introduction of personalised prostheses is challenging. There is, however, much effort currently in the area of computer assisted and image guided surgery, in order to improve consistency and alignment of the prosthesis to the individual patient geometry and anatomy. There is also considerable effort in terms of professional surgeon education and training to improve consistency, and an increasing recognition of the importance of centres of surgical excellence which undertake large volumes of surgery. Prostheses of different sizes and modular prostheses with a range of offsets are currently available to accommodate variations in patients anatomy. In the future, I would see stratified approaches becoming more common, with different types of surgical interventions being indicated for different diagnosis and disease states. This is consistent with earlier intervention strategies. However this is dependent on enhanced and earlier diagnosis.

Professor Klein commented: This comment follows on from my previous question regarding the use of chemical surface modifications of polyethylene components of implants (e.g. brush formation), which might make such implants the choice not only for older patients—the original Charnley idea—but also for younger ones. In subsequent discussion you mentioned 'disruptive technologies' which could lead to major changes in joint treatment. Tissue engineering for regenerative medicine is one of these 'disruptive approaches', and the idea of lubrication may well play a major role in improving scaffolds for such approaches, see *e.g.* Klein.[1]

1 J. Klein, *Science*, 2009, **323**, 47–48.

Professor Fisher answered: Thank you for your interesting comment. Biphasic biological scaffolds comprising a solid phase scaffold and a fluid phase offer considerable potential in tissue engineering and regenerative medicine. The chemical modification of these scaffolds to improve lubrication and to retain the fluid and fluid load support through biphasic lubrication is an interesting line of research in the area of cartilage tissue engineering.

Dr Mischler opened the discussion of the paper by Dr Myant: The electrochemical conditions established at the metal surface play a crucial role in tribocorrosion phenomena. They determine among others the corrosion rate, the surface chemical behaviour, the configuration and adsorption of ions and organic molecules. In tribological contacts they may significantly affect the surface mechanical behaviour (wear and friction) as well as the wear accelerated corrosion. In tribocorrosion the electrode potential is an experimental parameter as crucial as normal load or sliding velocity. In your experiments you investigated different chemical environments that most likely changed significantly the electrochemical conditions. I suggest to measure the electrode potential during your experiments. This is quite simple since only a reference electrode and an electrometer are needed. This measurement will probably help you in rationalizing your results and in correctly considering the role of pH and proteins.

Dr Myant responded: I totally agree with your comment and hope to implement these suggestions in the near future.

Professor Spencer said: In Fig. 2 in your paper, where you observe film-thickness increase at 10 mm s^{-1}, what is the effect of dropping the speed and starting again? Is the effect reversible? Local temperature increases in the contact could definitely be initiating reversible or irreversible protein degradation. This could be checked by circular dichroism spectroscopy.

Dr Myant answered: The film thickness profiles were observed not to be reversible and this behaviour was reported in an earlier paper of ours.[1] The film thickness behaviour was found to be complex, time-dependent and not characteristic of a simple Newtonian fluid.

Protein degradation is likely to be a combined result of microbial contamination, denaturation at the air–water interface, frictional heating and high shear rates. This is an interesting area which we hope to investigate further in the future. We are currently considering a number of vibrational spectroscopic techniques to achieve this.

1 J. Fan, C. W. Myant, R. Underwood, P. M. Cann and A. Hart, Inlet protein aggregation: a new mechanism for lubricating film formation with model synovial fluids, *Proc. Inst. Mech. Eng. Part H: J. Eng. Med.*, DOI: 10.1177/0954411911401306.

Dr Ratoi remarked: The proteins albumin and globulin are highly sensitive to changes in pH, concentration and electrolyte concentration. Has the effect of these factors on the proteins (especially their charge and state of dispersion/agglutination) been investigated? The maintenance of homeostasis inside the body is paramount. Was this taken into account when changing the pH and protein concentration? Has the adsorption of proteins on the lubricated parts under the studied conditions been investigated?

Dr Myant replied: There is a vast amount of work already on protein chemistry in solution, mostly under static conditions. In our work the protein behaviour was dominated by the flow aggregation—again there is a lot of work in the literature which we are drawing on. Protein adsorbance on static surfaces has already been studied extensively, however we are currently undertaking AFM work to complement the lubrication studies.

Dr Wahl enquired: How might the geometry of your contact influence the nature of the protein aggregate? Have you compared the aggregate in solution to what you find in the contact by FTIR or other means?

Dr Myant responded: The geometry of the contact may well affect the aggregation of the proteins, in particular the length of the new protein rich inlet phase. It is likely that a more conformal contact will increase the length of the inlet reservoir and may hinder larger proteins from entering the contact altogether. We hope to complete an investigation into the relationship between contact conformity and protein inlet aggregation in the near future, as this is an important step in validating our research for comparison to real artificial articular joints.

Aggregation both from solution and contact zone were studied using FTIR. We have recently completed a study into conformational changes in the protein aggregates which we hope to present soon.

Professor Klein said: I have two questions concerning your interesting paper. Did you observe any evidence of graphitic layers in the MoM surfaces, similar to that very recently reported by Liao *et al.*[1]? Secondly, it was not entirely clear to me why in your experiments you used pressures of 130 MPa, which is at least an order of magnitude or more larger than typical mean pressures in the major joints.

1 Y. Liao, R. Pourzal, M. A. Wimmer, J. J. Jacobs, A. Fischer and I. D. Marks, *Science*, 2011, **334**, 1687–1690.

Dr Myant answered: We did not observe any evidence of graphitic layers on the CoCrMo surface. That is not to say they were not present as the graphite could be inter-dispersed with the deposited proteins. IR spectroscopy was employed to identify the presence of organic deposits; consequently graphitic layers would not have been detected.

The comment on load is justifiable and is currently a limitation of our test device which we are working to rectify. However, whilst optimally aligned MoM hip components will produce a mean contact pressure in the region of 10–30 MPa, it is plausible for misaligned (edge loaded) components that the mean contact pressure will be an order of magnitude, or more, greater, particularly when we consider that the vertical force can be >4 times body weight in a simple gait cycle. This will be much greater during other types of articular motion, such as jogging or walking down stairs.

Mr Love communicated: In an infected joint (be it naturally caused or induced by debris) the temperature rises and it is observed that the pH shifts towards an acidic reading, not the slightly alkaline tests you performed. How would this affect your final result?

Dr Myant communicated in reply: For osteoarthritic joints there is an increase in the pH (alkaline shift) whilst for rheumatoid arthritis there is the opposite shift in pH, and for periprosthetic synovial fluid there have been both positive and negative pH shifts reported.[1-3] Any change in the solvent pH will affect the electrostatic attractions between the suspension's molecules and alter their solubility. A more acidic solution is therefore likely to have a similar effect on film thickness compared to the alkaline shift reported in this paper.

1 T. Kitano, G. A. Ateshian, V. C. Mow, Y. Kadoya and Y. Yamano, Constituents and pH changes in protein rich hyaluronan solution affect the bio-tribological properties of artificial articular joints, *J. Biomech.*, 2001, **34**, 1031–1037.
2 A. Wang, A. Essner and G. Schmidig, The Effects of Lubricant Composition on in Vitro Wear Testing of Polymeric Acetabular Components, *J. Biomed. Mater. Res. Part B*, 2003, **68B**, 45–52.
3 J. Delecrin, M. Oka, S. Takahashi, T. Yamamuro and T. Nakamura, Changes in joint fluid after total arthoplasty, *Clin. Orthop. Rel. Res.*, 1994, **307**, 240–249.

Professor Dr Franek continued the discussion of the paper by Professor Fisher: Patients are each a "tribosystem" of their own: should tribometrical investigations (here, of endoprostheses)—aberrant from standard tests—be personalised, in order to obtain proper results on the wear behaviour of implants (considering variants of stress conditions, such as weight of the patient, dynamics of movements, *etc.*)? Which modifications of such tests would be highly, which one less important?

Professor Fisher answered: We support the more widespread introduction of pre-clinical tribological testing under a wider set of conditions, including the testing of conditions reflecting variations found in individual patients, in addition to variations found in surgical positioning and variations found in individual activities. Clearly it is not possible to simulate every condition in every single patient. Our SAFER stratified approach for enhanced reliability, pre-clinical simulation methods, systematically addresses the range of variables found in the clinical tribological systems and the interactions between these variables on the wear rate of the joint replacement. We adopt a range of conditions for each of the variables, for example in the hip, we would test with a cup inclination position at 35, 45, 55 and 65°, with and without translational mal-positioning. It is not possible to generalise which set of conditions and modifications to tests are more or less important, as the response to the variation in conditions is dependent on individual bearing type.

For example, cup inclination did not affect wear in ceramic-on-ceramic bearings but did in metal-on-metal. In metal-on-metal, cup inclination had a smaller effect on wear in a 36 mm cup than in a 28 mm cup. Translational mal-position and medial lateral motion had an effect on wear on all sizes of metal-on-metal hip joints. The effect of third body particles and damage has a greater effect on wear in polyethylene bearings in both the hip and knee.

In our SAFER approach to pre-clinical simulation testing, it is important to use our knowledge of tribology as well as evidence from previous laboratory and clinical studies to select the most appropriate pre-clinical simulation tests for specific types of bearings. For example, we recently undertook pre-clinical simulation studies on a prototype surface engineered metal-on-metal bearing which was under commercial development. Based on my experience with metal-on-metal hips, we specified the SAFER pre-clinical test methods to include translational mal-position and edge loading. While this bearing produced substantially less wear and ion levels under ISO standard conditions, we were able to demonstrate accelerated wear and failure of the surface engineered bearing under conditions of translational mal-positioning, microseparation and edge loading, thus preventing it from being introduced into clinical trials.

Alternatively, we recently investigated the effect of the release of particles from a fixation coating on a prosthesis. In this case we chose to investigate the effect of these third body particles on metal-on-polyethylene bearings and found that they could cause third body damage and wear. Over the past ten years we have established a data bank of over 5 billion cycles of pre-clinical testing results, using our SAFER simulation methods, for a range of different bearing types. This data bank and information and our tribological knowledge allows us to effectively and efficiently apply SAFER pre-clinical simulation methods to support new product development and clinical introduction as well as to undertake fundamental and applied research.

Mr Love communicated: Alignment faults are typically caused by the surgeon not the design of the implant. Testing to quantify damage caused by misalignment (strike wear) is one aspect, but how could we prevent this from occurring? Is there a change in design to the implants themselves that could limit this induced damage?

Professor Fisher communicated in reply: We have to understand the range of accuracy of positioning and the tolerance band acceptable during surgery, recognising there will always be some variation in surgical positioning. For example we currently undertake simulator tests with cups inclined at 35, 45, 55 and 65°. We can then consider the tribological performance envelope under this range of conditions. In terms of design of implants we can evaluate the different designs and design variables under the different surgical positions. For example for metal-on-metal bearings, we get edge loading and stripe wear with increased wear rate with a 28 mm diameter bearing with a full hemisphere cup when it is inclined at 60°. However for a full hemisphere cup with a 36 mm diameter bearing, we do not get increased wear or stripe wear when the cup is inclined at 60°. Moving to a sub hemispherical cup we find we get edge loading, we get stripe wear and an increased wear rate when the cup is inclined at 60°.

Our stratified approach allows us to identify more robust designs, in terms of designs which tolerate variation in surgical positioning without causing an increase in wear rate. We have also used our approach to pre-clinically evaluate surface engineered bearings under a wider set of conditions, and identified clinical conditions which can cause failure of the surface layers.

Dr Cook communicated: Current pre-clinical tribological simulation testing of joint replacements uses 25% bovine serum as the lubricant, to simulate synovial fluid. In nature the viscosity of synovial fluid can vary from 0.4–0.001 Pa s when considering normal, osteoarthritic and inflammatory synovial fluids. 25% bovine serum has a viscosity of 0.001 Pa s which is at the extreme of the viscosity range. Given the importance of the lubricant in selection of clearance in the joints and the rate of synovial fluid recovery into the joint during service, should a more realistic viscosity fluid be used in pre-clinical tribological simulation testing of joint replacements, or should joints be tested over a range of viscosity lubricants?

Professor Fisher communicated in response: The 25% serum concentration was set by discussion of the ISO Committee in 2000. There is a range of protein concentrations and viscosities in the fluid surrounding joint replacements, and it is certainly not healthy synovial fluid. The viscosities you quote are of course shear rate dependent. The standard deliberately set the concentration at the low end of the spectrum in order to assess wear under this condition. Work we have published recently[1] investigates tribological performance under different concentrations of serum in different bearing types, and provides interesting results. Friction increases with decreasing serum concentration in metal-on-metal, but decreases in ceramic-on-ceramic and metal-on-polyethylene bearings. Wear increases with decreasing serum concentration in metal-on-metal, serum concentration has little effect on wear of ceramic-on-ceramic and in polyethylene the change in wear with decreasing serum concentration is dependent on the motion and kinematics. Our stratified approach indicates testing under different lubricant conditions.

1 C. Brockett, S. Williams, Z. M. Jin, G. Isaac and J. Fisher, Friction of total hip replacements with different bearings and loading conditions, *J. Biomed. Mater. Res. Part B*, 2007, **81B**(2), 508–515.

Predictive modelling of fatigue failure in concentrated lubricated contacts

H. P. Evans,* R. W. Snidle, K. J. Sharif and M. J. Bryant

Received 24th November 2011, Accepted 3rd January 2012
DOI: 10.1039/c2fd00116k

Reducing frictional losses in response to the energy agenda will require use of less viscous lubricants causing hydrodynamically-lubricated bearings to operate with thinner films leading to "mixed lubrication" conditions in which a degree of direct interaction occurs between surfaces protected only by boundary tribofilms. The paper considers the consequences of thinner films and mixed lubrication for concentrated contacts such as those occurring between the teeth of power transmission gears and in rolling element bearings. Surface fatigue in gears remains a serious problem in demanding applications, and its solution will become more pressing with the tendency towards thinner oils. The particular form of failure examined here is micropitting, which is identified as a fatigue phenomenon occurring at the scale of the surface roughness asperities. It has emerged recently as a systemic difficulty in the operation of large scale wind turbines where it occurs in both power transmission gears and their support bearings. Predictive physical modelling of these contacts requires a transient mixed lubrication analysis for conditions in which the predicted lubricant film thickness is of the same order or significantly less than the height of surface roughness features. Numerical solvers have therefore been developed which are able to deal with situations in which transient solid contacts occur between surface asperity features under realistic engineering conditions. Results of the analysis, which reveal the detailed time-varying behaviour of pressure and film clearance, have been used to predict fatigue and damage accumulation at the scale of surface asperity features with the aim of improving understanding of the micropitting phenomenon. The possible consequences on fatigue of residual stress fields resulting from plastic deformation of surface asperities is also considered.

1 Introduction

Lubricated concentrated contacts, such as those between gear teeth and in rolling element bearings, ideally operate in the regime of elastohydrodynamic lubrication (EHL) in which the combined effects of pressure upon the viscosity of the lubricant and elastic deformation of the surfaces lead to the generation of hydrodynamic films which can completely separate the surfaces.[1] In many demanding situations, however, the films generated can be of the same order or lower than the height of surface asperity features. Under these conditions significant asperity interactions can take place and the lubrication mechanism may be described as micro-EHL.[2] In the most severe cases of thin films/high roughness the local EHL mechanism may fail and transient direct solid contact occurs; this is the regime of mixed lubrication in which part of the load is carried by transitory boundary-lubricated contact.

Cardiff School of Engineering, Cardiff University, The Parade, Cardiff, CF24 3AA, UK. E-mail: evanshp@cf.ac.uk; Fax: +44 (0)29 2087 4716; Tel: +44 (0)29 2087 4266

As an engineering measure of the severity of surface roughness effects the lambda ratio, Λ, (defined as the ratio of calculated smooth surface lubricant film thickness to composite mean surface roughness) is often used, and for situations in which $\Lambda < 1$ mixed lubrication is predicted. Under mixed lubrication conditions friction and wear is increased and component surface failures take place predominantly in this regime.

The majority of power transmission gears have tooth surfaces that are rough compared to the EHL films which can be generated. Even the best quality gears finished by grinding have RMS roughness of the order 0.5 μm, with typical peak-to-valley roughness features of 2 μm. Under favourable conditions a calculated smooth-surface film thickness of 1.0 μm might be predicted, but under more severe conditions much thinner films are expected. It is clear that most types of practical gears operate in such conditions where significant asperity interactions occur, leading to micro-EHL effects and mixed lubrication.

Micropitting is a serious form of fatigue distress which is particularly associated with roughness effects in both gears and rolling-element bearings. It is characterised by the appearance of small surface pits 5–10 μm deep with a width corresponding to the roughness asperity features.[3] The benign initial appearance of micropitting, which may appear as "grey staining", belies the fact that crack branching can lead to large-scale pits and even tooth breakage.[4] It has become an endemic form of distress and failure in wind turbine speed-increasing gearboxes where it affects both gears and support bearings, and considerable efforts are currently being made to understand and overcome the problem in this particular application.[5]

The type of finish found on ground gear teeth has a characteristic "lay" in which close to two-dimensional grooves/ridges are aligned in a direction perpendicular to the sliding and entraining direction. Grinding produces an essentially random type finish and the distribution of surface heights of the ridges is Gaussian on newly finished parts.[6] However, when surfaces are put to work the running process exposes the most prominent asperities to significant local pressure and traction loading (either through micro-EHL films, or by direct contact) that exceed the elastic limit, so that the surface finish is modified significantly by plastic deformation in a process which may be described as a form of *running-in*. Experimental monitoring of this process in lubricated roller tests shows that surface modification takes place rapidly, within a few encounters between given parts of the two surfaces.[7] The resulting finish has a significantly skewed height distribution in which the valley features are re-tained and the asperities become less prominent, with their peaks more rounded in shape. Subsequent changes to surface finish as a result of mild wear processes take place on a much longer timescale.

From the foregoing it can be appreciated that the detailed analysis and prediction of the behaviour of lubricated rough contacts such as those in gears and bearings embodies aspects of surface mechanics, concentrated contact lubrication, elastic/plastic deformation and fatigue. Further complication is added due to the fact that in a real lubricated rolling/sliding contact between rough surfaces the problem is intrinsically time-dependent because of transient encounters between asperities on the two surfaces. Combining these features in a physical model of a gear tooth contact, for example, obviously presents a considerable challenge. Some progress is being made, however.[8–10]

2   Numerical analysis

Numerical method

The problem of rough surface EHL requires the simultaneous solution of the time-dependent Reynolds equation and the elastic deflection equation. This equation is made highly non-linear by the near exponential dependence of viscosity on pressure and the non-Newtonian lubricant behaviour exhibited at the strain rates of

$O(10^8\ s^{-1})$ experienced in thin films at high pressure. The novel methods used to solve the problem are described by the authors in detail elsewhere[11,12] and follow from casting the Boussinesq integral equation for the deflection of a semi-infinite body in a differential form which leads to pressure influence coefficients that are highly localised.[13] In this "differential deflection" approach the equations are solved as a simultaneous set in the two active variables, pressure and film thickness.

In a mixed lubrication environment the areas of the solution space where the fluid is unable to separate the surfaces and direct asperity interactions occur are not pre-determined and must be found as part of the solution procedure. Some approaches to this problem of predicting local film failure do so by plausible supposition, typically based on the assumption of dry contact when films less than a prescribed value are encountered in the solution.[14] The present authors have pursued an approach whereby the mathematical occurrence of transient surface interpenetration in the coupled solution of the elastic and fluid equations is replaced by the constraints imposed by contact mechanics. This algorithm ensures mass conservation and establishes direct contact conditions dynamically at each point in the computational mesh as the two fundamental equations are solved simultaneously.[15,16]

The results of analyses are transient evaluations of lubricant pressure, surface shear stress and film thickness at contact positions subject to a full lubricant film, and contact pressure at positions where asperity contact is calculated to occur. At these transitory asperity contacts the surface shear stress is determined from the contact pressure using a boundary lubrication friction coefficient. The time-dependent pressure and traction results thus predict the surface loading experienced by both contacting components. An evaluation of the time-varying surface and sub-surface elastic stress distribution may then be carried out which, when related to axes fixed in the moving surfaces, provide a stress history for a selected volume of each of the contacting components during their transit of the contact zone. These histories are subsequently used to evaluate the probability of localised surface fatigue using various classical fatigue models,[17–19] and the present authors have compared the results obtained using these different criteria.[20]

Application to gear experiments

The numerical procedures outlined in the previous section have been used to predict fatigue and damage in gears. Gear profile measurements were taken from test gears used for micropitting tests at the University of Newcastle using a form profilometer as illustrated in Fig. 1a. The tip of the gear tooth where the involute section meets the gear diameter is clearly evident and the coordinate x is measured from that point in a direction parallel to the profile trace direction, which is, in turn, parallel to the

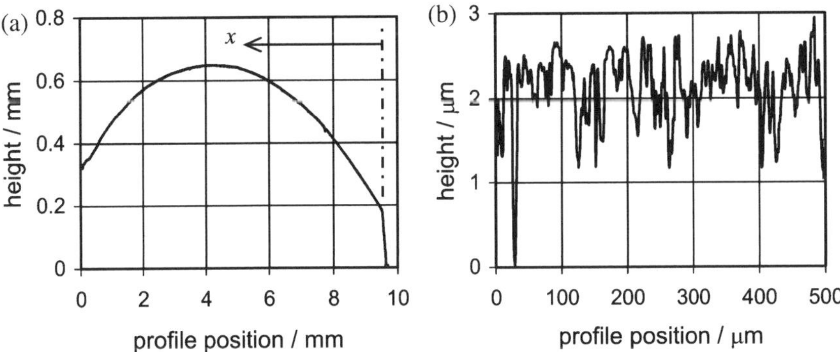

Fig. 1 (a) Form profilometer trace of gear tooth and (b) roughness profile at specified value of x (metal below profile).

tangent to the tooth at the pitch point. The value of x at any meshing point of the gear can then be obtained from involute curve geometry and is used to identify sections of interest in the filtered surface roughness profile for analysis as shown in Fig. 1b. A roughness profile with length $4a$, where a is the Hertzian contact dimension at the meshing position considered is selected. The representative profile section obtained in this way is then repeated successively to form a *multiprofile* with the joins between the repeated representative profiles effected at deep valley features so that no new artificial asperity features are introduced by the joining process. The purpose of using multiprofiles is to provide long representative profiles from the two surfaces for interaction during the simulation of the rolling/sliding contact of the gear tooth surfaces.

The mixed EHL analysis is then carried out using multiprofiles assembled in this way from the two surfaces at the meshing position of interest. The load and kinematic conditions (entraining and sliding speeds) specified are those corresponding to that particular meshing position. This analysis of the multiprofiles aims to reproduce all the asperity interactions that can take place between the representative profiles in the rolling/sliding motion of the contact surfaces.

Application to disc experiments

Further experiments are being carried out using a twin disc machine with crowned test discs on 76.2 mm centres with axial ground surface finish to replicate the kinematics and roughness orientation of gears.[21] The advantages of disc machine tests are the avoidance of dynamic loading and the potential to measure surface roughness profiles *in situ* without the need to dismount the test discs. In this way before and after profiles can be compared to quantify changes in the surface roughness profile. The disc crown radius is 304.8 mm so that the radii of relative curvature are in the ratio 8 : 1 which gives a Hertzian elliptical contact area with axis ratio of approximately 4 : 1. The direction of rolling/sliding is along the minor axis of the contact ellipse. This configuration avoids unpredictable edge loading stress concentrations which occur with cylindrical discs, and is intended as a realistic simulation of the gear tooth contacts. For disc experiments multiprofiles are again utilised for the analysis but are assembled in a different way. To illustrate the approach consider the discs illustrated in Fig. 2 in rolling/sliding contact. Position A, for example, of disc I will interact with all of the surface of disc II during running. Two kinds of multiprofile are constructed to model this process. For disc I a multiprofile consisting of repeated instances of the profile at A is constructed, and for disc II a composite multiprofile consisting of repeated instances of the sequence of profiles U,V,W,X,Y,Z is constructed. An analysis of the interaction of these two multiprofiles is taken to be representative of the experience of profile A during

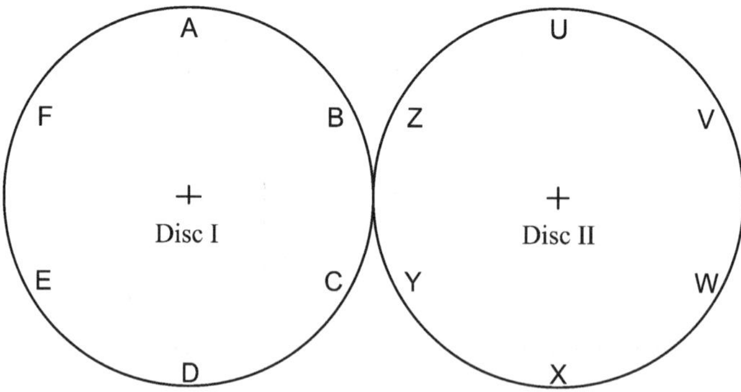

Fig. 2 Schematic of test discs with position of measured profiles A–F and U–Z indicated.

running. For analysis of a profile from disc II its multiprofile is run against a composite multiprofile constructed from profiles A to F.

3   Results

Results are presented taken from a study which compared two different gear manufacturing methods in micropitting tests where detailed fatigue calculations were compared to evaluate the finishing methods.[22] Gears of type A were finished by generation grinding and gears of type B were finished by form grinding. The analyses involved multiprofiles taken from four positions of interest over the gear meshing cycle with slide/roll ratios of ± 0.35 and ± 0.65 where negative slide/roll ratios correspond to contact in the pinion dedendum. Profiles from three different axial tooth positions were considered, giving a total of 24 multiprofile analyses (four kinematic conditions, two manufacturing processes and three axial positions). The main emphasis of the current contribution is on the extent of direct contact experienced by the surfaces and on modelling the running-in process, and results for the eight analyses of profiles on the gear centre plane are considered.

Contact and extreme pressure events

The transient contact events occurring during the mixed EHL analyses were counted and accumulated relative to the surface profile. In this way a count of the number of timesteps where contact incidents occurred was obtained at each position of the profile corresponding to the profile's traverse through the contact zone. Since the profile traverses repeatedly through the contact zone during the multiprofile analysis, counts for each traverse were obtained and an example of these calculations is given in Fig. 3 where results for eight traverses are given for a 1 mm length of the surface profile. The surface profile is illustrated as the lower of the curves in the figure with a dimension bar indicating its height scale. The eight traverse count curves are offset from each other by a 'count' value of 100. The number of timesteps taken for a point on the surface to traverse the Herzian contact zone is 800, so a profile position with a timestep count value of 100 corresponds to contact occurring for 12.5% of the transit time. Comparing the count curves it is clear that high count values occur at particular prominent asperity features with the asperities located at profile positions 576 and 777 μm experiencing contact for over 10% of the traverse time in some of the traverses. However for other traverses the counts at these positions are considerably fewer which emphasises the role of the counterface in determining the severity of loading. Fig. 4 shows the corresponding count of the number of timesteps where extreme contact pressure values ($p > 3$ GPa) were

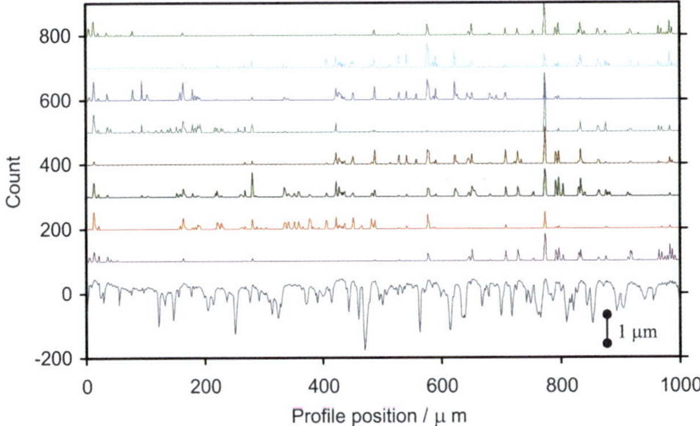

Fig. 3   Profile contact count for eight traverses of the contact zone.

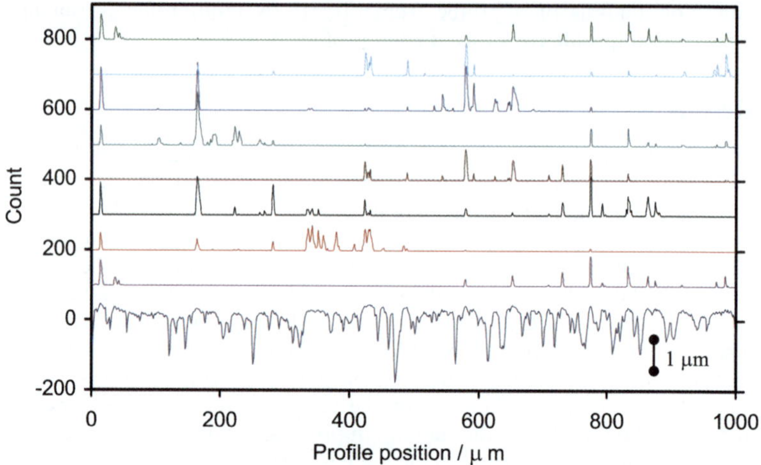

Fig. 4 Profile high pressure count ($p > 3$GPa) for eight traverses of the contact zone.

observed during the traverse. The same prominent asperities are seen to experience high count values as in Fig. 3 with those at positions 13, 161, 576 and 777 μm having values in excess of 10% for several of the traverses. It is clear from comparing the figures that these events are correlated in the sense that positions experiencing high contact counts also experience high extreme pressure counts, though not necessarily during the same timesteps because calculated contacts do not necessarily occur with high contact pressures.

The variability caused by the differences in the counterface asperities' relative positions for each traverse are clearly apparent, and it is possible to average the counts to obtain an indication of mean behaviour as shown in Fig. 5. This figure emphasises the association of both extreme events with profile position. The mean incidence for the prominent asperities is generally less than 7.5% of the contact transit time. When the average is taken for the whole profile the mean incidence falls to levels below 0.5% as is shown in Fig. 6 which compares these mean values for the

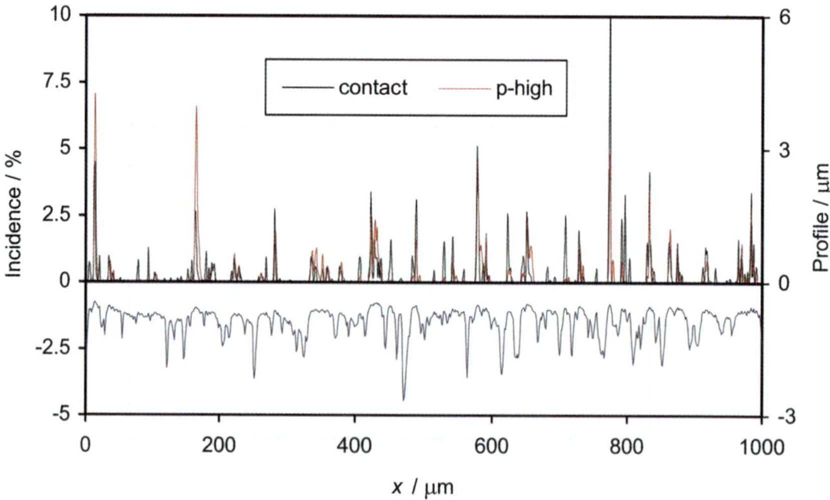

Fig. 5 Mean traverse contact and extreme pressure incidence.

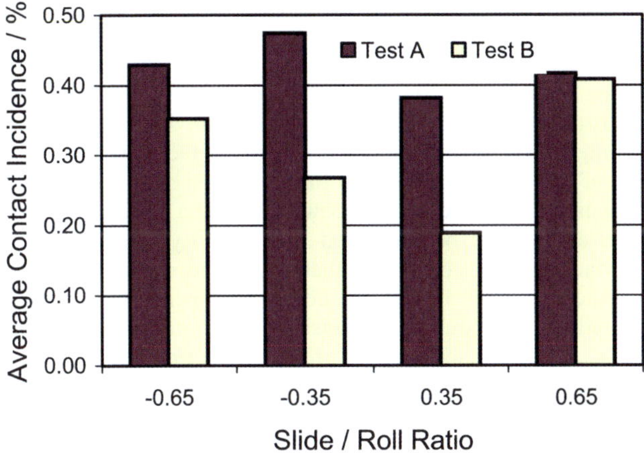

Fig. 6   Average contact incidence for the two tests at the four kinematic conditions.

two manufacturing processes (Test A and Test B) and the four kinematic conditions considered in the study.

Surface fatigue

Fig. 7 illustrates a typical pressure distribution generated at a single timestep obtained from a transient analysis of two rough surfaces. The individual surfaces are shown in their deflected configurations offset at the top of the figure so that the relative magnitudes of the surface roughness features and the lubricant film thickness can be appreciated. The pressure, p, is seen to be very different to the Hertzian semi-ellipse (shown as a broken line) that would occur for equivalent smooth surfaces and which has a maximum value of 1 GPa. In contrast the mixed EHL analysis has concentrated pressure spikes of 2, 3 and 4 GPa at positions $x/a = -1.1$, 0.52, -0.5, respectively, where surface asperity features can be seen to be in intimate interaction. Less aggressive, broader, pressure events occur at $x/a = -0.43$, -0.1, and 0.1,

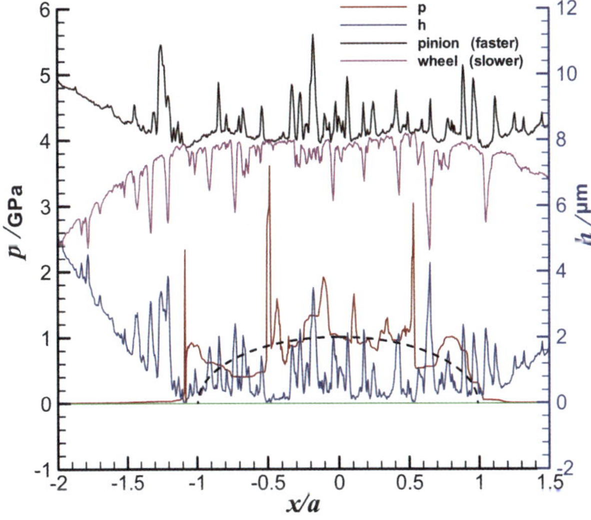

Fig. 7   Illustrative timestep result from mixed EHL analysis.

for example, and these are associated with thicker lubricant films as may be judged from the corresponding film thickness profile.

Gear contacts are generally designed based on smooth surface considerations but it is apparent that the real surface loading deviates considerably from this ideal when the roughness is taken into account. The lubricant film does not provide any significant "cushioning" of the asperity contacts due to the fact that it is very thin, but its presence does, of course, reduce the load that is carried by the asperity contacts due to the hydrodynamic pressure acting elsewhere on the surface. Since the extreme pressure events are seen to be correlated with asperity contact and near contact events, and surface asperities on the contacting surfaces move relative to each other at the sliding speed, it is clear that an individual asperity feature will experience a number of loading cycles during its transit of the contact area and the conditions for fatigue to occur at the asperity level are therefore present.

The mixed EHL timestep results also include surface shear stress distributions (not illustrated in Fig. 7) so that the surface loading history is known. This enables stress histories to be obtained for the contacting components. The ground surface roughness can be considered to be extruded perpendicular to the rolling sliding direction (at least as a first order approximation) so a plane strain stress field is assumed. In general, prominent asperity zones on the surface experience a series of elevated concentrated loading events whereas other areas have a less rapidly varying pressure commensurate with the smooth surface values.

In order to simulate the effect of this loading on the surface fatigue behaviour of the contacting components, classical models from the fatigue literature have been applied. Various critical plane models have been considered[20] but these have the disadvantage that they are driven by the most aggressive pressure events. Since these will occur for both surfaces simultaneously, such models tend not to distinguish between the slower moving surface and the faster moving one. This is in conflict with the observed pattern of micropitting development which occurs predominantly in the root of the gear tooth[23] *i.e.* the surface which moves more slowly relative to the contact. In response to this observation we prefer fatigue models in which the detrimental effect of all loading cycles are included, rather than that of only the most aggressive cycle.

The results presented here are obtained using the so called rainflow counting method[24] to determine a sequence of equivalent loading cycles at each point in the stressed volume considered from its loading history. These cycles correspond to strain hysteresis loops determined from the strain history. For each such cycle the number of repeated cycles that would result in fatigue, N, is determined from a (shear) strain–life model.[25] The damage associated with one such cycle is the reciprocal N^{-1} and the damage caused by a sequence of such cycles is given by the Palmgren Miner rule for linear damage accumulation as

$$D = \sum_{\text{all } i} N_i^{-1} \tag{1}$$

with a damage value $D = 1$ corresponding to predicted fatigue failure.

These methods were applied to the mixed EHL results obtained for the two test gears and Fig. 8 shows one such comparison which indicates that the Test B profile suffers a greater level of fatigue damage in each traverse of the contact zone. Areas coloured red correspond to damage values $D > 10^{-6}$ so that fatigue is predicted to occur at those positions in approximately 10^6 gear meshing cycles. In these simulations a friction coefficient of 0.1 was assumed at the transient "dry" contact events. An investigation in which the friction coefficient was varied from 0.1 to 1.0 did not show any significant effect on the predicted damage. This is due to the fact that the occurrence of contact events is infrequent in comparison to the stress cycling arising from lubricated asperity encounters. Dry contact events may, however, be of significance during initial running of surfaces where plastic deformation at asperity

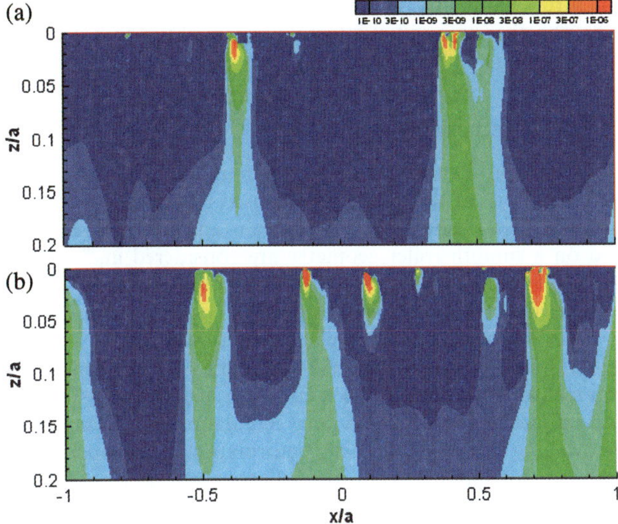

Fig. 8 Calculated fatigue damage for Test A (upper) and Test B (lower) pinions.

junctions may take place. Comparison of damage contour maps from pinion and wheel surfaces from the 24 simulations (*i.e.* a total of 48 damage maps) indicates a higher level of damage with gear set B in a significant number of cases. This shows that the line contact surface loading response is significantly different for the two surfaces which have nominally the same level of roughness. Reasons for these differences are being explored in the Newcastle University test program. In this respect it is important to recall that in the above simulations of damage accumulation the elastic stresses calculated are superimposed on stress-free bodies. The presence of significant residual stresses in the near-surface zone as a result of heat treatment, or plastic deformation during the initial running-in phase will clearly affect fatigue damage calculations. In an attempt to incorporate the appropriate residual stresses we have therefore carried out elastic/plastic contact simulations of rough surfaces in order to reveal the residual stress field at the asperity level.

4   Plastic deformation effects

Including a detailed elastic/plastic deflection calculation within the mixed EHL analysis is a very challenging objective that some researchers are currently attempting. However, as indicated above, experimental results strongly suggest that plastic deformation in gear tooth contacts is not a quasi-continuous process, but one that occurs predominantly during the initial encounters of asperities during a short-lived running-in phase. As an initial step we have therefore made the assumption that the residual stress and deformation fields may be approximated by consideration of corresponding dry contact of the surfaces. Since the asperity load depends on interaction of asperities correspondence will be based on the degree of residual deflection generated in the plastically deformed asperities. Clearly, in order to simulate plastic shakedown of the complete surface in contact, it would be necessary to simulate all possible encounters. However, by simulating the contact of a rough surface against a smooth surface at a range of interpenetrations it is possible to relate the residual stress and deformation fields to one another. Considerable progress has been made in the FEA modelling of *single* contacts ranging from early studies using bespoke software[26,27] to more recent work using commercial packages.[28,29] The current authors have made some progress in the FEA modelling of regular wavy surfaces, which reveals the interaction of stress and deformation fields of adjacent protuberances, together with initial attempts to model the elastic/plastic contact of real (measured) roughness.[30]

Contact modelling of real asperities

A surface roughness profile taken from the as-manufactured flank of the unloaded side of a tooth from one of the test gears was used to examine the effect of loading asperities beyond their elastic limit. Plane strain analyses where the roughness is superimposed on a smooth roller geometry are considered in,[30] and in the results reported here a 0.5 mm length of profile was mirrored repeatedly to form a rough nominally flat surface which is loaded against a rigid smooth surface using the ABAQUS FEA software system. The plane strain model has transverse deflection restrained at its (mirror image) transverse boundaries. The dimension of the model in a direction measured normal to the contacting surfaces was sufficient to ensure effective semi-infinite deflection behaviour. Simulation of repeated loading at the same load shows that the residual plastic deformation at an asperity occurs almost entirely in the first loading event. Further changes caused by subsequent load re-application were relatively small. Furthermore, during repeated loading with an increased load the final changes corresponded almost exactly to those occurring when only the higher load was applied. This behaviour is illustrated in Fig. 9. This shows results obtained for the last of a sequence of three load applications of 700 kN m^{-1} where this was the only loading, and where this was preceded by three load applications of 350 kN m^{-1}. Fig. 9a shows the contact pressures corresponding to the final load of each load sequence. The curves are almost identical and show that the contact pressure is essentially dictated by the largest load applied. The small differences due to different loading histories can be assessed more closely in Fig. 9b which shows the results of Fig. 9a for a 0.1 mm section in more detail. The figure shows two curves, one for the end load of each loading sequence, and it is clear that these are almost exactly superposed. Fig. 9c shows the resulting shape of the rough surface following plastic deformation, *i.e.* it illustrates the residual deflection after the final load of the sequence is removed. The green curve is again coincident with the blue one showing that the permanent set caused by plastic deformation is the same for both load sequences. The additional (red) curve in this figure shows the undeformed roughness profile so that the difference between the red and the coincident green and blue curves represents the residual deflection of the surface.

The von-Mises equivalent stress distribution at the final load in the sequence is illustrated in the upper part of Fig. 10a. The assumed yield stress value is 1.6 GPa and the red contour area indicates the zones where conditions are plastic. These can be seen to correspond to the areas of the profile illustrated in Fig. 9c where residual deflections have significantly modified the shape of asperity features. The residual deflection has a corresponding residual stress field associated with it. The tangential (*i.e.* the direction parallel to the contact plane) direct stress component of the residual stress is illustrated Fig. 10b. In general the residual tangential stress is compressive at and beneath the surface, but the figure also shows surface zones of high residual *tensile* stress aligned with the more highly modified asperities identified in Fig. 9c at $x/a = 0.324$, 0.336 and 0.341 together with a further subsurface tensile stress zone just below the compressive zone. It is tempting to speculate that this consequence of asperity plastic deformation during initial contact may be instrumental in encouraging fatigue cracks to initiate at the surface, or below the surface where the residual stress is tensile. Since the surface tensile zones are limited to the area of high plastic modification, such an initiation mechanism would be consistent with observed micropitting behaviour where the micropits are on the scale of the surface asperity features. Tensile stresses of this kind have been calculated using slip line field theory for the simplified model of a rigid-perfectly plastic body subject

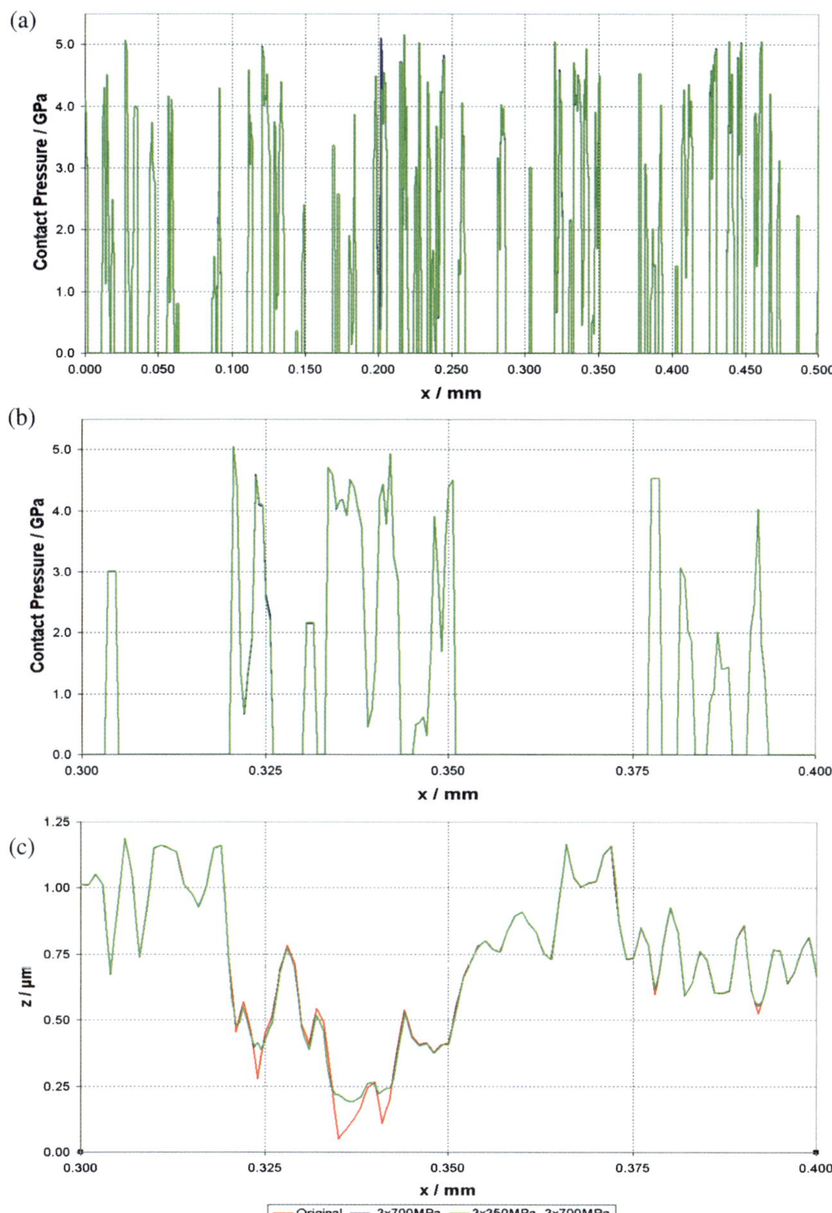

Fig. 9 FEA contact pressure (a), (b) and residual deflection (c) for repeated loads. Note that the profile of (c) has metal above the curve.

to normal-tangential load applied by a plane rigid die in plane contact with the surface.[31] The loading in the current model does not include a tangential component and is determined by the shape of the contacting asperity.

The residual stress pattern at plastically deformed asperities can also be observed in a different profile section in Fig. 11 where the residual deflection and residual tangential stress contours are shown. The highly modified asperity at $x/a = 0.122$ can be seen to be the site of a high tensile tangential residual stress at the surface together with an elevated subsurface tensile residual stress.

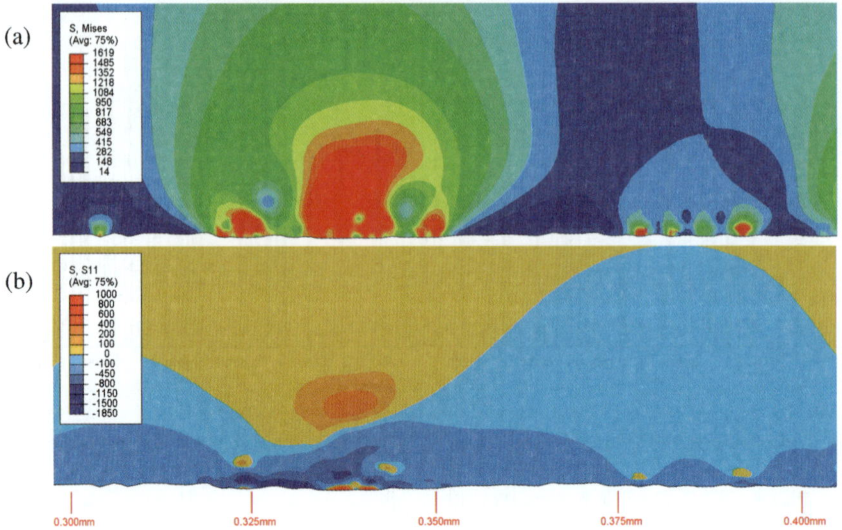

Fig. 10 Contours of (a) von-Mises equivalent stress under load, and (b) residual tangential direct stress when load is removed.

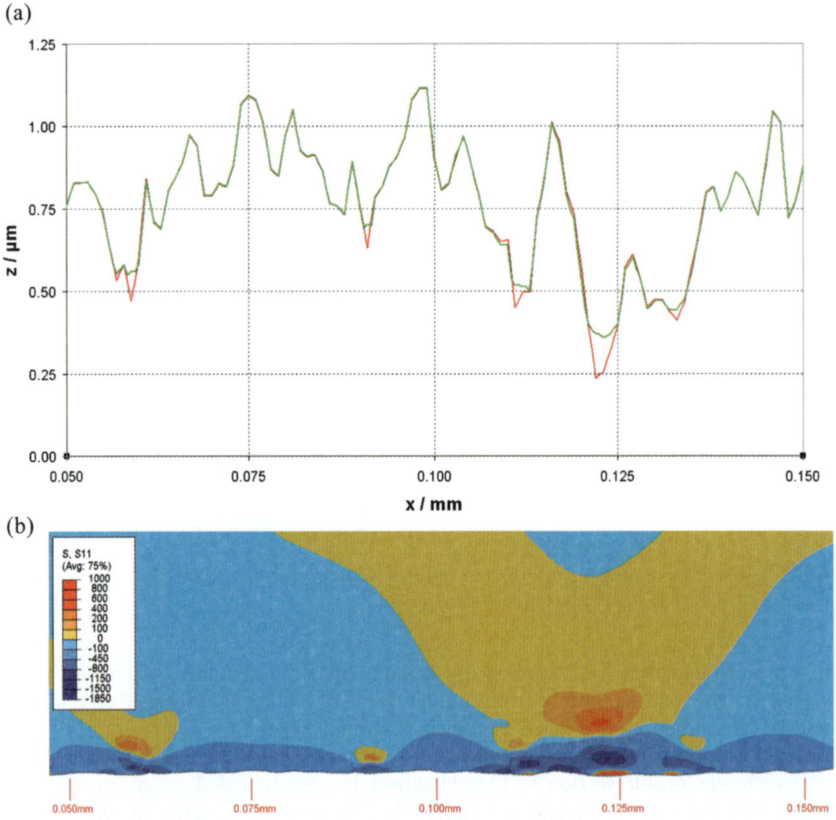

Fig. 11 (a) Original surface profile and post loading residual profile shape (with metal above the profile), and (b) residual tangential direct stress.

These predictions of significant residual stresses in the stressed zone are clearly of relevance to any subsequent elastic fatigue studies.[31] Work is therefore in progress to superpose such residual stress fields on the time-varying elastic stresses obtained during the mixed EHL simulations. In this way we aim to quantify the possible influence of initial contact on near-surface fatigue performance.

Mixed EHL analysis with consideration of running-in

The FEA residual stress results shown above suggest that the level of surface residual stress may be related to the extent of plastic deformation taking place in the initial running-in process when surfaces are first put to work. This initial "plastic shakedown" hypothesis is reinforced by the observation that when dry elastic contact simulation is applied to rough surfaces that have been run against each other (at the load used in the simulation) the maximum pressures observed are generally at the level of the surface hardness. This is in marked contrast to analyses using as-manufactured surfaces where elastic contact analysis gives unrealistic maximum asperity pressures of two or three times the hardness value. Running-in might therefore be viewed as a process which modifies the surface asperity shapes by the amount necessary to reduce the elastic pressures generated in contact to the hardness value.[6,7] This observation suggests a simplified, empirical means of representing the surface geometry effects of plastic deformation during the running-in process in a mixed EHL analysis procedure which can simulate running-in under lubricated (as opposed to dry contact) conditions. These ideas have been pursued in an EHL model in which the surface profile is dynamically modified to automatically satisfy a specified maximum pressure value.

Fig. 4 shows the positions at which extreme pressure events occur on a section of surface roughness in mixed EHL analyses of the profile's traverse of the contact zone. The value of the maximum mixed EHL pressure obtained at each position of the profile in ten such traverses is plotted in Fig. 12, and the maximum pressures for one particular traverse is given in Fig. 13. These pressures give a means to introduce surface asperity modifications to the multiprofiles as they interact with each other in their repeated traverses through the contact zone. In each traverse the information in Fig. 13 identifies the portions of the surface subject to mixed EHL pressures in excess of the assumed hardness value, and the counts of Fig. 4 indicate whether the extreme pressure was a frequent or isolated event during the traverse.

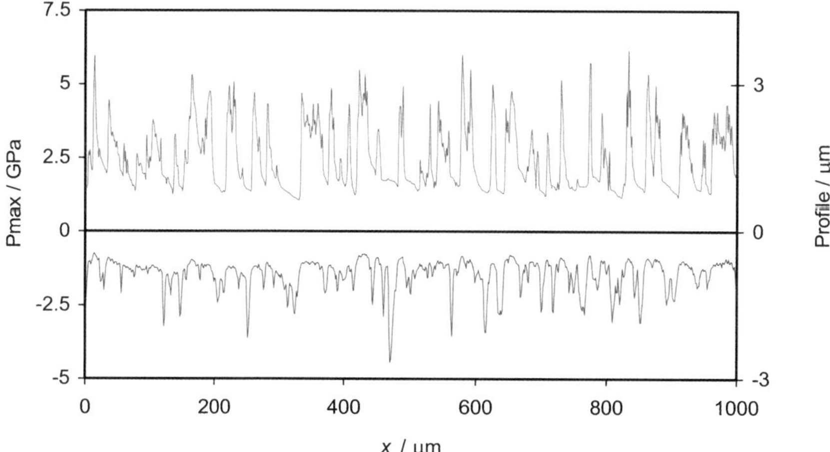

Fig. 12 Maximum mixed EHL analysis pressure obtained for the surface roughness profile over ten traverses of the contact zone.

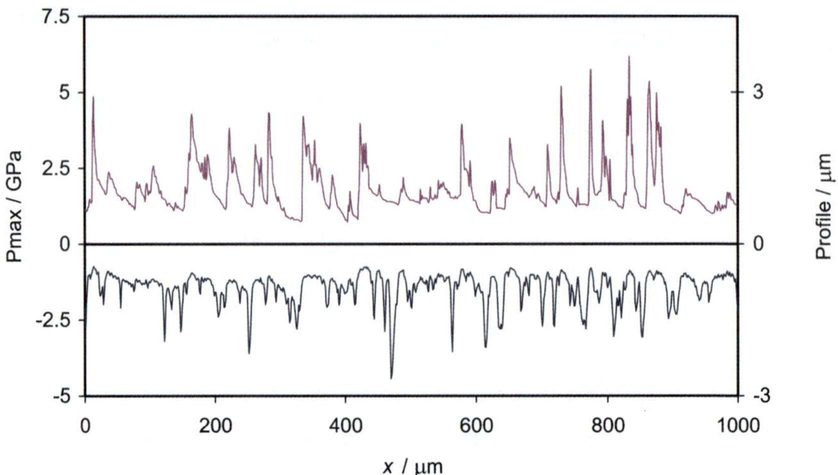

Fig. 13 Maximum mixed EHL analysis pressure obtained for the surface roughness profile for a single traverse of the contact zone.

This frequency information allows a distinction to be made between asperity features that are frequently subjected to high pressures, and points on the surface whose high pressure events correspond to single interactions with aggressive asperity features on the counterface.

Empirical numerical procedures to model the running-in process are being developed based on this information with the objective of specifying a surface hardness level and operating load, and allowing subsequent sustained multiprofile analysis to determine the surface profile modifications necessary to limit the maximum mixed EHL pressures experienced to be of the order of the specified hardness. Fig. 14 shows the changes obtained with such an analysis using a multiprofile analysis for one of the test gear cases considered above. The results presented here are for a profile taken after running, and work is in progress to extend the approach to the more aggressive as-manufactured surfaces. Fig. 14 shows an illustrative detail of the original and the evolved profile that emerges following the first 100 contact traverses of the multiprofile. This shows some asperity features that have been removed together with a general smoothing of small amplitude features on the rounded lands of the surface. The changes brought about by a second application of the procedure

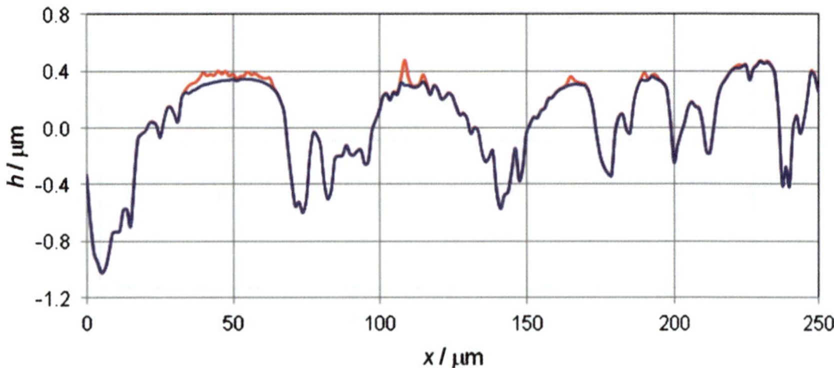

Fig. 14 Original profile (red) and evolved profile (blue) after 100 mixed EHL contact traverses.

over a subsequent 100 contact traverses are much smaller and the surface features have thus attained a stable shape consistent with repeated mixed EHL analyses giving peak pressures of the order of the specified hardness value.

This technique is in its infancy but shows promise as a means of including the observed running-in effect in an EHL simulation. It may be possible to develop the ideas aired in this section to produce an overall model in which a multiprofile mixed EHL analysis generates the stable "run-in" roughness profiles of contacting surfaces, and as part of the calculation determines the extent of a permanent set predicted for asperities. These asperity shape changes can then be associated with residual stress fields obtained from FEA contact and used for fatigue damage predictions.

5 Discussion and conclusions

The theoretical analyses described above attempt to bring together the major physical factors thought to be involved in micropitting failure. The EHL models which have been developed show that contact pressures well in excess of the corresponding smooth surface (Hertzian) values are generated and that the near-surface stress field is determined by the scale of surface asperities. The regions of high stress occur at a shallow depth consistent with the observed depth of micropits: this supports the view that micropitting is directly linked to surface roughness. Conventional high-cycle fatigue damage calculations based on the (assumed elastic) stress-cycling experienced by surface asperities as they traverse the overall contact zone and encounter asperities on the counterface further reinforces this conclusion. The earlier observation of the rapid initial surface modification during running-in leads to the idea that the plastic deformation and associated residual stresses may be of crucial importance in determining subsequent micropitting performance.

Incorporating the plastic deformation process into a full EHL solver presents a major challenge, however. We have therefore used a dry contact elastic/plastic simulation of rough surface contact to determine the asperity residual deformation and stress field which, in principle, can then be incorporated into the EHL and fatigue simulations. Detailed examination of the asperity residual stress contours reveals zones of high residual tensile stress which again points strongly to the observed location and size of micropits. Simulation of repeated elastic/plastic loading shows that asperity deformation shakes down rapidly and that the final condition is almost independent of loading history.

Experimental verification is clearly necessary in order to validate the predictions of the elastic/plastic contact simulations. Disc experiments will therefore be carried out in which rough surface profiles will be taken before and after loading in dry, static contact and the deformed profiles compared to the predictions using the FEA model. The elastic/plastic behaviour of surfaces under lubricated conditions is more complex because of multiple asperity/asperity encounters and the presence of a film. However, if correspondence can be found between the residual surface profiles after running under lubricated conditions and the results of the empirical pressure-limiting/profile-modifying model of lubricated running-in described above, then it will be possible (based on FEA modelling) to infer residual stresses under lubricated conditions from the degree of apparent plastic deformation taking place in the simulation.

The running-in process involving plastic deformation is rapid, and subsequent changes in surface finish occur on a much longer time scale, and in real machinery can be attributed to "mild" wear processes. A modified Archard-type model of mild wear based on the transient pressure experienced during running has been developed by the authors in previous work on wear prediction in worm gears[32] and will be assessed in terms of the measured wear changes in sustained running of test discs. The "mild wear" process could be viewed as a beneficial "running-in" effect which both improves the conformity of the surface profiles by removing prominent asperities without introducing serious plastic deformation, and it may also be helpful in removing the thin surface layer where micropitting may have begun to develop, but which has not progressed to the stage of deeper cracking.

The experimental program aimed at corroborating these theoretical developments is challenging and necessary in order to provide confidence that the approach can describe the key processes at work in mixed lubrication of rough surfaces. This is an essential step in building an understanding of micropitting failure in power transmission gears. A further reason to pursue this research is the need for condition monitoring systems that can detect the inherent changes in contact surface conditions and distinguish between the onset conditions for distress and surface failure on the one hand, and the continuous evolution of surfaces as a result of initial full load plastic deformation and long-term slow change due to mild wear processes on the other.

Being able to model the process, as is attempted using the methods described in this paper, will provide the tools to assess surface conditions and understand the transition between normal surface evolution and the conditions that develop in advance of failure.

Clearly, the paper is concerned with the physical phenomena of contact mechanics, hydrodynamic lubrication and fatigue behaviour of rough surfaces. Surface and lubricant additive chemistry undoubtedly have a significant influence in the way they affect what we have assumed to be the transient "dry" contact events predicted in the micro-EHL simulations both in terms of friction and the possible damage initiation and crack growth mechanisms. Such contacts are generally assumed to be protected by "boundary" films and the only way in which they can be incorporated into the physical model at this stage is in terms of an effective coefficient of friction, which is the approach we have taken in the paper. A greater understanding of boundary lubrication under the conditions of highly concentrated, transitory contacts is urgently required.

Acknowledgements

The research was supported by the UK Engineering and Physical Sciences Research Council with grant EP/G06024X/1, The British Gearing Association, and Rolls-Royce Goodrich Engine Control Systems Ltd.

References

1 D. Dowson and G. R. Higginson, *Elastohydrodynamic Lubrication*, Pergamon Press, Oxford, 1966.
2 C. C. Kweh, H. P. Evans and R. W. Snidle, *J. Tribol.*, 1989, **111**, 577–584.
3 B. R. Hohn, P. Oster and S. Emmert, *Proc. International Conference on Gears*, VDI Berichte Nr. 1230, 331–334, Dresden, Germany, 1996.
4 K. Brimble, I. Atkins, K. Blencoe, C. Aylott and B. A. Shaw, (2001), *Proc. BGA Annual Congress*, pp 44–50, London, 2001.
5 National Renewable Energy Laboratory, *Wind Turbine Micropitting Workshop: A Recap*, NREL Technical Report NREL/TP-500–46572, February 2010, (Shuangwen Sheng, Editor).
6 I. F. Bishop and R. W. Snidle, in *Studies of Engine Bearings and Lubrication*, Special Publication 539, Society of Automotive Engineers (SAE), Warrendale, 1983, 53–64.
7 I. F. Bishop, PhD Thesis, University of Wales, 1981.
8 J. Tao, T. G. Hughes, H. P. Evans, R. W. Snidle, N. A. Hopkinson, M. Talks and J. M. Starbuck, *J. Tribol.*, 2003, **125**, 267–274.
9 M. J. A. Holmes, H. Qiao, H. P. Evans and R. W. Snidle, *Proc 30th Leeds-Lyon Symp. On Tribology*, Elsevier, Amsterdam, 2004, 201–212.
10 M. J. A. Holmes, H. P. Evans and R. W. Snidle, *J. Tribol.*, 2005, **127**, 61–69.
11 M. J. A. Holmes, H. P. Evans and T. G. Hughes, *Proc Inst. Mech. Eng., Part J*, 2003, **217**, 289–303.
12 M. J. A. Holmes, H. P. Evans and T. G. Hughes, *Proc Inst. Mech. Eng., Part J*, 2003, **217**, 305–321.

13 H. P. Evans and T. G. Hughes, *Proc. Instn Mech. Engrs, Part C: Jn of Mechanical Engineering Science*, 2000, **214**, 563–584.

14 D. Zhu, *Tribol. Trans.*, 2002, **45**, 540–548.

15 H. P. Evans, R. W. Snidle and K. J. Sharif, *Tribol. Int.*, 2009, **42**, 1406–1417.

16 H. P. Evans, R. W. Snidle and K. J. Sharif, *Proc. World Tribology Congress*, Kyoto, Japan, 2009, 310.

17 W. N. Findley, *Trans ASME Journal of Engineering for Industry*, 1959, **81**, 301–306.

18 T. Matake, *Bulletin of JSME*, 1977, **20**, 257–264.

19 K. Dang Van, G. Cailletaud, J. F. Flavenot, A. Le Douaron and H. P. Lieurade, In: *Biaxial and Multiaxial Fatigue, EGF 3* (Edited by M. W. Brown and K. J. Miller), Mechanical Engineering Publications, London, 459–478, 1989.

20 H. Qiao, H. P. Evans and R. W. Snidle, *Proc Inst. Mech. Eng., Part J*, 2008, **222**, 381–393.

21 M. J. Patching, C. C. Kweh, H. P. Evans and R. W. Snidle, *J. Tribol.*, 1995, **117**, 482–489.

22 H. P. Evans, R. W. Snidle and K. J. Sharif, *Proc ASME 2011 International Design Engineering Technical Conferences & Computers and Information in Engineering Conference*, 2011.

23 W. Predki, N. Khashayar and G. Lutzig, *Proc International Conference on Gears*, VDI Berichte Nr. 2108,793–803, Dusseldorf, Germany, 2010.

24 C. Amzallag, J. P. Gerey, J. L. Robert and J. Bahuaud, *Int. J. Fatigue*, 1994, **16**, 287–293.

25 A. Fatemi and D. F. Socie, *Fatigue & Fracture of Engineering Materials and Structures*, 1988, **11**, 149–165.

26 C. Hardy, C. N. Baronet and G. V. Tordion, *Int. J. Numer. Methods Eng.*, 1971, **3**, 451–462.

27 C. H. Lee, S. Masaki and S. Kobayashi, *Int. J. Mech. Sci.*, 1972, **14**, 417–426.

28 L. Kogut and I. Etsion, *J. Appl. Mech.*, 2002, **69**, 657–662.

29 R. L. Jackson and I. Green, *J. Tribol.*, 2005, **127**, 343–354.

30 M. J. Bryant, H. P. Evans and R. W. Snidle, *Tribol. Int.*, 2012, **46**, 269–278.

31 A. V. Olver, H. A. Spikes, A. F. Bower and K. L. Johnson, *Wear*, 1986, **107**, 151–174.

32 K. J. Sharif, H. P. Evans, R. W. Snidle, D. Barnett and I. M. Egorov, *Proc Inst. Mech. Eng., Part J*, 2006, **220**, 295–306.

Physio-chemical hydrodynamic mechanism underlying the formation of thin adsorbed boundary films

W. W. F. Chong,[a] M. Teodorescu[*ba] and H. Rahnejat[c]

Received 24th November 2011, Accepted 20th January 2012
DOI: 10.1039/c2fd00118g

The formation of low shear strength surface-adhered thin films mitigates excessive friction in mixed or boundary regimes of lubrication. Tribo-films are formed as a consequence of molecular chemical reactions with the surfaces. The process is best viewed in the context of a lubricant-surface system. Therefore, it is usually surmised that the adsorption of lubricant molecular species to the contact surfaces is underlying to the formation of ultra-thin lubricant films. The paper considers contact between smooth surfaces at close separation. This may be regarded as the contact of a pair of asperity summits, whose dimensions, however small, are far larger than the size of fluid molecules within the conjunction. In such diminishing separations the constraining effect of relatively smooth solid barriers causes oscillatory solvation of fluid molecules. This effect accounts for the conjunctional load capacity but does not contribute to mitigating friction, except when molecular adsorption is taken into account with long chain molecules which tend to inhibit solvation. The paper presents an analytical predictive model based on the Ornstein–Zernike method with the Percus–Yevick approximation of a narrow interaction potential between conjunctional composition. The predictions confirm the above stated physical facts in a fundamental manner.

1 Introduction

Except for some occasions where friction is required for functional assurance such as locomotion and traction, in most other circumstances its reduction would improve energy efficiency. As far back as the 17th century the interaction of rough surface topography was understood to be the main underlying mechanism for friction both at the onset of motion (Amontons[1]) and in its pursuance (Coulomb[2]). Indeed there is compelling evidence that separation of rough surfaces by a film of low shear strength was intuitively understood even in the ancient times. Historical records show the use of water or vegetable oil between wooden sleds and wooden tracks or tree trunks, for example in the bas relief in the grotto of El Bersheh and vegetable grease or even mud in the bearings of the chariot of Ur in Mesopotamia.

In the 17th Century, Newton[3] described the slow viscous action in relative motion of *hard spherical* fluid molecules giving rise to shear resistance, which he used to define the concept of viscosity. This was the first tacit inference that, like solids, fluids also give rise to friction, enabling tractive motion. Later the concept of

[a]School of Engineering, Cranfield University, Cranfield, UK
[b]Baskin School of Engineering, University of California at Santa Cruz, CA, USA. E-mail: mteodorescu@soe.ucsc.edu
[c]Wolfson School of Mechanical & Manufacturing Engineering, Loughborough University, Loughborough, UK

viscosity and internal fluidic friction led to the works of Navier,[4] Poisson[5] and Stokes[6] and culminated in the fundamental equation for fluid flow (the Navier–Stokes equations). In the turn of 20th century Reynolds[7] modified the Navier–Stokes equations for narrow conjunctions where the effect of body, inertial and surface forces may be ignored. Reynolds[7] assumed the formation of a coherent film of lubricant between a pair of loaded contiguous surfaces in relative motion.

In hydrodynamics, the film thickness is inversely proportional to the applied load. It subsequently became apparent that a coherent film cannot be attained at all instances. The absence of wear in such circumstances was viewed as puzzling by Reynolds,[7] with ever decreasing predicted film thickness. This in time led to the understanding of the piezo-viscous action of lubricants, simultaneous with the localised elastic deflection of solids, noted many years earlier by Hertz.[8] The elastohydrodynamic regime of lubrication (EHL) was first declared by Grubin.[9] The key feature of EHL is the insensitivity of lubricant film thickness to increasing load.

By the turn of 20th century it was often noted that the break-down or breach of a coherent lubricant film does not lead to friction conditions pertaining to dry contact of solid boundaries in the form of dry friction which was noted by Coulomb.[2] In particular, Petrov[10] proposed a different form of lubricant viscosity: "stickiness", which he proposed was due to the preferential positioning of some molecules near surfaces. Following the same argument, Hardy and Doubleday[11] stated that "another kind of lubrication" exists when the solid faces are near enough to directly influence the chemistry of lubricants. They termed this as boundary lubrication. Hardy and Doubleday[11] noted the low shear strength of these chemical films.

As Dowson[12] has observed, the thickness of fluid films has spectacularly reduced since the time of Reynolds, where it may have been of the order of tens to hundreds of micrometres. The progressive reduction in film thickness throughout the 20th century has been partly the result of the miniaturisation of all forms of mechanisms and devices and partly because of a greater understanding of the role of boundary lubrication. Dowson states that talk of films of tenths of a micrometre and even nanometres is now commonplace.

In a pioneering paper, Bowden and Tabor[13] showed that a thin film of molecular dimensions can be adsorbed to the topographical surface features, whose summits are large compared with the dimensions of molecules. This confirmed Petrov's earlier supposition that the "stickiness" of the fluids near the surfaces is due to their increased viscosity there. At the relatively smooth summit of asperities the density of molecules is greater than in the bulk of any thin lubricating film as shown, for example by Israelachvilli.[14]

An experiment carried out by Chan and Horn[15] with ultra-smooth surfaces at vanishing separation of molecular dimensions showed discrete drainage of fluid molecules in a stepwise fashion from the conjunction. The phenomenon caused by the constraining effect of surfaces and the ensuing interactions with the intervening fluid molecules is known as solvation, where the packing order of molecules several molecular diameters in depth differs from that in the bulk of a fluid film (Israelachvilli,[14] Gohar and Rahnejat[16]). These findings are in accord with the suppositions put forward in the 19th century by Petrov[10] and later by Hardy and Doubleday.[11] The generated pressures in such conjunctions are subject to the attractive-repulsive solvation effect as the fluid film is successively discretised into rows of molecules which are drained from the conjunction in a stepwise fashion. Matsuoka and Kato[17] and Al-Samieh and Rahnejat[18,19] have shown that in tribological contacts where the entrainment of a fluid film is through hydrodynamic action by relative motion of surfaces, the solvation effect only dominates in gaps of several molecular diameters. They have also shown that its effect supersedes any van der Waals interaction between the fluid molecules and between those and the atoms of the bounding surfaces. Mutual approach of surfaces, promoting hydrodynamics in squeeze film motion was also found to inhibit molecular layering (Teodorescu et al.[20]) as well as the introduction of micro-meniscus effect, which sets the limit of adhesion at conjunction depths of the order of two molecular diameters of a non-polar mono-molecular idealised fluid (Al-Samieh and Rahnejat[21]). Using the same approach, in a recent contribution Chong et al.[22] considered idealised fluids of mono-molecular composition represented as spherical particles with different molecular diameters. The long chain molecules were represented with smaller cross-sectional diameters. The examples used were octamethycyclotetrasiloxane (OMCTS), an additive of silicone oil and hexadecane: a long chain thin molecule used as an additive boundary lubricant species. It was shown that the effect of solvation was significantly attenuated with the hexadecane when compared with OMCTS. This was in accord with the findings of Israelachvilli.[14] The long chain molecules reduced the load carrying capacity, but improved friction. The converse was found to be the case for small spherical molecules of OMCTS. The study of Chong et al.[22] also included hydrodynamic entrainment of the fluid into the conjunction of a pair of asperity summits, where the combined effect of hydrodynamics, solvation and van der Waals interaction accounted for the load carrying capacity. The effect of lubricant cavitation and inlet starvation were also taken into account.

All these contributions have used the empirical relationship proposed by Israelachvilli[14] for generated solvation pressures, which do not take into account the effect of molecular adsorption to the solid surfaces. Therefore, Petrov's so-called molecular "stickiness" and its effect upon shear characteristics of the lubricant was neglected. They also employed idealised fluids of mono-molecular composition. The study by Chong et al.[22] showed that shear characteristics of the contact closely resembled viscous shear of a thin lubricant film, with step-wise increases in shear as a form of work required to eject a layer of molecules from the conjunction.

Real fluids comprise a mix of molecular species in certain concentrations and packing fractions. The former corresponds to the concentration of various species. In particular, boundary lubricants as additive species represent a small proportion of the bulk lubricant volume; referred to as the base oil. The latter, packing fraction, acknowledges the state of the fluidic medium, with progressively lower dispositions corresponding to vapour or gaseous media. Chong et al.[23] extended their mono-molecular model to a bi-molecular mixture, with the spherical additive molecules possessing adsorption energy to stick to the bounding surfaces. The model is based on the solution of the Ornstein and Zernike[24] (OZ) integral equation, with an infinitely narrow, attractive well-potential represented by the Percus and Yevick[25] (PY) approximation. An analytical physio-chemical model was thus established which, unlike molecular dynamics, can be extended to broader contacting regions with significantly reduced computation.

It is natural to extend this work to hard long chain molecules, which is more representative of real boundary lubricant additive species. The Ornstein and Zernike[24] method can also be used to model the structure, molecular correlation, and thermodynamic properties of chain-like fluids.[26–31] For the hard chain spherical molecules, the model proposed by Baxter[32] is employed at the assumed sticky end of a long chain. This is the approach highlighted in the current study.

2 Mathematical model

As the initial investigation, a real fluid comprising two molecular species is assumed. One of these is a hard spherical molecule with no adsorption, as an allusion to the base lubricant molecular species. In practice oils have several species constituting the base oil. The other in a small percentage is a long chain molecule used as an additive, particularly as friction modifier for boundary lubrication. A model of a lubricant as a real fluid should comprise such a composition. A basic model is shown in Fig. 1, where both types of molecule are shown. They interact with each other as well as with the atoms of the bounding surfaces.

The interaction of hard molecules, confined by planar walls, can be modelled using the hard sphere model of Perram and Smith[33] (Fig. 1). For long chain

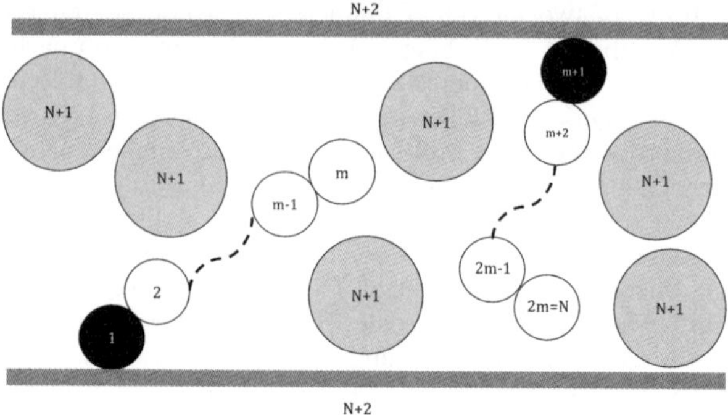

Fig. 1 Fluid mixtures of spheres/chains of *m*-mer with one end of the chain (represented by particle 1) adsorbing to the surface.

molecules, the concept of "sticky" hard spheres proposed by Baxter[32] is used, where adsorption (as the underlying mechanism for "stickiness") is assumed to occur at one end of the molecular chain. Furthermore, for molecular chains a connectivity constraint must be imposed (Chiew[34–36]).

2.1 Hard spheres

Initially, the fluid between two surfaces is modelled as a large number of interacting hard spheres.[17,32,37] These are impenetrable particles of diameter, σ_α and σ_β with a centre-to-centre distance of r^* (Fig. 2). To represent long chain molecules hard spheres can be linked *via* the connectivity constraints[34–36] (section 2.2).

The solvation pressure between approaching surfaces arises as a result of the fluid particles being constrained in a diminishing gap of the same scale as their molecular size. Using the Derjaguin approximation[14,38] for hard spheres confined by macroscopic flat bodies, the solvation pressure, p_s becomes:

$$p_s = -\frac{d^2}{dr^{*2}}\frac{1}{2\pi R_{eff}}[k_B T(g^*(r^*) - 1)] \tag{1}$$

where $R_{eff} = \sigma_\alpha \sigma_\beta / 2(\sigma_\alpha + \sigma_\beta)$ is the effective diameter, k_B is the Boltzmann constant, T is the temperature of the fluid system, α and β refer to the hard spherical species and $g^*(r^*)$ is the pair correlation function at distance r^* (described later).

The pair correlation function ($g^*_{\alpha\beta}$ in eqn (1)) describes the probability of finding a particle of species β at a distance, r^* from a referenced particle: species α. The particles (spheres) interact through central forces, thus the pair correlation function, $g^*_{\alpha\beta}$ is expressed as:

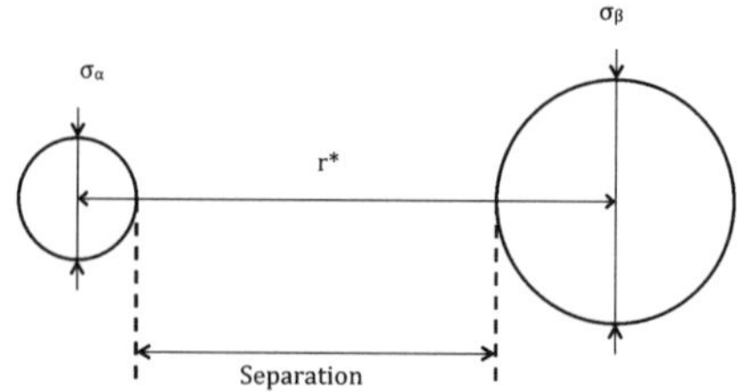

Fig. 2 Interaction between a pair of particles.

$$g^*_{\alpha\beta}(r^*) = h^*_{\alpha\beta}(r^*) + 1, \quad \alpha,\beta \in \{1,2,3\ldots(N+2)\} \tag{2}$$

where $h^*_{\alpha\beta}$ is the indirect correlation function, which describes the indirect influence of a particle of species α on another particle of species β through an intervening particle, which can be either of species α or β.

Ornstein and Zernike[24] proposed the following equation for the indirect correlation function ($h^*_{\alpha\beta}$):

$$h^*_{\alpha\beta}(r^*) = c^*_{\alpha\beta} + \sum_{\gamma=1}^{N+2} \rho^*_\gamma \int c^*_{\alpha\gamma}(|s|)h^*_{\gamma\beta}(|r^* - s|)ds \tag{3}$$

where $(N+2)$ is the total number of hard spherical species and s is the distance between any particle and a reference particle, where r^* is the centre-to-centre spacing. The direct correlation function, $c^*_{\alpha\beta}$ determines the interaction between the spherical particles of species α and β. The parameter ρ^*_γ refers to the number density or particle density for the hard spheres of species $\gamma \in \{\alpha, \beta\}$.

The Percus–Yevick[25] (PY) approximation (eqn (4)) is used in this study rather than the Convolution-Hypernetted Chain (CHNC) approximation, because the latter often causes divergence in solutions of multi-molecular fluids.[39] Additionally, the PY approximation is simpler to apply and suitable for strongly repulsive interactions (*e.g.* solvation) which leads to accurate results:[40]

$$c^*_{\alpha\beta}(r^*) = g^*_{\alpha\beta}(r^*)\left[1 - e^{\phi_{\alpha\beta}(r^*)/k_BT}\right] \tag{4}$$

The attractive potential $\phi_{\alpha\beta}$ in eqn (4) describes the adsorption between molecules α and β.[41] The adsorption refers to the adhesion of particles, which form a molecularly-thin layer, adhered to a surface. Baxter[32] describes the adsorption of molecules to surfaces based on infinitesimally short range potentials. He solves the Ornstein–Zernike equation analytically, using the Percus–Yevick approximation (OZ–PY) for a single component fluid. Perram and Smith[33] extended the work of Baxter to a fluid mixture. They defined the infinitely narrow well potential for a fluid mixture, $\phi_{\alpha\beta}$ as:

$$\phi_{\alpha\beta}(r)/k_BT = \begin{cases} log[12\overline{T}_{\alpha\beta}\delta / R_{\alpha\beta}] & r^* \leq R_{\alpha\beta} \\ 0 & r^* > R_{\alpha\beta} \end{cases} \tag{5}$$

where $R_{\alpha\beta} = (\sigma_\alpha + \sigma_\beta)/2$, $\overline{T}_{\alpha\beta}$ is the dimensionless temperature of the fluid and δ is the Dirac delta function, defining the limit of the infinitely narrow well potential. The adsorbent–adsorbate attraction described in this approach is characterised by a single energy parameter. Therefore, the particles coming into direct contact with the adsorbate planar surface are deemed as adsorbed.

Assuming $c^*_{\alpha\beta} = 0$ as $r^* > R_{\alpha\beta}$ and using Wiener–Hopf factorization,[42] eqn (3) becomes:[41,43]

$$r^*h^*_{\alpha\beta}(|r^*|) = -\frac{d}{dr^*}q_{\alpha\beta}(r^*) + 2\pi \sum_{\gamma=1}^{N+2} \rho^*_\gamma \int_{S_{\alpha\gamma}}^{R_{\alpha\gamma}} q_{\alpha\gamma}(s)(r^* - s)h^*_{\gamma\beta}(|r^* - s|)ds \tag{6}$$

where: $S_{\alpha\beta} = (\sigma_\alpha - \sigma_\beta)/2$ and
A) $S_{\alpha\beta} < r^* < R_{\alpha\beta}$,

$$q_{\alpha\beta}(r^*) = a_\alpha(r^{*2} - R^2_{\alpha\beta})/2 + b_\alpha(r^* - R_{\alpha\beta}) + \lambda_{\alpha\beta}R^2_{\alpha\beta}/12 \tag{7}$$

where
$$a_\alpha = (1 - \zeta_3 + 3R_\alpha\zeta_2)/(1 - \zeta_3)^2 - X_\alpha/(1 - \zeta_3)$$
$$b_\alpha = (-3R^2_\alpha\zeta_2)/2(1 - \zeta_3)^2 - R_\alpha X_\alpha/2(1 - \zeta_3)$$

$$X_\alpha = \frac{\pi}{6} \sum_{\gamma=1}^{N+2} \rho_\gamma^* \lambda_{\alpha\gamma} R_{\alpha\gamma}^2 \sigma_\gamma$$

$$\zeta_j = \frac{\pi}{6} \sum_{\gamma=1}^{N+2} \rho_\gamma^* \sigma_\gamma^j, \, j = 1, 2, 3$$

B) $r^* > R_{\alpha\beta}$,

$$q_{\alpha\beta}(r^*) = \frac{d}{dr^*} q_{\alpha\beta}(r^*) = 0 \tag{8}$$

Assuming planar or flat surfaces to be species $(N + 2)$, particle diameter $\sigma_{N+2} \to \infty$ and the number density or particle density $\rho_{N+2}^* \to 0$, eqn (6) can be now written as:

$$r^* h_{\alpha\beta}{}^*(|r^*|) = -\frac{d}{dr^*} q_{\alpha\beta}(r^*)$$

$$+ 2\pi \sum_{\gamma=1}^{N+1} \rho_\gamma^* \int_{S_{\alpha\gamma}}^{R_{\alpha\gamma}} q_{\alpha\gamma}(s)(r^* - s) h_{\gamma\beta}^*(|r^* - s|) ds \tag{9}$$

The $\lambda_{\alpha\beta}$ parameter can be related to the dimensionless temperature of the system $\bar{T}$ using the approximation proposed by Perram and Smith.[43] The relationship can be written as follows:

$$\lambda_{\alpha\beta} \bar{T}_{\alpha\beta} = a_\alpha + b_\alpha / R_{\alpha\beta} + \frac{\pi}{6} \sum_{\gamma=1}^{N+2} \rho_\gamma^* \frac{\lambda_{\beta\gamma} R_{\beta\gamma}^2}{R_{\alpha\beta}} q_{\alpha\gamma}(S_{\alpha\gamma}) \tag{10}$$

The hard spheres are initially considered not to adhere/adsorb to each other but only to the bounding solid wall.[40,43,44] The assumption provides a solution to $\lambda_{\alpha, \, N + 2}$ $(\alpha \in \{1, 2, 3...(N + 2)\})$. The sphere-to-sphere interaction, forming the hard chain is discussed in section 2.2.

With the wall species diameter, $\sigma_{N+2} \to \infty$, the adsorption parameter, d_α can be defined as:[40]

$$d_\alpha(T) = \int_0^\infty \left[e^{-\phi_\alpha(r^*)/k_B T} - 1 \right] dr^* \tag{11}$$

The corresponding infinitely narrow well potential, ϕ_α for hard spheres adsorbing to the planar wall in eqn (11) is:[40]

$$\phi_\alpha(r^*) = \begin{cases} -\varepsilon(\sigma_\alpha - r^*)/\sigma_\alpha & 0 < r^* < \sigma_\alpha \\ 0 & r^* > \sigma_\alpha \end{cases}$$

where ε is the adsorption energy per unit $k_B T$. Substituting a_α, b_α and S_α into eqn (10), $\lambda_{\alpha, \, M+1}$ can be determined using the following expression:[40]

$$\frac{\lambda_{\alpha,N+2} R_{\alpha,N+2}}{12 d_\alpha(T)} = \frac{1 - \zeta_3 + 3\sigma_\alpha \zeta_2}{(1 - \zeta_3)^2} - \frac{\pi \sigma_\alpha}{12(1 - \zeta_3)} \sum_{\gamma=1}^{N+1} \rho_\gamma^* \sigma_\gamma \lambda_{\gamma,N+2} R_{\gamma,N+2} \tag{12}$$

The pair correlation function, $g_{\alpha\beta}^*$ can be calculated once the indirect correlation function, $h_{\alpha\beta}^*$ is evaluated using eqn (9). The solvation pressure p_s generated by hard spheres confined by flat surfaces is computed from eqn (1), using a forward finite difference scheme.[17]

2.2 Molecular chains

Chiew[34–36] note that for a system of mono-molecular hard chain of a fixed length, m, the molecular density becomes:

$$\rho_c^* = \frac{N_c}{V} \tag{13}$$

where N_c is the total number of chains and V is the total volume of the system. The total number of hard spherical species (required to form chain-like molecules) present in the system is:

$$N = mN_c \tag{14}$$

and the packing fraction of these hard sphere species is

$$\eta^* = \frac{\pi \rho^* \sigma^3}{6} = \frac{\pi m \rho_c^* \sigma^3}{6} \tag{15}$$

where ρ^* is the number density of the hard spherical species. To represent molecular chains, the N_c chain system is viewed as a multi-component particle mixture in which the total number of hard spheres or segments in the chain is N ($=mN_c$). Thus, each particle in a multi-component mixture is regarded as a distinct species (Fig. 1).

The number density of species α is assumed to be $\rho_\alpha^o = 1/V$, because there is only one species α-type particle in the system. The superscript o denotes the distinct species of spheres forming the chain. Therefore, in the case of m-mer chains, as an example, molecule 1 is considered to be formed by particles of species 1, 2...m (Fig. 1). These constraints for the pair interactions between particles of species 1, 2...m, forming molecule 1 is required to fulfil the condition:[36]

$$\int_0^{R_{\alpha\beta}} \rho_\alpha^o 4\pi r^{*2} g_{\alpha\beta}^* \cdot dr^* = 1 \tag{16}$$

where $\beta = \alpha + 1$ for $\alpha = 1, 2...m - 1$ and $\beta = \alpha - 1$ for $\alpha = 2, 3...m$. For $0 < r^* < R_{\alpha\beta}$, the particle–particle pair correlation function, $g_{\alpha\beta}^*$ must take the form

$$g_{\alpha\beta}^*(r^*) = \frac{\lambda_{\alpha\beta}^o R_{\alpha\beta}}{12} \delta(r^* - R_{\alpha\beta}) \tag{17}$$

Eqn (16) and (17) require that the parameter $\lambda_{\alpha\beta}^o$ ($=\lambda_{\alpha\beta}$ in eqn (10)) to adopt the following form:

$$2\lambda_{\alpha\beta}^o \eta_\beta^o = 1 \tag{18}$$

where $\eta_\beta^o = \pi \rho_\beta^o \sigma_\beta^3 / 6$ and $\alpha, \beta \neq (N + 1)$ and $(N + 2)$. For example, the parameters $\lambda_{1,\beta}^o = 0$ except for $\beta = 2$ and so on.

Eqn (16)–(18) describe the connectivity constraints required to form a single hard chain molecule. Similar constraints should also be upheld for the formation of any subsequent chain molecules. For a mixture of chain molecules in a solvent of hard spherical molecules (e.g. base lubricants), the first particles of the N-species form the chain of molecules, while particle species ($N + 1$) is the hard sphere solvent. The planar walls are represented by particle species ($N + 2$). As a first approximation, particles of species i ($-1, m + 1, 2m + 1...$) are assumed to adsorb to the solid barriers. Now, $\lambda_{i,\,N+2}$ can be computed using eqn (12), where i ($=1, m + 1, 2m + 1...$). The described connectivity constraints can be applied to eqn (7)–(10) in order to predict the solvation pressure of a fluid mixture made of hard spheres/molecular chains confined by planar walls.

3   Conjunctional friction

Friction generated by the ultra-thin adsorbed films on nominally molecularly smooth surfaces follow a non-Newtonian shear due to chemical reactions which are based on the thermal activation energy. Eyring[45] developed a model which described the viscosity of fluids under such conditions. It assumes that the motion of a volume of fluid molecules taking place in the presence of a "cage-like" potential barrier by their mere closely- packed arrangement in the bulk. In order to overcome this potential and escape the cage, the fluid molecules strive to surmount the activation barrier potential. This is the thermal activation model which Eyring[45] modified to include the effects of prevailing pressure, p_s and shear, τ_y as:

$$E_y = Q_y + p_s\Omega_y - \tau_y\phi_y^* \tag{19}$$

where E_y is the barrier height for the Eyring model, Q_y is the process activation energy, Ω_y is the pressure activation volume where pressure, p_s is acting and ϕ_y^* is the shear activation volume. The shear activation volume, ϕ_y^* is interpreted as the size of segment that moves during any unit shearing process. This volume can be a part of a molecule or a dislocation line. The pressure activation volume, Ω_y is associated with a local increase in volume to permit the molecular motion to occur.

The applied pressure is due to solvation, as both hydrodynamic and van der Waals pressures are small in comparison. Therefore, the barrier height, E_y is equivalent to the solvation energy produced by the hard sphere particles. The barrier height, E_y can be expressed as:

$$E_y = \frac{1}{2\pi R_{eff}} \frac{d}{dr^*}[k_B T(g^*(r^*) - 1)] \tag{20}$$

By rearranging eqn (19), the shear stress, τ_y can be defined as:

$$\tau_y = \frac{Q_y + p_s\Omega_y - E_y}{\phi_y^*} \tag{21}$$

The parameters Q_y, Ω and ϕ_y^* must be obtained experimentally. As a first approximation, the values of these parameters are taken from the experimental measurements of He et $al.$[46] These are: $Q_y = 1.33 \times 10^{-20}J$, $\Omega_y = 1.93 \times 10^{-13}m^3 \ m^{-2}$ and $\phi_y^* = 1.21 \times 10^{-12}m^3 \ m^{-2}$. Therefore, the shear stress between planar walls can be predicted using eqn (21).

4   Results and discussions

For the purpose of simulation, hard spheres of 1 nm diameter are chosen as the base solvent molecules. These are supplemented by spherical chains of nominal diameter 0.5 nm. A total packing fraction of η_{tot}^* is assumed for the fluidic volume, constrained within nominally smooth planar walls, representing the flattened contact of a pair of opposing asperities. Therefore, for the fluid mixture, the packing fraction for the long chain and hard spherical molecules becomes:

$$\eta_{hs}^* = (1 - r_w)\eta_{tot}^*$$

$$\eta_{hc}^* = r_w\eta_{tot}^*$$

where r_w is the concentration ratio of the hard chain molecules added to the solvent's spherical molecules.

The two bounding solid surfaces are assumed at progressively diminishing separations. For a total packing fraction, $\eta^*_{tot} = 0.2$, Fig. 3 shows the generated solvation pressure and the corresponding shear stress, when the intervening fluid is assumed to comprise molecular chains only. The results in Fig. 3(a) and (b) discount adsorption potential of the molecules, whilst those in Fig. 3(c) and (d) include adsorption introduced to only one end of the molecular chains with the adsorption energy per unit $k_B T$. With adsorption taken into account a progressively larger number of molecules tend to stick to the bounding surfaces and a thin adsorbed film can result. The pressure increases due to a larger molecular content within the fluidic volume, as solvation attempts to drain layers of molecules from the contact with decreasing separations. This means that adsorption has effectively increased the molecular packing order and an additional energy is required to shear through the adsorbed film. The shear stress may be interpreted to be as the result of a "surface adhered viscosity" or Petrov's[10] "stickiness", but it is far less than that which would occur from direct interaction of rough solid surfaces, thus deviate from dry Coulombic friction as noted by Hardy and Doubleday.[11] It is interesting to note the reduced oscillatory solvation pressure with longer chain molecules, effectively indicating lower load carrying capacity, but reduced boundary friction.

As already noted, long chain molecules usually account for a small portion of the volume of lubricant. The case of a fluid with base spherical solvent molecules with no adsorption energy with various concentrations of a 4-mer chain as the additive is

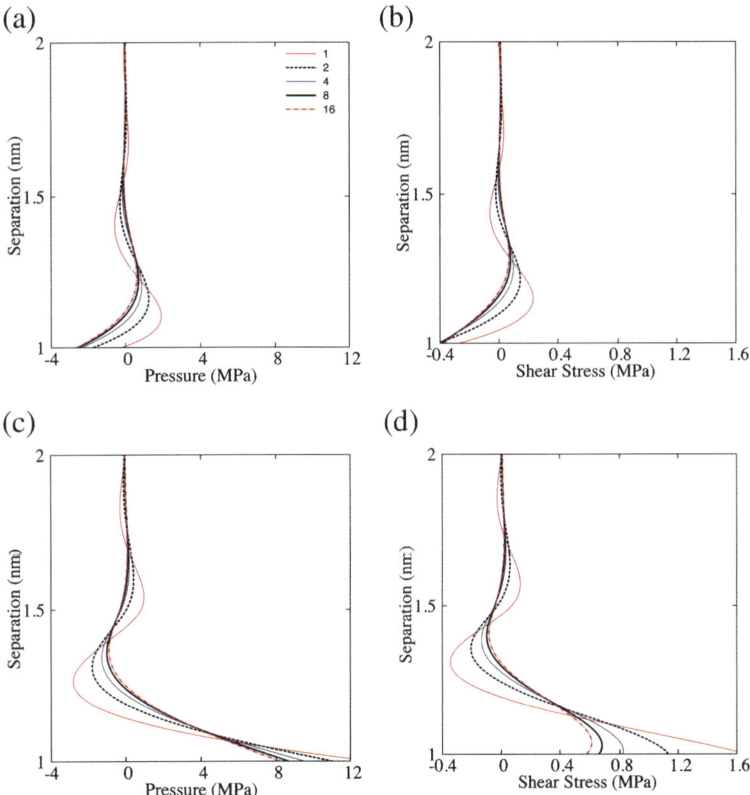

Fig. 3 Contact pressure and shear stress for various molecular chain lengths (*m*-mers) of hard chains confined by planar walls (with/without adsorption) ($\eta^*_{tot} = 0.2$).

considered next. Fig. 4 shows the normalised pressure (the ratio of the interfacial fluid-surface solvation pressure of the mixture to that with zero concentration of the additive molecule) and the corresponding shear characteristics. The adsorption energy of the long chain molecules (hc), in this case represented by 4-mer chains is 100 times larger than the base solvent spherical molecules (hs). Two points merit observation. Firstly, as the packing fraction within the volume increases at the same temperature, the fluidic environment tends to a liquid medium, increasing the number density of molecules near the solid barriers, thus enhancing the solvation pressure and the load carrying capacity of the conjunction. At the same time a larger number of long chain molecules adsorb to the boundary solids and form a thin film. Progressively lower packing fractions constitute a trend towards vapour or gaseous dominated media with reduced shear strength, but poorer load capacity.

Secondly, the result indicates that "optimum" conditions may be determined with sufficient load capacity and low shear characteristics by controlling the concentration of hc molecules in the mixture or its adsorption energy (Fig. 5). Fig. 5 shows that for the same concentration of 4-mer hc a higher adsorption energy results in a thicker surface adhered film. This constitutes a reduction in shear strength (Fig. 5(b)). At the same time a narrower conjunction results in which solvation of base molecule induces higher pressure (Fig. 5(a)). Referring back to Fig. 4, the results show that some small concentration of hc would be preferred, as indeed is the case in all boundary lubricants; a conclusion arrived at through long term empirical assessment, not because of any scientific rigour. With no concentration of hc molecules, the conjunction behaviour may be seen as that expected of a base fluid (a base lubricant of mono-molecular structure). The difference in shear characteristics between the base fluid and one with small concentrations of the hc additive is more pronounced for lower packing fraction of molecular content. In practice, this means that lower packing fractions should be used, with the significant part of the volume taken up by fillers, anti-oxidants, surfactants and other species, which is a common practice. The other extreme case corresponds to the active molecular mix which is dominated by the hc molecules. This is a rather theoretical scenario as any significant hc content tends to dramatically reduce the load capacity and cause gross slip at boundary solids.

Fig. 6 shows that when progressively longer chain molecules are used the boundary shear stress is reduced because of a larger coverage of the conjunctional surfaces. It is noteworthy that the same adsorption energy is assumed for all the *m*-mer chains.

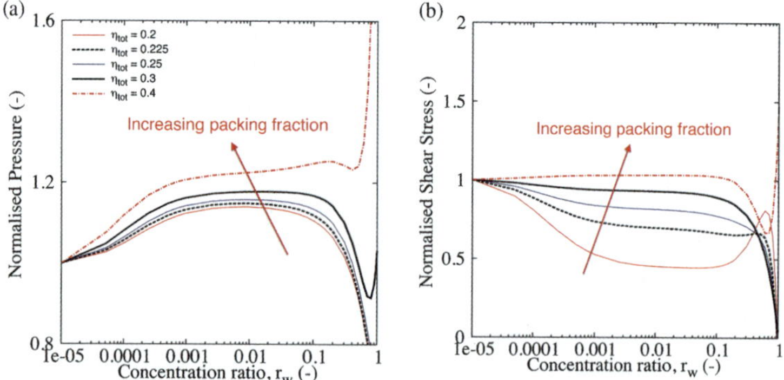

Fig. 4 Variation in total packing fraction, η_{tot}^* for hs and 4-mer hc composition considering different concentration ratio, r_w (ε_{hc} = 10, ε_{hs} = 0.1).

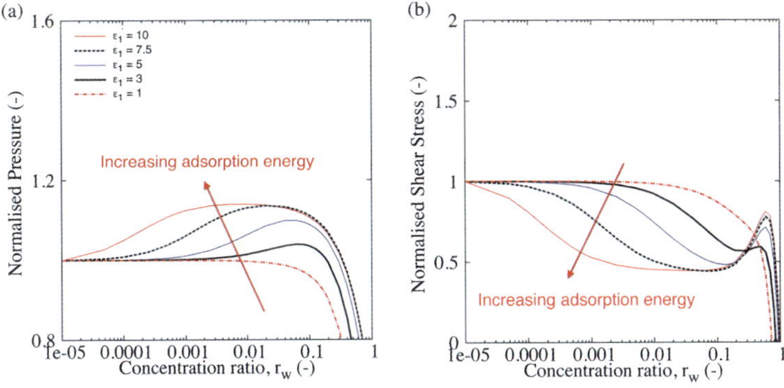

Fig. 5 Variation in adsorption energy, ε_{hc} for hs and 4-mer hc composition considering different concentration ratio, r_w ($\eta_{tot}^* = 0.2$, $\varepsilon_{hs} = 0.1$).

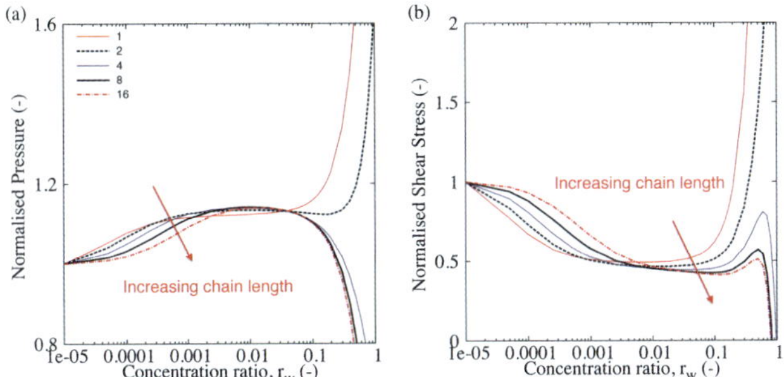

Fig. 6 Variation in molecular chain lengths of hard chains in a hard sphere solvent ($\eta_{tot}^* = 0.2$, $\varepsilon_{hc} = 10$, $\varepsilon_{hs} = 0.1$).

5 Conclusion

The method described predicts characteristic behaviour of real physical fluids, pertinent to typical composition of lubricants. Base oil molecules here represented as spheres account for the load carrying capacity of the conjunction even in nano-scale, similar to their behaviour in micro-scale, except that in ultra-thin conjunctions the generated pressures are due to the solvation effect. The long chain molecules with "sticky" ends adsorb to the bounding solids, thus affect the shear characteristics of thin films. These findings are in accord with knowledge which has been accumulated through experience. Thus, the expounded approach is an affirmation of the current practice, but through a fundamental study. The analytical nature of the OZ–PY method and its application to boundary lubrication represents the main contribution of this paper, an approach which has not hitherto been reported in literature. This initial study should be expanded to include branched molecular chains and a larger species of molecules to better represent real lubricants. In particular, the inclusion of surfactants and anti-oxidants would affect the mechanism of adsorption of molecular species to the bounding surfaces. These observation constitute the future directions of the current research. Another important consideration is formulation of the method for application to micro-scale contact of macroscopic solids through its integration with statistical representation of rough surface topography.

Nomenclature

E_y	Barrier height for Eyring model (J)
N	Number of molecule species (–)
N_c	Number of chain molecules (–)
Q_y	Process activation energy (J)
R_{eff}	Effective particle diameter (m)
$R_{\alpha\beta}$	Reduced particle diameter, $(\sigma_\alpha + \sigma_\beta)/2$, (m)
$S_{\alpha\beta}$	Average diameter difference between interacting particles, $(\sigma_\alpha - \sigma_\beta)/2$, (m)
T	Temperature of the fluid system (°C)
$\bar{T}$	Dimensionless temperature of the fluid system (–)
V	Total volume of the system (m³)
c^*	Indirect correlation function (–)
d_α	Adsorption parameter for particle species α (–)
g^*	Pair correlation function (–)
h^*	Direct correlation function (–)
hc	Hard chains (–)
hs	Hard sphere (–)
k_B	Boltzmann constant (m² kg s⁻² K⁻¹)
m	Chain length (–)
p_s	Solvation pressure (Pa)
$q_{\alpha\beta}$	Parameter for transformed Ornstein–Zernike (OZ) equation (–)
r^*	Distance between the centre of two particles (m)
s	Distance between the centre of a particle towards a reference particle (m)
t	Time step (s)
Δ	Step size (–)
Ω_y	Lubricant volume where pressure, p is acting on (m³)
α, β, γ	Particle species (–)
δ	Dirac delta function (–)
ε	Adsorption energy (–)
η^*	Particle packing fraction (–)
η°	Packing fraction for the particle forming the chain (–)
$\lambda_{\alpha\beta}$	Adsorption-temperature relation for the "sticky" hard sphere particle (–)
$\lambda_{\alpha\beta}^o$	Adsorption-temperature relation for the particle forming the chain molecule (–)
$\phi_{\alpha\beta}$	Interaction potential between particles (–)
ϕ_y^*	Activation volume (m³)
ρ^*	Density number of a particle (–)
ρ_c^*	Density number of a chain molecule (–)
ρ°	Density number of a particle forming the chain molecule (–)
σ	Particle diameter (m)

τ_y	Shear stress (Pa)
ζ_i	Parameter for variable $q_{\alpha\beta}$ where $i = 1, 2,$ and 3
	(–)

Acknowledgements

The authors acknowledge the support and sponsorship provided by the EPSRC through the ENCYCLOPAEDIC program grant.

References

1 G. Amontons, *Mem. Acad. R. A*, 1699, 275–282.
2 C. A. Coulomb, *Mem. Math. Phy. IX*, 1780, 166–342.
3 I. Newton, *The mathematical papers of Isaac Newton. Vol. III: 1670 to 1673*, Edited by D. T. Whiteside, with the assistance in publication of M. A. Hoskin and A. Prag. Cambridge University Press, London, 1969.
4 C. L. M. H. Navier, *Mem. Acad. R. Sci*, 1823, **6**, 389–440.
5 S. D. Poisson, *J. Ecole Polytech*, 1831, **13**, 1–174.
6 G. G. Stokes, *Trans. of Cambridge Phil. Soc.*, 1845, **8**, 287–319.
7 O. Reynolds, *Philos. Trans. R. Soc. London*, 1886, **177**, 157–234.
8 H. Hertz, *J. reine angew. Math.*, 1881, **92**, 156–171.
9 A. N. Grubin, *Central Scientific Research Institute for Technology and Mechanical Engineering*, Moscow (DSRI Translation, No. 337), 1949.
10 N. P. Petrov, *Friction in Machines and the Effect of the Lubricant*, Inzh. Zh., St. Peterb, 1883.
11 W. B. Hardy and I. Doubleday, *Proc. R. Soc. London, Ser. A*, 1921, **100**, 550–574.
12 D. Dowson, *Proc. 19th Leeds-Lyon Symp. on Tribology*, 1993, pp. 3–12.
13 F. P. Bowden and D. Tabor, *Nature*, 1942, **150**, 197–199.
14 J. N. Israelachvili, *Intermolecular and surface forces*, Academic press London, 1992.
15 D. Y. C. Chan and R. G. Horn, *J. Chem. Phys.*, 1985, **83**, 5311–5324.
16 R. Gohar and H. Rahnejat, *Fundamentals of tribology*, Imperial College Press, London, 2008, p. 391.
17 H. Matsuoka and T. Kato, *J. Tribol.*, 1997, **119**, 217–226.
18 M. Al-Samieh and H. Rahnejat, *J. Phys. D: Appl. Phys.*, 2001, **34**, 2610–2621.
19 M. F. A. Al-Samieh and H. Rahnejat, *Proc. Inst. Mech. Eng., Part C: J. Mech. Eng. Sci.*, 2001, **215**, 1019–1029.
20 M. Teodorescu, S. Balakrishnan and H. Rahnejat, *Proc. Inst. Mech Eng, Part N: J. Nanoeng and Nanosys*, 2006, **220**, 7–19.
21 M. Al-Samieh and H. Rahnejat, *J. Phys. D: Appl. Phys.*, 2002, **35**, 2311–2326.
22 W. W. F. Chong, M. Teodorescu and H. Rahnejat, *J. Phys. D: Appl. Phys.*, 2011, **44**, 165302.
23 W. W. F. Chong, M. Teodorescu and H. Rahnejat, *J. Phys. D: Appl. Phys.*, 2012, **45**, 115303.
24 L. S. Ornstein and F. Zernike, *Proc. Roy. Acad., Amsterdam*, 1914, **17**, 793–806.
25 J. K. Percus and G. J. Yevick, *Phys. Rev.*, 1958, **110**, 1–13.
26 M. S. Wertheim, *J. Stat. Phys.*, 1984, **35**, 19.
27 M. S. Wertheim, *J. Stat. Phys.*, 1984, **35**, 35.
28 M. S. Wertheim, *J. Stat. Phys.*, 1986, **42**, 459
29 M. S. Wertheim, *J. Stat. Phys.*, 1986, **42**, 477.
30 J. Chang and S. I. Sandler, *J. Chem. Phys.*, 1994, **102**, 437–449.
31 N. Wu and Y. C. Chiew, *Phys. Rev. E: Stat., Nonlinear, Soft Matter Phys.*, 2010, **81**, 041809.
32 R. J. Baxter, *J. Chem. Phys.*, 1968, **49**, 2770–2774.
33 J. W. Perram and E. R. Smith, *Chem. Phys. Lett.*, 1975, **35**, 138–140.
34 Y. C. Chiew, *Mol. Phys.*, 1990, **70**, 129–143.
35 Y. C. Chiew, *Mol. Phys.*, 1990, **73**, 359–373.
36 Y. C. Chiew, *J. Chem. Phys.*, 1990, **93**, 5067–5074.
37 P. Attard and J. L. Parker, *J. Phys. Chem.*, 1992, **96**, 5086–5093.
38 B. V. Derjaguin, *Kolloid-Z.*, 1935, **69**, 155–164.
39 F. Hirata, *Molecular Theory of Solvation*, Kluwer Academic Publishers, Dordrecht, 2003.
40 J. W. Perram and E. R. Smith, *Chem. Phys. Lett.*, 1976, **39**, 328–332.
41 R. J. Baxter, *J. Chem. Phys.*, 1970, **52**, 4559–4562.

42 M. S. Wertheim, *J. Math. Phys.*, 1964, **5**, 643–651.
43 J. W. Perram and E. R. Smith, *Proc. R. Soc. London, Ser. A*, 1977, **353**, 193–220.
44 P. T. Cummings, J. W. Perram and E. R. Smith, *Mol. Phys.*, 1976, **31**, 535–548.
45 H. Eyring, *J. Chem. Phys.*, 1936, **4**, 283.
46 M. He, A. S. Blum, G. Overney and R. M. Overney, *Phys. Rev. Lett.*, 2002, **88**, 154302.

Fate of methanol molecule sandwiched between hydrogen-terminated diamond-like carbon films by tribochemical reactions: tight-binding quantum chemical molecular dynamics study

Kentaro Hayashi,[a] Seiichiro Sato,[a] Shandan Bai,[a] Yuji Higuchi,[a] Nobuki Ozawa,[a] Tomomi Shimazaki,[a] Koshi Adachi,[b] Jean-Michel Martin[c] and Momoji Kubo[*a]

Received 6th December 2011, Accepted 23rd January 2012
DOI: 10.1039/c2fd00125j

Recently, much attention has been given to diamond-like carbon (DLC) as a solid-state lubricant, because it exhibits high resistance to wear, low friction and low abrasion. Experimentally it is reported that gas environments are very important for improving the tribological characteristics of DLC films. Recently one of the authors in the present paper, J.-M. Martin, experimentally observed that the low friction of DLC films is realized under alcohol environments. In the present paper, we aim to clarify the low-friction mechanism of the DLC films under methanol environments by using our tight-binding quantum chemical molecular dynamics method. We constructed the simulation model in which one methanol molecule is sandwiched between two hydrogen-terminated DLC films. Then, we performed sliding simulations of the DLC films. We observed the chemical reaction of the methanol molecule under sliding conditions. The methanol molecule decomposed and then OH-termination of the DLC was realized and the CH_3 species was incorporated into the DLC film. We already reported that the OH-terminated DLC film is very effective to achieve good low-friction properties under high pressure conditions, compared to H-terminated DLC films. Here, we suggest that methanol environments are very effective to realize the OH-termination of DLC films which leads to the good low-friction properties.

1. Introduction

Recently, from economical and environmental points of view, the development of new low-friction mechanical systems and the reduction of friction in present mechanical systems have been strongly desired, because energy loss by friction is very significant. Low friction also leads to a reduction of CO_2 emissions, which is of vital importance worldwide. Therefore it is essential to understand friction and wear behaviors at contact surfaces for the development of low-friction mechanical systems. Liquid lubricants are regularly employed to reduce friction at contact surfaces in many mechanical systems, such as vehicles and industrial robots.

[a]*Fracture and Reliability Research Institute (FRRI), Graduate School of Engineering, Tohoku University, 6-6-11 Aoba, Aramaki, Aoba-ku, Sendai, 980-8579, Japan*
[b]*Department of Nano-mechanics, Graduate School of Engineering, Tohoku University, 6-6-01 Aoba, Aramaki, Aoba-ku, Sendai, 980-8579, Japan*
[c]*Laboratory of Tribology and System Dynamics, Ecole Central de Lyon, 36 Avenue Guy de Collongue 69134, ECULLY Cedex, France*

On the other hand, solid lubricants have been recently used in precision mechanical equipment, such as microelectromechanical systems and aerospace instruments. Diamond-like carbon (DLC), which has an amorphous carbon structure, is one of the most promising solid lubricants because of its low abrasion, low friction and chemical resistance properties.[1-9] Diamond-like carbon is deposited on substrate surfaces by using various plasma and chemical vapor deposition processes. During the deposition of DLC films, some additives such as hydrogen and silicon are supplied in order to increase the tribological properties of the DLC film. For example, the addition of hydrogen atoms to the DLC during the synthesis of the DLC film improves its tribological characteristics.[10-16] More recently, nitrogen-doped DLC has gained much attention because of its low friction properties.[17-21] Furthermore, it is experimentally known that the DLC exhibits super-low friction characteristics under very specific conditions. Fontaine and co-workers experimentally performed rubbing tests of DLC against an iron surface under high-vacuum conditions and reported a super-low friction coefficient of 0.002.[22] They observed that a carbon-based transfer film is formed on the iron surface in the super-low friction state. However they also reported that the super-low friction state disappears when the transfer film is destroyed. On the other hand, it is experimentally well known that gas environments such as H_2, N_2, H_2O, O_2, and Ar significantly affect the tribological phenomena and properties, however its detailed mechanism has not been clarified.

Computational simulations are very effective for investigating the friction behaviors of DLC on an atomic scale, and many research groups have already reported the tribological phenomena of DLC films and other lubricants by various computational simulations.[23-26] We have also previously applied our classical molecular dynamics code to various tribological dynamics and very useful information on the friction mechanism on an atomic scale and the origin of the high or low friction coefficients has been obtained.[27-31] Recently, Schall and co-workers[32] have investigated the atomic-scale effects of adhesion and transfer film formation on DLC contacts using a classical molecular dynamics method. They employed reactive empirical bond-order potential (REBO) to describe the formation and cleavage of carbon–carbon bonds. From the simulation results, they reported that the addition of hydrogen to the DLC film decreases the friction coefficient by reducing the unsaturated carbon bonds at the contact surface.[32] However, classical molecular dynamics is insufficient for clarifying the chemical reaction dynamics accurately because electrons are not considered in this method. In order to reveal the chemical reaction dynamics accurately, a quantum chemical molecular dynamics method should be employed because the electron transfer is the origin of the chemical reactions. A first-principles molecular dynamics method is one of the candidates to investigate the chemical reaction and electron transfer dynamics under friction. We have previously applied our first-principles molecular dynamics code "Violet" based on our original Gaussian Fourier Transfer (GFT) method[33] to the friction behaviors of hydrogen-terminated DLC.[34] However, it is still very tough work to simulate a large DLC model by the first-principles molecular dynamics method, because the first-principles molecular dynamics method requires huge computational costs. Therefore, in order to simulate the large models by quantum chemical molecular dynamics method, we already developed our original tight-binding quantum chemical molecular dynamics (TB-QCMD) code "Colors" and successfully applied it to various tribochemical reaction dynamics phenomena.[35-38] Tribochemical reaction dynamics induced by the electron transfer were examined and the electronic-level friction mechanism were clarified using our TB-QCMD code.

Furthermore, we recently applied our TB-QCMD code to clarifying the low friction mechanism of hydrogen-terminated DLC[39] and clarified that the repulsion force between the terminated-hydrogen atoms on the upper and lower DLC films provides the low friction properties of the hydrogen-terminated DLC films. Moreover, we interestingly observed the generation of H_2 molecules at the DLC film interface by the tribochemical reactions of the terminated-hydrogen atoms. This chemical reaction was found to strongly affect the tribological characteristics of the hydrogen-terminated DLC films. Moreover, we also investigated the low friction mechanism of the OH-terminated DLC films by our TB-QCMD code.[40] We clarified that OH-termination suppresses the formation of C–C bonds at the friction interface and it leads to a low friction coefficient even at a high pressure of 7 GPa. H-termination leads to a high friction coefficient at a high pressure of 7 GPa because of the C–C bond generation at the friction interface and we concluded that the OH-termination solves the high friction coefficient problem of the H-terminated DLC films at high pressure. Therefore, we confirmed that our TB-QCMD simulator is very effective for simulating the friction process of DLC films and their chemical reaction dynamics and is very useful to clarify the low friction mechanism of the DLC films on the electronic- and atomic-level.

More recently, one of the authors in the present paper, J.-M. Martin, experimentally reported that alcohol environments such as ethanol and D-glycerol lead to low friction characteristics of DLC films.[41] However, the detailed mechanism on the low friction properties of DLC film under alcohol environments is not currently clarified. Therefore, in the present study we aim to clarify the reason why alcohol environments give a low friction coefficient of DLC films on an electronic- and atomic-level.

2. Method

We applied our TB-QCMD code "Colors" to the investigation of the tribochemical reaction dynamics of DLC films under methanol environments and to clarifying its low-friction mechanism on an electronic- and atomic-scale.[35–40] In the TB-QCMD method, the following Hamiltonian was used:[42]

$$H_{rs} = \frac{1}{2} K_{rs} S_{rs} (H_{rr} + H_{ss}) \tag{1-1}$$

$$K_{rs} = \{1 + \kappa_{rs}(1 - \Delta^4) + \Delta^2\} \exp[-\delta_{rs}\{r_{rs} - (d_r + d_s)\}] \tag{1-2}$$

$$\Delta = \frac{H_{rr} - H_{ss}}{H_{rr} + H_{ss}} \tag{1-3}$$

The diagonal matrix element, H_{rr}, is defined as the negative of ionization potential for valence electrons, I_r; that is, $H_{rr} = -I_r$. The off-diagonal term H_{rs} is calculated from formula (1-1), where S_{rs} is the overlap integral matrix. In formula (1-2), r_{rs} is the distance between two atoms to which the molecular orbitals belong, and κ_{rs} and δ_{rs} are the positive parameters for the tight-binding approximation. These parameters for the DLC films and methanol molecules were developed and are listed in Table 1. The radius of each orbital d_r is determined from the method reported by Calzaferri et $al.$[43] The total energy E_{total} of the system can be calculated from the eigenvalue ε_k and the repulsive potential E_{rep} as follows:[42]

$$E_{total} = \sum \frac{1}{2} m_i v_i^2 + \sum_k^{occ} \varepsilon_k + \sum_{i<j} E_{rep}(r_{ij}) \tag{2-1}$$

$$E_{rep}(r_{ij}) = b_{ij} \exp\left(\frac{a_{ij} - r_{ij}}{b_{ij}}\right) \tag{2-2}$$

Here, k is the index for the molecular orbital, and i and j are indices for the atoms in the system. a_{ij} and b_{ij} are the inter-atomic parameters, which are related to the size and stiffness of the atoms i and j (Table 1).

Table 1 Parameters for TB-QCMD simulation

Atom	I^a [eV]		ζ^b [Å^{-1}]	
	s orbital	p orbital	s orbital	p orbital
H	13.60	—	1.500	—
C	21.40	13.40	2.130	2.400
O	32.30	14.80	2.425	2.425

^{a} Ionization energy from the valence orbital. ^{b} Exponent of Slater-type atomic orbital.

Atom pair	a_{ij}	b_{ij}
H–H	0.844	0.024
H–C	1.480	0.092
H–O	1.255	0.092
C–C	2.306	0.160
C–O	2.011	0.119
O–O	1.142	0.160

Orbital pair	κ_{rs}	δ_{rs}
H(s)–H(s)	0.478	0.800
H(s)–C(s)	0.720	0.130
H(s)–C(p)	0.720	0.130
H(s)–O(s)	0.236	0.130
H(s)–O(p)	0.659	0.130
C(s)–C(s)	1.172	0.130
C(s)–C(p)	1.172	0.130
C(p)–C(p)	1.172	0.130
C(s)–O(s)	0.000	0.130
C(s)–O(p)	1.061	0.130
C(p)–O(s)	0.000	0.130
C(p)–O(p)	0.746	0.130
O(s)–O(s)	0.938	0.130
O(s)–O(p)	0.938	0.130
O(p)–O(p)	0.938	0.130

These parameters are determined so as to reproduce the binding energy and the bond distance of bulk diamond as well as of hydrogen, methanol, and water molecules. The TB-QCMD calculations using these parameters give the binding energy and the bond distance of bulk diamond as 7.36 eV and 1.546 Å, respectively, which are in good agreement with the experimental values of 7.37 eV and 1.546 Å. The calculated and experimental binding energies of a hydrogen molecule are 4.475 eV and 4.474 eV, respectively. The parameter sets give a bond length of 0.737 Å for a hydrogen molecule, which reproduces the experimental value of 0.741 Å. The calculated and experimental binding energies of a methanol molecule are 26.178 eV and 25.086 eV, respectively. The parameter sets give the C–H bond distance, O–H bond distance, and C–O–H angle as 1.092 Å, 0.993 Å, and 109.47° in a methanol molecule, respectively. These values reproduce the experimental values of 1.098 Å, 0.975 Å, and 107.6° well for the C–H bond distance, O–H bond distance, and C–O–H angle, respectively. Furthermore, the parameter sets give the O–H bond distance and H–O–H angle as 0.961 Å and 104.61° in a water molecule, respectively. These values also reproduce the experimental values of 0.960 Å and 104.45° well for the O–H bond distance and H–O–H angle, respectively.

In order to simulate the friction process, the upper substrate was forcibly slid, whereas the bottom atoms of the lower substrate were fixed (Fig. 1). According to previous simulation studies,[28,32] we also employed 100 m s^{-1} for the sliding speed. An MD time step of 0.1 fs was employed. The Verlet algorithm[44] was used for calculating the atomic motions under three-dimensional periodic boundary conditions. The temperature was maintained at 300 K by scaling the atom velocities.

3. Results and discussion

We constructed a simulation model in which one methanol molecule is sandwiched between two hydrogen-terminated DLC films. In this model, all the dangling bonds of the DLC films are terminated by hydrogen atoms. Then, we performed the sliding simulation of the DLC films to clarify the effect of methanol environments on the friction characteristics of the DLC films. The upper DLC film was slid with a velocity of 100 m s^{-1} under a load force of 1 GPa. Fig. 2 shows snapshots of the friction dynamics of the hydrogen-terminated DLC films between which one methanol molecule is sandwiched. At 0.35 ps, the formation of an O–C bond between the methanol molecule and the lower DLC film is observed and the methanol molecule is chemically adsorbed on the lower DLC film. At 4.7 ps, it is very interesting to see the formation of a C–C bond between the methanol molecule and the upper DLC film. It means that the methanol molecule binds with both the upper and lower DLC films through its C and O atoms, respectively. It is easy to imagine that one of these bonds will be dissociated soon because the upper DLC film is sliding. However, it is very interesting to see that the C–O bond in the methanol molecule is dissociated at 6.7 ps. This is completely different behavior from what we imagined. These results indicate that the methanol molecule makes O–C and C–C bonds with both the upper and lower DLC films and then the C–O bond in the methanol molecule is dissociated by the sliding. O-termination is then realized on the lower DLC film and the CH$_3$ species of the methanol molecule is incorporated into the upper DLC film at 6.7 ps. At 9.78 ps one hydrogen atom diffuses to the terminated O atom from the hydrogen-terminated DLC film and the OH-termination is accomplished. These chemical reactions are very complicated, especially the C–O bond dissociation in the methanol molecule at 6.7 ps is largely due to the sliding of the DLC film. Then, we confirmed the effectiveness of our TB-QCMD method to clarify the complicated chemical reaction dynamics under friction conditions. In order to

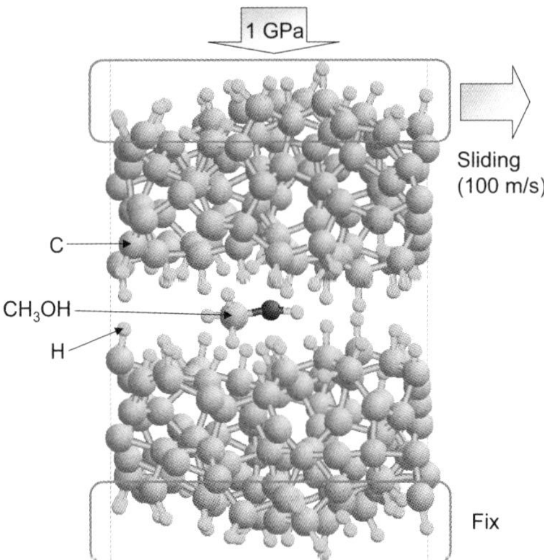

Fig. 1   Simulation model for the friction process of two DLC films between which one methanol molecule is sandwiched.

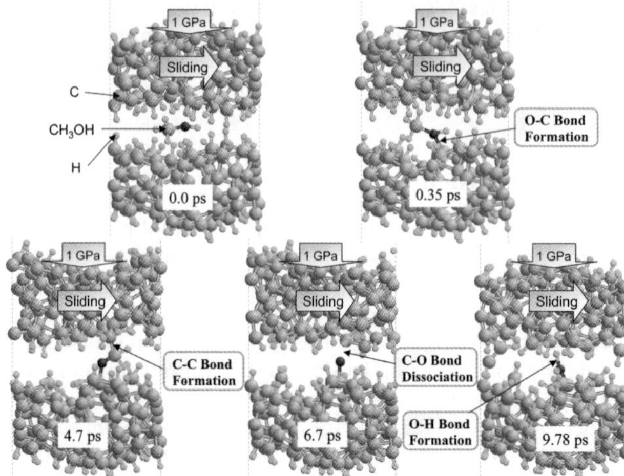

Fig. 2 Snapshots of the friction process of two DLC films between which one methanol molecule is sandwiched by TB-QCMD method.

confirm the origin of these complicated chemical reactions, we performed the TB-QCMD simulation without sliding (Fig. 3). In Fig. 3, even at 2.0 ps we still observed the existence of the methanol molecule between the two DLC films and we noticed that the chemical reaction of the methanol molecule does not occur at the interface under no friction condition. These results indicate that the sliding strongly induces the chemical reaction of the methanol molecule at the DLC–DLC interface.

Furthermore, in order to clarify the effect of the initial conditions on the tribochemical reactions of the methanol molecule at the DLC friction interface, we

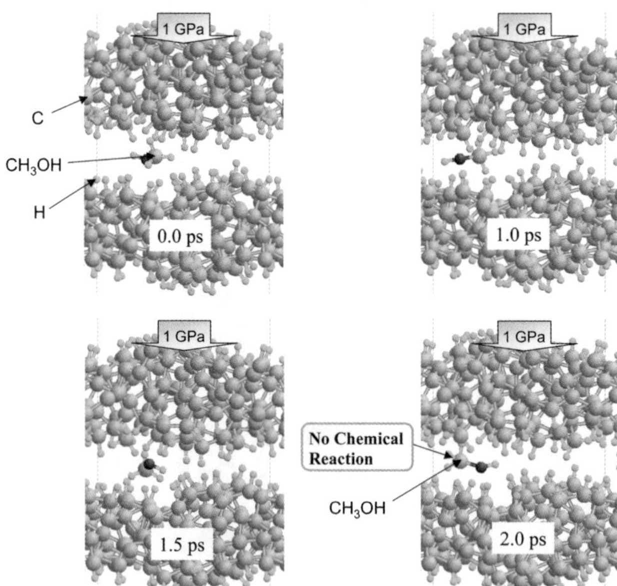

Fig. 3 Snapshots of the dynamic behaviors of two DLC films between which one methanol molecule is sandwiched under no friction condition by TB-QCMD method.

  This journal is © The Royal Society of Chemistry 2012

performed three further simulations with different initial conditions. We employed
the same model for the additional three simulations as for the first simulation
(Fig. 1). We only changed the initial velocity of each atom and then the additional
three simulations were performed. Our TB-QCMD simulations employ random
values of the initial velocity of each atom. We then produced three different initial
velocities of each atom in the same model (Fig. 1) and the sliding simulations
were performed. Here, the initial velocities of each atom in all the models were determined so as to set the temperature at 300 K. Fig. 4 shows the final structures of four
simulations with different random values of the initial velocity at 10.0 ps. Fig. 4 (a)
shows the final structure of the first simulation shown in Fig. 3, in which OH-termination of the DLC film is observed. Fig. 4 (b) shows that the methanol molecule is
decomposed and a C–O–C structure is generated on the DLC surface. It means that
O-termination is realized on the DLC surface. These results indicate that the
different chemical reactions occur depending on the initial velocity of each atom.
It suggests that different initial positions of the methanol molecule in the simulation
cell also gives different chemical reactions. In addition to the OH-termination, we
found that the O-termination (C–O–C structure) is another possible product after
the tribochemical reaction of the methanol molecule. Fig. 4 (c) shows that OH-termination is realized on the DLC surface and this is a similar result with that in Fig. 4
(a). Moreover, it is interesting to see the generation of a CH_4 molecule at the friction
interface. When the methanol molecule is decomposed, the CH_3 species of the methanol molecule abstracts the terminated-hydrogen atom of the DLC surface and the
CH_4 molecule is generated. Fig. 4 (d) shows that an H_2O molecule is generated by
the tribochemical reaction of the methanol molecule and a CH_4 molecule is also
generated at the DLC interface. This is a completely different structure from those
shown in Fig. 4(a)–(c). Finally, we conclude that depending on the random value of
the initial velocity of each atom, different chemical reactions occur and these lead to
OH-termination, O-termination (C–O–C structure), and water generation. It
suggests that the different initial positions of the methanol molecule in the simulation cell also give different final products such as OH-termination, O-termination
(C–O–C structure), and H_2O generation. Furthermore, although three types of final
products are obtained, we suggest that the OH-termination is most preferable as
a final product after the tribochemical reactions of the methanol molecule because

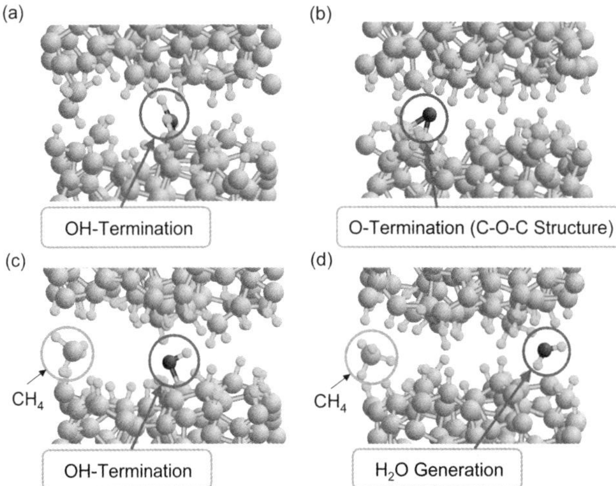

Fig. 4 Final structures of four different tribochemical reaction simulations of one methanol
molecule between two DLC films by TB-QCMD method: (a) OH-termination, (b) O-termination (C–O–C structure), (c) OH-termination, and (d) H_2O generation were observed.

50% of our sliding simulations on the DLC films with one methanol molecule result in OH-termination.

In order to confirm the higher possibility of the OH-termination after the tribochemical reaction of the methanol molecule, we compared the energies of the OH-termination, O-termination (C–O–C structure), and H_2O generation by first-principles calculations. For the simplification of the comparison, we employed the diamond(001) surface. The number of C, O and H atoms in all the calculation models is completely the same. The number of C, O and H atoms is 64, 8, and 16 in all the systems, respectively. In order to realize the same number of atoms in all the systems, the energies of diamond(001) surface and 8 H_2O molecules are summed for the H_2O generation model. First-principles density functional theory (DFT) calculations were performed within the generalized gradient approximation (GGA) by the Perdew–Burke–Ernzerhof functional (PBE)[45] using the "DMol³" code of Accelrys Inc.[46] The double-numerical polarized basis set is employed under the conditions of the octupole multipolar expansion with a global-space cutoff of 3.7 Å, and a Monkhorst–Pack grid of $4 \times 4 \times 1$ for the k-space representation. The surface species were optimized by first-principles calculations and the optimized structures are shown in Fig. 5. Fig. 5 (a), (b) and (c) show the OH-termination, O-termination (C–O–C structure), and H_2O generation models. The energies of the OH-termination, O-termination (C–O–C structure), and H_2O generation systems in Fig. 5 (a), (b) and (c) are −3047.817 Ha, −3047.710 Ha and −3046.947 Ha, respectively. These energy values indicate that the OH-termination is most stable. This result is in good agreement with the higher possibility of the OH-termination, obtained by our TB-QCMD simulations (Fig. 4). Therefore, we confirmed that the OH-termination is most preferable structure after the tribochemical reactions of the methanol molecule at the DLC–DLC interface.

4.   Summary

Recent experiments by one of the authors in the present paper, J.-M. Martin, show that alcohol environments lead to a low friction coefficient of DLC films. In the present study, we aim to clarify the low friction mechanism of the DLC films under alcohol environments on an electronic- and atomic-level. We investigated the friction dynamics of two DLC films under methanol environments by our TB-QCMD code. Our simulation results suggest that the methanol molecule is

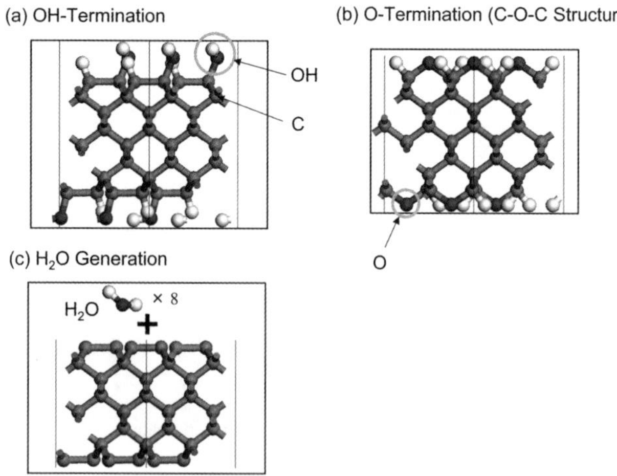

Fig. 5   First-principles calculation models for the energy evaluation of (a) OH-termination, (b) O-termination (C–O–C structure), and (c) H_2O generation.

decomposed by the friction and OH-termination of the DLC surface is realized. We already reported that the OH-termination of the DLC surface leads to the low friction properties. Then, we suggested that the OH-termination by the tribochemical reaction of alcohol molecules is the reason why the alcohol environments lead to low friction properties. Moreover, we performed three further TB-QCMD simulations using the same model to confirm whether the tribochemical reactions of the methanol molecule always lead to the OH-termination or not. We changed the initial velocity of each atom using the same model and then performed three further calculations. A total of four TB-QCMD calculations gives two OH-termination, one O-termination (C–O–C structure), and one H_2O generation by the tribochemical reaction of one methanol molecule. These results indicate that the OH-termination is highly possible, but O-termination (C–O–C structure) and H_2O generation are also possible. Next, we performed first-principles calculations to compare the energies of OH-termination, O-termination (C–O–C structure), and H_2O generation. The calculation results show that the OH-termination is energetically most stable, which is in good agreement with our TB-QCMD simulations on the tribochemical reaction dynamics of the methanol molecule. Finally, we concluded that the experimental low friction properties of DLC films under alcohol environments is due to the tribochemical reactions of the alcohol molecules at the DLC–DLC interface and to the realization of OH-termination on the DLC surfaces.

References

1 A. Erdemir and C. Donnet, *J. Phys. D: Appl. Phys.*, 2006, **39**, R311.
2 Y. Qi, E. Konca and T. Alpas, *Surf. Sci.*, 2006, **600**, 2955.
3 A. Erdemir, *Surf. Coat. Technol.*, 2001, **146–147**, 292.
4 A. Erdemir, *Tribol. Int.*, 2004, **37**, 1005.
5 J. C. Sanchez-Lopez, A. Erdemir, C. Donnet and T. C. Rojas, *Surf. Coat. Technol.*, 2003, **163**, 444.
6 A. Erdemir, O. L. Eryılmaz, I. B. Nilufer and G. T. Fenske, *Diamond Relat. Mater.*, 2000, **9**, 632.
7 K. Miyoshi, M. Murakawa, S. Watanabe, S. Takeuchi, S. Miyake and R. L. C. Wu, *Tribol. Lett.*, 1998, **5**, 123.
8 K. Miyoshi, R. L. C. Wu and A. Garscadden, *Surf. Coat. Technol.*, 1992, **54**, 428.
9 K. Yoshida, T. Horiuchi, M. Kano and M. Kumagai, *Plasma Process. Polym.*, 2009, **6**, 410.
10 S. G. Kim, S. W. Kim, N. Saito and O. Takai, *Diamond Relat. Mater.*, 2010, **19**, 1017.
11 C. Chouquet, G. Gerbaud, M. Bardet, S. Barrat, A. Billard, F. Sanchette and C. Ducros, *Surf. Coat. Technol.*, 2010, **204**, 1339.
12 J. Jiang, J. Hao, X. Pang, P. Wang and W. Liu, *Diamond Relat. Mater.*, 2010, **19**, 1172.
13 J. Jiang, J. Hao, P. Wang and W. Liu, *J. Appl. Phys.*, 2010, **108**, 033510.
14 F. Zhao, H. Li, L. Ji, Y. Wang, H. Zhou and J. Chen, *Diamond Relat. Mater.*, 2010, **19**, 342.
15 A. Erdemir, O. L. Eryilmaz and G. Fenske, *J. Vac. Sci. Technol., A*, 2000, **18**, 1987.
16 A. Erdemir, O. L. Eryilmaz, I. B. Nilufer and G. R. Fenske, *Surf. Coat. Technol.*, 2000, **133–134**, 448.
17 K. Kato, M. Bai, N. Umehara and Y. Miyake, *Surf. Coat. Technol.*, 1999, **113**, 233.
18 W. H. Kao, Y. L. Su, S. H. Yao and H. C. Huang, *Surf. Coat. Technol.*, 2010, **204**, 1277.
19 K. Kato, N. Umehara and K. Adachi, *Wear*, 2003, **254**, 1062.
20 F. Zhou, K. Adachi and K. Kato, *Thin Solid Films*, 2006, **514**, 231.
21 F. Zhou, K. Kato and K. Adachi, *Tribol. Lett.*, 2005, **18**, 153.
22 J. Fontaine, T. L. Mogne, J. L. Loubet and M. Belin, *Thin Solid Films*, 2005, **482**, 99.
23 M. Moseler, H. Riedel, P. Gumbsch, J. Staring and B. Mehlig, *Phys. Rev. Lett.*, 2005, **94**, 165503.
24 G. Zilibotti, M. C. Righi and M. Ferrario, *Phys. Rev. B*, 2009, **79**, 075420.
25 L. Pastewka, S. Moser and S. Moseler, *Tribol. Lett.*, 2010, **39**, 49.
26 G. T. Gao, P. T. Mikulski and J. A. Harrison, *J. Am. Chem. Soc.*, 2002, **124**, 7202.
27 C. Minfray, T. L. Mogne, J.-M. Martin, T. Onodera, S. Nara, S. Takahashi, H. Tsuboi, M. Koyama, A. Endou, H. Takaba, M. Kubo, C. A. Del Carpio and A. Miyamoto, *Tribol. Trans.*, 2008, **51**, 589.
28 Y. Morita, T. Onodera, A. Suzuki, R. Sahnoun, M. Koyama, H. Tsuboi, N. Hatakeyama, A. Endou, H. Takaba, M. Kubo, C. A. Del Carpio, T. Shin-yoshi, N. Nishino, A. Suzuki and A. Miyamoto, *Appl. Surf. Sci.*, 2008, **254**, 7618.

29 T. Onodera, Y. Morita, A. Suzuki, R. Sahnoun, M. Koyama, H. Tsuboi, N. Hatakeyama, A. Endou, H. Takaba, M. Kubo, C. A. Del Carpio, C. Minfray, J.-M. Martin and A. Miyamoto, *Appl. Surf. Sci.*, 2008, **254**, 7976.

30 T. Onodera, T. Kuriaki, Y. Morita, A. Suzuki, M. Koyama, H. Tsuboi, N. Hatakeyama, A. Endou, H. Takaba, C. A. Del Carpio, M. Kubo, C. Minfray, J.-M. Martin and A. Miyamoto, *Appl. Surf. Sci.*, 2009, **256**, 976.

31 T. Onodera, Y. Morita, R. Nagumo, R. Miura, A. Suzuki, H. Tsuboi, N. Hatakeyama, A. Endou, H. Takaba, F. Dassenoy, C. Minfray, L. Joly-Pottuz, M. Kubo, J.-M. Martin and A. Miyamoto, *J. Phys. Chem. B*, 2010, **114**, 15832.

32 J. D. Schall, G. Gao and J. A. Harrison, *J. Phys. Chem. C*, 2010, **114**, 5321.

33 T. Shimazaki and M. Kubo, *Chem. Phys. Lett.*, 2011, **503**, 316.

34 K. Hayashi, S. Sato, S. Bai, Y. Higuchi, N. Ozawa, T. Shimazaki, K. Adachi, J.-M. Martin and M. Kubo, unpublished results.

35 M. Koyama, J. Hayakawa, T. Onodera, K. Ito, H. Tsuboi, A. Endou, M. Kubo, C. A. Del Carpio and A. Miyamoto, *J. Phys. Chem. B*, 2006, **110**, 17507.

36 A. Endou, T. Onodera, S. Nara, A. Suzuki, M. Koyama, H. Tsuboi, N. Hatakeyama, H. Takaba, C. A. Del Carpio, M. Kubo and A. Miyamoto, *Tribol. Online*, 2008, **3**, 280.

37 T. Onodera, Y. Morita, A. Suzuki, M. Koyama, H. Tsuboi, N. Hatakeyama, A. Endou, H. Takaba, M. Kubo, F. Dassenoy, C. Minfray, L. Joly-Pottuz, J.-M. Martin and A. Miyamoto, *J. Phys. Chem. B*, 2009, **113**, 16526.

38 T. Onodera, R. Miura, A. Suzuki, H. Tsuboi, N. Hatakeyama, A. Endou, H. Takaba, M. Kubo and A. Miyamoto, *Modell. Simul. Mater. Sci. Eng.*, 2010, **18**, 034009.

39 K. Hayashi, K. Tezuka, N. Ozawa, T. Shimazaki, K. Adachi and M. Kubo, *J. Phys. Chem. C*, 2011, **115**, 22981.

40 K. Hayashi, S. Sato, S. Bai, Y. Higuchi, N. Ozawa, T. Shimazaki, K. Adachi, J.-M. Martin and M. Kubo, unpublished results.

41 J.-M. Martin, unpublished results.

42 K. Lassonen and R. M. Nieminen, *J. Phys.: Condens. Matter*, 1990, **2**, 1509.

43 G. Calzaferri, L. Forss and I. Kamber, *J. Phys. Chem.*, 1989, **93**, 5366.

44 L. Verlet, *Phys. Rev.*, 1967, **159**, 98.

45 J. P. Perdew, K. Burke and M. Ernzerhof, *Phys. Rev. Lett.*, 1996, **77**, 3865.

46 B. Delley, *J. Chem. Phys.*, 2000, **113**, 7756.

   This journal is © The Royal Society of Chemistry 2012

Anticorrosion imidazolium ionic liquids as the additive in poly(ethylene glycol) for steel/Cu–Sn alloy contacts

Meirong Cai,[ab] Yongmin Liang,[a] Feng Zhou[*a] and Weimin Liu[a]

Received 2nd December 2011, Accepted 17th January 2012

DOI: 10.1039/c2fd00124a

3-((1H-benzo[d][1,2,3]triazol-1-yl)methyl)-1-methyl-1H–imidazolium hexafluorophosphates ([BTAMIM][PF$_6$]) ionic liquids (ILs) were evaluated as friction reduction, antiwear (AW) and anticorrosion additives in poly(ethylene glycol) (PEG) for steel/Cu–Sn alloy contacts at 100 °C. The physical properties of PEG with the additive were measured. The anticorrosion properties of [BTAMIM][PF$_6$] was assessed *via* the accelerated corrosion test, which reveals the excellent anticorrosion properties in comparison with selected conventional ILs that have no benzotriazole group. Tribological results indicated that [BTAMIM][PF$_6$] as additives could effectively reduce the friction and wear of sliding pairs in PEG. The tribological properties were generally better than the normally used dibutyl phosphite (T304) and conventional ILs L-P108 in PEG. The wear mechanisms are tentatively discussed according to the morphology observation of worn surfaces of Cu–Sn alloy discs by scanning electron microscopy (SEM) and surface composition analysis by X-ray photoelectron spectroscopy (XPS), which revealed complex tribochemical reactions during the sliding process leading to a surface protective film composed of [Cu(–C6H5N3-R)], Cu$_2$O, CuF$_2$ and C–O bond containing compound is formed. A strong interaction between benzotriazole and the surface of the Cu alloy was proposed to account for the excellent friction reduction, anti-wear and anti-corrosion capability improvement.

1   Introduction

The discovery of ionic liquids (ILs) as high performance synthetic lubricants was initiated in 2001 and highlighted by Chemical & Engineering News.[1] Ionic liquids have fine tribological characteristics compared to ordinary synthetic lubricating oils. This may be attributed to the dipolar structure of ILs and their excellent physical properties such as extremely low volatility, nonflammability, high thermal stability and low melting points.[2,3] The outstanding characteristics of ILs also make them good candidates for high-performance lubricants,[4 21] as friction reduction and AW additives and as thin films.[8,15,22–29] In recent years, the publications on this topic have multiplied either within academic journals or in the form of patents, implying widespread interest from both fundamental and industrial aspects, but some problems have to be seriously considered and solved before putting to the real applications. For example, they have poor compatibility with the commonly used synthetic lubricating oils, and are liable to thermal oxidization and corrosion

---

[a]State Key Laboratory of Solid Lubrication, Lanzhou Institute of Chemical Physics, Chinese Academy of Sciences, Lanzhou 730000, China. E-mail: zhouf@licp.cas.cn
[b]Graduate School of Chinese Academy of Sciences, Beijing 100039, China

---

during the rubbing process particularly in the presence of moisture. The solution to these problems is to design task specific ionic liquid lubricants.[30]

ILs will turn to black after long time thermal stress probably due to the Hofmann elimination.[31] Substitution of H at the 2-position of the imidazolium ring can reduce its oxidation and so improve the tribological properties.[27,28] A sterically hindered phenol group was incorporated into ILs to improve their antioxidation capability. Corrosion is another problematic issue.[29] Corrosion largely comes from the hydrolysis of perfluoro-anions, or from impurities like halogens introduced during synthesis. To reduce corrosion, an alternative way is to replace the fluorine containing anion; for example, substitution of fluorine with fluoroalkyl chains from PF_6 to $(C_2F_5)_3PF_3$ can improve the IL friction reduction and AW properties and alleviate the corrosion.[10] Another way is to completely avoid use of fluorine containing anions; for example, a dialkylphosphate anion can be used and may have a synergistic effect with the imidazolium ring besides the corrosion resistance.[14,32] It is well known that benzotriazole and its derivatives are effective metal deactivators, especially for copper alloys.[33–35] This is attributed to the strong interaction of benzotriazole and its derivatives on a fresh copper surface *via* a nitrogen atom in triazole ring acting as the electron donor.[7] But benzotriazole has a relatively low sublimation temperature. Then we attached a benzotriazole moiety to ILs by molecule design. The functionalized ILs show good tribological properties and anticorrosion capability for steel/steel contacts.[36] In this context, functionalized ILs with the corrosion resistance functionalities were studied as the anticorrosion, friction reduction and antiwear additives in polyethylene glycol base oil for steel/Cu–Sn alloy contacts. The present paper is a continuity of previous work.[36,37] Together with this, more recent work will be delivered during the Faraday Discussion.

2   Experimental

2.1.   Chemicals

Fig.1 shows the chemical structures of [BTAMIM][PF_6], L-P108 and T304. 3-((1*H*-benzo[d][1,2,3]triazol-1-yl)methyl)-1-methyl-1H-imidazolium hexafluorophosphates ([BTAMIM][PF_6]) and 3-octyl-1-methyl-imidazolium hexafluorophosphates (L-P108) ILs were synthesized according to previously reported methods.[36–38] Dibutyl phosphite (T304) was purchased from LuBoRun Lanzhou LanLian Additive Co., Ltd. All other chemicals utilized in this work were of AR grade.

2.2.   Characterization

PEG was purchased from Shanghai Chemical Reagent Company. The average molecular weight was between 380–430 g mol^{-1}. It has kinematic viscosity of 40.10 mm^2 s^{-1} at 40 °C and 6.75 mm^2 s^{-1} at 100 °C. Base oil and additives were mixed thoroughly before testing. The IL [BTAMIM][PF_6] had a solubility over 10 wt% in PEG. The density, viscosity, and viscosity–temperature index of the ILs and T304 were measured by a SVM3000 Stabinger viscometer. The morphology and chemical

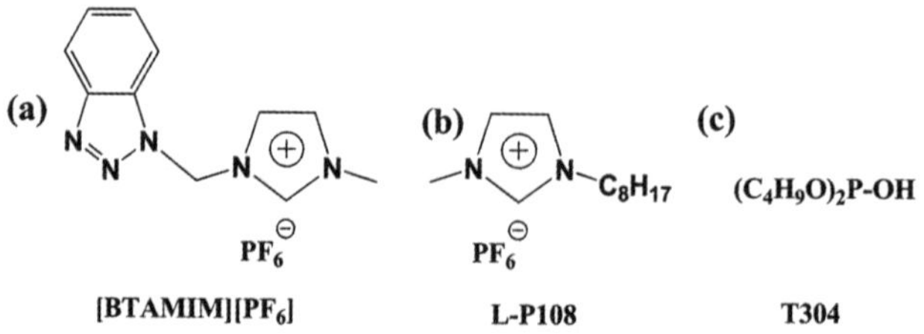

Fig. 1   Molecular structures of additives: (a) [BTAMIM][PF_6]; (b) L-P108; (c) T304.

   This journal is © The Royal Society of Chemistry 2012

composition of the worn surfaces were analyzed by JSM-5600LV SEM and Thermon Scientific–K-Alpha-surface Analysis XPS using Mg KR radiation as the excitation source.

2.3. Accelerated corrosion test

To make the test solution, the IL was dissolved in 25 mL of methanol and then added to 25 mL of saturated calcium hydroxide [$Ca(OH)_2$]. The copper piece specimens were incubated in IL solutions saturated with $Ca(OH)_2$ for 8 days.[39]

2.4. Tribological tests

The tribological behavior of the ILs as additives in PEG for steel/Cu–Sn alloy contacts was evaluated on an Optimol SRV-IV oscillating reciprocating friction and wear tester. Friction and wear tests were performed at 100 °C in a ball-on-block configuration. The contact between the frictional pairs was achieved by pressing the upper running ball (10 mm in diameter, AISI 52100 steel, hardness of approximately 59–61 HRC) against the lower stationary disk ($ø$ 24 mm × 7.9 mm, Cu–Sn alloy), hardness of approximately 120–140HV) in the reciprocating mode under a normal load of 20–120 N [corresponding to the maximum Hertzian pressure in the range of 1.32–2.39 GPa] at a frequency of 25 Hz, a sliding amplitude of 1 mm, a relative humidity of 30–35%, and for a duration of 30 min. The wear volume of the lower disk was measured using a MicroXAM 3D noncontact surface mapping profiler. Fig. 2a–5a shows the single friction curves under different lubrication conditions (note: the friction curves overlapped very well in different tests), whereas Fig. 2b–5b shows the averaged wear volume from 3 different tests.

3. Results and discussion

3.1. Physical properties of the synthesized ILs

Polyether lubricating oil has been widely used in industry. In the present work, we have used PEG with molecular weights of 380–430 g mol^{-1} as the model base oil for study. The density, viscosity and viscosity temperature index of PEG and PEG with ILs are shown in Table 1. The data have shown that the addition of ILs to PEG only slightly increases its viscosity both at room temperature and at 100 °C. Taking [BTAMIM][PF$_6$] as an example, the viscosity increases as the concentration increases. Obviously, the viscosity change is not that much and would have trivial impact on the lubricating properties, highlighting the effect of ILs themselves as lubrication additives as will be shown in the following.

Table 1 Physical properties of PEG and PEG with different additives

	Kinematic viscosity (mm^2 s^{-1})		Viscosity	Density
Lubricant	40 °C	100 °C	index	(kg m^{-3}) at 25 °C
PEG	40.10	6.75	130.6	1129.4
0.5% [BTAMIM][PF$_6$]	40.36	6.81	137.1	1131.1
1% [BTAMIM][PF$_6$]	40.69	6.89	137.7	1132.4
2% [BTAMIM][PF$_6$]	40.91	6.93	136.5	1137.6
3% [BTAMIM][PF$_6$]	41.35	6.96	135.4	1139.7
4% [BTAMIM][PF$_6$]	41.78	6.98	135.9	1142.6
2% L-P108	40.88	6.94	136.1	1138.4
2% T304	40.28	6.84	135.4	1126.3

3.2 Accelerated corrosion test

The accelerated corrosion test was carried out in a specially selected solution. Similar results have been reported previously and new data was presented here for integration.[36] The copper pieces were incubated in ILs solutions saturated with $Ca(OH)_2$ for 8 days, and made comparison with blank solution and the normal L-P108 IL. The anticorrosion behavior of the synthesized ILs is listed in Table 2. Table 2 shows the copper piece corrosion tests of ILs. It is seen that severe corrosion occurred on a copper piece soaked in a blank solution and that containing L-P108. The copper pieces in both solutions were seriously corroded and the color turned to black. The SEM morphologies of the copper pieces show that the copper top surface layer had been eroded away. However, under the same conditions, the copper piece colors in the solution containing $[BTAMIM][PF_6]$ or $[BTAMIM][PF_6]$ + L-P108 show a little change and the copper surfaces almost no corrosion, and the texture structure on steel surfaces due to mechanical polishing before is still clearly seen, indicating no obvious damage to the initial morphology. So the synthesized $[BTAMIM][PF_6]$ ILs have a significant anticorrosion capability for copper.

3.3 Friction and wear behavior

3.3.1. Effect of additive concentration.

Fig. 2a demonstrates the evolution of the friction coefficient with time at a constant load of 50 N and the frequency of 25Hz for $[BTAMIM][PF_6]$ + PEG with different additive concentrations and the wear volumes of the copper discs after testing. When the concentration of $[BTAMIM][PF_6]$ is 0.5 wt% and 1 wt%, in the initial friction stage, the $[BTAMIM][PF_6]$ additive may form a boundary lubricating film and the curve shape was stable for the initial 100 s and 600 s, respectively. Then the boundary film might be gradually worn away and could not complement rapidly, probably because of low concentration, so the friction coefficient gradually increased to 0.20, and afterward the value is comparable to the base oil. When the concentration of $[BTAMIM][PF_6]$ is above 2 wt%, the mixture not only has a very low and stable friction coefficient (Fig.2a), but also the lowest wear volume (Fig.2b). After increasing the concentration of $[BTAMIM][PF_6]$ to above 2 wt%, the AW property could not be improved any more (Fig.2b). The results show that the addition of 2 wt% $[BTAMIM][PF_6]$ can improve the AW properties of the base oil by 2 times and 1.9 times as compared with 0.5 wt% and 1 wt% $[BTAMIM][PF_6]$, respectively. So 2 wt% [BTAMIM][PF6] is the optimum concentration to provide significant friction and wear reduction.

3.3.2 Effect of kinds of additives.

Fig. 3 shows the tribological properties of 2 wt% $[BTAMIM][PF_6]$ at a constant load of 50 N and the frequency of 25Hz, and made comparison with pure PEG, T304 and the normal L-P108 IL. Pure PEG has relatively long running-in time, lasting for 300 s, and afterward stabilized when the friction coefficients reached 0.22. The friction behaviors of 2 wt% T304 and 2 wt% L-P108 were comparable to the base oil. Both have relatively long running-in time with larger friction coefficients. With the addition of 2 wt% $[BTAMIM][PF_6]$ as the additive in PEG, the running-in time is dramatically shortened, concomitant with very stable friction and a lower friction coefficient. It is seen that the friction coefficients of the four lubricants increase in the following sequence: $[BTAMIM][PF_6]$ < T304 | L-P108 < PEG, the wear volumes of the discs increase in the following sequence: $[BTAMIM][PF_6]$ < T304 < L-P108 < PEG. The results show that the addition of 2 wt% $[BTAMIM][PF_6]$ can improve the AW properties of the base oil by 2.3 times, 1.8 times and 1.9 times as compared with PEG, 2 wt% T304 and 2 wt% L-P108, respectively. The good tribological performance of the ILs has been attributed to the strong interaction of the benzotriazole group on the fresh copper surface *via* a nitrogen atom in triazole ring acting as the electron donor, and the polarity of $[BTAMIM][PF_6]$ IL molecules and their ability to form ordered adsorbed layers.[7,20]

Table 2 Accelerated copper corrosion tests of ILs

	Blank	0.01 mol L^{-1} L-P108	0.01 mol L^{-1} [BTAMIM][PF$_6$] + 0.01 mol L^{-1} L-P108	0.01 mol L^{-1} [BTAMIM][PF$_6$]
Copper (before corrosion)				
Copper (after corrosion)				
SEM(300X)				
SEM(1000X)				

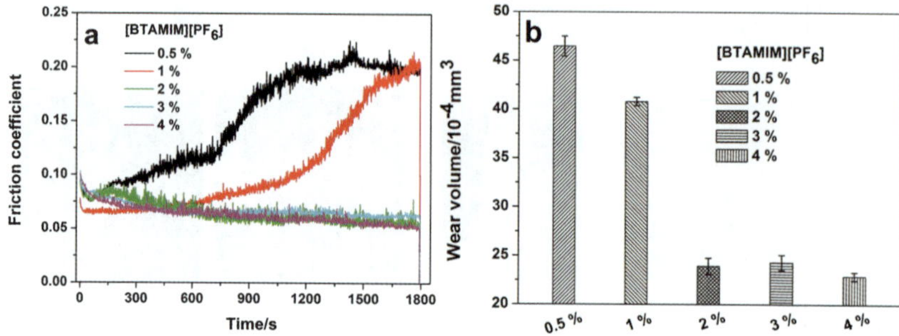

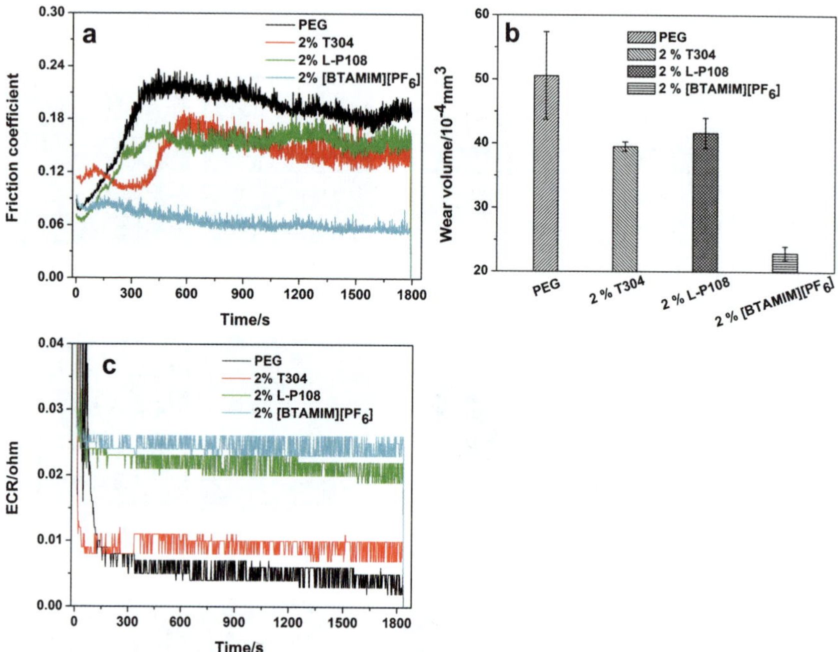

Fig. 2 (a) Evolution of friction coefficient with time at 50 N for PEG plus [BTAMIM][PF$_6$] additive at different concentrations; (b) wear volumes of the copper discs lubricated by PEG with [BTAMIM][PF$_6$] additive at different concentrations after the constant load tests. (SRV load: 50 N; stroke: 1 mm; frequency: 25 Hz; duration: 30 min; temperature: 100 °C.)

Fig. 3 (a) Changes in the friction coefficient relative to time at 50 N for PEG and different IL additives at 100 °C; (b) wear volumes of copper discs lubricated by PEG and different additives at 100 °C; (c) change in contact resistance during reciprocating friction test at 50 N. (SRV load: 50 N; stroke: 1 mm; frequency: 25 Hz; duration: 30 min.)

An efficient way of characterizing the boundary film is the *in situ* average contact resistance measurement. Fig.3c shows the electrical contact resistance change with the friction time under different lubrication conditions. In all the contact resistance is very low compared with that for steel/steel contacts[29] probably due to the better conductance of the copper alloy. However, an obvious difference was still discerned. Sliding contacts lubricated with pure PEG have the lowest contact resistance, while those lubricated with [BTAMIM][PF$_6$] IL additive in PEG have the highest contact resistance, indicating it forms a more efficient and robust boundary film.

3.3.3   Effect of the load. The boundary lubricating capability of an additive was further tested by varying applied loads and sliding speeds by changing the reciprocating frequencies. 2 wt% [BTAMIM][PF$_6$] lubricants will not change friction coefficient very much when varying loads and sliding speeds. Fig. 4a displays a load ramp test stepped from 20 N up to 120 N by 20 N intervals at a frequency of 25 Hz for three kinds of PEG + additive at 100 °C. The test duration for each load was 5 min. It is seen that all oils experience a running-in period. The friction coefficients of 2 wt% T304 and 2 wt% L-P108 were similar to the base oil, and gradually increased with increasing the load, fluctuating all the time. Upon the addition of 2 wt% [BTAMIM][PF$_6$], in the initial friction stage (at a load of 20 N), the friction coefficient reached 0.14, lasting for 300 s, and afterward stabilized at a value of 0.07. The wear volumes of the discs increased in the following sequence: [BTAMIM][PF$_6$] < T304 < L-P108 < PEG. The results show that the addition of 2 wt% [BTAMIM][PF$_6$] can improve the AW properties of the base oil by 16 times, 1.6 times and 1.7 times as compared with PEG, 2 wt% T304 and 2 wt% L-P108, respectively.

3.3.4 Effect of the frequency. Fig. 5 shows a frequency ramp test from 15 Hz up to 40 Hz by 5 Hz intervals at a load of 50 N for different additives and PEG at 100 °C. The test duration for each frequency was 5 min. All the lubricants experienced a running-in time, however; 2 wt% [BTAMIM][PF$_6$] experienced short running-in time, concomitant with very stable friction and a lower friction coefficient than 2 wt% T304, 2 wt% L-P108 and PEG during a frequency ramp test from 15 to 40 Hz. The wear volumes are presented in Fig. 5b. The wear volumes of the lubricants increased in the following sequence: [BTAMIM][PF$_6$] < T304 < L-P108 < PEG. This is consistent with the results shown in Fig. 3 and 4.

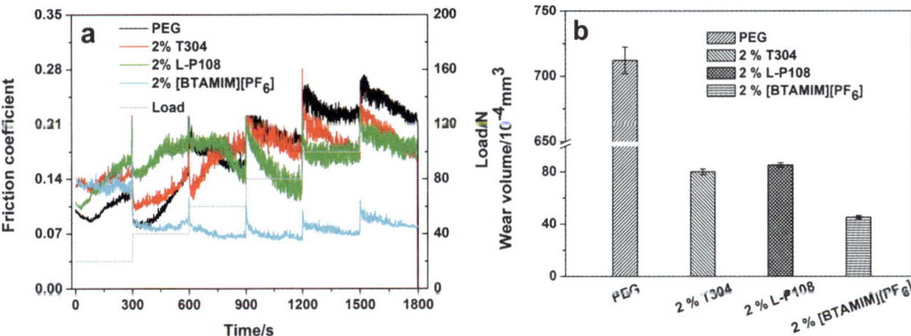

Fig. 4 (a) Evolution of friction coefficient with time during a load ramp test, (b) wear volumes of copper discs lubricated by PEG and different additives from 20 to 120 N at 100 °C. (SRV Load: 20–120 N; stroke: 1 mm; frequency: 25 Hz; duration: 30 min; temperature: 100 °C.)

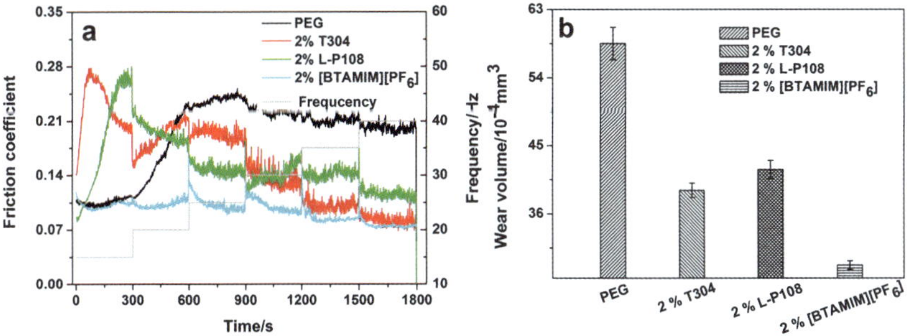

Fig. 5 (a) Evolution of friction coefficient with time during a frequency ramp test, (b) wear volumes of copper discs lubricated by PEG and different additives from 15 to 40Hz at 100 °C. (SRV Load: 50 N; stroke: 1 mm; frequency: 15–40Hz; duration: 30 min; temperature: 100 °C.)

[BTAMIM][PF$_6$] + PEG mixture as lubricant, both the friction reduction and AW wear capability were very prominent. The anticorrosive ILs had even lower friction coefficient and wear volumes than that lubricated by T304 and L-P108 under the same conditions. These results verify that ILs as additives in PEG both in the constant load, variable load, and variable frequency tests have better tribological performance for steel/copper contacts at 100 °C. This may be attributed to high thermal stability, and the strong interaction of benzotriazole group on the fresh copper surface, the capability to form effective boundary films.

3.4 Surface analysis

Fig.6 shows the SEM morphologies of the worn surfaces of the coppers lubricated with PEG, 2 wt% T304, 2 wt%L-P108 and 2 wt% [BTAMIM][PF$_6$] under the load of 2–120N at 100 °C, and all the wear scars were obtained under the same conditions. It is seen that the worn copper surface under lubrication of PEG displays severe scuffing, with a much wider and deeper wear scar as was measured with a 3D noncontact surface mapping profiler, and the wear volume is very large. For the copper lubricated with 2 wt% T304, 2 wt% L-P108, the wear scars are very rough, a lot of small furrows and scratches, but the diameter is considerably reduced compared with PEG. In marked contrast, the worn copper surface of 2 wt% [BTA-MIM][PF$_6$], the width of the wear scars were smaller, and the abrasions became smoother, and scuffing was greatly alleviated. This is consistent with the measured wear volume results in Fig. 4b.

In the region of boundary lubrication, the friction coefficient becomes significantly large and it requires effective additional additives for reducing friction and preventing severe wear of the metal surfaces. The additives can adsorb on the metal surfaces or react with the metal surface, particularly the chemical reaction of a lubricant or lubricant additive with the rubbing surface is very important. Indeed, the tribochemical reaction between active elements with contacts is too complicated to be disclosed satisfactorily.[7] XPS is a powerful tool to clarify the chemical states of elements within a boundary film on a wear scar. To gain further insight into the lubricating mechanism of ILs, Fig. 7 presents the XPS spectra of Cu2p, O1s, N1s and F1s on a worn copper surface lubricated by PEG, 2 wt% L-P108 and 2 wt% [BTAMIM][PF$_6$]. Fig. 7c shows that for N1s a strong peak appears at 400.1 eV, which differs from the binding energies of N1s in neat [BTAMIM][PF$_6$]

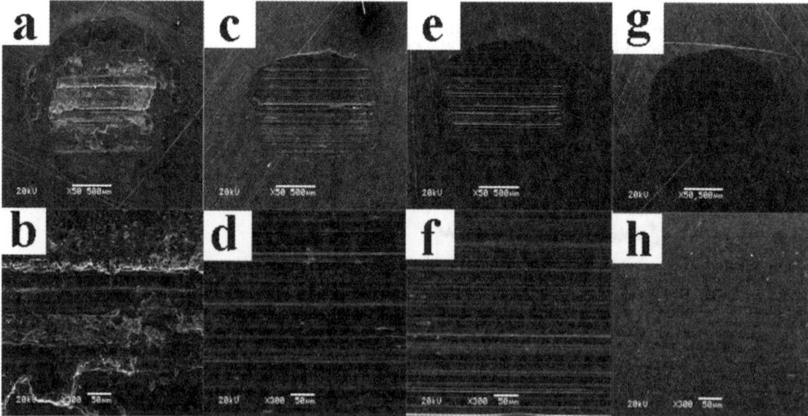

Fig. 6 SEM morphologies of worn surfaces lubricated by PEG and different IL additives: (a, b) PEG, (c, d) 2 wt% T304, (e, f) 2 wt% L-P108, and (g, h) 2 wt% [BTAMIM][PF$_6$]. (Magnification: top images, 50×; and bottom images, 300×; load, 20–120 N; stroke, 1 mm; frequency, 25 Hz; duration, 30 min; temperature, 100 °C.)

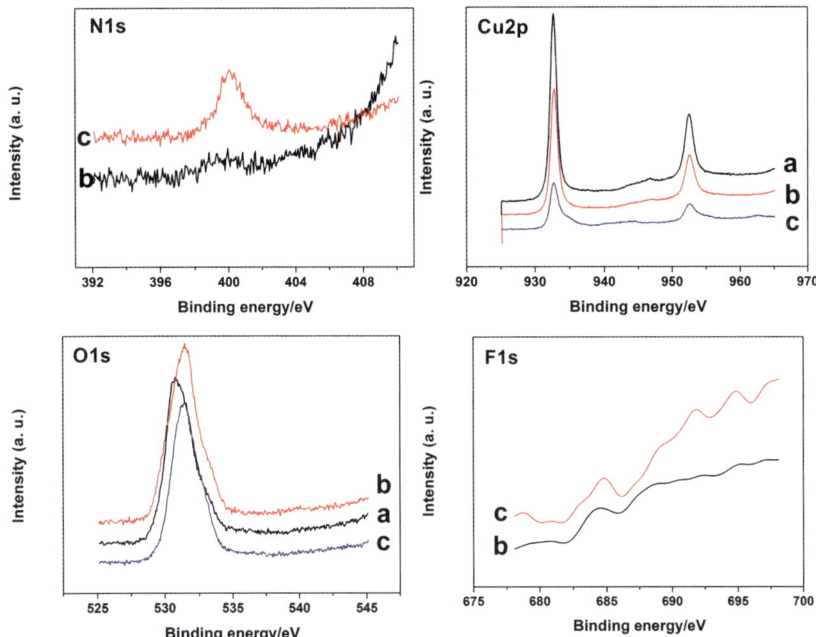

Fig. 7 XPS spectra of Cu2p, F1s, O1s, N1s, of worn surfaces lubricated by (a) PEG, (b) PEG + 2 wt% L-P108, (c) PEG + 2 wt% [BTAMIM][PF$_6$].

and is most possibly identified as [Cu(–C$_6$H$_5$N$_3$–R)].[7,36,40] Moreover, there is no detectable signal of N1s when it is lubricated by the 2 wt% L-P108. Therefore, it is possible that BTA formed a robust film on the surface of bronze when lubricated by 2 wt% [BTAMIM][PF$_6$]. The Cu2p peak at 932.7 eV can be ascribed to [Cu(–C$_6$H$_5$N$_3$)–R], Cu$_2$O and Cu; the peak at 952.5 eV can be identified as Cu$_2$O.[7,40] Fig. 7b and 7c reveal that the XPS peaks for F1s at 684.3 and 684.7 eV, respectively, may correspond to CuF$_2$.[40] O1s peak appear at 530.7 eV (Fig. 7a) on worn surface that can be identified as Cu$_2$O. The O1s peak (Fig. 7b, c) at approximately 531.5 eV, after comparing these against the standard spectra of the elements, can be assigned to C–O bonding.[40] From the above results, it can be concluded the tribochemical reaction occurred on the bronze surface. XPS spectra of the worn surface lubricated by PEG only have the signal of Cu$_2$O. When the worn surface was lubricated by 2 wt% L-P108, the compounds of Cu$_2$O, CuF$_2$ and compounds containing C–O bonds are formed on worn surface. A boundary film, containing [Cu(–C6H5N3-R)], Cu$_2$O, CuF$_2$ and a C–O bond-containing compound, formed on the surface of Cu when lubricated by the 2 wt% [BTAMIM][PF$_6$]. This film can protect against the corrosion and have better friction reduction and anti-wear properties. So [BTAMIM][PF$_6$] ILs have better tribological properties than other lubricants.

4. Conclusions and perspectives

[BTAMIM][PF$_6$] ILs bearing benzotriazole group has a significant anticorrosion capacity to copper when being used in PEG due to the presence of benzotriazole groups that can form strong interactions with copper. The addition of 2 wt% [BTAMIM][PF$_6$] in PEG dramatically reduced the friction coefficient and wear volume. XPS analysis revealed that tribochemical reactions occurred during the friction process. These reactions generated a surface protective film composed of

[Cu(–C$_6$H$_5$N$_3$–R)], Cu$_2$O, CuF$_2$ and C–O bond-containing compounds. Strong interactions between benzotriazole ILs and the surface of the Cu alloy were proposed to account for the excellent friction reduction, anti-wear and anti-corrosion improvement capability.

Tribology society has seen 10 years of research on IL lubricants.[1,30] It is time to think about their real applications. The area has seen random trials with different types of ILs, applicability to different substrates and applicability in different forms (base oils, additives, thin films).[30] What are the real problems ahead of application? Costs might be the primary concern for general industries, only probably not a question for aerospace industry or other high-tech industry where the use amount is very limited. High polarity and fluidity makes them have good lubricating properties as thin films.[41,42] Their uses as thin films reasonably reduce the cost by significantly lowering the applied amount. Or they can be used as additives.[8,25,27,29] They have poor miscibility with normally used lubricating oils. A tetraalkylphosphonium phosphonate type of ionic liquids has the enhanced miscibility with nonpolar lubricating oils[43–45] and should be studied further, however by achieving this, people have to sacrifice the polarity of ionic liquids, which is the basis for its excellent tribological performance. Corrosion and oxidation can be another two problems. By changing fluoro-anions to non fluoro-anions, corrosion can be alleviated. The incorporation of functional groups into ILs provides another synthetic route for solving problematic issues of ILs.[29,36,37] It is the right time to step from random study to designing "task-specific IL lubricants" that either target some special applications or aim to solve problems, for which the present work shows one example. These research directions should be stressed in the future and will be discussed in my presentation.

Acknowledgements

The authors thank the financial support from the NSFC(21125316, 21173243), Chinese Academy of Sciences (KJCX2.YW.H16 and "A Hundred Young Excellence" program).

References

1 C. Ye, W. Liu, Y. Chen and L. Yu, *Chem. Commun.*, 2001, 2244.
2 M. J. Earle and K. R. Seddon, *Pure Appl. Chem.*, 2000, **72**, 1391.
3 R. Hagiwara and Y. Ito, *J. Fluorine Chem.*, 2000, **105**, 221.
4 W. M. Liu, C. F. Ye, Q. Y. Gong, H. Wang and P. Wang, *Tribol. Lett.*, 2002, **13**, 81.
5 H. Wang, Q. Lu, C. Ye, W. Liu and Z. Cui, *Wear*, 2004, **256**, 44.
6 A. E. Jiménez and M. D. Bermúdez, *Tribol. Lett.*, 2006, **26**, 53.
7 X. Liu, F. Zhou, Y. Liang and W. Liu, *Tribol. Lett.*, 2006, **23**, 191.
8 J. Qu, J. J. Truhan, S. Dai, H. Luo and P. J. Blau, *Tribol. Lett.*, 2006, **22**, 207.
9 L. Weng, X. Liu, Y. Liang and Q. Xue, *Tribol. Lett.*, 2006, **26**, 11.
10 I. Minami, M. Kita, T. Kubo, H. Nanao and S. Mori, *Tribol. Lett.*, 2008, **30**, 215.
11 M. Yao, Y. Liang, Y. Xia, F. Zhou and X. Liu, *Tribol. Lett.*, 2008, **32**, 73.
12 A. E. Jiménez and M. D. Bermúdez, *Tribol. Lett.*, 2010, **40**, 237.
13 I. Minami, T. Inada, R. Sasaki and H. Nanao, *Tribol. Lett.*, 2010, **40**, 225.
14 D. Jiang, L. Hu and D. Feng, *Tribol. Lett.*, 2010, **41**, 417.
15 A. Jimenez, M. Bermudez, P. Iglesias, F. Carrion and G. Martineznicolas, *Wear*, 2006, **260**, 766.
16 X. Liu, F. Zhou, Y. Liang and W. Liu, *Wear*, 2006, **261**, 1174.
17 J. Sanes, F. Carrion, A. Jimenez and M. Bermudez, *Wear*, 2007, **263**, 658.
18 B. Yu, F. Zhou, C. Pang, B. Wang, Y. Liang and W. Liu, *Tribol. Int.*, 2008, **41**, 797.
19 J. Qu, P. J. Blau, S. Dai, H. Luo, H. M. Meyer Iii and J. J. Truhan, *Wear*, 2009, **267**, 1226.
20 M. Yao, M. Fan, Y. Liang, F. Zhou and Y. Xia, *Wear*, 2010, **268**, 67.
21 D. Li, M. Cai, D. Feng, F. Zhou and W. Liu, *Tribol. Int.*, 2011, **44**, 1111.
22 A. Jimenez and M. Bermudez, *Wear*, 2008, **265**, 787.
23 A. H. Battez, R. González, J. L. Viesca, D. Blanco, E. Asedegbega and A. Osorio, *Wear*, 2009, **266**, 1224.
24 A. Jimenez, M. Bermudez, F. Carrion and G. Martineznicolas, *Wear*, 2006, **261**, 347.

25 M. Cai, Z. Zhao, Y. Liang, F. Zhou and W. Liu, *Tribol. Lett.*, 2010, **40**, 215.

26 M. Zhu, J. Yan, Y. Mo and M. Bai, *Tribol. Lett.*, 2008, **29**, 177.

27 M. Yao, Y. Liang, Y. Xia and F. Zhou, *ACS Appl. Mater. Interfaces*, 2009, **1**, 467.

28 H. Zhang, Y. Xia, M. Yao, Z. Jia and Z. Liu, *Tribol. Lett.*, 2009, **36**, 105.

29 M. Cai, Y. Liang, M. Yao, Y. Xia, F. Zhou and W. Liu, *ACS Appl. Mater. Interfaces*, 2010, **2**, 870.

30 F. Zhou, Y. Liang and W. Liu, *Chem. Soc. Rev.*, 2009, **38**, 2590.

31 I. Minami, H. Kamimura and S. Mori, *J. Synth. Lubr.*, 2007, **24**, 135.

32 L. Zhang, D. Feng and B. Xu, *Tribol. Lett.*, 2009, **34**, 95.

33 A. Frignani, L. Tommesani, G. Brunoro, C. Monticelli and M. Fogagnolo, *Corros. Sci.*, 1999, **41**, 1205.

34 A. Frignani, M. Fonsati, C. Monticelli and G. Brunoro, *Corros. Sci.*, 1999, **41**, 1217.

35 N. K. Allam, E. A. Ashour, H. S. Hegazy, B. E. El-Anadouli and B. G. Ateya, *Corros. Sci.*, 2005, **47**, 2280.

36 M. Cai, Y. Liang, F. Zhou and W. M. Liu, *ACS Appl. Mater. Interfaces*, 2011, **3**, 4580.

37 M. Cai, Y. Liang, F. Zhou and W. M. Liu, *J. Mater. Chem.*, 2011, **21**, 13399.

38 P. BonhoÃte, A. P. Dias, N. Papageorgiou, K. Kalyanasundaram and M. Gratzel, *Inorg. Chem.*, 1996, **35**, 1168.

39 M. Sheban, M. Abu-Dalo, A. Ababneh and S. Andreescu, *Anti-Corros. Methods Mater.*, 2007, **54**, 135.

40 http://srdata.nist.gov/xps/.

41 B. Yu, F. Zhou, Z. Mu, Y. Liang and W. M. Liu, *Tribol. Int.*, 2006, **39**, 879.

42 M. Palacio and B. Bhushan, *Adv. Mater.*, 2008, **20**, 1194.

43 I. Minami, T. Inada, R. Sasaki and H. Nanao, *Tribol. Lett.*, 2010, **40**, 225.

44 T. Itoh, N. Watanabe, K. Inada, A. Ishioka, S. Hayase, M. Kawatsura, I. Minami and S. Mori, *Chem. Lett.*, 2009, **38**, 64.

45 R. G. Lu, H. Nanao, K. Kobayashi, T. Kubo and S. Mori, *J. Jpn. Pet. Inst.*, 2010, **53**, 55.

Does ultra-mild wear play any role for dry friction applications, such as automotive braking?

Werner Österle,[*a] A. I. Dmitriev[b] and H. Kloß[a]

Received 24th November 2011, Accepted 4th January 2012

DOI: 10.1039/c2fd00117a

Nanostructured third body films and/or storage of wear debris at the surfaces of the first bodies are deemed as prerequisites of sliding under ultra-mild wear conditions. Since such features have been observed experimentally on brake pads and discs, attempts were undertaken to study their sliding behaviour by modelling on the nanoscopic scale with an approach based on Movable Cellular Automata (MCA). The model rendered the possibility to study the influence of different nanostructures systematically and to assess the impact of different brake pad ingredients on the sliding behaviour, velocity accommodation and friction force stabilization at a sliding contact. Besides providing a review on previously published modelling results, some additional new graphs enabling better visualization of dynamic processes are presented. Although ultra-mild wear conditions were considered to be essential for achieving the desired tribological properties, transitions to mesoscopic and macroscopic wear mechanisms were studied as well. The final conclusion is that ultra-mild wear and corresponding smooth sliding behaviour play an important role during automotive braking, even though temporarily and locally events of severe wear may cause friction instabilities, surface damage and release of coarse wear particles.

Introduction

Ultra-mild wear is related to wear rates of less than 10 nm per hour. It is always associated with the formation of nanocrystalline surface films. Although wear rates of brake friction materials are usually much higher, we have frequently observed fragments of a nanocrystalline third body, either as films adhering to the surfaces or as loose wear particles.

Our hypothesis is that nanoparticles shearing or rolling along their contacting areas provide velocity accommodation at the interface of a sliding contact under dry friction conditions. If the zone of loose particles is restricted to a thin layer only, the situation is similar to liquid lubrication and the term quasi-fluid layer is justified.[1] Furthermore, if the particles after having been moved for some distance get trapped at the surface again, sliding without wear becomes possible. Since a disc brake is an open system, nanoscopic velocity accommodation will stabilize friction, although degradation of the third body film and partial release of wear particles to the environment will take place as well.

In order to visualize the mechanism of quasi-fluid layer formation and the corresponding velocity accommodation at the interface between a fixed brake pad and rotating brake disc it was necessary to implement the experimental findings of third

[a]BAM Federal Institute for Materials Research and Testing, Berlin, Germany. E-mail: Werner. oesterle@bam.de
[b]Institute of Strength Physics and Materials Science, Tomsk, Russia

body nanostructures to an appropriate model. The method of Movable Cellular Automata (MCA), developed by Psakhie *et al.*,[2] performs sliding simulations by considering the arrangement and mechanical properties of different materials which are involved in a tribological process. A great advantage of the MCA approach is that it can be adjusted to any desired length scale from nanometre to kilometre; the latter has been used for geological simulations.[3]

Since in our case the model is adjusted to describe mechanisms taking place at the nanometre scale within very small time intervals, it is not easy to judge whether such mechanisms play any role with respect to brake-performance properties realized at a macroscopic level. Therefore, it is important to discuss the limits of the modelling approach and possible interactions with mechanisms taking place at micro or macro levels.

Characterization of third body nanostructures

Although partly published in previous papers,[4,5] it is important for this discussion to show the essential features of the third body nanostructure which are similar in principle for all automotive brake applications involving cast iron brake discs and phenolic resin bound friction composites as pad materials. The main constituent is always magnetite-type iron oxide as shown by the green areas in Fig. 1a. Submicron-sized particles of all available pad constituents are embedded within this iron oxide matrix, which forms by tribooxidation of the cast iron disc and the steel fibres of the pad. Fig. 1a shows two types of soft particles, namely copper (red) and barite (blue). The Zr-map in Fig. 1b shows the distribution of hard zirconia particles within the same cross-section of the friction layer. At even higher magnification we detected that the iron oxide matrix consists of grains with diameters of the order of 10 nm

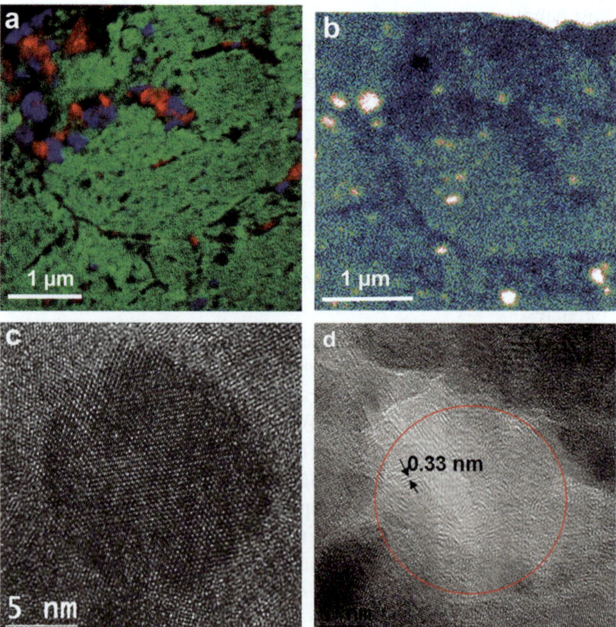

Fig. 1 Nanostructure of a third body film. **a)** Elemental map showing submicrometre-sized soft particles such as copper (red) and barite (blue) in an iron oxide matrix (green); **b)** white spots represent hard zirconia particles; **c)** HR-TEM image showing Fe_3O_4-nano-crystal (diameter 15 nm) with two sets of {220} lattice fringes indicating [111] zone axis; **d)** onion-like nanoparticles (diameters 5 nm) consisting of curved graphene sheets.

(Fig. 1c) and furthermore that the iron oxide is mixed with graphite-like particles of similar size (Fig. 1d).

The interesting point with these results is that, although most of the original pad constituents are rather large features ranging approximately from 10–1000 µm, the wear debris, or in other words the third body, contains all constituents mixed more or less on the nanoscopic scale. The mechanisms leading to fragmentation of the material seem to be similar to those of mechanical alloying during high energy ball milling[6] and tribologically induced oxidation of ferrous constituents seems to be the major mechanism for the formation of the third body matrix.[7]

Principles of modelling

The objective of the modelling was to simulate mechanisms of velocity accommodation between the first bodies after a running-in period when both surfaces are screened with third body films. The nanocrystalline structure of both the films and the loose wear particles that detached from the surfaces and were released to the environment suggest that the third body is an agglomerate of nanoparticles. The agglomerate may decompose under certain conditions and the particles will move relative to each other if stresses are acting on them. Periodic boundary conditions were assumed in the model, which means that granular material leaving the contact on the left side is entering it again on the right side. The modelling setup was designed as follows: the size of automata was adjusted to 10 nm according to the smallest grain size which was experimentally determined for typical third bodies formed during automotive braking (see Fig. 1). The conventional cellular automata approach was extended by introducing principles of particle-based modelling, *i.e.* equations of motion for each automaton and interaction laws between neighbouring automata. One of the essentials of the model is that all automata are initially linked to their neighbours, but that this linkage can be broken at a certain stress state and eventually may be activated again after coming into contact with another autom aton. In this respect, the model is similar to the one suggested by Fillot *et al.*,[8] who assumed attractive and repulsive forces between particles of the third body. In our model, tangential forces were used as well as normal interaction along the line connecting the mass centers. Furthermore, the MCA method uses multiple particle interaction, which means that the force calculation is based on the spatial configuration of nearest neighbours.

To express how the model works, the calculation tasks performed during a single time step are listed below. External stresses corresponding to the loading conditions

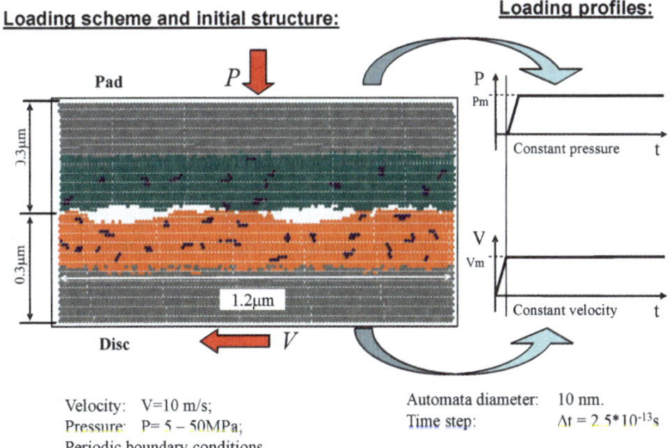

Fig. 2 Schematic of model structure and loading parameters; see Fig. 4 and 5 for colour code.

are depicted in Fig. 2. The response of each automaton during each time step was calculated in the following way: the strains and stresses of each pair of automata (which are arranged in a regular manner as described in previous papers[9-11]) are determined independently, assuming plane stress approximation (ref. 9, eqn 1 and 4). The stress σ_{xx} in the specimen coordinate system is calculated (ref. 9, eqn 3) taking into account the influence of neighbours. Using this value, the von Mises stress intensity σ_{int} is determined (ref. 9, eqn 5). After this, the criteria for the linked to unlinked transition (stress intensity σ_{int} = fracture stress σ_f) is checked and applied accordingly. Motion of the automata mass centers is governed by the Newton–Euler equation of motion (ref. 2, eqn 6). Small rearrangements of the automata continue as long as unbroken links to the neighbours exist. Larger movements become possible only if all links are broken. After coming into contact with another automaton, the unlinked–linked-transition may take place. The criteria for this transition are defined as follows:

i) $\sigma = \sigma_{pl}$, $\varepsilon_{pl} = 0.2$–0.4% is an adjustable parameter for different metals, ii) $\sigma > \sigma_f$ means that re-linking is quasi-forbidden for oxides (as a rule it is not allowed, but becomes possible at special conditions), iii) forbidden for graphite, iv) forbidden for pairs of metal with oxide or graphite.

Justification of these rules evolves from the following:

i) Compaction of metallic particles may occur under pressure at ambient temperature if a certain amount of plastic deformation takes place. ii) For the compaction of oxide particles both high pressure and elevated temperatures are needed. Since temperature is not considered in the model, re-linking was quasi-forbidden. iii) Graphite particles are assumed to degrade along their basal planes.

As a consequence, reformation of the nanocrystalline third body film from the quasi-fluid layer is not considered in the model. In reality such a mechanism must exist, because otherwise the third body film would exhaust very quickly.

The results of all calculations for one time step determine new positions and velocities for each automaton as starting points for the calculations of the next time step.

Only two dimensions defining a cross-section of the tribological interface are regarded in the model, although the automata are assumed as cylindrical units, thus being able to define shear stresses.[4,9] As shown schematically in Fig. 2, the basic modelling setup was chosen to be as simple as possible, although still resembling the main features of the pad–disc interface of a disc brake.

Four different materials were considered in the basic model structure: i) cold-worked ferritic steel representing a reinforcing ingredient of the brake pad and support for a stable third body film on the pad side, ii) pearlitic steel representing the major constituent of a gray cast iron brake disc and support for the third body film on the disc side, iii) magnetite representing the major phase of the third body, and iv) graphite representing a typical solid lubricant inclusion in the third body. Approximate stress–strain curves representing response functions of the four materials and some others, which will be considered later, are shown in Fig. 3. Although the properties were the same, two different colours were chosen for pad and disc oxide layers for better visualization of mechanical mixing during sliding simulation. The stress–strain curves of SiC at 20 °C and 800 °C shown in Fig. 3 were taken from the work of Milman *et al.*[12]

It is not claimed that the assumed stress–strain behaviours of bulk materials describe the response of corresponding nanoparticles correctly, because this could not be checked experimentally. The only justification for this choice is that the simulation results are plausible and provide an explanation of velocity accommodation between the rotating disc and fixed pad.

Rigney and coworkers used empirical pair atomic potentials and Molecular Dynamics (MD) to simulate atomic flow at sliding contacts.[13,14] Although the MCA approach is at a scale which is only one order of magnitude higher than for MD, the interaction of particles is considered like for a macroscopic system, such as, *e.g.*, sand particles in a soil. Interestingly, the automata size corresponds to

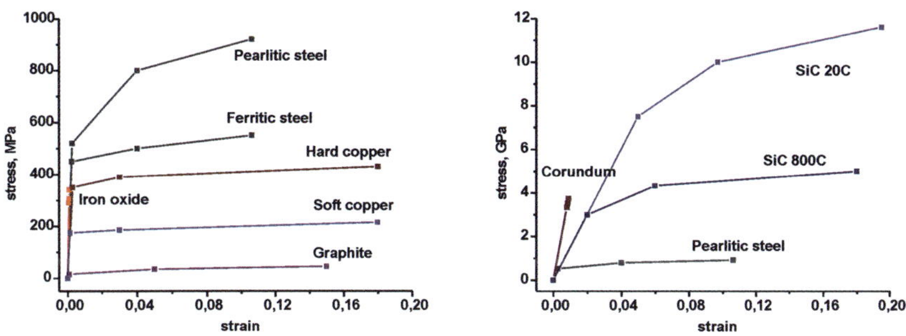

Fig. 3 Mechanical properties of materials considered for MCA modelling.

what Fedorov has termed "the elementary tribonanostructure",[15] the smallest unit in which dissipation of friction energy can take place. It should be made clear once more that the model does not consider chemical reactions. Our approach is first to determine the structure and composition of the third body experimentally and then to obtain an understanding of the sliding mechanism of the observed structures by modelling. Actually, the model provides a tool for visualization of the micro mechanisms that are assumed to take place if nanostructured materials are transformed into granular structures. The model supports our imagination of what could happen in reality, and adjustment of the model parameters in order to obtain certain simulation results helps us to learn which parameters are critical with respect to stable or unstable friction behaviour.

Prerequisites of smooth sliding behaviour and wear reduction

Mild wear of metallic materials is usually attributed to the formation of thin oxide layers that prevent adhesion and alloying of the first bodies. Initial modelling attempts assuming pure oxide layers on steel substrates revealed an unstable sliding behaviour.[16] It came out that during the sliding simulation the brittle oxide did not develop a mechanically-mixed granular layer but rather crack-like features, as shown in Fig. 4a. The coefficient of friction (COF) calculated for each time step showed very large fluctuations, indicating a stick-slip kind of sliding. Furthermore, the mean COF obtained by integrating over subsequent time steps did not saturate

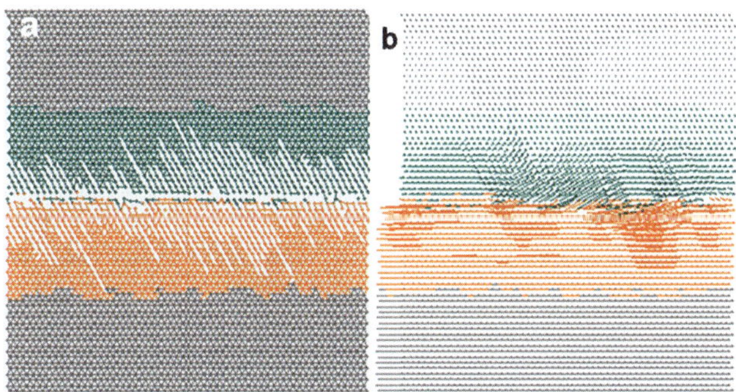

Fig. 4 Results of MCA modelling of a steel couple covered by oxide films. The materials involved are: steel as supporting substrate (grey) and oxide layers with the same mechanical properties shown in green and orange. The graphs depict the final structures after sliding of the lower part (disc) against the upper one (pad) for 10^{-7} s. **a)** Bonding states of neighbouring automata marked by lines. **b)** Momentary velocities of automata marked by lines (main direction from right to left, as shown in Fig. 2).

at a constant level (not shown here, but discussed in ref. 16). This type of behaviour is confirmed by the velocity pattern shown in Fig. 4b. Although the lines overlap completely in the centre of the graph, the abrupt change of automata velocites at the pad–disc interface is clearly visible at the left border. Darker contrasts at certain areas in the green and orange layers indicate that small rearrangements of automata are taking place.

It was observed that the sliding behaviour changed dramatically if a certain amount of a soft ingredient such as graphite was added to the model structure.[16] In that case, bonds between neighbouring automata are broken within a narrow zone on both sides of the interface and a granular layer, the quasi-fluid nanolayer according to Popov *et al.*,[1] is formed. Fig. 5a shows this situation for oxide layers containing 17.5 vol % graphite. Oxide particles from the top (green) and bottom (orange) are mixed within the granular layer. Therefore, the term mechanically-mixed layer (MML) was used in previous papers. A snapshot of the velocity field obtained during the simulation is shown in Fig. 5b. It not only reveals a velocity gradient within the MML between the moving bottom part and the fixed top (see the left border of the frame), but it also shows some vortex-like structures. Thus, we can conclude that the MML behaves similarly to a fluid layer and that velocity accommodation between the rotating disc and fixed pad takes place within this layer. Further systematic MCA simulations with oxide films containing different fractions of graphite particles revealed that at least 10% of graphite was needed to provide smooth sliding conditions with formation of a MML irrespective of the applied normal pressure.[16]

Adjustment of the model to more complicated experimentally-observed nanostructures

As is clearly visible in Fig. 1, the structure of real third body films obtained during braking contains more features than just iron oxide and graphite nanoparticles. Grains of recrystallized copper or other soft constituents of the pad material were frequently embedded in the third body matrix.[11] The characteristic size range of such soft inclusions was 50–100 nm. Hard grains of the same size range, such as ZrO_2 or SiC, were observed as well. Let us first consider the impact of additional soft grains with diameters three times larger than the graphite and iron oxide grains. The larger features were introduced into the modelling setup in the form of agglomerates formed from automata of the respective material, soft copper in this case. Furthermore, the model structure was designed in such a way that the overall volume fraction of soft components corresponded to 13%, a value which has been

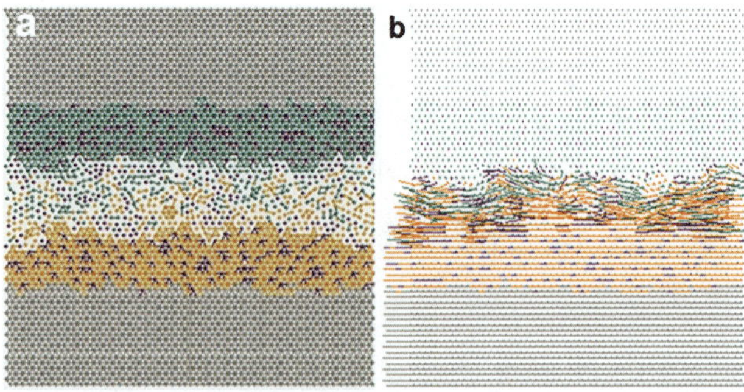

Fig. 5 Results of MCA modelling considering oxide films with 17.5 vol % graphite inclusions; graphite shown in purple; same colour code as in Fig. 4 for other materials. **a)** Bonding states of neighbouring automata marked by lines. **b)** Momentary velocities of automata marked by lines (main direction from right to left, as shown in Fig. 2).

     This journal is © The Royal Society of Chemistry 2012

identified to provide smooth sliding conditions over a wide range of applied normal pressures.[16,17] In other words, approximately half of the graphite automata of the basic model structure were substituted by the copper agglomerates. Thus, the new model structure fits much better with the experimentally-observed nanostructure (Fig. 1). The structure obtained after a sliding simulation is shown in Fig. 6a. Obviously a granular layer has formed at the interface and mixing of material from both sides of the interface has occurred. Furthermore, the soft agglomerates of copper, which are still visible within the unaffected third body film, have been decomposed completely and mixed with the other components within the MML. It should be mentioned here that only the combination of 5.5% graphite nanoparticles with 7.5% copper agglomerates results in MML formation and smooth sliding conditions, whereas the simple binary systems, iron oxide with 5.5% graphite, and iron oxide with 7.5% copper did not. This was shown in our most recent paper.[18] Thus, it can be concluded that the volume fraction of soft constituents in the third body is of major importance for MML formation and that the size and type of the inclusions seem to not be so critical as long as they are softer than the iron oxide matrix.

A further step toward considering the sliding behaviour of experimentally-observed third body nanostructures is to introduce a certain amount of hard particles into the model. Again, the hard particles were constructed as small agglomerates with diameters of approximately 50 nm. SiC was assumed to be a hard inclusion because the stress–strain curves of this material are available from the literature.[12] The matrix structure consisted of iron oxide with 13 vol % graphite inclusions and the hard agglomerates were distributed homogeneously in the oxide films. Fig. 6b shows this structure after a sliding simulation. A similar MML as for the same structure without hard inclusions was formed. Interestingly, the hard agglomerates are still visible – not only in the unaffected third body, but also within the MML.

The examples shown above (except Fig. 4) refer to simulations with MML formation. Since our hypothesis is that the MML is essential for smooth sliding behaviour (as desired for braking) it is important to know the critical conditions leading to a transition from smooth to stick-slip sliding. Taking into account all modelling results obtained thus far,[4,5,9–11,16–18] the critical features are the following:

i) Metal-on-metal contact does not provide smooth sliding conditions because unlinked automata can easily link again as soon as they come in contact with other automata.[5,9,17] ii) Pure oxides show crack-like features but no MML formation.[16] iii) An oxide with a certain amount of soft inclusions (at least 10 vol %) is needed to induce MML formation within a large range of applied normal pressures.[9,16,17] iv) Hard particles with diameters bigger than the thickness of the third body film will scratch off the film and thus lead to unstable behaviour of type i) or ii) (not simulated but observed experimentally[19]).

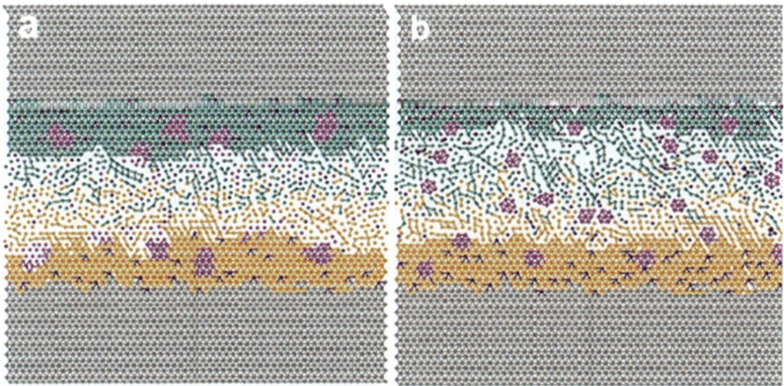

Fig. 6 Bonding states after sliding simulation with nanostructures containing additional coarse particles shown in magenta (size approximately 50 nm). **a)** 5.5% graphite + 7.5% coarse copper particles. **b)** 13% graphite + 4.5% coarse SiC particles.

The following conditions are not critical in respect to smooth sliding conditions but may exert an impact on COF level:

i) The type of soft inclusion is not critical as long as it is softer than the iron oxide. Little difference is observed between graphite and recrystallized copper.[4] ii) The size of soft inclusions is not critical because agglomerates are decomposed easily.[18] iii) Hard inclusions with diameters smaller than the thickness of the third body film are incorporated in the MML without changing sliding characteristics (smooth *versus* stick-slip). The friction level is increased compared to the same structure without hard inclusions.[18] iv) The type of substrate material is not critical as long as its strength is high compared to the strength of the oxide. Selecting cold-worked ferritic steel, cold-worked copper, pearlitic steel, or SiC at 20 °C or 800 °C makes no difference.[18]

All studies presented above were based on the assumption that the outermost surfaces of both first bodies are covered by a compact and well-adhering third body film. Despite the fact that it is still not understood how such a film may form, there is evidence that it may be unstable and prone to decomposition as soon as the normal pressure is released. Colleagues from Uppsala have observed wear debris flowing in the "labyrinth" between the so-called contact plateaux, and they also found evidence for the spreading of a film at contacting sites.[20] In the meantime, several studies have proven that dust particles emitted from brakes show the same nanostructure as third body films.[21–23] Therefore, it should be considered how loose wear debris flowing in the gap between pad and disc may contribute to friction and sliding behaviour of a brake.

A first step in this direction was undertaken with a slight modification of the MCA modelling setup, as shown in Fig. 7a. Links between automata were broken randomly along lines thus creating a layer of loosely packed agglomerates, resembling a layer of wear debris in the gap between first bodies. The most simple nanostructure, known to provide smooth sliding conditions (iron oxide + 12% graphite), was chosen for the third body.

Fig. 7b shows that, in this case, a MML was also formed during the simulation. Slight differences concerning the conditions under which this occurs were observed, but will not be discussed here. The important point is that a layer of loose wear debris may have a similar effect as a compact friction film with the same nanostructure.

In conclusion, it can be stated that the third body films and loose wear debris, which usually cover pad and disc surfaces during automotive braking, may readily form very thin quasi-fluid layers. Such layers can account for velocity accommodation between the rotating brake disc and fixed pad, and thus are an important prerequisite for smooth sliding conditions.

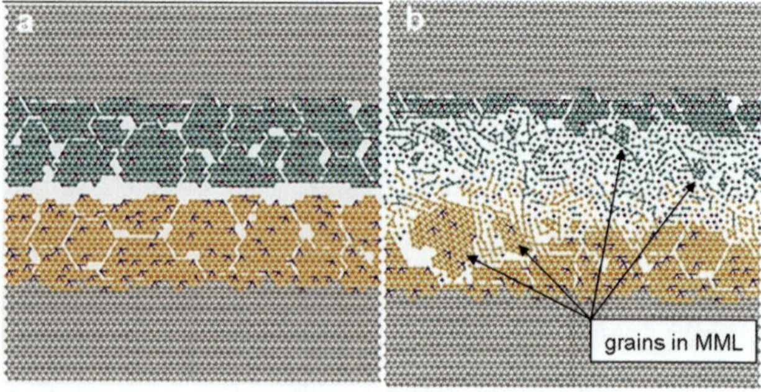

Fig. 7 Modelling setup for a third body (12% graphite) consisting of loosely packed agglomerates (wear debris); same colour code as in Fig. 5; **a)** initial structure; **b)** after simulation.

Impacts on wear

What can be learned from the modelling results with respect to wear? Neither any mechanism of third body formation nor wear was considered in our model. The only issue which has been studied intensively is a momentary sliding behaviour and corresponding COF of thin third body layers at an approximately micron-sized contact. On the other hand, the nanostructures of real third bodies could be reproduced quite well with the model, and the simulated sliding behaviour seems to be plausible. Furthermore, the mean COF values calculated with the model correspond very well to the range which is expected and demanded for automotive brake systems (not shown here, but in our previous papers). Therefore, it seems reasonable to assume that the nanomechanisms studied by modelling are realistic. One might expect that after a running-in period in which a sufficient amount of wear debris is provided, the surfaces of both first bodies are perfectly flat and covered with a stable third body film. In the ideal case, when the granular layer (corresponding to the MML in the model structure) remains at the tribological interface, no wear would occur. If we were to assume that the loose particulate material representing the MML will be ejected to the environment immediately after leaving the contact zone, the wear volume would still be quite low because of the small particle size (10 nm) and layer thickness (100 nm). Nevertheless, mechanisms must exist for retaining a major part of the third body at the tribological interface, because otherwise the structures providing smooth sliding and velocity accommodation would exhaust very quickly and the unscreened surfaces would result in unstable friction behaviour in terms of stick-slip and high friction force fluctuations. These considerations gave rise to the assumption that contact sites of brakes are usually sliding under conditions of ultra-mild wear, and provide smooth sliding at a constant coefficient of friction.

Transitions from nanoscopic to micro- and macroscopic wear

Unfortunately, a scenario with negligible wear is not realistic for real brake systems. Although some smoothening of disc surfaces is usually observed after running-in, ideal conditions are never reached and also are not really desired. This is so because some very important properties of brakes are related to mechanisms taking place at the mesoscopic and macroscopic scales. For example, the ability of the system to increase its macroscopic COF instantaneously with increasing applied pressure has been attributed to variable contact area due to anchoring of macroconstituents of the pad in a compliant matrix (phenolic resin), as described by Eriksson et al.[24] Considering wear, it should be kept in mind that most of the pad ingredients are large features with dimensions of 100 μm or more. During severe braking conditions, the temperature may rise well above 300 °C and the phenolic resin binder phase will start to degrade[25] leading to the release of such coarse particles from the pad surface. Although the coarse particles will gradually be fragmented and mixed with the other wear particles, they are present at the tribological interface for a certain time and may damage the surfaces or the third body films by third body abrasion, provided that they are harder than the substrate materials. A further source of coarse wear particles is severe plastic deformation of the cast iron disc which may occur when the third body film has been scratched off and a metal-on-metal contact is likely to form. Evidence for such a wear mechanism was observed several times by imaging micron-sized cross-sections with a Focused Ion Beam (FIB) instrument. Fig. 8a shows an example.

The formation of cracks preferentially at the graphite–pearlite interface of the cast iron microstructure was also revealed by MCA modelling,[9] as shown in Fig. 8b. It is quite clear that the damage mechanism visible in Fig. 8 may produce chip-like metallic wear particles with a thickness corresponding to the width of the plastically-deformed layer (approximately 4 μm in Fig. 8a). This mechanism explains

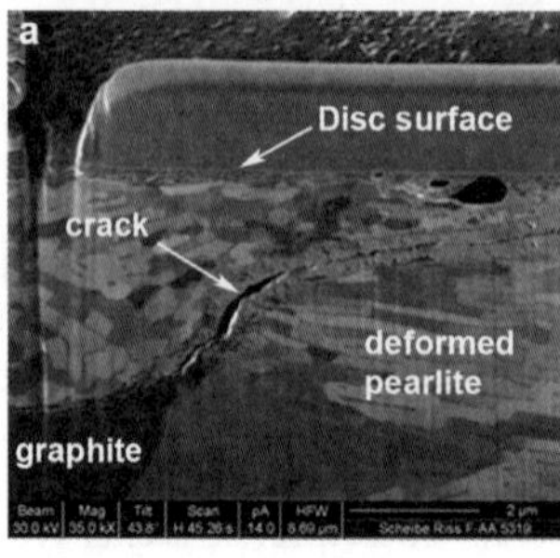

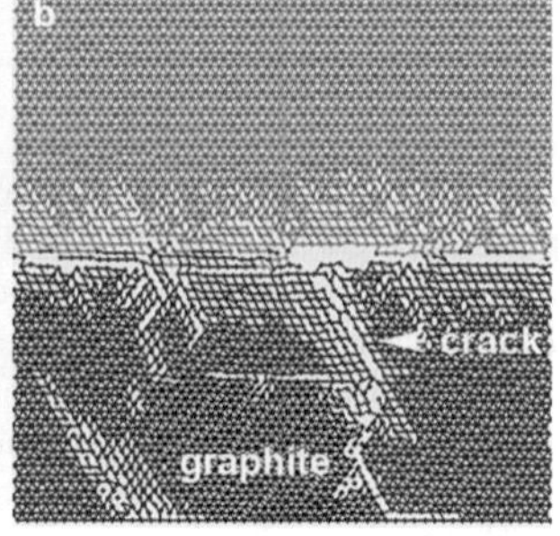

Fig. 8 Formation of micron-sized wear particle at a steel-on-steel contact; **a)** FIB-image at cross-section; **b)** after MCA simulation: cracks along graphite–steel interface in a superficial zone of the cast iron brake disc.

the origin of a well known albeit undesired phenomenon of braking praxis, namely metal pick-up at a pad surface.[26] Major problems arise if the width and length of a metallic chip approaches macroscopic dimensions. Since the crack visible in Fig. 8a runs almost parallel to the disc surface, the formation of a large and flat chip is quite likely.

Processes taking place at the micro- or mesoscopic scale play an important role as well. Such processes are related to secondary contact formation as a consequence of wear particle compaction. This was described phenomenologically by Eriksson *et al.*[24] and modelled by Ostermeyer and Müller.[27] A gradually changing coefficient of friction is attributed to the increase of contact area caused by wear particle compaction. A typical example is the so-called in-stop behaviour (continuously increasing COF during each stop braking event). Furthermore, formation of secondary contacts describes a mechanism of retaining wear debris at the pad surface. Whereas disc surfaces are usually flat and smooth, pad surfaces contain flat plateaux with troughs between them. The plateaux consist of both macroparticles of the pad and wear debris (primary and secondary plateaux, respectively). It is important that there exists a dynamic equilibrium of plateaux and troughs, thus providing enough wear debris (third body) to be spread over the contact sites in the form of a third body film, and enough space for storage of the nanoparticle agglomerates, which are assumed to form from the MML according to our nanoscopic model, respectively.

The examples shown above imply that a large variety of wear particles will be formed during braking. They will be stored partly at the pad surface and partly emitted to the environment. Thus, a broad size distribution of brake dust particles has to be taken into account. It is interesting to compare volume-based and number-based size distributions, as published by Kukutschová *et al.*[28] The data related to volume show a very broad maximum, around 100 μm, corresponding to macroconstituents of the pad and metal chips from the disc. The number-based size distribution shows its maximum in the submicron range. That means that, despite the negligible volume with respect to total wear, a large number of very small particles are emitted during braking. A more precise measurement of the fraction of small particles, undertaken by Gasser *et al.*, actually revealed that the major part of ultra-fine brake dust particles was smaller than 100 nm.[29] The latter result was corroborated by our own recently-published experiments,[30] and is shown in Fig. 9.

It is important to point out that both papers,[29,30] and also a previous study,[21] revealed significant nanoparticle emissions only under harsh braking conditions, such as when disc surface temperatures increased well beyond 300 °C.[21,30] Thus, one may conclude that third body films are no longer stable under such conditions, and lead to an increased release rate of film fragments to the environment. This also has consequences with respect to brake performance. It is well-known that highway

    This journal is © The Royal Society of Chemistry 2012

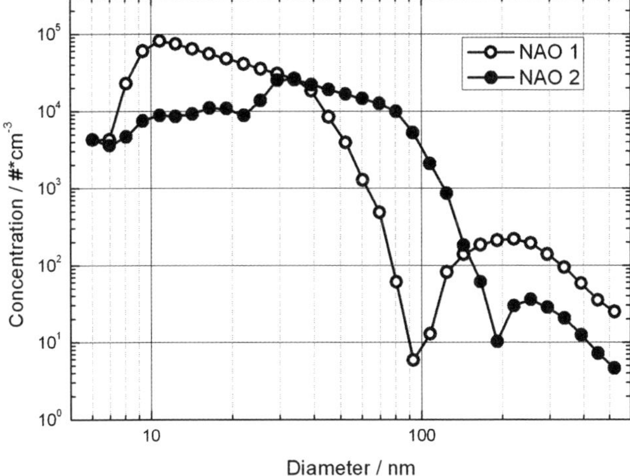

Fig. 9 Number-based size distribution of ultrafine brake dust measured during a test simulating severe braking conditions; NAO 1 and NAO 2 are two different brake pad materials.

emergency braking and continuous down hill braking may not only lead to momentary losses of friction properties, but also to long-term degradation of friction materials, although the latter may eventually recover during subsequent "normal" braking cycles.

Conclusions

Experimental observations with automotive brakes imply that wear mechanisms take place at the macroscopic, mesoscopic, and nanoscopic scale. In terms of wear volume, the formation of particles and chips in the size range 100–1000 μm play the most important role. Mesoscopic particles consisting either of not yet fully fragmented pad constituents or of third body particles have the ability to fill gaps and troughs, and thus contribute to smoothening of the surface and expansion of primary contact areas.

Nanoscopic particles are important for smooth sliding conditions and friction force stabilization at the desired level. Such kinds of behaviour could be simulated by MCA modelling provided that certain prerequisites of the nanostructure were met. Since the nanostructures considered during modelling were derived from experimentally-observed features, modelling results are well-suited to assess the impact of parameter variations and to define optimum structures. Efforts to verify modelling results by preparing and testing well-defined artificial third bodies are currently in progress.

Since it has been shown by modelling that velocity accommodation between sliding parts can be restricted to a very thin quasi-fluid layer under conditions that are relevant for braking, conditions of ultra-mild wear are fulfilled, although temporarily, while local events of severe wear may occur in parallel. Of course, wear volume and macroscopic appearance of the surfaces will be dominated by the latter. In spite of this, friction surfaces have the ability to regenerate as long as sufficient quantities of fully processed wear debris are available at the tribological interface.

Acknowledgements

Financial support from the German Research Foundation (grants OS77/9-1, OS77/14-1, OS77/18-1 and OS77/19-1) and program of the specialized branches of RAS,

project No. 13.13.3, program No. 127 of SB RAS with exterior organization is grate-
fully acknowledged. The authors would also like to thank Eric Payton for tidying the
English text.

References

1 V. L. Popov, S. G. Psakhie, A. Dmitriev and E. Shilko, Quasi-fluid nano-layers at the interface between rubbing bodies, *Wear*, 2003, **254**, 901–906.
2 S. G. Psakhie, Y. Horie, G. P. Ostermeyer, S. Korostelev, A. Smolin and E. V. Shilko, Movable cellular automata method for simulating materials with mesostructure, *Theor. Appl. Fract. Mech.*, 2001, **37**, 311–334.
3 D. O. Potyondy and P. A. Cundall, A bonded-particle model for rock, *Int. J. Rock Mech. Min.*, 2004, **41**, 1329–1364.
4 W. Österle, C. Prietzel, H. Kloß and A. I. Dmitriev, On the role of copper in brake friction materials, *Tribol. Int.*, 2010, **43**, 2317–2326.
5 W. Österle, C. Prietzel and A. I. Dmitriev, Investigation of surface film nanostructure and assessment of its impact on friction force stabilization during automotive braking, *Int. J. Mater. Res.*, 2010, **101**, 669–675.
6 D. Maurice and T. H. Courtney, Modelling of mechanical alloying: Part I Deformation, coalescence and fragmentation mechanisms, *Metall. Mater. Trans. A*, 1994, **25A**, 147–158.
7 S. Ilo, A. Tomala and E. Badisch, Oxidative wear kinetics in unlubricated steel sliding contact, *Tribol. Int.*, 2011, **44**, 1208–1215.
8 N. Fillot, I. Iordanoff and Y. Berthier, Modelling third body flows with a discrete element method-a tool for understanding wear with adhesive particles, *Tribol. Int.*, 2007, **40**, 973–981.
9 A. I. Dmitriev and W. Österle, Modeling of Brake Pad-Disc Interface with Emphasis to Dynamics and Deformation of Structures, *Tribol. Int.*, 2010, **43**, 719–727.
10 W. Österle, H. Kloß and A. I. Dmitriev, Friction control during automotive braking–Experimental observations and simulation at the nanometre scale. Tribology, Materials, *Tribol.-Mater., Surf. Interfaces*, 2009, **3**, 196–202.
11 W. Österle, C. Prietzel, H. Kloß and A. I. Dmitriev, On the role of copper in brake friction materials, *Tribol. Int.*, 2010, **43**, 2317–2326.
12 Y. V. Milman, I. V. Gridneva and A. A. Golubenko, Construction of stress-strain curves for brittle materials by indentation in a wide temperature range, *Sci. Sintering*, 2007, **39**, 67–75.
13 H. J. Kim, W. K. Kim, M. L. Falk and D. A. Rigney, MD simulations of microstructure evolution during high-velocity sliding between crystalline materials, *Tribol. Lett.*, 2007, **28**, 299–306.
14 H. J. Kim, S. Karthikeyan and D. Rigney, A simulation study of the mixing, atomic flow and velocity profiles of crystalline materials during sliding, *Wear*, 2009, **267**, 1130–1136.
15 S. V. Fedorov, The mechanical quantum of dissipative friction structures is the elementary tribonanostructure, *Proc. IV World Tribology Congress*, 2009, Japanese Society of Tribologists, Kyoto, p. 926.
16 A. I. Dmitriev, W. Österle and H. Kloß, Numerical simulation of mechanically mixed layer formation at local contacts of an automotive brake system, *Tribol. Trans.*, 2008, **51**, 810–816.
17 A. I. Dmitriev, W. Österle and H. Kloß, Numerical simulation of typical contact situations of brake friction materials, *Tribol. Int.*, 2008, **41**, 1–8.
18 W. Österle, A. I. Dmitriev and H. Kloß, Possible impacts of third body nanostructures on friction performance during dry sliding determined by computer simulation based on the method of movable cellular automata, *Tribol. Int.*, 2012, **48**, 128–136.
19 W. Österle, A. I. Dmitriev and H. Kloß, Basic considerations for the development of friction materials, *Proc. IWAAFC-2*, ed. J. Bijwe, published by ITMMEC, IIT, New Delhi, India, 2008, pp.24–51.
20 M. Eriksson, J. Lord and S. Jacobson, Wear and contact conditions of brake pads: dynamic in situ studies of pad on glass, *Wear*, 2001, **249**, 272–278.
21 W. Österle, H. Bresch, I. Dörfel, C. Prietzel and S. Seeger, Surface film formation and dust generation during brake performance tests, *Proc. IMECHE-Conference Braking 2009*, ed. D. Barton, Chandos Publishing, Oxford, UK, 2009, 29–38.
22 J. Wahlström, A study of airborne wear particles from automotive disc brakes, Doctoral thesis, KTH, Stockholm, Sweden, 2011 ISBN 978-91-7415-871-7.
23 R. Hinrichs, R. F. Soares Marcio, R. G. Lamb and R. F. Soares Marcos, Vasconcellos M.A.Z.: Phase characterization of debris generated in brake pad coefficient of friction tests, *Wear*, 2011, **270**, 515–519.

24 M. Eriksson, F. Bergmann and S. Jacobson, On the nature of tribological contact in automotive brakes, *Wear*, 2002, **252**, 26–36.
25 A. L. Bulthé, Y. Desplanques, G. Degallaix and Y. Berthier, Mechanical and chemical investigation of the temperature influence on the tribological mechanisms occurring in OMC/cast iron friction contact, *Wear*, 2008, **264**, 815–825.
26 F. Sanitate and O. Schmitt, An investigation of metal pick-up generation on passenger car brake pads in correlation with deep rotor scoring, *Proc. of the 26th Annual Brake Colloquium*, SAE International, Warrendale, PA, USA, 2008, pp. 65–70, ISBN 978-0-7680-2097-7.
27 G. P. Ostermeyer and M. Müller, New insights into the tribology of brake systems, *Proc. Inst. Mech. Eng., Part D*, 2008, **222**, 1167–1200.
28 J. Kukutschová, V. Roubíček, M. Mašláň, D. Jančík, V. Slovák, K. Malachová, Z. Pavlíčková and P. Filip, Wear performance and wear debris of semimetallic automotive brake materials, *Wear*, 2010, **268**, 86–93.
29 M. Gasser, M. Riediker, P. Gehr and B. Rutishauser, Toxic effects of brake wear particles on epithelial lung cells *in vitro*, *Part. Fibre Toxicol.*, 2009, **6**, 30.
30 W. Österle, H. Bresch, I. Dörfel, C. Fink, A. Giese, C. Prietzel, S. Seeger and J. Walter, Examination of airborne brake dust, *Proc. 6th European Conference on Braking JEF*, 2010, Lille, France, pp. 55–60; ed. G R R T, 20 rue Elisée Reclus-B.P.317, 59666 Villeneuve d'Ascq CEDEX-France.

On the three-term kinetic friction law in nanotribological systems

András Vernes,[*ab] Stefan Eder,[a] Georg Vorlaufer[a] and Gerhard Betz[b]

Received 25th November 2011, Accepted 23rd January 2012
DOI: 10.1039/c2fd00120a

A post-processing method, which maps the punctiform atoms in molecular dynamics (MD) simulations of boundary lubrication onto smoothed particles, is used to estimate the asperity contact area defined by the minimum cross-section of the formed solid bridges. It is then shown that this asperity contact area excellently agrees with the projected area resulting from a Voronoi tessellation of the corresponding contact zone, and that it can be applied to compute the constitutive system parameters of a three-term friction law, which is found to hold for any boundary-lubricated nanotribological system. Finally, an attempt is made to relate the load-independent friction offset observed in boundary-lubricated nanotribological systems without solid–solid contact to the structural order as measured by the entropy, which is estimated within the single macromolecule approach based on covariance (super)matrices of the carbon backbone atoms in the lubricant.

1   Introduction

According to the Amontons–Coulomb kinetic friction laws,[1,2] the kinetic coefficient of friction (CoF) is a dimensionless system parameter which is obtained as the ratio between the friction force observed for a given load and the applied load itself. Derjaguin[3] showed theoretically that the kinetic CoF beyond the Amontons–Coulomb term can also have a load-independent offset. If this occurs, the kinetic CoF is identified as the first derivative of the kinetic friction force with respect to the load. Due to the pioneering experimental work by Bowden and Tabor,[4] it is now well known that the kinetic friction force can also depend on the asperity contact area. So if the asperity contact area is found not to be proportional to the load, the first derivative of the kinetic friction force with respect to the load can no longer be used as a valid definition of the kinetic CoF because the so-resulting CoF would be load-dependent and hence not a system parameter.

In order to simultaneously access all the aforementioned friction force terms, the nanotribological simulation must be carefully designed ensuring that it takes place within the mixed lubrication regime of the corresponding Stribeck curve, where solid–solid contact can occur depending on the applied load and sliding velocity. Once such a nanoscopic setup is realized, one can expect that by increasing the sliding duration, the nanoasperities will wear to accommodate themselves to the sliding conditions. This material transfer between asperities can over time make the asperity contact subside, in which case the friction behaves according to full fluid lubrication. Exactly these aspects have motivated our present investigations, where

[a]Austrian Center of Competence for Tribology, Viktor-Kaplan-Straße 2, 2700 Wiener Neustadt, Austria. E-mail: vernes@ac2t.at
[b]Institute of Applied Physics, Vienna University of Technology, Wiedner Hauptstr, 8–10/134, 1040 Vienna, Austria

---

the transition between the mixed and fluid friction regimes as well as full fluid lubri-cation are separately considered.

In our previous molecular dynamics (MD) study of kinetic friction in boundary-lubricated nanotribological systems,[5] we found that all three terms, *i.e.*, the Derjaguin, Bowden–Tabor and Amontons–Coulomb, coexist simultaneously and completely explain the calculated friction-*versus*-load behavior in these systems. Furthermore, because our estimation for the asperity contact area yields that it does not linearly depend on the load, we concluded that the kinetic CoF at nanoscale cannot be straightforwardly extracted from the friction-*versus*-load curves without using various computational tools.

Therefore, in the first part of this paper, in Sec. 2, the main focus is on this three-term friction law, whose validity is proven for the case of two identical nanoasperities coming into contact several times, see Sec. 2.2. The asperity contact area is numerically estimated by post-processing the MD data, see Sec. 2.1.1, using a computational tool by the authors,[5] which is also compared with a Voronoi tessellation briefly explained in Sec. 2.1.2. Having estimated the asperity contact area, the constitutive system parameters involved in the three-term friction law are computed by applying a least squares fitting procedure described in Sec. 2.1.3. In addition, based on the time evolution of the asperity contact area, a geometrical description of asperity deformation is given in Sec. 2.3. The Derjaguin-form of the three-term friction law is separately considered in the second part of this paper, in Sec. 3, where the structural order dependence of the non-vanishing friction force offset is investigated if no asperity–asperity contact occurs, see Sec. 3.3. In order to relate the Derjaguin-offset to the entropy, its estimation within the single macromolecule approach is given in Sec. 3.1.

2 Three-term friction law

Using a smooth particle interpolation scheme by the authors,[5] it was recently proven by post-processing MD data obtained for boundary-lubricated nanotribological systems that a three-term friction law,

$$F(L) = F_0 + \tau A_{\mathrm{asp}}(L) + \mu L, \tag{1}$$

holds at any load considered and that this three-term friction law completely reproduces the observed friction-*versus*-load behavior in these nanotribological systems independently of the particular form of asperities and whether a solid–solid contact occurs or not, *i.e.*, for all values of the asperity contact area $A_{\mathrm{asp}}(L) \geq 0$. In this eqn (1), $F(L)$ is the load-dependent friction force, and the involved constitutive system parameters are as follows: F_0 is a load-independent Derjaguin-offset ascribed to the presence of the lubricant (discussed separately in Sec. 3), τ is the shear strength, and μ is the coefficient of friction. The Bowden–Tabor term $\tau A_{\mathrm{asp}}(L)$ in eqn (1) describes the adhesion-controlled friction, whereas the Amontons–Coulomb term μL describes the load-controlled friction.[6]

Note that the above three-term friction law obtained for boundary lubrication in nanotribological systems, formally comprises other long-standing friction laws well known in literature. The Derjaguin–Amontons–Coulomb friction law $F(L) = F_0 + \mu L$,[3] for example, directly results from eqn (1) by assuming $A_{\mathrm{asp}}(L) = 0$. The Bowden–Tabor friction law $F(L) = \tau' A_{\mathrm{asp}}(L)$,[4] on the other hand, immediately follows from eqn (1) when $F_0 = 0$, *i.e.*, $F(L) = \tau A_{\mathrm{asp}}(L) + \mu L$,[7] and by introducing $\tau' = \tau + \mu L/A_{\mathrm{asp}}(L)$.[8] From the latter particular form of eqn (1) also a generalized Amontons–Coulomb friction law $F(L) = \mu' L$ is reproduced considering $\mu' = \mu + \tau A_{\mathrm{asp}}(L)/L$.[9]

Clearly, in order to apply the three-term friction law given by eqn (1) in combination with MD simulations, one needs to numerically estimate the asperity contact area $A_{\mathrm{asp}}(L)$ as well as the system parameters F_0, τ and μ. In the following, two

  This journal is © The Royal Society of Chemistry 2012

different space-filling methods are presented for estimating $A_{\mathrm{asp}}(L)$, together with a standard fitting procedure to compute F_0, τ and μ. These numerical methods are then applied to two of the nanotribological systems from ref. 5, with improved MD setups and much longer sliding times than in ref. 5, in order to study the time evolution of the system parameters F_0, τ and μ.

2.1 Numerical methods

2.1.1 Smooth particle post-processing.

Originally, particle-based methods were developed to reduce the computational effort while solving either ordinary or partial differential equations in continuum mechanics (CM).[10] Although CM typically neglects any details regarding constitutive particles such as atoms or molecules, particle-based methods in CM in fact deal with macroscopic pseudoparticles which are indispensable for reducing the number of degrees of freedom *via* discretization from infinity, *e.g.*, in case of (in)homogeneous and (an)isotropic bulk systems, to a finite and numerically accessible number. Among other features, the smoothed particle method (SPM), well known from hydrodynamics,[11] is found to be a simple and very transparent computational scheme for smooth interpolation and differentiation on an irregular grid of moving pseudoparticles. Indeed, by partitioning the continuum into a finite number of representative subsystems of mass M_j and density ρ_j concentrated at $\vec{R}_j(t)$, the smooth-particle interpolation rule for an arbitrary quantity Q reads

$$Q(\vec{r}) = \sum_{j=1}^{\mathcal{N}} \frac{M_j}{\rho_j} Q_j w(\vec{r} - \vec{R}_j, h_j) = \sum_{j=1}^{\mathcal{N}} Q_j W(\vec{r} - \vec{R}_j, h_j), \tag{2}$$

where Q_j is the value of Q for the jth pseudoparticle temporarily situated at $\vec{R}_j$, w is the smoothing kernel (weight function) which has the dimension of an inverse volume and is supposed to rapidly fall with distance, $W(\vec{r} - \vec{R}_j, h_j) = w(\vec{r} - \vec{R}_j, h_j) M_j / \rho_j$, and h_j stands for the spatial smoothing length defining the influence domain of w. In eqn (2), the summation is performed over all pseudoparticles for which $\vec{r}$ is in their kernel support.

Exactly this ability of SPM to interpolate by smoothing point-like particles, was recently applied by the authors[5] by post-processing MD data in order to estimate the asperity contact area $A_{\mathrm{asp}}(L)$ at a given load L based on the momentary positions of selected atoms and hence bridge the gap between MD and CM as follows. Firstly, one identifies all the N_k atoms which form the two rough sliders ($k = 1, 2$) confining the lubricant within the MD simulation box, see the yellow and blue atomic spheres in Fig. 1. Knowing the mass m_i of each of these atoms and having determined their positions $\vec{r}_i(t)$ at a given moment t of an MD simulation ($i = 1, 2, \ldots, N_k$ and $k = 1, 2$), eqn (2) immediately yields the mass density $\rho(\vec{r})$ at any point $\vec{r}$ in space,[10]

$$\rho(\vec{r}) = \sum_{i=1}^{N_k} m_i w(\vec{r} - \vec{r}_i, h), \quad (k = 1, 2), \tag{3}$$

as the sum of partial densities $m_i w(\vec{r} - \vec{r}_i, h)$ of the atoms in one of the two solid sliders. Thus the so-resulting moving smoothed (pseudo)particles are continuously distributed material densities characterized by a threshold value ρ_0 and a dimensionless smearing factor c_{smear}, which determines the amount of smoothing applied to the interfaces by setting the spatial smoothing length to $h = c_{\mathrm{smear}} r_{\mathrm{LJ}}$, where r_{LJ} represents the Lennard–Jones radius of the atoms which are smoothed, for further details see ref. 5. Note that in eqn (3) it was assumed that the atoms which form the rough sliders are all identical, *i.e.*, $h_i = h = \text{const.}$ and hence the total mass of the solid part Ω of the entire system of interest,[11]

$$\sum_{l=1}^{N_1+N_2} m_l = \int_{\Omega} \rho(\vec{r}) d^3 r. \tag{4}$$

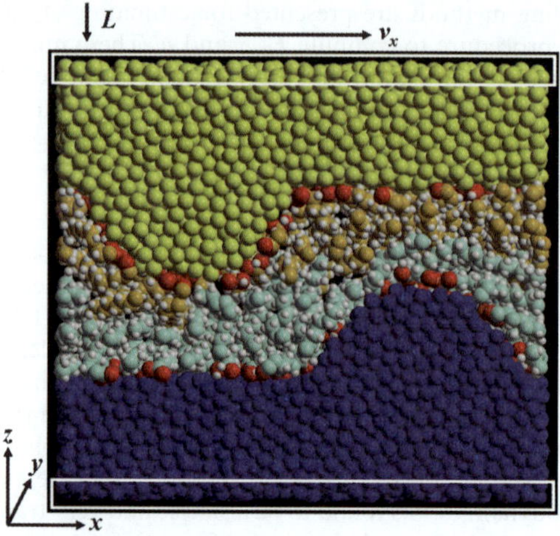

Fig. 1 Schematic MD-representation of the semi-spherical asperity system lubricated with stearic acid in its initial configuration before the equilibration period. The white boxes mark the atoms which are kept rigid throughout the simulations. The directions of load (L) and shear (v_x) are indicated as arrows. Colors: Fe (top)—yellow, Fe (bottom)—blue, C (top)—orange, C (bottom)—light blue, H—white, O—red. Different colours for Fe and C in the top and bottom halves of the system only serve to better show the sliding interface.

As illustrated in Sec. 3.3, $\rho(\vec{r})$ given by eqn (3) naturally envelopes the solid parts of a lubricated nanotribological system such that when solid–solid contact occurs, the solid parts fuse together into a single enveloped solid body. In our approach, the area corresponding to the minimal contour around the asperities in contact defines the instantaneous asperity contact area $A_{\mathrm{asp}}(L,t)$ at a given load L and moment t, of which the time average $\langle A_{\mathrm{asp}}(L,t)\rangle$, as it was shown in ref. 5 by using a third-order symmetric B-spline kernel $w(\vec{r} - \vec{r}_i,h)$ in eqn (3), yields a fairly good estimation for the asperity contact area $A_{\mathrm{asp}}(L)$ entering the three-term friction law from eqn (1).

2.1.2 Voronoi tessellation. An alternative to SPM, the Voronoi tessellation is another method to uniquely fill the space around some punctiform particles, called generators, based on their momentary positions.[12] The Voronoi cell (polyhedron) associated with a set of punctiform particles i ($i = 1, 2,..., N$) at a given moment t is the set of all spatial points $\vec{r}(t)$,

$$\Omega_i = \{\vec{r}(t) \in \mathbb{R}^3 \mid |\vec{r}(t) - \vec{r}_i(t)| \leq |\vec{r}(t) - \vec{r}_j(t)|, \quad \forall j \neq i\}, \tag{5}$$

which are at least as close to the position $\vec{r}_i(t)$ of the ith particle as to any other particle $j \neq i$ situated at $\vec{r}_j(t)$ ($j = 1, 2,..., N$). The union of all so-resulting closed and convex Voronoi polyhedra then defines the Voronoi tessellation,

$$\Omega_{\mathrm{tot}} = \bigcup_{i=1}^{N} \Omega_i, \quad \text{such that} \quad \bigcap_{i=1}^{N} \Omega_i = 0. \tag{6}$$

Among other properties, partitioning a finite spatial domain into Voronoi cells always provides information about the shape of dominant regions (aiming at pattern recognition, for example) and about the relationship between neighbors even when these are irregularly placed. These main features of the Voronoi tessellation make this construction method so successful in many research fields from natural to social sciences.[13] Particularly in condensed matter physics, the Voronoi construction is well established and has been widely used for eight decades leading to Wigner–Seitz cells in the real (direct) space and Brillouin zones in the reciprocal (inverse) space. Both cells are translationally and rotationally invariant unit cells centered around a single lattice node in one of the dual spaces.[14]

Thus, by performing a Voronoi tessellation of two asperities coming into contact, those nearest neighbors within the solid–solid interaction zone which belong to different asperities and share a common face can be immediately identified,

$$\Sigma_{ij} = \Omega_i \cap \Omega_j \neq 0; \quad \forall i = 1,\ldots, N^{(k)}_{\text{asp}}, \quad \forall j = 1,\ldots, N^{(l \neq k)}_{\text{asp}} \quad (k, l = 1, 2), \quad (7)$$

where $N^{(k)}_{\text{asp}}$ denotes the total number of particles in one of the two asperities. Having determined these common faces, the asperity contact area $A^{(V)}_{\text{asp}}(L)$ due to the Voronoi tessellation for a given load L is straightforwardly calculated as

$$A^{(V)}_{\text{asp}}(L) = \frac{1}{2} A\left(\bigcup_{i \neq j} \Sigma_{ij} \right) = \frac{1}{2} \sum_{i \neq j} A(\Sigma_{ij}), \quad (8)$$

with $A(\Sigma_{ij})$ denoting the area of Σ_{ij}.

Note that with the pairwise connection of the position of the punctiform particles whose Voronoi cells share a common edge, a dual structure of the Voronoi tessellation is obtained. This structure, apart from triangles, can also contain non-triangular polygons. If all these non-triangular polygons are then partitioned into triangles using line segments joining the vertices without intersecting each other, an additional tessellation called Delaunay triangulation results. Similarly to our post-processing SPM, see Sec. 2.1.1, the Delaunay triangulation can also provide a good estimate for the solvent-accessible surface around a solute and hence can be seen as a proper construction method to analyze contact areas in MD simulations.[15]

2.1.3 Least squares fitting of system parameters.

Assume that the friction force $F(L)$ as a function of the load L is known from MD simulations, *i.e.*, consider a finite set of values $F_i = F(L_i)$ ($i = 1, 2,\ldots, n$) together with their corresponding errors σ_i made while calculating the friction forces. Because these errors σ_i are normally distributed (not shown here), the χ-square merit function,[16]

$$\chi^2(F_0, \tau, \mu) = \sum_{i=1}^{n} \left[\frac{F_i - F_0 - \tau A_{\text{asp}}(L_i) - \mu L_i}{\sigma_i} \right]^2 \quad (9)$$

achieves its minimum with respect to the parameters F_0 (offset of the friction force), τ (effective shear strength) and μ (coefficient of friction), and for the given nanotribological system the three-term friction law in eqn (1) holds. This means that the partial derivatives of $\chi^2(F_0,\tau,\mu)$ with respect to F_0, τ and μ following from eqn (9) all vanish, and in order to determine these parameters one has to solve the system of linear equations

$$\begin{pmatrix} S_{11} & S_{12} & S_{13} \\ S_{12} & S_{22} & S_{23} \\ S_{13} & S_{23} & S_{33} \end{pmatrix} \begin{pmatrix} F_0 \\ \tau \\ \mu \end{pmatrix} = \begin{pmatrix} S_1 \\ S_2 \\ S_3 \end{pmatrix}, \quad (10)$$

for example by using Cramer's rule, where

$$\begin{cases} S_{11} = \sum_{i=1}^{n} \frac{1}{\sigma_i^2}, & S_{12} = \sum_{i=1}^{n} \frac{A_{\text{asp}}(L_i)}{\sigma_i^2}, & S_1 = \sum_{i=1}^{n} \frac{F_i}{\sigma_i^2} \\[2mm] S_{22} = \sum_{i=1}^{n} \frac{A^2_{\text{asp}}(L_i)}{\sigma_i^2}, & S_{13} = \sum_{i=1}^{n} \frac{L_i}{\sigma_i^2}, & S_2 = \sum_{i=1}^{n} \frac{F_i A_{\text{asp}}(L_i)}{\sigma_i^2} \\[2mm] S_{33} = \sum_{i=1}^{n} \frac{L_i^2}{\sigma_i^2}, & S_{23} = \sum_{i=1}^{n} \frac{L_i A_{\text{asp}}(L_i)}{\sigma_i^2}, & S_3 = \sum_{i=1}^{n} \frac{F_i L_i}{\sigma_i^2} \end{cases} \quad (11)$$

In addition, the error (variance) made by estimating F_0, τ and μ based on eqn (9) can be evaluated using eqn (11) and

$$\begin{cases} \sigma_{F_0}^2 = \sum_{i=1}^{n} \sigma_i^2 \left(\frac{\partial F_0}{\partial F_i}\right)^2 = \frac{1}{\Delta}\left(S_{22}S_{33} - S_{23}^2\right) \\[2mm] \sigma_{\tau}^2 = \sum_{i=1}^{n} \sigma_i^2 \left(\frac{\partial \tau}{\partial F_i}\right)^2 = \frac{1}{\Delta}\left(S_{11}S_{33} - S_{13}^2\right) , \\[2mm] \sigma_{\mu}^2 = \sum_{i=1}^{n} \sigma_i^2 \left(\frac{\partial \mu}{\partial F_i}\right)^2 = \frac{1}{\Delta}\left(S_{11}S_{22} - S_{12}^2\right) \end{cases} \qquad (12)$$

where $\Delta = S_{11}S_{22}S_{33} + 2S_{12}S_{13}S_{23} - S_{11}S_{23}^2 - S_{13}^2 S_{22} - S_{12}^2 S_{33}$ is the determinant of the system of linear equations in eqn (10). Apart from eqn (12), a further measure for the goodness-of-fit is provided directly by the χ-square merit function itself, recall eqn (9), when this $\chi^2(F_0,\tau,\mu)$ is determined for F_0, τ and μ obtained from eqn (10).

Note, however, that this least squares fitting of F_0, τ and μ properly works only as long as at least one load L_i exists such that $A_{\mathrm{asp}}(L_i) \neq 0$. If by chance, however, $A_{\mathrm{asp}}(L_i) = 0$ for all loads L_i considered, eqn (10) is replaced by

$$\begin{pmatrix} S_{11} & S_{13} \\ S_{13} & S_{33} \end{pmatrix} \begin{pmatrix} F_0 \\ \mu \end{pmatrix} = \begin{pmatrix} S_1 \\ S_3 \end{pmatrix}, \qquad (13)$$

which, once solved, provides F_0 and μ with an error (variance) of

$$\begin{cases} \sigma_{F_0}^2 = \sum_{i=1}^{n} \sigma_i^2 \left(\frac{\partial F_0}{\partial F_i}\right)^2 = \frac{S_{33}}{S_{11}S_{33} - S_{13}^2}, \\[2mm] \sigma_{\mu}^2 = \sum_{i=1}^{n} \sigma_i^2 \left(\frac{\partial \mu}{\partial F_i}\right)^2 = \frac{S_{11}}{S_{11}S_{33} - S_{13}^2} \end{cases} \qquad (14)$$

but the shear strength τ remains undefined. In this special case, one can also use the corresponding χ-square merit function,

$$\chi^2(F_0,\mu) = \sum_{i=1}^{n} \left(\frac{F_i - F_0 - \mu L_i}{\sigma_i}\right)^2 \qquad (15)$$

as an approach for measuring the goodness-of-fit, when no solid–solid contact occurs during the sliding.

2.2 Multiple asperity–asperity contact

The tribosystems studied in the first part of this work consist of two solid sliders with a single asperity, each covered with one monolayer of 66 molecules of stearic acid, for a model see Fig. 1. Two different asperity types are studied, one semi-spherical and one shaped like a slanted pyramid, both of which are initially 1.6 nm high. Each slider consists of 4050 atoms of amorphous Fe filling a volume of $7.42 \times 3.71 \times 2.00$ nm^3, of which the 670 furthest from the lubricant are kept rigid (white frames in Fig. 1). This number of atoms is equivalent to 12 monolayers of bcc (1 0 0) Fe and satisfies the requirement of having a substrate thickness equal to or greater than the asperity height.[17] The applied interatomic potentials, the propagating algorithm, the boundary conditions, the thermostatting scheme as well as the way the contact forces are calculated have been described elsewhere, *cf.* ref. 5.

The most important difference in the simulation procedure to previous work is the simulation duration Δt. While in ref. 5, Δt was 2.5 ns, allowing for a short equilibration period and a single asperity–asperity contact, in this work more than 19 ns are simulated for every load, allowing an asperity to pass an opposing one $p = 10$ times due to periodic boundary conditions in the x- and y-directions. At a sliding velocity of $v_x = 4$ ms^{-1}, one pass lasts approximately $T = 1.86$ ns. The subsequent nanoscopic run-in of the asperities is analysed at 16 loads ranging from 2.76–44.08 nN, which corresponds to 0.1–1.6 GPa measured over the nominal cross-section of the interface, for both examined systems. All simulations in this work were performed using the LAMMPS MD code.[18]

2.3 Sliding time dependence

2.3.1 Asperity contact area. At the beginning of the simulation, the lubricant molecules are evenly distributed over the substrate surfaces. As the two asperities approach each other during shear, the lubricant undergoes some initial restructuring, and if the local forces in the lubrication gap (which depend on load, shear velocity, asperity geometry, *etc.*) become sufficiently high, lubricant molecules situated on the asperities may be squeezed out and solid–solid contact occurs.

The momentary asperity contact area $A_{asp}(L,t)$ is calculated using the smooth particle post-processing scheme as introduced in ref. 5 and briefly described in Sec. 2.1.1. When superimposing these data for all calculated passes, it is evident that the time of the onset of contact $t_{cont}^{(p)}$ increases appreciably after the first pass. At loads where asperity contact occurs in almost every pass, $t_{cont}^{(p > 1)}$ fluctuates about a mean value greater than $t_{cont}^{(1)}$, whereas for loads where $A_{asp}(L,t)$ vanishes after several passes, $t_{cont}^{(p)} < t_{cont}^{(p + 1)}$ usually holds true, see Fig. 2.

As a general trend, it can be seen that the time-averaged contact area for a single pass

$$A_{asp}(L) = \langle A_{asp}(L,t) \rangle, \qquad \forall t \in [t_0^{(p)}, t_0^{(p)} + T], \tag{16}$$

where $t_0^{(p)}$ is the starting moment of pth pass of period T ($p = 1, 2,..., 10$), decreases with every pass irrespective of load. We have chosen to classify the types of asperity contact development as follows: (1) $A_{asp}(L) \approx 0$ for all L, (2) $A_{asp}(L)$ decreases monotonously with p, (3) $A_{asp}(L)$ decreases with p, but has a plateau for several passes, and (4) $A_{asp}(L)$ has a local maximum at $p > 1$. With the exception of the sporadic cases of the 3rd and the 4th type, asperity contact has virtually vanished after 5–6 passes.

This quite clear-cut behaviour of $A_{asp}(L)$ does not apply to the contact duration Δt_{asp}. Δt_{asp} and $A_{asp}(L)$ have a non-linear (approximately parabolic) relationship, meaning that even very small asperity surface areas can be in contact for considerable periods. Therefore, even after 7 passes, one may encounter values for Δt_{asp} which have only decreased to 30% of their initial or maximum values.

Fig. 3 shows complete maps of the asperity contact area as a function of time and load for both asperity types. The top map illustrates how even at medium to high loads, asperity contact may subside after the first pass (27.6 and 35.8 nN), whereas even for low loads, recurring asperity contact is possible (13.8 nN). In the bottom map it can be seen that for the slanted pyramid asperity there exist high loads (>38 nN) where, due to prior asperity deformation, no (or only negligible) asperity contact occurs, see Sec. 2.3.3. Interestingly, at the lowest load of 2.76 nN, asperity contact occurs only during the passes 4, 5, and 6.

2.3.2 Constitutive system parameters. The load dependence of the friction force differs considerably between the asperity types for $p = 1$, as can be seen in Fig. 4 (top). However, as p grows and the influence of solid–solid contact declines, the behaviour becomes almost identical, with the slope of the essentially linear load dependence for $p = 10$ leading to the same coefficient of friction μ for both systems.

The least squares fitting procedure described in Sec. 2.1.3 yields the system parameters as a function of the pass number p, shown in Fig. 4 (bottom). As in previous work by the authors,[5] here and in the following σ_i ($\forall i = 1, 2,..., n$) in eqn (11) is calculated based on the statistical inefficiency as introduced in ref. 19. The force

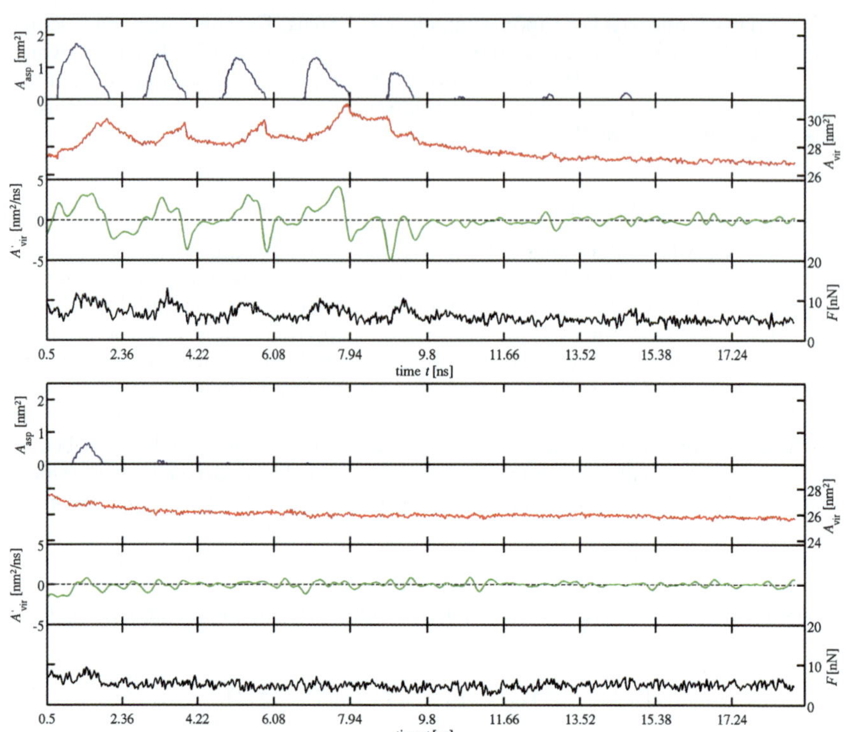

Fig. 2 Time development of the asperity contact area $A_{asp}(L,t)$, the "virtual asperity surface area" $A_{vir}(L,t)$ (see text), its filtered time-derivative $A'_{vir}(L,t)$ and the block-averaged friction force $F(L,t)$ for the semi-spherical (top) and the slanted pyramid asperity (bottom) at $L = 24.8$ nN. Tick marks along the time axis denote the beginning of a new pass. The equilibration period of 0.5 ns is not shown.

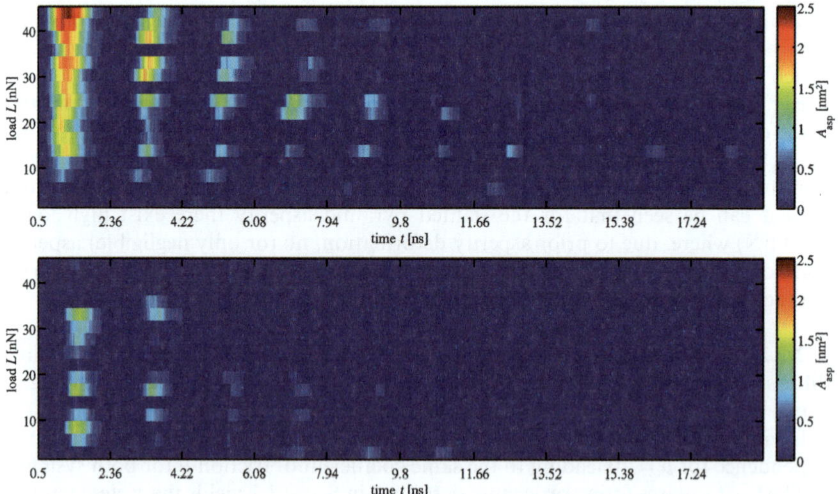

Fig. 3 Maps of the asperity contact area $A_{asp}(L,t)$ as a function of time and load for the semi-spherical (top) and the slanted pyramid asperity (bottom). The tick marks along the time axis denote the beginning of a new pass. The equilibration period of 0.5 ns is not shown.

offset F_0 and the coefficient of friction μ are well-conditioned and exhibit stable behaviour from one pass to the next. The shear strength τ, however, is more problematic since it becomes highly ill-conditioned for passes in which at none of the simulated loads appreciable contact $A_{\mathrm{asp}}(L)$ occurs, as already explained in Sec. 2.1.3. This becomes more and more likely for higher pass numbers, as the system has already run in and asperity tips have blunted, leading to values for τ either off by two orders of magnitude or even negative, with $\Delta\tau$ becoming very large accordingly. Therefore in practice the criteria which lead to the omission of τ from the fitting procedure have to be reformulated according to the following.

It was found that the system parameter τ starts becoming ill-conditioned (increased $\Delta\tau$, *etc.*) if any of the following occurs: (a) the number of loads for which $A_{\mathrm{asp}}(L) > 0$ drops below 3, (b) the maximum $A_{\mathrm{asp}}(L)$ for a given pass drops below 0.2 nm^2, or (c) the value for $A_{\mathrm{asp}}(L)$ averaged over all loads which have asperity contact drops below 0.03 nm^2. Moreover, τ diverges or becomes negative if any of the following occurs: (a) the number of loads for which $A_{\mathrm{asp}}(L) > 0$ drops below 2, (b) the maximum $A_{\mathrm{asp}}(L)$ for a given pass drops below 0.06 nm^2, or (c) the value for $A_{\mathrm{asp}}(L)$ averaged over all loads which have asperity contact drops below 0.022 nm^2. By comparison, with the potential parameters used, the cross-section of an Fe atom is roughly 0.064 nm^2. For these cases, it makes sense to perform the least squares fitting for F_0 and μ only, as described in Sec. 2.1.3, slightly altering the resulting values. In Fig. 4 (bottom), only those values are shown which meet the stricter of the criteria discussed, and ill-conditioned values of τ are omitted. The results shown there strongly suggest that F_0, τ and μ are indeed system parameters, namely

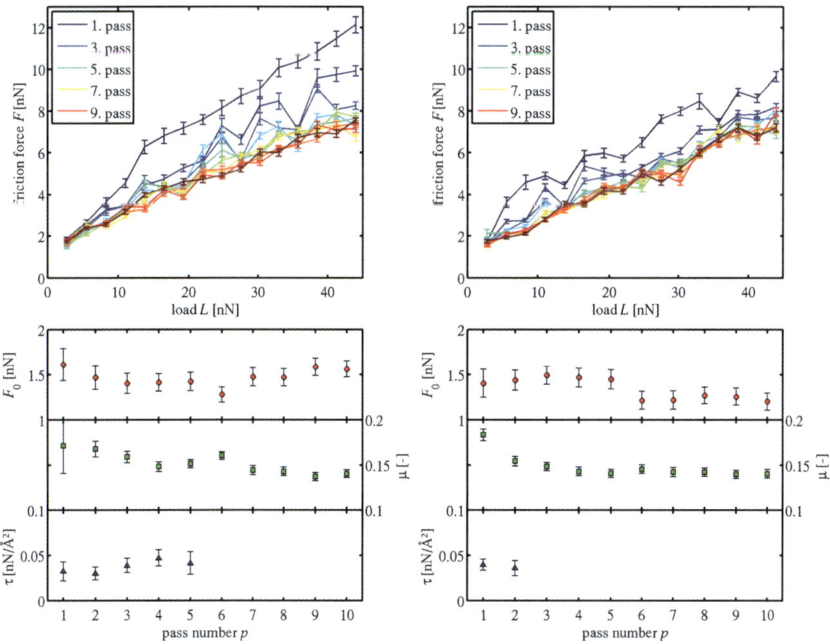

Fig. 4 Top: load-*versus*-friction behaviour of the semi-spherical (left) and the slanted pyramid (right) asperity. Results for the individual passes p are shown superimposed. The error bars represent the statistical inefficiencies of the MD friction force values. Bottom: development of the system parameters F_0, μ, and τ as a function of the pass number p for the semi-spherical (left) and the slanted pyramid (right) asperity. The error bars are ΔF_0, $\Delta\mu$, and $\Delta\tau$ from the least squares fitting procedure.

$$\begin{cases} F_0^{(p)} \simeq F_0 \\ \tau^{(p)} \simeq \tau \\ \mu^{(p)} \simeq \mu \end{cases}, \qquad \forall p = 2, 3..., 10. \tag{17}$$

Here, $p = 1$ was excluded since the first pass constitutes a nanoscopic run-in period where most of the asperity deformation occurs, which leads either to an outlying value for μ or a large $\Delta\mu$.

The relative standard deviations $\sigma_{F_0} = 6.8\%$, $\sigma_\mu = 7.8\%$, and $\sigma_\tau = 18.2\%$ for the semi-spherical asperity, and $\sigma_{F_0} = 8.8\%$, $\sigma_\mu = 8.9\%$, and $\sigma_\tau = 7.1\%$ for the slanted pyramid asperity. In the latter case, however, σ_μ falls to 3.3% when dropping the value at $p = 1$.

2.3.3 Asperity deformation. One quantity which is easily calculated using smooth particle post-processing is the total Fe surface area $A_{Fe}(L,t)$. During asperity contact, one can see the decrease of $A_{Fe}(L,t)$ due to the loss of $2A_{asp}(L,t)$. One may therefore be tempted to calculate $A_{asp}(L,t)$ from $A_{Fe}(L,t)$ directly, saving considerable computational effort, but this would only be accurate if $A_{Fe}(L,t)$ remains otherwise constant for the entire duration of contact, which is not the case. So by adding $2A_{asp}(L,t)$ to $A_{Fe}(L,t)$ and subtracting an estimate for the (constant) non-asperity Fe surface area ($2 \times xy$-cross-section $- 2 \times$ asperity base), we obtain the "virtual asperity surface area" $A_{vir}(L,t)$, which, assuming only very little compressibility of the iron and therefore nearly constant volume, is a reasonable measure for the surface-to-volume ratio and hence the shape of the asperities. This holds true if the non-asperity surface of the system does not appreciably change its shape throughout the simulation.

By numerically calculating the time-derivative of $A_{vir}(L,t)$,

$$A'_{vir}(L, t) = \frac{\partial A_{vir}(L, t)}{\partial t}, \tag{18}$$

one can now identify the times when the shape of the asperities changes the most, which may be interpreted as a geometrical indicator for asperity deformation.

Fig. 2 shows a side-by-side comparison of the time development of $A_{asp}(L,t)$, $A_{vir}(L,t)$, $A'_{vir}(L,t)$ and $F(L,t)$ for both systems with different asperity geometries at $L = 24.8$ nN. For clarity, $A'_{vir}(L,t)$ was filtered using a cubic B-spline kernel 600 ps wide, and $F(L,t)$ was block-averaged with a block size of 20 ps. Generally speaking, $A_{vir}(L,t)$ tends to decrease over time, which reflects the relaxation of the surface in order to minimise the surface-to-volume ratio. The decrease of $A_{vir}(L,t)$ is in the range of 0–7% and is greatest if there is little or no asperity contact. At high loads, deformation of both asperities may take place before contact would have occurred for the first time, sometimes preventing contact altogether. This can be seen clearly in the behaviour of $A_{asp}(L,t)$ and $A'_{vir}(L,t)$ for the slanted pyramid asperity at several loads greater than 12 nN. For example, looking at the top-left corner of the bottom map in Fig. 5, blue regions for the four highest loads indicate a considerable initial decrease of the asperity surface, while a comparison with the respective part in Fig. 3 shows that little to no asperity contact occurs during the first pass.

This surface relaxation is interrupted by local increases and sharp decreases of $A_{vir}(L,t)$ due to asperity contact. As can be expected, the local, usually linear increases coincide with the times of asperity contact, where the solid bridge is drawn out into a "wire", thus increasing the surface area. As soon as contact ends and the wire breaks, $A_{vir}(L,t)$ decreases, usually sharply at first as the two loose ends of the broken wire quickly retract, then more moderately as the shapes of the asperities relax.

In rare cases it can occur that $A_{vir}(L,t)$ decreases sharply not at the end but at the onset of asperity contact (*e.g.* semi-spherical, $L = 24.8$ nN, $p = 5$, *cf.* Fig. 2 and 6, center). Here, an unrelaxed dangling wire end snaps onto the opposing asperity, thus reducing the surface area very quickly.

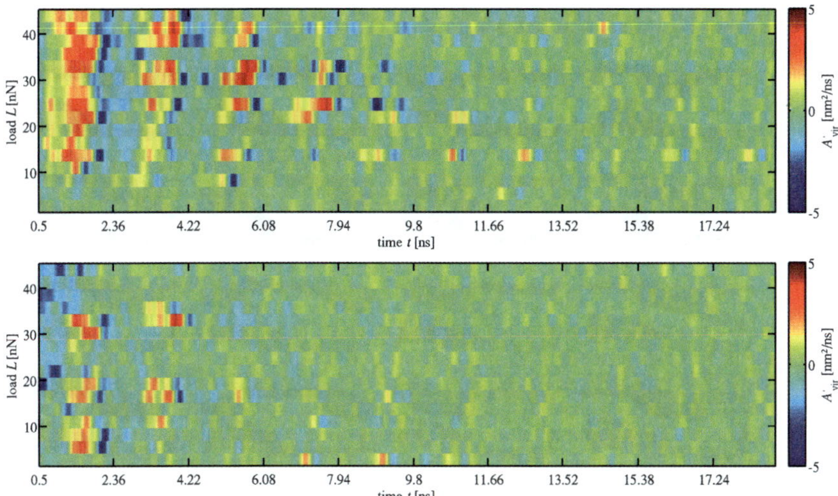

Fig. 5 Maps of the filtered time-derivative of the "virtual asperity surface area", $A'_{\mathrm{vir}}(L,t)$, as a function of time and load for the semi-spherical (top) and the slanted pyramid asperity (bottom). $A'_{\mathrm{vir}}(L,t)$ is a measure for the rate at which the asperities deform. The tick marks along the time axis denote the beginning of a new pass. The equilibration period of 0.5 ns is not shown.

Asperity contacts with maxima greater than 0.5 nm² are usually reflected as increases in the friction force $F(L,t)$, see Fig. 2. This applies to low and medium loads (up to 30 nN) in particular. At high loads, smaller increases are usually buried in the noisy $F(L,t)$-signal. Fig. 5 shows complete maps of the asperity deformation as a function of time and load for both asperity types. Yellow, orange and red areas denote loads and times where the surface-to-volume ratio of the asperities increases, as is typically the case when the two asperities are in contact, whereas light and dark blue areas are dominated by relaxation of the asperities, which occurs either after contact (when the drawn-out dangling ends of the broken solid bridge retract) or at the very beginning of a high-load simulation (*cf.* the bottom map), where high pressure and shear lead to asperity deformation without solid–solid contact. In the green parts of the maps, the virtual asperity surface area does not change. Note that the "creeping relaxation" of asperities (as can be seen for $t > 9.8$ ns in the top of Fig. 2) cannot be visualized in these maps due to the small gradients involved.

The development of the Fe surface geometries over time is illustrated in Fig. 6 for the semi-spherical asperity and in Fig. 7 for the slanted pyramid at a load of 24.8 nN. As can also be seen in Fig. 2 (top), the first five passes in Fig. 6 are dominated by intense asperity contact. The changes in the shape of the asperities over time are evident. Note the image of pass 5 at 1.0 ns, which shows the system shortly after the unrelaxed protrusion of the top asperity has snapped onto the lower one, instantly reducing A_{vir} by more than 1 nm². The final shape of the asperities is already visible after pass number 5, when asperity contact and plastic deformation have become negligible. It now looks very similar to the slanted-pyramid asperity in Fig. 7, where the two asperities engage in moderate contact only during the first pass, which blunts the tips sufficiently to prevent further contact. Therefore, the final configuration can already be seen during pass number 3. Note that the first 0.5 ns visible in Fig. 2 (bottom) indicate that deformation of the asperities already takes place before they first touch, which may reduce the overall intensity of asperity contact. The fact that the final shape of this asperity type does not differ very much from its initial one, and that the final geometries of both asperity types (semi-spherical and slanted pyramid) are more similar than they are different,

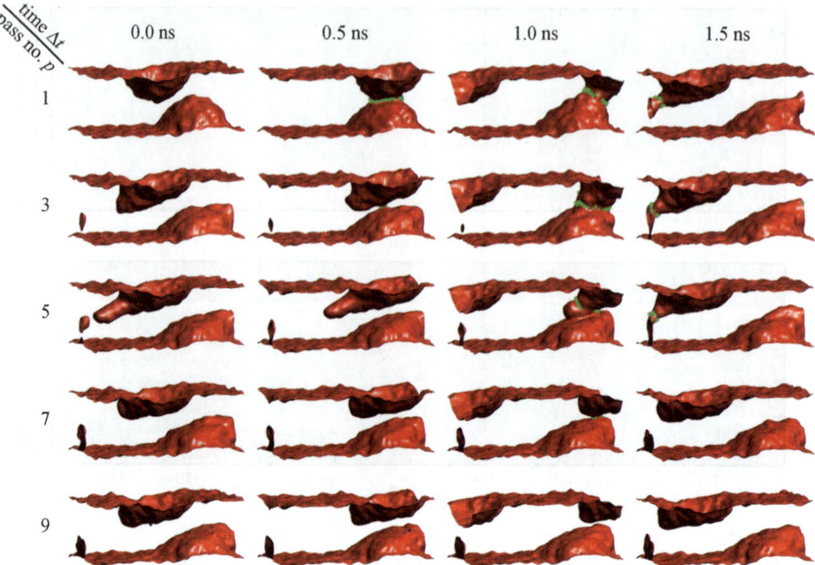

Fig. 6 Snapshots of an SPM-representation of the semi-spherical asperity system at $L = 24.8$ nN for sliding passes 1, 3, 5, 7, and 9, and at four equally spaced times during each pass. The lubricant molecules are not shown for clarity. The green bead chains mark the boundary of the contact zone calculated with SPM. The top left image shows the initial configuration after the equilibration period, and the bottom right one shows a configuration near the end of the simulation.

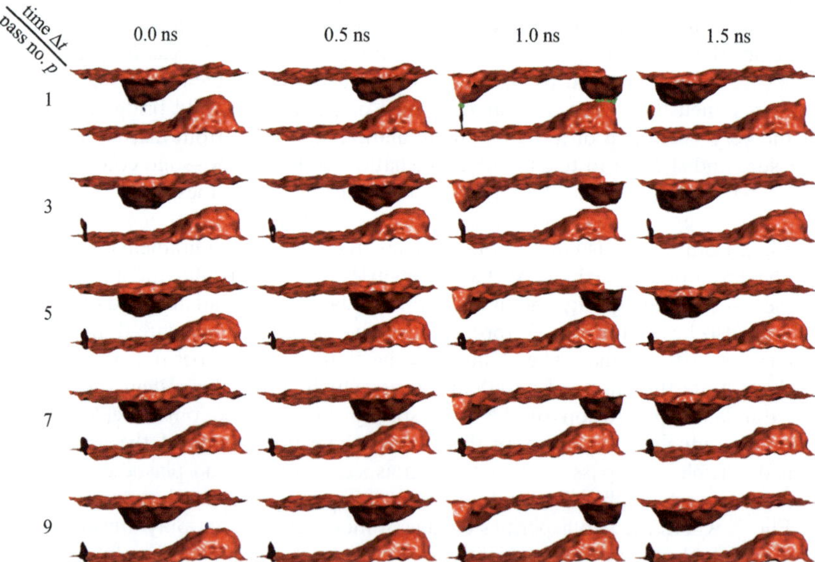

Fig. 7 Snapshots of an SPM-representation of the slanted pyramid asperity system at $L = 24.8$ nN for sliding passes 1, 3, 5, 7, and 9, and at four equally spaced times during each pass. The lubricant molecules are not shown for clarity. The green bead chains mark the boundary of the contact zone calculated with SPM. The top left image shows the initial configuration after the equilibration period, and the bottom right one shows a configuration near the end of the simulation.

suggests that the (blunted) slanted pyramid is the final asperity geometry in a unidirectional boundary-lubricated sliding simulation/experiment, regardless of the initial configuration.

2.3.4 Smooth particle post-processing *versus* Voronoi tessellation.

The results obtained for $A_{asp}(L,t)$ with SPM were compared with those from a Voronoi tessellation of the simulation cell.

For the Voronoi tessellation, the MD geometry data for each time step is modified in accordance with the contact atom counting procedure in ref. 5, changing the asperity affiliation of those atoms which migrate from one asperity to the other during contact at the appropriate time step. This ensures that single atoms or small groups of atoms which have left their initial asperity cannot falsely contribute to the contact area.

Next, a Delaunay triangulation of the simulation box is performed for each time step from which the Voronoi cells are calculated. Based on the modified affiliation tables mentioned above, those Voronoi cells are determined which belong to one asperity and neighbour a cell belonging to the other one.

When all contacting cells are known, the total Voronoi cell contact surface can be calculated. However, when comparing the time development of this quantity with the results obtained with SPM, one notices that the Voronoi method estimates the contact area $\sim 50\%$ higher on average and up to $\sim 250\%$ higher towards the end of contact, *cf.* Fig. 8 (a). This is hardly surprising, as the SPM-based $A_{asp}(L,t)$ is defined only by the contact zone's boundary, whereas the Voronoi-based $A_{asp}^{(V)}(L,t)$ is calculated taking into account the topography of the contact zone, where its roughness enters into the result.

The comparability between the results obtained with the two methods is greatly improved by calculating, weighting and averaging the normal vectors of all Voronoi cell faces contributing to the contact zone and then projecting the entire contact zone onto the average contact plane defined by the resulting normal vector. This eliminates the contact topography from the Voronoi approach. Fig. 8 (a) compares the results for the time development of the asperity contact area (for a load $L = 22.04$ nN and the semi-spherical asperity geometry) calculated with the Voronoi-method (total and projected) to those from SPM. On average, the asperity contact areas for the three methods are 2.009, 1.184, and 1.185 nm^2, respectively, so the relative difference between the projected Voronoi method and SPM is below 0.1% in this example.

Although the average and the maximum values for the asperity contact area in Fig. 8 coincide, one can see that at the onset of contact, SPM yields higher values than projected Voronoi, while from 1.5 ns on, the opposite is the case. This may be attributed to the increasing discrepancy between the position of the contact plane onto which the total Voronoi contact zone is projected and the position of the contact zone obtained with SPM, which does not take into account asperity affiliations, but only searches for the smallest solid cross-section. Fig. 8(b) and (c) compare the time development of the normal vectors defining the average contact planes yielded by the two methods. The average SPM contact plane is a best-fit plane of the bounding points. Evidently, the two normal vectors behave very similarly until maximum contact is reached, but as the solid bridge between the asperities is drawn out horizontally, the SPM normal vector starts rotating about the y-axis and ends up pointing in x-direction when contact ends, while the Voronoi normal vector, though also slightly rotating about the y-axis, remains virtually parallel to the z-axis (*cf.* Fig. 8(f)). The differences in definition of the asperity contact area between the Voronoi method and SPM are therefore most evident towards the end of contact, explaining the behavior of the curves in Fig. 8(a). The verticals in Fig. 8(a) through (c) indicate the points in time which are shown in the 3D illustrations in the right column of Fig. 8.

Taking into account that SPM can estimate $A_{asp}(L,t)$ ten times faster than the Voronoi method and that it does not require any asperity affiliation tables (which cannot always be reliably calculated, especially when considering multiple pass

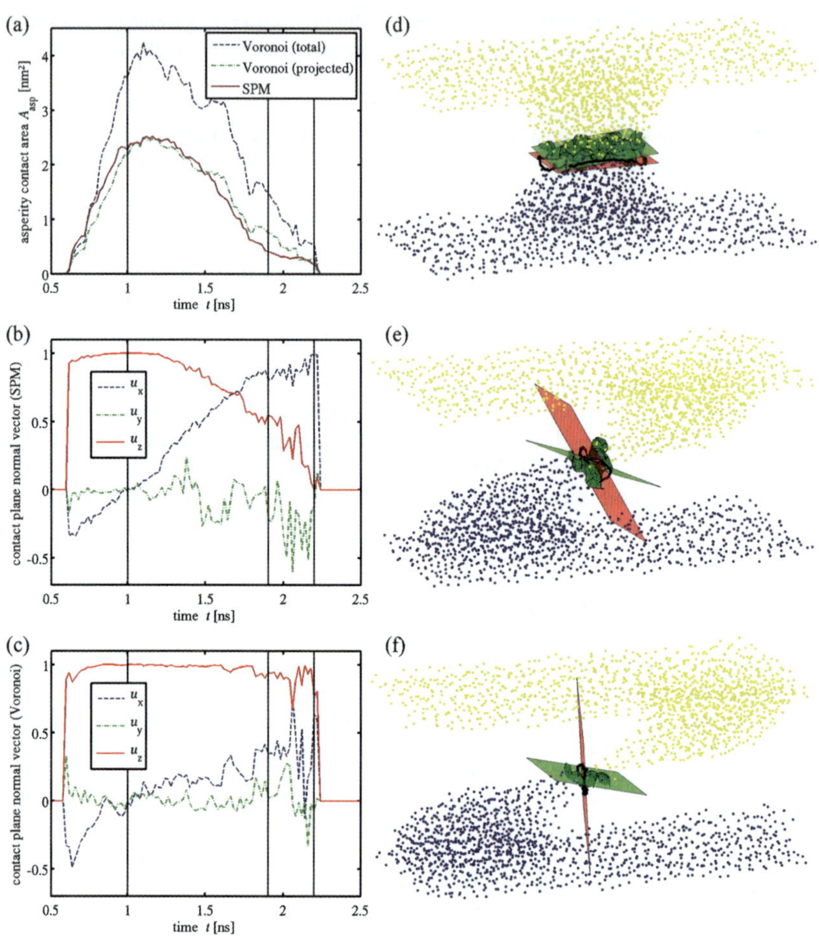

Fig. 8 (a) Comparison of the results for the asperity contact area for a semi-spherical asperity obtained with the Voronoi method (total and projected) and SPM. (b) Time development of the components of the normalized normal vector $\vec{u}$ of the average SPM contact plane. (c) Time development of the components of the normalized normal vector $\vec{u}$ of the average Voronoi contact plane. (d)–(f) 3D-illustrations of the boundary lubrication simulation at 1.0, 1.9 and 2.2 ns, respectively, as indicated by the verticals in (a)–(c). Lubricant molecules have been deleted for clarity. Fe atoms of the lower slider are shown in blue, those of the upper slider in yellow. The Voronoi contact area is shown as a set of dark green polygons, encompassed by the average Voronoi contact plane as a light green rectangle. The boundary of the SPM contact zone is shown as a black band, with the average SPM contact plane shown as a light red rectangle.

contact), it is absolutely feasible to calculate $A_{\mathrm{asp}}(L,t)$ with SPM if no information about the internal structure of the contact zone is required.

3 Derjaguin-form

An interesting particular form of the three-term friction law in eqn (1), when $A_{\mathrm{asp}}(L) = 0$ for all loads L considered, reads

$$F(L) = F_0 + \mu L \tag{19}$$

and comprises the Amontons–Coulomb term μL, which describes the load-controlled friction, as well as a non-vanishing load-independent friction force offset

F_0. This offset F_0 was first identified and introduced to tribology by Derjaguin in 1934 based on purely theoretical considerations.[3] He argued that the presence of $F_0 \neq 0$ in the friction law is a direct consequence of the cohesion forces between molecules within the lubricant, see also ref. 20.

Preliminary MD simulations by the authors on boundary-lubricated nanosystems, which obey the Derjaguin-form of the friction law, revealed that non-vanishing values for F_0 occur when the lubricant is less ordered within the nanotribological systems. Motivated by this visual finding, in the following, a first attempt is made to relate the friction force offset F_0 to variously estimated entropies of the lubricant, which are supposed to measure the structural disorder.

3.1 Entropy estimation

Beyond the contributions S_{tr} and S_{rot} arising from the translational and rotational motions of the entire system, the configurational entropy S_{config} also contributes to the total entropy S_{tot} of a given system. Being only related to the position of the constituent particles, the configurational entropy S_{config} can be seen as a measure of the structural order within the system and is decomposed into a conformational S_{conf} and vibrational S_{vib} part. Independently of which contribution S to S_{tot} is to be determined for a given positional configuration ξ of particles, this can be at least in principle directly obtained from the Shannon entropy of the joint probability density function (PDF) $\rho_\xi(\xi)$ assigned to ξ,[21]

$$S = -k_B \int d\xi \rho_\xi(\xi) \ln \rho_\xi(\xi), \tag{20}$$

where k_B is the Boltzmann constant. Note that for the sake of simplicity, in this expression of S the temperature-dependent constant occurring due to the integration of the PDF in the momentum space was omitted. Unfortunately, except for some model systems, $\rho_\xi(\xi)$ cannot be computed with sufficient accuracy using MD simulations,[22] and hence the expression on the right hand side of eqn (20) has to be approximated.

The most commonly used approach for the PDF in literature is the quasi-harmonic (Gaussian) one where the canonical PDF $\rho_\xi(\xi)$ of particle motion is assumed in the form of a multivariate Gaussian probability density,[23]

$$\rho_\xi(\xi) = \frac{1}{(2\pi)^{3N/2} \det C} \exp\left(-\frac{1}{2} \Delta \xi^{\mathrm{T}} C^{-1} \Delta \xi\right). \tag{21}$$

Here the $3N \times 3N$ covariance (super)matrix C is given by

$$C = \langle \Delta \xi \Delta \xi^{\mathrm{T}} \rangle, \quad \text{with} \quad \Delta \xi \, \Delta \xi^{\mathrm{T}} = \begin{pmatrix} C_{11} & C_{12} & \cdots & C_{1j} & \cdots & C_{1N} \\ C_{21} & C_{22} & \cdots & C_{2j} & \cdots & C_{2N} \\ \vdots & \vdots & \ddots & \vdots & & \vdots \\ C_{i1} & C_{i2} & \cdots & C_{ij} & \cdots & C_{iN} \\ \vdots & \vdots & & \vdots & \ddots & \vdots \\ C_{N1} & C_{N2} & & C_{Nj} & & C_{NN} \end{pmatrix} \tag{22}$$

and N being the total number of particles in the investigated system. The two-particle covariance matrix C_{ij}, on the other hand, is written as

$$C_{ij} = \Delta \xi_i \, \Delta \xi_j^{\mathrm{T}} = \begin{pmatrix} \Delta x_i \Delta x_j & \Delta x_i \Delta y_j & \Delta x_i \Delta z_j \\ \Delta y_i \Delta x_j & \Delta y_i \Delta y_j & \Delta y_i \Delta z_j \\ \Delta z_i \Delta x_j & \Delta z_i \Delta y_j & \Delta z_i \Delta z_j \end{pmatrix}, \quad (i,j = 1, \ldots, N) \tag{23}$$

by compacting the Cartesian components of the positional deviations into a single column matrix,

$$\Delta\xi = \xi - \langle\xi\rangle = \begin{pmatrix} \Delta\xi_1 \\ \vdots \\ \Delta\xi_i \\ \vdots \\ \Delta\xi_N \end{pmatrix}, \qquad \text{where } \Delta\xi_i = \begin{pmatrix} \Delta\xi_i^{(1)} \\ \Delta\xi_i^{(2)} \\ \Delta\xi_i^{(3)} \end{pmatrix} \equiv \begin{pmatrix} \Delta x_i \\ \Delta y_i \\ \Delta z_i \end{pmatrix}. \tag{24}$$

Thus any element of the covariance (super)matrix C reads

$$\langle\Delta\xi_i^{(k)}\Delta\xi_j^{(l)}\rangle = \langle\xi_i^{(k)}\xi_j^{(l)}\rangle - \langle\xi_i^{(k)}\rangle\langle\xi_j^{(l)}\rangle, \qquad \text{with } k,l = 1(x),\, 2(y),\, 3(z) \tag{25}$$

and the angle brackets denote time averages taken over the data acquisition period of the simulation.

Particularizing eqn (21) for the center of mass of the entire system consisting of N particles of different masses m_i $(i = 1,\dots, N)$,

$$\vec{R}_{\mathrm{CM}}(t) = \frac{1}{m}\sum_{i=1}^{N} m_i\vec{r}_i(t), \qquad \text{where } m = \sum_{i=1}^{N} m_i, \tag{26}$$

eqn (20) immediately yields for the translational contribution to the total molar entropy,[24]

$$S_{\mathrm{tr}} = R\ln\left[\prod_{k=1}^{3}\left(\frac{e^2 m k_{\mathrm{B}} T}{\hbar^2}\right)^{1/2}\sigma_{\xi^{(k)}}\right], \tag{27}$$

where $\hbar = h/(2\pi)$ stands for the reduced Planck constant, e denotes the Euler number, R is the universal (molar) gas constant, T the constant temperature, and σ_x, σ_y and σ_z are the principal root-mean-square (RMS) fluctuations of the center of mass. Similarly, the rotational contribution to the molar entropy S_{rot} is obtained as[25]

$$S_{\mathrm{rot}} = R\ln\left[8\pi^2\left(\frac{e k_{\mathrm{B}} T}{2\pi\hbar^2}\right)^{3/2}(I_x I_y I_z)^{1/2}\right] \tag{28}$$

by assuming a symmetry number of unit magnitude and inserting the principal moments I_x, I_y and I_z as eigenvalues of the inertia tensor I built up with the elements[26]

$$I_{kl} = \sum_{i=1}^{N} m_i\left(\langle\xi_i'\rangle^2\delta_{kl} - \langle\xi_i'^{(k)}\rangle\langle\xi_i'^{(l)}\rangle\right), \qquad \text{where } k,l = 1(x),\, 2(y),\, 3(z), \tag{29}$$

determined using the atomic positions ξ_i' with respect to the center of mass of the investigated system.

The common idea behind various estimations for S_{vib} known in literature is the mapping of each vibrational eigenmode of the analyzed system onto a well-defined frequency of a simple one-dimensional quantum harmonic oscillator.[27] In order to proceed in this manner, one has to first diagonalize the symmetric covariance (super)matrix C from eqn (22) using an orthogonal coordinate transformation, $i.e.$,

$$T^{\mathrm{T}}CT = \Lambda = \mathrm{diag}(\lambda_1, \lambda_2,\dots, \lambda_{3N}) \tag{30}$$

Here the diagonal matrix Λ consists of $3N$ eigenvalues $\lambda_J \equiv \lambda_j^{(l)}$ labelled with a composite index $J = 3(j-1) + l$, for example, such that the Jth column of the $3N \times 3N$ orthogonal matrix T is the eigenvector corresponding to λ_J, called the principal mode, and $\boldsymbol{T}^{\mathrm{T}}$ is the transpose of $\boldsymbol{T}$. Usually, the eigenvectors are also normalized, or alternatively one applies an orthonormal transformation in eqn (30) from the beginning to diagonalize $\boldsymbol{C}$.[28] At the end of the diagonalization, each eigenvector describes a single correlated displacement of particles relative to $\langle\xi\rangle$ in a multidimensional space, and the eigenvalue associated with this eigenvector gives the amplitude of the collective motion, *i.e.*, the mean-square fluctuation in the direction of that principal mode.[29] Commonly, eigenvalues are arranged in decreasing order $\lambda_1 \geq \lambda_2 \geq ... \geq \lambda_{3N} \geq 0$ and the corresponding normalized eigenvectors $\boldsymbol{V}_J$ ($J = 1,..., 3N$) as columns form the orthonormal matrix $\boldsymbol{V}$, which is equal to $\boldsymbol{T}$ only if the transformation in eqn (30) is an orthonormal one. Note that by diagonalizing $\boldsymbol{C}$ as defined in eqn (22), three eigenvalues will correspond to the collective translational motion, three more to the rotation, and only the remaining $3N - 6$ modes are purely vibrational.

Once the $3N - 6$ vibrational eigenmodes are identified, the frequencies ω_J of the associated one-dimensional quantum harmonic oscillators are calculated relating these to the classical variance $\langle\Delta\xi_J^2\rangle = \lambda_J$ of the uncorrelated particle coordinates using the equipartition theorem,

$$m_J\omega_J^2\lambda_J = k_{\mathrm{B}}T, \qquad (J = 1,2,...3N - 6), \tag{31}$$

which holds reasonably well as long as $\hbar\omega_J \ll k_{\mathrm{B}}T$. Summing up the analytically known vibrational entropies $S_{\mathrm{vib}}^{(J)}$ directly obtained from eqn (20) for all associated quantum harmonic oscillators $J = 1, 2,..., 3N - 6$, immediately results in the vibrational contribution to the total molar entropy within the quasi-harmonic approach as[30]

$$S_{\mathrm{vib}} = R\sum_{J=1}^{3N-6}\frac{\beta\hbar\omega_J}{\exp(\beta\hbar\omega_J) - 1} - R\sum_{J=1}^{3N-6}\ln[1 - \exp(-\beta\hbar\omega_J)], \tag{32}$$

where $\beta = (k_{\mathrm{B}}T)^{-1}$. Schlitter in his *ad hoc* quantum mechanical approximation[31] provided an upper bound to S_{vib} and hence to the configurational entropy in most systems with

$$S_{\mathrm{Schl}} = \frac{1}{2}R\sum_{J=1}^{3N-6}\ln\left[1 + \frac{e^2}{(\beta\hbar\omega_J)^2}\right] = \frac{1}{2}R\ln\left[\prod_{J=1}^{3N-6}\left(1 + \frac{k_{\mathrm{B}}Te^2}{\hbar^2}m_I\lambda_I\right)\right]$$

$$\approx \frac{1}{2}R\ln\det\left(1 + \frac{k_{\mathrm{B}}Te^2}{\hbar^2}\boldsymbol{M\Lambda}\right) = \frac{1}{2}R\ln\det\left(1 + \frac{k_{\mathrm{B}}Te^2}{\hbar^2}\boldsymbol{MC}\right) > S_{\mathrm{vib}}, \tag{33}$$

which correctly reproduces both the quantum and the classical mechanical limits of the entropy ($S_{\mathrm{Schl}} = 0$ if $T \to 0$, and $S_{\mathrm{Schl}} \propto \ln T$ if $T \to \infty$) and is not singular even if the $3N \times 3N$ covariance (super)matrix $\boldsymbol{C}$ is.[32] In eqn (33) $\boldsymbol{1}$ represents the $3N \times 3N$ unit matrix and $\boldsymbol{M}$ represents the mass (super)matrix introduced as formed with $\boldsymbol{M}_{ij} = m_i\delta_{ij}\boldsymbol{1}_{3 \times 3}$, δ_{ij} is the Kronecker symbol and $\boldsymbol{1}_{3 \times 3}$ the 3×3 unit matrix. Note also that $\boldsymbol{MC} = \boldsymbol{M}^{1/2}\boldsymbol{CM}^{1/2}$ is the mass-weighted covariance (super)matrix built up with the Cartesian components of the mass-weighted positional deviations, namely $\boldsymbol{M}_{ii}^{1/2}\boldsymbol{C}_{ij}\boldsymbol{M}_{jj}^{1/2} = \sqrt{m_i}\Delta\xi_i\left(\sqrt{m_j}\Delta\xi_j\right)^{\mathrm{T}}$,[28] which, once diagonalized, leads to mass-weighted mean-square fluctuations along the eigenvectors.[33] By removing the translational and rotational motions of the center of mass of the system by a least squares fit, for example, S_{Schl} will differ from that of the unfitted system, but its value may still be used for relative comparisons with S_{vib}.[34]

3.2 Substrate roughness, lubricant type and surface coverage

Snapshots of all systems analyzed in the second part of this work are shown in the insets of Fig. 9. They differ from those in the first part in several aspects, most notably in the lack of large asperities. In principle, the two opposing solid sliders each consist of 6 monolayers (ML) of bcc Fe exposing a (1 0 0) face with a square area of 3.71×3.71 nm^2. The topmost 3 ML of the top slider as well as the bottommost 3 ML of the bottom slider are kept rigid in order to account for the underlying bulk solid and to facilitate the movement control of the respective counteracting bodies. Each slider is covered with lubricant molecules of either stearic acid, oleic acid or methyl stearate. The functional groups are adsorbed to the solid surface, while the aliphatic tails extend away from the surface at an angle depending on the surface coverage, forming a close-packed monolayer. These systems are periodically replicated in the x- and y-directions to represent infinite surfaces, thus avoiding boundary effects.

The following variations of the basic models described above were considered: (1) introduction of nano surface roughness R_a in the form of small asperities ranging from 1 to 4 monolayers of Fe bcc (1 0 0) in height, (2) substituting the crystalline with an amorphous substrate, which implies a surface roughness R_a equivalent to $\sim$0.5 ML Fe bcc (1 0 0) roughness, and (3) variation of the lubricant surface coverage η (35 or 56 molecules/surface).

Shear simulations were carried out with the tribosystems described above, where the bottom substrate was kept fixed, and the sliding velocity v_x of the top substrate was ramped to 4 m s^{-1} and then kept constant. A Langevin thermostat kept all non-rigid Fe atoms at 300 K. An initial equilibration phase of 0.5 ns was followed by a data acquisition phase of 1.5 ns. The load was applied uniformly to the top three monolayers of Fe of the top slider in the $-z$-direction and varied within a range of 1.38–22.04 nN. At least three different loads were simulated per configuration. The friction force was calculated by determining the x-component of the force which the atoms of the top slider and the lubricant exert on the bottom Fe-substrate. Averaged over the entire data acquisition period, these friction forces are shown as a function of load in Fig. 9. The systems analyzed in the next section were chosen in such a way that all systems represented by squares in Fig. 9 have $F_0 \approx 0$, whereas all other systems have $F_0 > 0$.

3.3   Friction force offset *versus* lubricant order

The friction-*versus*-load data in Fig. 9 are used to fit the constitutive system parameters F_0 and μ for the nine analyzed tribosystems, shown in Fig. 10. The error bars are ΔF_0 and $\Delta \mu$ from the least squares fitting procedure. Notably, the highly ordered system with 56 molecules of stearic acid covering a smooth Fe surface has a coefficient of friction μ much lower than all other systems. In the following, an attempt will be made to link the behavior of F_0 to the lubricant order, which is quantified by various estimates for contributions to its entropy based on the $3N \times 3N$ covariance (super)matrix C introduced in eqn (22). These were obtained by time-averaging over the entire data acquisition period of 1.5 ns, based on the lubricant molecules' carbon backbone positions in the center-of-mass system.

The maps shown in Fig. 11 are representations of these covariance (super) matrices, which have been rearranged so that the nine sub-matrices constitute the Cartesian component-wise covariance matrices. All sub-matrices featuring the x-component show clear evidence of the dominant translation in x-direction. The remaining four sub-matrices reveal patterns according to the vibrational modes of the molecules, as will be shown below.

In order to estimate the contributions to the total entropy based on eqn (27), (28) and (32), the covariance (super)matrix C must be diagonalized, for example by using an orthonormal coordinate transformation, which yields eigenvalues λ_J ($J = 1,...,\, 3N$) in decreasing order. In an immediate next step, the translational, rotational and vibrational eigenmodes have to be identified among the normalized eigenvectors V_J ($J = 1,...,\, 3N$) which form the columns of the transformation matrix V in eqn (30). Although it is expected that the eigenvector corresponding to the

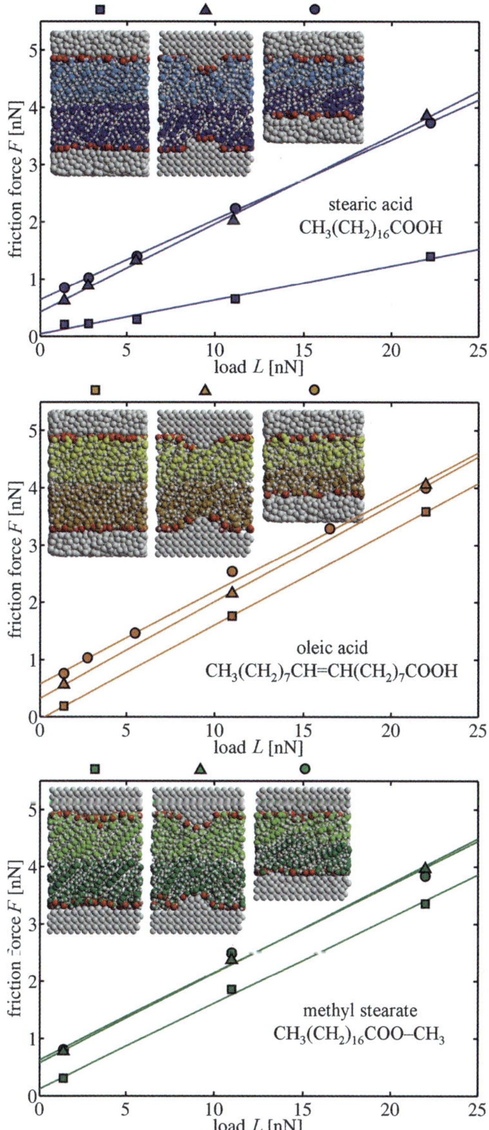

Fig. 9 Load-*versus*-friction behaviour of the nine analyzed nanotribological systems schematically shown in the insets (directions of load and shear are the same as in Fig. 1). They are ordered top-to-bottom by lubricant type: stearic acid (blue), oleic acid (orange), and methyl stearate (green). From left to right, the following parameters were varied: left (squares): low roughness $R_a \approx 0$–1 ML Fe bcc (1 0 0), high molecular surface coverage $\eta = 56$ molecules/surface; center (triangles): high roughness $R_a \approx 4$ ML Fe bcc (1 0 0), high molecular surface coverage $\eta = 56$ molecules/surface; right (circles): low roughness $R_a \approx 0$–1 ML Fe bcc (1 0 0), low molecular surface coverage $\eta = 35$ molecules/surface.

largest eigenvalue λ_1 describes the collective sliding motion along the x-axis in all of the nanotribological systems investigated here, a symmetry study of the other eigenvectors V_J ($\forall J \geq 2$) cannot be avoided because one has to distinguish between the other collective modes as well. Therefore one attempts to identify eigenvectors V_J stored in the transformation matrix V with a structure of, *e.g.*, (1 0 0 1 0 0...−1 0 0 − 1 0 0)$^\mathrm{T}$, with three possible permutations with respect to the Cartesian

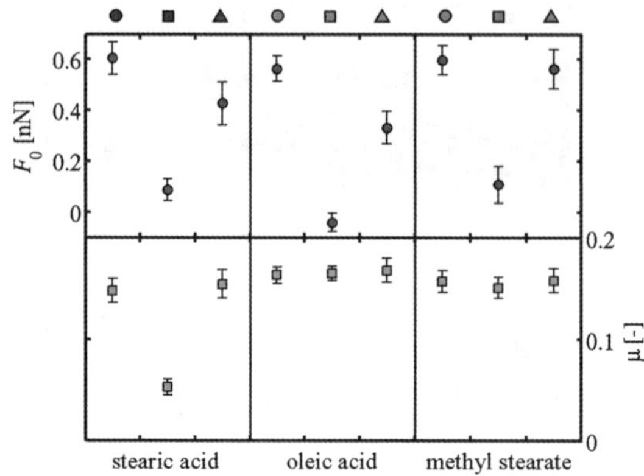

Fig. 10 The constitutive system parameters F_0 and μ in accordance with the linear load-*versus*-friction behaviour from Fig. 9.

components, knowing that each of them characterizes a purely collective translational motion along that axis for which the corresponding Cartesian component does not vanish. Three differently structured typical eigenvectors can stand for collective rotational motions in a given Cartesian coordinate plane about the center of mass. One of the easiest ways to figure out these six eigenvectors is to represent in a histogram the number of occurrences within the transformation matrix V of a given element, because for a purely collective translational motion, for example, ± 1 will be present in the histogram $N/2$ times and so on. Such a histogram formed with the elements of V and common to all the nanotribological systems considered in Fig. 9 is shown in Fig. 12 (top). In this figure, two tiny outlier peaks are present which were found to correspond to V_1. By drawing the Cartesian component-resolved histogram of V_1 in Fig. 12 (bottom), it becomes evident that V_1 describes the collective motion due to the sliding along the x-direction. Inspecting the values of the components, apart from the symmetry of V_1, one immediately concludes that this collective motion comprises also random fluctuations along the other two axes, and therefore as well as due to normalization, the repeated x-component value differs from unity. Furthermore, as can be seen in Fig. 12, there is no evidence of any other translational or rotational collective modes, which means that all the remaining ones are vibrational.

In view of these findings, it is now clear that for estimating the translational contribution S_{tr} to the entropy, eqn (27) is not directly applicable, but instead its 1D counterpart,

$$S_{tr} = R \ln\left[\left(\frac{e^2 m k_B T}{\hbar^2}\right)^{1/2} \sigma_x\right], \tag{34}$$

for which σ_x can be well approximated by the square root of the first eigenvalue λ_1, namely

$$\sigma_x = \sqrt{\lambda_1}. \tag{35}$$

Indeed, comparing the so-resulting estimate for S_{tr} with that obtained for σ_x determined as the square root of the corresponding eigenvalue obtained on the basis of the 3×3 covariance matrix constructed for the center of mass of the system (not shown here), it turns out that the former approach yields only slightly larger values than the latter. This difference is due to the small random y and z components in V_1, recalling Fig. 12. Accordingly, in the case of the vibrational contribution S_{vib} to the entropy, strictly speaking one has to deal with $3N - 1$ modes in eqn (32) and (33). In practice, however, it turns out that both S_{vib} and S_{Schl} converge slowly for small

   This journal is © The Royal Society of Chemistry 2012

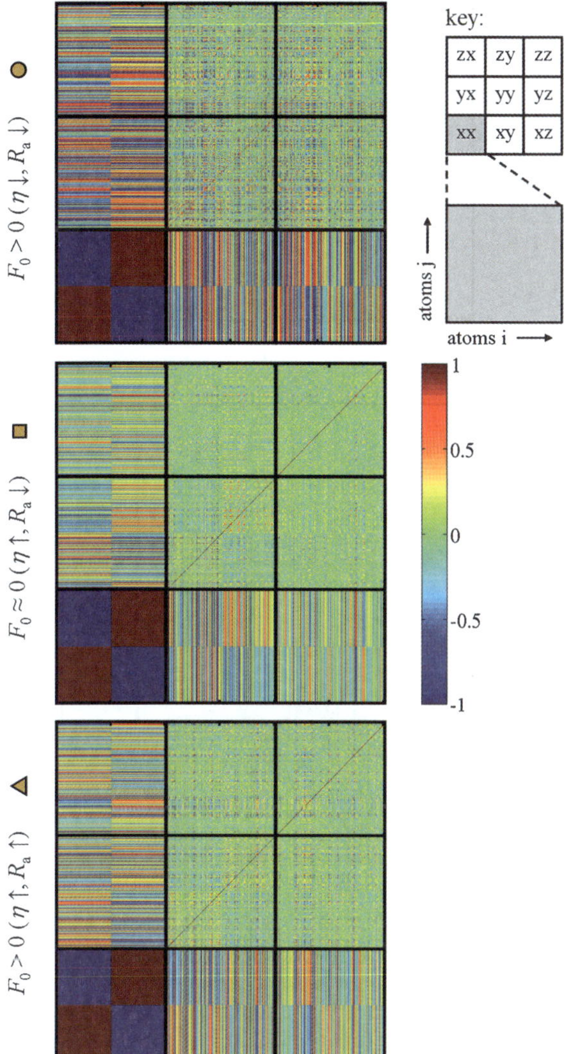

Fig. 11 Maps of the covariance (super)matrices of the three nanotribological systems from Fig. 9 with oleic acid as a lubricant at a load of $L = 11.02$ nN. The elements are calculated averaging over the entire data acquisition period of 1.5 ns and taking the Cartesian components of the atomic positions with respect to the momentary center of mass, see also key.

vibrational eigenvalues λ_J, *i.e.*, when the frequency ω_J of the associated one-dimensional quantum harmonic oscillator tends to be extremely large, see eqn (31). Fortunately, when $\lambda_J \to 0$ its contribution to the vibrational entropy S_{vib} vanishes, because

$$\lim_{\omega_J \to \infty} S_{\mathrm{vib}}^{(J)} = R \lim_{\omega_J \to \infty} \frac{\beta\hbar}{\beta\hbar \exp(\beta\hbar\omega_J)} - R \ln 1 = R \lim_{\omega_J \to \infty} \frac{1}{\exp(\beta\hbar\omega_J)} = 0, \quad (36)$$

and hence one can introduce a cut-off $\lambda_{\mathrm{cut}} \geq 0$ below which all the positive vibrational eigenvalues λ_J can be set to zero and not counted for S_{vib} and S_{Schl} without significantly altering their value.

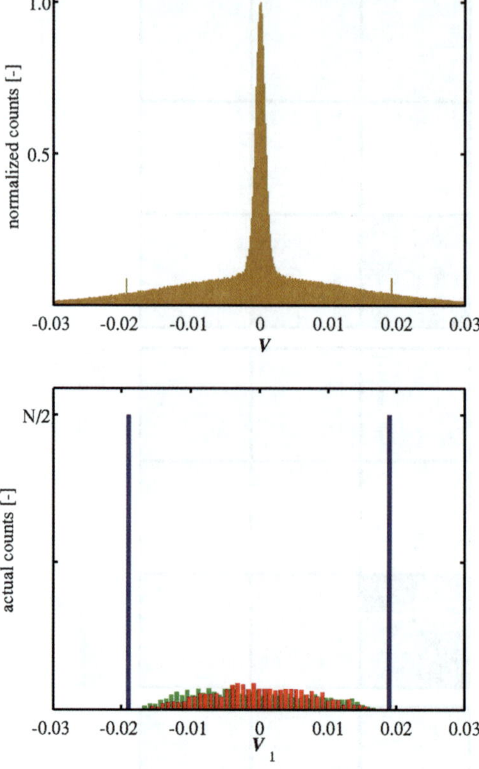

Fig. 12 Histogram of all components of all normalized eigenvectors corresponding to eigenvalues greater than $10^{-5}\mathrm{\mathring{A}}^2$ (top) and of the dominant one V_1 (bottom; blue—x, green—y, red—z) obtained by diagonalizing the covariance (super)matrix shown in Fig. 11 (middle). $N = 2016$ is the number of C-atoms in the system. The two peaks at $\sim\pm0.02$ hint at pure translation without rotation.

The results for the entropy contributions estimated in this manner are given as per-atom values in Fig. 13, where it can be seen that, to some extent, S_{tr} (right triangles, left axis) better follows the trend of F_0 in Fig. 10 than S_{vib} (diamonds, right axis). Both S_{tr} and S_{vib} correlate well with F_0 regarding changes in the lubricant surface coverage η, but do not reflect changes in F_0 due to an increase of surface roughness R_a. This could have two main reasons. On one hand, the individuality of the constitutive molecules is lost in the single macromolecule approach for the entropy, and so it seems to be unable to measure the change in the structural order due to the higher surface roughness. On the other hand, it could also be that, while the expressions for S_{tr} and S_{vib} are derived from the Shannon entropy, the quasi-harmonic (Gaussian) approach to the PDF considered here oversimplifies the inter-atomic potential by reducing it to an elastic one. The same holds for the Schlitter-entropy, recalling eqn (33), which by definition only sets an upper bound for S_{vib}—as confirmed by Fig. 13 (bottom).

4   Concluding remarks

Based on the momentary position of atoms in a molecular dynamics (MD) simulation, a smooth particle post-processing tool was recently developed by the authors for estimating the load-dependent asperity contact area in boundary-lubricated nanotribological systems. Here it was shown that this numerical tool yields the

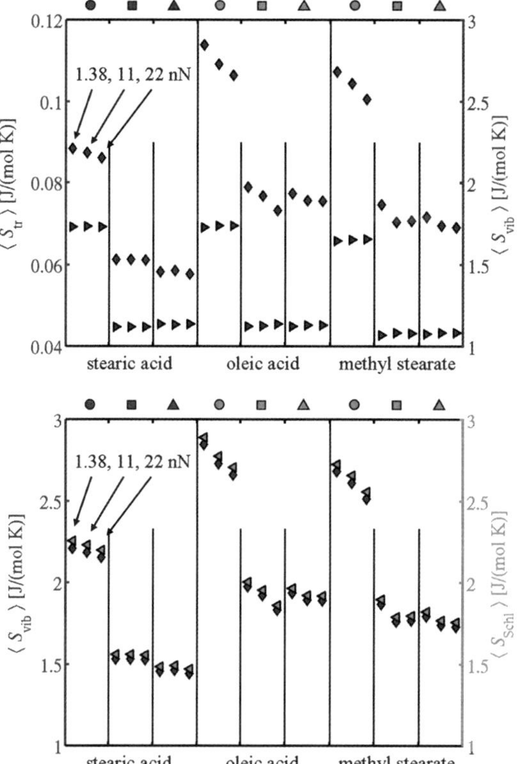

Fig. 13 Molar per-atom contributions to the entropy within the single macromolecule approach and following Schlitter's *ad hoc* approximation, for all nanotribological systems in Fig. 9. The translational entropy values are represented by right triangles, the vibrational ones by diamonds, and left triangles stand for the configurational entropy according to Schlitter.

time-dependence of the asperity contact area $A_{asp}(L)$ at a given load L, in excellent agreement with the projected asperity contact area $A_{asp}^{(V)}(L)$ calculated from a Voronoi tessellation of the same momentary contact zone. Compared to the Voronoi tessellation, however, our smoothed particle approach turned out to be computationally faster and more reliable, hence it is a proper tool to estimate the asperity contact area if one is not interested in additional geometrical details of the contact zone.

Considering $A_{asp}(L) \geq 0$ as given by the smooth particle post-processing tool together with the corresponding friction force $F(L)$, it was proven that the least squares fitting of these MD data using a three-term friction law always yields the involved constitutive system parameters, namely the friction force offset $F_0 > 0$, the shear strength τ and the coefficient of friction μ for any boundary-lubricated nanotribological system of interest. In addition, if no solid–solid contact occurs for any of the considered loads, *i.e.*, $A_{asp}(L)$ strictly vanishes and hence the Derjaguin-form of the three-term friction law holds, it was found that the same computational scheme yields only two constitutive system parameters, $F_0 \geq 0$ and μ.

In the former case, when $A_{asp}(L) \geq 0$ depends on L, it was demonstrated that the constitutive system parameters entering the three-term friction law are time-independent quantities, apart from a relatively short time interval at the beginning of sliding, which in turn can be seen as a nanoscopic run-in period. If $A_{asp}(L) \equiv 0$ for all L considered, on the other hand, it was found that the occurrence of the offset F_0 can be only partially related to the structural order of the system, at least when the load-dependent entropy is estimated using the single macromolecule approach based on covariance (super)matrices of the carbon backbone atoms in the lubricant.

Altogether one can conclude that with the careful design of nanoasperities, the run-in period of a nanotribological system can be optimized, and the friction regime in which the resulting device should work may be defined beforehand. In addition, if the working conditions of such a boundary-lubricated nano-device are known, the friction force at zero load might be also tuned.

Acknowledgements

This work was funded by the Austrian COMET-program (governmental funding program for pre-competitive research) *via* the Austrian Research Promotion Agency (FFG grant no.: 824187, project acronym: XTribology) and the TecNet Capital GmbH (Province of Niederösterreich) and was carried out at the Austrian Center of Competence for Tribology (AC^{2}T research GmbH). The authors would like to thank Nikolaj Kuntner for his implementation of the Voronoi method. Thanks are also extended to Herbert Störi and Friedrich Franek for reading through the manuscript, for fruitful discussions and their helpful ideas.

References

1 G. Amontons, *Mémoires de l'Académie Royale*, 1699, 257.
2 C. A. Coulomb, *Mém. Math. Phys. (Paris)*, 1785, 161.
3 B. Derjaguin, *Zeitschrift für Physik A*, 1934, **88**, 661.
4 F. P. Bowden and D. Tabor, *The Friction and Lubrication of Solids*, Oxford University Press, Oxford, 1950.
5 S. Eder, A. Vernes, G. Vorlaufer and G. Betz, *J. Phys.: Condens. Matter*, 2011, **23**, 175004.
6 J. G. W. D. Luedtke, D. Gourdon, M. Ruths, J. N. Israelachvili and U. Landman, *J. Phys. Chem. B*, 2004, **108**, 3410.
7 M. Ruths, *Langmuir*, 2003, **19**, 6788.
8 G. He and M. O. Robbins, *Tribol. Lett.*, 2001, **10**, 7.
9 G. He, M. H. Müser and M. O. Robbins, *Science*, 1999, **284**, 1650.
10 W. G. Hoover, *Smooth Particle Applied Mechanics – The State of the Art*, World Scientific, New Jersey, 2006.
11 J. J. Monaghan, *Rep. Prog. Phys.*, 2005, **68**, 1703.
12 A. Okabe, B. Boots, K. Sugihara and S. N. Chiu, *Spatial Tessellations: Concepts and Applications of Voronoi Diagrams* (2nd Ed.), J. Wiley & Sons, Ltd, Chichester, 2000.
13 G. Schliecker, *Adv. Phys.*, 2002, **51**, 1319.
14 M. P. Marder, *Condensed Matter Physics*, J. Wiley & Sons, Inc., New York, 2000.
15 P. F. B. Goncalves and H. Stassen, *J. Chem. Phys.*, 2005, **123**, 214109.
16 W. H. Press, S. A. Teukolsky, W. T. Vetterling and B. P. Flannery, *Numerical Recipes: The Art of Scientific Computing* (3rd Ed.), Cambridge University Press, Cambridge, 2007.
17 M. H. Müser, *Phys. Rev. Lett.*, 2008, **100**, 055504.
18 S. J. Plimpton, *J. Comput. Phys.*, 1995, **117**, 1.
19 M. P. Allen and D. J. Tildesley, *Computer Simulation of Liquids*, Clarendon Press, Oxford, 1987.
20 E. Barthel, *J. Phys. D: Appl. Phys.*, 2008, **41**, 163001.
21 P. H. Nguyen, *Chem. Phys. Lett.*, 2009, **468**, 90.
22 T. Lazaridis, A. Masunov and F. Gandolfo, *Proteins: Struct., Funct., Genet.*, 2002, **47**, 194.
23 C. W. Gardiner, *Handbook of Stochastic Methods for Physics, Chemistry and the Natural Sciences*, Springer Verlag, Berlin, 2004.
24 J. Carlsson and J. Åqvist, *Phys. Chem. Chem. Phys.*, 2006, **8**, 5385.
25 J. Carlsson and J. Åqvist, *J. Phys. Chem. B*, 2005, **109**, 6448.
26 H. Schäfer, A. E. Mark and W. F. V. Gunsteren, *J. Chem. Phys.*, 2000, **113**, 7809.
27 H. Meirovitch, *Curr. Opin. Struct. Biol.*, 2007, **17**, 181.
28 G. G. Maisuradze, A. Liwo and H. A. Scheraga, *J. Mol. Biol.*, 2009, **385**, 312.
29 M. Laberge and T. Yonetani, *Biophys. J.*, 2008, **94**, 2737.
30 I. Andricioaei and M. Karplus, *J. Chem. Phys.*, 2001, **115**, 6289.
31 J. Schlitter, *Chem. Phys. Lett.*, 1993, **215**, 617.
32 H. Schäfer, X. Daura, A. E. Mark and W. F. V. Gunsteren, *Proteins: Struct., Funct., Genet.*, 2001, **43**, 45.
33 A. L. Tournier and J. C. Smith, *Phys. Rev. Lett.*, 2003, **91**, 208106.
34 S.-T. D. Hsu, C. Peter, W. F. V. Gunsteren and A. M. J. J. Bonvin, *Biophys. J.*, 2005, **88**, 15.

General discussion

Professor Spencer opened the discussion of the paper by Professor Evans: Presumably the profilometry data were measured by some kind of mechanical profilometer, with a well-defined cutoff length corresponding to the size of the stylus. Of course you could have used other methods to include shorter size-scale roughness features. What is the sensitivity of your results to the value of this cutoff?

Professor Evans replied: The profilometer used was a Taylor Hobson Form Talysurf with a diamond stylus of 2 μm tip dimension. The trace is taken with a cut off length of 0.8 mm and is filtered to remove the form. The roughness profile is filtered to remove waviness. The profile ordinates are acquired by the instrument at a spacing of 0.25 μm.

The relationship between the computational mesh spacing and the roughness profile spacing is important. Because the surfaces are moving at different speeds relative to the contact it is necessary to interpolate surface heights from the profile information. Experience of various approaches to this aspect of the calculation has led us to define each surface using cubic splines in order to impose continuity of slope on the profile irrespective of its position relative to the computational mesh. It is also beneficial for the splines to be defined on a spacing that is the same order as the computational mesh spacing. Without this approach asperity features fall in and out of the computation as the feature moves through the mesh leading to spurious hydrodynamic squeeze film effects.

The question of what feature size is important is determined by the scale of the roughness. This is a mechanical analysis and the run-in asperity lands are typically 6 to 50 μm wide. The scale of resolution is typically 200 mesh points in a corresponding Hertz dimension giving a computational mesh spacing of 1.25 μm. The timestep adopted is such that the faster moving surface moves through half a mesh spacing in each timestep which was shown in ref. 11 in our paper to be the largest timestep that can be used that maintains numerical accuracy.

Finer surface features could be included in the analysis, but to do so would require commensurate spacing of the computational mesh. Such an approach is probably more realistic for an idealised contact of a pair of asperity features rather than the analysis of real gear profiles as presented in the paper.

Dr Wang said: It would be very useful if the model can incorporate the transient operation of wind turbine gearboxes, *e.g.* multiple directions of loading, torque reversal, rapid loading and acceleration *etc.*

Professor Evans responded: The model can include transient operation in the sense of a prescribed duty cycle. It is inherently transient because this is necessary to incorporate the "moving roughness" effect, but the timescale of the transient events to which you refer is completely different to those for the rough surface modelling. The transient events you list will change the gear pair loading and that would need to be considered in the context of a dynamic model of the whole machine. The output of that kind of evaluation for a gear pair would guide the way in which mixed EHL modelling could be applied to those components.

Dr Wang commented: We would be interested in applying the model your group developed in our RCF testing to predict the premature failures based on initial surface measurements.

Professor Evans replied: That is certainly possible in principle and a detailed discussion would be useful. The model is for ground surfaces with the grinding lay perpendicular to the rolling/sliding direction as is the case in most types of gears. If the RCF tests are conducted with cylindrical samples the surface finish would need to have an axial lay.

Professor Dowson asked: Were tests in Newcastle carried out at exceptionally high loads or at representative operating values?

Professor Evans responded: The tests were carried out at a series of load stages with nominal maximum Hertzian pressures in the range from 1.2 to 1.8 GPa. These conditions are not exceptionally high but are representative of high power density gears.

Professor Dowson commented: The detailed numerical analysis may be too daunting for designers in industry. The ratio of mean film thickness to composite surface roughness, known as the Λ ratio, is a useful, simple tool used to indicate the severity of contact during lubricated running. Has your detailed analysis indicated whether the concept is still useful? It has generally been accepted, following the work of Tallian[1] and Wellauer,[2] that pitting failure is significantly reduced and largely avoided if Λ falls in the range 3-5.

1. T. E. Tallian, The theory of partial elastohydrodynamic contacts, *Wear*, 1972, **21**, 49–101.
2. E. J. Wellauer, AGMA experience in establishing coordinated gear rating standards, invited paper presented to the Semi-International Symposium, *Japan Society of Mechanical Engineers*, 1967.

Professor Evans replied: This modelling work is aimed at improving fundamental understanding rather than as a design tool, and a Λ ratio approach is certainly relevant for gear designers. Experimental gear tests have established the improvements that can be obtained in terms of surface fatigue life as a result of improved surface finish.[1] Comparison of results obtained with the same rough surfaces operating with different values for the ambient pressure viscosity to produce different Λ values shows the sensitivity of contact incidence to Λ as illustrated in Fig. 1. The fatigue calculation results also show a progressive reduction in accumulated damage as the Λ ratio increases. These comparisons are for the same pair of rough surfaces

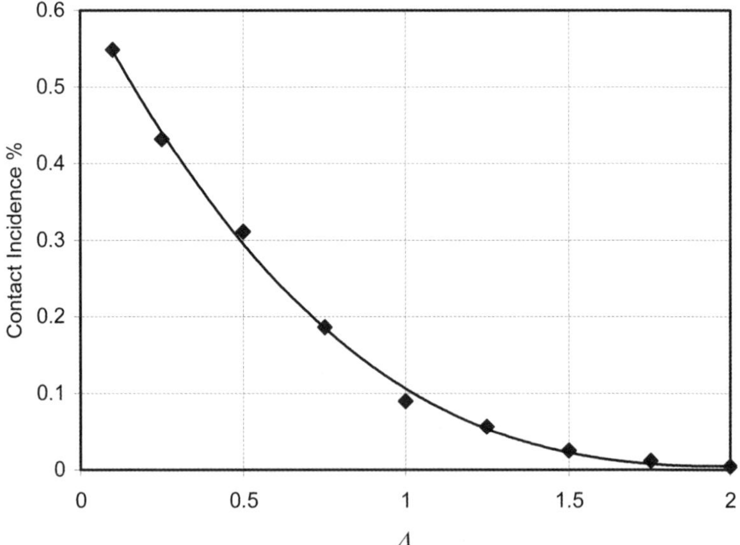

Fig. 1 Variation of contact incidence with Λ ratio based on roughness of run-in profiles.

and the Λ ratio is based on the roughness of the running profiles. However, comparisons with Λ ratios of results obtained with different rough surfaces are less clear cut. The Λ ratio used by designers is likely to be based on the manufactured roughness profiles or indeed as a basis for specifying the manufacturing roughness. Its relationship to the Λ ratio of the running profiles depends on the running in process. In practice the effect of specifying a high Λ ratio requires a fine finish of the gears which is beneficial but also has cost implications.

1. T. L. Krantz, *et al.*, *ASME J. Tribol.*, 2001, **123**, 709–716.

Dr Taylor queried: In your impressive simulations, the effect of rough surfaces in gear lubrication seems to result in peak stresses close to the surface. In some cases, failures seem to occur with cracks emanating from deeper below the surface, and it has been suggested this is due to weak points in the steel (such as inclusions). Is it possible to include such material imperfections in your model ?

Professor Evans answered: The peak stresses occur at the surface, but the conditions there are approximately hydrostatic. Peak shear stress values occur close to the surface, but not at the surface,[1] and this is picked up by the fatigue analysis as shown in Fig. 8 in our paper.

Including material imperfections in the transient EHL model is not realistic as the elastic behaviour is modelled as that of a homogeneous semi-infinite body, and this formulation is central to the solution technique. However the EHL model can generate realistic surface loading during asperity interactions for application to a detailed FE model. Such an FE analysis could include material imperfections as you suggest.

1. See J. Tao, *et al.*, *ASME J. Tribol.*, 2003, **125**, 267–274, for example.

Dr Limbert remarked: In the commercial finite element software package ABAQUS (Simulia, Dassault Systemes, Providence, RI, USA) contact interfaces are defined by contact pairs and interface laws. Generally, one can define a tangential law that characterises the shear behaviour between the two bodies in contact (friction or frictionless) and a normal law that characterises the normal behaviour. This latter law controls the evolution of contact pressure between the contacting bodies as a function of the overclosure at the contact interface.

What kind of normal law was used in the your finite element model? Linear? Exponential?

Professor Evans replied: The normal contact behaviour utilised in the finite element model presented uses the default "hard" contact pressure–overclosure relationship which minimises the penetration of the slave surface into the master surface at the constraint locations. The degree of penetration allowed within the model is governed by the constraint enforcement method. The default linear penalty method was modified to be used within an augmented iteration scheme, known as the augmented Lagrange method. This method works identically to the linear penalty method until a slave node penetrates the master surface by more than a specified penetration tolerance which can be manually set. The contact pressure is then "augmented" through a number of iterations until the required penetration tolerance is met and convergence can be achieved. This method can often require more iterations to provide a solution but can make the convergence of contact problems easier whilst ensuring that surface penetrations remain small. The results presented in the current paper were obtained with frictionless interface behaviour.

Dr Limbert asked: Have you ever thought to run probabilistic finite element analyses to capture the stochastic nature of surface roughness and assess the effect of particular statistical distributions of roughness measures on response variables such as shear forces, contact pressure, *etc.*?

Professor Evans answered: The paper describes an inherently deterministic model that runs measured roughness profiles against their counterfaces. Our standpoint is that specific asperities interact with a restricted set of counterface asperities in gear contacts with plastic modification of these asperity pairs occurring in response to their interface loading. These interactions are essentially localised and we have not therefore considered the suggested stochastic approach at this time.

Professor Williams commented: Could you comment on the ways in which fatigue or damage accumulation is incorporated into your thinking? The loading conditions of reversing shear to which the just sub-surface material is subjected occur under a very high hydrostatic stress-containing conditions which are different from those under which conventional fatigue data is amassed. How sensitive are the predictions to the particular model chosen?

Professor Evans responded: The approach adopted is to seek a plausible candidate amongst the large number of fatigue models in the literature with a view to testing its performance for rough surface mixed EHL conditions by comparison with twin disk experiments. The choice has been guided by the experimental observation that micropitting first appears in the root of the pinion tooth whilst the meshing tip of the wheel tooth is unaffected. This occurs in the Newcastle University test wheel and pinion gears that have 34 and 33 teeth, respectively, so that the gear meshing cycles of the gears differ by only 3%. In comparing the results of different fatigue models we have sought models that predict higher fatigue damage in the pinion root (*i.e.* the surface which moves more slowly relative to the contact) than in the faster moving wheel tip surface. This rules out critical plane models which are based on the maximum value of a function of the stress components, as both components will then experience the same maximum value. The cumulated damage approach does distinguish between the components as it can potentially respond to the fact that an asperity on the pinion root surface has a longer transit time through the contact and will encounter a greater number of counterface asperities during each meshing cycle than will an asperity on the faster moving surface. Comparisons of different fatigue models reported in ref. 20 in the paper indicate that the same asperities are identified as having the greatest vulnerability. This is not really surprising as the stress is produced by the surface loading predicted by the mixed EHL model and each fatigue model responds to the stress level. The predictions are not particularly sensitive to the particular model adopted as far as ranking contacting surfaces and asperities for fatigue vulnerability is concerned, as may be seen from the comparisons in ref. 20 in the paper.

The test conditions used to develop classical fatigue models are indeed very different from those occurring in the near surface material of the gear tests. The extent to which any of these models can be applied to lubricated rough surfaces needs to be established experimentally and the authors are open to suggestions regarding models that may be well suited to these conditions.

Professor Dr Rahnejat remarked: Does your analysis include non-Newtonian behaviour/adhesion/temperature effects?

Professor Evans replied: The analysis includes non-Newtonian behaviour. The results shown have been obtained with a shear thinning model, and limiting shear stress models have also been used. The model can include a thermal analysis but the results presented are isothermal. Including a thermal analysis is time consuming and we have found that there is no significant difference in terms of surface loading. The model does not include any adhesive effects other than in the coefficient of friction specified for direct asperity interactions.

Professor Dr Rahnejat queried: Are you meshing the entire rough surface, and therefore, what is the typical mesh density?

Alternatively, one can represent a typical region by flow factors, using the Patir and Cheng average flow model version of Reynolds equation. Is this the approach used?

Professor Evans responded: This is a deterministic analysis using measured surface roughness profiles. Details of the process and resolution are given in response to Professor Spencer's earlier question. The surfaces considered are assumed to be in line contact and the measured roughness structure is essentially extruded perpendicular to the rolling/sliding direction as is nominally the case for ground gears. Transient mixed EHL point contact results in ref. 10 from our paper show how transverse surface waviness can raise the severity of loading.

The suggested average flow model and more recent roughness homogenization techniques are an alternative approach but are not used in this work.

Professor Wood asked: Is there a role for the tribofilm in asperity to asperity contact and hence the surface and sub-surface stresses induced? If so, can your model accommodate a tribofilm effect (thin coating with different modulus *etc.*) at these scale lengths?

Professor Evans responded: There is clearly a role for a tribofilm at asperity to asperity contacts. In the current model this is no more than a coefficient of friction, μ, that controls the shear stress where there is no EHL film. We have experimented with different μ values and found the fatigue calculation to be relatively insensitive to the value adopted.

A low elastic modulus thin tribofilm could be added to the surfaces using the approach described by Professor Larsson,[1] for example, and that might be a useful development.

1. J. Andersson, R. Larsson, A. Almqvist, M. Grahn and I. Minami, *Faraday Discuss.*, 2012, DOI: 10.1039/C2FD00132B.

Professor Wood enquired: Is there a chemical effect here in the fatigue/pitting of gears? Or is it purely mechanical? If significant, can chemical aspects be modelled with your approach?

Professor Evans replied: The paper reports results of a purely mechanical model. As such its main contribution to evaluating any chemical effects is in determining the parameters under which any such effect would operate in terms of pressure and duration. It could also indicate the surface temperature, but that calculation would depend on the coefficient of friction applied at the asperity to asperity contacts. Whether or not chemical effects could be incorporated is unclear and would depend on the form taken by such effects under the conditions applicable to the asperity contacts.

Mr Evans remarked: Congratulations on a very interesting paper. In this study you have modelled the development of near surface residual stresses due to repeated contact of asperities in rolling contact. You noted that the subsurface zones which have developed a tensile residual stress would be detrimental to fatigue life in such modes as micropitting, where it is observed that a strong correlation exists between the size and location of pits and these tensile stress zones. It is mentioned that the application of this work is, for example, the gears, but also the bearings in wind turbine gearboxes which suffer the micropitting failure mode. A typical gearbox bearing is made from a tempered martensite 1–1.5% Cr bearing steel such as 100Cr6/52100 where the retained austenite content varies between approximately 10–15%. It is well established that under rolling contact loading some of the retained austenite decays to martensite with an associated volumetric expansion of 3–4%. This expansion results in a compressive residual stress development which can be substantial. The model presented in this paper does not take into consideration the metallurgical aspects such as retained austenite decay for some bearing materials, which could significantly influence the developed residual stress zones. Finding a way to incorporate metallurgical aspects into the model would be essential in advancing our understanding of the role of near surface tensile residual stress for the micropitting failure mode for bearing applications specifically.

Professor Evans responded: Martensite decay is certainly relevant to the practical problem and our collaborators at Newcastle University have also shown how metallurgical changes occur beneath plastically deformed asperity features.[1]

Metallurgical effects are not included in the current model. The mixed EHL analysis determines asperity loading conditions and this includes an elastic deflection analysis for isotropic semi-infinite bodies at the heart of the computation. The subsequent consideration of fatigue resulting from the asperity load histories is sensitive to residual stress. In principle any postulated, modelled or measured residual stress field can be incorporated at that stage of the analysis to include these effects. It is clear, however, that the residual stress information required needs to be sufficiently detailed to include differences occurring at the scale of the asperity features.

1. A. Oila *et al.*, *Proc. IMechE, J. Engng Tribology*, 2005, **219**, 77–83.

Professor Klein opened the discussion of the paper by Dr Teodorescu†: In your model the chains are end-adsorbed to the surfaces (Fig. 1 in your paper). Does your computational approach account for the configurational entropy of such chains?

Mr Chong responded: The chain molecules modelled in our paper are freely jointed chain molecules. As a simplified approach, the freely jointed chain molecules are ideal chain molecules, commonly used to simulate polymers as shown in ref. 30, 31 and 34–36 in our paper. The idealised molecules neglect the chain orientation, which means that the configurational entropy is not included in the model. These molecules are simple, but can still provide useful physical information (*e.g.* shearing and formation of surface films) about polymers, as shown in our paper.

Professor Klein asked: As a corollary to my previous question, were you able to control whether your computational approach enables known properties of polymers to be derived in a model setting (for example, properties such as chain dimensions)?

Mr Chong responded: The chain molecules consist of hard spheres linked through connectivity constraints. The current model considers the length and the cross-section nominal diameter of the chain molecules of interest as the input. It is shown in ref. 34–36 of the current paper that using a similar approach to the current paper, only the thermodynamic properties (*e.g.* gas-liquid transition phase) of the chain molecules can be derived from such models.

---

† Dr Teodorescu's paper was presented by Mr Chong, *Loughborough University, UK.*

   This journal is © The Royal Society of Chemistry 2012

Mr Chong answered: The current analysis attempts to understand only the kinetics influencing the formation and shear characteristics of adsorbed surface films. These are of primary importance in boundary lubrication. The proposed boundary film model can be integrated into a micro-scale tribology model (considering hydrodynamics/elastohydrodynamics), such as the conditions described in Prof. Evans' paper. The difference between the two analyses, therefore, is the question of scale. Referring to Prof. Evans' paper, please note that the measured typical asperity geometry included is shown in Fig. 1. These are measured using a profilometer, which has a typical measurement resolution of around the size of the probe (*i.e.* 2 micrometre or so). Roughness is hierarchical (see ref. 1 below). Our analysis is in the nano-scale, at the summit of much smaller asperities, many of which reside upon those in Prof. Evans' paper, and usually measured by an AFM. There are still finer features which may be ascertained by Fractal representation, and so *ad infinitum*.[1] The pressures generated are, therefore, progressively smaller (they can be viewed as the share of load per smaller feature projected area) at the lower scales. In our paper, the contact pressure for a diluted fluid (total packing fraction of 0.2) confined by smooth planar walls (representative of an asperity pair summit contact) is shown in Fig. 3 in our paper to be in the range kPa to MPa. Increasing the total packing fraction leads to a higher contact pressure as shown in ref. 23 in our current paper. The two lyses are fine by themselves. However, a challenge for all tribologists is to bridge the gap between them. This is an area of tribology which is receiving much attention.

1. Gohar and Rahnejat, *Fundamentals of tribology*, Imperial College Press, 2008.

Professor Spencer enquired: In your paper you claim that you are reproducing the behavior of real fluids, but on the other hand you are using a model—hard spheres and sticky chains—that does not really correspond to reality. Can you comment on the significance of the model for real systems? Chemistry seems to have been almost entirely omitted, for example.

Professor Dr Rahnejat responded: The answer unfortunately is quite long to this very good question.

There is currently no model for boundary lubricant shear near the surfaces. The boundary lubricant comprises additives, such as detergents/surfactants, friction modifier, anti-oxidants, *etc.* Therefore, there are a multitude of species within the lubricant. Also, the boundary species account for a small percentage of the base lubricant, itself made up of many species.

There are two approaches that one can adopt to create a boundary film model. One is through molecular dynamics, which is computationally very intensive and it is generally based on the electrostatic forces between pairs of molecules and between these with the atoms of the surfaces. The approach has two main problems; one is that only a few molecules may be included in a very small region of space and the other is that the chemical nature of the force is not usually taken into account (*i.e.* hydrophobic/hydrophilic, repulsive/attractive, based on any given chemically-based kinetic law).

The other approach is an allusion to Brownian-type dynamics, where the kinetic laws can be incorporated (*i.e.* more chemistry), but the actions of individual molecules, such as their inertial motion cannot be accounted for, nor it is necessary. For a successful boundary film model to be incorporated into a micro-scale tribology, such as in hydrodynamics/elastohydrodynamics, one would need to obtain some continuum measure from the predicted film, such as viscosity, or in this case, as Petrenko envisaged many years ago, a form of viscosity near the bounding surfaces: stickiness. In other words, we are interested in a shear model for surface adsorbed films.

Commencing with a smooth summit of asperities in nano-scale contact and at separations of the order of several molecular diameters of the average species, the dominant force has been found to be solvation. There are empirical approaches based on the density oscillations of an ideal fluid near solid barriers, which have been used, and are a function of separation, Boltzmann distribution and thermodynamic balance (so there is some rudimentary physical chemistry in such empirical methods). Moreover, there are experiments which underpin this approach in the absence of any significant meniscus effect.

A more appropriate way of dealing with physical chemistry near the surface is statistical mechanics, based on virial expansion, initially for hard sticky molecules with an appropriate distribution function. This is the approach that was used by Baxter (ref. 32 in the current paper) to solve the integral equation of Ornstein–Zernicke, and a potential such as Percus–Yevick may be assumed for a homogeneous fluid. The current paper is just an extension of this approach, using a connectivity constraint to extend the approach to long chain molecules as well as using Perram and Smith's method (ref. 33 in the paper) to take into account the inhomogeneous nature of the molecular mix. In this approach the assumed spherical molecule is just a representation of the base oil molecular mix which are "non-sticky" (*i.e.* have been assigned a low adsorption potential) and the long chain molecule represents the boundary active (adsorbing) species where a potential is assigned to it. So, there is some representation of a lubricant oil mix in this manner, because it alludes to a typical mix, although clearly there are limitations in this approach. It is important to include a larger number of species, particularly the branched variety. However, the approach is promising, because it allows stipulation of molecular level film formation and its shear characteristics based on the promotion or inhibition of the solvation effect: density variation near the surface of the molecular mix. How the adsorption takes place is not addressed in this approach, unlike molecular dynamics. All molecules, overcoming the potential well are considered as adsorbed. The advantage is a relatively quick and expandable model to larger surface domains from the nano-scale asperity pair to micro-scale contacts. It does not include all the chemistry which one would normally like, but has sufficient chemistry for tribological purposes. Also, it is noteworthy that in a typical micro-scale practical contact there may be as many as several million asperities.

Professor Dr Vernes opened the discussion of Professor Dr Kubo's paper: Why do the TB-QCMD data not directly confirm that the OH-termination (as a possible final structure of the observed tribochemical reaction) is energetically the most stable one?

Professor Dr Kubo answered: TB-QCMD can also directly confirm that the OH-termination is energetically the most stable one. However, the kinetics is also important for the discussion on the chemical reactions, in addition to the energetics. Our TB-QCMD simulator is very effective to discuss the kinetics of the chemical reactions in addition to the energetics. For the chemical reactions the addition of energy, which overcomes the activation barrier, is necessary. Then, if the energy, which overcomes the activation barrier, is not supplied, the chemical reaction does not occur. A static first-principles calculation only can discuss the energetics and cannot discuss the kinetics. However, our TB-QCMD can discuss the kinetics. Therefore, our TB-QCMD can discuss the by-products. Percentages of the by-products depending on the temperature can be investigated by our TB-QCMD. However, a static first-principles calculation can answer for only the most energetically stable structure.

Professor Dr Vernes asked: How do the observed tribochemical reactions (performing TB-QCMD simulations) depend on the applied load?

Professor Dr Kubo answered: We can add the load force perpendicular to the DLC substrate in the simulation model and the effect of the load force on the tribochemical reactions of the methanol molecules can be examined. However, I am very sorry that I have not simulated the effect of the load force on the tribochemical reactions of the methanol molecules at this moment. This is very interesting topic for me. Thank you very much for your useful comments.

Dr Polcar asked: You showed in the model that there was the possibility to generate water molecules. What would the effect of water be? Would it form similar OH-terminations on a DLC substrate?

Professor Dr Kubo replied: There are some possibilities for the fate of a water molecule at the DLC interface during the friction process:
1) OH-termination.
2) C–O–C structure formation.
3) No change—water molecules exist at the interface.
I have not calculated the chemical reactions of water molecules at the DLC interface yet, however I would like to do it as soon as possible. I think that all of the above three fates are possible. However, the total energy calculations will answer for the most energetically stable structure among the three possible structures.
In addition, the mixed structure of 1) OH-termination, 2) C–O–C structure formation and 3) no change—water molecules existing at the interface are also possible. Namely, the DLC surface is terminated by OH and C–O–C and still there are many water molecules at the DLC interface.

Dr Polcar asked: The results of the model, *i.e.* low friction due to the formation of OH-terminations on the DLC surface, are related with experimentally observed macroscopic friction. However, the scales of the model and experiment are significantly different. Could we relate atomistic simulation and real contact in this case in the suggested straightforward way?

Professor Dr Kubo replied: I agree that the scales of the simulation model and experiments are significantly different. Experimentally, the DLC surface is not flat and its surface roughness is over a μm-scale. However, I think that the experimentally observed macroscopic friction coefficient is mainly determined by very small contact area in nm-scale. During the friction processes, only very small area at the top of rough surfaces collide with each other and this nm-scale contact determines the macroscopic friction coefficient. Therefore, the friction coefficient obtained by our atomistic simulation method can well reproduce the experimentally observed macroscopic friction coefficient.

Professor Leggett remarked: It seems counter-intuitive that the introduction of oxygen-containing functional groups at the DLC surface leads to a decrease in the friction force, because one would expect that they would cause an increase in the interfacial free energy and, moreover, hydroxyl groups can form strong hydrogen bonds.
Can you explain how the polar groups cause a reduction in the friction force?
In your paper, you refer to "repulsion" between the hydroxyl groups. Can you please say more about the nature and origin of this repulsive interaction?

Professor Dr Kubo responded: I agree with you. Oxygen-containing groups at the DLC surface increase the friction coefficient compared to the H-terminated DLC. This is observed under 1 GPa load force condition by our quantum chemical molecular dynamics simulations. As you mentioned, this is due to the increase in the interfacial free energy and strong hydrogen bonds. Moreover the OH-termination increases surface roughness, which also leads to the increment of the friction coefficients. However, under very severe load force of 7 GPa, completely different phenomena are observed. The friction coefficient of the H-terminated DLC increases significantly, because many C–C bonds are formed at the DLC interface by the chemical reactions. These phenomena are observed by our quantum chemical molecular dynamics simulations.[1] However, for OH-terminated DLC the friction coefficient does not increase even under a severe load force of 7 GPa, because the C–C bonds are not formed at the DLC interface. This is due to the large distance between two OH-terminated DLC surfaces compared to that of two H-terminated DLC surfaces. Then, under a severe load force of 7 GPa, the OH-terminated DLC surface has a lower friction coefficient than the H-terminated DLC.

1. K. Hayashi, K. Tezuka, N. Ozawa, T. Shimazaki, K. Adachi and M. Kubo, *J. Phys. Chem. C*, 2011, **115**, 22981.

Professor Leggett asked: Are there any experimental data (for example from surface spectroscopic measurements) to support the hypothesis that oxygen-containing functional groups are formed at the DLC surface?

Professor Dr Kubo replied: It is very difficult to measure the formation of oxygen-containing functional groups at the DLC surface by experiments. There is no experimental technique to observe such small species at the friction interface. This is the reason why our quantum chemical molecular dynamics simulation method is essential to clarify the chemical reaction dynamics and mechanisms at the friction interface.

Professor Martin commented: I confirm that it is very difficult to analyze tribofilms on DLC surfaces by XPS. One solution is to use deuterated species as the lubricant and to analyze the surface by mass spectrometry (ToF-SIMS for example). This is why computer simulation has a huge advantage in these kinds of problems. My question is: relative to the formation of molecular hydrogen, which is shown on one of your slide and movie, what is the implication of dihydrogen formation on friction and wear of hydrogenated DLC friction pairs ?

Professor Dr Kubo replied: Thank you very much for your comments on the difficulties of the experimental measurements of DLC surfaces and the importance of the computer simulation for the surface analysis. Our quantum chemical molecular dynamics simulation shows that H_2 molecules are generated during the friction process at H-terminated DLC surfaces. This is due to the chemical reactions of terminated-hydrogen atoms at DLC surfaces. This result was published in ref. 1. The generation of H_2 molecules increases the distance between the two DLC surfaces and then leads to the decrement of the friction coefficients. It means that we successfully simulated that the chemical reactions at the friction interfaces strongly affect the macroscopic friction properties. However, I imagine that the generation of many many H_2 molecules at the friction interface increases the number of dangling bonds at the DLC surface. If the H_2 molecules escape from the interface, C–C bond formations may occur at the interface and it leads to the significant increase of the friction coefficient. Fontaine *et al.* reported that H-terminated DLC shows a very small friction coefficient at the initial stage, however the sudden and significant increment of the friction coefficient was observed later.[2] I think that our quantum chemical molecular dynamics simulations support the above experimental results. At the initial stage, H_2 generation leads to the increment of the distance between the two DLC surfaces and then the fiction coefficient decreases, however later the generation of C–C bonds occurs at the friction interface and then the friction coefficient increases because the generated H_2 molecules escape from the interface.

1. K. Hayashi, K. Tezuka, N. Ozawa, T. Shimazaki, K. Adachi and M. Kubo, *J. Phys. Chem. C*, 2011, **115**, 22981.
2. J. Fontaine, T. Le Mogne, J. L. Loubet and M. Belin, *Thin Solid Films*, 2005, **482**, 99.

Professor Williams remarked: As I understand it, you run your simulations under load control, so assume adequate compliance in the loading arrangement. Is it possible to run under fixed boundary compression or displacement so that pressure becomes an output—this might be more appropriate in models with a single asperity contact between interacting rough surfaces?

Professor Dr Kubo replied: Thank you very much for your important suggestion. I can perform the simulations under fixed boundary compression or displacement and then I can obtain the pressure as an output. I think that this output is also very interesting to discuss the friction properties of DLC. I will try to do it as soon as possible. I think that before the simulation I should obtain the experimental data of the distance between two DLC surfaces.

Mr Eder asked: Do you think that your combination of very high shear velocity and the crude thermostatting scheme may affect your results in an unforeseeable manner? Have you compared your results with those obtained using a common thermostat?[1]

1. Nosé-Hoover, Langevin, *etc.*

Professor Dr Kubo responded: I agree that we used very high shear velocity. This is necessary to accelerate the chemical reactions. Quantum chemical molecular dynamics methods can simulate only nano seconds and then very high shear velocity is essential to simulate the chemical reactions during nano seconds. I recently simulated 10 m s^{-1} velocity condition in addition to 100 m s^{-1} velocity in some cases in order to confirm the validity of the 100 m s^{-1} velocity. However, the simulation results are almost same. Therefore, we think that the high shear velocity of 100 m s^{-1} employed in the present paper does not significantly affect the summary of the simulation results. I am very sorry that I have not calculated the effect of the thermostat methods on the simulation results on the DLC friction system. However, previously we simulated the effect of the thermostat methods on the SiO_2 systems and we confirmed that the effect is not significant. I will investigate the effect of the thermostat methods on the DLC friction system also.

Mr Eder queried: Have you attempted to sandwich more than one methanol molecule between the DLC surfaces? Wouldn't this greatly improve your statistics of the chemistry which takes place in the lubrication gap? Have you done simulations with longer alcohols (such as the ones used experimentally)?

Professor Dr Kubo responded: Yes, I have calculated the system in which many methanol molecules are sandwiched between DLC surfaces. We observed many different chemical reactions:
1) OH-termination.
2) C–O–C structure formation.
3) H_2O formation.
Moreover, many methanol molecules did not react and then exist on the OH-terminated DLC surfaces. After, many OH-termination reactions occur, then methanol molecules did not react with the DLC surface because there are no dangling bonds on the DLC surfaces. It means that the chemical reactivity of the methanol

changes depending on the number of dangling bonds on the DLC surfaces. Moreover, the chemical reactivity of the methanol molecules decreases as time goes on because the number of dangling bonds decreases.

I also simulated ethanol and glycerol molecules sandwiched between two DLC surfaces. Ethanol and glycerol molecules also show the same chemical reactions with methanol molecules. This means that 1) OH-termination, 2) C–O–C structure formation, 3) H_2O formation, were observed.

Here, a methanol molecule produced CH_3 and it was incorporated into DLC surface, however, an ethanol molecule produced C_2H_5 and it was incorporated into DLC surface. This means that in the ethanol case, surface roughness slightly increases compared to the methanol case. Then the friction coefficient of the ethanol case is slightly larger than that of the methanol case. Glycerol also gives a slightly higher friction coefficient than methanol because of the same reason.

Mr Eder asked: How can you be sure that your systems are run-in after a simulation time of 10 ps? Could more tribochemistry occur after that period? Would the comparison of the formed/broken bonds at a different arbitrary point in time change your conclusion as to which final configuration of the system is most likely?

Professor Dr Kubo answered: I am very sorry that we have not performed longer calculations over 10 ps. However, our first-principles calculations show that OH-termination is most energetically favorable. It means that longer calculations may give OH-terminations in all cases. First-principles calculations are very effective to know the final structure of the systems, because it gives the most energetically stable structures.

Mr Gustavsson communicated: You mention several times in the paper that you want to clarify the mechanisms on an electronic and atomic scale, but in your results and conclusions you stick mainly to the atomic scale. Could you perhaps expand the conclusions so that the electronic transfer dynamics is explained more directly? I would find that interesting.

Professor Dr Kubo communicated in reply: Your comment is very very important. I calculated all the valence electrons in the simulation cell by our quantum chemical molecular dynamics method. Then, we can analyze the atomic charges, bond population, electron transfer and so on during the tribochemical reactions. However, these have not been done. I think that these are necessary to clarify the tribochemical reaction mechanism in detail. I will do it as soon as possible.

Dr Kobayashi opened the discussion of the paper by Professor Dr Zhou‡: In this work, the benzotriazole unit of the ionic liquid molecule effectively adsorbs on the Cu alloy surface to form a stable thin monolayer, reducing the friction and corrosion. Are there any contributions from the intermolecular interaction among the benzotriazol moieties to the stability of the ionic liquid monolayer?

Professor Dr Liu replied: Sorry, we really cannot answer the question. The strong interaction between benzotriazol moieties and copper will be the most important. There might be one hydrogen bonding intermolecular interaction.

Professor Klein asked: In this very nice work, were you able to measure the surface charge on the metal surfaces? And did you have any indication of layering of the ionic liquids (as for example in ref. 1)?

---

‡ Professor Dr Zhou's paper was presented by Professor Dr Liu, *Lanzhou Institute of Chemical Physics, CAS, China.*

     This journal is © The Royal Society of Chemistry 2012

1. S. Perkin *et al.*, *Phys. Chem. Chem. Phys.*, 2010, **12**, 1243–1247

Professor Dr Liu responded: Due to equipment limitations, we cannot directly measure the surface charge of the metal surface during friction. Normally, in a static state, metal surface may be negatively charged due to oxides on the outmost surface, but during friction it may be positively charged due to *exo*-electrons from the fresh metal surface. We really don't know the answer. We have noticed the reference you've mentioned. It provides some evidence of layering at extremely microscopic level. In fact, we have proposed a layering assembly model that contributes to the excellent tribological properties of ILs early in 2006 in our Wear paper.[1] Later, in a science paper, they provided direct characterization of layered structure of ILs at aluminum surface.[2] Continuous work should be further done to illustrate the issue.

1. X.-Q. Liu , F. Zhou, Y.-M. Liang, W.-M. Liu, *Wear*, 2006, **261**, 1174–1179.
2. M. Mezger, *et al.*, *Science*, 2008, **322**, 424.

Professor Spencer remarked: How many of the corrosion effects seen in your (non-imidazolium) experiments can be ascribed to the effects of water content in the ionic liquids?

Professor Dr Liu answered: It is true that BF_4- and PF_6-anions are chemically unstable in presence of water to produce highly corrosive HF gas under high temperature (such as 250 °C).[1] So the corrosion behavior of ILs largely comes from the hydrolysis of perfluoro-anions, generating fluoric acid that reacts with surfaces such as Cu or Fe. Therefore the water content in the perfluoro-anion ionic liquids plays a significant role in the corrosion behavior. But it is not quantitatively studied in the present work. According to our experiment, water will speed up corrosion when BF_4-and PF_6- are used as anions; for non-fluorine anions, water has less impact.

1. M. Yao, Y. Liang, Y. Xia, F. Zhou and X. Liu, *Tribol. Lett.*, 2008, **32**, 73–79.

Dr Ratoi commented: The base oil used on this study is highly polar and would compete with the ionic liquid additive for adsorption on the lubricated surfaces. What selection criteria have been employed for the base oil and have other oils of different polarities been investigated?

Professor Dr Liu answered: Yes, it is true that ILs have high polarity. It is the reason why ILs have both good lubrication and good antiwear properties. We have tried with some additives in ILs, and found that further improvement of their tribological properties is very limited, which means ILs can act as an additive free base oil, at least the friction modifier and antiwear additives are not actually required. On the other hand, since most additives are polar molecules, they will have some solubility with ILs and they don't have to adsorb on the surface through competitive action with the ILs.

Dr Craig said: Have you considered using Type II ionic liquids for your experiments as these are air and water tolerant?

Professor Dr Liu responded: We actually are carrying out the study. There will be several solutions to tackle the corrosion problems of ILs. The paper presents one of them. Another solution will be to use the fluorine-free anions. But it may sacrifice some lubrication or antiwear properties of fluoro-containing ILs. One task will be to find a balance.

Dr Wang asked: Are the ionic liquids conductive (or semi-conductive)? The ECR measurements seem to be very low compared with normal ECR measurements for oil lubricated contacts. Also, why were the ECR values at the beginning of the tests extremely high? Are you able to quantify the lubricant film thickness based on the level of resistance measured?

Professor Dr Liu replied: The ionic liquids are generally conductive, and the ionic conductivity is generally in the level of 10^{-3} s cm^{-1}. This is one reason that the ECR measurements seem to be very low compared with normal ECR measurements for oil lubricated steel/steel contacts, and the good conductance of the copper alloy compared to steel for another reason. For PEG, as an example to illustrate, in the initial friction stage, the lubricants may form boundary lubricating films and the friction coefficient was small at 0.12, then the boundary film might be worn away, so the friction coefficient suddenly increased to 0.22. We still cannot know how to quantify the film thickness using ECR, any theoretical work will be very useful to study boundary lubrication.

Professor Evans commented: One of the issues arising in the potential use of ionic liquids as lubricants or lubricant additives is the toxicity of the ionic compound. Your paper gives results for corrosion and lubricating characteristics of the liquids studied, but have you carried out any toxicity assessments for the ionic liquids considered and any of their relevant derivatives?

Professor Dr Liu responded: Actually most chemicals used are more or less toxic, especially some additives in base oils. ILs are not an exclusion to this. We have carried out some toxicity assessments for the ionic liquids. We found that the [BTA-MIM][PF6] ionic liquid can inhibit the growth of bacteria and fungi, having a good antibacterial (bacteria and fungi) properties.

Dr Mischler opened the discussion of the paper by Dr Österle: Which are the mechanical criteria or parameters considered for calculating deformation and break-down of the surface layers? Did you consider bulk materials properties? Are those properties the same as in nanocrystalline layers of very different structure?

Dr Österle responded: The stress–strain behaviour of each element (cell) of material was assumed as shown in Fig. 3 in the paper. According to this the iron oxide is a brittle material with a fracture stress of 340 MPa at an elastic strain of only 0.01. All the other materials (corundum was not considered in this paper) showed plastic or quasi-plastic behaviour with yield strengths either higher than iron oxide (work-hardened ferritic steel, pearlitic steel, SiC) or lower than iron oxide (soft recrystallized copper, graphite). The properties are not the same as for monolithic nanocrystalline structures. Nevertheless the sliding behaviour of the nano-composites could be modelled quite well because mainly the difference between hard and soft constituents seems to determine the formation and structure of the mechanically mixed layer, as shown for example in Fig. 6 in our paper.

Dr Mischler commented: How does the plastic flow of the nanocrystalline layer compare to the bulk material?

Dr Österle responded: We don't know the plastic flow behaviour of the nanocrystalline layers. We have tried nano-indentation, but the layers are not stable and thus are detached easily. On the other hand, the severe shear deformation which often is observed in superficial layers of tribologically stressed bodies can be related to the motion of unlinked particles in the mechanically mixed layer before they are again relinked to the third body layer.

Dr Polcar asked: Have you considered temperature in your model (*i.e.* frictional heating)?

Dr Österle replied: Temperature calculations in terms of energy dissipation processes are not included in the model. We could consider sliding behaviour at different temperatures by implementing the data of stress–strain curves for different temperatures, as the ones shown on the right side of Fig. 3 from our paper for SiC.

Mr Eder remarked: Do I have to imagine your simulation process with MCA as an iterative series of trial-and-error, where you start out from a first guess for an initial configuration and a first guess for the rules governing the behaviour of the MCA, and then keep altering configurations and rules until you reproduce an outcome that is observed experimentally? Were all the rules set from the beginning, or did they evolve?

Dr Österle replied: Yes, we tried out different rules and chose the ones which yielded the most plausible results (the applied rules are described in the paper). Besides yield or flow stress at a certain amount of plastic deformation, shear stress or interparticle distance could have been selected as well.

Mr Eder asked: How does the method of MCA compare to other coarse graining methods and why did you choose MCA for this work?

Dr Österle replied: Most discrete element methods use random element arrangements, but we used a regular arrangement of elements, as shown Fig. 2.

Mr Eder asked: How do two neighbouring MCA interact when they represent different materials? Are there schemes similar to the Lorentz–Berthelot mixing rules in molecular dynamics?

Dr Österle responded: The interaction is not comparable to MD-schemes.
First the stress intensity (von Mises stress) of the neighbouring pair of MCA is calculated, considering the impact of all other neighbouring MCAs. Then this value is compared to the flow stresses of material 1 and material 2. If it exceeds the flow stress of the softer material, the bond will be broken.

Professor Klein opened the discussion of Professor Dr Vernes' paper: Since in your study you have in principle—I presume—the capability of characterizing the

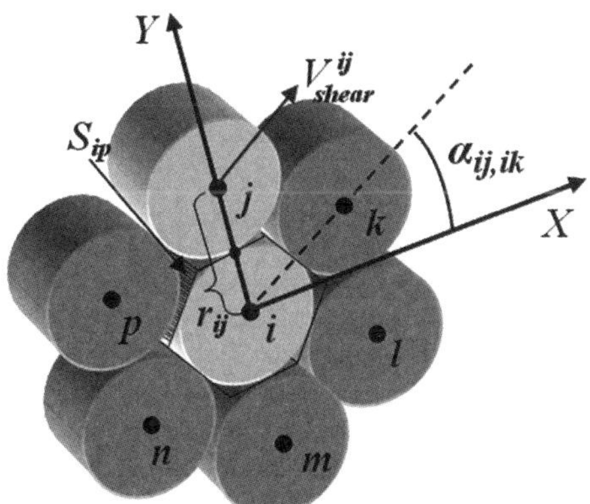

Fig. 2 Definition of the local coordinate system of automata pair *i-j* and its neighbourhood. (Reproduced with permission from ref. 4 in our paper. Copyright 2010 Elsevier.)

position and motion of every particle at all times, could that allow you to evaluate the detailed energy dissipation and then relate that to the coefficient of sliding friction?

Professor Dr Vernes answered: Commonly, in MD one simultaneously records at various moments of the simulation the position of particles and the force acting on these in order to closely follow the evolution of a given nanosystem in time. Therefore, in principle, the work done by the particles in the nanosystem can be straightforwardly determined. In our MD simulations, however, that part of the work which is guided to the thermostat was not explicitly considered. Thus only a gross estimation of the dissipated energy would be possible based on our MD data. This in turn would make the resulting correlation between the dissipated energy and the coefficient of friction entering the three-term friction law proposed in our paper extremely questionable.

Professor Williams remarked: The quantity τ in eqn (1) in your paper represents the shear strength of an asperity junction. Looking at Fig. 4 from the paper would suggest a value around 5 GPa—so am I correct in thinking that this is in effect the theoretical strength of the Fe substrate, so greater than might be expected from 'real' asperities? Given that the applied pressures are of the order of 1 GPa is this not likely to underestimate the effect of the adhesion term in eqn (1).

Professor Dr Vernes answered: The shear strength denoted by τ in eqn (1) in our paper is a constitutive system parameter characterizing the effective strength of shear within the entire nanotribological systems and therefore cannot be equal to or identified with the shear strength of Fe, known as being around 0.5 GPa. The adhesion-controlled friction force, as given by the Bowden–Tabor term, depends on this shear strength ascribed to the entire nanotribological system as well as on the contact area, which in turn is found to not necessarily increase linearly with the applied load.

Professor Dai addressed all participants in the discussion: I would like say that the main procedure of friction is the degeneration of energy, which can be presented by the entropy production, not the dissipation of energy. How is the friction coefficient correlated with dissipation of work?

Professor Dr Bhushan answered: It is commonly believed that friction is a measure of energy dissipation.[1]

1. B. Bhushan, *Principles and Applications of Tribology*, Wiley, 1999

Professor Martin replied: I agree with you. The production of entropy (or heat alternatively) in the interface region is necessary to decrease the Gibbs free energy to negative values. Then tribochemical reactions are made possible and a tribofilm will be generated.

Professor Leggett answered: When work is done, energy is dissipated as heat. The dissipation of energy as heat increases the entropy of the Universe. Entropy and the dissipation of energy in friction are thus processes that are related. It is customary to think about energy dissipation, because usually, from an engineering perspective, that is the focus (dissipation of kinetic energy in braking, for example). Thinking about entropic effects is certainly interesting but much more challenging.

Professor Dr Vernes replied: Tribological phenomena such as friction, wear and lubrication are typically non-equilibrium ones, and can be accurately described only within the framework of non-equilibrium thermodynamics. Therefore a study of entropy production and entropy current whilst a tribological phenomenon occurs

    This journal is © The Royal Society of Chemistry 2012

should be mandatory. Due to the diversity of transport processes accompanying a given tribological phenomenon, however, it is almost impossible to accurately access these thermodynamical quantities in their entire complexity. Nevertheless, by adopting a near-equilibrium approach it was shown in the literature that the coefficient of friction as we know it cannot provide energetical insights into friction.

Professor Williams reopened the discussion of the paper by Dr Österle: What is the force–distance relationship between the automata—is it a Lennard–Jones type relation? How do you decide when two automata become dissociated or reconnected?

Dr Österle responded: A Lennard–Jones type potential would only describe the interaction of a pair of particles. Our approach was to consider multi-particle interactions. Instead of a theoretical pair of potentials we preferred to relate particle interactions to the stress–strain behaviour of the different involved materials.

Professor Dr Rahnejat asked: In the paper there are various rules with regard to bonding and debonding of material from and to the surfaces. There's no mention of what forces may be responsible for/underlying to this process. A mechanical model based on mechanical properties is alluded to. You have described debonding based on shear or yield stress. What would account for the bonding of two particles together? What force/kinetics is involved? Is it adhesion?

Dr Österle answered: Firstly, it is not chemical bonding, neither covalent nor van der Waals.

What can be observed experimentally is that airborne nanoparticles of a critical concentration are not stable but form agglomerates. The third body layers we have observed experimentally are agglomerates of nanoparticles of different chemical species. Some colleagues have termed this tribo-sintering. In the model we have considered tribo-sintering for the metallic species by introducing the rule, that when two particles start to touch each other and a certain amount of plastic deformation has occurred, the agglomerate will form. For the iron oxide species it is more complicated. Since it cannot deform plastically, elevated temperature would be necessary to initiate sintering. Since heat production is not implemented in the model, re linking of oxide nanoparticles is not simulated. Thus the model shows only the initial reaction of an already existing third body layer, but not the regeneration of the third body from the mechanically mixed granular layer. The latter mechanism must exist, because otherwise the third body would exhaust rapidly, although a certain fraction of the loose particles may be ejected to the environment as well.

Dr Polcar continued the discussion of the paper by Professor Dr Vernes: Why should the Amontons–Coulomb term (*i.e.* friction times load) be valid at nanoscale contact?

Professor Dr Vernes replied: When the friction is completely load-controlled, the Amontons–Coulomb friction law is valid even on the nanoscale. There exist boundary lubricated nanotribological systems where the Derjaguin-form of the Amontons–Coulomb friction law describes the friction, depending on the surface roughness of the solid sliders as well as the chemistry and the density of the lubricant. In the mixed lubrication regime, on the other hand, where solid–solid contact also occurs, a three-term friction law holds—as we showed in our paper—which involves the Derjaguin-offset, the load-controlled term, as well as the Bowden–Tabor term providing the adhesion-controlled part of the friction. In the latter case, we demonstrated that the Derjaguin-offset, shear strength and coefficient of friction are all system parameters, *i.e.*, they are independent of the loading conditions, but do depend on the set-up of the nanotribological systems.

Professor Williams remarked: Our explanation, at least to undergraduates, of the physical origin of the observed constancy of the coefficient of friction on the macro-scale—conventionally defined as the ratio of the tangential to the normal loading of a sliding pair—inevitably involves the distinction between the 'real' and 'apparent' or geometric areas of contact and so to the notion of populations of asperities, although we are usually rather reticent about specifying their precise number or sizes. Once we get to the nano-scale these arguments become less easy to maintain as the number of asperities dwindles—perhaps, in the extreme case of an AFM tip, to one. The effects of adhesion become apparent as is evident from your own numerical models and the work presented in Professor Leggett's paper[1] to this meeting and it must be true that at the micro-scale we need a more sophisticated picture which, in a sense, revives the Bowden and Tabor friction model of deformation plus adhesion terms. You advocate a three term model separating out the Derjaguin term—as we move from the nano to the micro will this not become effectively subsumed into the adhesion term?

1. K. Busuttil, N. Nikogeorgos, Z. Zhang, M. Geoghegan, C. A. Hunter and G. J. Leggett, *Faraday Discuss.*, 2012, DOI: 10.1039/C2FD00133K.

Professor Dr Vernes responded: We think that the three-term friction law as we proposed results not just from a formal separation of various terms, but is consistent with the physics and chemistry behind the friction in nanotribological systems. It is true that both the Derjaguin-offset and the Bowden–Tabor term ascribed to the adhesion-controlled friction originate from the adhesion between the constitutive particles of the investigated nanotribological systems. In our present interpretation, however, they differ in their consequences. As long as the Derjaguin-offset survives at vanishing load, the occurrence of the Bowden–Tabor term depends on the actual load-dependent solid–solid contact area, and hence, loosely speaking, it is a more dynamical term than the former.

Professor Dr Rahnejat addressed all participants: Friction is a question of scale. The coefficient of friction has no specific definition at the nanoscale. Amontons' rules are only true for pure sliding condition. Therefore, the Amontons–Coulomb approach does not apply to stick-slip motion or adhesion, causing cold-welded asperity pair junctions . It is far better to look at friction in terms of energy dissipation.

Professor Leggett answered: The question of the relationship between nanoscale contacts and continuum models for contact mechanics remains unanswered, and is undoubtedly one of the central problems in nanotribology. I would suggest that "pure" sliding, or any other type of "pure" phenomenon is uncommon! Phenomenologically, one observes friction behaviour in many circumstances that are consistent with Amontons' law. Our own view is that this represents a limit, when adhesion becomes weak. Certainly it is helpful to think about this in terms of dissipative processes: a linear friction–load relationship represents a limit in which dissipation occurs primarily through ploughing effects, while a non-linear relationship implies that energy is dissipated in the shearing of contacts.

Professor Dr Bhushan responded: I totally agree. We need to give up the archaic definition of the coefficient of friction although it makes life simpler while reporting data as a nondimensional number.

Professor Dr Vernes replied: There is no doubt that friction at all length scales should be thermodynamically monitored. In this regard, it is known from literature that an energetical description of friction makes the definition of the coefficient of friction commonly used to interpret tribological results highly questionable.

Professor Dr Bhushan communicated: When Amontons observed that friction force was proportional to load, it made sense to define the proportional constant as coefficient of friction which is nondimensional. It has been convenient to make friction measurements at a range of loads and report the value of a coefficient of friction which had been believed to be a material property. It is now widely known that the coefficient of friction is not a material property but system response.[1] Among other things, it depends upon operating conditions. Nanoscale measurements clearly show scale dependence and it changes as, for example, load and speeds change.[2] It is now the time to divorce this antiquated term and describe friction force at given operating conditions for a material pair.

1. B. Bhushan, *Introduction to Tribology*, John Wiley, New York, 2002.
2. Z. Tao, and B. Bhushan, *Rev. Sci. Instrum.*, 2006, **77**, 103705; B. Bhushan, *Nanotribology and Nanomechanics—An Introduction*, Springer-Verlag, Heidelberg, Germany, first edition, 2005; second edition, 2008; third edition—*Nanotribology and Nanomechanics I—Measurement Techniques and Nanomechanics, II—Nanotribology, Biomimetics, and Industrial Applications,* 2011.

Professor Dr Vernes communicated in response: Our nanoscopic coefficient of friction should not be confused with its macroscopic counterpart. When considering nanoscopic systems, the naïve division of the friction force by the applied load will usually lead to a load-dependent specific friction force which in some cases is erroneously identified with the coefficient of friction. We agree that the frictional response of a tribosystem will likely depend on boundary and operating conditions. However, when applying our three-term-friction law, we do find our system parameters, *e.g.*, the resulting coefficient of friction, to be independent of load, so we are convinced that these parameters can be used to predict friction forces for certain system classes.

Hydration lubrication: exploring a new paradigm

Anastasya Gaisinskaya,† Liran Ma,†‡ Gilad Silbert,† Raya Sorkin,†
Odeya Tairy,† Ronit Goldberg, Nir Kampf and Jacob Klein*

Received 9th December 2011, Accepted 22nd December 2011
DOI: 10.1039/c2fd00127f

Lubrication by hydration shells that surround, and are firmly attached to,
charges in water, and yet are highly fluid, provide a new mode for the extreme
reduction of friction in aqueous media. We report new measurements, using
a mica surface-force balance, on several different systems which exhibit hydration
lubrication, extending earlier studies significantly to shed new light on the nature
and limits of this mechanism. These include lubrication by hydrated ions trapped
between charged surfaces, and boundary lubrication by surfactants, by poly-
zwitterionic brushes and by close-packed layers of phosphatidylcholine vesicles.
Sliding friction coefficients as low as 10^{-4} or even lower, and mean contact
pressures of up to 17 MPa or higher are indicated. This suggests that the
hydration lubrication mechanism may underlie low-friction sliding in biological
systems, in which such pressures are rarely exceeded.

1 Introduction

Attempts to reduce the friction between sliding surfaces have been documented since
antiquity.[1,2] Modern insight into the nature of friction has emerged through understanding the dissipative processes that take place between rubbing surfaces,[3,4] while
the main modes of lubrication are often considered in terms of hydrodynamic and
boundary processes (or a combination of these), as well as processes such as plastic
deformation and those that result in wear.[5] Boundary lubrication involves thin films
of lubricant materials that are firmly attached to the underlying substrates, so that
when the surfaces slide past each other the slip occurs at the interface between these
layers. This generally results in lower sliding friction, but particularly in much
reduced wear of the underlying substrate surfaces. A common approach to
boundary lubrication utilizes amphiphilic surfactant molecules whose polar headgroups attach to the solid substrate, forming monolayers with the alkyl tails
exposed. When these slide past each other, the relatively weak van der Waals adhesion between the opposing alkyl tail layers may be overcome at low shear stresses,
leading to low friction coefficients. At the same time the presence of the boundary
monolayers greatly reduces substrate–substrate contact, resulting in much reduced
wear.[6–9]

In recent decades the use of polymers and other soft materials adsorbed or grafted
as boundary lubricants on surfaces has been explored, particularly when considering
friction in liquid environments.[10–15] The way in which the chain-like nature of polymeric layers—in particular the configurational entropy of chains—affects frictional

Weizmann Institute of Science, Rehovot, 76100, ISRAEL. E-mail: Jacob.klein@weizmann.ac.il

† These authors contributed equally to this paper.
‡ Present address: State Key Laboratory of Tribology, Tsinghua University, Beijing 10084,
China.

forces, as in suppressing interpenetration of opposing layers at moderate compressions or leading to entanglement effects at high compressions, is reasonably well understood. Friction in a *water* environment is of special interest, in the context of biological lubrication processes and of biomedical devices, and may have implications also for tissue engineering in regenerative medicine.[16]

Recently several studies have revealed a remarkable mode of lubrication in aqueous systems, termed hydration lubrication.[17–22] This originates in the hydration layers that form about charges as a result of the large dipole of the water molecule. A sheath of such molecules surrounding a charge (such as an ion, see inset cartoon in Fig. 1, or the charges on a zwitterion) reduces its self-, or Born-energy substantially, and so may be tenaciously attached, requiring considerable energy to remove.[23] At the same time the *exchange* of such hydration water molecules with adjacent free water molecules can be extremely rapid (depending on the precise ion enclosed), with exchange rates ω up to 10^9 s^{-1} (for the common alkali metal ions such as Na$^+$ and K$^+$).[24] The exchange rate ω may be viewed as effectively the relaxation rate of the hydration sheath. Thus such a hydrated charge between sliding, confining surfaces can sustain a large normal load while maintaining its strongly-attached hydration layer; however, under shear the compressed hydration layer responds in a fluid manner as long as its relaxation rate ω exceeds the shear rate $\dot{\gamma}$. This combination of sustaining a large normal load, together with a fluid response to shear, results in striking lubrication properties, as first revealed in the study of Raviv and Klein,[20] illustrated in Fig. 1.

In that study, two charged solid surfaces were made to approach across a salt solution at high concentration ($\sim$0.1 M NaCl). The trapped counterions resulted in the well-known hydration repulsion between the surfaces. At mean contact pressures up to *ca.* 0.4 MPa—the highest reported in that work—the sliding friction force was lower than could be measured even using the state-of-the-art sensitivity available with the surface force balance used (SFB, see later). This corresponded to an effective friction coefficient μ with an upper limit of *ca.* 0.0002 at these pressures. Later

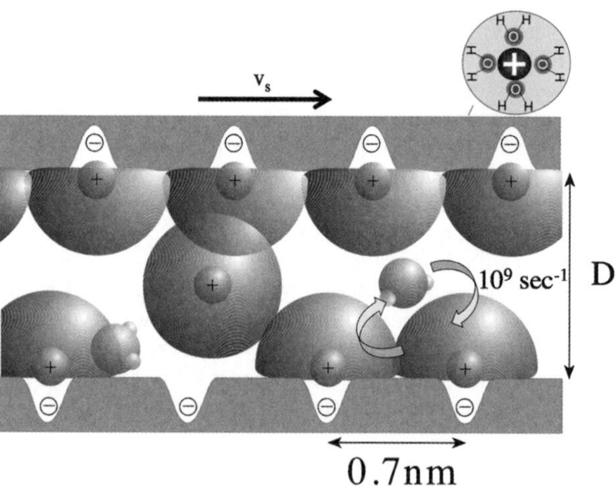

Fig. 1 Schematically illustrating the hydration lubrication mechanism when two (negatively) charged surfaces confining hydrated counterions slide past each other: as long as the shear rate (v_s/D) is less than the hydration shell relaxation rate—indicated here as similar to the exchange rate 10^9 s^{-1} as for alkali metal ions—the response to shear will be fluid. At the same time the hydration layers are tenaciously attached—dehydration energies can be very large, *e.g.* some 400 kJ mol^{-1} for the hydration shell surrounding the Na$^+$ ion.[23] Dimensions in the cartoon, including free water molecules for perspective, are roughly to scale for charged mica surfaces (top and bottom, green online) and Na$^+$ counterions surrounded by hydration shells (blue online, see also top right inset) for $D \approx 1$ nm.

   This journal is © The Royal Society of Chemistry 2012

measurements showed similar behaviour when different alkali metal ions were used[25] (Na[+], K[+], Li[+]—though the case of Cs[+], whose hydration layer is much less tenacious, was very different[26]), up to pressures as high as 1 MPa (*ca.* 10 atm),[27] and also when one mica surface was replaced by a smooth gold surface.[28]

The central idea of lubrication being provided by the hydration layers surrounding charges or zwitterions proved fruitful in understanding the very low sliding friction observed in several other systems. These include sliding between silica surfaces across different salt solutions;[29] friction between supported lipid[30] and surfactant[31] bilayers; the unusual behaviour of surfactant boundary layers under water, when the slip plane shifts from the usual midplane separating the alkyl tail layers, to the substrate/polar-headgroup interface as the latter becomes hydrated;[17] the case of charged[19] and, particularly, of highly hydrated polyzwitterionic[18] brushes; and the very recent observation of remarkable lubrication by close-packed surface layers of gel-phase liposomes,[22,32] where the outer liposome surfaces expose dense highly-hydrated phosphocholine layers. Hydration lubrication indeed appears to be a central mechanism for low-friction of sliding surfaces in biological systems, and may explain the very low friction observed in synovial joints.[33]

This novel insight into lubrication processes in aqueous media immediately raises several basic questions as to the nature of the hydration lubrication process itself. How does it depend on the identity of the enclosed charges or on the macromolecular vectors (surfactants, polymers, liposomes) delivering the boundary lubrication? How robust is it, both with respect to the maximal pressures sustainable and to long sliding times? How does the frictional dissipation depend on the sliding velocity? In this study we extend our measurements of sliding friction, using the surface force balance, to explore several different configurations where hydration lubrication is implicated. By going to much higher pressures we are able, for the first time, to measure explicitly the friction coefficient between smooth charged (mica) surfaces sliding across hydrated ions, and to identify factors that may limit this mechanism. We connect the known rearrangement of surfactant monolayers into bilayer domains[34–37] to their boundary lubrication properties, demonstrating how this breaks down as the domain density decreases. We extend earlier work[18] on grafted-from, highly-hydrated poly-zwitterionic brushes to much thicker, denser brushes and higher pressures, and, finally, we examine different liposome surface layers at both higher pressures and, importantly, at extended sliding times to demonstrate the robustness of this mecha-nism. Our studies shed light on the limits and applicability of the emerging hydration lubrication paradigm, and provide new insight into its nature.

2 Experimental

Materials

Water used in all cases was purified in either a Milli-Q Gradient purification system (total organic content, TOC 4 ppb or better) or in a Barnstead Nanopure Diamond system (TOC 1 ppb), conductivity 18.2 MΩ cm. Mica was ruby muscovite grade I (S&J Trading, NY, NY). Salts were 99.99% purity (Merck KGaA). Cetyltrimethy-lammonium bromide (CH$_3$(CH2)$_{15}$N(Me)$_3$Br), CTAB, was purchased from Fluka (puriss grade p.a.) and used as received. Monomers of 2-(methacryloyloxy)ethyl phosphorylcholine (MPC) were kindly donated by Biocompatibles (UK), and mac-roinitiator for the grafted-from pMPC polymerization was obtained from S. Armes (and described previously[38]). Catalysts Cu(I)Br (99.999%), Cu(II)Br$_2$ (99.999%) and 2,2'-bipyridine (bpy, 99+%) for the ATRP of the pMPC were purchased from Sigma-Aldrich and used as received. 1,2-distearoyl-*sn-glycero*-3-phosphocholine lipids (DSPC, liquid-crystalline-to-gel transition temperature $T_m = 55.5$ °C), were purchased from Lipoid, Ludwigshafen, Germany, for the liposome preparation. Epoxy resin ("EPON 1004", Shell Chemicals) was used in all cases to glue the mica sheets onto the cylindrical glass lenses in the surface forces balance.

Methods

Surface forces. The surface force balance (SFB) used has been described in detail earlier[39] and is shown schematically in Fig. 2. It measures the absolute surface separation between two molecularly smooth mica surfaces to $\pm(3\text{–}5)$ Å in the present experiments (and somewhat lower absolute precision in cases where surfaces need to be dismounted after calibration to attach surface layers prior to remounting and measuring). The surfaces are mounted in a crossed cylinder configuration and may be made to move normally or laterally relative to each other *via* a sectored piezoelectric tube (P, Fig. 2). Direct measurement of the bending of two orthogonal springs K_n and K_s (Fig. 2) enables the monitoring of normal and shear forces respectively as the surfaces move normally or slide past each other.

Dynamic light scattering (ALV-NIBS High Performance Particle Sizer (Langen, Germany)) was used to characterize liposome dimensions as described earlier.[22,32]

Cryo-scanning electron microscopy (cryoSEM) on the liposome-coated surfaces was carried out using an Ultra 55 SEM (Zeiss) as described earlier.[22,32]

3   Results and discussion

Hydrated ions trapped between charged solid surfaces

Fig. 3 shows the normal force $F_n(D)$ *vs.* surface separation D profile between mica surfaces in (nominal) 0.01 M KCl solution (normalized in the standard Derjaguin approximation as $F_n(D)/R$ to enable comparison between different contact points with different radii R). The profile shows the characteristic exponential increase in the repulsion at decreasing D, as in the Derjaguin–Landau–Vervey–Overbeek (DLVO) relation[40]

$$F_n(D)/R = 128\pi c k_B T \kappa^{-1}\tanh^2(e\psi_0/4k_B T)\exp(-\kappa D) - A_H/6D^2 \tag{1}$$

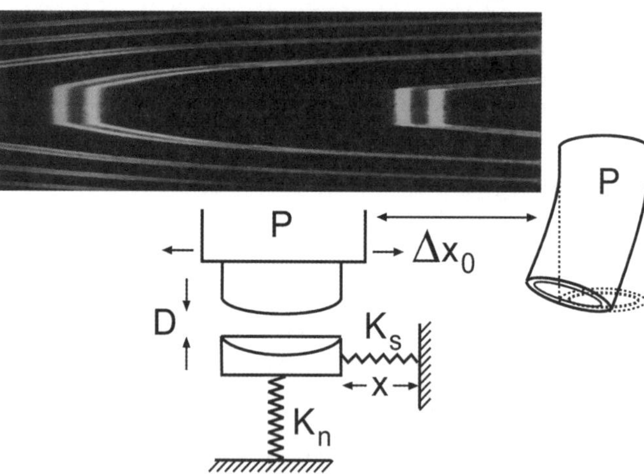

Fig. 2 Schematic of the surface force balance (SFB) used in these experiments. The interaction of two mica surfaces (in a crossed cylindrical configuration, mean radius R (≈ 10 mm) and a closest distance D apart) with relevant surface attached species is measured directly by the bending of two sets of springs, K_n and K_s respectively for the normal and shear (frictional) forces. Fringes of equal chromatic order between two mica surfaces in contact are shown, as is the lateral bending (by Δx_0) of the piezo-tube P when opposing sectors are made to expand/contract by application of opposite voltages. The bending x of the shear spring is monitored *via* changes in an air-gap capacitor.

   This journal is © The Royal Society of Chemistry 2012

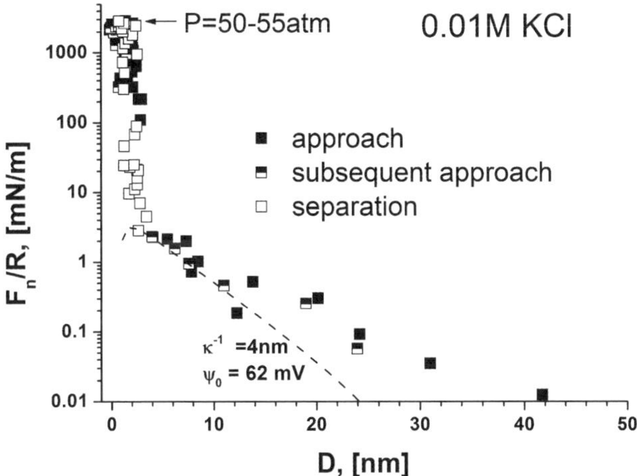

Fig. 3 Normal force F_n vs. surface separation D profiles between mica surfaces, normalized as $F_n(D)/R$ where R is the mean curvature of the mica surfaces, across (nominal) 0.01 M KCl solution. The broken line is the DLVO fit (eqn (1) in text) to the data, with Debye screening length κ^{-1} and surface potential ψ_0 as indicated, showing the deviation due to hydration repulsion at $D < ca.$ 3 nm. The value of $\kappa^{-1} = 4$ nm corresponds to a 1 : 1 electrolyte concentration 0.6×10^{-2} M, rather than the nominal 10^{-2} M).

where c is the ion concentration, T is the temperature (296 K), k_B is Boltzmann's constant, A_H is the Hamaker constant (2×10^{-20} J), ψ_0 is the effective (far-field) surface potential, κ^{-1} is the Debye screening length, and e is the electronic charge. The strong repulsion commencing at $D < ca.$ 2–3 nm, deviating from the predicted van der Waals attraction at that separation, is due to the well-documented hydration repulsion[11][43] arising from the tenaciously-attached hydration shells about the trapped K^+ ions (see also Fig. 1) at concentrations higher than the critical hydration value of $ca.$ 10^{-3} M for K^+ salts. The normal forces were increased by progressive compression of the normal springs (K_n in Fig. 2), to values that are one to two orders of magnitude greater than in earlier studies. Both approach and separation runs are shown in Fig. 3, as well as a second approach following separation at the same contact point.

In general, if no shear was applied (up to the highest pressures) or if, when applying shear, the normal loads (pressures) did not exceed $ca.$ 20–30 mN m^{-1} ($ca.$ 1 MPa) the normal force profiles were reproducible on second and subsequent approaches of the surfaces, indicating that the mica–mica contact region remained undamaged. For the shear forces, this is consistent with earlier shear experiments across aqueous salt solutions,[20,25,27] where the normal mean contact pressures P never exceeded 0.5–1 MPa. Both here and subsequently, the mean pressures P are evaluated as $P = (F_n/A)$ where $A = \pi r^2$. Here r is the radius of the flattened region determined either directly from the flattened tip of the fringes (e.g. see fringes in Fig. 2) or from the Hertzian relation $r = (F_n R/K)^{1/3}$, where K is the effective modulus of the mica/glue combination determined separately[44] (and is of order 10^9 N m^{-2}). For normal compression to the highest pressures, the question of damage or no damage to the mica surfaces depended to some extent on the provenance and purity of the salts used, the thickness of the mica sheets, the actual ions investigated (Li^+, Na^+ or K^+), and the specific orientation of the contacting mica sheets. When shear was applied at the higher pressures (> $ca.$ 50–100 mN m^{-1}, or > $ca.$ 1.5 MPa), there was, in some of the runs, indication of damage to the surfaces as a result of the shear motion. Such damage was indicated when, on separation and a subsequent approach, a long-ranged repulsion was noted and the surfaces could not be approached close to their original (undamaged) contact position. Rarely, such damage was also indicated on approach to the highest pressures even in the absence of applied shear (we note that some slight shear motion may occur during the application of normal pressure alone, due to vibrations and/or to mechanical coupling arising as the normal spring is progressively compressed). However, in very many cases—including those shown in Fig. 3–5—there was no sign of such surface damage when sliding motion was applied, even at pressures of up to 10^7 N m^{-2} (corresponding to $F/R > ca.$ 10 N m^{-1}) or more, indicating that the surfaces retained their structural integrity and smoothness even when sliding under these pressures. The implications of these results is discussed below; a full description of these results with different salts and other conditions is beyond the scope of this paper and is described elsewhere (A. Gaisinskaya *et al.*[45] and L. Ma *et al.*[46]). Here we focus on the typical new features revealed, showing only data where no surface damage was indicated up to the highest compressions and subsequent decompressions.

At progressive compressions (and, for some of the runs, de-compressions) a lateral motion was applied to the top mica surface *via* the sectored piezo-electric tube (P in Fig. 2), and the force F_s transmitted to the lower surface was monitored *via* the bending of the shear springs K_s (Fig. 2). In some of the experiments the normal load was increased to a given value, shear forces measured, then the surfaces were well separated and made to approach again to a higher normal load, and the procedure repeated until the highest pressures attained (the normal force profiles of Fig. 3 were measured in this way). Typical shear force traces are shown in Fig. 4 for sliding mica surfaces compressed to different pressures as indicated (across 0.1 M NaNO$_3$ for these traces). Trace 4a is the back and forth motion of the upper surface, while

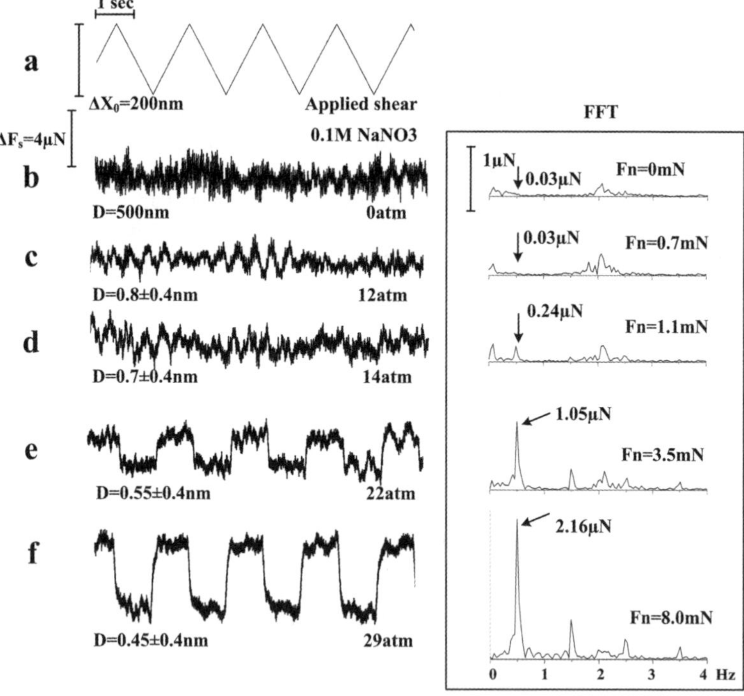

Fig. 4 Typical shear force F_s *vs.* time traces (b–e) for mica surfaces across confined hydrated ions at different pressures as shown (the data are for a 0.1M NaNO$_3$ solution), in response to a back-and-forth lateral motion, trace a, of the piezo-tube-mounted upper surface (Fig. 2). The panel on the right shows the corresponding fast-Fourier transform (FFT) frequency analysis of the forces, with the drive frequency marked by an arrow, which enables the detection of weak frictional forces (*e.g.* trace d).

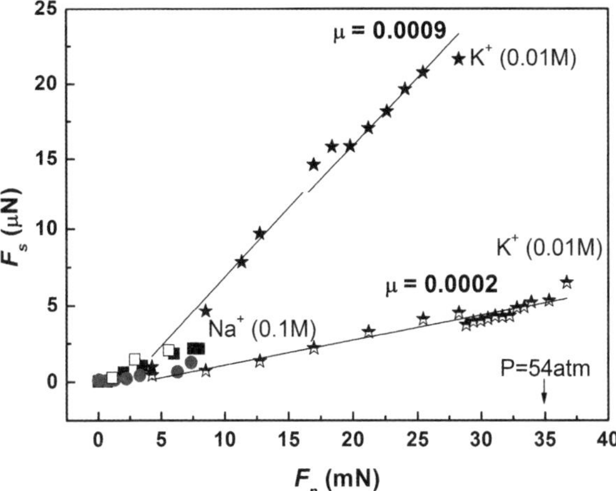

Fig. 5 Variation of shear (frictional) forces F_s with load F_n between mica surfaces across 0.01 M KCl solution (corresponding to the $F_n(D)$ profiles in Fig. 3) star data symbols; and across 0.1 M $NaNO_3$ solutions, circles and squares (taken from traces of Fig. 4). Filled stars correspond to the 17th approach, and half-filled stars to the 19th approach at a given contact point. Filled squares are for approach of the surfaces, while empty squares are taken during separation.

traces 4b–f are the corresponding frictional or shear force response. The right hand panels show a frequency analysis of the transmitted forces, revealing more clearly the onset of measurable forces at the drive frequency (marked with arrow). These show – again, in agreement with the earlier studies where pressures of at most 1 MPa were achieved[20,25,27] – that up to *ca.* 1.2 MPa (~12 atm) pressure (trace 4c) the sliding friction force was within the large-separation systematic signal level, trace 4b (arising from the weak coupling to the PZT wires[39]).

The variation of friction force F_s with normal load F_n, extracted from traces such as in Fig. 4, is shown for typical cases in Fig. 5. The data in Fig. 5 relates to friction across 0.1 M NaNO3 (circles and squares, corresponding to the traces in Fig. 4) and across 0.01 M KCl solutions (stars), corresponding to the normal force profiles in Fig. 3. Fig. 5 illustrates well some of the main new features arising as the mica surfaces are compressed to many tens of atmospheres and made to slide across trapped, hydrated alkali metal ions. The effective friction coefficient, taken as $\mu = (\partial F_s/\partial F_n)$, is low, in the range 0.0009 to 0.0002 in Fig. 5. Friction across the $NaNO_3$ solution, for which $\mu \approx 0.0002$–0.0003, ranges up to 29 atm (*ca.* 2.9 MPa) while that across the KCl solution ranges up to *ca.* 55 atm (the corresponding *ca.* 5-fold difference in the range of F_n for the two cases arises from the fact that, according to Hertzian contact mechanics, the mean pressure P varies only as $F_n^{1/3}$). The two sets of data for the K⁺ solution were both taken at the same contact point, on different approaches: the top data set ($\mu = 0.0009$) was for the 17th approach, while the lower data set ($\mu = 0.0002$) was for the 19th approach, following the proce dure described earlier. We note also that the hydration layers between the sliding surfaces could be robust for long periods; back and forth sliding for up to 60 min at high compressions (*e.g.* for 0.01 M KCl, at *ca.* 55 atm for the 19th approach for the contact point measured in Fig. 5) showed the friction to be stable at its very low values, indeed decreasing slightly after 60 min sliding.

Several new features emerge from these results, which probe the limits of lubrication by hydrated ions. For the first time, we are able not only to demonstrate that friction across hydrated charges can be extremely low but to determine the friction coefficient μ itself. In earlier studies the maximum mean pressures P applied on the contact area across the confined charges ranged from 0.3 MPa to *ca.* 1 MPa (*ca.* 10 atm) at most,[20,25,27] and the frictional force was below the noise level of the

SFB, allowing only an upper limit on μ to be determined. In the present studies, the maximal pressures were 5-fold (*e.g.* 55 atm in Fig. 5) and even 10-fold or more greater (not shown), ranging to over 100 atm (>10MPa), and a relatively linear relation between load and friction yields a clear value of μ. The friction coefficient μ was generally lower than 10^{-3} for the K^+ and Na^+ salts above their critical hydration concentration, as seen in Fig. 5 where the range of values was $\mu = 0.0009$–0.0002 up to $P = 55$ atm. It is worth emphasizing that because of the weak variation of P with load ($\sim(load)^{1/3}$) a 10-fold increase in pressure across the contact region in the SFB requires a 1000-fold increase in the load.

One result that emerged clearly following a large number of experiments was that at higher pressures ($P > P_0 \approx ca.$ 1–1.5 MPa) the friction forces were sensitive to small differences arising from the nature of the salt used and the contact between the mica surfaces. Up to mean pressures P_0, which is roughly the maximum contact pressure probed in previous studies,[20,25,27] all salts used at all contact points between the surfaces yielded very low friction in line with the earlier reports, attributed to the hydration lubrication mechanism. For pressures higher than this, we found that only salts from a particular company (Merck KGaA) yielded generally satisfactory results, while the same salts with similar or even higher nominal purity (>99.99%) obtained from other companies (*e.g.* Sigma, Alfa Aesar) often gave results indicating tearing of the mica on shear at high pressures ($P > P_0$). We attribute this to sensitivity to differing contaminants in the 'unsuccessful' salts, which may be present in trace amounts (ppm) and yet, if they are surface active, result in significant perturbation to the mica surfaces when they are pressed very close together. This is because at the high pressures reached in our study the mica surfaces are expected to separated by an order of an Å or so (lower than the spatial resolution in determining D). Indeed, extrapolating from the earlier exponential increase of the hydration repulsion with decreasing D, as revealed in earlier studies,[20,43,47] to the large normal forces ($F_n/R \approx 3$ N m^{-1} in Fig. 3) in our experiments, would lead to an unphysical negative separation. It is likely that the mean mica–mica separation in the case of our highest pressures would, rather, be of order of the size of the enclosed ions themselves (*ca.* 2 Å) or possibly slightly larger if water of hydration is considered. In that case surface perturbations that may arise from adsorption of species even at ppm levels or less could result in higher friction and a tearing of the mica. Moreover, at such Å-level separations, any steric forces between the mica outer lattice structure and the confined hydrated ions are likely to depend on the detailed relative crystallographic orientation of the mica sheets themselves.

Relaxation of the hydrated ions into a more favourable orientation with respect to the confining mica lattice may also be important at the small surface separations arising at the highest pressures. The observation in Fig. 5 that at the 17th approach to high pressures in the 0.01 M KCl solution (filled stars) the friction is somewhat larger ($\mu = 0.0009$) than on a subsequent approach (19th approach, half-filled stars, $\mu = 0.0002$) at the same contact point may indicate that the trapped hydrated ions have adopted a more favourable orientation with respect to sliding of the confining mica surfaces. A similar conclusion may be drawn from the observation that following an hour of continuous back-and-forth shear motion at high pressures ($\sim$5 MPa) across the 0.01 KCl solution, the friction force (and thus the friction coefficient) decreased slightly. It seems reasonable to assume that these effects—limitations arising from trace surface perturbations, or the relative orientation of the mica sheets or of the confined ions—are not intrinsic to the hydration lubrication mechanism itself. Thus we may conclude that this mechanism, at least in the case of some of the alkali metal ions, is effective at least up to 10 MPa or more.

Boundary lubrication with bilayer domains of polar surfactants

As noted in the Introduction, the slip plane between boundary layers of polar surfactants sliding in air, or in organic solvents and oils, is at the midplane interface

   This journal is © The Royal Society of Chemistry 2012

between the exposed alkyl-tail surfaces, while, as recently revealed, under water the slip plane shifts to the hydrated polar-headgroup/substrate interface. This effect was demonstrated with uniform monolayers of a double-tailed C_{11}-quaternary ammonium surfactant. Here we extend this to monolayers of CTAB surfactants, which are known to rearrange with time into bilayer domains.[35,36] Following calibration of the mica contact position in water, a CTAB monolayer was created on one of the mica surfaces by incubation for two hours in a CTAB solution above its c.m.c. and subsequent rinsing (details in G. Silbert *et al.*[48]). Subsequently both normal and shear interactions between the CTAB-coated and the bare mica surface were measured. From the normal force profiles (not shown), as well as from earlier studies on CTAB monolayers on mica, we deduce that the original monolayer broke up into bilayer domains on the mica, separated by bare mica patches, and that with time these domains became smaller as CTAM molecules dissolved from the surface. Here we focus on the frictional forces between the two surfaces immersed in water.

Fig. 6 shows typical lateral motion (upper trace) and friction force trace (lower) as the surfaces slide during the initial period (up to some 7 h) after the CTAB monolayer is first immersed in water. The sliding stress is in the range 10–20 kPa. If we take the pull-off force between the adhering surfaces as giving a rough measure of the effective 'load' between them then an effective friction coefficient of *ca.* 0.004 may be evaluated (we emphasize however that there is no applied load, and only adhesive forces which pull the surfaces together).

In order to relate the lubrication to the nature of the CTAB-coated surface, where bilayer domains form, initially covering about 50% of the surface but contracting as the CTAB molecules desorb from the surface, we measured the variation in sliding stress as a function of time. This was done by measurements such as in Fig. 6, separating the surfaces—immersed in water—for an additional period, then measuring again and so forth, and the data are shown in Fig. 7.

We see that within the scatter the stress required for sliding the adhered mica surfaces does not change for around 7 h (*ca.* 400 min) of immersion time, following which it rises sharply (arrow in Fig. 7) to the point where the surfaces become rigidly coupled over the maximal applied lateral motion Δx_0 (Fig. 2). That is, the frictional force exceeds the maximal applied shear force $K_s \Delta x_0$. This constancy of the sliding stress can be understood as follows. Within the initial immersion period (up to 7 h) contact between the opposing surfaces is across the bilayer domains ($D \approx 3$ nm with respect to bare-mica/bare-mica contact), with the intervening regions separated, as shown schematically in the left inset to Fig. 7. Sliding then takes place *via* slip of the bilayer domains against the bare mica surface. As they decrease in size with

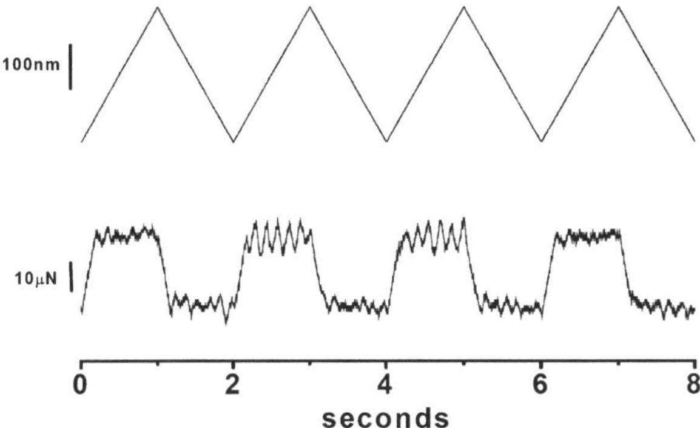

Fig. 6 Typical shear force F_s trace (lower) for sliding between a CTAB-coated mica surface in adhesive contact with a bare mica surface, taken about 3 h following water immersion. The upper trace indicates the lateral motion applied to the upper surface. The lower curve indicates the corresponding shear force F_s transmitted to the lower surface.

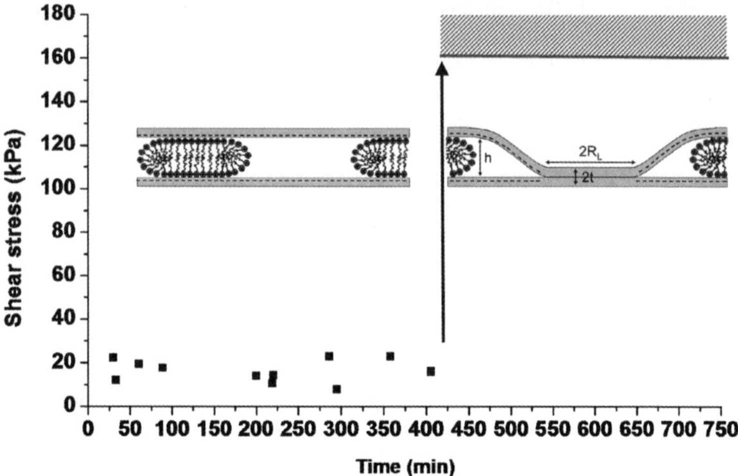

Fig. 7 Sliding frictional stress between a bare mica surface in contact with a CTAB-coated mica surface as function of immersion time prior to adhesion in water. The arrow indicates the abrupt increase of the frictional stress to values (grey region) larger than could be measured in the SFB. Left and right insets schematically illustrate the contact configuration to which the different regimes of, respectively, low and high sliding frictional stress are attributed, as detailed in the text.

time, there are two opposing effects on the sliding shear stress σ_y. On the one hand, reduction of the effective contact area due to bilayer-domain shrinkage should lead to a higher normal stress for a given load, which might be expected to increase the sliding friction. On the other hand the load itself is proportional to the adhesion force which depends on the contact area, so it decreases with bilayer-domain shrinkage. This compensates for the previous effect, and since both effects are expected to vary linearly with the bilayer-domain area, σ_y remains roughly constant. The low value of σ_y itself may be attributed to the hydration lubrication mechanism which enables easy sliding of the hydrated headgroups exposed by each bilayer domain on the mica.

We note that normal force profiles $F_n(D)$ (not shown) after shear are mostly very similar to those before shear, even when the shear amplitude is much larger then the dimension of the bilayers domains. This suggests that the bilayer patches retained their integrity following the shear, and that material was not transferred between the surfaces either on jump-in to adhesion or following the sliding, a conclusion which is also consistent with a slip at the mica–headgroup interface, in agreement with previous conclusions. In these earlier studies[17] with the C_{11} double-tailed surfactants, the values of σ_y, *ca.* 1–5 kPa, were significantly smaller than the values obtained in our work, *ca.* 15 kPa. This is attributed to the double-tail on the C_{11} surfactants, which results in a significantly larger area per head-group, and so a better extent of hydration under water at the mica–headgroup interface, leading to more efficient lubrication by the hydrated headgroups.

The abrupt increase in the frictional stress—to values larger than can be measured in the SFB—shown in Fig. 7 is attributed to the progressive reduction of areal density of the bilayer patches (by loss of surfactant molecules to solution). Eventually the bare-mica gaps between them become large enough to come into adhesive contact *via* vdW attraction. This is schematically illustrated in the right inset to Fig. 7. Once bare-mica/bare-mica contact occurs, water is completely excluded from the mica contact region and hydration lubrication no longer plays a role; as a consequence the friction rises sharply. It may be shown[49] that such contact is expected whenever the extent of the bare mica region exceeds $2R_L$, where

    This journal is © The Royal Society of Chemistry 2012

$$R_L^4 = \frac{h^2 t^3 E}{6(1 - \nu^2)w}$$

Here ν is Poisson's ratio, E is the mica modulus and w is the adhesion energy for mica–mica contact. For $h = 3$ nm, corresponding to the thickness of a bilayer domain, and typical values of t, E, w and n for mica,[49] the calculated separation between the domains is $2R_L \approx 2$ μm. *i.e.* when the bilayer domains have shrunk sufficiently that the bare mica regions between them exceed 2 μm in size, mica/mica contact, as in inset B to Fig. 7, forms a stable configuration.

Finally, we note that at the same time as the jump-in to contact results in the sharp rise in friction, attributed to the mica–mica contact as in inset B to Fig. 7, the bilayer domains compress down from 3 nm (bilayer thickness) to 1.5 nm, a monolayer thickness, over some 15 s. This is attributed to the 'squeezing' effect on the bilayers arising from the tendency of the adhered mica regions (right inset to Fig. 7) to expand, driven by the gain in their adhesive energy, which presumably squeezes the top monolayer away from the bilayer domain, leaving just the lower monolayer behind.

Polyzwitterionic brushes

Earlier work[38] showed that polymer brushes consisting of the polyzwitterion poly[2-(methacryloyloxy)ethyl phosphorylcholine] (pMPC) could lead to extremely efficient lubrication, with friction coefficients—at pressures up to 7.5 MPa—down to 0.0004 in no-salt-added water (and somewhat higher values with added salt). This very low friction was attributed to the hydration lubrication mechanism, arising from the highly hydrated pMPC chains as they are compressed and made to slide against each other. The brushes in those earlier studies were somewhat sparse on the surface (typically $(1/s^2) \approx 1$ chain/12 nm^2, where s is the mean interchain spacing on the surface), and relatively short (molecular weight M estimated at 26×10^3). We have now extended the range of these brushes, using a slightly modified surface ATRP synthesis approach for the grafting-from of the pMPC brushes (O. Tairy *et al.*[50]), which enables a much more efficient polymerization from the initiation sites on the adsorbed macroinitiator molecules. Thus we now obtain significantly longer and denser pMPC brushes in a fraction of the polymerization time compared with the earlier studies. Normal force profiles (normalized as F/R) between two such pMPC brush coated surfaces are shown in Fig. 8. Comparison with the Alexander–de Gennes model for brush interactions[51] (solid line in Fig. 8, fitted to the most relevant region of the data) enables estimation of the unperturbed brush thickness, $L_0 = 63$ nm, and mean grafting density $(1/s^2) \approx 1$ chain/(6 nm^2). From the dry thickness of the brushes of Fig. 8, a molecular weight $M \approx 37{,}000$ could be extracted. These values, for a polymerization time of 15 min, compare with $L_0 \approx 37$ nm, $(1/s^2) \approx 1$ chain/(12 nm^2), and $M \approx 26{,}000$ for brushes following 1.5 h of polymerization in the previous studies, emphasizing the much more efficient pMPC grafting-from process in the present work.

The denser, thicker brushes enable an even more efficient lubrication at yet higher pressures than before. This is shown in Fig. 9, where, for the brushes whose normal interactions are shown in Fig. 8, the normal load is plotted against the sliding friction forces determined from traces such as in Fig. 4 (though at much higher sliding amplitudes, up to *ca.* 1 μm). A sliding friction coefficient $\mu = 9 \times 10^{-5}$ is indicated up to the maximal pressures reached, $P > 10$ MPa, compared with $\mu = 4 \times 10^{-4}$ up to $P \approx 7.5$ MPa with the shorter, less dense brushes of the earlier study.[18] The low friction may, as before, be attributed largely to the hydration lubrication mechanism. The MPC monomers, which have the same phosphocholine structure as the headgroups of phosphatidylcholine lipids (inset to Fig. 8), are known to be exceptionally highly hydrated, with up to 20 or so water molecules in the primary hydration shells (depending on the method of measurement[52-56]). The lower values of the friction coefficients relative to those in the earlier studies (which were themselves remarkably

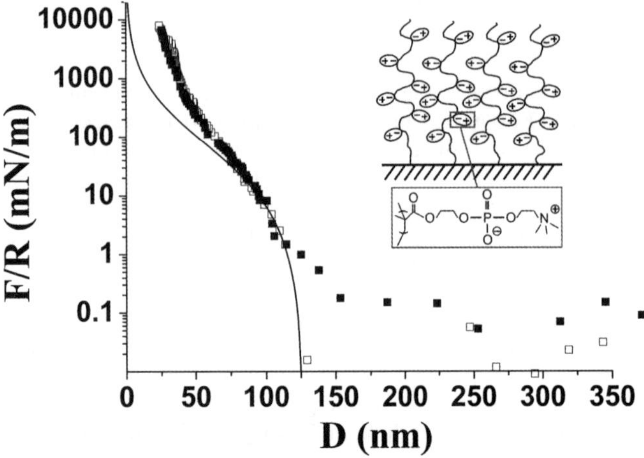

Fig. 8 Normal interactions across water between pMPC brushes after 15 min polymerization by surface-ATRP, following 20 min incubation in a macroinitiator solution (20–15 pMPC). The cartoon inset shows the MPC monomer structure on the brush chains. The solid line demonstrates the fit to the data of the Alexander–de Gennes model at regions well above the noise level (> *ca.* 0.1 mN m^{-1}) but below volume fractions of 0.15 (beyond which scaling models are less valid), enabling an unperturbed brush thickness $L_0 \approx 63$nm and a mean interanchor spacing $s \approx 2.5$nm to be estimated.

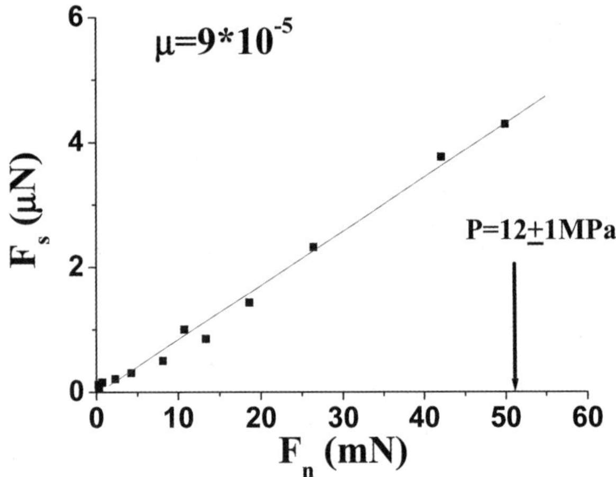

Fig. 9 Variation of shear (frictional) forces F_s with load F_n between mica surfaces bearing 20–15 pMPC brushes, for which the $F_n(D)$ profiles are shown in Fig. 8. The friction coefficient indicated is the slope of the straight line; the arrow indicates the pressure at the highest load reached in this run.

low) may be attributed to the substantially larger areal density of the brush chains: this may suppress brush interpenetration and, in consequence, the associated frictional dissipation as brushes slide past each other.

Surface layers of phosphatidylcholine (PC) liposomes

Exploitation of the strong hydration of phosphocholine groups for friction reduction *via* the hydration lubrication mode—as indicated in the previous section—was, very recently, implemented using surface boundary layers of PC liposomes.[22,32]

    This journal is © The Royal Society of Chemistry 2012

Such liposomes expose a dense phosphocholine layer at the outer surfaces of their bilayer membranes. In those studies small unilamellar vesicles (SUVs) of hydrogenated soy phosphatidylcholine (HSPC) adsorbed spontaneously from dispersion onto (negatively charged) mica surfaces, forming close packed surface layers. These provided outstanding lubrication, with friction coefficients down to $\mu = 2 \times 10^{-5}$ at mean pressures up to 12 MPa. The HSPC liposomes, with a liquid-crystalline-to-gel phase transition temperature $T_m(\text{HSPC}) = 53\,^\circ\text{C}$ were in their gel phase at the room temperature of the measurements. This was believed to be an important factor in the robustness of the surface assemblies of the vesicles to pressure and shear. This was particularly in comparison to liposomes of another common PC, 1-palmitoyl-2-oleoyl-sn-*glycero*-3-phosphocholine (POPC) which was in the liquid-crystalline phase at room temperature, and was a rather poor lubricant at these pressures.[22] We have now extended these earlier studies to several different PC liposome systems to examine in more detail the relation of their liquid-crystalline/gel-phase transitions to their lubricating properties (R. Sorkin *et al.*[57]).

Here we present new data on SUV liposomes from a common high T_m phospholipid, DSPC, well into its gel phase at the room temperature of our measurements ($T_m(\text{DSPC}) = 55.5\,^\circ\text{C}$), revealing not only very low friction coefficients up to higher pressures than previously attained, but also a remarkable robustness at very long sliding times. Surfaces were prepared by overnight incubation in a 0.3 mM dispersion of the DSPC-SUVs in purified water, followed by rinsing to remove excess material by placing them in a beaker containing 300 ml water for 30 min, along with a delicate shaking motion. The inset in Fig. 10 is a cryo-SEM image of such a DSPC-SUV-coated surface, showing clearly a densely packed, flattened liposome layer on the underlying mica, with an overlayer of free liposomes, a configuration similar to that seen earlier for HSPC-SUVs on mica. The driving force for the adsorption of the vesicles is the dipole-charge interaction between the (dipolar) zwitterionic phosphocholine groups and the charged mica surfaces, noted—and measured—earlier.[22] The main Fig. 10 shows the variation of friction force with applied load between two such DSPC-coated mica surfaces, revealing a friction

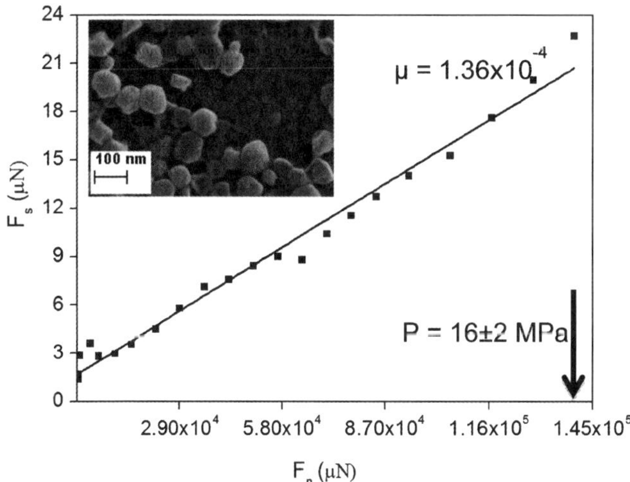

Fig. 10 Variation of shear force F_s as a function of applied load F_n between two DSPC-coated mica surfaces. The indicated friction coefficient m is the slope of the data, *i.e.* $F_s = \mu F_n$. The maximal applied pressure for this contact position is marked with arrow. Inset: Cryo-SEM micrograph of DPPC-SUVs spontaneously adsorbed on mica. The darker region on the right shows clearly the close packed nature of the liposomes flattened by adsorption on the mica surface, while the lighter vesicles are those in the looser overlayer.

coefficient $\mu \approx 1.4 \times 10^{-4}$, up to mean pressures $P = 16 \pm 2$ MPa. This pressure, and even higher pressures (see Fig. 11 below) compares with the maximal pressures of 12 MPa for which sliding across the HSPC-SUV layers was measured.[22] The actual value of μ (Fig. 10), while low, is slightly higher than the lowest measured friction coefficient with the HSPC-SUVs (for which $\mu = 2 \times 10^{-5}$), though lower values were measured with the DSPC-SUV coating in other experiments, as seen below. As for the case of the HSPC-SUVs studied earlier, we attribute the low friction to the hydration lubrication mechanism operating at the outer surfaces of the liposomes, which expose the highly hydrated, densely packed phosphocholine groups, as they slide past each other. This is augmented by the robustness to pressure and shear of the liposomes themselves, which are well into their gel phase. The slightly higher value of μ relative to the earlier work with the different gel-phase liposomes may arise from a residual overlayer of DSPC-SUVs (seen in the micrograph inset to Fig. 10). The extent of this overlayer may differ from contact point to contact point, and from experiment to experiment, depending on the thoroughness of the rinsing and local surface heterogeneities. As the surfaces slide past each other, the presence of trapped liposomes in the overlayer may increase the frictional dissipation as they are compressed and sheared. If this is indeed a dissipative mechanism, it may be transient following longer sliding as the overlayer liposomes in the contact region may be removed or 'massaged' into a different, lower-dissipation configuration.

Some evidence for this idea is provided when examining the trend following sliding for extended periods, as shown in Fig. 11. The friction force *vs.* time traces in Fig. 11 show the friction response both initially, and following one hour of back and forth applied lateral motion at high pressures (for a different contact point to the data in Fig. 10). The important feature to be emphasized is that the friction remains low following this extended sliding: this reveals the long-term robustness of the DSPC-SUVs as boundary lubricants. Two other points in Fig. 11 are of interest: even on initial sliding the effective friction coefficient (taken as $\mu = F_s/F_n \approx 1.1 \times 10^{-4}$) is somewhat lower than that indicated in Fig. 10 (possibly due to fewer liposomes in the overlayer at this different contact point). Following 1 h sliding it has decreased to $\mu = F_s/F_n \approx 5.5 \times 10^{-5}$, not far above the lowest values seen earlier[22] with the HSPC-SUVs. This indicates that the liposome layers have undergone some modification during the long sliding period which reduces the frictional dissipation, possibly removal of the liposomes in the overlayer or 'massaging' of the adsorbed vesicle layers to a less dissipative conformation.

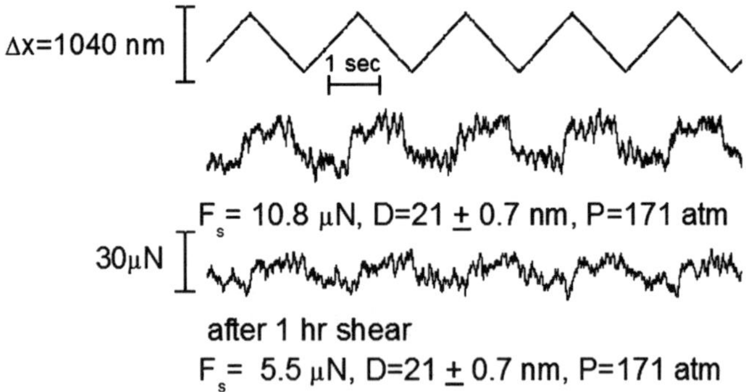

Fig. 11 Typical shear force *versus* time traces for the DSPC system taken directly from the SFB at a given contact position. The top trace shows the applied back and forth lateral motion of the upper surface Δx. The middle trace shows the response motion at the indicated compression, while the lower trace shows the response motion at the same compression after applying continuous shear motion for one hour. Calculated friction forces F_s are also indicated, showing that the shear force following an hour of back-and-forth sliding is reduced by *ca.* 50%.

  This journal is © The Royal Society of Chemistry 2012

4 Summary and conclusions

In this paper we explore some of the implications and limits of lubrication by hydration layers, extending earlier studies to different systems and a larger parameter space. The 'simplest' configuration, that of hydrated alkali metal ions trapped between molecularly-smooth charged surfaces, should be the most revealing in terms of the basic mechanism. According to this the hydration layers surrounding charges are tenaciously held—so resisting removal under normal loading—yet labile, so that they are fluid at shear rates lower than their (fast) relaxation rates. We have accessed contact pressures an order of magnitude or more higher than previous studies, and shown that the friction coefficient can remain as low as $\mu \approx O(10^{-4})$ up to mean contact pressures of order 10 MPa. A limitation of such studies is that at such pressures the mica surfaces confining the hydrated ions approach to mean separations of order an Å. At such separations the details of the mica surface lattice structure, including relative orientations of the confining surfaces and trace surface-adsorbed species, if any (which are difficult to control for), may play a role and cause locally-high friction (*e.g.* if the hydration layer is removed) and tearing of the mica. This is manifested by a relatively large variation of the maximal pressures that could be applied across the trapped ions before surface damage occurred on sliding followed by separation.

The finding[17] that classical boundary lubrication by surfactant molecules reverted—under water—from slipping at the midplane between the surfactant-coated surfaces, to slipping at the substrate interface (due to hydration of the substrate-attached polar headgroups) is now extended to an additional common surfactant, CTAB. For the (usual) case that such surfactant monolayers broke up into bilayer domains, which shrunk with time as surfactants evaporated into the surrounding water, we demonstrate that hydration lubrication breaks down when the density of (lubricating) bilayer patches becomes small enough. At that point the underlying substrate surfaces come into adhesive contact with an abrupt rise in the friction.

By modifying the ATRP surface polymerization protocol, highly hydrated pMPC brushes were covalently grafted-from substrate surfaces to densities and thicknesses significantly higher than in previous studies on such chains.[38] The resulting brushes provided levels of lubrication ($\mu \approx 10^{-4}$ or less) even better than the very efficient lubrication seen earlier with the sparser brushes,[18] up to significantly higher mean contact pressures $P \approx 12$ MPa. In addition to the hydration lubrication mechanism, the lower μ values may be attributed to weaker interpenetration between the compressed brushes due their higher density—and thus lower frictional dissipation when sliding.

Finally, very recent work demonstrating highly efficient lubrication by gel-phase liposomes, boundary layers of HSPC-SUV,[22,32] is extended to different surface-attached liposomes, DSPC-SUVs, also in their gel phase. Comparably low friction coefficients ($\mu \approx 10^{-4}$–5×10^{-5}) are measured also for this system, though to pressures—P up to 17 MPa—significantly higher than before, and, moreover, robustness to extended shear periods at these high compressions was demonstrated.

The common thread running through all these different systems—hydrated ions, amphiphilic surfactants, polymer brushes and phosphatidylcholine bilayers 'delivered' by liposomes—is the lubrication afforded by tenaciously attached yet fluid hydration layers which they expose at the slip plane between two sliding surfaces. Our new findings shed light on the detailed nature of this hydration lubrication paradigm—which differs from the classic modes of friction and lubrication—as well as its limits. We note in particular that our results are relevant up to pressures of *ca.* 20 MPa, though this is not necessarily the limiting pressure for this mechanism. Such pressures are clearly much lower than in classical engineering tribology between hard surfaces (metals, ceramics), where contact pressures may reach hundreds of MPa or even GPa. At the same time, the intrinsic sliding friction coefficients for our systems, down to order 10^{-4}–10^{-5}, are many orders of magnitude lower than for classic boundary lubrication. The lower pressures we describe ($P < ca.$ 20 MPa) are however very relevant in the context of biomedical devices (prosthetic implants, stents, catheters), as well as for tissue engineering in regenerative medicine,[16] and particularly in biological systems (*e.g.* synovial lubrication at the major joints). For these reasons we believe that such hydration lubrication is important not only for understanding frictional processes in aqueous media, but may play a central role also in modulating friction in living systems.

Acknowledgements

We thank Y. Barenholz and his colleagues for providing liposomes (R. Sorkin *et al.*[57]), and S. Armes for providing macroinitiator (O. Tairy *et al.*[50]). The European Research Council (Advanced Grant), the Israel Science Foundation and the Charles W. McCutchen Foundation are thanked for their financial support.

References

1 D. Dowson, *History of Tribology*, Longmans, London, 1979.
2 M. Nosonovsky, *Tribol. Online*, 2007, **2**, 44–49.
3 B. Bhushan, *Fundamentals of Tribology and bridging the gap between Macro- and Micro/ nanoscales*, Kluwer Academic, 2001.
4 I. L. Singer and H. M. Pollock, in *NATO ASI series*, Kluwer Scientific, Dordrecht, 1991.
5 D. Tabor, *J. Lubrication Technology*, 1981, **103**, 169–179.
6 F. P. Bowden and D. Tabor, *The Friction and Lubrication of Solids I*, Clarendon Press, Oxford, 1950.
7 F. P. Bowden and D. Tabor, *The Friction and Lubrication of Solids II*, Clarendon Press, Oxford, 1964.
8 F. P. Bowden and D. Tabor, *Friction: An introduction to tribology*, Anchor Press/ Doubleday, New York, 1973.
9 H. Yoshizawa, Y.-L. Chen and J. Israelachvili, *J. Phys. Chem.*, 1993, **97**, 4128–4140.
10 F. Brochard and P. G. de Gennes, *Langmuir*, 1992, **8**, 3033.
11 J. Klein, *Annu. Rev. Mater. Sci.*, 1996, **26**, 581–612.
12 J. Klein, E. Kumacheva, D. Mahalu, D. Perahia and L. Fetters, *Nature*, 1994, **370**, 634–636.
13 P. Schorr, T. Kwan, M. Kilbey, S. G. Shaqfeh and M. Tirrell, *Macromolecules*, 2003, **36**, 389–398.
14 A. Halperin, M. Tirrell and T. Lodge, *Adv. Polym. Sci.*, 1991, **100/1**, 31.
15 L. Leger, E. Raphael and H. Hervet, *Adv. Polym. Sci.*, 1999, **138**, 185–225.
16 J. Klein, *Science*, 2009, **323**, 47–48.
17 W. H. Briscoe, S. Titmuss, F. Tiberg, R. K. Thomas, D. J. McGillivray and J. Klein, *Nature*, 2006, **444**, 191–194.
18 M. Chen, W. H. Briscoe, S. P. Armes and J. Klein, *Science*, 2009, **323**, 1698–1702.
19 U. Raviv, S. Giasson, N. Kampf, J.-F. Gohy, R. Jerome and J. Klein, *Nature*, 2003, **425**, 163–165.
20 U. Raviv and J. Klein, *Science*, 2002, **297**, 1540–1543.
21 U. Raviv, P. Laurat and J. Klein, *Nature*, 2001, **413**, 51–54.
22 R. Goldberg, A. Schroeder, G. Silbert, K. Turjeman, Y. Barenholz and J. Klein, *Adv. Mater.*, 2011, **23**, 3517–3521.
23 P. P. S. Saluja, *Int. Rev. Sci. Electrochemistry, part 1, Physical Chemistry Series2*, 1976, **6**, 1–51.
24 F. A. Cotton and G. Wilkinson, *Advanced Inorganic Chemistry*, Wiley, NY, 1998.
25 L. Chai, R. Goldberg, N. Kampf and J. Klein, *Langmuir*, 2008, **24**, 1570–1576.
26 R. Goldberg, L. Chai, S. Perkin, N. Kampf and J. Klein, *Phys. Chem. Chem. Phys.*, 2008, **10**, 4939–4945.
27 S. Perkin, R. Goldberg, L. Chai, N. Kampf and J. Klein, *Faraday Discuss.*, 2009, **141**, 399–413.
28 L. Chai and J. Klein, *Langmuir*, 2009, **25**, 11533–11540.
29 B. C. Donose, I. U. Vakarelski and K. Higashitani, *Langmuir*, 2005, **21**, 1834–1839.
30 A.-M. Trunfio-Sfarghiu, Y. Berthier, M.-H. Meurisse and J.-P. Rieu, *Langmuir*, 2008, **24**, 8765–8771.
31 C. Drummond, J. Israelachvili and P. Richetti, *Phys. Rev. E: Stat. Phys., Plasmas, Fluids, Relat. Interdiscip. Top.*, 2003, **67**, 066110.
32 R. Goldberg, A. Schroeder, Y. Barenholz and J. Klein, *Biophys. J.*, 2011, **100**, 2403–2411.

33 J. Klein, *Proc Inst. Mech. Eng., Part J*, 2006, **220**, 691–710.
34 E. E. Meyer, Q. Lin, T. Hassenkam, E. Oroudjev and J. N. Israelachvili, *Proc. Natl. Acad. Sci. U. S. A.*, 2005, **102**, 6839–6842.
35 S. Perkin, N. Kampf and J. Klein, *J. Phys. Chem. B*, 2005, **109**, 3832–3837.
36 S. Perkin, N. Kampf and J. Klein, *Phys. Rev. Lett.*, 2006, **96**, 038301.
37 J. Zhang, R.-H. Yoon, M. Mao and W. A. Ducker, *Langmuir*, 2005, **21**, 5831–5841.
38 M. Chen, W. H. Briscoe, S. P. Armes, H. Cohen and J. Klein, *ChemPhysChem*, 2007, **8**, 1303–1306.
39 J. Klein and E. Kumacheva, *J. Chem. Phys.*, 1998, **108**, 6996–7009.
40 B. V. Derjaguin, N. V. Churaev and V. M. Muller, *Surface Forces*, Plenum Publishing Corporation, 1987.
41 R. M. Pashley, *Adv. Col. Int. Sci.*, 1982, **16**, 67–62.
42 R. M. Pashley, *J. Colloid Interface Sci.*, 1981, **83**, 531–546.
43 R. M. Pashley, *J. Colloid Interface Sci.*, 1981, **80**, 153–162.
44 The effective modulus K is determined by measuring the flattening of the curved surfaces directly as a function of the load, and fitting the data (not shown here) to the Hertz relation with the modulus K as a fit parameter.
45 A. Gaisinskaya *et al.*, to be published.
46 L. Ma *et al.*, to be published.
47 J. N. Israelachvili, *Intermolecular and Surface Forces*, Academic Press Limited, London, 1992.
48 G. Silbert *et al.*, submitted.
49 S. Perkin, L. Chai, N. Kampf, U. Raviv, W. H. Briscoe, I. E. Dunlop, S. Titmuss, M. Seo, E. Kumacheva and J. Klein, *Langmuir*, 2006, **22**, 6142–6152.
50 O. Tairy *et al.*, to be published.
51 P. G. de Gennes, *Adv. Colloid Interface Sci.*, 1987, **27**, 189–209.
52 E. A. Disalvo, F. Lairion, F. Martini, H. Almaleck, S. Diaz and G. Gordillo, *J. Argent. Chem. Soc.*, 2004, **92**, 1–22.
53 L. J. Lis, M. McAlister, N. Fuller, R. P. Rand and V. A. Parsegian, *Biophys. J.*, 1982, **37**, 657–665.
54 J. F. Nagle, R. Zhang, S. Tristram-Nagle, W. Sun, H. I. Petrache and R. M. Suter, *Biophys. J.*, 1996, **70**, 1419–1431.
55 G. Pabst, M. Rappolt, H. Amenitsch and P. Laggner, *Phys. Rev. E: Stat. Phys., Plasmas, Fluids, Relat. Interdiscip. Top.*, 2000, **62**, 4000–4009.
56 M. Yaseen and J. R. Lu, *Langmuir*, 2006, **22**, 5825–5832.
57 R. Sorkin *et al.*, to be published.

Fabrication and characterization of multi-level hierarchical surfaces

Bharat Bhushan* and Hyungoo Lee

Received 23rd November 2011, Accepted 12th December 2011
DOI: 10.1039/c2fd00115b

A nanostructured surface may exhibit low adhesion or high adhesion depending upon fibrillar density, and it presents the possibility of realizing eco-friendly surface structures with desirable adhesion by mimicking the mechanics of fibrillar adhesive surfaces of biological systems. The current research uses a patterning technique to fabricate smart adhesion surfaces: one-, two- and three-level hierarchical synthetic adhesive structure surfaces with various fibrillar densities and diameters. The contact angles and contact angle hysteresis were measured to characterize the wettability. A conventional and a glass ball attached to an atomic force microscope (AFM) tip were used to obtain the adhesive forces *via* force–distance curves and to study the buckling behavior of a single fiber on the hierarchical structures.

1. Introduction

The mechanics of the fibrillar adhesive surfaces of biological systems such as a Lotus leaf and a gecko are widely studied due to their unique surface properties. The Lotus leaf is a model for superhydrophobic surfaces due to its extreme water-repellent properties, as well as self-cleaning properties and low adhesion. These properties are achieved by having a hydrophobic surface and a hierarchical structure with both micro- and nanoscale dimensions.[1–4] The contact angle depends on several factors, such as surface energy, surface roughness, and its cleanliness.[3,5–8] For hierarchical structures, the contact angle is dependent upon the heterogeneous (composite) interface present. For the heterogeneous interface, the contact angle is given by the Cassie–Baxter equation[9]

$$\cos\theta = R_f\cos\theta_0 - f_{LA}(R_f\cos\theta_0 + 1) \tag{1}$$

where θ is the contact angle on a rough surface, θ_0 is the contact angle on a smooth surface, f_{LA} is the fractional contact area of the liquid–air interface, and R_f is the surface roughness factor (>1) equal to the ratio of the real interface surface area (A_{SL}) to its geometric interface area (A_F), $R_f = A_{SL}/A_F$.

Geckos are well known for their exceptional ability to climb any wall and ceiling due to the micro/nano fibrillar hierarchical structure on their feet with about a billion fibers.[10–12] A nanostructured surface may exhibit low adhesion or high adhesion depending upon fibrillar density, and it presents the possibility of realizing eco-friendly surface structures with desirable adhesion. The adhesion mechanism of geckos is based on so-called division of contacts.[11,13] Cumulative van der Waals attraction results in strong adhesion. The adhesive force of a single contact, F_{ad}, based on the so-called Johnson–Kendall–Roberts (JKR) theory is given by[14]

Nanoprobe Laboratory for Bio- & Nanotechnology and Biomimetics, The Ohio State University, Columbus, OH, 43210, USA. E-mail: Bhushan.2@osu.edu

$$F_{ad} = \frac{3}{2}\pi W_{ad} R \tag{2}$$

where R is the radius of a spatula hemisphere tip, and W_{ad} is the work of adhesion (units of energy per unit area). It shows that the adhesive force of a single contact is proportional to the linear dimension of the contact. For a constant area divided into a large number of contacts or setae, n, the radius of a divided contact, R_1, is given by[13]

$$R_1 = \frac{R}{\sqrt{n}} \tag{3}$$

Therefore, the total adhesive force (F'_{ad}) for multiple contacts can be given by

$$F'_{ad} = \frac{3}{2}\pi W_{ad}\left(\frac{R}{\sqrt{n}}\right)n = \sqrt{n}F_{ad} \tag{4}$$

Thus, the total adhesive force increases linearly with the square root of the number of contacts. Based on this analysis, one needs to develop structures with a high density of nanofibers. A hierarchical structure is needed to provide adaptability to a variety of rough surfaces.[12]

In the present study, hierarchical-structured superhydrophobic surfaces have been fabricated using a porous membrane as a template. It is shown that one-, two-, and three-level fiber structures can be fabricated. Contact angle and AFM adhesion measurements were made. The buckling behavior of a single fiber on hierarchical structures was investigated.

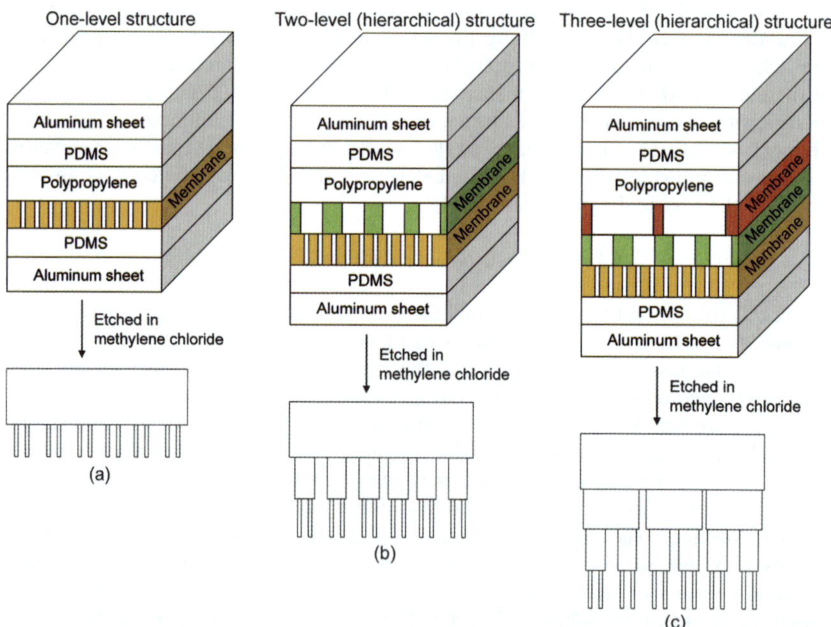

Fig. 1 Sample fabrication processes for (a) the one-level, (b) the two-level, and (c) the three-level fiber structures using one, two and three membranes in the stack, respectively. After heating the stacks in an oven, the membranes are etched using methylene chloride, to obtain the fibrillar samples.

2. Experimental

Polycarbonate (PC), a porous membrane with three pore sizes (600 nm, 5 μm, and 12 μm diameter), was used to create structures with different diameters and densities of fibers. All samples were fabricated using polypropylene (PP), a thermoplastic polymer. Fig. 1 shows the stacks used to fabricate one-, two-, or three-level structures. For the samples with a one-level structure (Fig. 1a), a PP film and a PC membrane were sandwiched between two polydimethylsiloxane (PDMS) disks, and the whole stack was again sandwiched between two aluminum sheets to provide support.[15,16] For fabricating the two- or three-level structures (Fig. 1b and 1c), a PP film was placed on two or three PC membranes with different sizes corresponding to two or three levels. The stacked layers were placed in an oven at 200 °C for 40–50 min with a weight of 1 kg in order to melt the PP and fill the pores in the membrane. The sandwiched samples were dipped into methylene chloride or a mixture of methyl chloride and chloroform for 1 h to etch the membranes to realize the polypropylene fibers. The controlled sample (flat surface) of PP was fabricated with no PC membrane by undergoing all steps used in processing the structured samples.

The wetting properties of the samples were characterized by contact angle measurement. The static contact angle (CA) was measured by placing a DI water droplet of about 5 μL on the samples using a microsyringe. Contact angle hysteresis (CAH) was also obtained by measuring the contact angle using a tilting stage with an automated goniometer (290-F4, Rame-Hart Instrument, Succasunna, NJ). The experiments were carried out at room temperature (21 °C) and in 45–55% relative humidity.

A commercial AFM (Nanoscope IIIa, Bruker, Santa Barbara, CA) was used for adhesion measurement and study of the buckling behavior of a single fiber. The AFM tip with 30 nm of nominal diameter (DNP, spring constant k of 3 N m^{-1}) was used to obtain the force–distance curves for each sample. To measure the adhesive force, a glass ball with a 30 μm diameter (dry soda lime glass microspheres, Duke Scientific, Palo Alto, CA) was attached to the AFM tip and used to obtain the force–distance curves.[3,12] The experiments were performed at room temperature (21 °C) and 45–55% relative humidity.

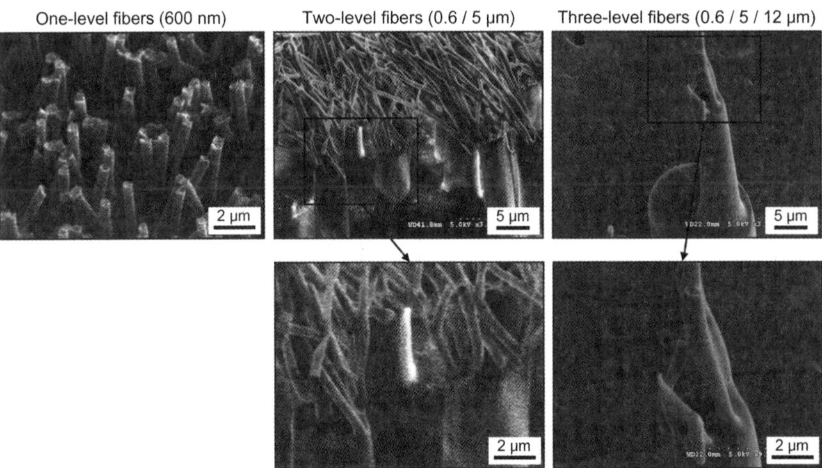

Fig. 2 SEM images of the samples. The one-level structure of 600 nm diameter fibers, the two-level structure of 600 nm diameter with 5 μm diameter fibers, and the three-level structure of 600 nm diameter with 5 μm diameter fibers on 12 μm diameter fibers, are shown.

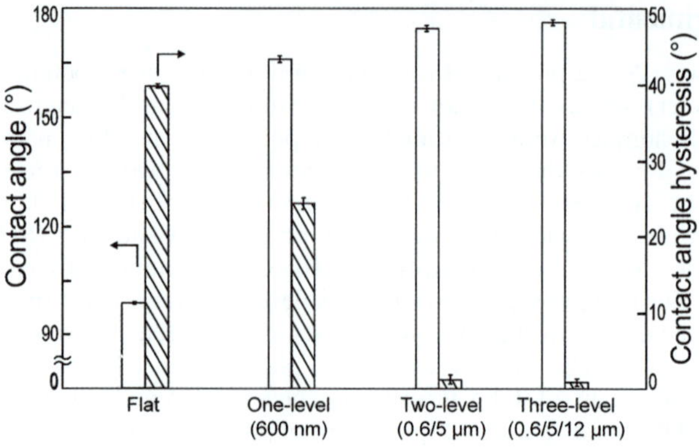

Fig. 3 The measured CAs and CAHs on the flat sample, and the one-, two-, and three-level fibers.

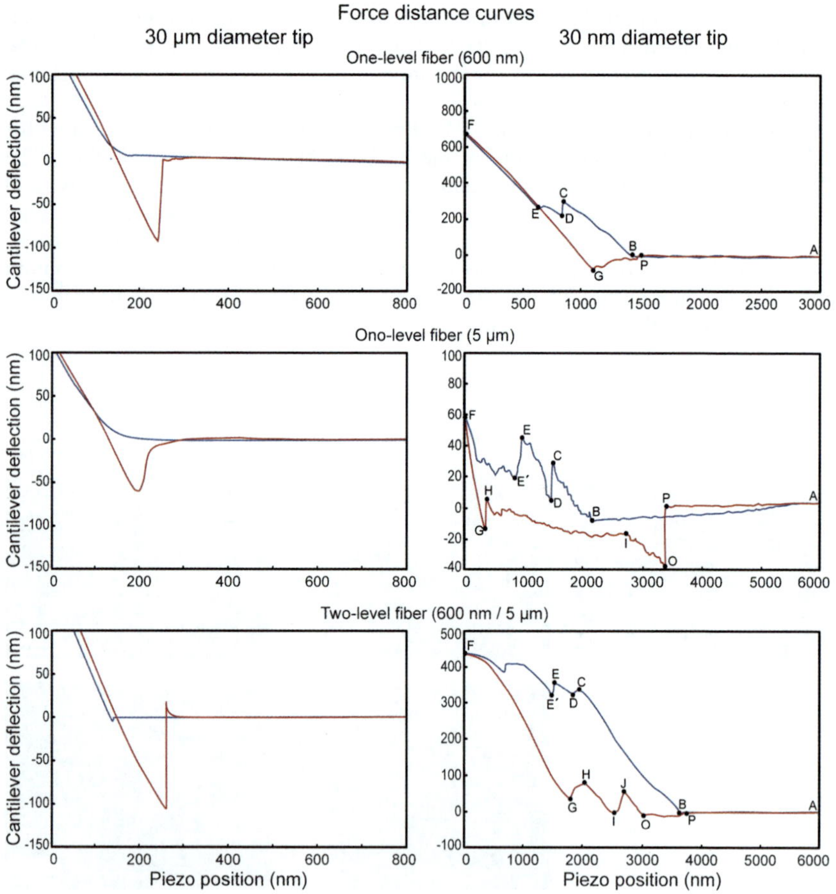

Force distance curves

30 μm diameter tip   30 nm diameter tip

One-level fiber (600 nm)

Ono-level fiber (5 μm)

Two-level fiber (600 nm / 5 μm)

Fig. 4 Representative force–distance curves for the samples with the one-level (600 nm and 5 μm) and the two-level single fibers (600 nm/5 μm) obtained using the 30 μm diameter AFM tip (left column) and the 30 nm diameter AFM tip (right column).

3. Results and discussion

Using a polypropylene film and PC membranes with different pore sizes, the one-, two- and three-level fibrillar structures have been fabricated. The SEM images of the fabricated samples are shown in Fig. 2.

The wetting properties of the samples were characterized by the static contact angle (CA) and contact angle hysteresis (CAH) of a water droplet on each sample, as shown in Fig. 3. The CA (99°) of the flat (control sample) surface of PP indicates that PP is hydrophobic itself due to its low surface free energy (about 30 mJ m^{-2}). As the order of the fiber structure level increases, the CA increases due to the increase in surface roughness (R_f) and the formation of air-pockets (f_{LA}) under the water droplet. Increasing R_f and f_{LA} also leads to a decrease of the CAH.[1] The results show that the one-, two- and three-level fibrillar structures are superhydrophobic.

Adhesive forces (F_{ad}) of the one-level (600 nm and 5 µm) and two-level fibers were measured using the AFM tips. Representative force–distance curves are shown in Fig. 4. The left column is for data obtained using the 30 µm diameter tip, and the right column is for the 30 nm diameter tip. Bending or buckling behavior of the fibers was not observed in the force–distance curves in the left column.

In the right column in Fig. 4, bending and buckling behaviors of a one- and two-level fibers are shown while the 30 nm diameter tip travels downward. Fig. 5 shows the behavior of the two-level single fiber with the AFM tip. Schematics of the fiber behavior at each point as the AFM tip travels are also shown. The tip approaches the fiber (point A to B), and the tip touches the fiber at point B. From point B to C, the tip presses the fiber and is deflected so that the fiber is gradually bent and remains pressed. From point C to D, the fiber buckles. However, the tip keeps pressing the fiber from point D to E, inducing more compression of the fiber.

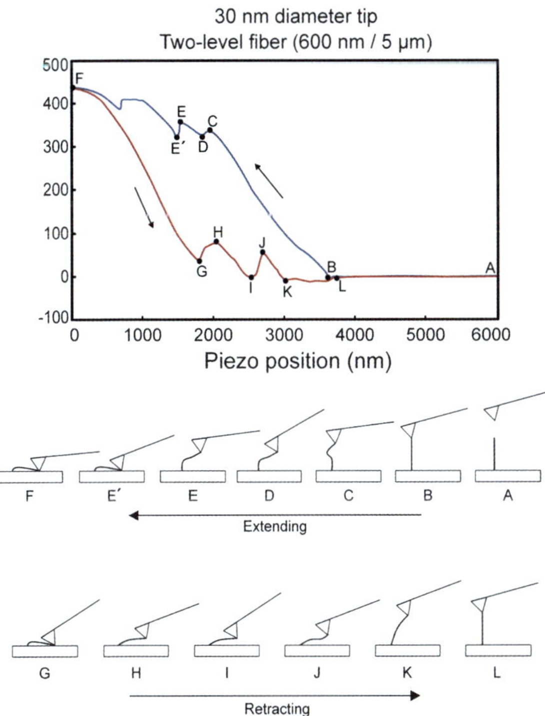

Fig. 5 The force–distance curve for the two-level single fiber (600 nm/5 µm) obtained using the AFM tip of 30 nm diameter. Schematics of the fiber behavior at each point as the AFM tip travels are shown.

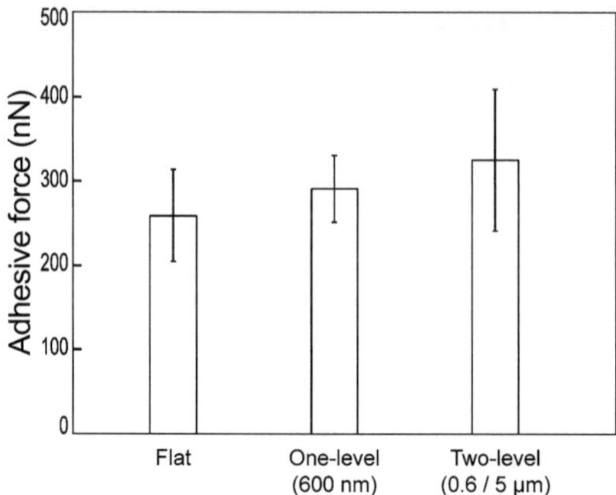

Fig. 6 Adhesive force of the flat sample, and the one- and two-level fiber samples measured using the 30 µm diameter tip. The measurements were performed at room temperature (21 °C) and 45–55% relative humidity.

From point E′ to F, even though the tip keeps pressing, the fiber is not bent or buckled any more so the tip is deflected. From point F, the tip retracts upward. Even though the tip retracts, the fiber does not stand back up (from point F to G). At point G, the fiber stands. From point H to I, the tip retracts, but the fiber does not move. From point I to J, the fiber stands up again. This phenomenon repeats at point K to L.

From the force–distance curves obtained using the 30 µm diameter tip (Fig. 4), the adhesive forces for the samples are calculated. The adhesive force values are plotted in Fig. 6. The force on the flat surface is 260 nN, but those on the one- and two-level fibers are 290 and 326 nN, respectively. This is attributed to the number of fibers. The flat surface can be considered as a fiber with a diameter larger than the real contact area between the AFM ball tip and the flat surface. As shown in eqn (4), with an increase in the number of fibers (n) the adhesive force increases in proportion to the square root of n. Moreover, it is expected that the AFM tip travels deeper into the fiber structures than for the flat sample as shown in the buckling experiment on the fibrillar structures (Fig. 5). It results in an additional increase of the adhesive force. The two-level fibrillar structures have an adhesive force slightly larger than the one-level structures. Although the density of the two-level fibrillar structures is lower than that of the one-level, the two-level structure is more compliant which leads to a larger number of fibers coming in contact with the tip, increasing the adhesive force.

4.   Conclusions

In this study, a simple way to fabricate one-, two-, and three-level fiber structures has been developed. The wetting properties and the adhesive forces on the samples have been investigated. By measuring the CA and CAH of the samples, it is shown that the fiber structures exhibit superhydrophobicity. It is observed that the CA increases and CAH decreases with increasing R_f and f_{LA}.

The adhesive forces (F_{ad}) of the one- and two-level fibers are higher than that of the flat surface due to the increase of the number of fibers on the surfaces. It is shown that the more compliant the fiber structures are, the higher the adhesive forces are.

References

1 M. Nosonovsky and B. Bhushan, *Multiscale Dissipative Mechanisms and Hierarchical Surfaces: Friction, Superhydrophobicity, and Biomimetics*, Springer, Heidelberg, Germany, 2008.

2 *Springer Handbook of Nanotechnology*, ed. B. Bhushan, Springer, Heidelberg, Germany, 3rd edn, 2011.

3 *Nanotribology and Nanomechanics I – Measurement Techniques and Nanomechanics, II – Nanotribology, Biomimetics, and Industrial Applications*, ed. B. Bhushan, Springer-Verlag, Heidelberg, Germany, 3rd edn, 2011.

4 B. Bhushan and Y. C. Jung, *Prog. Mater. Sci.*, 2011, **56**, 1–108.

5 A. W. Adamson, *Physical Chemistry of Surfaces*, Wiley, NY, 1990.

6 J. N. Israelachvili, *Intermolecular and Surface Forces*, Academic, London, 2nd edn, 1992.

7 B. Bhushan, *Principles and Applications of Tribology*, Wiley, NY, 1999.

8 B. Bhushan, *Introduction to Tribology*, Wiley, NY, 2002.

9 A. B. D. Cassie and S. Baxter, *Trans. Faraday Soc.*, 1944, **40**, 546–541.

10 R. Ruibal and V. Ernst, *J. Morphol.*, 1965, **117**, 271–294.

11 K. Autumn, M. Sitti, Y. A. Liang, A. M. Peattie, W. R. Hansen, S. Sponberg, T. W. Kenny, R. Fearing, J. N. Israelachvili and R. J. Full, *Proc. Natl. Acad. Sci. U. S. A.*, 2002, **99**, 12252–12256.

12 B. Bhushan, *J. Adhes. Sci. Technol.*, 2007, **21**, 1213–1258.

13 E. Arzt, S. Gorb and R. Spolenak, *Proc. Natl. Acad. Sci. U. S. A.*, 2003, **100**, 10603–10606.

14 K. L. Johnson, K. Kendall and A. D. Roberts, *Proc. R. Soc. London, Ser. A*, 1971, **324**, 301–313.

15 M. Sitti, "High aspect ratio polymer micro/nano-structure manufacturing using nanoembossing, nanomolding and directed self-assembly", *Proc. IEEE/ASME Advanced Mechatronics Conference*, July 2003, pp. 886–890.

16 J. Lee, R. S. Fearing and K. Komvopoulos, *Appl. Phys. Lett.*, 2008, **93**, 191910.

Friction on ice: stick and slip

Jane R. Blackford,* Gerasimos Skouvaklis, Marc Purser
and Vasileios Koutsos

Received 9th December 2011, Accepted 16th January 2012
DOI: 10.1039/c2fd00128d

Faraday made investigations into behaviour of ice and snow. He was ahead of his
time. Our paper briefly describes the current state of knowledge in ice friction and
adhesion and its historical development. Important aspects of these phenomena
in engineering, winter sports and the natural environment are considered. We
report new results for static and dynamic friction of a metal (steel) and a polymer
(PMMA) on ice over a range of temperatures (−3 to −13 °C), and interpret the
behaviour by considering processes that operate at the interface and in the bulk
of the materials. Clearly the chemical and thermomechanical properties of steel,
PMMA and ice differ. The thermomechanical properties of ice itself also vary
within the temperature range examined. We find higher static friction with
increasing time, and a curious difference in the behaviour of the metal and
polymer with temperature. We explain the results by considering the materials'
stiffness, plastic deformation and creep, the ductile/brittle transition in ice,
thermal properties, physicochemical properties of the surfaces and the real area
of contact.

1. Introduction

Faraday made early experiments essentially by pressing two ice cubes together and
observing that when left in contact they stuck together (he termed this regelation; it
is now known as sintering). He developed ideas of how melting and freezing are
influenced by interfaces. Around the same era, with work on the effect of pressure
on phase transformations, it was proposed that the adhesion occurred because of
the reduction in melting temperature due to the increase in pressure between the
asperities on the contacting surfaces. This became the accepted interpretation for
sintering (even though Faraday suggested more subtle experiments for verification),
and also for the low coefficient of friction on ice. A review of friction on ice up to the
1970s can be found in *Ice Physics* by Hobbs,[1] and a review from Kietzig *et al.*[2]
provides a good introduction to the topic and details of recent studies.

Bowden and Hughes, in 1939,[3] proposed that the low friction of ice is because of
frictional heating that melts a layer of water on the ice surface. This finding was
based on experiments and a simple calculation that indicated how tiny the temperature increase is from pressure melting (typically <0.1 °C under a ski). Frictional
heating has remained as the most prominent and accepted explanation for the slip-
periness of ice. Numerous studies since Bowden and Hughes have used the same
interpretation—our group included—and in an engineering sense it works well.
However, the deeper we delve scientifically into the nature of the materials and tribological processes, the more details, subtleties and questions appear. For example:
how does the layer form, and what else can we determine about it and the make-
up of the interface? The surface of ice is a "hot" topic in physical chemistry[4-6] and

*Institute for Materials and Processes, School of Engineering, The University of Edinburgh,
King's Buildings, Edinburgh, EH9 3JL, UK*

its role in friction is not clear. The surface is covered in a pre-melting layer that has an atomic arrangement between that of liquid water and solid ice. This is a difficult subject—in part because, as with much science, the way you examine it affects what you find.

Sliding on snow and ice has applications in winter sports: skiing,[7–10] skating,[11] bobsleigh,[12] luge and curling;[13,14] vehicle traction in cold climates;[15–17] and ice–ice[18,19] and snow–snow friction in the natural environment, for example in avalanches.[20] Interestingly, and very fortunately for those involved, there have been a number of cases when an avalanche has been triggered but instead of the upper snow slab sliding it has rapidly stuck to the underlying snow resulting in no avalanche. Sticking of ice—adhesion and static friction—is a significant concern in de-icing aircraft[21] and power lines.[22]

Sticking and sliding on ice is an important, interesting and difficult subject. In many applications the number of interacting variables is huge and they are hard to control. In this paper we present new experimental results of static and dynamic friction of steel and poly(methyl methacrylate) (PMMA) on ice. The tests are conceptually simple but it is not trivial to make good and reliable measurements in systems involving ice as the structure and surface of ice are not stable at the temperatures of interest. We use a new large scale tribometer in a specifically designed cold room.[16] This machine is based on pneumatically controlled application of load, precise control of movement and measurement of forces, for macroscopic distances (*ca.* 0.2 to 0.5 m). Carefully prepared ice surfaces are used for the tests. This set up gives us an excellent opportunity to revisit this notoriously difficult system involving ice. Our aim is to conduct reliable experiments under the same conditions for different "model" materials over a range of sub-zero temperatures to elucidate the behaviour of the system and to explain what behaviour stems from the ice properties and what comes from the other materials' properties. This underlies the choice of "simple" sliding materials, steel and PMMA, whose thermomechanical properties are essentially constant during the tests.

2.   Experimental

Static and dynamic friction tests on ice were made with a metal (mild steel AS3679 grade 250) and a polymer (poly(methyl methacrylate) PMMA) on a linear friction test machine in a temperature-controlled cold room. The linear tribometer has been described in detail elsewhere by Skouvaklis *et al.*[16]

The steel and PMMA samples were machined on an automatic milling machine and finished on a lathe. The rectangular test section protruded from the original block 100 mm length and 60 mm width. The dimensions of this test region were 50 mm length and 35 mm width with a height of 22 mm. The 35 mm leading edge of each sample was then rounded off to a diameter of approximately 2 mm to reduce the effect of ploughing of the ice. The samples were bolted (through holes made in corners of the original blocks of the materials) to stainless steel sample holders that were then attached to the friction machine.

The ice was made at a cold room temperature of $-3.5\ ^\circ$C in an aluminium tray of dimensions $0.9 \times 0.4 \times 0.03$ m by freezing several layers of deionised water (resistivity of 18 MΩ cm at 25 $^\circ$C). Each layer of water, of approximately 1 litre, was boiled to remove any dissolved air and then poured into the tray and allowed to freeze entirely before adding the next. Once the ice was frozen, a milling cutter was used to machine a recess to create a level track of approximately 0.7 m in length in the ice surface. The temperature in the cold room was then adjusted to test desired test temperature and ice left for approximately 15 h before testing.

A series of experiments were made to investigate key parameters for steel and PMMA slider materials. The following parameters were used for the tests: temperatures -3.5, -8.5 and $-13.5\ ^\circ$C; loads 0.45, 0.7 and 1.5 kN (these correspond to nominal stresses of 0.26, 0.40, and 0.86 MPa); dwell times (the time the slider material is left in contact with the ice before beginning the test) 5, 15, 60 and 150 s; velocities 0.1 m s^{-1} (with 1 m s^{-2} initial acceleration) and 1 m s^{-1} (with 10 m s^{-2} initial acceleration). Each test, for a given set of parameters, was repeated at least four times.

The friction force is measured in the direction of sample travel. Typical plots of friction force against distance are shown in Fig. 1 for PMMA, speed 0.1 m s^{-1}, load 1.5 kN and temperature -13.5 °C. Near the beginning of the test there is a peak in friction force that corresponds to the static friction. The friction force then decreases and shows a plateau. The dynamic friction force for each test was obtained by averaging data from the plateau region where both speed and friction force were stable.

3.   Results

The results were reproducible for every combination of velocity, load and temperature tested, although more scatter was observed in the static friction test data compared with the dynamic friction data. No macroscopically visible ploughing of the ice surface was seen (after the leading edges of the samples were rounded).

3.1   Static friction

Static friction test results for steel and PMMA on ice are plotted in Fig. 2 to 4. Increasing static friction force is measured with increase in dwell time (Fig. 2),

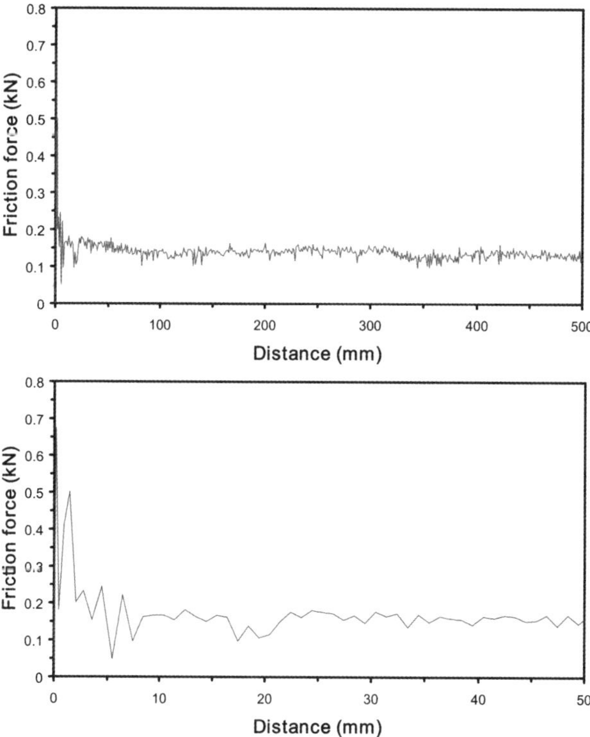

Fig. 1 A typical plot of friction force against distance for PMMA, speed 0.1 m s^{-1}, load 1.5 kN and temperature -13.5 °C. The upper plot indicates the total distance, while the lower plot shows an expanded view of the first 50 mm of the test. There is an initial peak that corresponds to static friction force followed by a plateau for the sliding friction force. The dynamic friction force is obtained from the plateau.

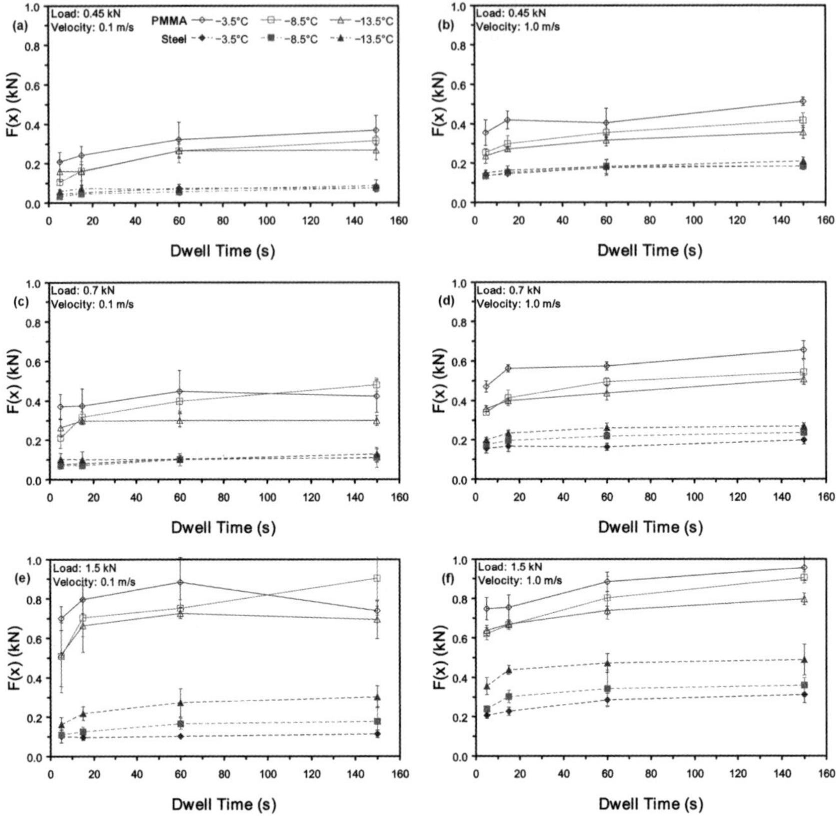

Fig. 2 Friction force against dwell time for steel and PMMA on ice, at temperatures of −3.5, −8.5 and −13.5 °C for the following velocities and loads: (a) 0.1 m s^{-1} and 0.45 kN; (b) 1 m s^{-1} and 0.45 kN; (c) 0.1 m s^{-1} and 0.7 kN; (d) 1 m s^{-1} and 0.7 kN; (e) 0.1 m s^{-1} and 1.5 kN; and (f) 1 m s^{-1} and 1.5 kN.

though the rate of increase becomes less with time. PMMA always shows significantly higher static friction forces on ice than steel. The only exceptions to this increasing trend with time are for PMMA (−3.5 °C, 0.7 and 1.50 kN, 0.1 m s^{-1}) at 60 s the static friction force is higher than at 150 s. To visualise the trends of static friction force against temperature and normal load we plot the average of the static friction results from 60 and 150 s in Fig. 3 and 4 respectively. The static friction force for steel increases with decreasing temperature, though this effect is more pronounced at the high load and the high speed. Conversely for PMMA the static friction force decreases with decreasing temperature. As normal load increases the static friction force increases, and the rate of increase for PMMA is higher than for steel. The static friction force tends to increase slightly when the test is carried out at a high velocity (the high velocity 1 m s^{-1} corresponds to a higher initial acceleration, 10 m s^{-2}; *cf.* low velocity 0.1 m s^{-1} and acceleration of 1 m s^{-2}).

3.2 Dynamic friction

Dynamic friction force is plotted against normal force for steel and PMMA, at velocities of 0.1 and 1 m s^{-1} for the three temperatures in Fig. 5. The results show notably less scatter than the data for static friction force. The increase in dynamic friction force for both materials with increasing normal force is approximately linear thus under these conditions the behaviour is consistent with Amontons' law. There

   This journal is © The Royal Society of Chemistry 2012

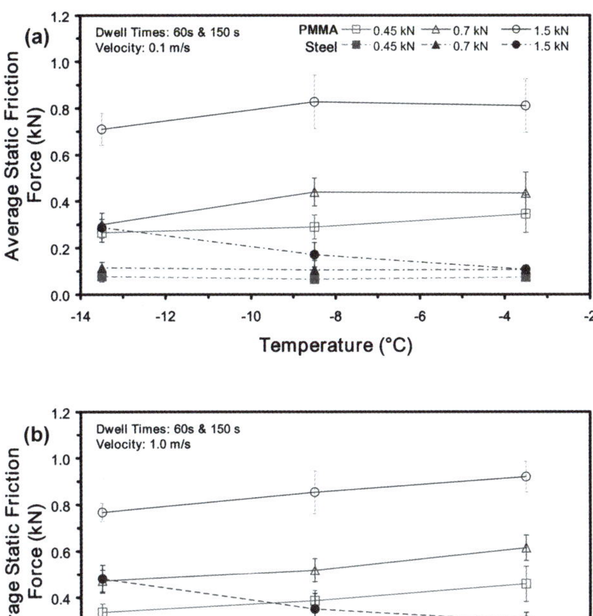

Fig. 3 Average static friction force (from 60 and 150 s) against temperature for steel and PMMA on ice for loads of 0.45, 0.7 and 1.5 kN and velocities of (a) 0.1 and (b) 1 m s^{-1}.

are clear trends of higher dynamic friction force with lower temperature and lower velocity for both steel and PMMA. Steel exhibits lower dynamic friction force than PMMA for all conditions tested.

4. Discussion

4.1 Static friction

The static friction force depends on the interactions that occur between the materials that are in contact and on the real contact area, which in turn depends on load. These interactions can occur at several scales and depend on the materials' properties. To interpret the behaviour of the steel–ice and PMMA–ice static friction tests we discuss the likely effects of material properties and test parameters, and aim to elucidate what mechanisms operate to produce the observed behaviour.

For this system knowledge of the properties of ice is particularly important as they cause the ice to alter during the test, whereas it is reasonable to assume the properties of steel and PMMA are constant during the test. In the tests ice is at high homologous temperatures, $T/T_{\mathrm{m}} = 0.99$ to 0.95. This results in a number of effects: the ice is prone to melting which is important for dynamic friction, as discussed later; deformation over time, creep, is significant; and sublimation occurs because of the unusually high vapour pressure of ice. In addition ice exhibits a ductile–brittle transition: ductile behaviour is promoted by higher temperatures and/or lower strain rates, and brittle fracture becomes more prevalent as the temperature is reduced and strain rate is increased. On a microscale brittle fracture and plastic deformation are not independent—with rapidly applied stresses cracking is more important, while during

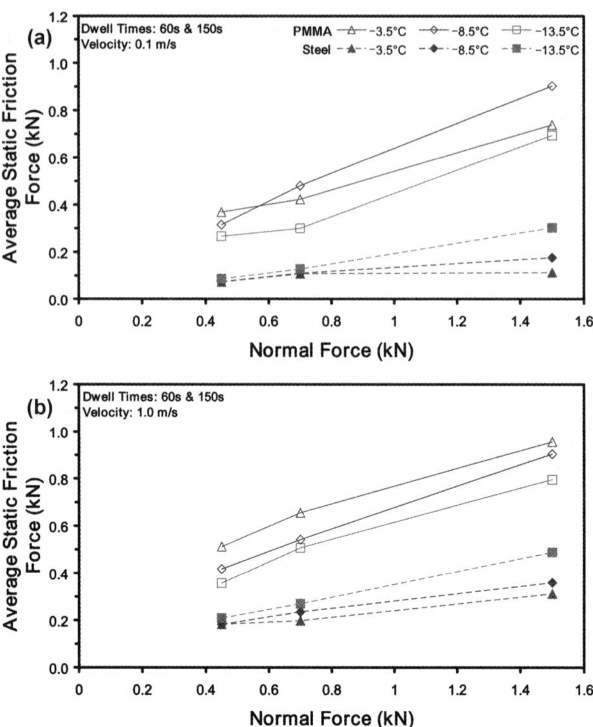

Fig. 4 Average static friction force (from 60 and 150 s) against normal force for steel and PMMA on ice for loads of 0.45, 0.7 and 1.5 kN and velocities of (a) 0.1 and (b) 1 m s^{-1}.

deformation (particularly in compression) the cracks can be rather stable and lead to ductile deformation, although *via* cracking processes.[23,24]

The real area of contact between the materials at the start of the static friction tests depends on their surface roughness; as is well known in tribology, typically only a small fraction of the apparent contact area is in intimate contact—at the tips of adjoining asperities. In our experiments, for both steel and PMMA on ice, the static friction force increased with increasing load. This can be explained by an increase in real area of contact at the interface that occurs as the load increases, which clearly leads to higher static friction. The initial deformation of the materials is elastic, and once the yield strength of one of the materials is reached further deformation continues *via* plastic deformation, or brittle fracture. This behaviour is generically applicable to all solid materials. However, for materials that exhibit time dependent behaviour in their mechanical properties (over the time duration of interest), the static friction force can change with time.

It is important to explain the behaviour of ice asperities as much of the observed behaviour in our experiments can be related to their properties. The contact between ice asperities and how they develop over time is of much interest and importance to the ice and snow research communities.[25] For example the bond strength between snow particles determines the stability of snow on the ground that is important for understanding and predicting avalanches, and the densification of highly porous snow to ice at the polar ice caps is important for better modelling of climatic processes. When two particles of ice contact each other a cohesive bond forms between them; with time this bond increases in size. This is sintering; generally in sintering the surface area of the system reduces and the bonds between particles grow. To understand sintering processes it is important to know about the mass transport paths, and their kinetics relative to each other, that operate and lead to bond growth

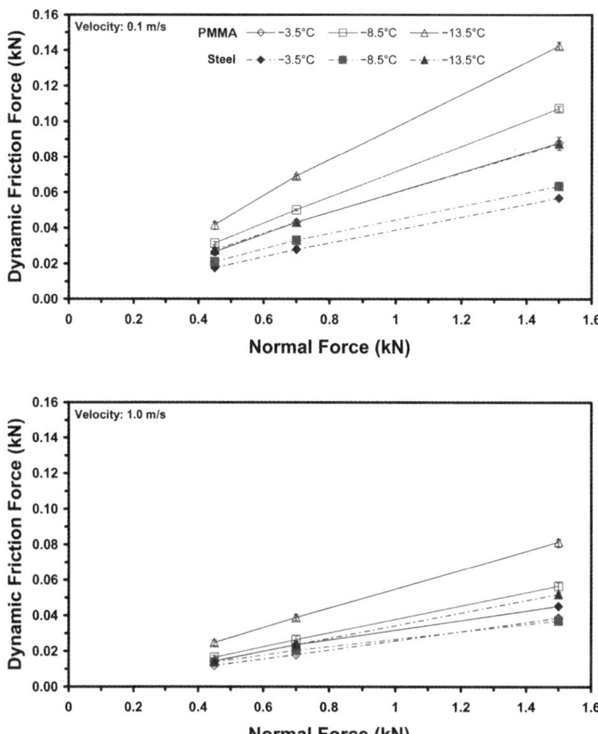

Fig. 5 Dynamic friction force against normal force for steel and PMMA on ice for loads of 0.45, 0.7 and 1.5 kN, temperatures −3.5, −8.5 and −13.5 °C, and velocities of (a) 0.1 and (b) 1 m s⁻¹.

(Fig. 6). For ice particles at ambient pressure, and high homologous temperatures mass transport by sublimation and condensation dominates. From this we can reason that connections (bonds) between ice and steel or PMMA asperities will grow in size over time; however with a sublimation–condensation sintering

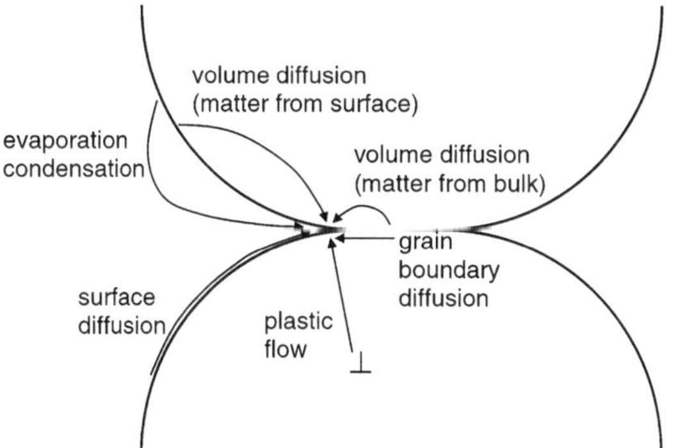

Fig. 6 Transport mechanisms in solid state sintering: plastic flow, volume diffusion, grain boundary diffusion, surface diffusion, and evaporation–condensation. In the initial loading phase of the friction tests plastic flow (accompanied by micro-cracking) is likely to be the main transport mechanism. Note: densification of the system occurs only with plastic flow, volume diffusion (matter from bulk), and grain boundary diffusion.

Table 1 Mechanical and thermal properties of steel,[27] PMMA[28] and ice[29,30]

Material	Stiffness GPa	Yield strength MPa	Ultimate strength MPa	Thermal conductivity W mK^{-1}	Glass transition temperature °C
Steel[27]	210	275	430–580	52	—
PMMA[28]	3.1–3.3	60–80		0.19	105–120
Ice[29,30]	9.7–11.2 at −10 °C[29]	Plastic flow from 0.2 to 10 MPa at −10 °C[30] (behaviour depends strongly on temperature and strain rate)	0.7–3.1 (tension) 5–25 (compression)[29]	2.30[29]	—

mechanism although some bonds grow larger with time this occurs at the expense of smaller bonds shrinking, the density of the system remains constant, and the total bond area does not actually increase with increasing time. However if pressure is applied to the system, as it is in static friction tests, mass transport by plastic deformation will be strongly activated and will play a much more significant role than vapour transport. Plastic deformation leads to densification of the system and consequently an increase in the real area of contact at the interface.

The ice microstructure changes in response to creep; plastic deformation mechanisms *e.g.* by dislocation slip (on particular crystallographic systems; ice exhibits extreme anisotropy in its plastic deformation) and recrystallisation have been studied extensively.[23] This is an important topic in the ice research community and recent work using electron backscatter diffraction to quantify crystallographic changes in ice post deformation indicates significant heterogeneity within the microstructure.[26] The nature of the deformation within the ice may be significant for our study, however as the results of the static friction tests are reproducible, it is likely a stable deformation structure develops in testing. It appears that any microstructural changes within the ice are of secondary importance compared with other factors.

To summarise: under the conditions of the static friction tests ice deforms plastically with time (creep) and this increases the real area of contact with the steel or the PMMA. This deformation behaviour of ice correlates with the higher static friction observed as load and time increase, for both steel and PMMA. However it does not explain why PMMA exhibits significantly higher static friction, for all test conditions, than steel. A closer examination of the mechanical properties of all three materials may go some way to answering this. In addition the physicochemical properties at the interface of the ice–steel or ice–PMMA may be important, as discussed later.

Let us consider the interaction of asperities of ice and PMMA or steel during a static friction test. Table 1[27–30] includes mechanical properties of the materials, and our hypothesis of the sequence of behaviour is shown schematically in Fig. 7. When the asperities first come into contact they deform elastically (Fig. 7B); a material with a higher stiffness will indent a material of lower stiffness. Given the elastic moduli of the materials (Table 1): steel will indent ice (Fig. 7B, steel), while ice will indent PMMA (Fig. 7B, PMMA). During the application of load on the system, after the initial elastic deformation, either the ice deforms plastically or it fractures. As the ice is more than an order of magnitude weaker than steel or PMMA, both steel and PMMA will indent the ice (Fig. 7C). We propose that this creates a rather complicated interface between the ice and the PMMA, because of the "reversal" of indentation direction (Fig. 7C, PMMA). (The load is applied over a few seconds so

   This journal is © The Royal Society of Chemistry 2012

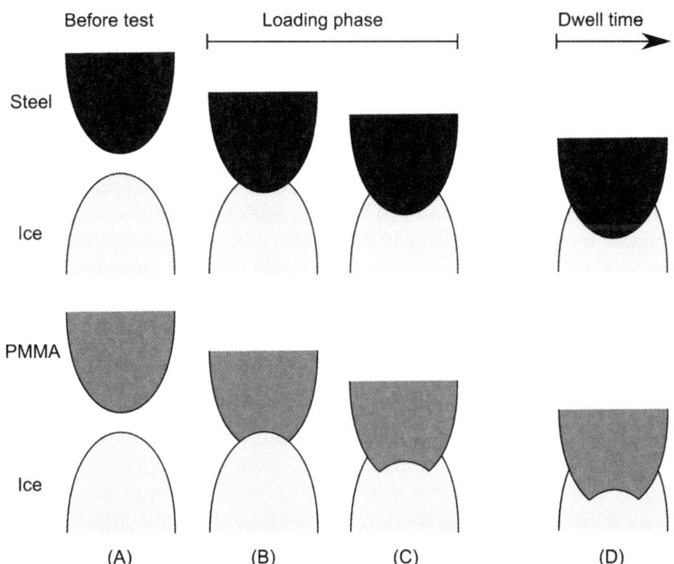

Fig. 7 The proposed sequence of behaviour for single asperities of ice and steel or PMMA that occurs during the test before the static friction force is measured (*cf.* properties given in Table 1). (A) Before the test, (B) elastic deformation at the start of the loading—note that steel indents ice whereas ice indents PMMA, (C) plastic deformation during loading—this occurs either by plastic flow or by fracture, and (D) further plastic deformation during the dwell time.

the strain rates—in this initial loading phase—may be relatively high and the fracture of ice asperities is likely to be brittle; for ice in tension brittle fracture is always at strain rates above 10^{-6} s^{-1}.[24] However we should keep in mind that because of the nature of the contact, stresses and strain rates will not be homogeneous across the whole interface, so the system may exhibit different behaviour locally). The intimate contact at the interface continues to increase with increasing dwell time and load because of the continued deformation of ice (Fig. 7D), and it is also possible that healing of any micro-cracks in the ice can occur during this time. But this alone does not explain why the ice–PMMA static friction becomes so much higher than for steel. Examining the effects of other parameters leads to insights.

The difference in static friction behaviour of steel and PMMA with temperature is intriguing: static friction of ice–steel becomes higher as the temperature decreases while that of ice–PMMA becomes lower (although the ice–PMMA static friction force is always notably higher than that of ice–steel). As mentioned above the mechanical properties of the metal and polymer (well below the glass transition temperature) are essentially independent of temperature, while the ice is not. For ice there are two competing factors as the temperature decreases that will either produce lower or higher static friction: creep rates decrease resulting in less plastic deformation and lower real area of contact—this decreases static friction force. Conversely ice becomes stronger as it gets colder (by approx. 0.3 MPa °C^{-1},[23]) so this acts to increase static friction force. This second factor appears to explain the behaviour of steel on ice, and this behaviour is in agreement with the steel–ice static friction measurements of Raraty and Tabor.[31] In addition steel has a high stiffness its asperities will not have blunted during the loading phase. Thus when the friction test begins the stress concentrations coupled with the strain rates imposed by the test lead to local failures at the interface (because of these factors and the material properties the failure is likely to be predominantly brittle).

The static friction of ice–PMMA becomes higher as the temperature increases, which suggests the behaviour is dominated by a different mechanism: we hypothesise that the higher plastic deformation of the ice at higher temperatures and the resulting increase in real area of contact underlies this behaviour. (As an extreme it is possible the ice–PMMA real area of contact is higher than the apparent area—more work needs to be carried out to determine the nature of the contact). The asperities of the PMMA are likely to be blunted in the test compared with steel because of the lower stiffness of PMMA, which leads to an increase in real area of contact. Local viscoelastic effects of PMMA asperities and chemical interactions at the molecular scale between the polar groups of the PMMA and water/ice could also play a role.

Static friction for both steel and PMMA increases as the initial acceleration (strain rate) of the test increases from 1 to 10 m s^{-2}. For compression testing of ice typically higher strain rates produce higher strengths and fracture then proceeds by more dense micro-cracking;[32] in our system such behaviour will increase the static friction force. For PMMA, viscoelastic effects at the micro-asperity scale, or even at a larger scale, could also contribute to increased friction.

Both steel and PMMA are hydrophilic (with contact angles smaller than 90°);[3,33] the steel will have an oxide film on its surface (there were no obvious indications of rust on the steel in testing). The wetting behaviour of the materials would be important when there is liquid in the system, so it is of more significance in dynamic friction, however it is possible that a small volume of liquid is produced in the static friction tests. During the initial loading phase of the tests the asperities of the steel or PMMA and ice connect and deform. This in itself can be seen as a mini-friction test in the loading direction; it is feasible that liquid could be produced, especially at higher temperatures. This then gives potential for liquid phase sintering, and "healing", at the interface. Further work is needed to determine the significance of this.

From our experiments is it not possible to know whether the failure at the interface is cohesive (in the ice) or adhesive (at the interface); typically cohesive breaks are stronger. Our interpretation is based on qualitative arguments of what is happening at the microscale. An actual microscale investigation of an ice system is not trivial even if we restrict it to examining the ice only after the tests *e.g.* with cryo-scanning electron microscopy as rapid quenching of the microstructure and transfer to the instrument is critical to ensure minimal alteration of the ice. With our new tribometer this is difficult as the ice would need to be cut form the main ice sheet. Our previous small-scale pin-on-disc tribometer enabled this much more easily as the ice sample had the correct dimensions for direct transfer to the cryo-SEM.[15] In the future, we plan to design a micromechanical device with *in situ* high resolution imaging tools to visualise the contact region directly during and after the tests in order to directly observe the underlying deformation mechanisms, devise new experiments to isolate the different hypotheses and develop quantitative models.

4.2 Dynamic friction

The dynamic friction behaviour measured on our new linear tribometer is highly consistent and shows very little scatter, as we have seen with previous measurements on rubbers.[16] This repeatability also provides hints about the nature of the processes in static and dynamic friction. It appears the processes that operate during sliding, once steady state is established, are—for some reason—more amenable to very stable measurement. The increase in dynamic friction force for both materials with increasing normal force is approximately linear thus under these conditions the behaviour is consistent with Amonton's law. The trends in the behaviour of the sliding materials with increasing friction with decreasing velocity and decreasing temperature can be explained with frictional heating that can create a melt water layer. Typically the higher the velocity and temperature the thicker the lubricating melt water layer and the lower the friction (up to a certain thickness, then increasing amounts of heating and melt water lead to higher friction, but we do not reach this regime in these tests). This behaviour is consistent with the observations of Evans *et al.*[34] who also measured the friction of both steel and PMMA in the study. However their test rig was different: it consisted of a rotating ice cylinder and a rod of the slider material resting on the top, balanced by counter weights below, and the slider runs over the same ice repeatedly. Other studies of ice–steel dynamic friction show the same trends over these comparable parameter ranges, although the friction test equipment in each study differs.[2,35-37] Steel exhibited significantly lower dynamic friction force than PMMA under all conditions tested. Evans *et al.*[34] found slightly lower values for the friction of PMMA compared with steel, while we found the reverse and the difference was considerably larger. However the normal stress in their tests was higher (*ca.* 15 MPa *cf.* 0.26 to 0.86 MPa in our tests) so the real area of contact will be higher with both slider materials, and they report that the ice is worn in the test and a steady state is achieved creating an indent in the ice surface. The behaviour of our tests cannot be explained by considering the heat flow at the slider material–ice interface, as the thermal properties of the materials are inconsistent with this hypothesis. The thermal conductivity, and thermal diffusivity, of steel is higher than that of ice, which is higher than that of PMMA (Table 1). Heat generated at the interface flows preferentially into the material with higher conductivity. Clearly a simple analysis using this approach indicates that most heat flows into the steel whereas very little heat flows into the PMMA, so for PMMA there should be more heat available at the interface to melt the ice and cause lower friction, which is not the case. This simple approach however assumes perfect (or exactly the same) thermal contact between the pairs of materials. As we have discussed above the PMMA is considerably less stiff than the steel and this led to a higher real area of contact with the ice that we correlated with its higher static friction force, so it is highly probable that this increased real area of contact is a significant cause of the higher dynamic friction force. We have found analogous behaviour with rubber friction on ice, we found higher dynamic friction with more compliant rubbers.[16] These softer, compared with harder, rubber compounds (with low glass transition temperatures, *e.g.* −50 °C) have increased real area of contact with a surface; in addition they dissipate energy by bulk dissipation within the rubber itself (internal friction). Bulk dissipation may be possible with PMMA, however as it is well below its glass transition temperature, we do not consider this to be the primary mechanism for the increased friction. We plan to use the new micromechanical tester that was mentioned above to probe the mechanisms and nature of the interfaces further.

5. Conclusions

We present new results of the static and dynamic friction behaviour of steel and PMMA on ice. We explain much of the static friction of steel and PMMA on ice by considering the processes that occur at the interface and within the materials. Our interpretation of the results relies strongly on understanding the intricacies of the mechanical behaviour of ice and how this affects the nature of the contacts. We believe the elastic deformation, ductile deformation, by dislocation movement and micro-cracking, fracture, and ductile/brittle behaviour for ice are significant over a range of length scales.

Static friction increases with increasing time and with increasing load because of the increase in real area of contact for both materials. The PMMA always exhibits higher static friction than steel and we explain this by considering the lower stiffness of the polymer; this results in a larger real area of contact and potentially a rather intricate interface with the ice (because of the polymer's lower stiffness but higher strength than ice). In addition physicochemical interactions between the ice and PMMA at the molecular scale may play a role in increasing static friction. Static friction increases with decreasing temperature for steel and we explain this because of the increase in strength of ice. However for PMMA curiously the static friction decreases with decreasing temperature which we explain with the increase in real area of contact, as there is more creep at higher temperatures, and because of the failure processes that occur at the interface.

The dynamic friction of steel and PMMA on ice decreases with increasing velocity and increasing temperature as more lubricating melt water forms because of frictional heating. The PMMA has higher friction, for given sliding conditions, than steel—this effect cannot be explained by considering heat flow at the ice–slider material interface. In sliding the real area of contact is likely to be higher for PMMA than for steel, as PMMA has lower stiffness. We propose this is the primary explanation for the higher friction though further studies are needed to confirm this.

Acknowledgements

We wish to thank Michelin for funding our cold room and the friction machine. We are grateful to Tamas Parkanyi for enthusiastic discussions and help with the manuscript preparation.

References

1 P. V. Hobbs, *Ice Physics*, Oxford University Press, 1974.
2 A. M. Kietzig, S. G. Hatzikiriakos and P. Englezos, *J. Appl. Phys.*, 2010, **107**, 081101.
3 F. P. Bowden and T. P. Hughes, *Proc. R. Soc. London, Ser. A*, 1939, **172**, 280–298.
4 J. S. Wettlaufer, *Proc. R. Soc. London, Ser. A*, 1999, **357**, 3403–3425.
5 Y. Li and G. A. Somorjai, *J. Phys. Chem. C*, 2007, **111**, 9631–9637.
6 C. L. Bishop, D. Pan, L. M. Liu, G. A. Tribello, A. Michaelides, E. G. Wang and B. Slater, *Faraday Discuss.*, 2009, **141**, 277–292.
7 S. C. Colbeck, *J. Sports Sci.*, 1994, **12**, 285–295.
8 L. Bäurle, D. Szabó, M. Fauve, H. Rhyner and N. D. Spencer, *Tribol. Lett.*, 2006, **24**, 77–84.
9 L. Bäurle, T. U. Kaempfer, D. Szabó and N. D. Spencer, *Cold Reg. Sci. Technol.*, 2007, **47**, 276–289.
10 J. L. Giesbrecht, P. Smith and T. A. Tervoort, *J. Polym. Sci., Part B: Polym. Phys.*, 2010, **48**, 1543–1551.
11 S. C. Colbeck and G. C. Warren, *J. Glaciol.*, 1991, **37**, 228–235.
12 A. M. Kietzig, S. G. Hatzikiriakos and P. Englezos, *J. Appl. Phys.*, 2009, **106**, 024303.
13 B. A. Marmo, I. S. Farrow, M.-P. Buckingham and J. R. Blackford, *Proc. Inst. Mech. Eng., Part L*, 2006, **220**, 189–197.
14 M.-P. Buckingham, B. A. Marmo and J. R. Blackford, *Proc. Inst. Mech. Eng., Part L*, 2006, **220**, 199–205.
15 D. D. Higgins, B. A. Marmo, C. E. Jeffree, V. Koutsos and J. R. Blackford, *Wear*, 2008, **265**, 634–644.
16 G. Skouvaklis, J. R. Blackford and V. Koutsos, *Tribol. Int.*, 2012, **49**, 44–52.
17 S. Ella, P.-Y. Formagne, V. Koutsos and J. R. Blackford, *Tribol. Int.*, 2012, DOI: 10.1016/j.triboint.2012.01.017, *accepted for publication*, special issue for Leeds–Lyon 38th Symposium.
18 F. E. Kennedy, E. M. Schulson and D. E. Jones, *Philos. Mag. A*, 2000, **80**, 1093–1110.
19 P. Oksanen and J. Keinonen, *Wear*, 1982, **78**, 315–324.
20 J. Heierli, P. Gumbsch and M. Zaiser, *Science*, 2008, **321**, 240–243.
21 R. W. Gent, N. P. Dart and J. T. Cansdale, *Philos. Trans. R. Soc. London, Ser. A*, 2000, **358**, 2873–2911.
22 J. L. Laforte, M. A. Allaire and J. Laflamme, *Atmos. Res.*, 1998, **46**, 143–158.
23 P. Duval and E. M. Schulson, *Creep and fracture of ice*, Cambridge University Press, 2009.
24 V. F. Petrenko and R. W. Whitworth, *Physics of Ice*, Oxford University Press, 2002.
25 J. R. Blackford, *J. Phys. D: Appl. Phys.*, 2007, **40**, R355–R385.
26 S. Piazolo, M. Montagnat and J. R. Blackford, *J. Microsc.*, 2008, **230**, 509–519.
27 *Smithells Metals Reference Book*, ed. E. A. Brandes and G. B. Brook, Butterworth Heinmann Ltd, 7th edition, 1992.
28 G. W. Ehrenstein, *Polymeric Materials*, Hanser, Munich, 2001.
29 J. J. Petrovic, *J. Mater. Sci.*, 2003, **38**, 1–6.
30 P. Duval, M. F. Ashby and I. Anderman, *J. Phys. Chem.*, 1983, **87**, 4066–4074.
31 L. E. Raraty and D. Tabor, *Proc. Roy. Soc.*, 1958, **245A**, 184–201.
32 M. A. Rist and S. A. F. Murrel, *J. Glaciol.*, 1994, **40**, 305–318.
33 Y. Ma, X. Cao, X. Feng, Y. Ma and H. Zou, *Polymer*, 2007, **48**, 7455–7460.
34 D. C. B. Evans, J. F. Nye and K. J. Cheeseman, *Proc. R. Soc. London, Ser. A*, 1976, **347**, 493–512.
35 B. A. Marmo, J. R. Blackford and C. E. Jeffree, *J. Glaciol.*, 2005, **51**, 391–398.
36 A. M. Kietzig, S. G. Hatzikiriakos and P. Englezos, *J. Glaciol.*, 2010, **56**, 473–479.
37 M. Akkok, C. M. M. Ettles and S. J. Calabrese, *J. Tribol.*, 1987, **109**, 552–561.

Sliding friction at soft micropatterned elastomer interfaces

Elise Degrandi-Contraires,[ab] Christophe Poulard,[a] Frédéric Restagno[a] and Liliane Léger[*a]

Received 25th November 2011, Accepted 19th January 2012
DOI: 10.1039/c2fd00121g

In this paper, we present an experimental study of the friction between a smooth elastomer lens and an elastomer substrate micropatterned with hexagonal arrays of cylindrical pillars. Depending on the normal load, the surfaces can be in top or mixed contact. The friction force can be interpreted in terms of friction stresses in the full contact and top contact zones. The latter is higher than that on smooth surfaces evidencing the role of the elastic deformations of the surfaces in the dissipation processes.

Introduction

Roughness is known to deeply influence the contact mechanics of elastic bodies and to drastically affect properties such as adhesion and friction.[1] Due to roughness, only partial contact is usually established between two solids. The real area of contact is then smaller than the apparent one, and depends on experimental and material parameters such as the applied normal load, the geometrical characteristics of the roughness, and the mechanical properties of both solids.[2] As a result, molecular forces do not usually produce a noticeable adhesion between solids, except in the case of molecularly smooth solids (the so called molecular adhesion, used to hold together optical parts without the help of any adhesive layer).[3–7] Concerning friction, roughness is thought to be at the origin of Amonton's law[1,8,9] which specifies that the friction force is proportional to the normal load, independently of the real surface of contact. This allows one to characterize a sliding contact by a friction coefficient, *i.e.* the proportionality factor between the friction force and the normal load. Although widely observed and used, this law is not established on a firm microscopic basis. Fuller and Tabor,[3] Greenwood,[10] and more recently, Persson[11] *et al.*, have shown theoretically through an analysis of the friction between a smooth glass plate and solids with specific roughness distributions (gaussian and fractal respectively) that it was possible to give a microscopic interpretation of Amonton's law: due to plastic (or elastic) deformation of the top of the asperities at contact, increasing the load changes the real contact area, leading to the observed proportionality between the friction force and the normal load. This proportionality is not however a general rule for all sliding contacts, and the development of experimental tools such as the atomic force microscope (AFM) or the surface force apparatus (SFA) has shown that one has to distinguish two different situations: single full contact in the case of negligible roughness (mono-contact) (this can indeed be attained for small enough contacts, for example with an AFM tip, or when particular care is taken to work with large atomically smooth surfaces, in a SFA machine) and multi-contact between rough surfaces. For a situation of mono-contact, the friction

[a]Laboratoire de Physique des Solides, Université Paris-Sud & CNRS, Bat. 510 – Campus universitaire d'Orsay, F-91405 Orsay cedex, France. E-mail: liliane.leger@u-psud.fr
[b]SVI, CNRS-Saint-Gobain Recherche, BP 135, 93303 Aubervilliers Cedex, France

force is dictated by the real area of contact (identical to the apparent one), usually not proportional to the load, as is the case for example in the JKR sphere–plane contact.[12,13] For a situation of multi-contact between rough surfaces Amonton's law is generally observed even in the case of elastomers.[14] There is however at present no real understanding of how one can go from the mono- to the multi-contact behavior when changing the roughness or the load, despite the obvious practical importance of being able to adjust and control friction. How does the applied normal load affect the nature of the contact between two solids? What are the combined impacts of geometry, roughness and mechanical properties of the solids on the contact mechanics?

The recent development of microfabrication techniques[15] allows the relatively easy preparation of surfaces with well controlled micro-patterns having specific geometrical characteristics. Such surfaces provide unique tools to experimentally try to provide answers to the above questions.

A first exploration of the incidence of micro-patterning on sliding friction for elastomer–elastomer contacts has been reported recently[16] and has pointed out the complexity of the problem: for a smooth surface in contact with a surface covered with hexagonal arrays of cylindrical elastic micro-pillars, two different states of contact were observed, depending on the height of the pillars (at fixed spacing between pillars). Tall pillars were leading to partial contact, with the contact only established on the top of the pillars, while short pillars were not able to prevent the two surfaces from establishing full contact, due to adhesion forces and despite the elastic energy penalty resulting from the deformation of both solids. As a consequence, the interpretation of sliding friction data appears complex, with various sliding friction regimes, depending on the nature of the contact, or, for a given surface geometry, depending on the applied load.[17]

We have recently conducted a series of experiments aimed at understanding the formation of the static contact between a smooth polydimethylsiloxane (PDMS) elastomer lens and series of patterned PDMS elastomer substrates.[18] The patterns consisted of hexagonal arrays of cylindrical micro-pillars with various diameters, d, various relative distances, i, and a given height, $h = 2.2$ μm. These experiments allowed us to establish that there exists a critical normal load for which one goes from a purely top contact in the whole zone of contact for low normal loads to a situation

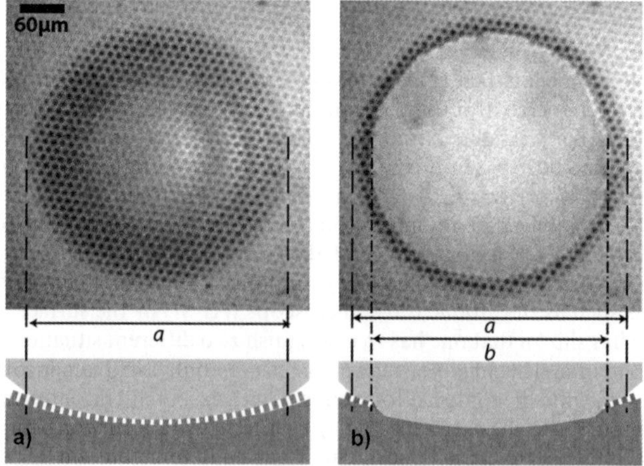

Fig. 1 Observation of the zone of contact, as a function of the applied load: a) purely top contact at low applied load; b) mixed contact at higher applied loads, with a central full contact in which the lens touches the substrate in between the pillars which then are hardly visible optically, surrounded by a corona of top contact. ($d = 6$ μm, $i = 12$ μm).

   This journal is © The Royal Society of Chemistry 2012

of mixed contact above this critical load, with a zone of full contact appearing in the center of the contact, surrounded by a corona of top contact (Fig. 1).

We have investigated how that critical load was varying with the pattern geometry, and how the geometry of the pattern was affecting the way the area of full contact was growing above the critical load. Benefiting from the simple elastic response of both the lens and the substrate, we proposed mechanical criteria for the onset of full contact, and rationalized through a mechanical model the evolution of the area of full contact above threshold, as a function of the pattern geometry. We thus essentially understand how the patterning impacts the formation of a static contact between soft deformable elastic bodies.

In the present paper, we present an experimental investigation of the behavior of these same patterned substrates in sliding friction, and show that the understanding of the evolution of the nature of the contact *versus* the pattern geometry provides a firm framework to analyze friction data.

More precisely, from an image of the contact similar to that shown in Fig. 1, one can define an apparent contact area (A_{app}) and a real contact area (A_{real}):

$$A_{\mathrm{app}} = \pi a^2$$

$$A_{\mathrm{real}} = \pi b^2 + \pi\left(a^2 - b^2\right)\frac{2d^2}{\pi\sqrt{3}i^2}$$

assuming that when in top contact, the surface of contact between the lens and the pillars remains that of the top of the undeformed pillars, which is indeed compatible with the optical observations.

Materials and experimental techniques

Patterned substrates

Patterned surfaces were produced by classical molding techniques using a silicon wafer with an etched resist layer as a mold. This mold was obtained by electronic lithography techniques: a thin layer of positive resist (MicroChem PMMA 950k) was spin-coated at 4000 rpm for 60 s onto a silicon wafer. The thickness of the resulting film fixes the height h of the pillars. This resist layer was then locally exposed to an electron beam (30 kV, 13 nA) in a field emission scanning electron microscope (FESEM) (Zeiss SUPRA 55VP) controlled with NPGS V9.0.190 to write the pattern, first designed with DesignCAD Express V16.2. After irradiation, the exposed parts of the resists were developed for 60 s under agitation in a (3 : 1) solution of methyl isobutyl ketone (MIBK)–isopropyl alcohol (IPA). PDMS replicas were obtained by pouring into this mold a millimeter thick layer of PDMS mixed with a crosslinker with a 10 : 1 ratio (Sylgard 184, Dow Corning), curing at 50 °C for 24 h, and finally peeling off the crosslinked PDMS elastomer from the mold. The patterned PDMS elastomer films were finally fixed on a carefully cleaned (UV–ozone) silicon wafer. The elastic modulus of the films, measured by a classical JKR test on a smooth PDMS substrate was found to be $E = 1.8 \pm 0.1$ MPa. All data presented in this paper have been obtained with patterned surfaces made of regular hexagonal arrays of cylindrical pillars, with a fixed height, $h = 2.2$ μm, diameter, d, and spacing, i, as summarized in Table 1.

Lens fabrication: the same Sylgard 184 batch was also used to make small smooth spherical lenses. They were obtained by depositing droplets of the reactive mixture on a glass slide previously treated with a perfluoro-silane, in order to obtain a partial wetting substrate for PDMS.[19] It is worthwhile to notice that due to smoothening of the free surface of the droplets under the effect of surface tension, the roughness of the lenses, as seen through AFM imaging of the upper part of the crosslinked drops, had a typical RMS roughness of 0.3 nm.

Table 1 Geometrical characteristics (diameter and spacing of the cylindrical pillars) of the patterned substrates used in the present study

Diameter/µm	Spacing/µm
1	[2;3;4;5;6;7;8;9;10]
1.5	[3;3.5;4]
2.5	[3;4;6;8;10]
4	[5;6;7;8;9;10;11;12;16;20]
6	[10;12;18;24]
8	[16;24;32]

Friction test

The friction force has been measured with a homemade JKR apparatus, equipped to work as a micro-tribometer which has previously been described in detail.[20,21] Its principle is schematically presented in Fig. 2.

An elastomer microlens, (L), is made adhere to a glass plate inserted into a mechanical holder (H), which can be translated vertically with a micrometric screw (not presented in Fig. 2), with a micrometric resolution. This lens is brought into contact with the substrate (S) covered with the elastomer sheet to be investigated. This elastomer sheet consists of successive sequences of square patterned zones and smooth zones, with a lateral size of the patterned squares of 8 mm, so that the friction on both the smooth and patterned substrate can be characterized in the same experiment. The substrate is fixed at the free end of a double cantilever spring, (K) (stiffness $k = 240$ N m^{-1}), able to slide with respect to the lens, as driven at chosen velocities by a micro-step motor connected to the other extremity of the spring. The range of available velocities is 3 nm s^{-1} < V < 330 µm s^{-1}. A capacitive displacement gauge (model S601-0.2 from Micro-Epsilon, France, equipped with DT610 electronic control) measures the spring bending, x, and allows one to access

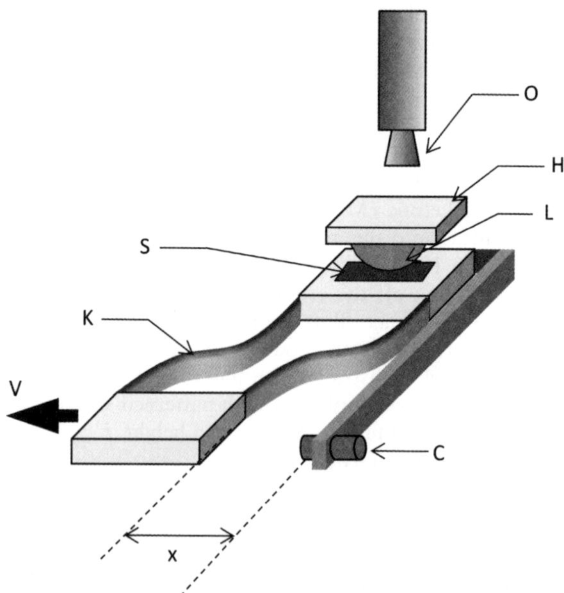

Fig. 2 Schematic representation of the JKR-like micro-tribometer used to measure the sliding friction force on patterned substrates (see text for explanations).

  This journal is © The Royal Society of Chemistry 2012

the friction force, in the range 50 μN to 50 mN. The linearity of this capacitive sensor is better than 1% on the full range used in the present experiments, so that no linearity corrections need be implemented, contrary to what is usually done in the case of piezoelectric actuators in AFM or SFA machines. The normal force cannot be measured directly in this setup, but, as an indication of the normal load, the size of the contact area between the lens and the substrate is monitored optically, through a long working distance microscope, (O), (Questar, QM100). During a sliding experiment, the sphere/substrate indentation depth is fixed. As reported in Degrandi-Contraires *et al.*[18] for all patterned substrates investigated here, the contact was observed to obey JKR contact mechanics, whatever the pattern, and whatever the nature of the contact (top or mixed) with an elastic stiffness of the contact given by that of the corresponding smooth contact, and an effective work of adhesion given by that on the smooth substrate times the fraction of area occupied by the top of the pillars.

Results

It at first appears obvious that the change in nature of the contact when increasing the applied load (or equivalently the contact area) deeply affects the friction response of the system, in a way which in turn depends on the geometry of the pattern. For example, when a mixed contact is formed, and then put into sliding motion, the full contact area may remain essentially that without sliding, at low sliding velocity, or strongly evolve at higher sliding velocities, as shown in Fig. 3.

What is then the meaning of the measured friction force? How far is it possible to analyze the friction response in terms of friction stress, like in mono-contacts or in terms of a friction force which then depends in a complex manner on both the pattern geometry and on the applied load?

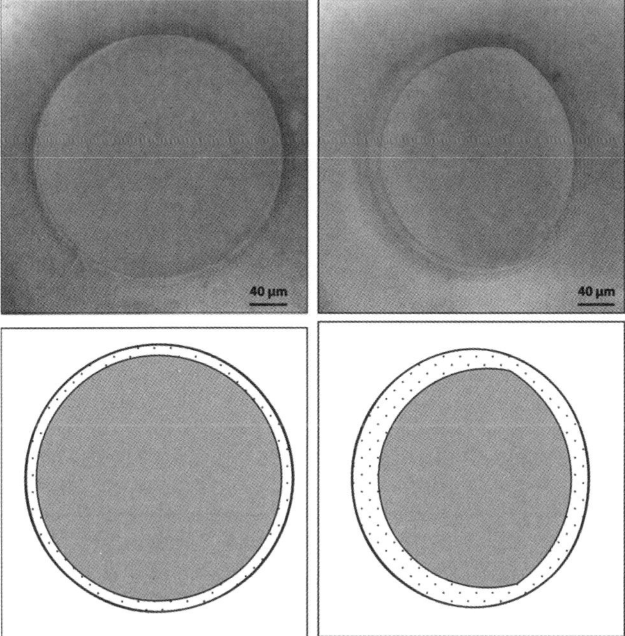

Fig. 3 Evolution of the relative amount of top and full contact with the sliding velocity, at fixed distance between the lens and the substrate. Left: contact at $V = 0.1$ μm s^{-1}; right: $V = 10$ μm s^{-1}. Bottom: corresponding drawings of the two zones inside the contact.

In order to make these questions more precise, a series of friction data analyzed in terms of friction force as a function of the contact area is reported in Fig. 4, choosing as area either the apparent contact area (squares) or the real contact area (diamonds) which can be precisely evaluated as explained before. A reference curve obtained between a lens and a flat elastomer surface is also reported.

Two important conclusions can be drawn from these data. First, the smooth substrate indeed leads to a friction force proportional to the real contact area, as expected for such smooth elastomer contacts which indeed behave as mono-contacts.[16,21,22] Second, when the data are reported in terms of the apparent area of contact (square symbols), the friction force appears smaller than on the smooth one. Indeed, this is a trivial effect due to the contact surface reduction. A more interesting result can be extracted from an analysis in terms of real contact area: when the contact is purely a top contact, the friction force appears proportional to the real contact area, with a slope larger than that observed for the same smooth contact, meaning that the pattern indeed contributes to an increase of friction stress.

Another interesting result is obtained when the lens displacement direction is not parallel to the substrate. In this situation, when the lens is displaced on the surface the normal load is not constant and the friction force can be analyzed during a constant loading or unloading phase depending on the sliding direction.

The friction force as a function of the apparent area of contact (which is fixed by the normal load) is plotted in Fig. 5. The friction force on the patterned substrate is clearly small as long as one remains in top contact (due to the reduction of the area of real contact) and jumps rapidly close to that of the smooth substrate when entering into the mixed contact regime. Interestingly enough, the friction data exacerbate the fact that the transition from pure top to mixed contact displays hysteresis, as shown by the very large difference between the two curves corresponding respectively to loading and unloading, in the vicinity of the transition. This shows that knowing the normal load and the sliding velocity between these kinds of surfaces does not allow a precise prediction of the friction force which depends on the history of the contact. Understanding in more detail what parameters of the system affect this hysteresis is certainly an important direction for further research.

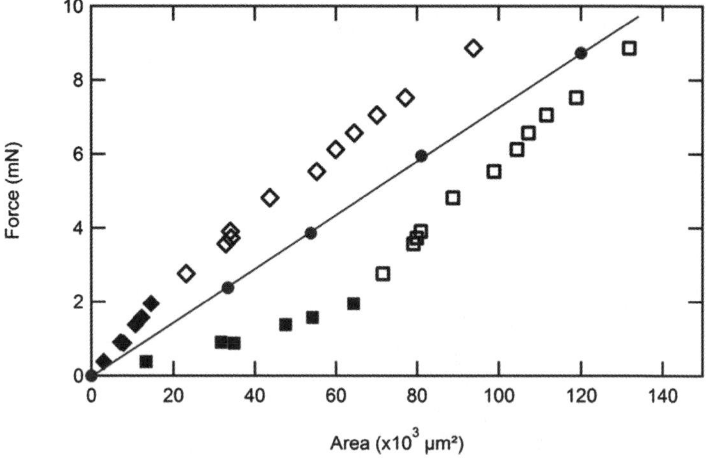

Fig. 4 Evolution of the friction force with the contact area for both top (filled symbols) and mixed contact (open symbols) and for $d = 8$ μm, $i = 16$ μm and sliding velocity $V = 2.5$ μm s^{-1}. Squares: apparent contact area, diamonds: real contact area. The circles and the line correspond to the friction force measured on the corresponding smooth substrate at the same velocity.

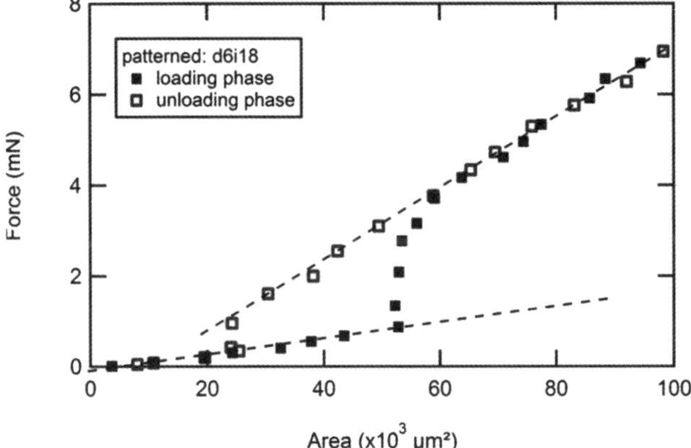

Fig. 5 Typical evolution of the friction force as a function of the apparent area of contact when crossing the transition between pure top and mixed contact, upon loading or upon unloading for $d = 6$ μm, $i = 18$ μm and sliding velocity $V = 2.5$ μm s^{-1}.

In order to go a step further in the understanding of the impact of the patterning on the friction behavior, we have decided to focus on the regime of pure top contact. We present below some first systematic results in this regime of pure top contact, along with first ideas on their possible interpretation in terms of mechanical deformation of the pillars inside the contact zone under the effect of the friction force.

In Fig. 6, the evolution of the friction force with the real area of contact is reported for four different diameters of pillars, and for a spacing defined by a constant ratio $i/d = 2$, along with the curve of the corresponding smooth substrate. As shown in the insert in Fig. 6, the spacing has only a very weak influence on the friction stress (comparable to the dispersion of the data at fixed i), while the diameter of the pillars fixes the level of friction stress enhancement compared to the smooth surface. This dependence in the pillar diameter is best seen in Fig. 7, where the friction stress τ is reported as a function of the diameter of the pillars d.

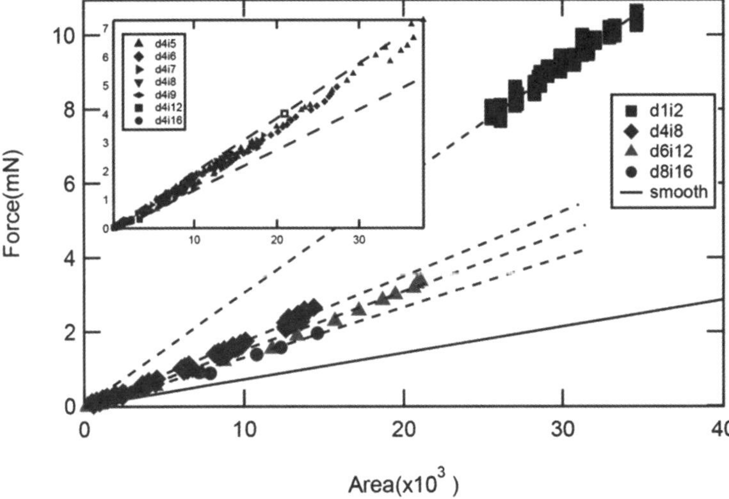

Fig. 6 Friction force *versus* the real area of contact for different diameters keeping the ratio $i/d = 2$ (see corresponding symbols in the figure). Insert: friction force *versus* the real area of contact for $d = 4$ μm and different spacing varying from 5 μm to 16 μm.

The error bars for each diameter include the spreading of the stress values due to the change in pillar spacing. The power law dependence, $\tau = \tau_0 + Ad^{-\alpha}$ with $\alpha = 0.998$ (indeed very close to 1), $A = 412.2 \times 10^{-3}$ N m^{-1} and $\tau_0 = 73$ kPa, the value of the friction stress obtained on the smooth substrates accounts very well for these data, evidencing a simple $1/d$ dependence for the friction force enhancement due to the patterning. The question is then to try to understand the origin of this d^{-1} dependence.

We have recently reported adhesion experiments showing that the elastic deformation of both the pillars and the underlying substrate were responsible for the enhancement of adhesion at such patterned PDMS–acrylic adhesive interfaces.[18,23,24] It is then plausible to assume that, similarly, when sliding takes place between the patterned PDMS substrate and the smooth PDMS lens, the pillars are elastically deformed under the effect of the friction force, and that they can transmit stress to the underlying substrate and to the lens, which in turn are deformed. When going out of the contact zone, the elastic penalty associated with these deformations is lost and thus contributes an additional energy dissipation to be paid to allow for the sliding motions.

Generally speaking, the energy dissipation can be written as:

$$T\dot{S} = \tau V = \frac{E_{el}}{t} \tag{1}$$

with τ the friction stress, V the sliding velocity, E_{el} the total elastic energy associated with the contact, and t a characteristic time for the relaxation of this stored elastic energy when emerging from the contact. Several contributions to such a total elastic energy can easily be identified. We have shown in ref. 24 that in the absence of sliding motion, for pillars separated by large enough distance so that their contributions were not coupled through the deformations of the underlying substrate, the elastic energy stored per unit area of contact when the pillars were under the contact could be written as:

$$E_{el} = \frac{2}{\sqrt{3}}\frac{1}{i^2}\frac{1}{E}\left[\frac{32}{3\pi}\frac{h^3}{d^4}F_t^2 + \frac{2}{\pi}\frac{h}{d^2}F_n^2 + \frac{8}{\pi^2}\frac{1}{d}F_n^2\right] \tag{2}$$

where E is the young modulus of the elastomer, and F_t and F_n are respectively the tangential and normal force exerted on top of the pillars. The first term in the bracket on the right hand side of eqn (2) is the bending elastic energy stored by one pillar, the second term is associated with the compression or the pulling

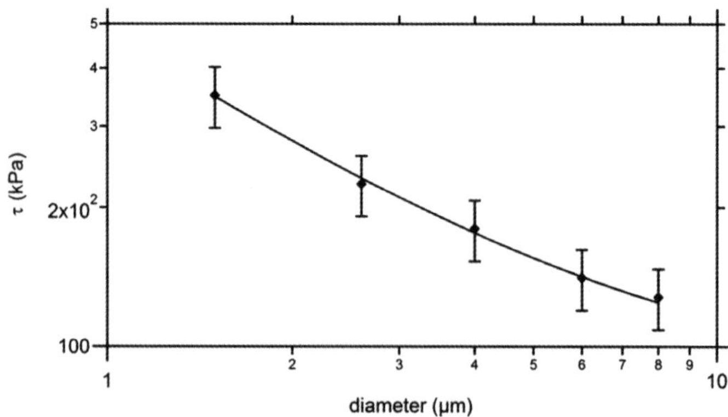

Fig. 7 Friction stress *versus* diameter of the pillars d in log–log representation deduced from the data presented in Fig. 6. The line corresponds to a power law $\tau_0 + Ad^{-\alpha}$ with $\tau_0 = 73$ kPa, the measured friction stress on a smooth substrate, $A = 412.2 \times 10^{-3}$ N m^{-1} and $\alpha = 0.998$.

     This journal is © The Royal Society of Chemistry 2012

(depending on the direction of F_n) of one pillar, and the third one is associated with the deformations of both the substrate and the lens locally imposed by one pillar. If the tangential force can easily be assumed to be related to the friction stress on the smooth substrate through $F_t = \tau_0 \pi d^2/4$, the identification of the normal component of the force is more delicate to evaluate: we have shown that without sliding, the stress repartition inside the contact could be described by a JKR[12] distribution of stresses, and that, when pulled off, the criterion of rupture on top of a pillar could be given by $F_n = W\pi d$.[18,24,25] If one can reasonably still assume that if a pillar is pulled off when emerging from the contact, such a rupture criterion can be postulated, it is not obvious at all that the stress profile under the contact can still be described by the symmetric JKR one when sliding takes place. Contact zones as highly deformed as the one shown in Fig. 3 are indeed clear evidence that the stress distribution for high enough velocities is deeply affected by the sliding motion. Another delicate question is that of the evaluation of the contribution of the tangential force transmitted by the pillars on the substrate and lens, which is far more difficult to calculate than that resulting from the normal component of the force (last term in the bracket of eqn (2)). We are presently working on these evaluations. We know however that without sliding, the dominant contribution to the elastic energy is that associated with the bending of the pillars, and this is especially true for the smaller diameters. It is then tempting to check if that dominant term can be compatible with the $1/d$ dependence observed experimentally. Injecting $F_t = \tau_0 \pi \, d^2/4$, and dropping all other terms in the bracket, one obtains:

$$\tau V = \frac{E_{el}}{t} = \frac{2}{\sqrt{3}}\frac{1}{i^2}\frac{1}{E}\left[\frac{32}{3\pi}h^3\tau_0^2\right]\frac{1}{t} \tag{3}$$

In order to recover the $1/d$ dependence, one needs to assume that the relaxation time t is proportional to d. A reasonable guess is $t = \alpha d/V$, with α a numerical factor. If one injects in eqn (3) the experimental values for all known quantities, one is left with a quite small value for $\alpha \cong 10^{-2}$. Such a small value is in itself not really surprising as, omitting all other contributions in the stored elastic energy under contact except the bending of the pillars, we have in fact artificially decreased the numerator in eqn (1) and 2, and as a consequence, the denominator needed also to be decreased to adjust to the measured friction stress. Much more work is needed to fully account for the observed friction behavior. In particular, in addition to the fact that we have at present no full description of the elastic deformations of the substrate and lens under the contact, we do not either know what the relaxation time t is, and how it could be related to the details of the detachment process, at the edge of the contact. Studies of systematic velocity dependences of the friction, as a function of both the geometry of the pattern and the nature of the adhesion forces at contact, in the top contact regime of contact, are presently under way in order to gain a better understanding of these complex phenomena, and have at our disposal firm guides to develop a full mechanical description of the contribution of elastic deformations to friction.

Conclusion

We have presented an experimental investigation of the incidence of patterning on friction at elastomer–elastomer sliding contacts. The test geometry chosen was a JKR like contact between a small smooth elastomer lens and various substrates made of the same elastomer, but patterned with hexagonal arrays of cylindrical micro-pillars, with diameters in the 1–10 μm range, and a fixed height of 2.2 μm. The relative distance between pillars was varied from two to ten times the pillar diameters. The nature of the contact (pure top contact or mixed one) was found to drastically affect the friction behavior. In the *a priori* simpler regime of pure top contact, we have shown that the friction force was proportional to the real area of contact between the lens and the top of the pillars, so that the friction could be characterized by a friction stress. This friction stress was observed to be higher on the patterned substrates than on the smooth one, and mainly driven by the diameter of the pillars (the pillar spacing was essentially without any effect on the friction stress). Relying on a recently developed mechanical analysis of the non-sliding JKR contact on such patterned substrates, we propose that this enhancement of the friction stress is associated with the elastic energy stored in the deformations of both the pillars themselves and the underlying substrate and the lens, energy which is released and lost when the pillars emerge out of the contact. Among the various contributions to that elastic energy, the bending energy of the pillars under the effect of the friction stress is rather easy to estimate and was shown to dominate the elastic contributions in the case of static JKR contact. Then focusing on that bending term, we were able to make plausible the fact that the enhancement of friction stress is observed to be inversely proportional to the diameter of the pillars. Among the additional elastic contributions involved in the description of this sliding contact, two appear delicate to evaluate: the deformation of the underlying substrate under the effect of the tangential friction force transmitted locally by each pillar, and the deformation of the stress distribution under the contact associated with the sliding motion. The sliding induced dissymmetry of the stress profile under the contact rules the distribution of local normal loads exerted on each pillar, and thus the cycle of compression–decompression of the pillars and substrates. It is thus important to correctly evaluate it to estimate the elastic energy dissipated during the sliding motion and its dependence upon normal load. We think that the systematic investigations of both normal load and velocity dependences of the friction stress enhancement presently under way should provide firm guidelines to develop such mechanical analysis.

Acknowledgements

We thank the C-Nano program "Nanofric" and the ANR MERIG for financial support. We benefited from discussions with E. Barthel, R. Weil. Some of the experiments have been performed by A. Beaumont.

References

1 F. P. Bowden and D. Tabor, *The Friction and Lubrification of Solids*, Clarendon Press, Oxford, 1950.
2 E. Verneuil, B. Ladoux, A. Buguin and P. Silberzan, *J. Adhes.*, 2007, **83**, 449–472.
3 K. N. G. Fuller and D. Tabor, *Proc. R. Soc. London, Ser. A*, 1975, **345**, 327–342.
4 K. Autumn, Y. A. Liang, S. T. Hsieh, W. Zesch, W. P. Chan, T. W. Kenny, R. Fearing and R. J. Full, *Nature*, 2000, **405**, 681–685.
5 K. Autumn, M. Sitti, Y. C. A. Liang, A. M. Peattie, W. R. Hansen, S. Sponberg, T. W. Kenny, R. Fearing, J. N. Israelachvili and R. J. Full, *Proc. Natl. Acad. Sci. U. S. A.*, 2002, **99**, 12252–12256.
6 A. Jagota and S. J. Bennison, *Integr. Comp. Biol.*, 2002, **42**, 1140–1145.
7 A. J. Crosby, M. Hageman and A. Duncan, *Langmuir*, 2005, **21**, 11738–11743.
8 T. Baumberger and C. Caroli, *Adv. Phys.*, 2006, **55**, 279–348.
9 Z. Burton and B. Bhushan, *Nano Lett.*, 2005, **5**, 1607–1613.
10 J. A. Greenwood, *J. Lubr. Technol.*, 1967, **1**, 81–91.
11 B. N. J. Persson, *Eur. Phys. J. E*, 2002, **8**, 385–401.
12 K. L. Johnson, K. Kendall and A. D. Roberts, *Proc. R. Soc. London, Ser. A*, 1971, **324**, 301–313.
13 A. Chateauminois and C. Fretigny, *Eur. Phys. J. E*, 2008, **27**, 221–227.
14 O. Ronsin and K. L. Coeyrehourcq, *Proc. R. Soc. London, Ser. A*, 2001, **457**, 1277–1294.
15 J. C. McDonald, D. C. Duffy, J. R. Anderson, D. T. Chiu, H. K. Wu, O. J. A. Schueller and G. M. Whitesides, *Electrophoresis*, 2000, **21**, 27–40.
16 F. Wu-Bavouzet, J. Cayer-Barrioz, A. Le Bot, F. Brochard-Wyart and A. Buguin, *Phys. Rev. E*, 2010, 82.

17 E. Wandersman, R. Candelier, G. Debrégeas and A. Prevost, *Phys. Rev. Lett.*, 2011, **107**, 164301.

18 E. Degrandi-Contraires, C. Poulard, F. Restagno, R. Weil and L. Léger, submitted, 2011. Available online: http://arxiv.org/abs/1201.1719.

19 M. K. Chaudhury and G. M. Whitesides, *Langmuir*, 1991, **7**, 1013–1025.

20 L. Bureau and L. Leger, *Langmuir*, 2004, **20**, 4523–4529.

21 C. Cohen, F. Restagno, C. Poulard and L. Leger, *Soft Matter*, 2011, **7**, 8535–8541.

22 A. Casoli, M. Brendle, J. Schultz, P. Auroy and G. Reiter, *Langmuir*, 2001, **17**, 388–398.

23 M. Lamblet, E. Verneuil, T. Vilmin, A. Buguin, P. Silberzan and L. Leger, *Langmuir*, 2007, **23**, 6966–6974.

24 C. Poulard, F. Restagno, R. Weil and L. Leger, *Soft Matter*, 2011, **7**, 2543–2551.

25 C.-Y. Hui, N. J. Glassmaker, T. Tang and A. Jagota, *J. R. Soc. Interface*, 2004, **1**, 35–48.

Why can TiAlCrSiYN-based adaptive coatings deliver exceptional performance under extreme frictional conditions?

Ben D. Beake,[*a] German S. Fox-Rabinovich,[b] Yannick Losset,[a] Kenji Yamamoto,[c] Myriam H. Agguire,[d] Stephen C. Veldhuis,[b] Jose L. Endrino†[e] and Anatoliy I. Kovalev[f]

Received 21st December 2011, Accepted 2nd February 2012
DOI: 10.1039/c2fd00131d

Adaptive TiAlCrSiYN-based coatings show promise under the extreme tribological conditions of dry ultra-high-speed (500–700 m min^{-1}) machining of hardened tool steels. During high speed machining, protective sapphire and mullite-like tribo-films form on the surface of TiAlCrSiYN-based coatings resulting in beneficial heat-redistribution in the cutting zone. XRD and HRTEM data show that the tribo-films act as a thermal barrier creating a strong thermal gradient. The data are consistent with the temperature decreasing from ~1100–1200 °C at the outer surface to ~600 °C at the tribo-film/coating interface. The mechanical properties of the multilayer TiAlCrSiYN/TiAlCrN coating were measured by high temperature nanoindentation. It retains relatively high hardness (21 GPa) at 600 °C. The nanomechanical properties of the underlying coating layer provide a stable low wear environment for the tribo-films to form and regenerate so it can sustain high temperatures under operation (600 °C). This combination of characteristics explains the high wear resistance of the multilayer TiAlCrSiYN/TiAlCrN coating under extreme operating conditions. TiAlCrSiYN and TiAlCrN monolayer coatings have a less effective combination of adaptability and mechanical characteristics and therefore lower tool life. The microstructural reasons for different optimum hardness and plasticity between monolayer and multilayer coatings are discussed.

1   Introduction

Hard and wear-resistant coatings have been successfully applied to cutting tool inserts to prolong tool life in machining applications. Trends currently driving the development of advanced coatings include (1) cutting faster to increase productivity (2) cutting dry (coolant free) for environmental reasons and (3) machining

[a]Micro Materials Limited, Willow House, Yale Business Village, Ellice Way, Wrexham, LL13 7YL, UK
[b]Department of Mechanical Engineering, McMaster University, 1280 Main St. W., Hamilton, Ontario, L8S 4L7, Canada
[c]Materials Research Laboratory, Kobe Steel Ltd., 1-5-5 Takatsuda-dai, Nishi-ku, Kobe, Hyogo 651-2271, Japan
[d]EMPA, Solid State Chemistry and Catalysis, CH-8600, Dübendorf, Switzerland
[e]Department of Surfaces and Coatings, Instituto de Ciencia de Materiales de Madrid (ICMM), Cantoblanco, 28049 Madrid, Spain
[f]Surface Phenomena Research Group, CNIICHERMET, 9/23, 2nd Baumanskaya St., Moscow 105005, Russia

† Current address: Abengoa Research S. L., Campus Palmas Altas, 41014 Seville, Spain.

hard-to-cut materials such as hardened steels, or advanced Ti alloys and Ni-based superalloys due to their increasing usage in aerospace applications. The heavy mechanical loads applied (1–5 GPa) on the cutting edge and friction generated heat from adhesive interaction at the tool/chip interface lead to intensive wear of the cutting tools.[1-3] The severity of the mechanical contact conditions is increased by cutting fast and dry, resulting in high temperature (*e.g.* 1000 °C) in the contact zone due to friction between the tool and the workpiece.[4] The combination of heavy loads and high temperatures results in extreme tribological conditions during operation. To achieve long tool life under these conditions coatings need to be multifunctional and display several interlinked characteristics to minimise wear.[3,5,6] For high performance machining applications high aluminium fraction TiAlN coatings are widely used. The coatings are thermally insulating so heat flow to the substrate is impeded.[7] More heat remains in the chip and dissipates *via* chip removal. Nevertheless, with the high temperatures at the cutting edge hardness and yield stress can decrease and this thermal softening can influence tool life. The coated components operate in the region of the elastic limit, and in some cases even above it, so plasticity can also become important, particularly for interrupted cutting operations.[8] Coatings that display adaptive behaviour forming highly protective and/or lubricious tribo-oxides during cutting can prolong tool life.[3,5,6,9] Differences in the composition and mechanical properties of the coatings at operating temperatures both affect the formation and stability of these protective and lubricating tribo-films.

A mechanical property approach to minimising wear has been shown to be highly effective in more general tribological applications such as sliding or abrasion.[10,11] However, in-depth studies of the interplay between the high temperature nanomechanical properties of thin coatings and the formation and stability of tribo-films and the resultant tool life in extreme frictional conditions have been stymied by lack of suitable instrumentation with sufficient stability and resolution to obtain accurate data at higher temperatures. With the advent of a commercial high temperature nanoindentation instrument (NanoTest) it is now possible to test directly on thin coatings, at least up to 750 °C. In addition to hardness (H) and reduced elastic modulus (E_r), other parameters such as H/E_r, plasticity index and H^3/E_r^2 can be determined from the high temperature nanoindentation data.

Different cutting conditions require coatings to have various combinations of mechanical properties such as hardness and plasticity. A microstructural design to reduce wear in one situation will not necessarily be optimum for another. By correlating room and high temperature nanoindentation test data on a range of advanced monolayer multicomponent nitride coatings deposited on cemented carbide inserts with tool life data from cutting tests it has been possible to show that there exists optimum combinations of hardness and plasticity for these monolayer coatings to achieve longer tool life in different cutting conditions.[8]

In this current paper we have studied two more complex high Al-fraction nitride coatings, a TiAlCrSiYN monolayer and a TiAlCrSiYN/TiAlCrN multilayer, that have recently shown promise in dry machining of hardened tool steels and turning Ni-based aerospace alloys.[3,5] Their behaviour has been compared with that of a TiAlCrN monolayer coating previously shown to have well-optimised composition and mechanical properties for ball nose end milling hardened steel, capable of outperforming other TiAlN-based coatings at 200 m min^{-1}.[12] Si and Y additions are thought to work synergistically in these coatings. Si is believed to refine grain size, and yttrium to prevent grain size coarsening at elevated temperatures, segregating to grain boundaries to block diffusion paths, and to increase phase stability.[13-15] Nano-multilayer coatings have been reported to improve coating properties and machining performance.[13-16] Various strategies have been employed, in particular in microstructural design to increase hardness.[17] In contrast, the nano-multilayer coating studied here is comprised of nano-layers with modulating composition, similar crystal structure and hardness. The resultant multilayer coating does not display superhardness at room temperature.

The interplay between the high temperature nanomechanical properties of these coatings and the formation and stability of tribo-films and the resultant tool life has been investigated. Nanomechanical properties (H, E_r, H/E_r, plastic work, elastic work, plasticity index and H^3/E_r^2) were determined from the nanoindentation testing at 25–600 °C. Data was correlated with results from surface analytical and high resolution transmission microscopy techniques to estimate the temperature at the coating/tribo-film interface.

2 Experimental

The nano-multilayered $Ti_{0.2}Al_{0.55}Cr_{0.2}Si_{0.03}Y_{0.02}N/Ti_{0.25}Al_{0.65}Cr_{0.1}N$ coating (TiAlCrSiYN/TiAlCrN) was deposited using $Ti_{0.2}Al_{0.55}Cr_{0.2}Si_{0.03}Y_{0.02}$ and $Ti_{0.25}Al_{0.65}Cr_{0.1}$ targets fabricated by powder metallurgical process on a mirror polished cemented carbide WC–Co substrate and ball nose end mills in a R&D-type hybrid PVD coater (Kobe Steel Ltd.) using a plasma-enhanced arc source. The $Ti_{0.2}Al_{0.55}Cr_{0.2}Si_{0.03}Y_{0.02}$ target was used for the $Ti_{0.2}Al_{0.55}Cr_{0.2}Si_{0.03}Y_{0.02}N$ (TiAlCrSiYN) monolayer and a $Ti_{0.1}Al_{0.7}Cr_{0.2}$ target for the $Ti_{0.1}Al_{0.7}Cr_{0.2}N$ (TiAlCrN) monolayer. Samples were heated up to $\sim$500 °C and cleaned through Ar ion etching process. Ar-N_2 mixture gas was fed to the chamber at a pressure of 2.7 Pa with a N_2 partial pressure of 1.3 Pa. The arc source was operated at 100 A for a 100 mm diameter $\times$ 16 mm thick target. Other deposition parameters were: bias voltage: 100 V; substrate rotation: 5 rpm. The thickness of the coatings was around 3 microns for the film characterization and cutting test work.

Nanomechanical properties were measured on coated WC–Co tool inserts using a Micro Materials NanoTest system. Nanoindentation was performed at room and elevated temperatures up to 600 °C. For the high temperature experiments both the sample and indenter were heated separately to ensure isothermal contact. For the testing on the monolayers a diamond indenter was used but for the testing on the multilayer a c-BN indenter was used as the maximum test temperature of 600 °C was above the oxidation onset temperature for diamond. It was checked that both indenters gave the same results at room temperature. Nanoindentation was performed in a load controlled mode with Berkovich indenters calibrated for load, displacement, frame compliance and indenter shape according to an ISO14577-4 procedure. The area function for the indenters were determined by indentations to 0.5–500 mN into a fused silica reference sample. For the nanoindentation into the coatings, the peak load was 40 mN and up to 40 indentations were performed for each coating at each temperature. This load was chosen to minimize any influence of surface roughness on the data whilst ensuring that the indentation contact depth was under 1/10 film thickness so that a coating-only (load-invariant) hardness could be measured in combination with coating-dominated elastic modulus.[5,6] The high roughness resulted in scatter in the data of around 15%. For the multilayer coating the scatter did not increase significantly with increasing test temperature.

Cutting tests have been performed during dry ball-nose end milling (Mitsubishi carbide end mills, $D-10$ mm) of hardened AISI H13 tool steel under strongly intensifying cutting conditions. The cutting experiments were carried out on a three-axis vertical milling center (Matsuura FX-5). The cutting parameters were: speed 300–700 m min^{-1}; feed: 0.06 mm tooth^{-1}; axial depth: 5.0 mm; radial depth: 0.6 mm. The coated tool flank wear was measured using an optical microscope (Mitutoyo model TM). At least three cutting tests were performed for each coating for each cutting speed and the scatter in the tool life measurements was in the region of 10%.

Cross-sectional Transmission electron microscopy (TEM) observation was employed in combination with FIB (focused ion beam) for investigation of the coatings on the cemented carbide WC/Co substrates. The TEM and selected area electron diffraction (SAED) were performed in a JEOL FS2200 microscope at an acceleration voltage of 200 kV. The structural and phase transformations at the cutting tool/workpiece interface and the chemical composition of the tribofilms formed were studied by X-ray photoelectron spectroscopy (XPS) with a ESCALAB MK2 (VG) electron spectrometer equipped with a hemispherical energy analyzer. The X-ray tube with monochromatic Al K_{α} radiation ($hv = 1486.6$ eV) was used as an excitation source. The sector 0.5×5.0 mm was selected for surface analysis. The XPS signal was recorded in the mode CAE = 50.0 V at 0.25 eV s^{-1}. X-ray absorption near-edge structure (XANES) experiments were carried out at the SGM beamline at the Canadian Light Source.

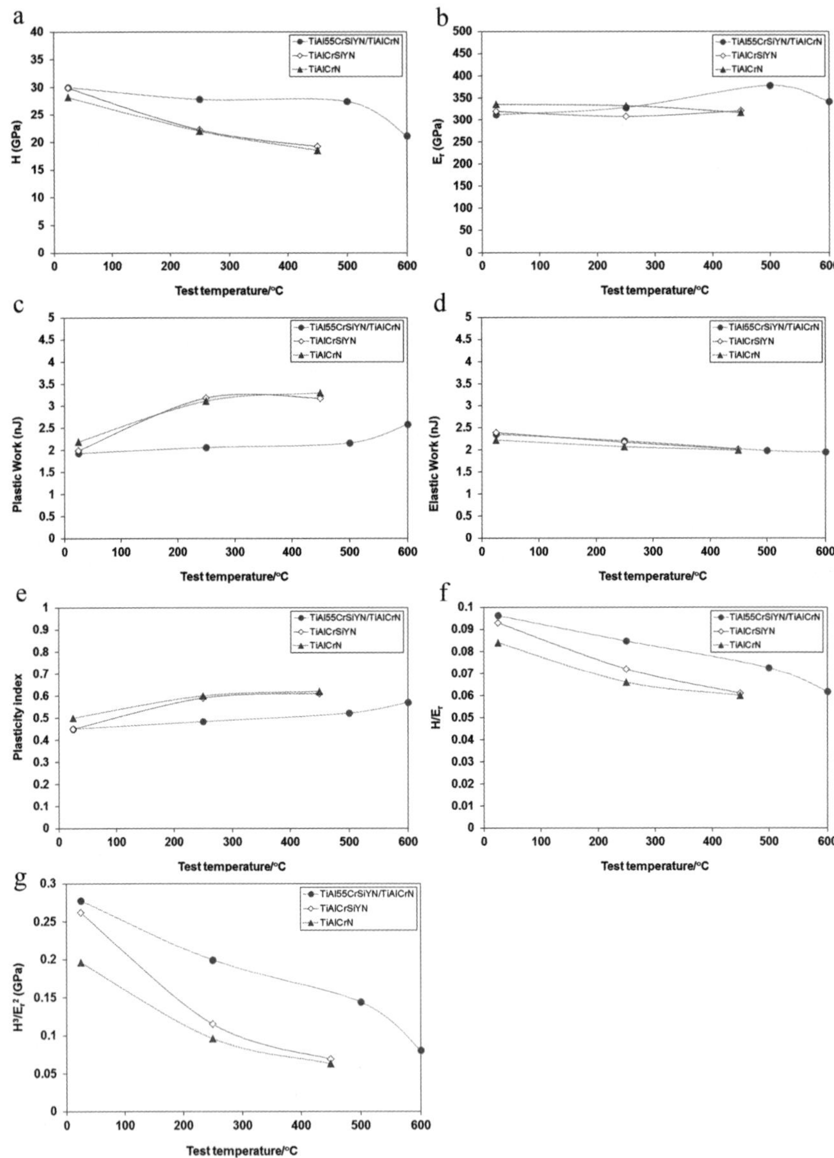

Fig. 1 Nanomechanical properties of TiAlCrSiYN/TiAlCrN multilayer, TiAlCrSiYN monolayer and TiAlCrN coatings measured at 25–600 °C a) hardness, H; b) reduced elastic modulus, E_r; c) plastic work, d) elastic work, e) plasticity index, f) H/E_r, g) H^3/E_r^2.

   This journal is © The Royal Society of Chemistry 2012

3 Results

The variation in micro-mechanical properties with temperature in the range 25–600 °C of the multilayer TiAlCrSiYN/TiAlCrN, monolayer TiAlCrSiYN and monolayer TiAlCrN coatings is shown in Fig. 1. With increasing test temperature there was no change in the relative ranking of H, H/E, plasticity index and H^3/E_r^2 between the coatings. The differences between the multilayer and the monolayers persist at high temperature. Although the hardness of all the coatings decreased with temperature, the reduction was much less pronounced for the multilayer TiAlCrSiYN/TiAlCrN. It decreased from 30 GPa at room temperature to 28 GPa at 500 °C, retaining relatively high hardness (21 GPa) at 600 °C. The average indentation depth at the peak load of 40 mN increased from 280 nm at 25 °C to 313 nm at 600 °C on this sample. Plastic work increased markedly on the multilayer TiAlCrSiYN/TiAlCrN only above 500 °C whereas only a temperature of 250 °C was required for a similar increase in plastic work on the monolayers. Elastic modulus varied relatively little with temperature. There was a slight decrease in elastic work with temperature for all three coatings. The plasticity index increased with temperature, similarly to the plastic work. For all the coatings H/E and H^3/E_r^2 decreased with increasing temperature. For all temperatures the multilayer TiAlCrSiYN/TiAlCrN showed the highest H/E and H^3/E_r^2 of three coatings.

The tool life of the three coatings has been compared during high speed ball nose end milling of hardened H 13 tool steel. The variation in tool life with cutting speed (300–700 m min⁻¹) is shown in Fig. 2. The data show that the TiAlCrSiYN/TiAlCrN multilayer coating significantly outperforms the TiAlCrSiYN monolayer coating within the range of cutting speeds of 500–700 m min⁻¹. However, the TiAlCrSiYN monolayer coating dramatically outperforms the TiAlCrN monolayer which cannot sustain speeds over 300 m min⁻¹.

XPS analysis of the worn tool surface of multilayer TiAlCrSiYN/TiAlCrN and monolayer TiAlCrSiYN coatings after machining at 500 m min⁻¹ is shown in Table 1.[6] Data were only on TiAlCrSiYN/TiAlCrN and the TiAlCrSiYN monolayer as the TiAlCrN coating cannot sustain cutting speeds above 300 m min⁻¹. The XPS data revealed a complex phase composition in the tribo-films formed on the friction surface with the presence of protective sapphire (Al_2O_3) and mullite ($Al_6Si_2O_{13}$) tribo-ceramics; lubricating polyvalent chromium oxides, non-protective TiO_x and TiO_2 tribo-films. TEM showed that the deformation is localised within a thin layer with an amorphous structure around 10 nm thick (Fig. 3). TEM/SAED of the worn sample of the TiAlCrSiYN/TiAlCrN multilayer coating did not clearly show the presence of AlN_{hex} phase within the surface layer at 40 nm (Fig. 4, a–b), with

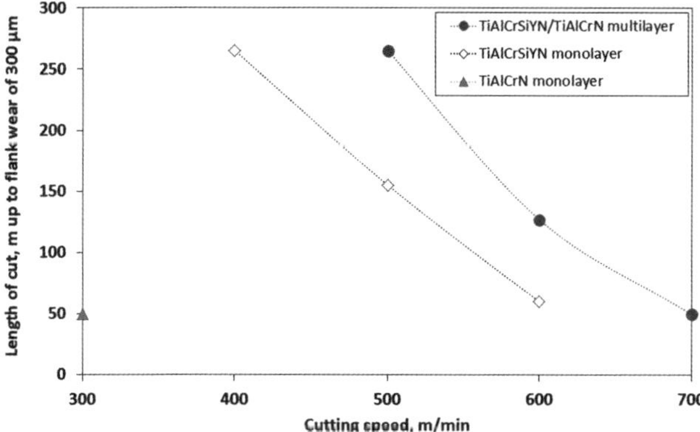

Fig. 2 Tool life *vs.* cutting speed at 300–700 m min⁻¹ in dry ball-nose end milling of hardened AISI H13 tool steel.

Table 1 XPS data of phase and chemical composition of the worn surface of the TiAlCrSiYN/TiAlCrN multilayer and the TiAlCrSiYN monolayer coatings after machining at 500 m min:[6] Al–O, Ti–O and Cr–O tribo-films, N = composition in nitride coating

Coating	at% Al			at% Ti			at% Cr	
	Al_2O_3	Mullite	N	TiO_x	TiO_2	N	Cr_xO_y	N
TiAlCrSiYN/TiAlCrN	29.1	6.6	19.3	7.3	5.5	7.2	15.9	4.1
TiAlCrSiYN	8.8	17.6	28.6	6.8	7.2	6.0	16.0	4.0

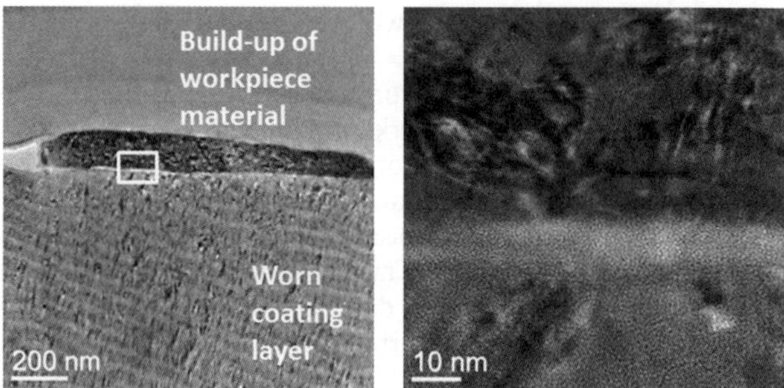

Fig. 3 TEM images of the worn tool with TiAlCrSiYN/TiAlCrN multilayer coating; FIB cross-sectional views.

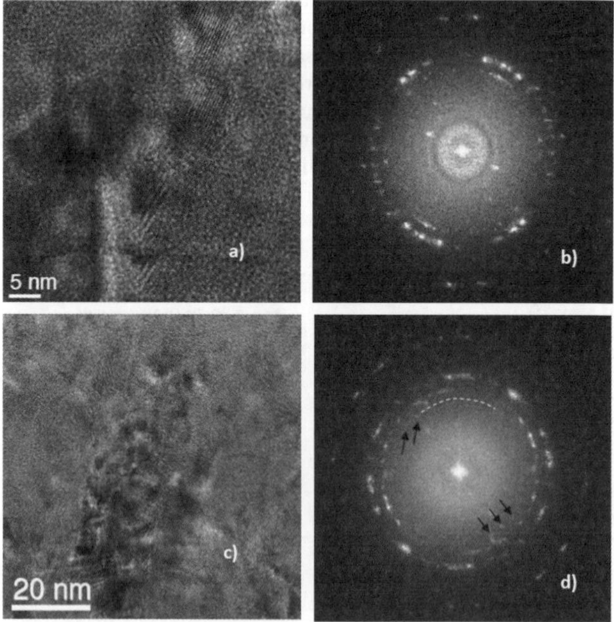

Fig. 4 Zero loss HRTEM image with SAED pattern inset of the worn TiAlCrSiYN/TiAlCrN coating layer. a–b) 45 nm from the surface, no evidence of AlN_{hex}; c–d) 85 nm from the surface, small amount of the AlN_{hex} phase.

  This journal is © The Royal Society of Chemistry 2012

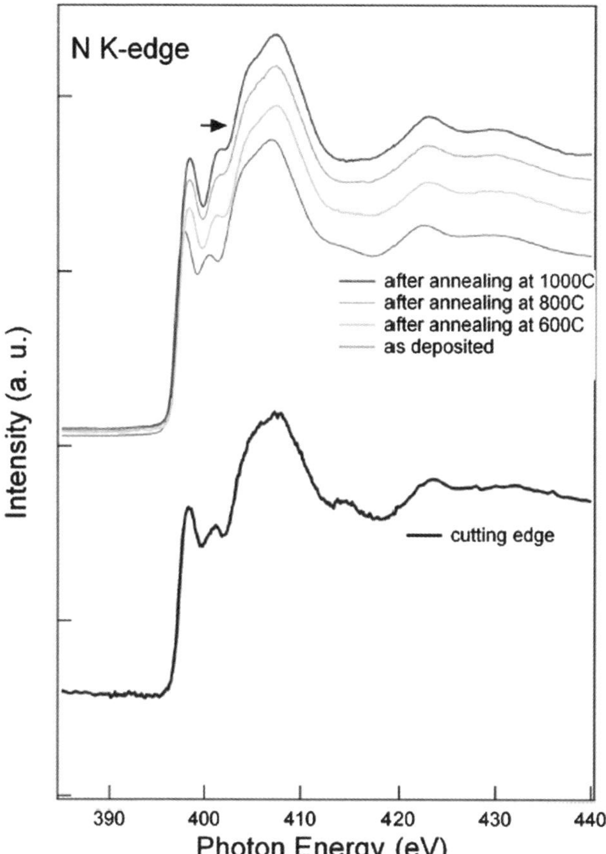

Fig. 5 Partial fluorescence yield X-ray absorption spectra of N–K edge after thermal annealing in-vacuum of the TiAlCrSiYN/TiAlCrN multilayer coating. N–K edge standards are presented here for comparison purposes in order to show the evolution in thermal decomposition of the TiAlCrSiYN/TiAlCrN multilayer coating.

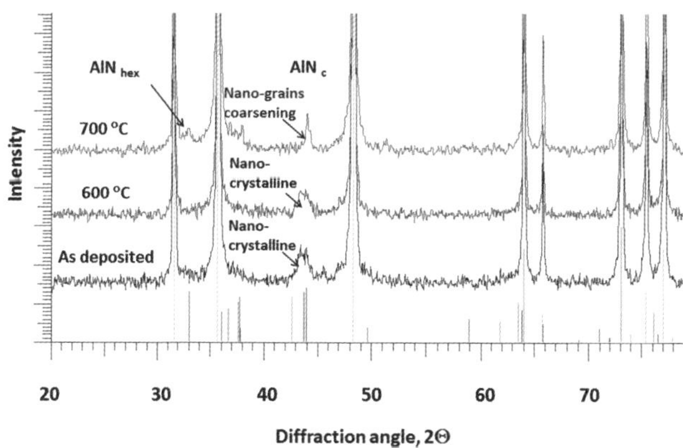

Fig. 6 XRD data on TiAlCrSiYN/TiAlCrN multilayer coating before and after annealing at 600 and 700 °C correspondingly.

only a small amount of AlN_{hex} (100) $\sim$0.268 nm found at greater depth ($\sim$80 nm) (Fig. 4, c–d). XANES analysis shows that the formation of AlN_{hex} phase is quite marked during *in situ* heating of TiAlCrSiYN/TiAlCrN above 600 °C (Fig. 5). XRD data of the TiAlCrSiYN/TiAlCrN multilayer coating annealed in vacuum for 0.5 h at 600 and 700 °C (Fig. 6) confirm XANES data presented in Fig. 5. The XRD spectra show the onset of phase decomposition at 700 °C with AlN_{cubic} and AlN_{hex} phase formation.

4   Discussion

The TiAlCrSiYN/TiAlCrN multilayer showed a considerably smaller decrease in several key mechanical properties (H, H/E and H^3/E_r^2) with increasing temperature than either of the TiAlCrSiYN and TiAlCrN monolayer coatings and it retained a high hardness of around 20 GPa at 600 °C. Both monolayer coatings have better high temperature mechanical properties than AlTiN or TiAlN studied previously by similar methods.[8,18–20]

The approximately inverse correlation observed between H/E_r (Fig. 1f) and the plasticity index (Fig. 1e) was expected from previous studies at room temperature.[18] Using finite element analysis Cheng and Cheng showed that the relationship for an ideal Berkovich indenter follows the apparent linear form[21,22]

$$\text{Plasticity index} = 1 - x(H/E_r) \tag{1}$$

where x is a constant and E_r is the reduced indentation modulus. From a simple examination of Cheng and Cheng's data the proportionality constant appears to be in the range $x = 4.5–5$.[23] More recently it has been noted that this equation is only approximately linear, particularly for $H/E_r > 0.1$, and although $x \sim 5$ on glasses, other samples such as metals ($x \sim 6–7$) and thin coatings ($x \sim 6.4$) showed different proportionality constants.[18,23,24] Nevertheless, eqn (1) provides a readily accessible way to interpret nanoindentation data in terms of the partitioning of elastic and plastic deformation energies. For the TiAlCrSiYN/TiAlCrN multilayer coating the values of x range from 5.7 at 25 °C to 6.6 at 500 °C and 7.0 at 600 °C. For the monolayer coatings they ranged from 5.9–6.0 at 25 °C to 6.3–6.4 at 450 °C. The observed slight upward trend with temperature might be due to the increasing contribution of the WC–Co substrate, as cemented carbide typically has values around 6.5–6.8. The small decrease in the elastic work done with increasing temperature is also likely to be due to the increasing contribution from the stiffer substrate as the coating softens, since the elastic modulus of WC–Co varies little in the temperature range studied.

It is interesting to investigate how these high temperature nanomechanical properties are related to tool life under increasingly severe conditions. Previously it has been shown that tool life and the evolution of wear in the machining of H13 steel was similar for TiAlCrSiYN at 600 m min^{-1} and TiAlCrN at 300 m min^{-1}.[3] Although the TiAlCrSiYN/TiAlCrN multilayer coating has higher hardness than either of these monolayer coatings the difference is not too great at room temperature and it is clearly not superhard. Room temperature coating hardness is not the best predictor of tool life. The high temperature properties are of more interest as they influence the stability of the environment where the tribo-films form. The simultaneous formation of the refractory sapphire and mullite compounds leads to excellent surface thermal protection under severe frictional conditions. TEM of the workpiece/tool interface after machining at 500 m min^{-1} showed that grain size coarsening on the TiAlCrSiYN monolayer was not observed for TiAlCrSiYN/TiAlCrN.[5,6,25] Being chemically stable the sapphire and mullite compounds in the tribo-films can reduce the adhesive interaction at the workpiece/tool interface. The reduction in surface damage strongly influences the phase transformation within the layer of the coating during friction. In the as-deposited state it has been shown that the TiAlCrSiYN/TiAlCrN multilayer coating has only a very small amount of the non-beneficial AlN_{hex} phase present.[6] Its presence/absence in worn surfaces may be correlated with tool life as an indicator of the temperature of the coating/tribo-film interface, and the effectiveness of the tribo-films as a thermal barrier. Previous studies have reported the presence of a tetragonal martensite structure in EDX spectra of adhered workpiece material, so locally the temperature at the outer surface must be above the phase transformation temperature of the H13 steel ($\sim$1000 °C).[3] The tribo-films act as a thermal barrier creating a strong thermal gradient. The XANES and XRD results indirectly indicate that the temperature of the coating below the layer of the protective tribo-films is strongly reduced to $\sim$600 °C. This is a cause of low surface damage and low intensity of phase decomposition (Fig. 4) within the coating. The reduced formation of non-beneficial AlN_{hex} phase helps prevent intensive coating damage under high temperatures.

By correlation of (room and) high temperature nanoindentation test data on a range of advanced monolayer multicomponent nitride coatings on cemented carbide substrate with the tool life results from cutting tests it has been possible to determine optimum combinations of hardness and plasticity consistent with longer tool life in different cutting conditions.[8,18] For the monolayer coatings the optimum values of hardness and plasticity at 450–500 °C to achieve longer tool life in interrupted cutting conditions such as end milling were found to be $H \sim 20$ GPa and plasticity index ~ 0.6,[8] with coatings exhibiting values far outside of these having significantly lower tool life under these conditions.

Compared to the optimum values determined from monolayer coatings, the multi-layer TiAlCrSiYN/TiAlCrN has higher hardness (27 GPa) and slightly lower plasticity (0.52) at the same temperature. A monolayer coating with similarly high hardness and low plasticity at temperature, $Al_{0.67}Ti_{0.33}N$ after 2 h vacuum annealing at 900 °C, has shown excellent performance in turning[26] but been considerably less successful in interrupted cutting tests,[27] where it was out-performed by as-deposited AlTiN and AlTiN coatings annealed at lower temperatures (700 or 800 °C) which show greater ductility at the expense of high temperature hardness.

It is interesting to investigate the causes for this improved behaviour in comparison with these state of the art Al-rich monolayer nitride coatings. At room temperature both nano-impact and micro/nano-scratch and wear tests have revealed that the multilayer TiAlCrSiYN/TiAlCrN can deform by a different mechanism to the mono-layer coatings under severe conditions. It has the capacity for crack deflection through the nano-layer interfaces which improves energy dissipation, so leaving less energy for surface damage and reducing the build-up of elastic strain that can result in the abrupt failures more typically observed for the monolayer films. In impact its higher H^3/E_r^2 minimizes the probability of initiating cracks in the first place. For monolayers with similarly high H^3/E_r^2 this would potentially result in abrupt failure. The multilayer film combines very high H^3/E_r^2 with a route–crack deflection through the inter-faces—to achieve stability under severe conditions. Chen and co-workers recently reported that a nano-multilayered TiAlSiN coating on high speed steel (HSS) showed better nano-impact resistance than a hard TiN coating with lower H/E and H^3/E_r^2 on the same substrate tested under the same conditions.[28] They noted that for the high H^3/E_r^2 multilayer (i) the critical impact load for cracking was increased and (ii) the spallation at high load was lessened. The more ductile HSS substrate in this case may have been beneficial in spreading the impact load. Hassani and co-workers have noted the ability of high H^3/E_r^2 coatings to spread the load in impact and erosive wear conditions that are not dissimilar to those in the interrupted cutting conditions of end milling may be a factor in their low wear rate.[29]

There is a strong correlation between the different damage mechanisms observed on the multilayer compared to the TiAlCrSiYN monolayer in the severe nano-scale wear tests (impact and scratch) and the cutting tests.[6] TEM images of the cutting edge show that the TiAlCrSiYN monolayer coating is more susceptible to cracks and the coating is removed from the very cutting edge after only 1.9 m of cutting whereas for the multilayer TiAlCrSiYN/TiAlCrN a stable wear stage continues up to 100 m. Bull,[23] Hassani *et al.*[29] and Beake *et al.*[30] have reported improved erosion and impact resistance by increasing H/E or H^3/E_r^2.

However, coatings design for very high H^3/E_r^2 cannot by itself improve either (i) nano-impact resistance (ii) erosion resistance or (iii) tool life in interrupted cutting (interrupted high speed turning or end milling) and it is vital to consider the microstructure. An excellent example of this is the influence of thermal annealing (1100–1500 °C) on the erosion and nano-impact performance of YSZ (8 wt% yttria stabilised zirconia) EB-PVD thermal barrier coatings (TBCs). Thermal annealing increases H/E by a factor of ~2 and H^3/E_r^2 by x5–x8. There is an excellent correlation between the results of the nano-impact test and the bulk erosion test.[31] As-deposited, TBCs show excellent erosion resistance but after thermal annealing the erosion resistance decreases by a factor of x2–x4[32,33] despite the large increases in H^3/E_r^2. The reason is the microstructure. As deposited the TBCs possess a pronounced complex and highly heterogeneous columnar microstructure which stops erosive impact-induced cracks from propagating across columns and large sections of coating being removed. This beneficial microstructure is degraded by the thermal annealing, particularly at 1500 °C where pronounced sintering across the columns is observed so each impact can result in more coating loss.[32]

The TiAlCrSiYN/TiAlCrN multilayer has a good combination of properties for high speed machining of hardened steel. Although it has rather limited plasticity this is offset by the crack deflection mechanism under severe conditions. For machining of Inconel DA 718 alloy we have recently reported that compositional tuning of this multi-layered structure to increase the % Al in the Si + Y containing layers has promise.[6] The higher % Al multilayer coatings show noticeably lower hardness (24.5 GPa at room temperature) but greater plasticity and other characteristics related to the coating's ability to dissipate energy during friction. For this application plasticity appears a more dominant factor than maximising elevated temperature H/E and H^3/E_r^2.

5   Conclusions

Multilayered TiAlCrSiYN/TiAlCrN coatings showed longer tool life in dry ultra-high-speed machining of hardened tool steel due to the formation of protective sapphire and mullite-like tribo-films on the surface resulting in beneficial heat-redistribution in the cutting zone. XRD and HRTEM data show the tribo-films act as a thermal barrier creating a strong thermal gradient. The data are consistent with the temperature decreasing from ~1100–1200 °C at the outer surface to ~600 °C at the tribo-film/coating interface. The mechanical properties of the multilayer TiAlCrSiYN/TiAlCrN coating were measured by high temperature nanoindentation. It retains relatively high hardness (21 GPa) at 600 °C. The nanomechanical properties of the underlying coating layer provide a stable low wear environment for the tribo-films to form and regenerate so it can sustain high temperatures under operation (600 °C). The microstructure and mechanical properties of the multilayer are important factors in its ability to sustain the extreme frictional conditions. It has very high H^3/E_r^2 which gives high resistance to plastic deformation and crack formation in the first place. The nano-laminated structure enables crack deflection along interfaces providing an additional route to relieving strain accumulation in heavy loaded cutting. In contrast, the microstructure of the monolayer coatings means they cannot readily combine high H^3/E_r^2 with a mechanism that avoids large scale fracture under increasingly severe conditions.

References

1 P. Wright and E. Trent, *Metal Cutting*, 4th edition, Boston, Butterworth–Heinemann 2000.
2 J. Loffler, *Surf. Coat. Technol.*, 1994, **68–69**, 729.

3 G. S. Fox-Rabinovich, S. C. Veldhuis, G. K. Dosbaeva, K. Yamamoto, A. I. Kovalev, D. L. Wainstein, I. S. Gershman, L. S. Shuster and B. D. Beake, *J. Appl. Phys.*, 2008, **103**, 083510.

4 L. Ning, S. C. Veldhuis and K. Yamamoto, *Int. J. Mach. Tools Manuf.*, 2008, **48**, 656–665.

5 G. S. Fox-Rabinovich, K. Yamamoto, B. D. Beake, A. I. Kovalev, M. H. Aguirre, S. C. Veldhuis, G. K. Dosbaeva, D. L. Wainstein, A. Biksa and A. Rashkovskiy, *Surf. Coat. Technol.*, 2010, **204**, 3425–3435.

6 G. S. Fox-Rabinovich, B. D. Beake, K. Yamamoto, M. H. Aguirre, S. C. Veldhuis and G. Dosbaeva, *Surf. Coat. Technol.*, 2010, **21–22**, 3698–3706.

7 W. Kalss, A. Reiter, V. Derflinger, C. Gey and J. L. Endrino, *Int. J. Refract. Met. Hard Mater.*, 2006, **24**, 399–404.

8 Using nanomechanics to optimise coatings for cutting tools, B. D. Beake, S. R. Goodes, J. F. Smith, G. S. Fox-Rabinovich and S. C. Veldhuis, in *Handbook of Nanostructured Thin Films and Coatings, Mechanical Properties*, Chapter 6, pp205–244, Ed. S Zhang, CRC Press (2010).

9 Physical and Mechanical Properties to characterize Tribological Compatibility of Heavy Loaded Tribo-systems (HLTS), G. S. Fox-Rabinovich, L. S. Shuster, B. D. Beake, S. C. Veldhuis, pp121–150, In: *Self-organization during friction: Advanced surface engineered materials and systems design*, G. S. Fox-Rabinovich, G. Totten (ed.) Taylor and Francis Books/CRC Press LLC, 2007.

10 A. Leyland and A. Matthews, *Wear*, 2000, **246**, 1–11.

11 A. Leyland and A. Matthews, *Surf. Coat. Technol.*, 2004, **177–178**, 317–24.

12 G. S. Fox-Rabinovich, A. I. Kovalev, M. H. Aguirre, B. D. Beake, K. Yamamoto, S. C. Veldhuis, J. L. Endrino, D. L. Wainstein and A. Y. Rashkovskiy, *Surf. Coat. Technol.*, 2009, **204**, 489–496.

13 K. Yamamoto, S. Kujime and K. Takahara, *Surf. Coat. Technol.*, 2005, **200**, 1383.

14 Q. Luo, P. Eh. Hovsepian, D. B. Lewis, W.-D. Münz, Y. N. Kok, J. Cockrem, M. Bolton and A. Farinotti, *Surf. Coat. Technol.*, 2005, **193**, 39.

15 L. A. Donohue, I. J. Smith, W.-D. Münz, I. Petrov and J. E. Greene, *Surf. Coat. Technol.*, 1997, **94**, 226.

16 D. B. Lewis, S. Creasey, Z. Zhou, J. J. Forsyth, A. P. Ehiasarian, P. Eh. Hovsepian, Q. Luo, W. M. Rainforth and W.-D. Munz, *Surf. Coat. Technol.*, 2004, **177–178**, 252–259.

17 M. Kong, X. Wu, B. Huang and G. Li, *J. Alloys Compd.*, 2009, **485**, 435–438.

18 B. D. Beake, G. S. Fox-Rabinovich, S. C. Veldhuis and S. R. Goodes, *Surf. Coat. Technol.*, 2009, **203**, 1919–1925.

19 B. D. Beake, J. F. Smith, A. Gray, G. S. Fox-Rabinovich, S. C. Veldhuis and J. L. Endrino, *Surf. Coat. Technol.*, 2007, **201**, 4585.

20 G. S. Fox-Rabinovich, B. D. Beake, S. C. Veldhuis, J. L. Endrino, R. Parkinson, L. S. Shuster and M. S. Migranov, *Surf. Coat. Technol.*, 2006, **200**, 5738.

21 Y.-T. Cheng and C.-M. Cheng, *Appl. Phys. Lett.*, 1998, **73**, 614.

22 Y.-T. Cheng and C.-M. Cheng, *Mater. Sci. Eng., R*, 2004, **44**, 91.

23 S. J. Bull, *J. Phys. D: Appl. Phys.*, 2006, **39**, 1626.

24 Y. Choi, H.-S. Lee and D. Kwon, *J. Mater. Res.*, 2004, **19**, 3307.

25 G. S. Fox-Rabinovich, J. L. Endrino, M. H. Agguire, B. D. Beake, S. C. Veldhuis, A. I. Kovalev, I. S. Gershman, K. Yamamoto, Y. Losset, D. L. Wainstein and A. Rashkovskiy, *J. Appl. Phys.*, 2012, **111**, 064306.

26 G. S. Fox-Rabinovich, J. L. Endrino, B. D. Beake, A. I. Kovalev, S. C. Veldhuis, L. Ning, F. Fotaine and A. Gray, *Surf. Coat. Technol.*, 2006, **201**, 3524.

27 G. S. Fox-Rabinovich, J. L. Endrino, B. D. Beake, M. H. Aguirre, S. C. Veldhuis, D. T. Quinto, C. E. Bauer, A. I. Kovalev and A. Gray, *Surf. Coat. Technol.*, 2008, **202**, 2985.

28 J. Chen, R. Ji, R. H. U. Khan, X. Li, B. D. Beake and H. Dong, *Surf. Coat. Technol.*, 2011, **206**, 522.

29 S. Hassani, M. Bielawski, W. Beres, L. Martinu, M. Balazinski and J. E. Klemberg-Sapieha, *Surf. Coat. Technol.*, 2008, **203**, 204–210.

30 B. D. Beake, V. M. Vishnyakov and J. S. Colligon, *J. Phys. D: Appl. Phys.*, 2011, **44**, 085301.

31 J. Chen, B. D. Beake, R. G. Wellman, J. R. Nicholls and H. Dong, submitted.

32 R. G. Wellman and J. R. Nicholls, *Surf. Coat. Technol.*, 2004, **177–178**, 80–88.

33 R. G. Wellman, M. J. Deakin and J. R. Nicholls, *Tribol. Int.*, 2005, **38**, 798–804.

Mechanism of ultra low friction of multilayer graphene studied by coarse-grained molecular simulation

Hitoshi Washizu,[*a] Seiji Kajita,[a] Mamoru Tohyama,[a] Toshihide Ohmori,[a] Noriaki Nishino,[b] Hiroshi Teranishi[b] and Atsushi Suzuki[b]

Received 25th November 2011, Accepted 9th December 2011
DOI: 10.1039/c2fd00119e

Coarse-grained Metropolis Monte Carlo Brownian Dynamics simulations are used to clarify the ultralow friction mechanism of a transfer film of multilayered graphene sheets. Each circular graphene sheet consists of 400 to 1,000,000 atoms confined between the upper and lower sliders and are allowed to move in 3 translational and 1 rotational directions due to thermal motion at 300 K. The sheet–sheet interaction energy is calculated by the sum of the pair potential of the sp2 carbons. The sliding simulations are done by moving the upper slider at a constant velocity. In the monolayer case, the friction force shows a stick-slip like curve and the average of the force is high. In the multilayer case, the friction force does not show any oscillation and the average of the force is very low. This is because the entire transfer film has an internal degree of freedom in the multilayer case and the lowest sheet of the layer is able to follow the equipotential surface of the lower slider.

1 Introduction

Lamellar materials, such as graphite, often show low friction in air. Graphite and molybdenum disulfide are typical low friction materials, while mica is not.[1] These materials are used as solid lubricants in an artificial satellite in which liquid lubricants, such as hydrocarbons, are not used because of the high vacuum environment. Some additives are mixed into automotive lubricants in order to generate a solid lubricant film in the sliding contact area due to the heat and shear which often undergo tribochemical reactions.[2]

The mechanism of low friction in such lamellar materials, whether the interlayer actions are due the van der Waals interactions or Coulomb ion pair interactions, is commonly explained by the slip generated between the layers. When we put the pile of papers on the desk and slide the uppermost paper, it appears that the inner paper slipping generates the low friction. However, this macroscopic mechanism is not confirmed to occur in the nanoscopic range.

Assume that a steel ball with a radius of several millimetres is sliding on an infinitely long graphene[3] sheet on the graphite. In this case, the graphene cannot slide as the pulling force will be infinitely high when the pulling force is finite per unit length. The effect of bending should also be considered in the realistic case as the shearing between the layers is hard to put into practice for geometrical reasons.

[a]Toyota Central R&D Labs., Inc., Nagakute, Aichi 480-1192, Japan. E-mail: h@washizu.org; Fax: +81 561 63 6920; Tel: +81 561 71 7531
[b]Toyota Motor Corporation, 1 Toyota-cho, Toyota, Aichi 471-8572, Japan

To consider the realistic phenomena, the low friction should be due to the sliding motion between the small pieces of graphene layers which are transferred to the steel ball and the lower substrate graphite. The surface has a roughness of a micron order and the transfer film is assumed to be physically adsorbed. Some transfer films are visualized by a Transmission Electron Microscope.[4] Recently, the molecular dynamics simulations concerning interactions between a graphite surface and the rigid pyramidal nanoasperity have shown the cleavage and flake formation of graphite.[5]

The question is then the mechanism of friction between the transfer film and the graphite surface. Does the friction occur inside the transfer film similar to the macroscopic friction of the pile of papers? If not, what is the difference in the friction mechanism between general solid materials and lamellar materials? In general crystal materials, sliding between the same materials produces a high friction.[1] The case of low friction is attributed to the incommensurate systems in which the rotation (yaw) angles of two surfaces are twisted.[6,7] The physically adsorbed transfer film may rotate in a commensurate condition for a long time due to the stability of the thermal equilibrium structure. Therefore, the macroscopically observed low friction of lamellar materials is not totally understood from the viewpoint of an incommensurate friction mechanism.

From a molecular point of view, the most underlying problem when investigating these phenomena is the size of the transfer film. The transfer film consists of a huge number of atoms[4] which is difficult to treat by an atom based simulation, such as molecular dynamics (MD) or molecular mechanics (MM). Based on this difficulty, MD and MM simulations are either performed for a small flake of graphene,[8,9] or for an infinitely large sheet by adopting periodical boundary conditions.[10] A coarse-grained molecular simulation is needed to overcome this difficulty.

The transfer film consists of graphene sheets. One concept is to model each graphene sheet as a rigid body. The covalent bond of the carbon atoms is on the order of 100 $k_B T$ and the van der Waals interlayer interaction is on the order of $k_B T$,[11] where T is the absolute temperature and k_B is the Boltzmann constant. This can be one foundation to support such a rough molecular model. Each graphene sheet has several internal vibration modes. The fluctuation of the sp2 electron cloud due to this internal vibration can be the source of the thermal fluctuation of the van der Waals force which affects the thermal motion of neighboring graphene sheets. The rigid body has 3 translational and 3 rotational degrees of freedom. The important degrees of freedom are the 3 translational and yaw rotational angles which are the motion around the axis in the direction of the film thickness. Based on these assumptions, the sliding dynamics of a transfer film can be described as the motion of a set of rigid graphene sheets which move by thermal brownian motion in 4 degrees of freedom.

In this study, coarse-grained Metropolis Monte Carlo Brownian dynamics (MCBD)[12–14] simulations are employed to investigate the friction dynamics of the transfer film of multilayered graphene sheets. MCBD was first introduced by Kikuchi *et al.*[12] in order to calculate the dynamics of colloid suspensions. This method is mathematically the same as Langevin dynamics, but has advantages in calculation stability and speed. MCBD is suitable for a system for which the effect of the thermal fluctuation and the inner sheet interactions are comparable in order.

2 Simulation method

2.1 Monte Carlo Brownian dynamics

The MCBD is the numerical solver of the Fokker–Plank diffusion equation and physically equal to the Langevin dynamics.

The Metropolis Monte Carlo (MC) method,[15] when applied to part of the degrees of freedom of a system, *e.g.*, the center of graphene sheets, turns into a simulation procedure for the Brownian motion of the sheets. The Metropolis MC was originally developed as a method for calculating statistical mechanical configuration integrals. Since the MC sampling is a Markovian process, if we introduce a "time" scale t which actually labels the order of subsequent configurations X, the "dynamic" evolution of the probability distribution function is governed by the master equation[16]

$$\frac{\partial P(X,t)}{\partial t} = \int \left\{ W(X|X'X')P(X',t) - W(X'|X)P(X,t) \right\} dX' \tag{1}$$

where $W(X|X')$ is the transition probability per unit "time" for a transition from configuration X' to X. The master equation may be approximately solved by an expansion method in powers of a parameter Ω, the size of the system. Given that $W(X|X')$ has the canonical form

$$W(X|X') = \Phi_0(x';r) + \Omega^{-1}\Phi_1(x';r) + \Omega^{-2}\Phi_2(x';r) + \ldots \tag{2}$$

with $x' = X'/\Omega$ and $r = X - X'$, the jump moments are defined by

$$\alpha_{\nu,\lambda}(x) = \int r^{\nu} \Phi_{\lambda}(x;r) dr \tag{3}$$

When $\alpha_{1,0} = 0$, the Ω expansion yields the lowest approximation of a nonlinear Fokker–Planck equation:

$$\frac{\partial P(X,\tau)}{\partial \tau} = -\frac{\partial}{\partial x}\alpha_{1,1}(x)P + \frac{1}{2}\frac{\partial^2}{\partial x^2}\alpha_{2,0}(x)P \tag{4}$$

with $\tau = \Omega^{-2}t$. In the Metropolis MC, the reciprocal of the maximum displacement allowed for an MC move during a "time" interval Δt may be taken as the parameter Ω. The transition probability then has the canonical form with

$$\Phi_0(x;r) = \frac{1}{2\Delta t} \quad \text{for} \quad |r| \le 1$$

$$\text{and} \qquad\qquad = 0 \quad \text{for} \quad |r| > 1$$

and, supposing, for example, the derivative of the potential energy of the system $U(x)$ with respect to x is negative, *i.e.*, $U(x) < 0$, with

$$\Phi_1(x;r) = -\frac{1}{2k_B\Delta t}U'(x)r \quad \text{for} \quad -1 \le |r| < 0$$

$$\text{and} \qquad\qquad = 0 \quad \text{for} \quad r < -1 \quad \text{and} \quad r \ge 0$$

for a sufficiently large Ω. From these one obtains

$$\alpha_{1,0} = 0, \alpha_{2,0} = \frac{1}{3\Delta t}, \alpha_{1,1} = -\frac{1}{2N_f k_B T\Delta t}U'(x) \tag{5}$$

where N_f is the number of the degree of freedom, so that eqn (4) reduces to the diffusion equation

$$\frac{\partial P(X,t)}{\partial t} = \frac{D}{k_B T}\frac{\partial}{\partial x}U'(x)P + D\frac{\partial^2}{\partial x^2}P \tag{6}$$

where the diffusion constant D is defined by

$$2N_f D\Delta t\Omega^2 = 1 \tag{7}$$

Thus, by making the size of the maximum allowed displacement Ω^{-1} in the Metropolis MC very small the forces acting on a particle remain essentially constant during the Monte Carlo "time" step, the method turns into a Brownian dynamics simulation.

The merit of MCBD compared to a molecular dynamics based simulation is that the calculation of the forces acting on each sheet is not needed and only the calculation of the potential energy $U(x)$ is needed so that the calculation remains stable. Compared to the general Monte Carlo method, MCBD provides the time evolution of a physical quantity, where averaging of multiple trajectories is needed.

As described above, the reality of the MCBD simulation relies on the reality of the interacting energy $U(x)$ and the diffusion coefficients D. In this paper, we constructed $U(x)$s from a widely used pairwise potential parameter proposed by Girifalco et $al.$[17] The potential is used in sp2 carbons, such as graphites, carbon nanotubes, and C60 and evaluated in elastic and thermal properties. In order to obtain the diffusion coefficients, D, ether experiments and atom-based simulations are available. The parameters can be more precisely obtained from ab $initio$ quantum calculations.

2.2 Potential between graphene sheets

In the structure of graphites under a thermal equilibrium stable AB stuck structure, the distance between carbon atoms l_a is 1.42 Å, and the average distance between sheets l_z is 3.35 Å. The interaction between graphene sheets calculated and stored during the simulation are taken from the literature.[17] This potential reproduces the stable AB stuck structure and the stress during separation of the two graphene sheets. Using this pairwise potential for the interactions between rigid sheets, the anisotropy of potential landscape due to the motion of sheets is obtained.

The potential between the sp2 carbon atoms $U_{\text{atom–atom}}(r_a)$ is described by the following Lennard–Jones type function

$$U_{\text{atom–atom}}(r_a) = -\frac{A}{r_a^6} + \frac{B}{r_a^{12}} \tag{8}$$

where r_a is the distance between carbon atoms, A and B are constants. This function can be written using the parameter which describes the depth of the potential ε and the equilibrium distance σ.

$$U_{\text{atom–atom}}(r_a) = 4\varepsilon\left[-\left(\frac{\sigma}{r_a}\right)^6 + \left(\frac{\sigma}{r_a}\right)^{12}\right] \tag{9}$$

ε, and r_{a0} are rewritten as follows:

$$\varepsilon = \frac{A^2}{4B}, \tag{10}$$

$$r_{a0} = 2^{1/6}\sigma = \left(\frac{2B}{A}\right)^{1/6}. \tag{11}$$

We used the pairwise inter atom potential on the graphene sheets as A = 15.2 eV Å⁶, B = 24.1 × 10⁻³ eV Å¹², r_0 = 3.83 Å, ε = 2.89 meV.

We then calculated the potential between a carbon atom and a graphene sheet by the following equation using eqn (8).

$$U_{\text{atom–sheet}}(x,y) = \sum U_{\text{atom–atom}}(r_a) \tag{12}$$

We set x as the sliding direction in Cartesian coordinates, y as the perpendicular direction to the sliding direction, and the summation at the rhs as the sum of the interactions between a set of carbon atoms in a honeycomb structure of unit

   This journal is © The Royal Society of Chemistry 2012

length l_a in the $z = 0$ plane and a carbon atom at $z = \Delta z$. During the simulation, we employed the coordinate system based on the vectors $a = ((\sqrt{3}/2)l_a, (1/2)l_a), b = (0, l_a)$ considering the symmetry and calculated $U_{\text{atom–sheet}}$ before the simulation on the lattice point divided by 100 in the a,b directions, and returned to the Cartesian coordinates during the motion of the sheets in order to calculate the potential energy between the sheets.

Each $U_{\text{atom–sheet}}$ on the lattice points are calculated until the difference in the energy converges to $\Delta U_{\text{atom–sheet}} < 10^{-6}$ eV from the neighbor to farther atoms. Fig. 1 shows the $U_{\text{atom–sheet}}(x,y)$ in the Cartesian coordinates.

As two carbon atoms, which are facing each other on the honeycomb structures, can be geometrically distinguished by the periodicity, the potential between the sheets $U_{\text{sheet–sheet}}$ is calculated using $U_{\text{atom–sheet}}(x, y)$.

$$U_{\text{sheet–sheet}} = (U_{\text{atom–sheet}}(\Delta x, \Delta y) + U_{\text{atom–sheet}}(\Delta x, \Delta y - (1/2)l_a)) \cdot S(\Delta x, \Delta y) \quad (13)$$

where Δx and Δy are the distances between center of two circle shaped sheets in the x and y directions respectively, and $S(\Delta x, \Delta y)$ is the number of the carbon atoms in an overlapped area of two circles in a position Δx and Δy. By eqn (13), the end effect which is the effect of the finite size of the graphene sheets is able to be included in the simulation. The potential surface $U_{\text{sheet–sheet}}$ of the system is plotted in Fig. 2. $\Delta x = 0$ and $\Delta y = 0$ correspond to the AB stuck structure and the interaction between the sheets decreases when two sheets are in separated positions.

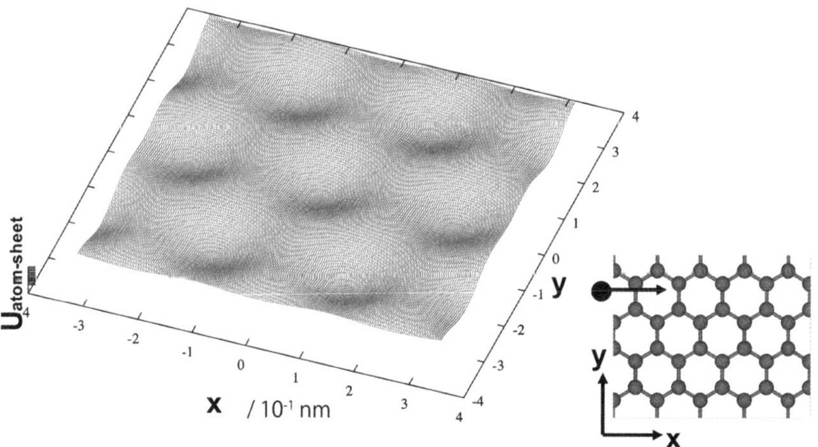

Fig. 1 Potential between a carbon atom and a graphene sheet $\Delta U_{\text{atom–sheet}}$ (x,y plane).

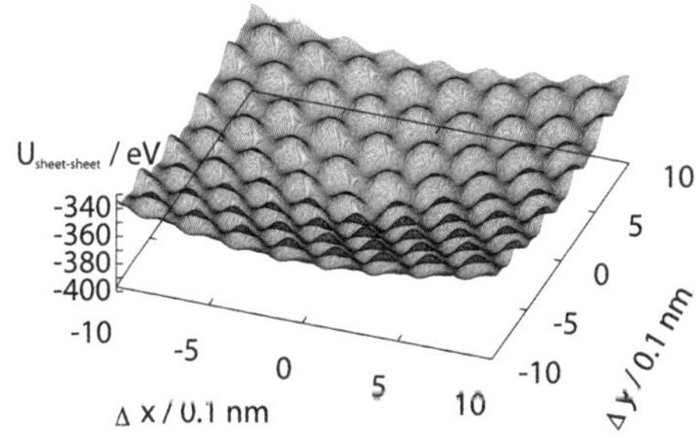

Fig. 2 Potential between two graphene sheets $\Delta U_{\text{sheet–sheet}}$ (x, y plane).

The interaction between a graphene sheet and an infinitely large graphite plate $U_{\text{sheet–plate}}$ is described as follows:

$$U_{\text{sheet–plate}} = (U_{\text{atom–sheet}}(x,y) + U_{\text{atom–sheet}}(x,y - (1/2)l_a)) \cdot N_{xy}/2 \qquad (14)$$

where x,y are the coordinates of the sheet, and N_{xy} is the number of atoms in the sheet. During this interaction, the inclined baseline shown in Fig. 2 does not exist and the potential becomes a periodical function.

The effect of the incommensurate surface interaction is included by adopting a smooth energy surface when two sheets are twisted at the yaw angle θ. The effect of the yaw angle is included as follows. The potential between graphene sheets $U_{\text{sheet–sheet}}$ is set to an average value $U_{\text{sheet–sheet}} = U_{\text{ave}}$ when the difference between the sheet rotation angles becomes 0.1 degree. In Fig. 3, this simulation condition is plotted using the direct calculation due to the interactions of the finite number of carbon atoms. Although the direct calculation shows cyclic functions, this effect is neglected for simplicity.

For the z direction, which is the direction of load and the film thickness, each potential energy is already calculated $U_{\text{sheet–sheet}}(x,y)$ as a summation of each atom pair potential $U_{\text{atom–sheet}}$ for the distance between both sheets Δz. During the simulations, $U_{\text{sheet–sheet}}(x,y)$ is stored as a table calculated before the MC simulation run starts. The values of $U_{\text{sheet–sheet}}(x,y)$ is linearly complemented from the mesh value.

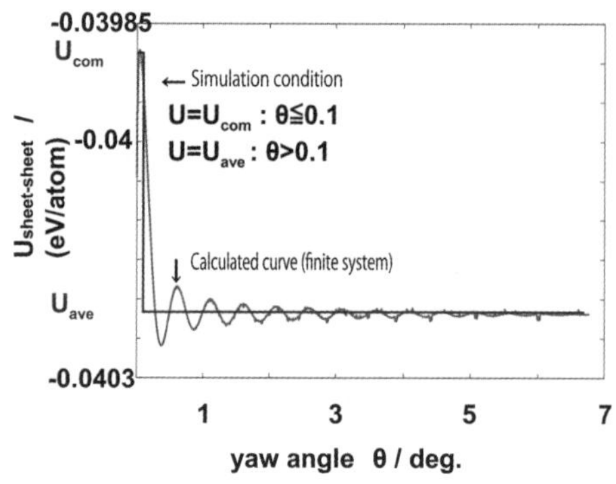

Fig. 3 Potential between two graphene sheets $\Delta U_{\text{sheet–sheet}}$ as a function of the yaw angle θ.

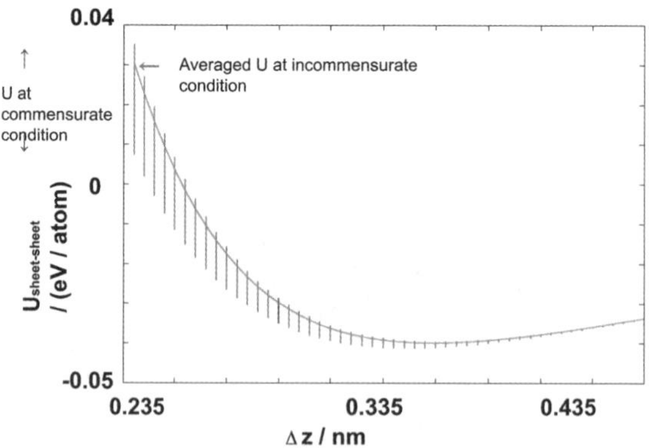

Fig. 4 Potential between two graphene sheets $U_{\text{sheet–sheet}}$ as a function of z.

   This journal is © The Royal Society of Chemistry 2012

Fig. 4 shows the sheet potential $U_{\text{sheet-sheet}}$ as a function of Δz under a commensurate condition. The averaged U under the incommensurate condition is also plotted as a curve. Each bar shows the range of the $U_{\text{sheet-sheet}}$ distribution in the (x, y) plane. A small Δz corresponds to a high pressure under a heavy load which shows a large range of energy in the commensurate condition. As Δz increases, which corresponds to a lower pressure, the range of $U_{\text{sheet-sheet}}$ decreases and when over the equilibrium width of 0.335 nm, $U_{\text{sheet-sheet}}$ does not significantly change.

2.3 Simulation conditions

The MCBD simulation conditions are described as follows. Each circular graphene sheets consist of 400 ($N_{xy} = 20 \times 20$) to 1 000 000 ($N_{xy} = 1\,000 \times 1\,000$) atoms allowed to move in 3 translational and 1 rotational directions due to thermal motion at 300 K. The transfer layer consists of N_z graphene sheets piled in the z direction.

The initial conditions of the graphene sheets are set for the AB stuck structure at the origin and confined by the upper and lower sliders. The lower slider is set to an infinitely wide plane. The interaction between the lowest confined graphene sheet and the lower slider is set to the same interaction without the end effect. The upper slider is fixed to the same size as the confined graphene sheets. The interaction between the top confined graphene sheet and the upper slider is set to the same interaction including the end effect. The effect of the load in the z direction is given by setting the total width of the upper and the lower sliders to a fixed value $l_z \times (N_z + 1)$ where $l_z = 0.330$ nm is the average of the interlayer distance.

The sliding simulation is done by moving the upper slider in the x direction 1.0×10^{-8} nm MC^{-1} step. In the heaviest case $N_{xy} = 1\,000 \times 1\,000$, $N_z = 1$, the number of atoms is 1 000 000 which may take a huge amount of time for an all atom molecular dynamics simulation. In this method, the total simulation time depends on N_z and not on N_{xy} due to the calculation method described in the former subsection $i.e.$, we first calculate the potential table $U_{\text{atom-sheet}}$ in the infinite system, then calculate $U_{\text{sheet-sheet}}$ by multiplying the number of atoms N_{xy} including the end effect. The radius of the transfer film on $N_{xy} = 100 \times 100$, $N_z = 10$ is equivalent to the flake diameter of 18.2 nm and thickness of 3.7 nm which is almost as the same scale as the transfer film observed on the AFM tip.[4]

The maximum allowed displacement is set to $\Omega_x^{-1} = \Omega_y^{-1} = 0.01$ Å for the x,y direction, $\Omega_z^{-1} = 0.001$ Å for the z direction and $\Omega_\theta^{-1} = 0.01$ for the θ direction. Each Monte Carlo time step in the MCBD method and physical time Δt is related to using the diffusion coefficient D in eqn (4). Although the correlations between the directions of fluctuations are assumed to be independent in this study, the correlation between the x,y directions should be considered in the future.

3 Results and discussions

The sliding simulations are done by moving the upper slider at a constant velocity. Fig. 5 shows the typical time developments of the x coordinates of the graphene sheets. As the upper slider moves in the x direction, the graphene sheets follows the upper slider. The lower the sheet number N_z, the larger the delay in the motion of the sheets and the curve shows a wavy pattern.

The trajectory during the sliding motion of the lowermost sheet $N_z = 10$ is plotted $vs.$ the potential surface between the lower slider and the 10th sheet in Fig. 6. It is clearly shown that even the upper slider moves against the potential hill, and the lowest sheet slides toward the valley of the potential surface. More precisely, a stay motion at the bottom of the potential surface is also shown. Apart from the stay, the trajectory shows that the motion of the lowermost sheet is almost on the plane energy surface.

Time development of the friction forces $F_x = \Delta U/\Delta x$ is plotted in Fig. 7 for $N_z = 1$ and $N_z = 10$, where ΔU is the difference in the total potential energy of transfer film

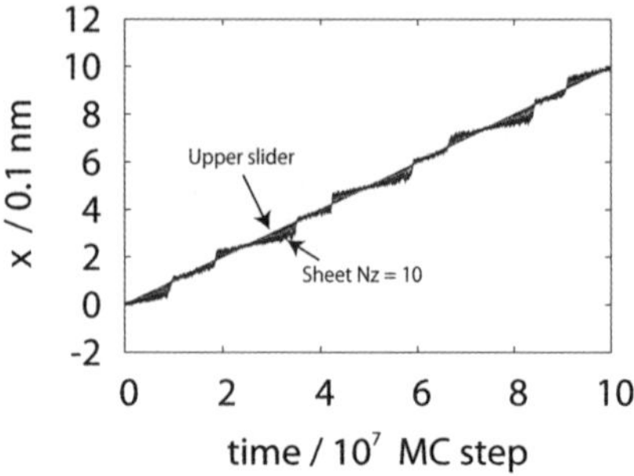

Fig. 5 Motion of each graphene sheet in x direction under sliding condition. The lowest curve is the 10th layer. $N_{xy} = 10{,}000$, $N_z = 10$, Degrees of freedom: x,y,z,θ, $l_z = 0.330$ nm.

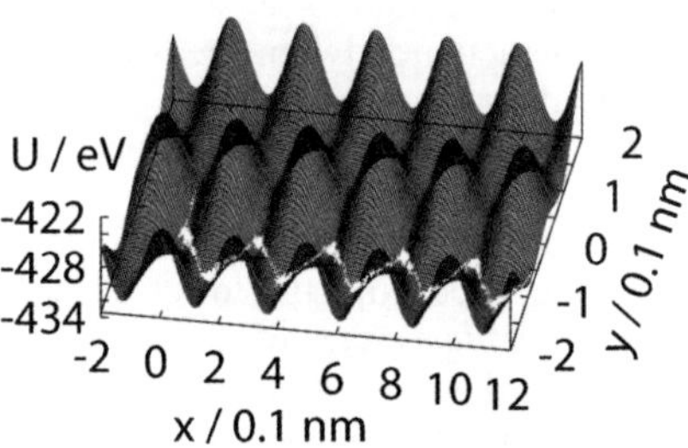

Fig. 6 Trajectory of the center of the 10th sheet of the transfer layer and the potential surface between the lower slider and the 10th sheet.

and Δx is the motion in the x direction. In the $N_z = 1$ system, the stick-slip like oscillation of the friction force is found. On the other hand, in the $N_z = 10$ system, the friction force fluctuates around zero and no oscillation is found. This is due to the motion shown in Fig. 6 that the lowest sheet moves the plane, which is almost equal to $\Delta U = 0$, and the friction force, which is calculated from this quantity, becomes very small. We call this motion of multilayer graphene sheets which generates a low friction as the thermal escaping motion.

In order to quantitatively discuss the low friction force due to the thermal escaping motion, the averaged friction forces F_x in several N_{xy} and N_z are plotted in Fig. 8. When the sheets are large enough ($N_{xy} \geq 60^2$), the large friction force F_x is found when $N_z = 1$ and decreases when $N_z > 1$ which is due to the thermal escaping motion. The friction force F_x increases as the number of N_{xy} increases when $N_z = 1$. The friction force F_x slightly increases as N_z increases in $N_z \geq 3$ and does not show any sheet size N_{xy} dependence. This may be due to the friction between the inner sheets; in other words, the weakening of the spring constant of a whole transfer film. When the sheets are small ($N_{xy} \leq 40^2$), the friction forces monotonously increase with the increase in N_z and the two curves are different in $N_z \geq 3$ which suggests the lack of any thermal escaping motion.

Considering the mechanism of the thermal escaping motion, a conceptual illustration is shown in Fig. 9. The confined graphene sheet interacts with both the upper slider and the lower slider shown in Fig. 9(a). When the upper slider moves right, the interaction region of the upper side decreases whereas the lower side does not change. The graphene sheet moves in the right direction in order to compensate for the lost interacting region and the stability recovers (Fig. 9(b)). This is the end effect which is the basic reason that the graphene sheet follows the upper slider. In other words, an asymmetric situation due to the existence of the ends of the upper and the lower sliders makes the basic motion. In realistic sheets, the potential energy

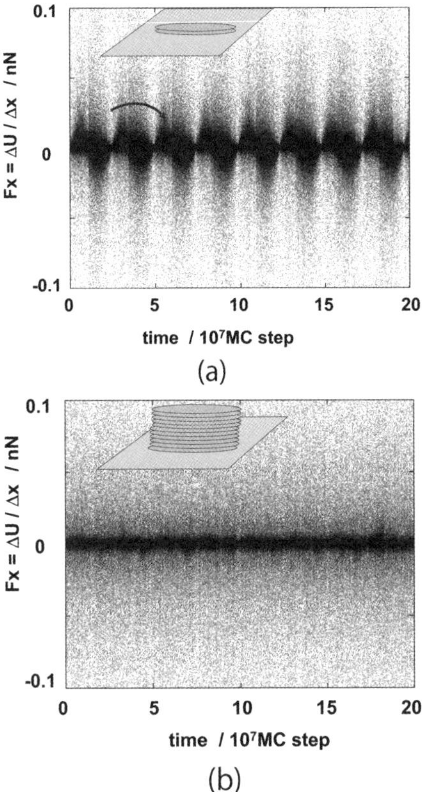

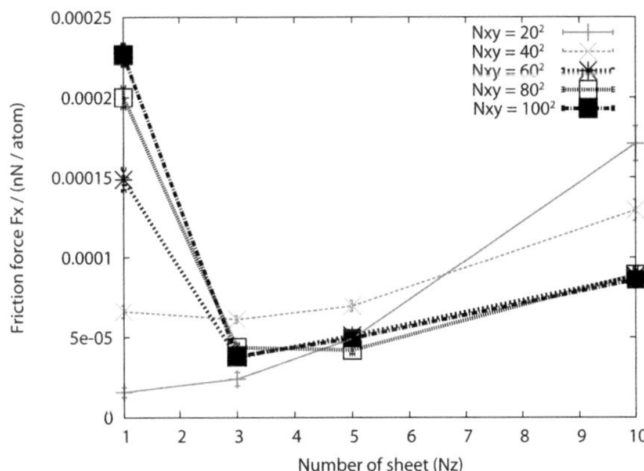

Fig. 7 Time development of the friction force for a number of sheets $N_z = 1$ (a), $N_z = 10$ (b).

Fig. 8 Dependence of the size of the sheets (N_{xy}), the number of sheets (N_z) on friction force F_x. The friction force is averaged by the MCBD simulation of 2×10^8 MC step at 16 calculations under independent initial conditions. The error bars are almost within the size of the markers.

function drawn in Fig. 9(b) has the landscape precisely shown as $U_{\text{sheet–sheet}}$ in Fig. 3 which has local minima (Fig. 9(c)). In order to move out from the local minima, thermal fluctuation is necessary. This is strongly related to the size N_{xy} and number of sheets N_z dependence on the friction force F_x found in Fig. 8.

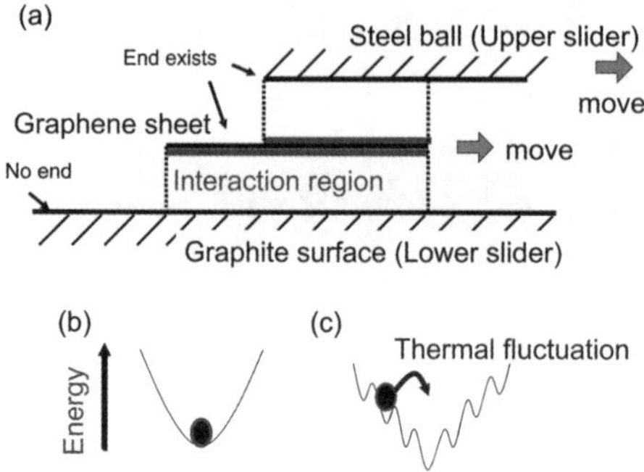

Fig. 9 A conceptual illustration of the end effect.

The trajectories on the xy plane under the three different sheet numbers $N_z = 1, 3,$ 10 are plotted in Fig. 10. In the $N_z = 1$ system, because of the restricted free lateral motion, the trajectory is narrow in the y direction and the graphene sheet climbs the potential hill. In the $N_z = 3, 10$ systems, the widths of the fluctuation range in the y direction are almost the same and thermal escape is found. Note that due to the stochastic motion of the sheets, the sheets randomly move both positively and negatively in the y direction when $N_z = 3, 10$.

From an energetic point of view, the time evolution of the total energy U_t of the three different sheet numbers $N_z = 1, 3, 10$ are plotted in Fig. 11. In the $N_z = 3, 10$ systems, the fluctuation of U_t is very small and almost used as a single quantity. In the $N_z = 1$ system, the U_t separates into two quantities and the fluctuation of each quantity is high. This means that when $N_z = 1$, the confined graphene sheet must move to two stable points which are made by the upper and lower sliders. The binary energy difference ΔU_B is about 20 meV and the transfer motion between the two stable points generates a large hysteresis which causes a high energy dissipation. The increase in the friction force F_x on N_{xy} when $N_z = 1$ shown in Fig. 8 can be explained from this point of view, *i.e.*, the increase in ΔU_B causes an increase in the friction.

The friction behavior of a small flake of a sheet ($N_{xy} = 20^2, 40^2$) shown in Fig. 8 is different compared to that of a larger sheet. This can be understood by the thermal fluctuation. Fig. 12 shows the fluctuation of the total energy U_t for different sheet sizes N_{xy}. In the $N_{xy} = 20^2$ system, it shows a very large fluctuation with the range $\Delta U_t = 0.5$ meV. For $N_{xy} = 40^2$, it also show a large fluctuation which is smaller than the $N_{xy} = 20^2$ system whereas the larger system shows almost the same range of fluctuation. In the $N_{xy} = 20^2$ system, it does not show any oscillation of the energy which

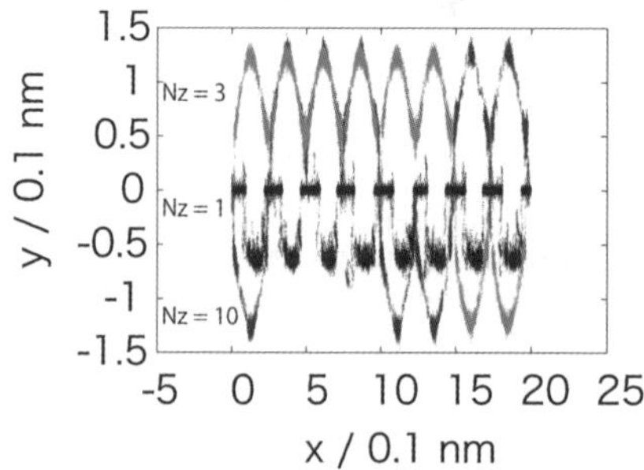

Fig. 10 The trajectories on xy plane under three different sheet numbers N_z ($N_{xy} = 100^2$). Each sheet moves from the origin at time $t = 0$ to the positive direction of the x axis.

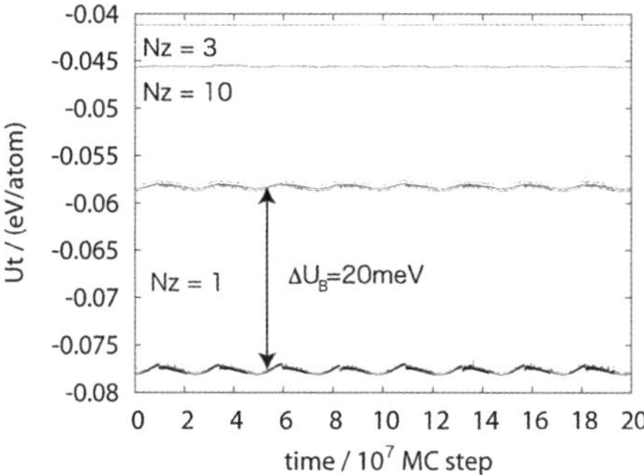

Fig. 11 The time evolution of the total energy U_t of the three different sheet numbers N_z ($N_{xy} = 100^2$).

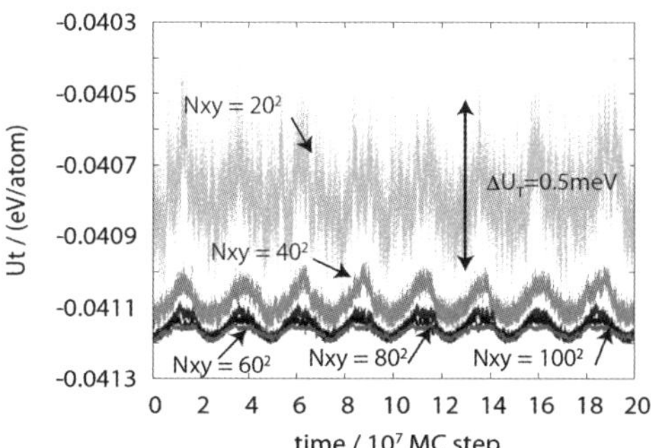

Fig. 12 The time evolution of the total energy U_t of the five different sheet sizes N_{xy} ($N_z = 10$).

is found in the others. This means that in the $N_{xy} = 20^2$ system, the thermal fluctuation exceeds the depth of the periodical potential well in the potential landscape of the lowermost sheet and the lower slider. A sufficient depth of the potential well is needed to stick the graphene sheets together. For this reason, the small sheets cannot exhibit the thermal escape motion found in the larger sheet systems.

In contrast, when the sheet size is very large, the depth of the potential well in each graphite interaction exceeds the thermal fluctuation. The friction behavior of a very large system $N_{xy} = 1\,000^2$ is plotted in Fig. 13 with the potential surface of the potential between the sheet and the lower slider. When compared to the trajectory for $N_{xy} = 100^2$ shown in Fig. 10, the motion in the y direction is completely suppressed and the sheet climbs the potential hill. In this case, the friction may be due to the energy dissipation of the atom vibration. This is same as in the case for phonon dissipation in general solid materials.[18,19]

Using the coarse-grained Metropolis Monte Carlo Brownian Dynamics simulations, we found a low friction behavior in multilayer graphene sheets which we called the thermal escape motion. The low friction of lamellar materials has been explained by the weak interaction between the layers. However, even if the interaction is weak in a commensurate system, the atoms must overcome the potential hill which produces a large energy dissipation.[18,19] Note that the van der Waals interaction energy is on the same order for the graphite sp2 carbon and the other elements. The weakness of the interlayer bond in the depth direction should cause a weak spring constant, then the energy dissipation becomes high. Therefore, we cannot directly understand the low friction of lamellar materials from this point of view.

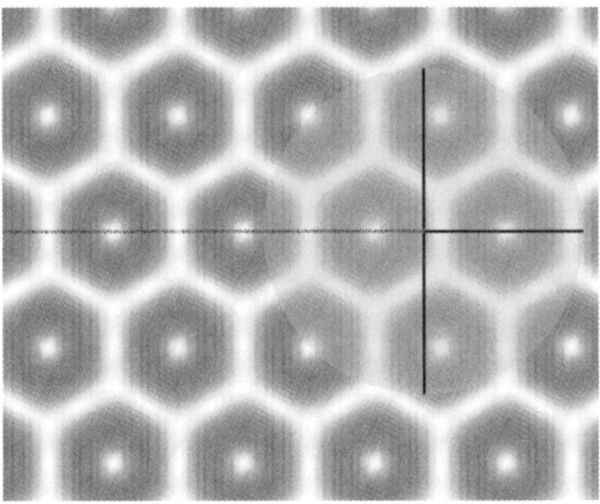

Fig. 13 Trajectory of the very large single sheet ($N_{xy} = 1\,000^2$, $N_z = 1$).

The largest difference between general solid materials and lamellar materials is that, in the transfer film of lamellar materials, each sheet has high translational and rotational degrees of freedom. Due to the flexibility of the whole transfer film by this degree of freedom, the sheet can escape the potential hills. This is the only situation for the multilayer case already shown in our simulation. This motion also occurs only when the potential well depth and the degree of thermal fluctuation are comparable. If the thermal fluctuation is high in a small flake, the upper slider cannot hold the film. If the potential well depth is high in the very large sheet, the sheets cannot escape the potential hill by thermal fluctuation. This thermal escape motion has not been reported as far as the authors know by a study using an all-atom simulation such as MD or MM. This can be explained by the restriction of the MD or MM the precise simulation can treat a very small flake,[8,9] or infinitely large sheet by adopting periodic boundary conditions.[10]

The total friction force due to the sliding is the sum of the energy dissipation due to the atomistic lattice vibration[18,19] and the energy dissipation due to the conformational change in the entire transfer film which is calculated in this paper. To compare it with the experiments, the effect of the atomistic lattice vibration should be included for a precise discussion. We have, however, already found the difference between the single layer and the multilayer case for the amount of energy dissipation due to the conformational change. By including the atomistic lattice vibration, the thermal escaping motion will decrease the impulse of atoms on the opponent surface so that the difference between the single and the multilayer case will become larger.

Our simulation also shows that the very low friction of the lamellar materials is able to exist even in the commensurate system. We think that the low friction of the lamellar materials obtained from macroscopic experiments can be explained by this mechanism.

The effects of the chemical nature at the edge[20] are not included in our rough simulation. Also, the effect of a vacancy and defect are not included.[21] In another study, these can be treated using a modified potential surface. The effect of the internal atom vibration should also be studied by using direct all-atom simulations. In these means, the all-atom simulations and our coarse-grain simulation are complementary in each other. A comparison with the experiments is also desired. This can be realized by fixing the size and the number of graphene sheets on the atomistic friction experiments such as by the atomistic force microscope. Recently, the friction of a fixed number of graphene sheets was measured,[22–24] whereas the size of the sheets was obviously larger than the transfer film which is our concern. We would verify the mechanism for the thermal escape motion by measuring the friction force of a transfer film for a fixed size and number of graphene sheets.

4 Conclusions

The Monte Carlo Brownian Dynamics simulation was used to investigate the friction motion for a transfer layer of graphite. In the monolayer case, the friction force showed a stick-slip like curve and the average of the force was high. In the multilayer case, the friction force did not show any oscillation and the average of the force was very low. This is because the entire transfer film obtained the internal degree of freedom in the multilayer case and the lowest sheets of the layer were able to follow the equipotential surface of the lower slider which is called the thermal escape motion. The low friction of lamellar materials obtained in macroscopic experiments is able to be explained by this mechanism.

Acknowledgements

This study was partially supported by the Next Generation Super Computing Project, Nanoscience Program, MEXT, Japan. We also thank Dr Shoichi Shirai, Prof. Shi-aki Hyodo, Prof. Kazuo Kikuchi and Prof. Mark Robbins for their useful discussions.

References

1 F. Bowden and D. Tabor, in *The friction and lubrication of solids*, Oxford: Clarendon Press, Oxford, 1964.
2 A. Erdemir and E. J.-M. Martin, in *Superlubricity*, Elsevier Science, Amsterdam, 2007.
3 A. Geim and K. Novoselov, *Nat. Mater.*, 2007, **6**, 183.
4 M. Dienwiebel, *et al.*, *Surf. Sci.*, 2005, **576**, 197.
5 A. Khomenko and N. Prodanov, *Carbon*, 2010, **48**, 1234.
6 M. Hirano and K. Shinjo, *Phys. Rev. B: Condens. Matter*, 1990, **41**, 11837–11851.
7 K. Shinjo and M. Hirano, *Surf. Sci.*, 1993, **283**, 473–478.
8 N. Sasaki, K. Kobayashi and M. Tsukada, *Phys. Rev. B: Condens. Matter*, 1996, **54**, 2138–2149.
9 G. S. Verhoeven, M. Dienwiebel and J. W. M. Frenken, *Phys. Rev. B: Condens. Matter Mater. Phys.*, 2004, **70**, 165418.
10 N. Itamura, K. Miura and N. Sasaki, *Jpn. J. Appl. Phys.*, 2009, **48**, 060207.
11 Israelachvili, in *Intermolecular and Surface Forces*, Third Edition, Academic Press, Burlington, 2010.
12 K. Kikuchi, M. Yoshida, T. Maekawa and H. Watanabe, *Chem. Phys. Lett.*, 1991, **185**, 335–338.
13 H. Washizu and K. Kikuchi, *J. Phys. Chem. B*, 2002, **106**(43), 11329.
14 H. Washizu and K. Kikuchi, *J. Phys. Chem. B*, 2006, **110**(6), 2855–2861.
15 N. Metropolis, A. W. Rosenbluth, M. N. Rosenbluth, A. H. Teller and E. Teller, *J. Chem. Phys.*, 1953, **21**, 1087–1092.
16 N. G. van Kampen, in *Stochastic processes in physics and chemistry*, revised and enlarged edition, North-Holland, Amsterdam, 1992, ch. 11.
17 L. Girifalco, M. Hodak and R. S. Lee, *Phys. Rev. B: Condens. Matter*, 2000, **62**, 13104.
18 S. Kajita, H. Washizu and T. Ohmori, *Europhys. Lett.*, 2009, **87**(6), 66002.
19 S. Kajita, H. Washizu and T. Ohmori, *Phys. Rev. B: Condens. Matter Mater. Phys.*, 2010, **82**, 115424.
20 N. Sasaki, H. Okamoto, S. Masuda, K. Miura and N. Itamura, *Journal of Nanomaterials*, 2010, 742127.
21 Y. Guo, W. Guo and C. Chen, *Phys. Rev. B: Condens. Matter Mater. Phys.*, 2007, **76**, 155429.
22 C. Lee, Q. Li, W. Kalb, X.-Z. Liu, H. Berger, R. Carpick and J. Hone, *Science*, 2010, **328**, 76–80.
23 C. Lee, X. Wei, Q. Li, R. Carpick, J. W. Kysar and J. Hone, *Phys. Status Solidi B*, 2009, **246**, 2562–2567.
24 T. Filleter and R. Bennewitz, *Phys. Rev. B: Condens. Matter Mater. Phys.*, 2010, **81**, 155412.

General discussion

Dr Mischler opened the discussion of the paper by Professor Klein: The effect of solvated cations should depend very much on the concentration. At low concentration the effect on friction should be negligible as few solvated ions reach the contacting surface. At higher concentration solvation may be incomplete and interactions with other ions may interfere with surface attraction. Did you investigate the effect of salt concentration on friction?

Professor Klein answered: This is a good point. We find—and others have found earlier[1]—that below a certain salt concentration in water, which has been called the critical hydration concentration and which varies, depending on the salt, but is around 10^{-3} M for the alkali metal salts, there is no short-ranged hydration repulsion as the negatively-charged mica surfaces approach. They jump into adhesive van der Waals contact at relatively low compressions. What you suggest might happen at very high salt concentrations (say in the range 1–5 M) is intriguing, though we have not yet tried such high concentration. Some indication about the effect of incomplete hydration at high salt concentration comes from experiments showing that adding 0.1 M salt to a highly hydrated surface layer leads to an increase in the friction, possibly because of competition for the water of hydration (see ref. 18, 26 in our paper).

1. See: R. M. Pashley, *J. Colloid Interface Sci.*, 1981, **80**, 153.

Dr Ratoi asked: Is mica a good surrogate for bodily tissues in term of both surface roughness and polarity (hydrophilicity/hydrophobicity)?

Professor Klein responded: Of course the mica sheets we use—hard, molecularly smooth single crystals, exposing their {001} surface, that become negatively charged under water—aren't exactly identical to relatively soft articular cartilage surfaces, where the morphology of the very outer surface is complex and likely to consist of different macromolecular species (see *e.g.* ref. 33 in our paper for a review of this). However, there are two aspects which make the results of the SFB experiments more instructive for understanding biological lubrication processes than the difference between mica and cartilage would suggest. As far as polarity goes, both have a negative surface charge—as indicated by ζ potential measurements on cartilage surfaces, and by other considerations.[1] Concerning the smoothness of the mica, it is particularly important to bear in mind that, at the pressures in the major joints and given the modulus of the articular cartilage, two compressed cartilage surfaces are in fact in molecularly affine contact (this point is considered in detail in Fig. 1 of ref. 33 of our paper). When they slide past each other, the shear interactions of the two opposing soft layers are then expected to be quite similar to the interactions between compressed, sliding, similar soft layers on the mica surfaces, which are also in molecularly smooth contact over their region of contact.

1. A. Minassian *et al.*, *J. Orthop. Res.*, 1998, **16**, 720–725.

Professor Bartlett remarked: From classical studies of the double layer at electrode surfaces it is well known that cations such as Na^+ or K^+ are strongly solvated in water whereas anions such as Cl^- or Br^- are much less strongly solvated so that in the Helmholtz layer at the electrode surface the cations remain fully solvated whereas the anions, under suitable conditions, can be partially desolvated leading to specific anion adsorption and the formation of an inner Helmholtz layer. I wonder if you have looked at positively charged surfaces in your experiments and whether you see any evidence for desolvation of the anions within the gap as the pressure increases?

Professor Klein replied: You have raised a suggestive point which indeed may account for some of our earlier observations. Firstly, concerning your immediate point: we have looked at mica surfaces coated with a thin adsorbed layer of chitosan, a positively charged naturally-occurring polyelectrolyte which reverses the charge on the mica from negative to positive.[1] The interaction between two such surfaces is typical of a double-layer interaction, presumably with negatively charged counter-ions (anions) trapped between the positively-charged, chitosan-coated mica surfaces. Unfortunately, the macromolecular nature of the adsorbed chitosan phase makes it difficult to interpret the resulting normal and frictional interactions in terms of simple hydration repulsion or hydration lubrication, as we do for the case of bare mica with trapped cations as the counter-ions (as in Fig. 3 and 5 of our paper). This is because of the steric interaction between the adsorbed chitosan layers, and means that I cannot give a direct answer to your question. However, the point you make that hydration layers about anions are, effectively, much less strongly attached than the hydration layers about cations may explain some of our earlier results on lubrication by negatively charged polyelectrolyte brushes (ref. 19 in our paper). We found in these experiments that the hydration lubrication was effective only up to quite low pressures, after which the friction increased greatly and indeed sheared the (physisorbed) brushes off the surfaces. The weakness of hydration of negative charges on the polyelectrolyte-brush monomers may well account for this, since then these hydration layers would be removed under shear at relatively low pressures.

1. See: N. Kampf *et al.*, *Macromolecules*, 2004, **37**, 1134–1142 and N. Kampf, *Phys. Rev. Lett.*, 2009, **103**, 118304.

Mr Snow said: Mica exhibits a remarkable basal cleavage with the ability to provide molecularly smooth surfaces over large areas, however it is not alone in this property; would substitution with another mineral, such as gypsum or rhodochrosite, provide the ability to reverse the surface charge? Alternatively, do you think that another compound could be used for the surface, for example graphene or diamond which could then be charged?

Professor Klein answered: Mica is in fact pretty unique in being able to provide (with practice!) large area (up to several cm^2), micron-thin films which are molecularly smooth on both sides. This makes mica especially suitable for the surface force balance (SFB) method. For that reason, neither gypsum nor (as far as I am aware) other crystals, which cannot be cleaved into such large films, would be suitable. That said, it is possible to modify mica *via* LB or other methods to change the surface charge to positive while largely retaining the large area molecular smoothness. It is also possible[1] to create large (cm^2) thin sheets of gold that are smooth to ± 2 Å over their entire area and suitable for the SFB; the potential of the gold (and its charge state) may then be controlled externally to provide a positively charged surface. Your suggestion of using graphene is intriguing—though I believe it is difficult to get large area (cm^2), defect-free sheets of graphene.

1. See: L. Chai and J. Klein, *Langmuir*, 2007, **23**, 7777–7783 and Research Highlight in *Nature*, 2007, **447**, 889.

Dr Taylor asked: In engineering contacts, water is not generally considered a good lubricant since its pressure viscosity coefficient is approximately zero. Do you know what the pressure viscosity coefficient of the hydrated shells is, and does this help explain the good lubrication properties of these shells ?

Professor Klein replied: You raise an interesting point. The simple answer is that the pressure viscosity coefficient of the hydrated shells, or some corresponding quantity, has not, to my knowledge, been measured. My own feeling is that it might not be useful to think about the pressure viscosity coefficient of a single layer of water molecules, such as those that form the hydration sheath about charges, in the same way as one thinks about pressure viscosity coefficients of much thicker lubricating films. It might be more instructive rather to consider in detail the relaxation times and the energetics of the dipole–charge interactions which lead to the hydration layers forming in the first place. Detailed molecular dynamics studies might shed some light on this.[1] Experimentally, a direct measure of this would be to compress a hydration layer to different pressures and measure its effective viscosity; in principle one could make such measurements in the surface force balance—and indeed Fig. 4 and 5 in our paper show a version of this—but the interpretation of the data in terms of a pressure viscosity coefficient of the hydration layers is far from straightforward. I should also say, since you mention engineering contacts, that at the very high pressures typical of contacts in machine tribology water molecules in the hydration layers are likely to be squeezed out (in physiological systems, where hydration lubrication is more likely to occur, the pressures are much lower, up to *ca.* 10 MPa rather than GPa, and so the hydration layers will be quite stable).

1. See *e.g.* Y. Leng and P. T. Cummings, *J. Chem. Phys.*, 2006, **124**, 074711, as well as more recent papers by Leng and co-workers.

Professor Martin commented: At the end of your presentation, you mentioned the possibility of hydration lubrication at high contact pressures (in the GPa range). We recently observed the possibility for water to lubricate such hard contact (especially EHL contacts[1]). However, in this case it is the water molecules produced by decomposition of polyhydric alcohols (glycerol for example) that provide the very low friction coefficients (well below 1%). Because the water is produced inside the contact, molecules cannot escape and lubricate till they find the exit place.

1. W. Habchi *et al.*, *Tribol. Lett.*, 2011, **42**, 351–358.

Professor Klein responded: That is an interesting observation. The effect you describe arises from the *in situ* production of water within a confined space. It differs of course from what I call hydration lubrication, which is the retention of a lubricating water sheath held in place by virtue of the dipolar water molecules surrounding and reducing the free energy of the enclosed charge, polar group or zwitterion.

Professor Spencer asked: In your modified version of Hill's phospholipid lubrication mechanism, to what are the phospholipid tails connected?

Professor Klein responded: Hill's phospholipid lubrication mechanism resembles the classical machine-engineering boundary lubrication ideas, where extended, surfactant-like phospholipid monolayers form on the opposing cartilage surfaces to expose their hydrophobic alkyl tails. According to Hills, these tails slide past each other at the slip plane, much as W. B. Hardy proposed almost 100 years ago (see *e.g.* Fig. 1(A)). I think this mechanism is unlikely to be correct, as it would lead to friction coefficients, around 0.05–0.1, that are orders of magnitude higher than observed in actual joints (where the friction coefficient can go down to around 0.001). Thus Hill's picture bears little relation to our ideas, which are based on the hydration-lubrication mechanism. In this, the lubricating elements at the sliding interface are strongly-hydrated *hydrophilic* groups, as illustrated schematically in Fig. 1(B).

The highly-hydrated phosphocholine groups indicated in Fig. 1(B) are good candidates for this, as we have shown them to lubricate well at physiologically

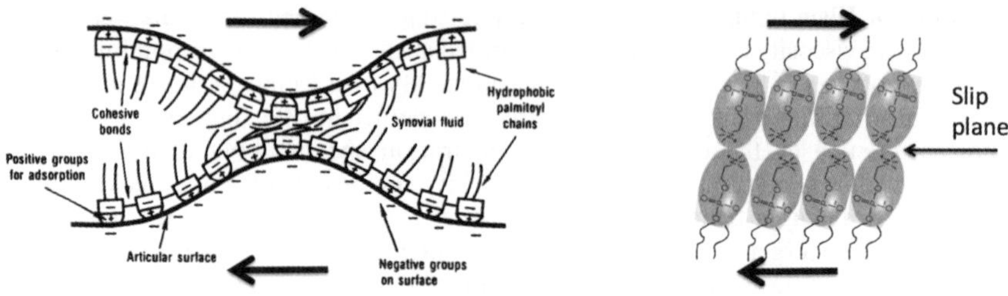

Fig. 1 (A) Hill's mechanism.[1] (B) Hydration lubrication by phosphocholine groups.

high pressures both when forming part of a polymer brush and when exposed at the outer-surfaces of liposomes (see Fig. 9 and 10, as well as ref. 18 and 22, respectively, in our paper). Such phosphocholines are ubiquitous in joints as the headgroups of phophatidylcholine lipids; they may be exposed at the surface of cartilage as the outer-surfaces of liposome-like structures,[2] or be attached to macromolecular species emanating from the cartilage surface—this is an important issue which is unresolved as yet, and is part of our current investigations.

1. B. A. Hills and B. D. Butler, *Ann. Rheum. Dis.*, 1984, **43**, 641–648.
2. See *e.g.* M. Watanabe *et al.*, *Med. Electron Microsc.*, 2000, **33**, 16–24.

Dr Wang opened the discussion of the paper by Professor Dr Bhushan: Do the heights of the features on the surface affect its hydrophobicity? Does the two or three-level structure essentially produce an angle of contact or a slope (compared to the straight trenches in the one-level structure) which helps to increase the hydrophobicity of the surface? If so, would it be better to design patterns with non-straight angle protrusions?

Professor Dr Bhushan replied: Height and pitch of the features very much affect the hydrophobicity based on Wenzel and Cassie–Baxtor regimes.[1] Regarding the answer to the second question related to hierarchical structures, formation of a composite interface is a multiscale phenomena which depends upon the relative sizes of the liquid droplets and roughness details. A composite interface is metastable and the mechanisms that lead to its destabilization are also scale-dependent. Hierarchical structures help in stabilizing the composite interface.

1. B. Bhushan, *Biomimetics: Bioinspired Hierarchical-Structured Surfaces for Green Science and Technology*, Springer, 2012.

Dr Wang asked: Is the adhesion force on patterned surfaces affected by the rigidness or stiffness of the features?

Professor Dr Bhushan responded: Adhesion on the patterned surface will primarily depend upon the surface structure at low loads in AFM measurements. However the value will increase at high loads.[1] If the data on various samples is taken at a given load, it serves a useful purpose in comparing the adhesion of various samples.

1. B. Bhushan, *Nanotribology and Nanomechanics*, Vols. 1 and 2, Springer, 2011.

Professor Spencer noted: In your figure showing contact angles and contact-angle hysteresis (CAH), there is a very large CAH for flat polypropylene. This is rather surprising, isn't it?

Professor Dr Bhushan answered: The contact angle hysteresis for the flat sample has to do with the morphology of the sample. The purpose of the contact angle

   This journal is © The Royal Society of Chemistry 2012

and contact angle hysteresis of the flat sample is to have the data which serves as a benchmark to compare with that of structured data. The data clearly show that structuring increases the contact angle and reduces contact angle hysteresis, as expected.

Dr Ratoi asked: What happens when the superhydrophobic nanostructured surfaces get soiled, for example by organic vapours?

Professor Dr Bhushan replied: If the surface is only superhydrophobic and it gets contaminated then it may not be effective in repelling water. A surface has to be designed for a given liquid. The surface energy of the surface and that of liquid needs to be optimized.[1]

1. Y. C. Jung and B. Bhushan, *Langmuir*, 2009, **25**, 14165.

Dr Zekonyte said: Explanation of the force *vs.* displacement curves during fibre bending experiments might be somewhat debatable. When bending the fibre there is possibility that it will meet the neighbouring fibre and so the kicks observed in the *F vs. D* curves may be the result of fibre–fibre interaction, especially in the cases when you claim that by pushing the tip into the surface, or removing it, the fibre in contact with the tip does not move.

Professor Dr Bhushan replied: Interactions between adjacent fibers are dependent upon the fiber diameter, pitch and sidewise deflections. In the structures studied here, it is not probable that inter-fiber interaction occurs. If the such interactions occurred, we would see discontinuity in the force-deflection curve which is not observed. Furthermore repeated experiments show that data is reproducible

Dr Zekonyte commented: Fig. 4 in your paper, right column, middle force–displacement curve that shows the bending of a 5 μm diameter fibre. Here you state that you bend the fibre of this size with an AFM tip, the radius of which is 30 nm. But, according to the graph, you apply an order of magnitude lower maximum load than the one you exert on the 600 nm fibre. How is this possible?

Professor Dr Bhushan answered: Regarding the plots of the 5 micron and 600 nm fibers deformed using 30 nm AFM tip in Fig. 4, it is possible that the 5 micron fiber could be elastically squeezed (or deformed) only on the area where the sharp (30 nm) AFM tip stressed it. On the other hand, the 600 nm fiber couldn't be squeezed but bent because it is too thin to be squeezed. The figure shows the clue for this explanation. The plot of the 500 micron fiber exhibits vibrations while the tip travels from B to C, D to E, and E′ to F. The vibration phenomenon is not observed in the plot of the 600 nm fiber. The deformation was analyzed by imaging the top surface of the 5 micron fiber. Finally, cantilever deflection can be calculated for load, but piezo position should be considered for a given load.

Professor Williams remarked: Natural adhesive structures such as, for example, that on the gecko foot are often inclined to the plane of attachment and so provide a directional response to imposed shear. Can you readily adapt your fabrication route for hierarchical surfaces to generate non-normal geometries?

Professor Dr Bhushan responded: Yes we can. All we need to do is to orient the fibrous array at an angle before the fibers cool off. Simply by gravity, they will orient.

Professor Dr Vernes asked: Is the assumed JKR-scaling law confirmed by your AFM experiments?

Professor Dr Bhushan answered: The JKR-scaling law assumed in the hypothesis proposed is based on the model alone.

Dr Stoodley commented: In your paper you conclude that the governing variables in the adhesion strength to your hierarchical surfaces were 1) the number of contact points between the surface and the attaching object and 2) the compliance of the asperities. Tony Brennan's group using materials based on shark skin has reported that the patterning is also important.[1] How do you explain the difference between Brennan's conclusions and your conclusions regarding patterning?

1. *i.e.* J. F. Schumacher, M. L. Carman, T. G. Estes, A. W. Feinberg, L. H. Wilson, M. E. Callow, J. A. Callow, J. A. Finlay and A. B. Brennan, Engineered antifouling micro-topographies—effect of feature size, geometry, and roughness on settlement of zoospores of the green alga Ulva, *Biofouling*, 2007, **23**(1–2), 55–62.

Professor Bhushan replied: The low drag of a fast moving shark in turbulent flow is dependent upon lifting the vortices at the apex of the riblets, allowing normal fluid flow at the shark skin surface. Thus the relevant mechanism in shark skin is entirely different from that in the lotus leaf.[1]

1. B. Dean, and B. Bhushan, *Philos. Trans. R. Soc., A*, 2010, **368**, 4775–4806; B. Dean, and B. Bhushan, *Philos. Trans. R. Soc., A*, 2010, **368**, 5737; B. Bhushan, *Langmuir*, 2012, **28**, 1698–1714.

Dr Stoodley added: The material has also been tested for low shear applications such as wound dressings.[1] I also note that some of the work that was done with marine fouling was low shear larval settling studies.

1. *i.e.* K. K. Chung, J. F. Schumacher, E. M. Sampson, R. A. Burne, P. J. Antonelli and A. B. Brennan, Impact of engineered surface microtopography on biofilm formation of *Staphylococcus aureus*, *Biointerphases*, 2007, **2**(2), 89–94.

Dr Stoodley communicated: To what extent are your conclusions generalizable given the testing procedure? You used an AFM with a glass sphere of 30 μm diameter. The size scale of the attaching particle and the density (and possibly patterning) of the asperities will both determine the number of contact points. And leading on from that is it possible to tailor your surfaces to favor the attachment of certain sized objects over others—*i.e.* create a selective surface?

Professor Dr Bhushan communicated in response: Regarding the influence of test method on the data, the actual data will be dependent upon the test method. For a specific application, an appropriate test method needs to be used. For the purpose of the paper to demonstrate the role of texturing on adhesion, general trends are valid.

Dr Stoodley asked: You mentioned the antifouling properties of superhydrophobic materials which you have created based on the hierarchical structure of the lotus leaf. It is my understanding that the antifouling effect is mainly due to the "self-cleaning" as water droplets roll off of the surface entrapping particles in them as the air/water interface travels over the solid surface. For example, in bacteria Gómez-Suárez *et al.*[1] experimentally confirmed the predicted effect that an air bubble moving across a surface colonized with bacteria under aqueous flow would be removed by the passage of a bubble since the detachment force caused by the surface tension associated with the moving interface was greater than the adhesion force. In my own experiments I have grown bacteria on submerged superhydrophobic surfaces, under flow—including lotus leaves themselves. If the cleaning effect of these surfaces requires the passage of an air/water interface, can you speculate how

   This journal is © The Royal Society of Chemistry 2012

your technology might have application on completely submerged surfaces such as marine coatings?

1. C. Gómez-Suárez, H. J. Busscher and H. C. van der Mei, Analysis of bacterial detachment from substratum surfaces by the passage of air-liquid interfaces, *Appl. Environ. Microbiol.*, 2001, **67**(6), 2531–2537.

Professor Dr Bhushan answered: First off, I agree with you that the rolling of water droplets on the lotus surface would provide anti-biofouling. However in underwater marine applications, one may use the shark skin effect to provide anti-fouling.[1]

1. B. Dean, and B. Bhushan, *Philos. Trans. R. Soc., A*, 2010, **368**, 4775–4806; G. D. Bixler, and B. Bhushan, Biofouling: Lessons from Nature, *Philos. Trans. R. Soc., A*, in press.

Professor Dai enquired: When you measured the adhesion force of the gecko-mimicking hairy structure, how much preloading force was applied on the samples? And how was the adhesion force measured?

Professor Dr Bhushan replied: The adhesion force is measured by obtaining a force–distance curve with an AFM with colloidal AFM probe.[1]

1. B. Bhushan, *Nanotribology and Nanomechanics I—Measurement Techniques and Nanomechanics, II—Nanotribology, Biomimetics, and Industrial Applications*, Springer, 2011.

Professor Dai remarked: Both the lotus effect and gecko adhesion are dependent on the hierarchical hairy structure of surface; where is the boundary of the transfer from self-cleaning or anti-adhesion to adhesion properties?

Professor Dr Bhushan responded: Nature has a limited toolbox. It uses hierarchical and multilayered structures and commonly found materials such as calcium and silica to provide functionality of interest.[1] It is clever in using these structures. In the lotus leaf, nature uses the hierarchical structure to provide superhydrophobicity and self-cleaning whereas for the gecko, it uses it to provide high adhesion and adaptability to variety of surfaces. Of course the mechanisms responsible in these two cases are entirely different.

1. B. Bhushan, *Biomimetics: Bioinspired Hierarchical-Structured Surfaces for Green Science and Technology*, Springer, 2012.

Professor Spencer opened the discussion of the paper by Dr Blackford: In the paper by Giesbrecht *et al.* (ref. 10 in your paper), the authors demonstrated that surface structuring dominates over all surface-energy effects for materials sliding on ice. Although you describe the preparation of your PMMA and steel surfaces in detail, what was the roughness of the two surfaces? Did you look at the effects of varying roughness?

Dr Blackford answered: As you say we prepared the steel and PMMA surfaces with the same procedure, however we have not yet quantified their surface roughness. We plan to do this in the near future. This will aid in quantifying the behaviour in our system. The study by Giesbrecht and co-workers revisits and further develops some of Bowden's classic experiments made on snow. They have made some elegant findings. Our experiments are in a different "parameter space" compared with Giesbrecht's. Their study is made at lower pressures (*ca.* 1.3 kPa) and on snow—it is designed to represent the behaviour of skis, whereas our study is made at higher pressures (0.26 to 0.86 MPa)—these pressures are representative of tyre pressures though clearly the materials are rather different to rubbers. In addition to the work we reported in the paper, we have made measurements with steel and PMMA samples of different surface roughnesses. Our analysis of the static friction behaviour indicates that the static friction of steel increases as surface roughness increases, while for PMMA we find the opposite behaviour.

Professor Klein asked: In this very interesting study, do you have any idea whether the ice surface beneath the thin water layer is charged?

Dr Blackford answered: This is a good and difficult question. Probably, yes, the surface is charged. We have not examined surface charge in any of our experiments. A number of studies have been made on this topic, many by Petrenko.[1] He has shown that charge is generated during sliding, and also that friction can be modified by the application of a potential to the system. In the book "Physics of Ice" (Ref. 24 in our paper) Petrenko considers surface potential and surface charge—the subject appears to be complex with some experiments showing conflicting results (in the book, p240, he states "…the whole topic of surface potentials, which must include the free surface and the ice-metal contact, is very hard to interpret"). Based on my simplistic understanding of this it seems likely that charge is present before contact, once we initiate contact, and during sliding, however the magnitude of the effect caused by charge may be very small compared with other effects. And in many engineering systems it is not a parameter we can easily manipulate.

1. For example: V. F. Petrenko, *J. Phys. D.: Appl. Phys.*, 1994, **76**, 1216–1219; V. F. Petrenko and S. C. Colbeck, *J. Phys. D.: Appl. Phys.*, 1995, **77**, 4518–4521.

Professor Williams noted: A key parameter in friction models is always the so-called 'real' area of contact. At the nano-scale this isn't always that easy to define but at the macro-scale I think most would agree that it remains a very useful notion—if not always that easy to measure. But given that ice is transparent—and so is PMMA come to that—would it not be feasible to optically observe the number and nature of the contact asperities in some of your experiments?

Dr Blackford responded: This is a very nice idea. Using the linear tribometer we used for the study in this paper such observations are not easily possible. However we are currently building a new device that should enable us to observe the contact directly. Based on a similar idea, in other studies we have made observations of ice wear surfaces in a low temperature scanning electron microscope after the passage of steel and rubber on a small ice dome (radius about 5 mm) (ref. 35 and 15 in our paper). Although this doesn't show the contact directly, it gives useful information about the nature of the wear surfaces and indicates, for example, whether the surface melted or fractured.

Dr Harvey commented: I noticed you used deionised water in your experiments and was wondering what effect you would get with the use of tap water or rain water?

Dr Blackford replied: We have made tests using ice made from tap water and rubber samples. This work is reported in a paper by Skouvaklis *et al.* (ref. 16 in our paper). We found that the dynamic friction was always slightly lower with tap water. Tap water and rain water tend to contain various impurities such as salts. The salts often result in a liquid phase being present in the ice; this will occur at temperatures above the eutectic temperature for a particular salt (for example $-22\,°C$ for NaCl). The presence of a liquid phase means that there is already a lubricant in the system that can reduce friction before heat is generated from sliding. Experiments of the friction of rubber on ice containing various quantities of potassium chloride showed similar results: lower friction with salt than without, and also lower friction with higher salt contents.[1] The study of friction on ice containing impurities is interesting and important, however for us it is also important to use deionized water as a model system.

1. A. D. Roberts and J. D. Lane, *J. Phys. D.: Appl. Phys.*, 1983, **16**, 275–285.

Dr Koutsos remarked: Compared to rubbers, working with PMMA and steel has the advantage of minimising bulk dissipation effects so that one can concentrate on the study of the interface contribution to friction with ice. Actually, to some extent this was the original incentive for this work. In view now of the results, do you think we have attained this goal?

Dr Blackford responded: Yes and no. Yes, I believe that we focus on interface effects much more with these more rigid materials than with rubber. As you said an original aim was to simplify the system by using "simple" materials as the sliders (in the paper we discuss why these are potentially much simpler than rubber—as the mechanical properties of rubber change with temperature and strain rate), and at the outset I thought we would get results that would be simpler to interpret. But also no, I do not think we have attained this goal fully (and on reflection with this set up I don't think it's possible). When we look at the behaviour of the system more closely we could still have deformation and dissipation contributions in the PMMA, and particularly in the ice—it is not only the interface that plays a role in generating the forces we measure. As discussed in the paper the behaviour of the systems turned out to be non-trivial, we showed the interplay of the yield point and elastic modulus between the materials (PMMA, steel and ice) can induce very different behaviour. And when movement is initiated in the tests the fracture and then melting behaviour of the ice is complex. As with other topics I have worked on in science it seems like the deeper you probe into a subject the more you realise how much more there is to discover, and often in answering one question many more questions arise. But that's a good thing.

Dr Walker communicated: Your ice counterface was made by freezing of a number of layers of deionised water. If the structure of the ice counterface was prepared such that a dendritic or single crystal structure was present instead, would this affect the static coefficient of friction which you measured during your experimental procedure?

Dr Blackford communicated in response: Possibly! These could be interesting—though not trivial—experiments to do. Ice, as with many crystalline materials, has different surface energies on different crystallographic planes. And in the lab it is relatively straightforward to make columnar-grained ice by directional solidification. Growing single crystals is rather more difficult. A question we posed, but did not answer, in our paper was whether the break that occurs in the test is adhesive—that is, at the interface between the ice and steel or PMMA, or is cohesive—that is, in the ice itself, or is a mixture of both. If the failure is adhesive the surface energy of the ice can have an influence on the behaviour. If the failure is cohesive the fracture behaviour of the ice itself is important. Tensile tests on single crystals of ice show a significant variation of strength with crystallographic orientation (a study by Carter[1] (1971 Ph.D. thesis, University of Laval) reported in Erland Schulson and Paul Duval's book on Creep and fracture of ice (ref. 23 in our paper) shows the tensile strength of single crystals of ice depend on orientation, with a minimum when the basal planes are inclined at 45° to the tensile axis). Also the creep deformation of ice varies substantially with crystallographic orientation, so altering the ice structure will affect how the interface develops and the real area of contact during the dwell time of the tests as the ice will creep different amounts. Considering all these effects it seems likely that the static friction behaviour of ice is affected by its crystallographic structure. But it is possible these effects are rather subtle and difficult to detect in tests. For comparison it is worth noting that for dynamic friction experiments of ice on ice reported by Maurine Montagnat and Erland Schulson[1] no significant effects between the behaviour of polycrystalline ice and directionally solidified columnar ice were found. However, tests using a steel ball sliding on ice single crystals under certain conditions, particularly at rather low velocities (10^{-5} m s^{-1}), showed the friction on the prismatic plane was twice that on the basal plane.[2]

1. M. Montagnat and E. M. Schulson, *J. Glaciol.*, 2003, **166**, 391–396.
2. K. Tusima, *J. Glaciol.*, 1977, **19**, 225–235.

Mr Eder continued the discussion Professor Bhushan's paper by communicating: If a gecko ran on a wet lotus leaf, would it slip?

Professor Dr Bhushan communicated in response: Gecko feet are designed for dry surfaces. If there is tiny amount of liquid present on the surface from condensation of water vapor from humid environment, adhesion in fact can be enhanced by meniscus formation.[1] However, they will not produce strong adhesion in wet or flooded environments. On the other hand some amphibians, such as tree and torrent frogs and arboreal salamanders, are able to attach to and move over wet or even flooded environments without falling.[2] Tree frog toe attachment pads consist of a hexagonal array of flat-topped epidermal cells about 10 μm in size separated by approximately 1 μm wide mucus-filled channels; the flattened surface of each cell consists of submicron array of nanopillars or pegs of approximately 100–400 nm diameter. The toe pads are made of an extremely soft, inhomogeneous material; epithelium itself has an effective elastic modulus of about 15 MPa, equivalent to silicone rubber. The pads are permanently wetted by mucus secreted from glands that open into the channels between epidermal cells. They attach to mating surfaces by wet adhesion. They are capable of climbing on wet rocks even when water is flowing over the surface. The pad structure is believed to produce high adhesion and friction by conforming to the mating rough surface at different length scales and by maintaining a very thin fluid film at the interface, responsible for animal locomotion and manoeuvrability. Adhesion is believed to occur primarily by a meniscus contribution, resulting from menisci formed around the edges of the pads. The presence of static friction suggests that the fluid film is very thin in order to have some dry contact between the tips of the nanopillars and the mating surface. The dry contacts between the pad and the mating surfaces are produced by squeezing out the fluid film from the interface. Hierarchical structure and material properties facilitate the squeezing and avoid the formation of trapped liquid islands during draining, which would favor sliding. During walking, the squeezing is expected to occur rapidly. Torrent frogs can resist sliding even on flooded surfaces. The surface of their toe pads is similar to that of tree frogs with some changes in the structure to handle the large flow of water.

1. B. Bhushan, *Introduction to Tribology*, Wiley, 2002.
2. W. Federle *et al.*, *J. R. Soc., Interface*, 2006, **3**, 689; B. Bhushan, *Philos. Trans. R. Soc., A*, 2009, **367**, 1445.

Dr Zekonyte communicated: A missing detailed experimental explanation: What was the real spring constant of AFM cantilever, especially of the modified cantilevers? How was it determined? What was the maximum applied load in adhesion and fibre bending measurements?

Professor Dr Bhushan communicated in reply: We used a standard force–distance curve approach previously described for fiber bending experiments.[1]

1. B. Bhushan, Nanotribology of Carbon Nanotubes, *J. Phys.: Condens. Matter*, 2008, **20**, 365214; B. Bhushan, *Nanotribology and Nanomechanics*, Vol. I and II, Third edition, Springer, 2011

Dr Mischler opened the discussion of the paper by Professor Dr Léger: During sliding the pillars are likely to bend under the effect of the tangential force. This deformation may modify the real area of contact. Did you observe such an effect ?

Professor Dr Léger responded: Yes, indeed this is an important and obviously crucial question for the determination of the friction stress, which necessitates the knowledge of the exact real area of contact. We have carefully observed the images of the pillars during sliding when in top contact to see whether or not the size of the contact between the pillars and the lens was affected by the sliding. We have not been able to put into evidence such a change, at the accuracy of our optics (long working distance telescope, Questar QM 100) except maybe for the largest sliding velocities used. In fact we think that this absence of a noticeable change of area of contact results from the flat top of the pillars and also from their relatively high bending rigidity as their aspect ratio h/d always remains of order one or smaller in all experiments reported here. The situation would certainly be quite different for pillars with hemi-spherical tops or a larger aspect ratio.

Professor Williams queried: When sliding is initiated, does the whole surface slide at the same time or is a wave of detachment initiated at one edge or a set of pillars— akin to a Schallamach wave—or are the velocities of your experiments below the threshold of such phenomena?

Professor Dr Léger responded: It seems that we are at too low a sliding velocity to see detachment waves. Indeed, we have been looking for them and have never seen them, except maybe at the highest sliding velocities we can reach. From the inspection of many images, all pillars under the contact seem deformed in the same way and smoothly relax their deformation when emerging from the contact. They all behave the same. The sliding velocity range we can explore at present is between 10 nm s^{-1} and 300 μm s^{-1}. For PDMS this is too low for Schallamach waves.

Professor Williams asked: Your experiment and observations are made using a PDMS lens on PDMS structure, could you use a glass lens for one so that the deformation is only in pillars?

Professor Dr Léger answered: Yes, the experiment with the patterned substrate pressed against a rigid surface (glass lens) is feasible and will result in deformations confined in the pillars and the underlying PDMS film. We have investigated the static contact between a rigid glass lens and a patterned substrate using JKR test, but not the sliding behaviour. The interest of the system we presently use (soft elastomer lens against elastomer patterned substrate) is that we know the level of adhesion (PDMS against PDMS) which is a rather weak adhesion (thermodynamic work of adhesion $W = 43$ mJ m^{-2}) and also the level of friction on the smooth PDMS/PDMS substrate. Because PDMS has a low surface energy, it hardly pollutes, and the PDMS/PDMS system is a remarkably stable one, which would not be the case for a PDMS/glass interface. As far as we can say our present understanding of our results is that all three elastic deformations, pillars, underlying PDMS film and lens, all contribute to the additional friction stress. If we were using a rigid lens, the only possible deformations would be confined in the pillars and underlying substrate, but would not be more or less complicated to estimate.

Professor Klein commented: Detachment (Schallamach) waves are a feature of sliding across soft elastic surfaces, but in a recent study by Varenberg and co-workers[1] they found that surface patterning—similar to your system but on a larger scale—substantially modulated this effect. Did you find a similar behaviour in your study, *i.e.* modification of the detachment waves as a function of the patterning?

B. Murarash, Y. Itovich and M. Varenberg, *Soft Matter*, 2011, **7**, 5553–5557.

Professor Dr Léger replied: As previously said, we hardly see any detachment wave. It may well be that the bending rigidity of the pillars needs be much larger to start to see what is reported in the paper by Varenberg *et al.*

Professor Dr Vernes enquired: How did you verify that there was no wear during the sliding on the patterned substrates?

Professor Dr Léger responded: We have two ways of checking for possible wear during sliding: first, we can observe the sliding track after sliding (both optically and by scanning electron microscopy), and second we check for the reproducibility of the sliding friction stress, when sliding again at the same place on the substrate. We can also observe, by the same techniques, the surface of the lens. When wear or any damage of the surfaces is observed, we change both lens and substrate.

Professor Bartlett asked: Can you also pattern the surface with an array of shallow cylindrical pits rather than pillars so you effectively have the inverse of the structure? Does this give any further insights?

Professor Dr Léger replied: Yes, it is quite as easy to make surfaces with regular arrays of cylindrical pits as with arrays of pillars: one just needs to use the arrays of pillars as a mold to form a negative. We have not tried doing so because we wanted to find evidence for the role of the elastic deformations of the features formed on the surface on the friction. The substrate with pits will be less deformable than that with pillars. The pit geometry can however be very interesting for other purposes: for example to use the pits as reservoirs of a liquid and look for a transition between a contact with isolated patches of lubricated contact to a fully lubricated one, just by changing the level of liquid in the pits. This is quite an interesting route, and I would be pleased to try and see what it gives.

Dr Wang queried: Have you translated the patterns produced on the PDMS surface to surface roughness values, *e.g.* R_a, R_q, R_{sk} *etc.*, and do the friction levels measured in your study based on the surface patterning agree with measurements using real surfaces under similar roughness?

Professor Dr Léger answered: The geometry of the pattern is fully controlled at the size of the pillars: all pillars are cylinders with a flat top, they all have the same height $h = 2.2$ μm, and they are regularly displayed on a hexagonal lattice. We call i the closest distance between pillars which is always larger than the diameter of the pillars, d. If we take as the reference surface the plane of the substrate in between pillars, we can quite easily estimate all usual numbers characterizing a roughness: $R_a = R_q = R_t = h$, the height of the pillars. Indeed we know much more about the topography of our surfaces than is usually known on a surface when one specifies series of roughness parameters: these parameters are only averages of height distribution around a reference surface and can thus be the same for very different geometries of surfaces. Concerning the second part of the question, I do not know what would be the real surface you have in mind: a surface of the same elastomer with a random roughness in the micrometer range? We are indeed preparing such surfaces in order to try understanding the impact of the order of our pillars on the measured friction. The only thing we can say for sure at present is the fact that the friction stress appears larger on the patterned surface than on the smooth one.

Dr Marinov asked: Do you think that a local deformation of the lens due to the pillars can lead to an increase in the contact area that is sufficient to shift the force data so that they can actually match the straight line obtained with a smooth surface, as shown in Fig. 4 in your paper? I envisaged the increase in the surface area resulting from the curvature formed around the pillar tops as they indent the smooth surface of the lens.

Professor Dr Léger replied: As said previously in response to Dr Mischler's question, we have not been able to see any noticeable change in the area of contact between the pillars and the lens during sliding. Of course the exact shape of the top of the pillars is certainly crucial and a sharp edge will help to maintain the surface of contact. We have used a finite element analysis, without sliding, to model the deformations of the film beneath the pillars, the lens and of the pillars themselves, as a function of the applied normal load. Then the shape of the pillars appears quite sensitive to the exact boundary condition imposed at the pillar/lens interface (fully adhesive or full slip). More work clearly needs to be done, especially varying the shape of the top of the pillars. When observing the passage from top to full contact, one can see that some air tends to remain trapped along the edges of the pillars. This is coherent with the fact that we can explain the transition from top to full contact when increasing the normal load by assuming that the full contact forms when the lens and the film beneath the pillars start to touch in the middle of the spacing between pillars near neighbors. It thus seems quite difficult for the lens (and the substrate) to adapt to the sharp edge of the pillars. However, again we need additional work (and observations) to be more precise on the important question of the real area of contact, especially when close to the threshold between top and full contact.

Professor Dr Bhushan communicated: You perform experiments using two compliant surfaces which means that both surfaces will deform under load. It may be instructive to perform some experiments with micropatterned polymer surface pressed against a rigid surface.

Professor Dr Léger communicated in reply: The answer to the previous question by Professor Williams regarding using a glass lens in experiments also answers this question.

Dr Österle opened the discussion of the paper by Professor Beake: My question is related to tribofilm formation.
Could it be that the coating has already been removed from the cutting edge before the protective film could form on the monolayer coatings, and only the bilayer coating had a chance to survive because of its better mechanical properties?

Professor Beake responded: The protective film does form on the monolayers as well, but not as effectively. Early in the cutting process it can be removed from the very cutting edge on the monolayers. We do think that the better mechanical properties at the cutting temperature are a key factor in enabling the tribo-film to form more easily on the multilayer. The mechanical properties might be especially critical at the "running in" stage of tribofilm dynamics.

Dr Österle asked: Why was the film structure not revealed by TEM, but only by XPS?

Professor Beake answered: Recently[1] we have also reported TEM data with EDAX (1 nm spot size) that are in agreement with the data presented in this paper.

1. G. S. Fox-Rabinovich *et al.*, *J. Appl. Phys.*, 2012, **111**, 064306.

Dr Harvey commented: I noticed in Fig. 1 of your paper that the nanohardness measurements are shown as single points; from experience these are usually the average of many measurements and I was wondering what the error was or why there was no error bar on the graphs?

Professor Beake replied: These are averages from up to 40 measurements at each temperature, with typical standard deviation of 15% in H and E, as mentioned in the experimental section. The source of the variability is the high surface roughness of these coatings rather than any marked intrinsic variability in their properties or inaccuracy in the measurements. By taking a large number of measurements we increase the confidence (standard errors are much lower, at typically ~3%, which are virtually within the symbols), though the error bars were not included on Fig. 1 simply for clarity.

Dr Harvey queried: Fig. 2 in your paper shows the length of a cut that produces 300 microns of wear and I was wondering how this was measured; was it an on-line technique or an off-line technique (did you stop cutting periodically and measure the wear)? If it is an off-line approach, do you think this will influence the results and how?

Professor Beake answered: It was an off-line approach using an optical microscope with a special set up to measure flank wear according to ISO 368. The worn ball nose end mill tooling was fitted in a special holder in the microscope. This is a standard procedure. It does not affect the results in significant way because: 1) we are dealing with interrupted cutting, and dry conditions. When the tool comes to the end of the block during the testing it cools anyway. So, stopping the testing for measurements does not much affect the wear rate (this has been checked it experimentally). 2) We reported comparative results, in our case mono-layer *vs.* multilayer coatings. Flank wear data were collected in the same way on all the coatings.

Professor Dr Vernes asked: How were the points distributed for nanoindentation in order to obtain the nanomechanical characterisation of the entire surface?

Professor Beake replied: Indentations were spaced 40 microns apart. For this type of hard coatings we have never observed any trend in lateral variation in mechanical properties across the surface. The variations observed (SD ~ 15% in H and E) are due to high surface roughness (typical for these coatings) and do not reflect any compositional differences across the surface of the coated inserts. A relatively high load of 40 mN was chosen to ensure a fully plastic response and, together with the large number of repeat indentations, to minimise the influence of the high roughness.

Mr Polcar noted: It is speculated that a 10 nm thick tribolayer causes a significant decrease of temperature (about 500 °C). Could you comment on the physical process behind this, *i.e.* explain the main features of such an unusually effective thermal barrier? How precise is the indirect measurement of temperature using structural analysis?

Professor Beake responded: Temperature dependence of the heat conductivity coefficient mainly determines the thermal barrier properties of the coating and the tribo-oxide films. In general nitride coating layers raise their own heat conductivity during heating,[1] but in contrast, the alumina dramatically reduces its own heat conductivity from 40 (W m^{-1} K^{-1}) up to 3 (W m^{-1} K^{-1}) as the temperature is increased from 293 to 1393 K.[1] Aluminium oxide in the tribo-film therefore efficiently protects the tool surface from overheating. For mullite tribo-films this trend is even stronger. This thermal conductivity coefficient for mullite thin films decreases from 6.86 (W m^{-1} K^{-1}) at 100 K down to 0.19–0.26 at high temperatures.[2]

Regarding the precision of the indirect temperature measurement, we do not observe AlN-hex phase formation at 600 C (*e.g.* Fig. 6 in our paper) but we do see this phase formation at 700 °C, so our accuracy is around 100 °C. Indirect evidence for the temperature at the tool/chip interface has similar precision. Literature data show that the temperature at the tool/chip interface during cutting of steels is above 1000 °C [3] and during ball nose end milling conditions it is above 1100 °C.[4] The formation of α alumina (sapphire) tribo-films on the friction surface also indicates that temperature is above 1000 °C because this phase is forms at 1000 °C.

1. D. A. Ditmars, S. Ishihara, S. Chang, G. Bernstein and E. West, *J. Res. Natl. Bur. Stand.*, 1982, **87**, 159–163.
2. H. Schneider, J. Schreuer and B. Hildmann, *J. Eur. Ceram. Soc.*, 2008, **28**, 329–344.
3. P. Wright and E. Trent, *Metal Cutting*, 4th edition, Boston, Butterworth-Heinemann, 2000
4. L. Ning, S. C. Veldhuis and K. Yamamoto, *Int. J. Mach. Tools Manuf.*, 2008, **48**, 656–665.); Y. Ning, M. Rahman and Y. S. Wong, *J. Mater. Process. Technol.*, 2001, **13** 360–367.); V. C. Venkatesh, D. Q. Zhou and W. Xue, Annals of the CIRP, 1993, **42**(1), 631–636.

Dr Mischler remarked: You deduced the occurrence of surface temperature in excess of 1000 °C from the presence of martensite within the contact. Indeed such temperatures are necessary to form martensite under standard conditions. However, extremely high pressures and shear rates are established in tribological contacts. This may introduce metallurgical modifications, such as martensite formation, without the need of thermal activation. Thus your estimation of contact temperature may be incorrect. Have you considered this point?

Professor Beake replied: Its an interesting point. High pressures and shear rates probably do influence transformation temperatures to some extent but the >1000 °C temperature is supported by the presence of alumina in the tribo-film as well. Typical reported temperatures in the interrupted cutting of steels are >1100 °C.

Professor Martin opened the discussion of the paper by Dr Washizu: Your computer simulations are made without any environment and then would correspond to an "*in vacuo*" experimental test. However, all tests performed in vacuum with any of the forms of pure carbon (diamond, graphite, nanotubes, carbon onions, fullerenes...*etc.*) always gave very high friction and amorphisation in the interface zone. In particular for graphite, no basal plane sliding was observed by HRTEM. Only the presence of water molecules can decrease the friction. How do you explain these experimental facts with your calculations ?

Dr Washizu responded: The whole friction reduction mechanism should consist of: (1) the formation of a transfer graphite layer, (2) friction between the transfer layer and the graphite substrate and (3) repetition of the process (physico-chemical stability of the transfer layer). In our simulation, we are calculating only the process (2) in vacuum, similar to many other molecular simulations. We think the environmental water and oxygen affects mainly process (1). For example, when steel is sliding on graphite in open humid air, graphite is transferred to the steel surface, while in vacuum metal is transferred to the graphite surface.[1] For process (3) we can calculate the relaxation process after sliding using our simulator. Some other atmosphere effects in process (2), such as the effect of functional groups on the end of graphene, are able to be treated by modifying the interaction energy function U in our method. Process (1) is the open question and should be solved by a simulation including chemical reactions and the motion of massive water molecules. We think the reduction of friction after the formation of the transfer layer can be understood by the mechanism described in this paper.

1. M. El Mansori, M. Schmitt, D. Paulmier, *Surf. Coat. Technol.*, 1998, **108–109**, 479.

Professor Dr Vernes asked: Based on your MCBD simulations, you concluded that a very low friction occurs even for commensurate systems. What are the reasons for this?

Dr Washizu answered: This is because the entire transfer film obtained the internal degree of freedom in the multilayer case and the lowest sheets of the layer were able to follow the equipotential surface of the lower slider. This means that how the atom on the lowest sheet hits the atoms on the lower slider changes. To obtain the exact friction force in this system, the energy dissipation due to atom vibration (phonon) must be included, which we have published previously (see ref. 18, 19 from our paper). The hit is weakened in the multilayer case; the difference in the friction force between the monolayer case and multilayer case shown in Fig. 8 in our paper will be larger. However, the existence of a thermal escaping motion depends on the pressure. Under high pressure (*e.g.* $l_z = 3.20$ nm), the atomistic lock motion due to an emphasis of the depth of the potential well causes a high friction force.

Professor Dr Vernes queried: You explained your findings in terms of a concept called by you as the thermal escape motion. How does this differ from the thermal lubricity well known in literature?

Dr Washizu replied: S. Yu. Krylov *et al.*[1] introduced the concept of thermolubricity for the friction of graphene. The theoretical model well described the experimental results. We agree with their concept but have some difference. In their model, the system is characterized by one effective spring constant K (eqn (1) in their paper). It is the tradition to model for both the flexibility of the cantilever and that of the tip of friction force microscope (FFM). To describe the friction of FFM, in some cases, *e.g.* the case where only single graphene is adsorbed on the tip, this is correct. However, many TEM observations have shown that the transfer layer consists of multilayer graphene sheets for friction tests of graphite substrates. Moreover, for the usual mechanical engineering situation for a steel ball with a radius of more than some millimeters rubbing on graphite, there is no cantilever or tip which has the weak spring constant K. In these situations, the role of the multilayer graphene is to be the molecular origin of the weak spring constant in the thermolubricity model. From another point of view, there are many Langevin dynamical treatments of friction models. The origin of the thermal fluctuation force in the Langevin equation is not clear in many cases. In our MCBD simulation, the origin of the thermal fluctuation force is due to the fluctuation of the sp^2 electron cloud between graphene sheets. Even in this paper we only treat the force as an isotropic force; this can be modelled more precisely in future.

1. S. Yu. Krylov *et al.*, *Phys. Rev. E*, 2005, **71**, 065101(R).

Professor Dr Franek continued the discussion of Professor Beake's paper: For the presented multilayer coating you pointed to the steep slope of temperature. Did you consider (calculate or estimate) thermal stresses due to those temperature differences?

Professor Beake responded: They have not been taken into account. Tribo-films are dynamically re-generated films on the friction surface, being continually created and destroyed, and their thermal barrier properties are of critical importance as shown by FEM modelling[1] for example.

1. G. S. Fox-Rabinovich *et al.*, *J. Appl. Phys.*, 2012, **111**, 064306.

Dr Harvey communicated: If your coatings are only 3 microns thick, how much influence is the substrate having when you are looking at 300 microns of flank wear (see Fig. 2 in your paper)?

Professor Beake communicated in reply: 300 microns typically marks the point at which the tool becomes too worn. We have previously investigated the surface morphology of the cutting edge[1] by SEM and shown that the multilayer is more effective at stabilising the wear. The load support of the substrate is important, but these very thin coatings do dramatically improve tool life over uncoated tools, reducing rake and flank wear.

1. G. S. Fox-Rabinovich, K. Yamamoto, B. D. Beake *et al.*, *Surf. Coat. Technol.*, 2010, **204**, 3425.

Dr Harvey communicated: You stated in the paper that the martensitic transformations in the tool steel indicate that locally the temperature must have been above ~1000 °C, this was discussed during the meeting and somebody mentioned that strain can affect the transformation temperature. I would like to say that we have observed martensitic transformation in stainless steel 316L in erosion experiments at 40 °C and concluded this was due to the high strain rates involved producing a strain-induced transformation, thus the localised temperature is likely to be a lot lower than you think.

Professor Beake communicated in response: It is an interested observation in your erosion tests. We do think the temperature is in the 1000–1200 °C range that is typical for cutting steels. The presence of alumina in the tribo-film also supports a temperature >1000 °C. The effective thermal barrier properties are due to the trends in thermal conductivity with the temperature of the sapphire and mullite phases in the tribofilms.

The origin of anti-wear chemistry of ZDDP

Jean Michel Martin,*[a] Tasuku Onodera,†[b] Clotilde Minfray,[a] Fabrice Dassenoy[a] and Akira Miyamoto[c]

Received 8th December 2011, Accepted 16th January 2012
DOI: 10.1039/c2fd00126h

Molecular Dynamics has been used to simulate the anti-wear chemistry of zinc dialkyl dithiophosphate (ZDDP). The model simulates the digestion of abrasive particles into the zinc polyphosphate glass. The main result is that the driving force for the tribochemical reaction is not temperature but entropy due to mechanical mixing at the atomic scale.

Introduction

The role of chemical hardness in predicting tribochemical reactions in the liquid phase has already been highlighted in the literature[1] and a general survey on ZDDP mechanisms can also be found.[2] The chemical hardness model applied to ZDDP tribochemistry in the solid phase has been described about ten years ago.[3] Here we give a summary of the main properties of the ZDDP tribofilm and the mechanism of anti-abrasive action based on the HSAB principle.

The ZDDP tribofilm has a gradient structure and is several tens of nanometres thick. It is generally composed of a short-chain phosphate layer, itself covered by a thin, long-chain polyphosphate one. There is no carbon in the bulk of the tribofilm. This has been strongly evidenced by AES profiling on the tribofilm (Fig. 1). Sulphur may partially substitute for oxygen in the polymer chain backbone (O–P–S instead of O–P–O). However, XPS core level data on the film show that some sulphur is in the sulphide form (S^{2-}), but XPS cannot easily separate the metal sulphide from the thiophosphate due to the small chemical shift that is expected. When the phosphate film is formed on a steel surface from the thermo-oxidative decomposition of ZDDP, a reaction between the phosphate and the iron oxide native layer is likely to occur. This reaction certainly takes place between the phosphate and Fe_2O_3, predominantly leading to an inter-grown layer, due to the acid–base chemical reaction. Little is known about the mechanical properties of zinc phosphates, but these glasses have a low transition temperature (softening point around 200 °C) compared to silicate or borate glasses. Nano-hardness measurements carried out on ZDDP films[4] showed that the hardness of the tribofilm increases with penetration depth and this has been interpreted as a smart behaviour of the ZDDP tribofilm material. Unfortunately, it has not been verified if the top layer (long-chain polyphosphates) was softer than the bulk (short-chain phosphates). This could be another explanation to the hardness

[a]Laboratory of Tribology and System Dynamics, Ecole Centrale de Lyon, 69134 Ecully, France. E-mail: jean-michel.martin@ec-lyon.fr
[b]Department of Applied Chemistry, Graduate School of Engineering, Tohoku University, 6-6-10 Aramaki Aoba Aobaku, Sendai 980-8579, Japan; Fax: +81-22-795-7235; Tel: +81-22-795-7233
[c]New Industry Creation Hatchery Center and Graduate School of Engineering, Tohoku University, 6-6-10 Aramaki Aoba Aobaku, Sendai 980-8579, Japan. E-mail: miyamoto@aki. che.tohoku.ac.jp; Fax: +81-22-795-7235; Tel: +81-22-795-7233

† Present affiliation. Hitachi, Ltd., Hitachi Research Laboratory, 7-1-1 Omika-cho, Hitachi, Ibaraki 319-1292, Japan, Tel: +81-294-52-5111, Fax: +81-294-52-7622, E-mail: tasuku.onodera.qp@hitachi.com

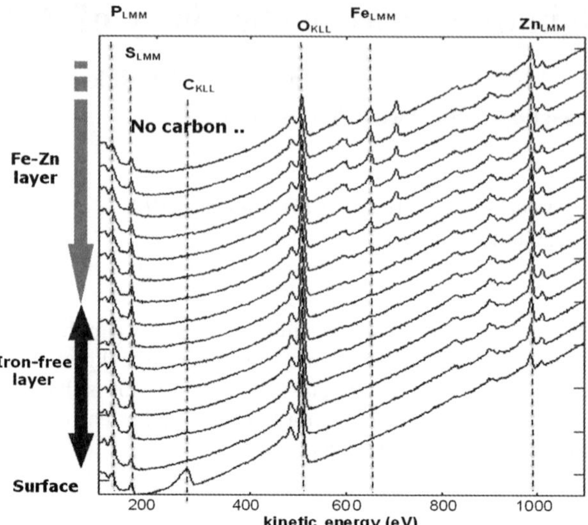

Fig. 1 Auger Electron Spectroscopy (AES) profile on a ZDDP tribofilm. The top layer contains only zinc polythiophosphate. There is no carbon in the film (except contamination at the outmost surface).

results. Additionally, the existence of a soft viscous surface layer overlying the tribofilm has been shown by AFM force–distance curves.[5] During the wear process, iron oxide particles can be readily formed when the thermal film is disrupted and when oxygen dissolved in the lubricant attacks the nascent surface that is generated.

It is also possible that iron oxide particles originate from other parts of the mechanical system. Iron oxide particles, and particularly hematite (Fe_2O_3), can cause severe damage by abrasive wear of the film. This is due to the hardness of the crystallized oxide and its relatively high melting point (>1200 °C). Abrasive wear itself produces a lot of debris due to plastic deformation and also large nascent surfaces that quickly oxidize. This usually results in catastrophic abrasive wear, eventually leading to scuffing. An important aspect of the anti-wear mechanism of ZDDP has been recognized to be the ability of phosphate glasses to "digest" any abrasive particles of iron oxide by means of tribochemical reactions.[2] Here we give more details about the chemical reactions that are thought to be responsible for this basic effect. Typically, the hard acid–hard base reaction between phosphates and iron oxides stems from the fact that the Fe^{3+} ion is a harder Lewis acid than the Zn^{2+} ion and that the cation exchange is energetically favourable from the point of view of the HSAB principle as proposed originally by Pearson.[6] Starting from the polymer-like zinc metaphosphate for example, a possible route for the elimination of 1 mole of Fe_2O_3 would be as follows:

$$5Zn(PO_3)_2 + Fe_2O_3 \longrightarrow Fe_2 Zn_3 P_{10} O_{31} + 2\,ZnO$$
$$(ZnO, P_2O_5) \qquad\qquad (Fe_2O_3,\, 3\,ZnO,\, 5\,P_2O_5)$$

This reaction is an illustration of the cation exchange process between iron (as in Fe_2O_3) and zinc (as in ZnO). The digestion of the hard oxide in the phosphate glass (having a low transition temperature) can already explain the benefit in terms of wear protection. Moreover, hematite, and more generally all iron oxides, are much harder than zinc oxide (approximately twice in Moh's scale). However, the reaction needs the friction process (pressure, shear and temperature) in order to be initiated because the Fe dissolution in the phosphate is not considered to be exothermic and cannot be very favourable from the point of view of energy. As

   This journal is © The Royal Society of Chemistry 2012

the reaction proceeds, the reservoir of polyphosphate decreases and the exchange reaction is certainly stopped at a certain degree of the digestion process. We will discuss this situation later with the help of computer simulation. From this model, several important conclusions can be drawn:

(1) It is known that glasses have some universal properties which means that their physical and mechanical properties do not depend much on the exact chemical composition to a certain extent (here the Fe_2O_3/ZnO ratio). Therefore, we may first assume that the elimination of some abrasive oxide does not strongly modify the rheological properties of the glass at low Fe : Zn ratios.

(2) It is important to notice that as the reaction proceeds, the chain length of the phosphate decreases and a depolymerisation process is engaged. This is because the exchange of Zn^{2+} with Fe^{3+} needs more negative charges to balance the reaction, and this is obtained by shortening the chain length. Short-chain mixed Fe/Zn polyphosphates become concentrated in the bulk of the tribofilm whereas a thermal film from the original ZDDP is continuously deposited on the surface. Therefore, the result of the tribochemical process is a layered structure: the tribofilm is composed of Fe/Zn short-chain polyphosphates covered by a zinc polymer-like phosphate (see Fig. 1). Actually, the anti-wear mechanism is very adaptable: in certain cases the bulk film is free of iron because no abrasive wear occurs. But in more severe cases, the film can contain large proportions of iron. This dual mechanism to protect a steel surface both against adhesion and abrasion is thought to be the reason for the excellent performance of ZDDP additives. The model described above is mainly supported by XANES experiments.[7] Interestingly, other very hard metal oxides can be digested in the polyphosphate elements in steels. For example, chromium, nickel and manganese oxides are known to diffuse to the surface of steels and to cause severe abrasive wear.

The need for computer simulation stems from the fact that we would like to know how the properties of the glass are changed *in situ* with the incorporation of iron in the network and what the consequence of that is on friction and wear. This is hardly attainable with experiments without synthesizing a series of mixed glass. Also the kinetics of iron digestion is not known and the driving force is not known. In this work, we choose here classical Molecular Dynamics (MD) approach in a first step.

Computational details

The analysis at atomistic and molecular level is often difficult only for experimental techniques. Moreover, *in situ* analytical methods in tribology are in the limits of experimental equipment at hand. Computational chemistry methods provide us with information at these levels and permit *in situ* observation and quantitative measurements, and therefore have been extensively applied to the field of nanotribology (see for example Mosey *et al.*,[8–10] Gao *et al.*,[11,12] and Onodera *et al.*[13–15]).

For the study of the anti-abrasive action of polyphosphates, we prepared a simulation model simplifying the complex realistic system. This model was already described in detail in a previous paper[13] and was used to show that a zinc polythiophosphate behaves in the same manner as the corresponding zinc polyphosphate (in the mild wear regime). We report here MD simulations on the shear properties of a zinc metaphosphate layer placed between two Fe substrates and containing an embedded iron oxide nanoparticle located in the centre of the phosphate layer. We choose this model because it is very close to the situation observed in some high resolution TEM images of a FIB preparation of the ZDDP tribofilm (Fig. 2).

In this image, nano-grains of iron oxide are embedded in the glass matrix. The size of the crystallized particles is a few nanometres. We performed EDS analyses on this ZDDP tribofilm with an electron probe of 1 nm diameter. We detected a very small quantity of sulphur and the atomic ratio Fe : Zn was about 4. A zinc metaphosphate matrix was formed by compaction of $Zn(PO_3)_2$ clusters of atoms (Fig. 3). This is a good compromise to study the anti-wear mechanism of ZDDP in the mild wear

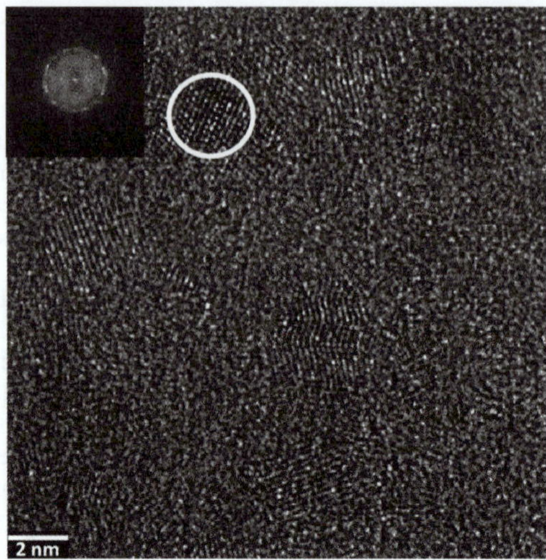

Fig. 2 High Resolution TEM image of a ZDDP tribofilm (prepared by focused ion beam FIB). Nano-crystalline oxide particles are embedded in the amorphous zinc thiophosphate matrix. Some of them look like they are being digested into the glassy structure.

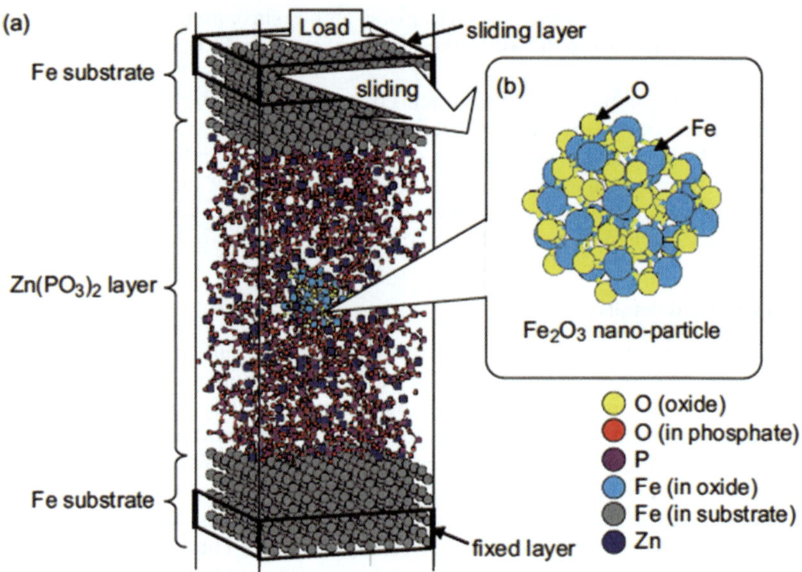

Fig. 3 Model for MD simulation of digestion of an iron oxide nanoparticle embedded in zinc metaphosphate matrix under the combined effects of pressure and shear. Temperature is fixed at 353 K.

regime. The details of the simulation model are described in the following: the phosphate layer contains 432 phosphorous atoms, 1296 oxygen atoms and 216 zinc atoms. The Fe substrates contain 648 iron atoms each. A non-equilibrium MD program, "NEW-RYUDO"[14,15] was used for all the simulations. We prepared the calculation models including two types of iron oxide particle: hematite (Fe_2O_3) and magnetite (Fe_3O_4). Two hematite particle sizes have been used: a large one (1 nm diameter) containing 75 atoms and a smaller one (0.7 nm diameter) containing

40 atoms. In the same way, the 1 nm diameter magnetite particle contains 10 Fe^{2+}, 20 Fe^{3+} ions and 40 O^{2-} ions. The magnetite particle (0.7 nm diameter) contains 5 Fe^{2+}, 10 Fe^{3+} and 20 O^{2-} atoms. In all simulations, the particle was located in the centre of the cell. The cell size is $25.8 \times 25.8 \times 100.0$ Å^3.

To simulate the friction condition, a constant load was applied to the top layer of the upper iron substrate in a vertical direction and simultaneously the substrate was forced to horizontally slide with a constant velocity. The position of the bottom substrate was fixed at the beginning of simulations.

In the MD simulation, a selection of interatomic potential model is usually important. In this work, the MD simulation for a zinc phosphate system had already been studied in several papers.[13] Hence the following two-body potentials were employed to study the shear properties of zinc phosphate and iron oxide interface, referring to the works by Boiko *et al.*[16] The interatomic potential between atoms in $Zn(PO_3)_2$ and Fe_2O_3 can be expressed by:

$$U = \sum_i \sum_{j>i} \left[\frac{Z_i Z_j e^2}{r_{ij}} + f_0 (b_i + b_j) \exp\left(\frac{a_i + a_j - r_{ij}}{b_i + b_j} \right) \right]$$

where the terms in the right hand of the equation correspond to long-range Coulombic interaction and exchange repulsion energy, respectively. r_{ij} is the inter-atomic distance between atoms i and j. Atomic charge Z_i, and coefficients a and b are the values specific to each atom. f_0 is a constant for unit conversion. A long-range Coulombic interaction was calculated by using the Ewald method.[17] The conventional Lennard–Jones type potential describes the interaction between the Fe atoms constituting the iron substrate and above atoms.

$$U = \sum_i \sum_{j>i} \left(\frac{A_{ij}}{r_{ij}^{12}} - \frac{B_{ij}}{r_{ij}^{6}} \right)$$

Parameters A_{ij} and B_{ij} are the specific values for each type of atom, and are referred from the consistent valence force-field.[18] The validity of such a model and parameters was shown in our previous paper.[19] A periodic boundary condition is applied in horizontal directions. Verlet algorithm[20] was used to solve the equation of motion and we set the integration time to 0.5 fs. MD simulations were carried out for 1 000 000 steps except at low sliding speeds.

In this work, we used zinc metaphosphate or zinc orthophosphate as specific materials representing the tribofilm composition. Note that any base oil molecules were not included in the model as a first step to investigate the complex tribology phenomena under the boundary lubrication condition. The pressure value was varied from 1 MPa to 1.0 GPa assuming the boundary lubrication condition, and horizontal velocity was varied between 0.1 m s^{-1} and 100 m s^{-1} to simulate the shear properties of zinc phosphate in presence of iron oxide within a reasonable computation time. The temperature was controlled to be 353 K (80 °C) by scaling the atomic velocities. Both Fe substrates are excluded from the temperature control scheme except in a specific simulation where thermostats were used. We also performed experiments by heating the glass up to 3000 K at atmospheric pressure. Finally, we studied the effect of the incorporation of iron in the zinc phosphate on the ability to digest new iron oxide particles.

Results and discussion

1 Effect of pressure at 353 K

In this first simulation, we studied the effect of pressure on the composite sandwich system. Fig. 4 shows the effect of a pressure of 1 GPa (maximum pressure investigated) on the behaviour of the system. As can be shown, even after 1 000 000 steps (corresponding to simulation time of 500 ps), the particle is not destroyed and is only elastically deformed. Note that for clear understanding, the zinc phosphate atoms have been omitted in the figure. Therefore, the particle cannot be eliminated under the effect of hydrostatic pressure only.

2 Effect of temperature at atmospheric pressure

To study the effect of heating, we kept the pressure constant at atmospheric conditions and we increased the temperature with time step of 2.5 fs for 100 000 steps. We fixed constant values of 300 K, 500 K, 1000 K, 1500 K, 2000 K and 2500 K, successively. The force fields were the same as before. Results showed that the nanoparticle was dismantled at about 2000 K (not shown). Lower temperature conditions than 2000 K could not induce any changes in the iron oxide nanoparticles.

In another experiment, the temperature was increased gradually from 300 K to 3000 K with a rate of 0.05 K step^{-1} (equivalent to 2.0×10^{13} K s^{-1}). The result in Fig. 5 shows the evolution of the mean square displacement in nm^2 (MSD), (which expresses a degree of movement of the atoms of Fe in the oxide particle) as a function of temperature. The graph clearly confirms that the "digestion" of the iron oxide particle in the glassy phosphate matrix starts at about 1700 K, in agreement with data from the literature.[21]

3 Combined effects of pressure and sliding speed at 353 K

For sliding experiments, we used three different contact pressures of 1 MPa, 10 MPa and 1000 MPa, respectively, and a temperature of the cell fixed at 80 °C (353 K) every 100 steps in the simulation. The sliding speed was adjusted to 2.5×10^{-5} nm step^{-1} (equal to 10 m s^{-1}) for a reasonable computational time. Both pressure and sliding speed were applied to the topmost atomic layer of the upper iron substrate. Fig. 6 shows what happens to the iron oxide nanoparticle in these friction conditions. There is diffusion of iron and oxygen atoms into the zinc phosphate matrix

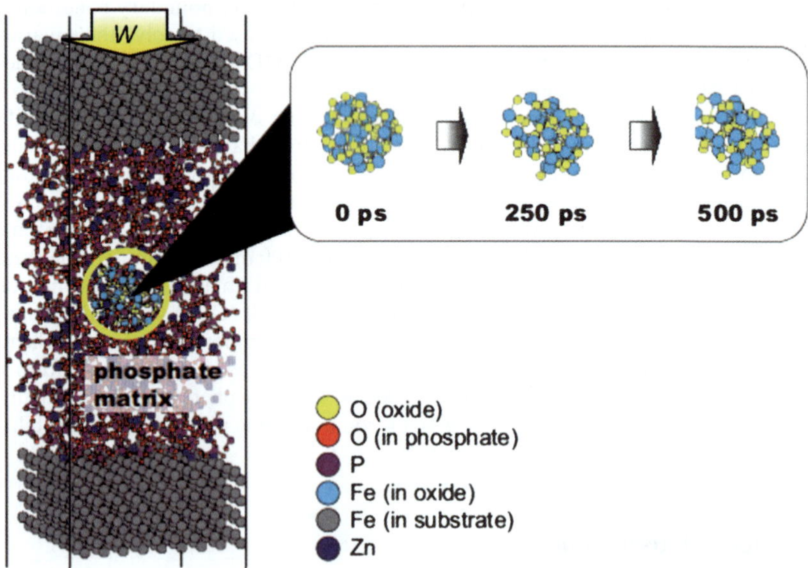

Fig. 4 Effect of pressure only (1 GPa) on the shape of the iron oxide nanoparticle in the polyphosphate glass. No significant change was observed, only a slight elastic deformation after 500 ps.

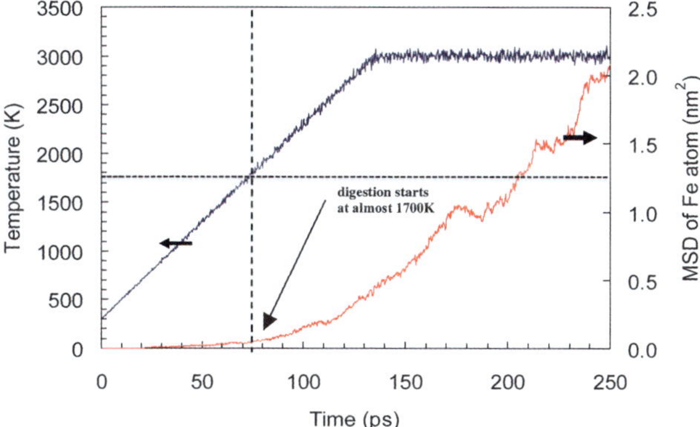

Fig. 5 Heating experiments for a mixture of zinc metaphosphate and hematite nanoparticles by MD simulation. The diffusion of iron in the phosphate (corresponding to the digestion of the particle and the formation of mixed Fe : Zn polyphosphate) starts at about 2000 K.

and the particle is thus progressively digested. More quantitatively, Fig. 7 shows the radial distribution function (RDF) of Fe–O_{PO_4} pairs as a function of the different pressures after 2.5 ns duration. We remind here that the intensity of the peak at 0.2 nm corresponds to the degree of digestion of the iron oxide species in the phosphate matrix. Whatever the pressure in the sliding simulation, the particle is digested, because the intensity of this peak increases in all cases compared to the initial structure. However, as expected, the digestion is more significant at the highest contact pressure (1 GPa).

We also studied the effect of sliding speed at 1 GPa maximum contact pressure. We used three sliding speeds: 2.5×10^{-5} nm step^{-1} (equal to 10 m s^{-1}), duration: 1 000 000 steps; 2.5×10^{-6} nm step^{-1} (equal to 1 m s^{-1}), duration: 10 000 000 step and 2.5×10^{-7} nm step^{-1} (equal to 0.1 m s^{-1}), duration: 20 000 000 steps. Of course, for the lowest sliding speed, the calculation time drastically increases and we were obliged to stop the experiment after only 50 ns of duration. Results are summarized in Fig. 8, showing the RDF of Fe–O_{PO_4} pairs. Results show that the digestion occurs in all cases, including the lowest sliding speed (0.1 m s^{-1}), which is very close to practical cases in thermal engines, for example (ring/lining system).

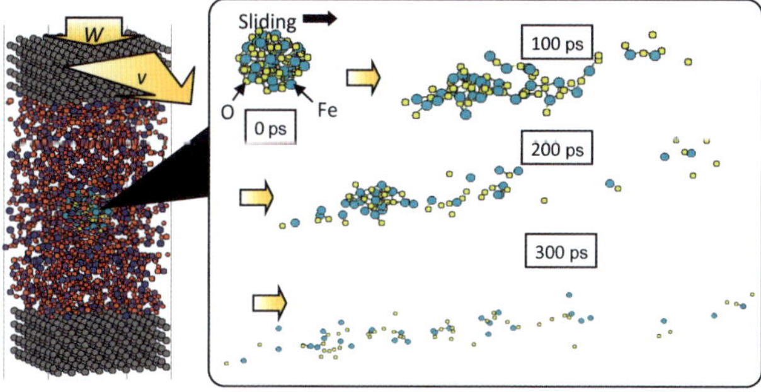

Fig. 6 The combined effects of pressure and shear on the behaviour of the iron oxide nanoparticle embedded in the zinc metaphosphate by MD. After 300 ps of simulation, the iron and oxygen atoms diffuse into the phosphate glass. The particle is thus completely digested by the tribochemical reaction.

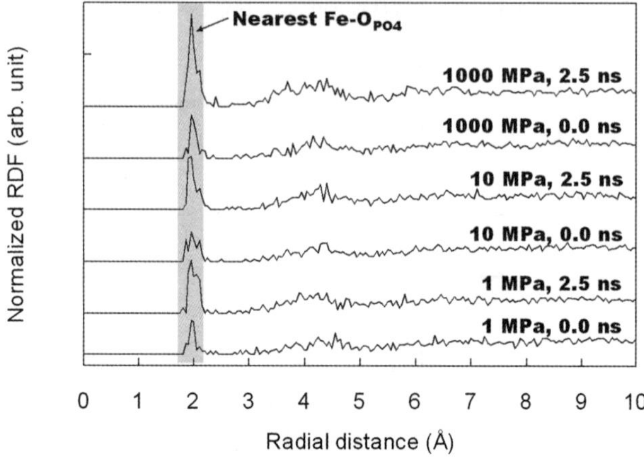

Fig. 7 The effect of contact pressure on the Radial Distribution Function of Fe–O$_{PO_4}$ pairs in the MD simulation. The particle is digested after 2.5 ns of simulation, even at the lowest contact pressure (1 MPa).

To study in more detail the origin of the mixing between the two species, we focused again on the role of the temperature during the friction process. In previous experiments, the temperature was fixed at 353 K in the cell (phosphate + oxide), and this was done for every 100 steps of the simulation. We also checked that the temperature did not increase significantly during this integration without controlling the temperature in the cell itself. In another experiment, we used a part of the Fe substrates as a thermostat at a fixed temperature. The rest of the cell was without temperature control. This last case is more realistic compared with the practical case where the steel substrates evacuate heat by thermal conductivity. Results are compared in Fig. 9. As can be seen from the evolution of the Fe–O$_{PO_4}$ pairs, digestion of the oxide always occurs even with the thermostat.

Then the question arising is: what is the driving force for the chemical reaction between iron oxide and zinc phosphate under the combined effects of pressure and shear? There are three possibilities to answer this question: the first one is the result of only heating at temperatures above 2000 K (due to dissipation of

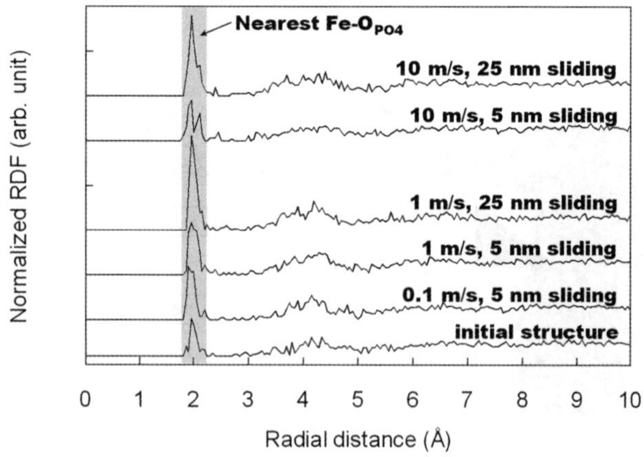

Fig. 8 The effect of sliding speed on the Radial Distribution Function of Fe–O$_{PO_4}$ pairs in the MD simulation. The particle is digested after 5 nm of sliding distance, even at the lowest sliding speed (0.1 m s^{-1}).

mechanical energy into heat in the cell), the second is mechanical mixing at low temperature and the flow of the glass under shear. The third one is the mixing entropy effect: the effect of shear produces disorder in the cell and increases the entropy of the system. Even if the enthalpy ΔH is not negative (that is probable here), the effect of increasing the entropy ΔS can result in a negative free energy ΔG and a possibility for the reaction to initiate, and this according to the thermodynamic relation:

$$\Delta G = \Delta H - T\Delta S$$

Because there is no significant temperature increase observed in all our simulations, the third explanation is the most probable in our opinion.

Another prediction of the Chemical Hardness model (based on HSAB principle) is the depolymerisation of the polyphosphate when oxygen atoms become mixed in the zinc phosphate.[3]

Then we compared the results of two simulations: one performed with zinc metaphosphate $Zn(PO_3)_2$ as a matrix in the cell and a second with zinc orthophosphate $Zn_3(PO_4)_2$. The iron oxide particle was Fe_2O_3 of 1 nm diameter. The contact pressure was 1 GPa, sliding speed 100 m s^{-1}, the temperature was fixed at 353 K with an integration time of 0.5 fs. Fig. 10 shows what happened to the particle after 250 ps of simulation: in the case of zinc orthophosphate in the cell, the digestion of the oxide particle becomes much more difficult because oxygen atoms from the particle cannot migrate.

It is made clear that the digestion of the oxide is easier in the case of the metaphosphate and oxygen can contribute to decrease the chain length of the polyphosphate. In Fig. 11, we show the RDF of P atoms, surrounded by oxygen atoms originating from the Fe_2O_3 particle. The results clearly show that oxygen atoms diffuse into the metaphosphate and consequently decrease the chain length (between PO_3 and orthophosphate PO_4). Fig. 12 presents a high resolution TEM image (FIB cross-section) of the tribofilm formed during a friction experiment on steel substrates in the presence of zinc orthophosphate on the surface (as a powder). This result shows that the oxide particles are not digested (compared to the image in Fig. 2). Once more, this demonstrates the validity of our MD simulation model. To confirm this effect of the polyphosphate metallic composition, we performed simulations of digestion experiments by increasing the iron content in the zinc metaphosphate matrix (this actually

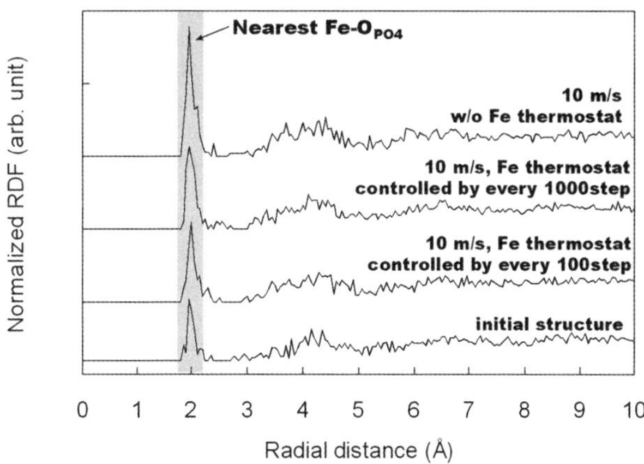

Fig. 9 The effect of using thermostats in the Fe substrates on the Radial Distribution Function of Fe–O$_{PO_4}$ pairs in the MD simulation.

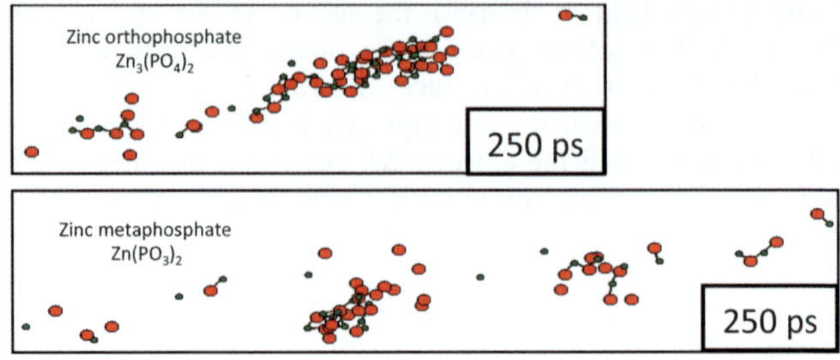

Fig. 10 Comparison of the digestion of iron oxide particle into zinc metaphosphate and zinc orthophosphate. It is clear that the long-chain polyphosphate is more efficient.

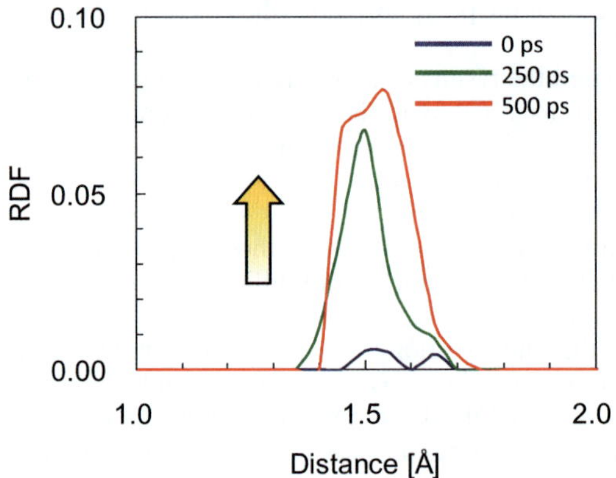

Fig. 11 Radial Distribution Functions of P–O$_{particle}$ pairs in the MD simulation at the end of experiment Fig. 6. The decrease of the RDF as a function of time indicates the diffusion of oxygen atoms into the metaphosphate glass (PO$_3$)$_n$ and consequently a shortening of the phosphate chain length (towards orthophosphate PO$_4$).

corresponds to a reduction of the phosphate chain length). The conditions of simulation were the same as previously described.

We used different Fe : Zn ratios in the polyphosphate glass; 2 : 8, 4 : 6, 5 : 5, 6 : 4 and 8 : 2. Results in Fig. 13 clearly show that the reaction strongly depends on the presence of iron in the glass matrix, as expected from the HSAB principle. With a ratio of Fe : Zn above 1, the digestion becomes difficult. In Fig. 13, we also show a TEM image and corresponding electron diffraction pattern of a fragment of ZDDP tribofilm (collected from a lubricated test carried out in mild wear conditions). The diffraction shows the amorphous state and the X-ray analysis of the transparent area (not shown here) indicates a ratio Fe : Zn of about 1 and the presence of a very small amount of sulphur. This demonstrates the validity of the MD approach to simulate the anti abrasive mechanism of ZDDP.

From the MD simulation we can also obtain information on the hardness of the polyphosphate glass and its shear properties. The accumulated frictional work can also be calculated and it is shown to increase with the Fe^{3+} content in the glass (not shown here). Also the hardness of the glass is increased with the Fe content.[19] This indicates that the friction coefficient of the ZDDP tribofilm is expected to increase as the iron oxide digestion proceeds. Fig. 14 presents details of atom trajectories during the shear experiment for two compositions of the phosphate matrix (corresponding to atomic ratios Fe : Zn of 0 : 10 and 6 : 4, respectively. It is clear from the figure that the rheological properties of

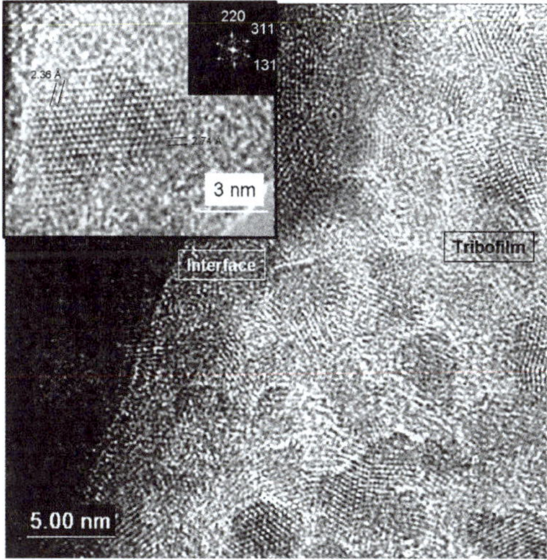

Fig. 12 High resolution TEM image of a tribofilm on steel formed starting from zinc ortho-phosphate powder as a lubricant. It is clear that iron oxide particles (indexed by the electron diffraction pattern) are hardly digested in the zinc phosphate.

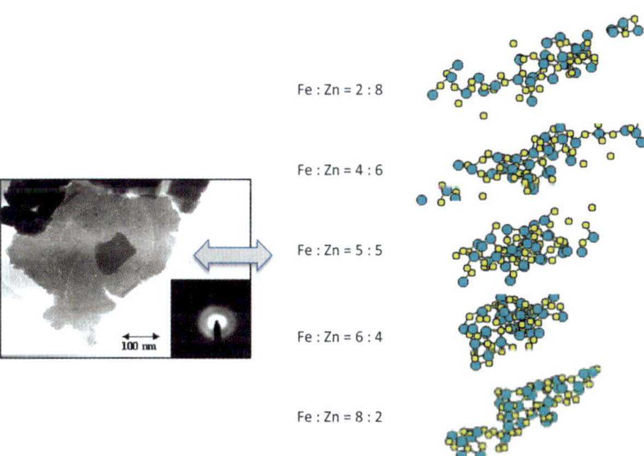

Fig. 13 The effect of the matrix composition (Fe : Zn ratio) on the efficiency of the polyphosphate to digest more iron oxide. It is clear that digestion does not occur once the Fe : Zn atomic ratio goes above unity. The TEM image of the amorphous polyphosphate corresponds to Fe : Zn = 1 (as measured by EDS in the TEM).

the glass are deeply modified by its chemical composition. An absence of shear planes and slips at the boundary are also seen when iron atoms are mixed with zinc phosphate.

4 Influence of the nature and size of the iron oxide particle

MD simulations have been performed on two crystalline forms of iron oxides, hematite (Fe_2O_3) and magnetite (Fe_3O_4). The nanoparticles had the same size in the simulation (1 nm diameter). As a result, we did not detect any difference between the behaviours of the two species. They are digested in the same way and at the same kinetics (no results shown here). Also, there was no significant difference between the two sizes of the particles.

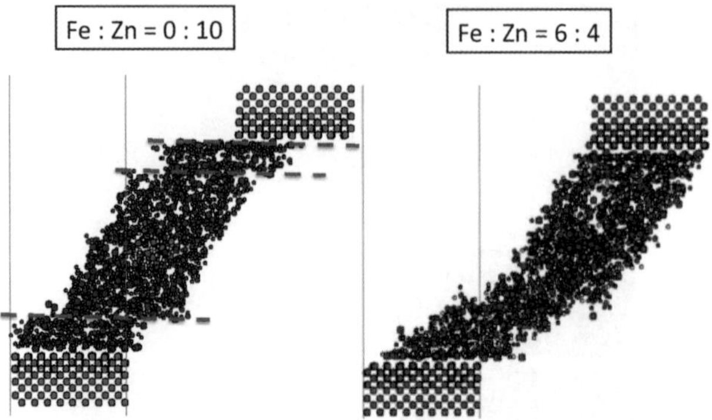

Fig. 14 Flow behaviour (atoms trajectories) of the polyphosphate glass during friction MD simulations. Shear planes and slip at the boundary are observed in the pure zinc polyphosphate. Rheological properties of the glass depend strongly on chemical composition and particularly the Fe content of the polyphosphate.

Conclusions

We have used a classical Molecular Dynamics simulation to study one of the basic tribochemical reactions of the anti-wear chemistry of ZDDP: the hard acid-hard base reaction between the glassy zinc phosphate and crystalline iron oxide nanoparticles. This particular reaction is known to be responsible from the elimination of the abrasive material in the contact area of a lubricated tribological system.

The overall results of the MD simulation (and the choice of the different force fields) are in excellent agreement with experimental findings and particularly *post mortem* surface analysis (AES) and TEM images carried out in wear scar or on wear debris. Moreover, the MD approach gave us more insights into the kinetics of the reaction and the following points have been addressed:

1–The combined effect of pressure and shear is necessary for the reaction to occur in the contact (temperature controlled at 353 K). Only pressure is not sufficient to initiate the reaction and to eliminate the particle.

2–The reaction can be initiated even at very low contact pressure (1 MPa) and in a very short time (2.5 ns) in the simulation, (temperature controlled at 353 K).

3–At 1 GPa contact pressure, the reaction starts even at low sliding speeds (0.1 m s^{-1}), after 5 nm sliding (temperature controlled at 353 K).

4–The reaction is made possible without sliding at atmospheric pressure, by heating the mixture at elevated temperature. However, the MD simulations show that a temperature above 1700 K is necessary to digest the particle, in agreement with the synthesis of mixed phosphate glass described in the literature.

From this set of results, we suggest that the driving force of the tribochemical reaction of ZDDP (dissolution of Fe atoms and migration of oxygen atoms in the zinc metaphosphate decreasing the chain length) is not temperature, but preferentially an increase of the entropy mixing contribution ΔS (contributing to a decrease the total free Gibbs energy ΔG).

Concerning the influence of the nature of the polyphosphate glass, quantitative data were obtained from the MD simulation whereas the HSAB principle can only give general trends and preferences. The following points have been shown in this work:

1–Zinc metaphosphate is more chemically reactive with iron oxide than zinc orthophosphate.

2–Hematite and magnetite have similar reaction kinetics with zinc polyphosphate.

3–As the reaction of digestion proceeds; the zinc polyphosphate becomes progressively enriched in oxygen and iron atoms. As a result, its ability to eliminate iron oxide drastically decreases. When the ratio Zn : Fe is about 1, the reaction is stopped. Moreover, it has been shown (in a previous paper[19]) that the effect of iron in the phosphate is to harden the polyphosphate. This can explain a hardness gradient in the ZDDP tribofilm that was observed experimentally, and this permits the material to adapt the contact pressure to a certain extent.

All these MD simulations are in excellent agreement with the observed composite and multilayer structure of the ZDDP tribofilm: a zinc polyphosphate layer covering a mixed iron and zinc polyphosphate with a gradient of Fe content (and then a gradient of hardness).

Next study is the use of computational quantum chemistry simulation (QCMD) to confirm the results of the Molecular Dynamics simulation.

Notes and references

1 P. A. Willermet, D. P. Dailey, R. O. Carter, P. J. Schmidt, W. Zhu, J. C. Bell and D. Park, *Tribol. Int.*, 1995, **28**, 163.
2 H. Spikes, *Tribol. Lett.*, 2004, **17**, 469.
3 J. M. Martin, *Tribol. Lett.*, 1999, **6**, 1.
4 S. Bec and A. Tonck, *Proc. of Leeds-Lyon Symposium*, 1995, 173.
5 A. J. Pidduck and G. C. Smith, *Wear*, 1997, **212**, 254.
6 R. G. Pearson, *Chemical Hardness*, (Wiley-VHC, New York), 1996.
7 Z. Yin, M. Kasrai, M. Fuller, G. M. Bancroft, K. Fyfeand and K. H. Tan, *Wear*, 1997, **202**, 172.
8 N. J. Mosey and T. K. Woo, *J. Phys. Chem*, 2003, **107**, 5058.
9 N. J. Mosey, M. H. Müser and T. K. Woo, *Science*, 2005, **307**, 1612.
10 N. J. Mosey, T. K. Woo, M. Kasrai, P. R. Norton, G. M. Bancroft and M. H. Müser, *Tribol. Lett.*, 2006, **24**, 105.
11 T. G. Gao, P. T. Mikulski and J. A. Harrisson, *J. Am. Chem. Soc.*, 2002, **124**, 7202.
12 T. G. Gao, P. T. Mikulski, G. M. Chateauneuf and J. A. Harrisson, *J. Phys. Chem.*, 2003, **107**, 11082.
13 T. Onodera, Y. Morita, A. Suzuki, M. Koyoma, H. Tsuboi, N. Hatekeyama, A. Endou, H. Tabaka, M. Kubo, C. A. Del Carpio, C. Minfray, J. M. Martin and A. Miyamoto, *Appl. Surf. Sci.*, 2008, **254**, 7976.
14 T. Onodera, Y. Morita, A. Suzuki, M. Koyoma, H. Tsuboi, N. Hatekeyama, A. Endou, H. Tabaka, M. Kubo, F. Dassenoy, C. Minfray, L. Joly-Pottuz, J. M. Martin and A. Miyamoto, *J. Phys. Chem. B*, 2009, **113**, 16526.
15 T. Onodera, Y. Morita, R. Nagumo, R. Miura, A. Suzuki, H. Tsuboi, N. Hatekeyama, A. Endou, H. Tabaka, M. Kubo, F. Dassenoy, C. Minfray, L. Joly-Pottuz, J. M. Martin and A. Miyamoto, *J. Phys. Chem. B*, 2010, **114**, 15832.
16 G. G. Boiko, N. S. Andreev and A. V. Parkachev, *J. Non-Cryst. Solids*, 1998, **238**, 175.
17 P. P. Ewald, *Ann. Phys.*, 1921, **64**, 253.
18 P. Dauber-Osguthorpe, V. A. Roberts, D. J. Osguthorpe, J. Wolff and A. T. Hagler, *Proteins: Struct., Funct., Genet.*, 1988, **4**, 31.
19 C. Minfray, T. Le Mogne, J. M. Martin, T. Onodera, S. Nara, S. Takahashi, H. Tsuboi, M. Koyoma, A. Endou, H. Tabaka, M. Kubo, C. A. Del Carpio and A. Miyamoto, *Tribol. Trans.*, 2008, **51**, 589.
20 L. Verlet, *Phys. Rev.*, 1967, **159**, 98.
21 M. Crobu, A. Rossi, F. Mangolini and N. D. Spencer, *Trib. Letters*, 2010, **39**, 121.

  www.rsc.org/faraday_d | Faraday Discussions

The mechanics of nanometre-scale molecular contacts

Katerina Busuttil,[a] Nikolaos Nikogeorgos,[a] Zhenyu Zhang,[a] Mark Geoghegan,[b] Christopher A. Hunter[a] and Graham J. Leggett[*a]

Received 23rd December 2011, Accepted 3rd February 2012
DOI: 10.1039/c2fd00133k

The adhesive interactions and friction–load relationships have been investigated in liquid mixtures. For hydrogen bond-forming monolayers in acetone–heptane mixtures a linear friction–load relationship is observed at compositions that yield extensive surface solvation. As the concentration of the hydrogen bond acceptor in the liquid medium is reduced, non-linear friction–load relationships are observed that may be modelled using DMT mechanics. These observations are rationalized by assuming, as others have previously suggested, that the friction force is the sum of a load-dependent term and a shear term. The load-dependent term is found to be invariant with the adhesion force and represents energy dissipation in molecular ploughing (conformational disruption of the surface). The shear term results from adhesive interactions between the probe and the surface and correlates closely with the free energy of interaction between hydrogen bonding functional groups. A non-linear friction–load relationship is "normal", with linearity representing a limiting form of behaviour where unusually weak adhesion occurs (e.g. a highly solvated surface). Observations of the solvent-dependence of the pull-off force and the surface shear strength enable the prediction of thermodynamic properties of the interacting functional groups.

1 Introduction

The atomic force microscope (AFM) has been used to study nanoscale tribological phenomena for two decades. In friction force microscopy (FFM),[1,2] the lateral deflections of an AFM cantilever are measured either as a function of position (to yield an image) or as the probe sweeps back and forth across a line (a friction loop) to yield quantitative data. The lateral force is the sum of the frictional resistance to motion at the tip–sample contact and the component of the load resolved in the plane of the surface on a sloped substrate. For relatively smooth surfaces, the topographical contribution to the lateral force can be removed by subtracting line scans acquired with opposing directions of motion, yielding the friction force.[2–4]

There has been a significant amount of interest in the use of FFM to study tribological interactions between nanoscale molecular contacts, driven both by an interest in the fundamental nature of interactions at interfaces and also by the emergence of new technologies, such as microelectromechanical systems, which have necessitated the exploration of new lubrication schemes for very small sliding contacts. Developments in organic film chemistry have enabled control of the chemical functionality of both the probe and the counterface. Nakagawa et al. first reported the

[a]Department of Chemistry, University of Sheffield, Brook Hill, Sheffield, S3 7HF, UK. E-mail: Graham.Leggett@sheffield.ac.uk; Fax: +44 114 222 9346; Tel: +44 114 222 9556
[b]Department of Physics and Astronomy, University of Sheffield, Sheffield, S3 7RH, UK

functionalisation of an AFM tip with an organic layer; they functionalised a silicon nitride probe with a film of alkylsilanes and compared interaction forces for surface films containing molecules of differing alkyl chain lengths.[5] Frisbie *et al.* reported the use of alkylthiolate self-assembled monolayers (SAMs) to functionalise gold-coated AFM probes and coined the term "chemical force microscopy" (CFM) to describe their approach.[6,7] They measured adhesion forces for hydrogen-bonding systems, and also mapped surface friction. Subsequently, a large number of papers has been published that report the use of either FFM or a combination of FFM and CFM to investigate molecular surfaces. Alkylthiolate SAMs, which offer a great deal of versatility in the design of molecular interfaces, have attracted a great deal of interest. Friction forces measured by FFM have been found to be influenced by the nature of the adsorbate tail group,[8–12] acid–base interactions,[13] the chain-length,[14] packing and order in monolayers,[15] phase-separation,[16,17] the nature of the substrate–adsorbate interaction,[18,19] intra-monolayer hydrogen bonding interactions[20,21] and surface chemical reactivity.[22,23]

In order to interpret FFM measurements on organic films, it is necessary to have a model for the contact mechanics. However, a unified model for the mechanics of the tip–sample interaction in FFM is elusive. Fundamental questions remain unanswered. Remarkably, many authors have modelled FFM using Amontons' law (in which the friction force is proportional to the load), despite its being based on a macroscopic, multi-asperity model for sliding contacts. Intuitively, one might expect that single asperity mechanics approaches, such as the Johnson–Kendall–Roberts (JKR) and Derjaguin–Muller–Toporov (DMT) models (in which there is a sub-linear relationship between the friction force and the load), would be a better choice; certainly there are also data that support the use of such models. However, it has been unclear why such different approaches may apparently claim support from experimental evidence. Indeed, some authors have used Amontons' law and single asperity approaches in different papers on similar materials, or even in the same paper, with no better justification than that a particular data set can be fitted most conveniently in a certain way. There have been two notable attempts to resolve this conflict previously. Marti *et al.*[24] and Carpick and Salmeron[3] have suggested that the friction force may be treated as the sum of a pressure-dependent term and an area-dependent shear term. Under certain circumstances, they have argued, a dominant pressure-dependent term may yield an apparently linear friction–load relationship. Hence friction in a nanoscale contact is explained by single asperity models, except in exceptional circumstances. An alternative approach has been proposed by Gao *et al.*[25] They have argued that while the friction force may often vary with the area of contact (an assumption that underpins the use of single asperity approaches), there is no *a priori* reason why this should be the case; a linear friction–load relationship is thus normal, and single asperity mechanics represent a limiting situation where the sliding interaction is dominated by adhesion.

While the role of surface adhesion is dominant in nanoscale molecular contacts, there is currently no clear understanding of the correlation between molecular interactions in single asperity contacts and in the bulk-phase. There is an abundance of data demonstrating that changes in intermolecular bonding influence the sliding contact between tip and surface, but little insight into the mechanistic basis for these correlations. For chemists, the promise of access to quantitative data on intermolecular interactions has been a central motivation for exploring scanning probe techniques.

There is an urgent need to develop a unified approach to understanding data from FFM measurements on molecular systems. Here we attempt to establish a direct link between solution-phase thermodynamics and hydrogen bonding in nanoscale molecular contacts. A distinctive feature of these studies has been the systematic investigation of the correlation between contact mechanics and the composition of the liquid medium. There is some evidence that not only the strengths of adhesion and friction forces, but also the contact mechanics, may be influenced by the nature of the liquid medium.[26–28] Previous work in the field has, in general, paid too little attention to the role of the medium in determining nanoscale tribological phenomena; here we show that by using liquid mixtures with systematically varying composition, the role of interfacial thermodynamics in controlling friction may be made explicit.

2 Experimental

Monolayers were formed on glass slides (Menzel-Gläser 22 mm × 64 mm, # 1.5) that were cleaned with piranha solution (H_2SO_4/H_2O_2, 70 : 30 v/v; caution! piranha solution is a strong oxidizing agent and should be handled with care). The slides and probes were rinsed with deionised water (18.2 MΩ cm) and dried in an oven at 150 °C.

Commercial V-shaped Si_3N_4 AFM probes (Veeco Instruments, Santa Barbara, CA) with a nominal spring constant of 0.06 N m^{-1} were used. These were also cleaned in piranha solution prior to use, because they were found to be heavily contaminated with polydimethylsiloxane (PDMS) contaminant. The probes were supplied packaged in "gel pack", thought to be the source of contamination. Imaging SIMS revealed high levels of PDMS contamination both directly after removal of probes from the packaging, and after deposition of a gold film and over-night immersion in solutions of alkylthiols. The problem of probe contamination has been reported previously by Beebe and co-workers.[29] In the studies reported here, probes that were contaminated with PDMS were found to yield very different, and much less reliable, data than clean probes. Cleaning in piranha solution was found to cause insignificant change in the radius of the tip, and SEM confirmed that there was little evidence for roughening of the tip surface. The SPM community rarely uses surface spectroscopy to characterise probes. The widespread use of gel packs in the supply of SPM probes may mean that a significant fraction of published adhesion measurements are influenced by the presence of PDMS contamination.

Probes and substrates for alkylthiolate SAM formation were coated with a 1 nm Cr layer at a rate of 0.03 nm s^{-1} (Cr chips, 99.99% purity, Agar Scientific), followed by a 10 nm Au layer (Au wire, 99.99% purity, Advent Research Materials Ltd) deposited at 0.03 nm s^{-1} in an Edwards Auto 306 bell jar vacuum coater system.

11-Mercaptoundecanoic acid (MUA), 99% purity, Sigma-Aldrich, 11-mercapto-1-undecanol (MUL), 99% purity, Sigma-Aldrich, and diethoxy-phosphatoethyl-trie-thoxysilane (DPTS), ≥92%, Acros Organics, were used as received. Thiolate monolayers were prepared immediately after gold deposition by immersion of the freshly-coated SFM probes and slides in 1 mM solutions of thiol in degassed ethanol for approximately 18 h at room temperature. Modified probes and slides were rinsed in copious amounts of degassed ethanol and dried in a stream of N_2 gas.

Silane films were prepared by immersion of clean glass slides in a 1 mM solution of DPTS in dry toluene in a Schlenk tube for 48 h. Samples were removed from the tubes, rinsed in toluene and sonicated for a further 10 min in toluene. Subsequently they were rinsed with toluene, acetone and ethanol and were sonicated for another 10 min in ethanol. After having been rinsed again they were dried thoroughly in a stream of nitrogen and placed in a vacuum chamber at 150 °C for 1 h. Once they were slowly cooled down at room temperature under vacuum, they were taken out of the oven and stored in 33 mL sample vials fitted with polyethylene stoppers. The samples were used within 10 days after preparation. Prior to use, they were rinsed with ethanol and thoroughly dried in a stream of nitrogen gas.

n-Heptane (HPLC, Fisher Scientific), ethyl acetate (HPLC, Fisher Scientific), n-hexadecane (99%, Sigma-Aldrich), toluene (HPLC, Fisher Scientific), acetone (HPLC, Fisher Scientific), cis,trans-perfluorodecalin (95%, Sigma-Aldrich), ethanol (HPLC, Fisher Scientific), n-decane (≥99% Sigma Aldrich) and n-dodecane (≥99% Sigma Aldrich) were all used as received and injected into the AFM fluid cell using a disposable 1 mL syringe.

Calibration of normal forces was carried out in a two-step procedure. The normal spring constant of the cantilever was obtained from the power spectral density of its thermal fluctuations in the resonant frequency domain, at room temperature, according to the method introduced by Hutter and Bechhoefer.[30] This was achieved with the use of a routine implemented contained within the Digital Instruments Picoforce software, and a correction factor of 0.764.[31-33] The normal photodetector sensitivity (nm V^{-1}) was acquired from the slope of the linear part of a force curve at the repulsive regime, obtained on the flat regions of a silicon calibration grating (TGF11, Mikromash, Eesti, Tallinn, Estonia). Calibration of lateral forces was achieved using the 'wedge calibration method', introduced by Ogletree *et al.*,[34] as developed by Varenberg *et al.*[35] who took adhesion into consideration. A commercially available silicon grating was used, the TGF11 (Mikromash), while the method was applied *in situ*. The tip radius of curvature was determined by imaging of the TGG01 (Mikromash) calibration grating at 0° and 90° scanning angles. The geometric mean radius of the tip was calculated by fit of a circle at the top of each image's profile and application of the Zenhausern model of deconvolution.[36] All calibration procedures, as well as the tip radius determination, were performed right after the experiments so as to reduce the possibility of probe contamination. Tip radii were found to be in the range 61–68 nm. At the loads used here, there was no evidence for plastic deformation of any of the SAMs studied.

Force curves were obtained at 200 locations on each sample, while two samples of each monolayer were examined with two different cantilevers in each environment. The pull-off forces were extracted from the unloading force curves using Carpick's Toolbox.[37] For friction measurements the instrument was operated in contact mode with the long cantilever axis perpendicular to the fast scanning direction (2 Hz scanning speed), over areas of 1×1 μm^2. The normal applied load was being decreased stepwise in increments of *ca.* 0.7 nN, varying from *ca.* +15 nN down until the tip broke out of contact with the sample, while the friction force was recorded in each step. Friction forces were determined from trace–retrace loops acquired along single lines; the mean signals in opposing directions were subtracted and, subsequently, halved.[1,2] Three to five different locations were examined on each sample, while two samples and two different cantilevers were used in each environment. The lateral deflection was carefully adjusted so that it was zero with the tip out of contact with the surface prior to commencing data acquisition.

3   Results and discussion

Dielectric properties of the medium

In previous studies, it was reported that poly(ethylene terephthalate) and SAM surfaces yielded large adhesion forces, and fitted JKR mechanics, in perfluorodecalin, while in ethanol, small adhesion forces were measured and the friction–load relationship was found to be linear. It was hypothesised that because all of the contributions to the van der Waals interaction depend upon the dielectric constant of the medium, there may be a correlation between the adhesion force and the relative dielectric constant of the liquid in which measurements were made. Heptane–acetone mixtures and heptane–ethyl acetate mixtures yield smooth relationships between the liquid composition and the relative dielectric constant, enabling the relationship between the pull-off force and the liquid phase dielectric constant to be explored in a systematic fashion. Fig. 1 shows data for carboxylic acid-terminated probes and surfaces in a range of liquid mixtures and for a selection of pure liquids.[38] It is clear that there is a large number of liquids with very different dielectric constants that yield very similar, small adhesion forces, and a number of liquids with very similar dielectric constants that yield widely differing adhesion forces. It seems unlikely that variations in the adhesion force for hydrogen bonding interactions in different media may be explained in terms of the dielectric properties of the medium.

     This journal is © The Royal Society of Chemistry 2012

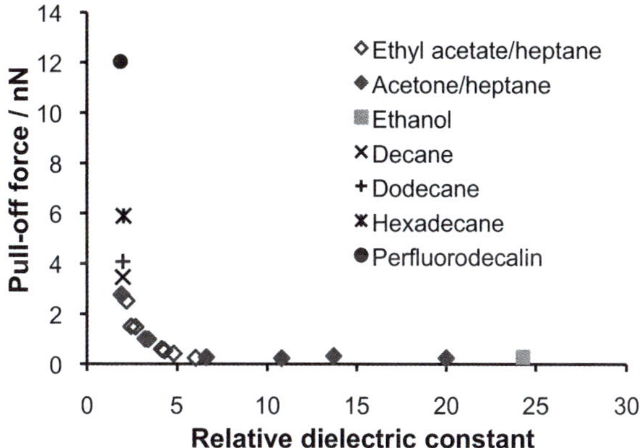

Fig. 1 Variation in the pull-off force with the relative dielectric constant for liquid mixtures containing heptane and a more polar solvent (ethyl acetate, open blue diamonds, or acetone, filled red diamonds), together with data for pure ethanol and four non-polar liquids. The error bars are smaller than the size of the symbols used to mark points. Reproduced from Busuttil et al.[38]

Hydrogen bond thermodynamics

In single asperity mechanics models, the adhesion force is determined by the tip radius and the work of adhesion W at the tip–sample contact ($F_a = 2\pi RW$ in the DMT model and $3/2\pi RW$ in the JKR model). At the tip–sample contact, there is a three-phase equilibrium, and the solvent interactions with the surfaces of the tip and the substrate might reasonably be expected to influence the magnitude of γ. It was hypothesised that the thermodynamics of solvent–surface interactions may determine the pull-off force.

Hydrogen bond interactions were modelled using an approach developed by one of us (CAH) in which the solvation state of a molecule is determined, at the molecular level, by the relative concentrations and the polarities of the molecules in the surrounding medium. For a hydrogen bonding interaction between a donor (D) and an acceptor (A), in a solvent that is a mixture of a hydrocarbon (S1) and a hydrogen bond acceptor (S2), the equilibrium constant K_a for the formation of a 1 : 1 association complex is given by:

$$K_a = \frac{K_1}{1 + K_S[\text{polar solvent}]} \tag{1}$$

where K_S is the equilibrium constant for solvation of D by S2 in solvent S1. Measurements in the bulk phase using a variety of techniques have provided strong support for this approach. Moreover, it is possible to estimate values for both K_1 and K_s based on the polarities of the functional groups. The free energy of interaction is calculated as the sum of the pairwise interactions between solute and solvent:

$$-RT\ln K_1 = -(\alpha - \alpha_{S1})(\beta - \beta_{S1}) + 6 \text{ kJ mol}^{-1} \tag{2}$$

$$-RT\ln K_S = -(\alpha - \alpha_{S1})(\beta_{S2} - \beta_{S1}) + 6 \text{ kJ mol}^{-1} \tag{3}$$

Here, α is the H-bond donor parameter for D, β is the H-bond acceptor parameter for A, α_{S1}, β_{S1} and β_{S2} are the corresponding solvent H-bond parameters,[39] and the constant of 6 kJ mol^{-1} is the free energy penalty for formation of a bimolecular complex between two solutes.

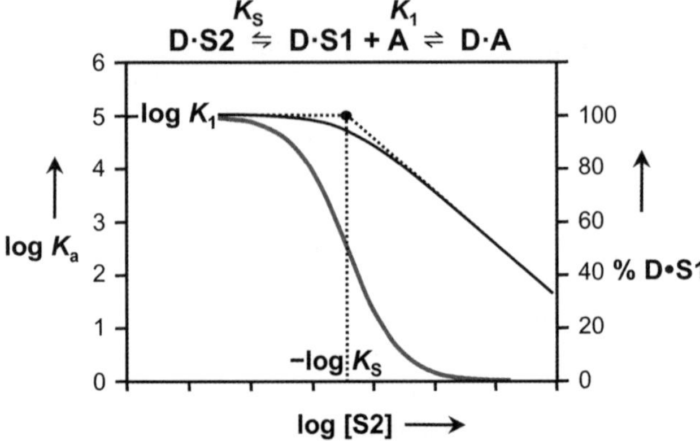

Fig. 2 Black line: variation in $\log K_a$ for the formation of a 1 : 1 complex between two solutes, D (a H-bond donor) and A (a H-bond acceptor) in mixtures of a non-polar solvent (S1) and a polar solvent (S2) that is a strong H-bond acceptor but a weak H-bond donor. Grey line: variation in solvation state of D (% D•S1).

Fig. 2 shows the general form of the relationship between $\log K_a$ and the concentration of the polar component in a binary liquid mixture. It can be seen that for concentrations of the polar solvent smaller than K_S, the free energy of interaction is invariant with the composition of the medium. However, as the concentration of the polar solvent increases above K_S, the free energy of interaction decreases linearly. This decrease in the interaction free energy results from the increasing solvation of the surface by the hydrogen bond acceptor S2 in solution.

Adhesion measurements

Four systems were investigated: symmetrical interactions between a tip and a surface each coated with either a carboxylic acid-terminated (mercaptoundecanoic acid, MUA) or a hydroxyl terminated monolayer (mercaptoundecanol, HUT), in heptane/acetone and heptane/ethyl acetate mixtures; and an asymmetric interaction between a hydrogen bond acceptor (DPTS) and a hydroxyl-functionalised probe (acting as a hydrogen bond donor, only) in heptane/acetone mixtures.

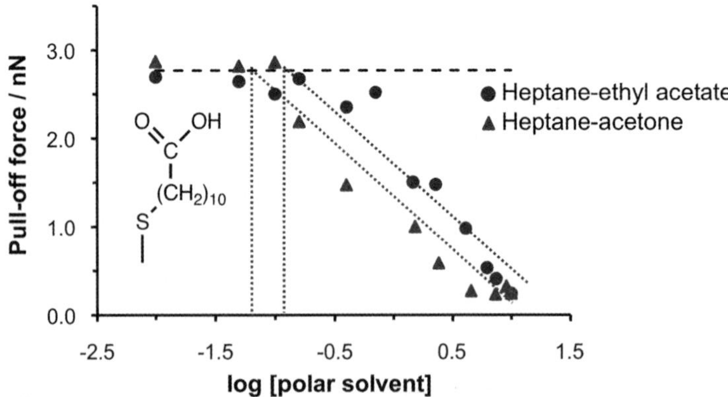

Fig. 3 Variation in the pull-off force with log[polar solvent], where [polar solvent] is the concentration of polar solvent for an MUA functionalised probe interacting with an MUA functionalised surface. The horizontal line corresponds to the pull-off force in pure heptane. The error bars are smaller than the size of the symbols used to mark points. Reproduced from Busuttil *et al.*[38]

The adhesion forces are shown in Fig. 3 for MUA–MUA interactions as a function of the composition of the liquid medium. Data for DPTS–HUT interactions have been submitted for publication elsewhere.[40] For all of the systems studied, the relationship was in good agreement with the general form of behaviour shown in Fig. 2. At low concentrations of the polar solvent, the adhesion force was invariant with composition, and equal to the value measured in pure hydrocarbon. At higher concentrations of the polar solvent, the adhesion force was found to decrease with the concentration of the hydrogen bond acceptor in the liquid medium, consistent with the hypothesis that solvation of the interacting surfaces leads to a reduction in the free energy of interaction. The transition from concentration-invariance to concentration-dependence occurred at similar liquid compositions for heptane/acetone and heptane/ethyl acetate mixtures, despite the fact that the dielectric constant of acetone is over three times that of ethyl acetate. However, the hydrogen bond acceptor characteristics of the two liquids are quite similar, confirming that the solvation behaviour of the liquid medium plays a more significant role in determining the magnitude of the pull-off force than do its dielectric properties.

If our hypothesis is correct, the transition from concentration-invariance to concentration-dependence in the adhesion force should correspond to K_S. This can be readily tested using the pull-off force data. Table 1 shows values for K_S that have been calculated using eqn (1)–(3), and experimental values, determined by finding the intersection between the horizontal and sloped portions of the graphs shown in Fig. 3 and submitted for publication elsewhere.[40] Given that the range of concentrations covered spans four orders of magnitude, the agreement is remarkably close. These data suggest very strongly that the pull-off force for surfaces functionalised with hydrogen-bonding functional groups is determined by the thermodynamics of the three-phase equilibrium at the tip–sample contact. Large adhesion forces are measured in media in which the tip and sample are not solvated; however, as the degree of solvation increases, the adhesion force is reduced.

Contact mechanics

Friction–load plots were acquired for all four systems. Fig. 4 shows some representative data. In pure polar solvents, linear friction–load relationships were observed, consistent with Amontons' law:

$$F_F = \mu F_N \tag{4}$$

where F_F is the friction force, F_N is the normal force and μ is the coefficient of friction. When these were fitted by linear regression, the slopes were found to pass through the origin, or close to it. The small positive intercept with the vertical axis observed for the data acquired in pure acetone and shown in Fig. 4(b) is attributed to uncertainty in the position of zero in the lateral photodetector signal. In general, we have found that for SAM systems that exhibit linear friction–load behaviour, the slope to the friction–load plot tends to pass through the origin, provided the cantilever deflection is properly zeroed at the outset. In the literature, there

Table 1 Equilibrium constants, K_S, calculated using eqn (1)–(3) and determined experimentally from plots of the pull-off force against the solution composition

	COOH in heptane/ ethyl acetate	COOH in heptane/ acetone	HUT in heptane/ acetone	DPTS in heptane/ acetone
Calculated value/mol dm^{-3}	0.07	0.05	0.30	0.30
From pull-off data/mol dm^{-3}	0.14	0.06	0.28	0.40

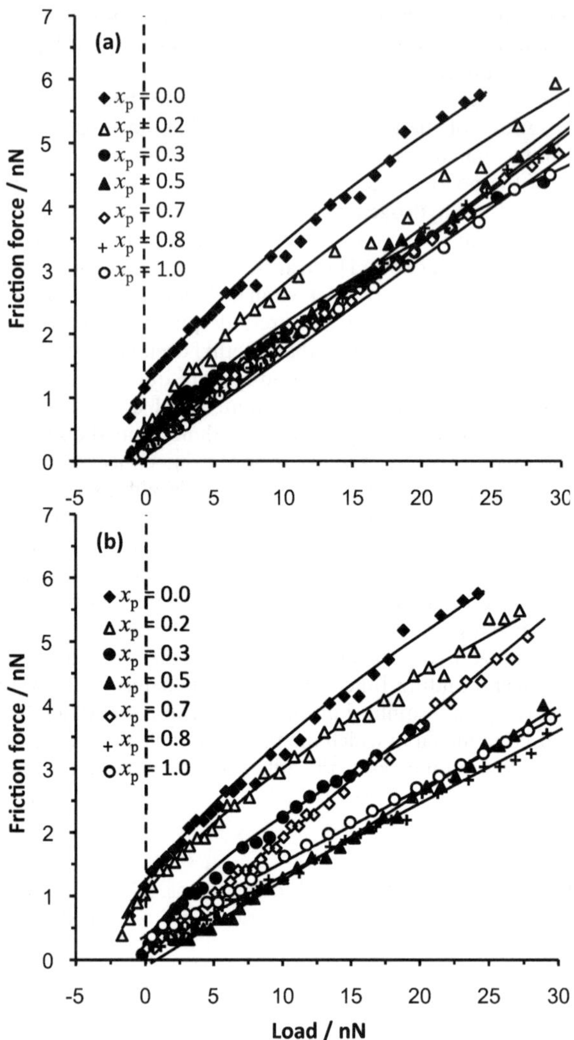

Fig. 4 Friction–load plots in (a) ethyl acetate/heptane mixtures and (b) acetone/heptane mixtures of varying composition, where mole fraction $x_p = 0$ corresponds to pure heptane. The error bars are smaller than the size of the symbols used to mark points. Reproduced from Busuttil *et al.*[38]

has been much discussion of the non-zero intercepts observed in friction–load plots for some SAM systems. However, assuming that the very real possibility of calibration errors has been eliminated, it is the considered view of the authors that large, positive intercepts with the friction force axis reflect the onset of behaviour that is better described by single asperity mechanics (see below).

As heptane was added to the liquid medium there was a change in behaviour. For approximately $1:1$ mixtures of acetone and heptane and of ethyl acetate and heptane, the behaviour was found to be non-linear. The friction–load plots were analyzed using the General Transition Equation (GTE) developed by Carpick *et al.*[41] Analysis using the GTE yields a "transition parameter", α_{GTE}, that may be used to gauge whether DMT or JKR mechanics fits the behaviour best. In general, values of α_{GTE} close to zero were obtained, suggesting that the data fitted DMT mechanics.

The transition from linear to non-linear behaviour corresponds to a decrease in the extent of solvation of the hydrogen bond-forming groups at the sample surface, according to the thermodynamic calculations. For fully, or nearly fully, solvated surfaces, linear behaviour was observed. However, non-linear friction–load relationships were observed for liquid mixtures in which the surface was not expected to be fully solvated. Solvated surfaces yielded weak adhesion forces, and as the surface became increasingly less well solvated, as a consequence of the addition of heptane to the medium, the adhesion force was found to increase. The most natural explanation for these observations is that a linear friction–load relationship reflects an anomalous situation in which the surface is very highly solvated by molecules in the liquid medium. For other circumstances, single asperity contact mechanics were found to fit the data very well.

It is notable that in all cases studied to date, with the exception of perfluorodecalin, it has been DMT mechanics, and not JKR mechanics, that have been found to fit the data. Perfluorodecalin yielded extremely large pull-off forces (over twice the magnitude of those measured in heptane). However, for the other liquids studied, the "hard-contact, weak adhesion" regime associated with the DMT model appears to apply. It is significant, in this context, to note the prevalence with which JKR mechanics have been used in the literature to model tip–sample contacts in AFM. While it cannot be excluded that the mechanical analysis of pull-off and sliding phenomena requires a different analysis, it seems unlikely. Previous applications of the JKR model have, in general, been founded largely on the assumption that it was the appropriate model to use, rather than any empirical data. An advantage of measuring forces in liquid mixtures is that by controlling the medium in which interactions occur, one is able to test hypotheses concerning the tip–sample interaction in a more rigorous fashion.

Although it appears surprising that friction–load relationships may be either linear or sublinear depending on the solvation state of the surface, it was postulated some time ago by others that it may be appropriate to treat the friction force as the sum of a pressure-dependent term and an area-dependent shear term:[3,24]

$$F_F = \mu F_N + \sigma A \tag{5}$$

Here, A is the area of contact and σ is the surface shear strength. In DMT mechanics, the area of contact between a sphere and a plane is given by:

$$A = \pi \left(\frac{R}{K}\right)^{\frac{2}{3}} (F_N + 4\pi\gamma R)^{\frac{2}{3}} \tag{6}$$

where R is the radius of the probe, K is the modulus, γ is the surface free energy, and the term $(4\pi\gamma R)$ is equal in magnitude to F_a. Combining this with eqn (5) we arrive at:

$$F_F = \mu(F_N + F_a) + \left(\frac{\sigma}{K^{2/3}}\right)\pi R(F_N + F_a)^{2/3} \tag{7}$$

The DMT model effectively applies a correction to the load that results from adhesive interactions. Eqn (7) applies the same correction to the load-dependent friction term too, in the interests of consistency. In the limit of low adhesion, the shear term is expected to become vanishingly small and the load-dependent term is expected to dominate, yielding a linear friction–load relationship and a zero intercept with the friction axis in a friction–load plot. As the degree of surface solvation is reduced, and the adhesive force increases, the area-dependent shear term is expected to become dominant and the friction–load relationship to become non-linear.

To test this explanation further, experimental friction–load data were modelled using eqn (7). The modulus was not known, and for monolayer samples may be difficult to determine. Hence the fitting of the second term on the right-hand side of eqn (7) yielded a parameter $\sigma/K^{2/3}$. Nevertheless, assuming that the moduli of the SAMs do not change with the composition of the liquid medium, this quantity should be proportional to the surface shear strength. The data are shown in Fig. 5(a), as a function of the pull-off force F_a, for carboxylic acid-terminated SAMs. There is a very clear correlation between the surface shear strength and the pull-off force: $\sigma/K^{2/3}$ increases with the pull-off force. This is exactly as might be expected for the area-dependent shear term in eqn (5), which reflects the energy dissipated in the shearing of adhesive interactions between the tip and surface as the probe is scanned across the sample. The limiting value of the surface shear strength, in pure heptane, was *ca.* six times larger than the value obtained in pure acetone.

It is striking that for both heptane/acetone mixtures and heptane/ethyl acetate mixtures, the coefficient of friction was invariant with the strength of adhesion between the tip and the sample. Very similar results were obtained in studies of HUT and DPTS films.[40] For polar SAMs on Au the value of μ was *ca.* 0.1 for all of the hydrogen bonding systems studied, but for dodecanthiol SAMs on Au, the value of μ was *ca.* half this. For DPTS films, the coefficient of friction was significantly larger than those of the alkylthiolate SAMs.

Much previous literature has reported that polar and non-polar SAMs yield different coefficients of friction. For example, detailed quantitative studies have

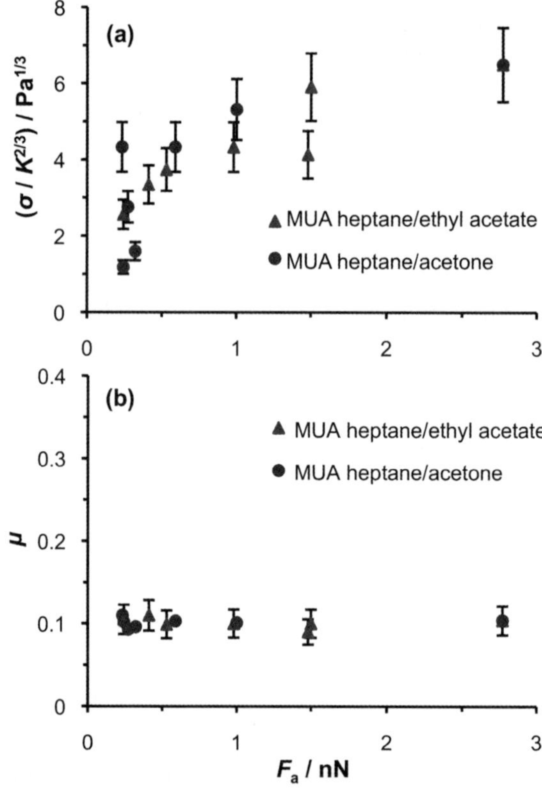

Fig. 5 Results of fitting of friction–load data to eqn (7). (a) Variation in the surface shear strength with F_a for carboxylic acid terminated SAMs in contact with a carboxylic acid functionalised probe in heptane/ethyl acetate and heptane/acetone mixtures. (b) Variation in μ with F_a for the same systems.

been reported on the kinetics of surface reactions, and good evidence has been provided for a close correlation between the variation in the coefficient of friction and changes in surface composition measured by X-ray photoelectron spectroscopy.[23] The explanation that has been invoked previously is that the AFM probe adheres more strongly to polar surfaces than to non-polar ones, and that this gives rise to a higher rate of energy dissipation and hence a larger coefficient of friction. However, the data in Fig. 5 refute such an explanation: despite very large changes in the strength of the pull-off force, the polar SAMs show no differences in their coefficients of friction.

There are two alternative explanations for these observations. First, it is possible that polar solvent molecules physisorb strongly to polar SAMs, forming an organised surface boundary layer. The shearing of this boundary layer gives rise to the load-dependent term in eqn (5), in a molecular equivalent of a ploughing process. This is certainly plausible under circumstances where the surface is highly solvated, but seems unlikely in other media where the surface is weakly solvated, when the friction coefficient remains unchanged. Second, many polar materials form intra-film non-covalent interactions. There is evidence for strong lateral stabilisation of carboxylic acid and hydroxyl terminated SAMs on gold through hydrogen bonding.[42] Kim and Houston demonstrated that odd and even length carboxylic acid terminated SAMs yielded different frictional behaviour,[20] and that this could be explained in terms of their differing propensities to form intra-monolayer hydrogen bonds. Brewer *et al.* studied the rate-dependence of friction forces in a variety of SAMs with polar and non-polar terminal groups, and suggested that intra-monolayer hydrogen bonding accounted for the unexpected velocity-dependence of friction forces for carboxylic acid and hydroxyl terminated SAMs.[12] The smaller coefficient of friction observed for dodecanthiol SAMs[40] is thus attributable to the absence of lateral hydrogen bonding interactions within the monolayer.

These explanations are consistent with the attribution of the load-dependent components of eqn (5) and (7) to molecular deformations. Carpick and co-workers have suggested that "molecular ploughing" phenomena may occur in monolayers.[43,44] While such processes would not necessarily involve plastic deformation as might ordinarily be expected,[45] they would involve the non-recoverable dissipation of energy in molecular deformations, *via* mechanisms like those modelled by Harrison and co-workers.[46–49] We hypothesise that the load-dependent terms in eqn (5) and (7) are due to such ploughing phenomena. It is significant that while the adhesion forces measured for the DPTS films were smaller than those measured for the HUT SAMs, the coefficient of friction was much larger. The smaller pull-off force for DPTS may be attributed to the lower density of hydrogen bond acceptors at the surface of the disorganised silane film than is the case for the close-packed alkylthiolate films. This same disorganisation would be expected to facilitate more extensive energy dissipation through molecular ploughing mechanisms, however, and this appears to be reflected in the much larger coefficient of friction observed.

Mixed surfaces

It is tempting to conclude that the type of contact mechanics is determined by the size of the pull-off force. To examine this hypothesis further, mixed self-assembled monolayers were formed by carrying out partial photo-oxidation of alkylthiolate SAMs. In an earlier study,[17] it was demonstrated that while single component SAMs exhibit symmetrical distributions of pull-off forces, mixed SAMs formed by the coadsorption of thiols from solution exhibit poorly defined distributions of forces. These observations were attributed to the formation of phase-separated domains of the order of a few nm (or perhaps 10s of nm in size).[17] However, it was conjectured that exposure of SAMs to UV light from a frequency-doubled argon ion laser would cause photo-oxidation at random locations on the sample surface.[50,51] On immersion of the sample in a solution of a contrasting thiol in ethanol, the oxidation products would be displaced from the surface by the second thiol, leading to the formation of a mixed surface.

Fig. 6 shows the variation in the advancing water contact angle with the time of UV exposure for SAMs of MUA that have been immersed in a solution of dodeca-nethiol (DDT) following exposure. It can be seen that the contact angle increases as a function of exposure, reaching 90° after 30 J cm^{-2} exposure (slightly smaller than is measured for a SAM formed on a clean gold surface because the solution-phase displacement process tends to yield a more disordered film than is formed by adsorption onto clean gold). Further exposure yielded little increase in the contact angle beyond this value. As the polar, hydroxyl terminated thiolates are increasingly photo-oxidised at increasing exposures, the fraction of the monolayer replaced by DDT in the solution-phase immersion step increases, until eventually the entire MUA acid film has been replaced.

To examine whether phase separation was occurring, histograms of adhesion forces were acquired. Fig. 7 shows representative data, after exposures of 10 and 20 J cm^{-2} (sufficient to cause extensive but still only partial photo-oxidation and replacement of MUA). In both cases, a smooth Poisson distribution of pull-off forces is obtained, in contrast to the irregular distributions reported for mixed SAMs formed in a solution-phase process,[17] giving confidence that the mixed SAMs consist of a random mixture of methyl and hydroxyl terminated adsorbates.

Pull-off forces were measured in heptane, using a carboxylic acid terminated probe, as a function of the UV exposure time (Fig. 8). Heptane was selected as the medium because it yielded a larger free energy of interaction than did the polar solvents. It can be seen from Fig. 8 that as photo-oxidation progresses, the pull-off force declines from the value of 2.77 nN measured in pure heptane to less than 1 nN at an exposure of 1 J cm^{-2}, and *ca.* 0.5 nN at an exposure of 10 J cm^{-2}. This dramatic reduction in the pull-off force is consistent with the change in composition indicated by the increase in the advancing water contact angle.

The pull-off force measured after an exposure of 10 J cm^{-2}, 0.5 nN, was similar to the pull-off forces reported previously for MUA SAMs in liquids that were rich in acetone/ethyl acetate, *i.e.* media in which the surface was expected to be highly solvated. In heptane, however, there will be negligible solvation of any carboxylic acid groups present at the surface; the carboxylic acid groups are present at very low abundance, rather than being "blocked" by bound solvent molecules. For the single-component SAMs in heptane/acetone mixtures that yielded similarly low pull-off forces, linear (or transitional) friction–load relationships were observed.

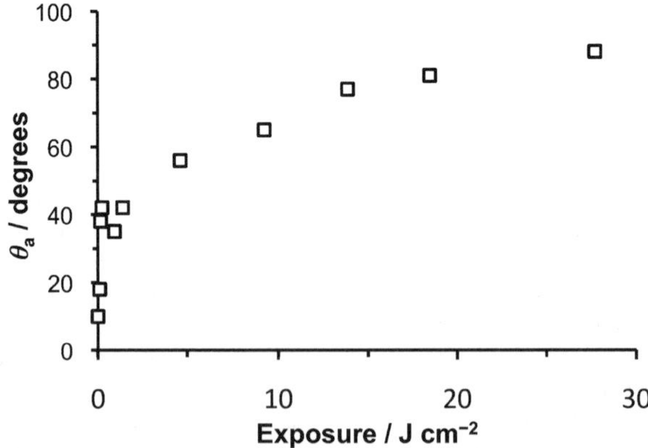

Fig. 6 Variation in the advancing water contact angle of mercaptoundecanoic acid SAMs with UV exposure time, following immersion in a solution of dodecanethiol in ethanol.

 This journal is © The Royal Society of Chemistry 2012

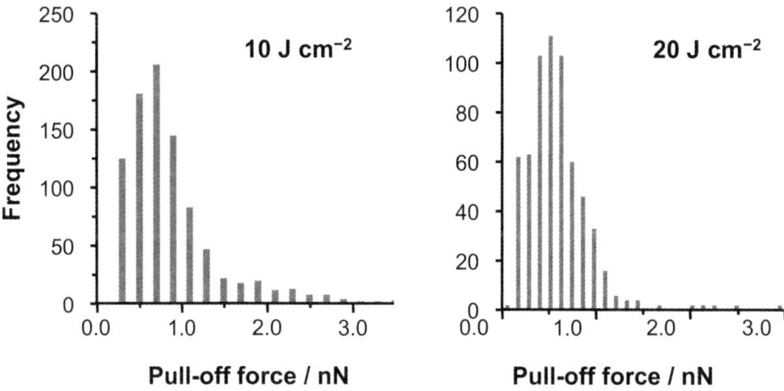

Fig. 7 Histograms of pull-off forces measured for SAMs of mercaptoundecanoic acid on Au following exposure to UV light for different times and immersion in a solution of dodecanethiol.

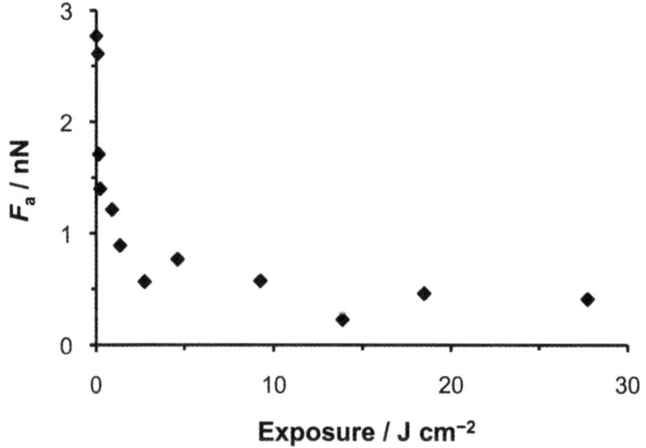

Fig. 8 Variation in the pull-off force with UV exposure for mercaptoundecanoic acid films following immersion in a solution of dodecanethiol.

Friction–load relationships were measured for the mixed monolayer samples in heptane. Fig. 9 shows data for three samples, that have been subjected to UV exposures of 14, 18 and 28 J cm^{-2}. For all three systems, non-linear friction–load relationships were observed. Fitting of the data using the GTE suggested that they were consistent with DMT mechanics; the curves shown in Fig. 9 are DMT fits to the data. The longest exposure yielded an adhesion force similar to that measured in pure acetone. However, a linear friction load relationship was not observed. These data indicate that the absolute magnitude of the adhesion force is not the most significant factor in determining the type of mechanics observed; it is the thermodynamics of the interaction between the probe and the surface.

For the high exposures used in preparing these samples, precise quantification of the surface composition is difficult. Normally X-ray photoelectron spectroscopy (XPS) would be the method of choice for quantification of surface composition, but its sensitivity is *ca.* 0.1 atomic %. We must therefore speculate a little concerning the sublinear friction–load relationships in Fig. 9. If the surface density of carboxylic acid groups is as low as *ca.* 1 : 100, a sweep of the AFM probe across a region 1 μm wide during a friction measurement will yield 20 binding sites with which the probe may interact (assuming an alkyl chain diameter of 0.5 nm). In heptane, where the

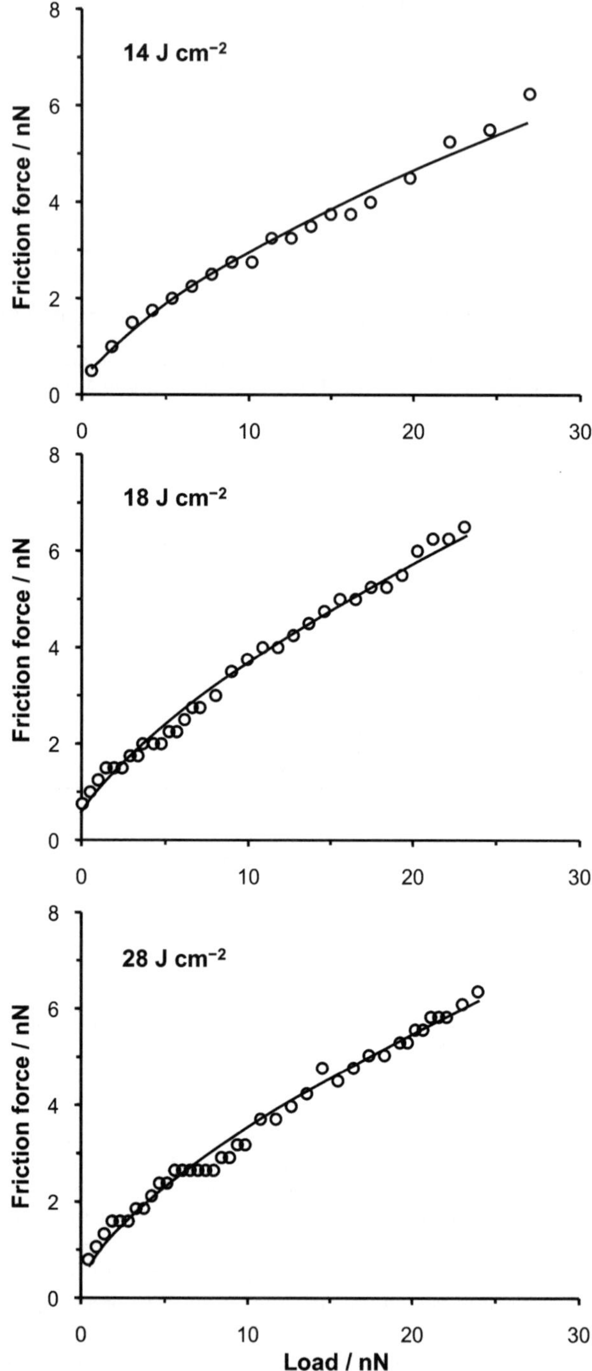

Fig. 9 Friction–load relationships for mixed SAMs formed by UV-modification of MUA SAMs at exposures between 14 and 28 J cm^{-2} and subsequent immersion in dodecanethiol solutions.

carboxylic acid groups are not solvated, the interaction is a strong one at the molecular level, and even at such low concentrations, the strong unbinding thermodynamics influence the shear force sufficiently to yield a non-zero shear term in eqn (7) and render the overall friction–load relationship sublinear.

These data suggest that nanoscale molecular contacts may conveniently be analysed using the concepts of single asperity contact mechanics. Given that monolayers are rather thin (typically less than 2 nm thick), the volume that can be perturbed by molecular ploughing effects is extremely small and the amount of energy dissipated in this way is rather modest. The tip–sample interaction is thus dominated by adhesion in all cases save those where the surface is highly solvated. The free energy of interaction between the tip and surface in the presence of the liquid medium is proportional to the interaction force, consistent with the usual approaches to single asperity contact mechanics, in which the interfacial tension is used to calculate the adhesion force. The most significant advance in the present study is the use of liquid mixtures as the media in which interactions are measured, thus enabling these adhesion forces to be varied in a controlled fashion.

While monolayers have finite depth, and offer few pathways for energy dissipation in molecular ploughing, polymer brushes present much thicker films. Recent work in the authors' laboratories has addressed the tribological behaviour of films of poly(2-(methacryloyloxy)ethylphosphorylcholine) (PMPC) brushes. In methanol, which solvates the polymer strongly, adhesion is weak and a linear friction–load relationship results. In propanol, the brush structure is collapsed, and the tip–sample interaction is dominated by ploughing, leading to a linear friction–load relationship. PMPC brushes exhibit co-nonsolvency behaviour in 90 : 10 ethanol : water mixtures, undergoing a collapse that yields a linear friction–load relationship and a very large coefficient of friction because of the large number of pathways available for energy dissipation.[52] However, in pure water, when the brush layer is solvated, a non-linear friction–load relationship is observed. Water solvates the brush less well than does methanol, however, and while the mean free energy of interaction per repeat unit is small, force curves suggest that the AFM probe is able to penetrate deep into the brush layer; the area of contact may be very large, therefore, yielding a substantial interaction. Under these conditions, JKR mechanics were found to apply. Such studies may help to illuminate the connection between the DMT and JKR regimes, with the brushes offering a convenient model for the soft-contact regime where the SAMs that have been the principal focus of the present work represent the hard-contact regime that is better modelled by the DMT theory.

4   Conclusions

A rigorous approach to the thermodynamics of non-covalent interactions is required to address the mechanics of nanoscale molecular contacts. The use of liquid mixtures for experimental measurements enables careful comparison between tribological observations and thermodynamic data. Based on the work reported here, we can suggest the following features that a unified model for the mechanics of nanoscale molecular contacts should exhibit.

1. The friction force is the sum of load-dependent and area-dependent terms.

2. The load-dependent term dominates in the limit of very low adhesion (for example, when the surface is highly solvated). It results from "molecular ploughing" phenomena – the non-recoverable dissipation of energy in molecular conformational changes.

3. Under "normal" conditions, a non-linear friction–load relationship is expected.

4. A coefficient of friction may be associated with the load-dependent term. This constant is invariant with the strength of tip–sample adhesion, and predominantly reflects energy dissipation in tip-induced molecular conformational change.

5. The area-dependent term is strongly dependent on the strength of tip–sample adhesion. It is the product of the surface shear strength and the area of contact.

6. "Strength of adhesion" needs to be understood in thermodynamic terms: even small densities of hydrogen bond-forming functional groups at a surface are capable of causing a transition from a linear to a sublinear friction–load relationship.

7. The pull-off force and the surface shear strength are proportional to the free energy of interaction of the functional groups attached to the tip and surface in the medium selected.

8. Thermodynamic quantities, such as the equilibrium constant for the solvation of the surface by a hydrogen bond acceptor in solution, may be determined from analysis of plots of either F_a or σ against the composition of the medium.

A number of questions still need to be resolved. First, if the "coefficient of friction" is invariant with the pull-off force, it may be useful to re-evaluate some of the large body of work that has been published that correlates μ with the surface composition. Viewed as a molecular ploughing parameter, it may provide valuable insights into surface molecular organisation. Second, the conditions under which the transition from DMT to JKR type behaviour need to be identified. As noted here, studies of polymer brushes may be helpful in this regard. For example, is there a continuum of behaviour or is there a sharper transition? Measurements for single component monolayers yielded JKR behaviour in perfluorodecalin. However, caution must be exercised in specifying a threshold for the transition as an adhesion force, given that for mixed monolayers, DMT behaviour is observed where there are very low densities of hydrogen bonding functional groups.

Acknowledgements

The authors thank EPSRC (Grant EP/039999/1) for financial support.

References

1 R. Overney and E. Meyer, *MRS Bull.*, 1993, 26–34.
2 S. Grafstrom, M. Neitzert, T. hagen, J. Ackerman, R. Neumann, O. Probst and M. Wortge, *Nanotechnology*, 1993, **4**, 143–151.
3 R. W. Carpick and M. Salmeron, *Chem. Rev.*, 1997, **97**, 1163–1194.
4 E. Gnecco, R. Bennewitz, T. Gyalog and E. Meyer, *J. Phys.: Condens. Matter*, 2001, **13**, R619–R642.
5 T. Nakagawa, K. Ogana, T. Kurumizawa and S. Ozaki, *Jpn. J. Appl. Phys.*, 1993, **32**, L294–L296.
6 C. D. Frisbie, L. F. Rozsnyai, A. Noy, M. S. Wrighton and C. M. Lieber, *Science*, 1994, **265**, 2071–2074.
7 D. V. Vezenov, A. Noy and P. Ashby, *J. Adhes. Sci. Technol.*, 2005, **19**, 313–364.
8 E. W. van der Vegte and G. Hadziioannou, *Langmuir*, 1997, **13**, 4357–4368.
9 H. I. Kim, T. Koini, T. R. Lee and S. S. Perry, *Langmuir*, 1997, **13**, 7192–7196.
10 J. E. Houston, C. M. Doelling, T. K. Vanderlick, Y. Hu, G. Scoles, I. Wenzl and T. R. Lee, *Langmuir*, 2005, **21**, 3926–3932.
11 H. I. Kim, M. Graupe, O. Oloba, T. Koini, S. Imaduddin, T. R. Lee and S. S. Perry, *Langmuir*, 1999, **15**, 3179–3185.
12 N. J. Brewer, B. D. Beake and G. J. Leggett, *Langmuir*, 2001, **17**, 1970–1974.
13 D. V. Vezenov, A. Noy, L. F. Rozsnyai and C. M. Lieber, *J. Am. Chem. Soc.*, 1997, **119**, 2006–2015.
14 M. T. McDermott, J.-B. D. Green and M. D. Porter, *Langmuir*, 1997, **13**, 2504–2510.
15 B. D. Beake and G. J. Leggett, *Langmuir*, 2000, **16**, 735–739.
16 W. A. Hayes, H. Kim, X. Yue, S. S. Perry and C. Shannon, *Langmuir*, 1997, **13**, 2511–2518.
17 N. J. Brewer and G. J. Leggett, *Langmuir*, 2004, **20**, 4109–4115.
18 E. W. van der Vegte, A. Subbotin, G. Hadziioannou, P. R. Ashton and J. A. Preece, *Langmuir*, 2000, **16**, 3249–3256.
19 T. T. Foster, M. R. Alexander, G. J. Leggett and E. McAlpine, *Langmuir*, 2006, **22**, 9254–9259.
20 H. I. Kim and J. E. Houston, *J. Am. Chem. Soc.*, 2000, **122**, 12045–12046.
21 J. E. Houston and H. I. Kim, *Acc. Chem. Res.*, 2002, **35**, 547–553.
22 K. S. L. Chong, S. Sun and G. J. Leggett, *Langmuir*, 2005, **21**, 3903–3909.
23 T. J. Whittle and G. J. Leggett, *Langmuir*, 2009, **25**, 9182–9188.

24 A. Marti, G. Hähner and N. D. Spencer, *Langmuir*, 1995, **11**, 4632–4635.
25 J. Gao, W. D. Luedtke, D. Gourdon, M. Ruths, J. N. Israelachvili and U. Landman, *J. Phys. Chem. B*, 2004, **108**, 3410–3425.
26 C. R. Hurley and G. J. Leggett, *Langmuir*, 2006, **22**, 4179–4183.
27 T. J. Colburn and G. J. Leggett, *Langmuir*, 2007, **23**, 4959–4964.
28 M. Ruths, *J. Phys. Chem. B*, 2006, **110**, 2209–2218.
29 Y.-S. Lo, N. D. Huefner, W. S. Chan, P. Dryden, B. Hagenhoff and T. P. Beebe, *Langmuir*, 1999, **15**, 6522–6526.
30 J. L. Hutter and J. Bechhoefer, *Rev. Sci. Instrum.*, 1993, **64**, 1868–1873.
31 H. J. Butt and M. Jaschke, *Nanotechnology*, 1995, **6**, 1–7.
32 R. W. Stark, T. Drobek and W. M. Heckl, *Ultramicroscopy*, 2001, **86**, 207–215.
33 B. Ohler, *Rev. Sci. Instrum.*, 2007, **78**, 063701.
34 D. F. Ogletree, R. W. Carpick and M. Salmeron, *Rev. Sci. Instrum.*, 1996, **67**, 3298–3306.
35 M. Varenberg, I. Etsion and G. Halperin, *Rev. Sci. Instrum.*, 2003, **74**, 3362–3367.
36 F. Zenhausen, M. Adrian, B. T. Heggeler-Bordied, L. M. Eng and P. Descouts, *Scanning*, 1992, **14**, 212–217.
37 Carpick's Toolbox, http://nanoprobenetwork.org/welcome-to-the-carpick-labs-software-toolbox.
38 K. Busuttil, M. Geoghegan, C. A. Hunter and G. J. Leggett, *J. Am. Chem. Soc.*, 2011, **133**, 8625–8632.
39 C. A. Hunter, *Angew. Chem., Int. Ed.*, 2004, **43**, 5310–5324.
40 N. Nikogeorgos, C. A. Hunter and G. J. Leggett, 2011, submitted.
41 R. W. Carpick, D. F. Ogletree and M. Salmeron, *J. Colloid Interface Sci.*, 1999, **211**, 395–400.
42 E. Cooper and G. J. Leggett, *Langmuir*, 1999, **15**, 1024–1032.
43 E. E. Flater, W. R. Ashurst and R. W. Carpick, *Langmuir*, 2007, **23**, 9242–9252.
44 M. J. Brukman, G. O. Marco, T. D. Dunbar, L. D. Boardman and R. W. Carpick, *Langmuir*, 2006, **22**, 3988–3998.
45 F. P. Bowden and D. Tabor, *The Friction and Lubriction of Solids*, Oxford University Press, Oxford, 1950.
46 A. B. Tutein, S. J. Stuart and J. A. Harrison, *J. Phys. Chem. B*, 1999, **103**, 11357–11365.
47 A. B. Tutein, S. J. Stuart and J. A. Harrison, *Langmuir*, 1999, **16**, 291–296.
48 P. T. Mikulski and J. A. Harrison, *J. Am. Chem. Soc.*, 2001, **123**, 6873–6881.
49 P. T. Mikulski, L. A. Herman and J. A. Harrison, *Langmuir*, 2005, **21**, 12197–12206.
50 N. J. Brewer, S. J. Janusz, K. Critchley, S. D. Evans and G. J. Leggett, *J. Phys. Chem. B*, 2005, **109**, 11247–11256.
51 G. J. Leggett, *Chem. Soc. Rev.*, 2006, **35**, 1150–1161.
52 Z. Zhang, A. J. Morse, S. P. Armes, A. L. Lewis, M. Geoghegan and G. J. Leggett, *Langmuir*, 2011, **27**, 2514–2521.

Semi-deterministic chemo-mechanical model of boundary lubrication

Joel Andersson,[a] Roland Larsson,[*a] Andreas Almqvist,[a]
Mattias Grahn[b] and Ichiro Minami[ac]

Received 22nd December 2011, Accepted 1st February 2012
DOI: 10.1039/c2fd00132b

A model for tribofilm growth is developed. The model is used in combination
with numerical contact mechanics tools to enable evaluation of the combined
effects of chemistry and contact mechanics. The model is tuned with experimental
data and is thereafter applied to rough surfaces. The growth of the tribofilm is
evaluated for 3 different contact cases and short-term tribofilm growth behaviour
is analyzed. The results show how tribofilms grow in patches. The model is
expected to be used as a tool for analysis of the interaction between rough
surfaces.

1   Introduction

Boundary lubrication is the lubrication regime where hydrodynamic action is negligible. Only a fraction of the nominal contact area supports the applied load.
Extreme pressures occur at the contacting asperities when surfaces slide relative to
each other. The contact temperature may reach several hundred degrees if contact
time is sufficiently long. The base fluid of the lubricant has an important role even
if it cannot provide hydrodynamic lift and load support. In the boundary lubrication
regime, the base fluid acts a carrier of surface active components (additives) that
adhere to, or react with, the surfaces and form a thin protective layer—*a tribofilm*.
   Fig. 1 shows a snapshot of two surfaces in sliding contact. Three layers are indicated schematically. More precisely, on top of the base material there is an oxide film
and on top of the oxide there is a reacted film. This film is formed from a reaction
between lubricant components and the base material or its oxide. The top layer is
a physically adsorbed, easily sheared, layer.[1]
   Asperities will collide as the surfaces slide and all layers may be sheared off if the
collisions are severe. This will cause scuffing and may give rise to serious surface
damage. The ultimate design of a boundary lubricated system would rely on physical
adsorption only. In such a case, the adsorbed molecules provide sufficient load
carrying capacity without causing any damage to the reacted layers. This is,
however, normally not possible to obtain for engineering surfaces under normal
operating conditions. The successful design of a boundary lubricated system is therefore based on a balance between wear and growth of the reacted layers. It is thus
important to avoid very severe collisions and it is important to have access to lubricant components that can react with surfaces and reform the layers as soon as they
are worn off. The severity of collisions is controlled by surface roughness, sliding
speed and applied load while lubricant-surface reaction kinetics control the growth
of tribofilms.

[a]Division of Machine Elements, Luleå University of Technology, Sweden
[b]Division of Sustainable Process Engineering, Luleå University of Technology, Sweden
[c]Department of Chemistry and Bioengineering, Iwate University, Japan

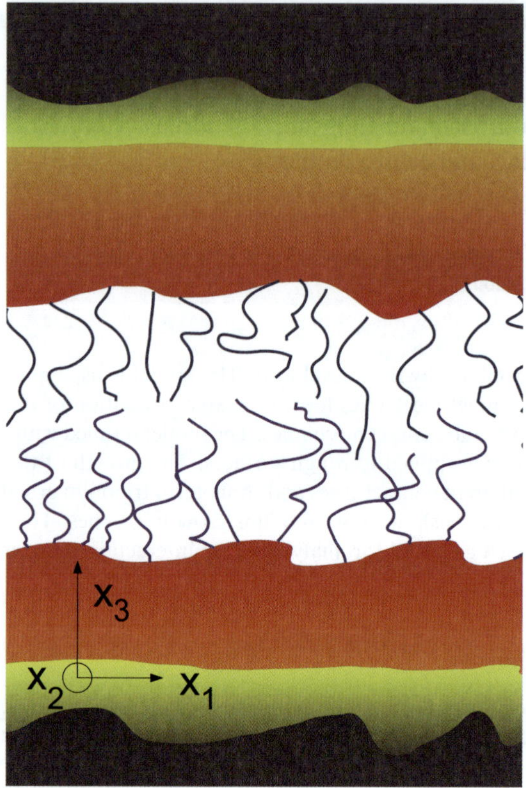

Fig. 1 Two surfaces with 3 layers each are in contact. The base of each surface is the substrate material, steel in this case. An oxide layer has been formed on top of the steel layer. On top of the oxide layer a chemisorbed layer is illustrated. The spaghetti like strings on top illustrates a physisorbed easy-to-shear layer. Coordinate directions are indicated, with x_1 representing sliding direction.

The vast majority of boundary lubrication studies are experimental and surface analytical and there are many thousands of publications from the past 50 years. Typically, the growth and removal of the reacted layers are studied first by employing tribotests with subsequent (post-mortem) surface analysis using techniques such as Scanning Electron Microscopy (SEM) and X-ray Photoelectron Spectroscopy (XPS), see for instance Spikes.[2] The outcome is detailed knowledge about individual systems and a general understanding of some of the processes. There are, however, very few attempts to describe these complex processes in mathematical terms (for implementation on the continuum level). Given the pair of materials, operating conditions, surface roughness and lubricant type there are very few models available which can predict risk of wear under boundary lubrication conditions.[3] Indeed, even the most basic type models can contribute significantly to the understanding of the complex processes governing the growth and removal of tribofilms. Moreover, it would be beneficial to enable predictions of system performance without running an experiment first.

Boundary lubrication has often been said to be too complex to enable modelling and this is most probably the explanation for why there are relatively few publications available. Sullivan[4] derived a model for oxidational wear under boundary lubrication conditions. The model was based on the Quinn and Sullivan oxidational wear theory[5] with the addition of a model for the physical adsorption

   This journal is © The Royal Society of Chemistry 2012

of a boundary film. No detailed contact mechanics model was included. Stolarski[6] derived a similar model for the tribofilm considering the contact mechanics by adding a statistical Greenwood and Williamson[7] type of contact model. Chang and co-workers[8] developed a physicochemical micro-contact model. They studied colliding asperities and determined contact pressure and temperature deterministically and they developed a statistical model for physically adsorbed and chemically reacted layers. Their model is based on the Volmer adsorption isotherm for physical adsorption. The reacted layer growth was modelled by an empirical law and Archard's wear equation was used to describe the wear of the reacted layer. Fujita and Spikes[9] presented another model for growth and removal of reacted films. The model was experimentally validated. They did, however, only study the growth on the global scale not on the roughness scale. Recently, Bosman and Schipper[10] presented a deterministic model of wear in boundary lubricated contacts with rough surfaces. Their wear modelling strategy was based on the Podra and Andersson time stepping technique[11] for numerical wear predictions.

This paper presents a new model for the growth and removal of the reacted layer. Contact mechanics is deterministic and quasi-transient. This means that real rough surfaces are brought into contact and that these are moved relative to each other to simulate a sliding interface.[12] This means that the contact pressure and deformation distributions are time dependent. An experimentally validated model for growth of the reacted tribofilm is developed and layer thickness is updated after every time step. The varying properties of the layer itself does, in turn, influence the contact mechanics. The effect of different surface roughness on running-in and wear risk is studied for a given combination of materials and lubricant. The underlying motivation of the work is to generate knowledge about the micro level mechanical processes of tribofilms in between rough surfaces in sliding contact. The focus is on the contact mechanics of tribofilms. These studies are believed to be helpful in designing better tribological systems. This model will also be a platform for further improvement of the physico-chemical model of additive-surface interaction.

2   Nomenclature

$u_3(x_1, x_2)$ = the out of plane deformation of a surface [m].
E^*, E_1 and E_2 = elastic modulii [Pa].
x_i = spatial coordinates [m].
y_i = spatial coordinates [m].
$f_3(x_1, x_2)$ = stress distribution [Pa].
$G(x_1, x_2)$ = the out of plane gap between the surfaces [m]
v = Poisson ratio.
V = complementary potential energy [J].
A, B and C = substances' concentration [mol m^{-3}].
t = time [s].
$k(T)$ = reaction rate [mol s^{-1}].
m and n = order of chemical reaction.
C_i and D = constants related to chemical reactions [varies]
T, T_{bulk} and T_{flash} = temperatures [K].
B_0 = concentration of substance [mol m^{-2}].
h_{max} = highest allowed tribofilm height (x_3 direction) [m].
h and h_n = tribofilm height (x_3 direction) [m].
μ = friction coefficient.
p and $p(i, j)$ = contact pressure [Pa].
v = relative surface velocity [m s^{-1}].
p_y, p_{ys} and p_{yfm} = plastic deformation pressures [Pa].

h_1 and h_2 = tribofilm height on surface 1 and 2 [m].
h_t = the thicker of two tribofilm elements in contact [m].
U_p = plastic deformation of a surface [m].
Q = wear volume per sliding distance [m^3 m^{-1}]
K = dimensionless wear constant.
H = hardness [Pa]
F_N = normal force [N].
s = sliding distance [m].
h_w = height (x_3 direction) change due to wear [m].
κ = dimensional wear constant K/H [Pa^{-1}].

3   Numerical model

The novelty of this work lies in the growth and removal of the tribofilm layer and how it is combined with contact mechanics. The model consists of four parts:
- contact mechanics to find contact pressure and elastic/plastic deformations
- tribofilm growth model
- tribofilm mechanics model
- wear model

The components of the model are described in the following sections.

3.1   Contact mechanics

The first step is to find out the pressure as this gives much information about contact severity. In combination with the friction coefficient the pressure gives rise to tangential tractions and therefore friction work in the sliding direction. Friction energy is a key component in the current model for chemical activation of the tribofilm growth.

The contact mechanics calculation seeks the distribution of pressure due to a given load. In turn this is controlled by how the surfaces deform in the contact. An overview of the numerical procedure can be found in Fig. 2. For the contact mechanics to agree with reality the correct material model must be employed. Most materials have elastic behaviour up to some plastic deformation pressure where the material begins to deform plastically, and when the strains becomes too high the material will fail. The transition between elastic and plastic behaviour is governed by plasticity functions in theoretical contact mechanics. A simple form of elastic–plastic behaviour is elastic-perfectly plastic. This stress–strain behaviour will resemble the behaviour of steel surfaces.

The stress–strain mechanics of tribofilms has been investigated by Demmou *et al.*[13] ZnDTP tribofilm experiments and simulations have indicated that the tribofilm hardness varies with the height of the film with high values near the substrate underlaying the film and low values at top of the film.[14] The variation of hardness with penetration depth has also been investigated.[13]

The elastic properties of tribofilms are not very well established. For this reason, the elastic modulus of the tribofilm was chosen to be the same as for the steel substrate. This will also keep the model uncomplicated. The model applied here is elastic, perfectly plastic, with the hardness of the tribofilm depending on the thickness of the film while the modulus of elasticity is assumed to be the same for the tribofilm and the steel substrate. Plastic deformation is assumed to occur when pressure reaches the same magnitude as the tribofilm hardness.

The half-plane assumption is used to describe the elastic deformation, *i.e.* the contacting bodies are assumed to have infinite support. Small asperity angles and negligible influence of tangential tractions are assumed. In this case the deformation $u_3(x_1, x_2)$ due to stress distribution $f_3(x_1, x_2)$ in x_3 direction (perpendicular to the contact plane) is given by

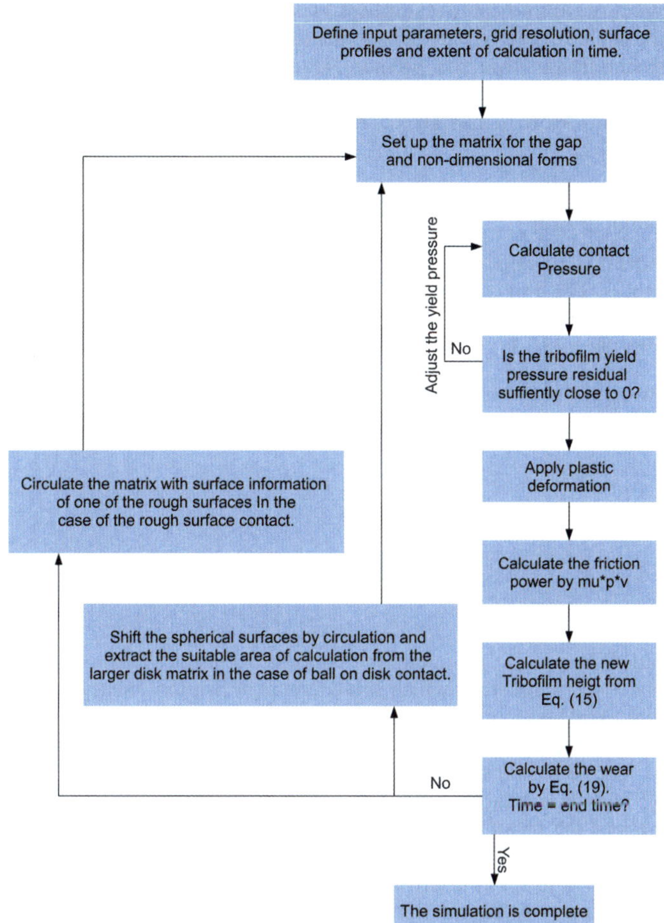

Fig. 2 Flowchart of the numerical procedure implemented in the boundary lubrication model.

$$u_3(x_1, x_2) = \frac{1}{\pi E^*} \cdot$$

$$\int_{-\infty}^{\infty} \int_{-\infty}^{\infty} \frac{f_3(y_1, y_2)}{\sqrt{(x_1 - y_1)^2 + (x_2 - y_2)^2}} dy_1 dy_2. \tag{1}$$

Here,

$$E^* = \frac{1}{((1 - \nu_1^2)/E_1 + (1 - \nu_2^2)/E_2)} \tag{2}$$

is the reduced elastic modulus of the materials, with E_1 and E_2 the as elastic moduli and ν_1 and ν_2 the Poisson ratios of the two materials. According to the variational principle developed for contact mechanics by Kalker,[15] the corresponding static solution is found by minimizing the functional

$$V = \frac{1}{2} \iint_S f_3(x_1, x_2) u_3(x_1, x_2) dS - \iint_S f_3(x_1, x_2) G(x_1, x_2) dS. \tag{3}$$

Here, $G(x_1, x_2)$ denotes the separation distance between two surfaces before deformation. Eqn (1) may be recognized as a convolution. Once discretized, this type of equation allows for the application of a Fourier transformation and the numerical evaluation can be reduced significantly by employing the FFT (Fast Fourier Transformation). Once the pressure reaches the predefined value for plastic deformation, the node in question is taken out of the calculation as well as the corresponding load. More details about the elastic plastic calculation can be found in Sahlin *et al.*[16]

3.2 Tribofilm growth

In this model it is assumed that a film is formed due to a chemical reaction between two substances. The film is assumed to grow only in the contact spots where rubbing takes place, *i.e.* it is a tribofilm. One attempt to model tribofilm growth was presented by So and Lin.[17] Their model is based on the Arrhenius equation. The reaction rate $\frac{\mathrm{d}}{\mathrm{d}t}$ for a chemical reaction where substances A and B react to produce substance C depends on the temperature T and is given by:[18]

$$\frac{\mathrm{d}C}{\mathrm{d}t} = k(T)A^m B^n.$$

(4)

where

$$k(T) = C_1 e^{-C_2/T}$$

(5)

A, *B* and *C* in eqn (4) represent the concentrations of substances A, B and C respectively. C_2 is a constant which includes the activation energy of the reaction and the universal gas constant. In the present model, C_2 must be found from curve-fits to experiments. C_1 is the pre-exponential factor which tells us about the probability that a reaction occurs. Assume that the concentration A is constant and always equally available in the contact area. The concentration B depends on the thickness of the tribofilm, as this substance is related to elements present near the substrate surface. When the tribofilm becomes thicker it will act as a barrier and there will be a lower concentration B available at the top of the layer slowing down the reaction. Assuming that the growth completely stops at a thickness h_{max}. A first approximation for the variation of the concentration by height h is linear:

$$B = \begin{cases} B_0(h_{max}-h) & \text{if } h < h_{max}, \\ B = 0 & \text{if } h < h_{max} \end{cases}$$

(6)

Where B_0 is the concentration of reaction substance B at the surface. This means that we have

$$A^n B^n = C_3(h_{\mathrm{max}} - h)^n \text{ for } h < h_{\mathrm{max}}$$

(7)

where $C_3 = B_0 A^n$. The expression is finally simplified by setting the order of the relevant reaction to 1, that is $n = 1$. The rate of change of reaction product C is proportional to the film height. Eqn (4) and (7) can now be combined to:

$$\left(\frac{\mathrm{d}h}{\mathrm{d}t}\right)_{growth} = C_4(h_{max} - h)k(T).$$

(8)

where C_4 is a proportionality constant that includes constants B_0 and C_3 plus the transformation of concentration C into film thickness h.

The temperature T can be divided into flash temperature and bulk temperature according to,

$$T = T_{\mathrm{flash}} + T_{\mathrm{bulk}}.$$

(9)

                This journal is © The Royal Society of Chemistry 2012

where the bulk temperature can be obtained from experiment or predictions. The flash temperature is proportional to the (local) friction heating μvp, see for instance ref. 1. The bulk temperature is proportional to the global friction heating from the whole contact area. The reaction rate can thus be written as:

$$k(T) = C_1 e^{\frac{-C_2}{D(\mu pv)^r + T_{bulk}}}. \tag{10}$$

where D is a proportionality constant and the exponent r is 1 for Péclet numbers below 5. In this case eqn (10) can be simplified to:

$$k(T) = C_1 e^{\frac{-C_5}{(\mu pv)^r}}. \tag{11}$$

where C_5 is a new constant that could be found from curve-fits to experiments. The final expression for the tribofilm growth is given by combining eqn (11) and eqn (8),

$$\left(\frac{dh}{dt}\right)_{growth} = C_6 (h_{max} - h) e^{\frac{-C_5}{\mu pv}}. \tag{12}$$

Where $C_6 = C_1 C_4$. A finite difference formulation of the height of the tribofilm has the form

$$h_{n+1}(i, j) = h_n(i, j) + \Delta h. \tag{13}$$

A discrete equivalent of eqn (12) is

$$\Delta h = \Delta t C_6 \left(h_{max} - h_n(i,j)\right) e^{\frac{-C_5}{\mu p_n(i,j)v}} \tag{14}$$

Combining eqn (14) and eqn (12) gives the height of the tribofilm in the numerical model:

$$h_{n+1}(i,j) = h_n(i,j) + \Delta t C_6 \left(h_{max} - h_n(i,j)\right) e^{\frac{-C_5}{\mu p_n(i,j)v}}. \tag{15}$$

3.3 Tribofilm mechanics

The mechanics of the tribofilm are certainly important for its anti-wear properties. The 'smart' behaviour of the tribofilm formed by Zinc dialkyldithiophosphate (ZDDP) under pressure, possibly related to pressure induced crystallization as shown by Mosey *et al.*[19] and observed as a variation in the elastic modulus[13] is a phenomenon which should optimally be studied in combination with the contact mechanics. Unfortunately the variation in elastic modulus does not allow for the same numerical efficiency for calculating contact pressure, thus reducing the time-range of the calculation of contact pressure to levels too far from a tribological time-span, such as the time it takes for a contact to be considered run-in. The plastic deformation pressure variation with film height and penetration depth, however, has been incorporated in the model. This is done by assuming a linear variation of plastic deformation pressure p_y with height. The plastic deformation pressure will vary from bulk hardness p_{ys} of 4 GPa to a minimum p_{yfm} value of 1 GPa at the top of the fully developed tribofilm of height h_{max}. Notice that in practice this height of film will never be reached as the tribofilm grows asymptotically toward this value. Concerning plastic penetration depth U_p, the tribofilm will carry load as if it was the height of the deformed film. This is achieved by iterative minimization of the residual

$$
p_y = \begin{cases} p_{ys} - \dfrac{p_{ys} - p_{yfm}}{h_{max}} \left(h_t - U_p \right) & \text{if} \quad U_p < |h_1 - h_2|, \\[3mm] p_{ys} - \dfrac{p_{ys} - p_{yfm}}{2h_{max}} \left(h_1 + h_2 - U_p \right) & \text{if} \quad |h_1 - h_2| \leq U_p < (h_1 + h_2), \\[3mm] p_{ys} & \text{if} \quad (h_1 + h_2) \leq U_p. \end{cases} \tag{16}
$$

where h_t is the thicker of h_1 and h_2. This way of varying the plastic deformation pressure, or hardness, is an approximation that does not fully mimic stress and deformations of the film and the substrate. It is, however, believed that the approximation is sufficiently good for the purpose of getting representative prediction of contact pressure and real area of contact.

3.4 Wear model

The nature of wear is all but simple. Plastic deformation, oxidational wear, corrosion, delamination wear and seizure are some examples of wear modes, which are triggered for different reasons and cause different damage. For this reason the universal wear laws lack general accuracy, and understanding wear in an engineering component often requires a vast number of experiments.

The Archard wear equation is often used to estimate the sliding wear. In this equation the wear volume is proportional to the sliding distance and pressure. This type of wear model is easily included in the present model since local pressures are computed. The drawback is the non-constancy of the proportionality constant. Indeed, factors other than sliding distance and normal pressure influence wear. But starting with this simple relation between pressure and wear, and excluding effects one by one, a more accurate picture of how a contact wears takes form. In this work, plastic deformation is included separately in the contact mechanics model while all other wear effects are included in the Archard model. Historically, Holm[20] proposed that wear volume Q, is proportional to the normal force F_N times sliding distance s, for each material pair according to:

$$
Q = K \frac{F_N}{H} s, \tag{17}
$$

where H is the hardness. The wear constant K was interpreted by Holm as number of abraded atoms per atomic collision. Eqn (17) is normally referred to as the "Archard wear equation". Archard[21] re-interpreted the constant in the equation as the probability that an asperity collision would lead to the formation of a wear particle. The model has been used to predict wear due to many different wear mechanisms, thus being used as a rough wear predictor for wear types other than from delamination wear. In this work, wear is included in the form of the Archard equation and plastic deformation. In the model applied here, the wear depth at each point on the surface is denoted h_w. Rewriting eqn (17) results in

$$
h_w = \kappa p s. \tag{18}
$$

The dimensional Archard wear coefficient $\kappa = K/H$ is used as the proportionality constant to the pressure p times the sliding distance s. A local discrete version of eqn (18) is used. This means that the wear rate is constant during the sliding.

Wear rate dh/dt can be obtained as the time derivative of eqn (18)

$$
\frac{dh}{dt} = \kappa p v. \tag{19}
$$

3.5 Full numerical model

The calculation procedure can be illustrated by a flowchart, see Fig. 2. The calculations in each step described in the numerical model are represented in this flowchart.

When making calculations on real measured surfaces the resolution needed to include a significant amount of asperities quickly becomes too high. Furthermore, as the length scale becomes smaller, not only lengths but also times become short. For example if a grid of 64 × 64 is chosen to resolve a rough surface of area 62 × 53 μm and the surfaces move at a velocity of 0.25 m s^{-1}, one contact calculation corresponds to a time step of about 3 μs and a travel distance of 0.83 μm. The tribofilm growth rate is considered to occur slowly in this work, meaning that such small timescales will produce tribofilms of physically insignificant thicknesses.

For the interest of studying how the tribofilm grows on asperities a method based on averaging the influence from the contact pressure is introduced. It is a two step method, were first the contact mechanics are deterministically solved and the pressure for each contact case which arises is calculated. More precisely, a procedure where one surface is moved across the counter surface and the points on the surface exiting the contact over the right boundary, is assumed to re-enter the contact from the left, is employed. The next step involves time averaging of the pressure for each separate node on the surface. In the second step, the averaged pressure at each node is considered constant for about 0.2 s, corresponding to a sliding distance of 53 mm. The constant pressure conditions are used to calculate how the tribofilm grows and the system wears. The process is repeated until the tribofilm behaviour has been sufficiently established. Fig. 3 illustrates the schematics of the averaging method.

Concerning the choice of the resolution of the surfaces, a few aspects should be taken into account. First, in the case of the ball on disk contact, the symmetry of the geometry gives fairly quick grid convergence which means that a less dense grid can be successfully implemented, without severe loss of accuracy. In the case of rough surfaces the issue is more complicated. As the geometry itself is measured with a limited number of data points this sets an upper limit of what we can say is the measured surface. A lower resolution limit is found when contact mechanics change severely due to changes in roughness. In this work the chosen compromise between calculation efficiency and resolution is including all measured points over a small area.

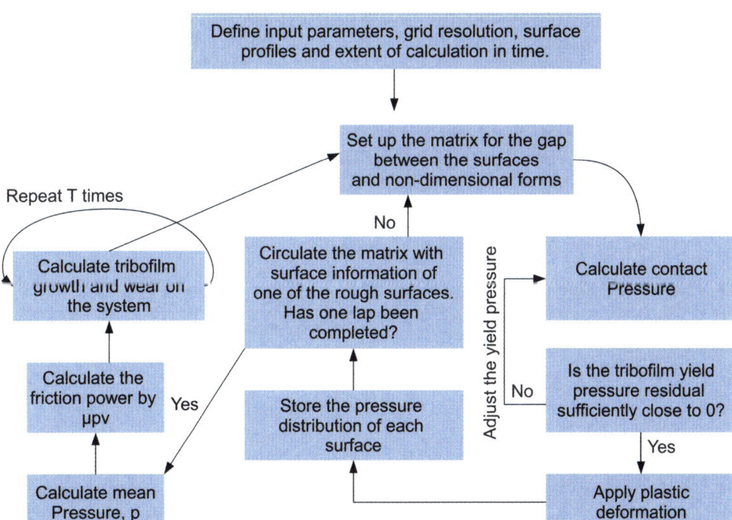

Fig. 3 Flowchart illustrating the numerical procedure used for evaluation of tribofilm growth on rough surfaces.

4 Simulation details

The simulation is run in two stages. First a calibration with experiments is performed in order to establish the set of constants in eqn (19) and (15) and then utilization of this set of constants for real rough surfaces in sliding contact. The calibration is expected to be valid for all cases with the same surface materials and same lubricant.

4.1 Calibration

The surfaces used for calibration is a sphere and a flat. These surfaces are generated on a calculation mesh of 32×32 elements. The spherical surface is set to have a radius of 1 cm. Furthermore, the wear scar on the disk is assumed to be located at a distance of 5 cm from the centre of the disk. This means that a point on the ball is in contact 1/5 as long as a point on the disk. The effect of this is achieved by storing the disk surface as a matrix containing 3×160 elements. The size of the calculation grid corresponds to a square area of 0.7×0.7 mm. The surfaces are loaded with 300 N.

To achieve movement through time the matrices containing surface data are shifted one step at a time in one direction. The predefined Slide-Roll-Ratio (SRR) determines how many steps the surfaces will be shifted. For instance, when the SRR is 5% the ball surface will be shifted 21 times when the disk surface is shifted 20 times. The pressure is solved for in every 5th shift using the same pressure value to calculate film growth and wear. To minimize computation time, the geometry matrices are circulated. The material and tribofilm parameters are chosen to resemble bearing steel with a tribofilm formed by poly-α-olefin 2 wt% ZDDP. The material and tribofilm parameter values are listed in Table 1. The tribofilm simulation data was adapted so that agreement is found to an experiment by Naveira-Suarez *et al.*[22] at an SRR of 0.5%. The constants found from curve-fit to experiments are presented in Table 1. Fig. 4 shows the experimental data used to calibrate the parameters.

4.2 Rough surfaces

As the model has been calibrated it is of interest to measure its usefulness on rough surfaces and evaluate how the tribofilm grows in a sliding contact with rough surfaces. Contact between four rough surfaces is evaluated with the numerical model. The surfaces are once again adapted to behave as bearing steel—no parameter values will be different from those listed in Table 1.

The surfaces are optically measured real surfaces. The smooth surfaces are balls from a Wedeven Associates Tribology Research Machine (WAM) which have been optically measured in an optical profiler. The rough surfaces are taken from the same unidirectionally ground steel sample measured with the same equipment.

A two step processing of the surface is employed. First, tilt is removed based on the acquired surface heights. Then possible missing data is restored by the

Table 1 Parameter values in the simulation

Parameter	Value	Explanation
E_1, E_2	207 GpA	Young's modulus
ν_1, ν_2	0.3	Poisson ratio
h_{max}	70 nm	max local tribofilm height
C_6	160 kW	exponential constant of eqn (15)
C_5	0.3 1/s	linear constant for reaction rate equation
κ	1.63×10^{-15}	dimensionless Archard wear coefficient
y_{ps}	4 GPa	the limiting pressure of the (steel) substrate
y_{pfm}	1.5 GPa	the limiting pressure of a 70 nm tribofilm

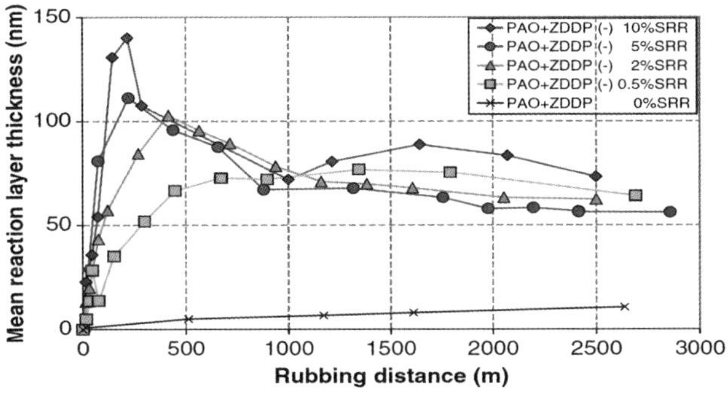

Fig. 4 Mean PAO + ZDDP-derived reaction layer thickness with rubbing distance and negative SRR at 1.9 GPa, 0.25 m s^{-1}, and 90 °C. The case of 5 wt% was used for calibrating the numerical parameters. Reprinted from ref. 23.

application of a Delaunay triangulation based interpolation technique; *TriScatteredInterp* function in MATLAB.[24]

After this the surfaces are cut of to preserve a suitable amount of asperities. 64 × 64 grid points are preserved corresponding for all surfaces to an area of 62μm × 53μm. Surface data can be found in Table 2.

Short length and time scale simulations applying the technique illustrated in Fig. 3 are run on the 64 × 64 grid for the S1–S2, the S1–R1, and the S1–R2 contact cases.

5 Results and discussion

The calibration of constants C_4, C_5, max tribofilm height h_{max} and wear coefficient κ were first adapted to an experiment as described above. The resulting values on the parameters were used to predict different cases of SRR in the ball on disk contact. Checking how well the predicted film thickness agrees with the measured mean film thickness from the experiment is seen as a measure of the quality of the model. The values and how they change is then used to test different rough surfaces, which are compared in terms of tribofilm quality and contact severity.

5.1 Calibration of the growth model

The calibration was done by adjusting parameters until the agreement with experiments was considered to be sufficient and the values of the constants of the tribofilm growth were balanced against the sliding wear constant. The resulting curve, which was adapted to 0.5% SRR, is seen in Fig. 5. Comparing with the experimental curve of Fig. 4 we can say that the agreement is sufficient. The problem now is that for different SRRs other than 0.5% there is an overshoot of tribofilm height above the set value for h_{max}, which means the model will not be able to reconstruct the experimental results completely. In fact, we need a different model to achieve this. This will be discussed in the discussion section.

Table 2 Surface roughness parameters. The bearing steel balls are of the type used in the WAM

Surface	Surface information	Sq
R1	Unidirectionally ground sample	96 nm
R2	Unidirectionally ground sample	53 nm
S1	Bearing steel ball (WAM)	21 nm
S2	Bearing steel ball (WAM)	20 nm

5.2   Model evaluation

Once the model was calibrated to agree with one case of SRR, other SRR cases were tried out. Results from choosing 10%, 5%, 2% and 0.5% SRR are seen in Fig. 5. Corresponding experimental measurements are shown in Fig. 4. A quick growth in the beginning of the numerical experiment can be observed, with a faster growth for higher SRR, as also observed in the experiment. The domination of wear against tribofilm growth for the higher SRR seems to indicate a model weakness. Although an exact match was not achieved, the parameter values will be considered accurate enough for use on the small scale with rough surface contacts.

5.3   Rough surfaces contact

Results from the deterministic technique for studying rough contacts are presented here. The results are presented case wise and each contact pair is discussed separately.

The first contact case is between two smooth surfaces (S1 and S2). Fig. 6 shows the mean film height against time.

It can be seen that the two surfaces develop tribofilms in a similar fashion. This is expected as the surfaces are of similar quality and geometry. It can also be seen that the growth process is random. There are ups and downs of the tribofilm height and the tribofilm height is initially higher on the surface S1, while after some time this is switched around in favour of the S2 surface. This chaotic behaviour indicates that the solution can not be interpreted exactly but rather phenomenologically, due to measuring equipment and numerical limitations.

One of the qualities of the numerical model is that we can observe the geometrical shape of either surface or tribofilm at any time of it's development. Fig. 7 shows the profile of the tribofilm after 0.2, 4 and 20 s. Fig. 7A–C is the tribofilm on surface S1, and Fig. 7D–F is the tribofilm on surface S2 as its counter surface.

Having observed already how the mean tribofilm thickness develops, the distributions provide a more detailed perspective. It can be seen that ridges of the tribofilm are formed in the sliding direction. These ridges are due to asperities on the counter surface, generating the amount of activation energy necessary to activate tribofilm growth, without wearing down too much film and substrate. With the new insight of wear and tribofilm growth in the specific case an explanation of the average

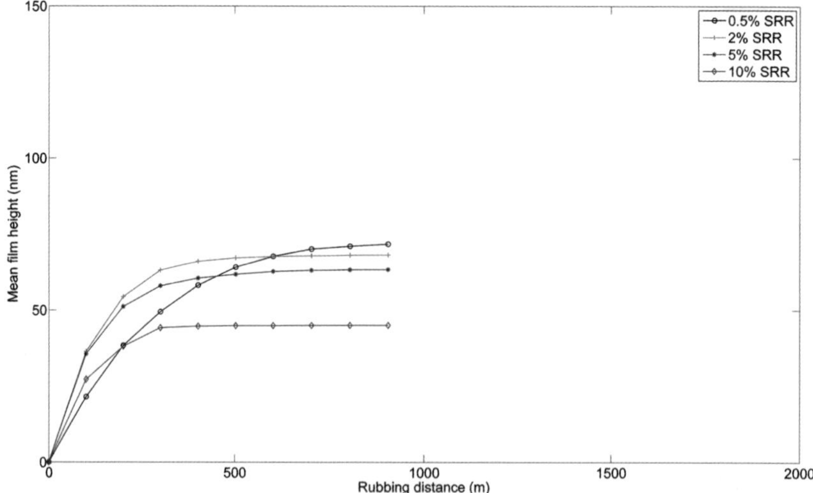

Fig. 5   Mean tribofilm height as a function of time numerically calculated with SRR of 0.5%, 2%, 5% and 10%.

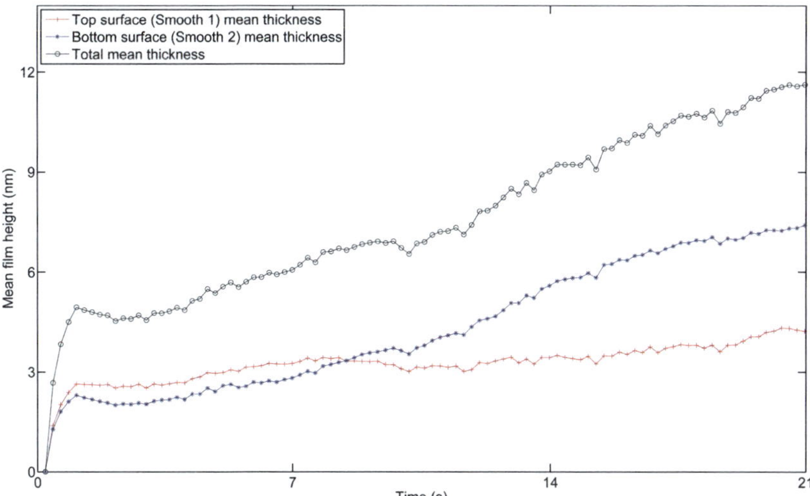

Fig. 6 Mean tribofilm height from the numerical simulation. The contact is between two smooth balls exhibiting the surface roughness S1 and S2, respectively. The height is measured by summing up the nodal tribofilm height of each surface and dividing over surface area. The circled line (black) shows the sum of both surfaces' tribofilm height. The line with plus signs (red) shows the mean tribofilm height on the surface S1 and the line with asterisks (blue) shows the mean tribofilm height on the surface S2.

tribofilm behaviour is suggested. It can be seen in Fig. 7B and D, that the ridge behaviour is more established on surface S2. This is noteworthy, as at this point of tribofilm formation the average height is lower on this surface. But, as these ridges are developed sooner and at least one of them seems to survive, the long-term effect is that this surface gets a thicker tribofilm.

The mean film thickness of the rough(R1)–smooth(S1) contact can be seen in Fig. 8.

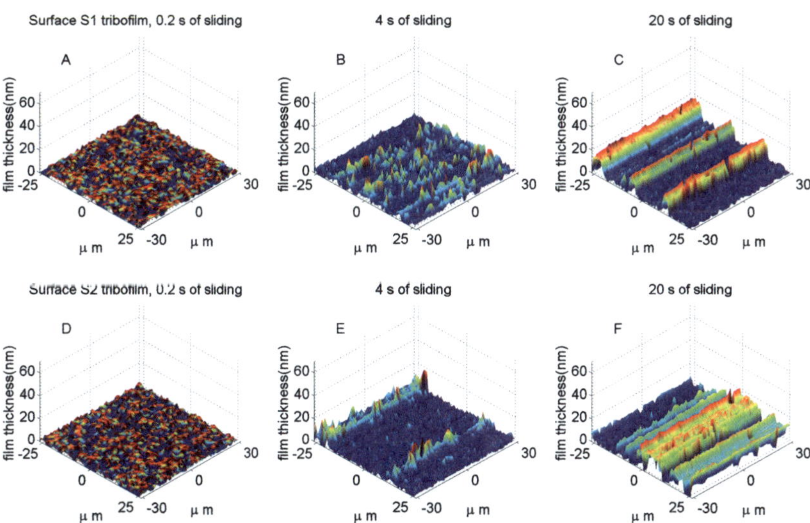

Fig. 7 A–C shows the development of tribofilm on the surface S1, after 0.2, 4 and 20 s while rubbing against surface S2. D–F shows the development of tribofilm on surface S2.

It is noteworthy that the tribofilm of S1 grows faster in contact with the rougher surface R1 than with the smoother surface S2. It seems that the higher contact pressure caused by the rougher surface is, at least on average, a better initiator of tribofilm growth.

The formation of ridges is in line with this hypothesis in the sense that the rougher surface will produce a wider span of contact pressures on the counter surface, resulting in more possibilities for generating the conditions required for tribofilm growth.

Fig. 9 shows the development of a tribofilm for the S1–R1 contact pair. A–C depicts the tribofilm on surface S1 and D–F is the one on R1, after 0.2, 4 and 20 s from left to right.

The initial growth of tribofilm on the rough surface, R1, that is seen in Fig. 10D, is different from the growth of tribofilm on the smooth surface S1. The coverage is initially poor, indicating that there are many grooves on this surface, which initially do not come into contact at all. Even after 4 s not much has happened with the tribofilm on the R1 surface. It is only after 20 s, Fig. 10F, that some ridge like formation of tribofilm can be observed.

The contact pair S1–R1 was analyzed using the same procedure as for the other contact pairs (S1–S2 and S1–R2). Fig. 10 illustrates the mean film height for S1–R1 and Fig. 11 shows the tribofilm on each surface after 0.2, 4 and 20 s.

The surface R2, which is smoother, in the sense that it exhibits a smaller S_q-value, than R1 and rougher than S2 promotes a fast tribofilm growth on its counter surface while also providing a decent ground for growing a tribofilm on itself. Therefore, the contact pair S1–R2 produces the thickest accumulated tribofilm of the contact pairs studied here. Unlike the situation on the surface R1, the mean film height enters a stage of tribofilm growth which seems faster than just linear growth. By comparing Fig. 9F and Fig. 11F it is also observed that the S1–R2 contact pair produces more ridges than S1–R1.

In the present model, the tribofilm is assumed to behave as a linear elastic–perfectly plastic material. It is obvious that the outcome would have been different

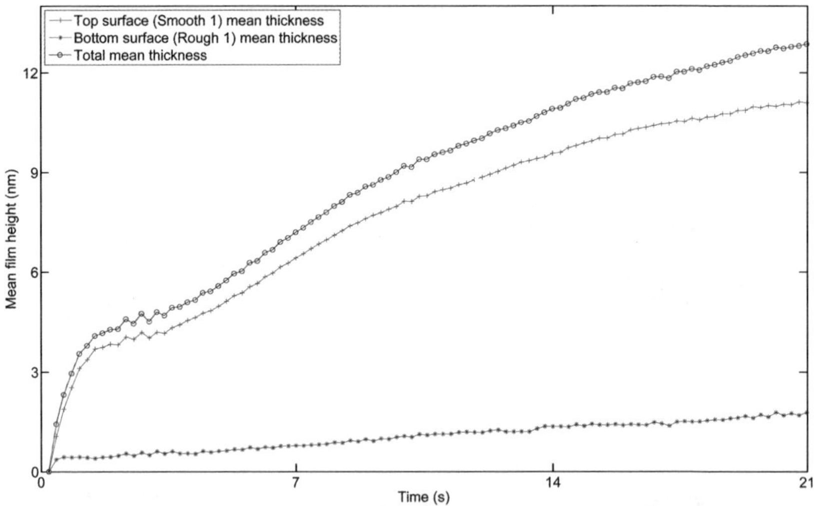

Fig. 8 Mean tribofilm height from the numerical simulation. The contact is between one smooth ball exhibiting the surface roughness S1 and one rougher ground surface exhibiting the surface roughness R1. The height is measured by summing up the nodal tribofilm height of each surface and dividing over surface area. The circled line (black) shows the sum of both surfaces' tribofilm height. The line with plus signs (red) shows the mean tribofilm height on the surface S1 and the line with asterisks (blue) shows the mean tribofilm height on the surface R1.

     This journal is © The Royal Society of Chemistry 2012

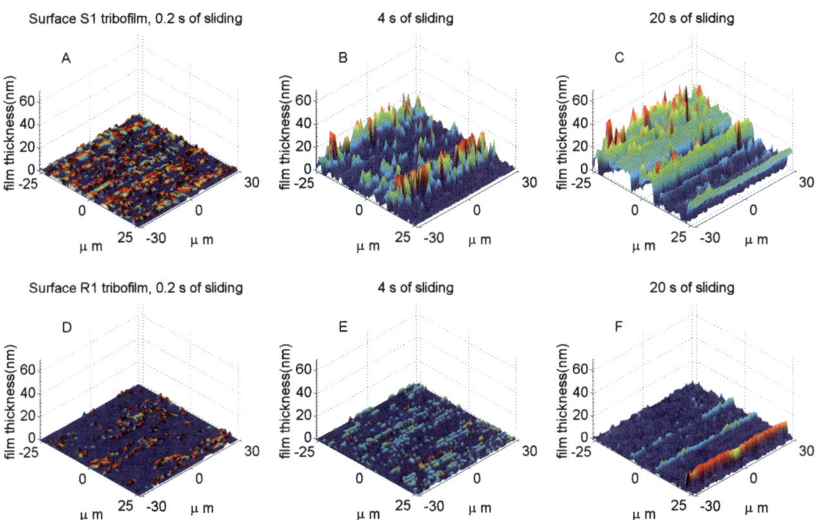

Fig. 9 A–C shows the development of tribofilm on the surface S1, after 0.2, 4 and 20 s while rubbing against surface R1. D–F shows the development of tribofilm on surface R1.

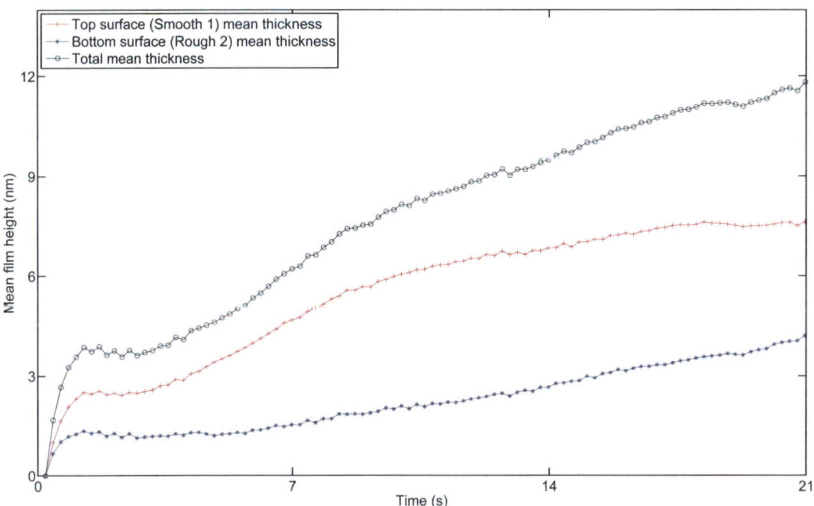

Fig. 10 Mean tribofilm height from the numerical simulation. The contact is between one smooth ball exhibiting the surface roughness S1 and one rougher ground surface exhibiting the surface roughness R2. The height is measured by summing up the nodal tribofilm height of each surface and dividing over surface area. The circled line (black) shows the sum of both surfaces' tribofilm height. The line with plus signs (red) shows the mean tribofilm height on the surface S1 and the one with asterisks (blue) shows the mean tribofilm height on the surface R2.

if a more realistic material model, considering possible variations in modulus of elasticity with composition of the tribofilm, would have been employed.

Summarizing the results for the different contact pairs some common trends on the tribofilm growth for all surfaces can be identified. All tribofilms seem to start out with a quick growth period during the first 1–2 s of sliding. After this, the growth

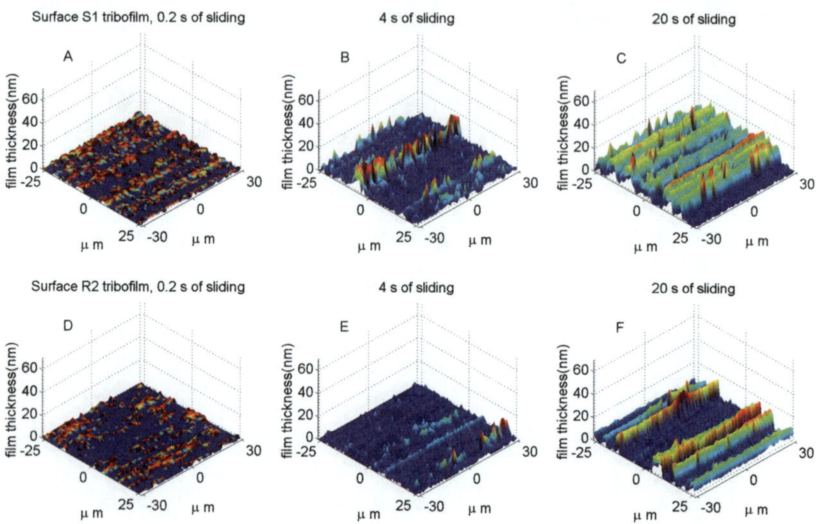

Fig. 11 A–C shows the development of tribofilm on the surface S1, after 0.2, 4 and 20 s while rubbing against surface R2. D–F shows the development of tribofilm on surface R2.

rate reduces significantly, and the average film thickness even reduces for the S1–S2 and S1–R2 contact pairs. After this a transition to increased growth occurs for all contact cases, on surface S2 in the contact pair S1–S2, on both surfaces in the contact pair S1–R1 and on surface S1 in the S1–R2 contact pair. The film growth after this approaches a steady state for S2 in the S1–S2 contact pair and for S1 in the S1–R1 and S1–R2 contact cases.

6   Discussion on an alternative empirical model

The model applied so far has been derived from an Arrhenius equation type of reaction building tribofilm. From a mechanist's point of view, it may be tempting to simply postulate a tribofilm growth model based on friction work which gives a good result for the tribofilm thickness. Clearly work will partially lead to heat development and plastic deformation in the contact and partially to chemical energy. The heat developed will also increase the probability for molecular collisions which will grow the tribofilm. A polynomial expression is numerically convenient. If the global behaviour of the experiments by Naveira-Suarez[22] is transferred to a smaller scale a simple model for the tribofilm height is easily implemented. For instance the expression

$$h = h_{max} \frac{W_{tot}}{W_{tot} + C_e},$$ (20)

can be adapted and applied locally to match the average tribofilm height. In this equation h_{max} is the highest allowed film thickness, W_{tot} is the total friction work following a node and C_e is a constant which determines the required energy for growing the tribofilm of dimension energy. The numerical application of such an expression leads to a form

$$h_{n+1} = h_{max} \frac{h_n C_e + W_{n+1}(h_{max} - h_n)}{h_{max} C_e + W_{n+1}(h_{max} - h_n)}$$ (21)

for tribofilm growth due to the work

$$W_n = p\Delta x \Delta y \mu \Delta s. \tag{22}$$

during the timestep n, with Δx and Δy as the lengths of the computational cell and Δs as the sliding distance, i.e. $u\Delta t$. This model was adapted to match the 5% SRR case of Fig. 4. To achieve a match of the overshoot, the growth constant C_e needs to vary, decreasing over the first 1000 m of sliding distance.

Making a similar investigation for this model as was done with the chemically derived one, resulted in much better matching with the mean film height of the varying SRR experiments. Fig. 12 shows results from this model. The agreement between this model and the WAM experiments indicate a predictive ability for SRR effects on the poly-α-olefin and 2% ZDDP system. It also indicates that in fact a chemical running in, occurring slowly over the first hour of running the experiment, is taking place. The causes for the chemical running in could be for instance reduction of reactant concentration with time, a slower ZDDP action due to draining of some catalytic chemical component or oxidation of the Fe surface. However, as for predicting the reaction energies of the chemical reactions (and thus aiding in finding them), the model is insufficiently anchored to chemical theory to be useful, as far as the authors can see.

7 Conclusions

A model for a deterministic chemo-mechanical modelling of boundary lubrication has been successfully implemented. The module for tribofilm growth has been adjusted to agree with measured mean tribofilm height from experiments in a system of ZDDP in poly-α-olefin for different SRR. Evaluation on rough surfaces shows clear differences in the protection of different contact cases. The method developed could be used to predict the tribofilm protection efficiency for different surfaces designs.

On the asperity scale, the roughness of the surfaces in contact has large effect on the tribofilm coverage and contact severity. Because of higher contact pressures the tribofilm growth may be overpowered by wear leading to lower tribofilm coverage on a rougher surface. The effects considered in the present model indicate that

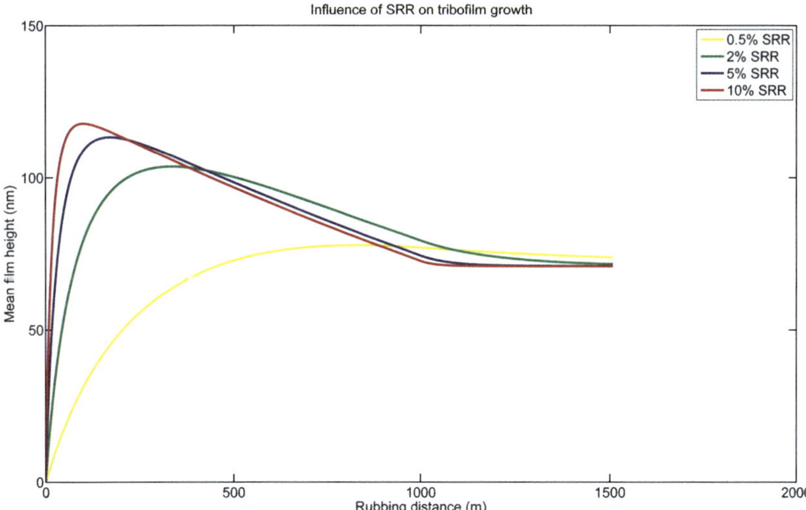

Fig. 12 Mean tribofilm height as a function of time numerically calculated with SRR of 0.5%, 2%, 5% and 10%.

smoother surfaces form more tribofilm, while inducing less film growth on their countersurface.

Acknowledgements

The authors would like to thank Marcus Björling for providing surface data and Andrew Spencer for proofreading this article.

References

1 G. W. Stachowiak and A. W. Batchelor. *Engineering tribology.* Referex Engineering. Butterworth–Heinemann, 2000.
2 H. Spikes, The history and mechanisms of zddp, *Tribol. Lett.*, 2004, **17**(3), 469–489.
3 S. M. Hsu and R. S. Gates, Boundary lubrication and boundary lubricating films, *Modern tribology handbook*, 2000, 1, 455–492.
4 J. L. Sullivan, Boundary lubrication and oxidational wear, *J. Phys. D: Appl. Phys.*, 1986, **19**(10), 1999–2011.
5 T. F. J. Quinn, J. L. Sullivan and D. M. Rowson, Origins and development of oxidational wear at low ambient temperatures, *Wear*, 1984, **94**(2), 175–191.
6 T. A. Stolarski, A system for wear prediction in lubricated sliding contacts, *Lubr. Sci.*, 1996, **8**(4), 315–350.
7 J. A. Greenwood and J. B. P. Williamson, Contact of nominally flat surfaces, *Proc. R. Soc. London, Ser. A*, 1966, **295**, 300–319.
8 H. Zhang, L. Chang, M. N. Webster and A. Jackson, A micro-contact model for boundary lubrication with lubricant/surface physiochemistry, *J. Tribol.*, 2003, **125**(1), 8–15.
9 H. Fujita and H. A. Spikes, Study of zinc dialkyldithiophosphate antiwear film formation and removal processes, part ii: Kinetic model, *Tribol. Trans.*, 2005, **48**(4), 567–575.
10 R. Bosman and D. J. Schipper, Mild wear prediction of boundary-lubricated contacts, *Tribol. Lett.*, 2011, 1–10.
11 Priit Podra and Sren Andersson, Simulating sliding wear with finite element method, *Tribol. Int.*, 1999, **32**(2), 71–81.
12 J. Andersson, A. Almqvist and R. Larsson, Numerical simulation of a wear experiment, *Wear*, 2011, **271**(11–12), 2947–2952.
13 Karim Demmou, Sandrine Bec, Jean-Luc Loubet and Jean-Michel Martin, Temperature effects on mechanical properties of zinc dithiophosphate tribofilms, *Tribol. Int.*, 2006, **39**(12), 1558–1563. Interactions of Tribology and the Operating Environment: Proceedings of the 32nd Leeds-Lyon Symposium on Tribology (Lyon, 2005).
14 Andrew J. Gellman and Nicholas D. Spencer. *Surface chemistry in tribology. Technical report*, Department of Chemical Engineering, Carnegie Institute of Technology, 2002.
15 J. J. Kalker, A minimum principle for the law of dry friction, with application to elastic cylinders in rolling contact—Part 1: Fundamentals—application to steady rolling, *J. Appl. Mech.*, 1971, **38**(4), 875–880.
16 F. Sahlin, R. Larsson, A. Almqivst, P. M. Lugt and P. Marklund, A mixed lubrication model incorporating measured surface topography. Part 1: Theory of flow factors, *Proc Inst. Mech. Eng., Part J*, 2010, **224**(4), 335–351.
17 H. So and Y. C. Lin, The theory of antiwear for zddp at elevated temperature in boundary lubrication condition, *Wear*, 1994, **177**(2), 105–115.
18 S. Arrhenius, Uber die reaktionsgeschwindigkeit bei der inversion von rohrzucker durch sauren, *Z. phys. Chem*, 1889, **4**(26), 226–248.
19 Nicholas J. Mosey, Martin H. Muser and Tom K. Woo, Molecular mechanisms for the functionality of lubricant additives, *Science*, 2005, **307**(5715), 1612–1615.
20 Ragnar Holm, *Electric contacts handbook*, Springer, 1958.
21 J. F. Archard, Contact and rubbing of flat surfaces, *J. Appl. Phys.*, 1953, **24**(8), 981–988.
22 A. Naveira-Suarez, A. Tomala, M. Grahn, M. Zaccheddu, R. Pasaribu and R. Larsson, The influence of base oil polarity and slide-roll ratio on additive-derived reaction layer formation, *Proc Inst. Mech. Eng., Part J*, 2011, **225**(7), 565–576.
23 A. Naveira-Suarez. The Behaviour of Antiwear Additives in Lubricated Rolling-Sliding Contacts. PhD thesis, Luleå University of Technology, 2011.
24 Mathworks. Matlab R2011b Documentation.

Tribology and energy efficiency: from molecules to lubricated contacts to complete machines

Robert Ian Taylor*

Received 25th November 2011, Accepted 11th January 2012
DOI: 10.1039/c2fd00122e

The impact of lubricants on energy efficiency is considered. Molecular details of base oils used in lubricants can have a great impact on the lubricant's physical properties which will affect the energy efficiency performance of a lubricant. In addition, molecular details of lubricant additives can result in significant differences in measured friction coefficients for machine elements operating in the mixed/boundary lubrication regime. In single machine elements, these differences will result in lower friction losses, and for complete systems (such as cars, trucks, hydraulic circuits, industrial gearboxes *etc.*) lower fuel consumption or lower electricity consumption can result.

1 Introduction

There is currently great interest in improving the energy efficiency of machines. This is partly due to high fuel prices (gasoline, diesel, and electricity) and partly due to government legislation designed to limit CO_2 emissions from vehicles. For example, in the European Union, it is proposed that the fleet average CO_2 emissions from cars should be less than 130 gCO_2 km^{-1} in 2015, with a very challenging target of 95 gCO_2 km^{-1} set for 2020.[1] (For gasoline engined vehicles, 130 gCO_2 km^{-1} is equivalent to a fuel consumption of 5.6 litres/100 km, or 50.4 miles per imperial gallon and 95 gCO_2 km^{-1} is equivalent to 4.1 litres/100 km, or 67.3 miles per imperial gallon.) Manufacturers that do not meet these limits with their vehicles will face stiff financial penalties. Other regions of the world (the US, Japan, China, India *etc.*) are also introducing fuel consumption targets for their vehicles, and there are also proposals to apply fuel consumption targets to heavy duty diesel trucks in the US from model year 2014.[2]

Engine, gearbox and axle lubricants can be developed that reduce a vehicle's fuel consumption.[3–10] Compared to vehicle hardware changes that impact fuel economy, changing the lubricant is cost effective, and can be implemented quickly.[11] Clearly, if there is a move to a lower viscosity lubricant, tests will need to be carried out to ensure the new lubricants do not cause any durability issues. For passenger cars, industry standard tests are available (in the US and Europe)[12,13] that are used to quantify an engine oil's fuel economy potential. Many Original Equipment Manufacturers (OEMs) also have their own tests. However, for heavy duty trucks, gearboxes, axles, and industrial systems, there are currently no such industry standard tests for lubricant energy efficiency.

A lubricant consists of a mixture of base oils (comprising 80–95% of a lubricant) together with a mixture of lubricant additives (viscosity index improvers, anti-wear additives, antioxidants, friction modifiers, dispersants, detergents, corrosion inhibitors, anti-foam additives, pour point depressants *etc*). A wide range of base oils are

Shell Global Solutions (UK), Shell Technology Centre Thornton, PO Box 1, Chester, CH1 3SH, UK. E-mail: robert.i.taylor@shell.com

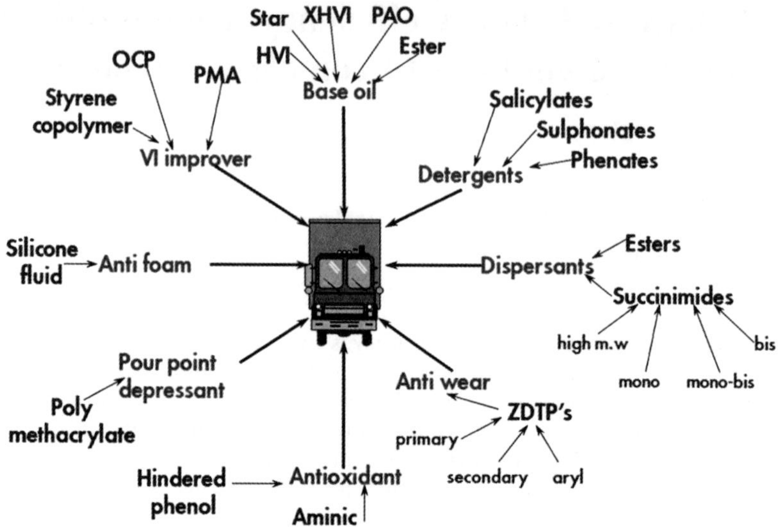

Fig. 1 Showing the range of lubricant additive chemistries available to a lubricant formulator.

available for a lubricant formulator to choose from. Fig. 1 gives an indication of the wide range of lubricant additive chemistries that are available.

The precise molecular composition of a lubricant base oil has a major influence on how lubricant viscosity varies with temperature and pressure. The precise molecular structure of a Viscosity Index (VI) improver impacts on how lubricant viscosity varies with shear rate. The molecular details of the surface active additives present in a lubricant have a large impact on the friction coefficient measured in the mixed and boundary lubrication regimes. These detailed differences, at the molecular scale, result in reduced friction in individual machine elements (such as journal bearings) and reduced energy consumption in complete systems. This paper will discuss in more detail these various effects.

2   Impact of molecular structure on lubricant friction

Base oils

In general, lubricant formulators use two or more base oils in a finished lubricant. The choice of base oil viscosity, and the proportion of base oils used, are chosen by the lubricant formulator to give the correct lubricant viscosity, and the correct variation of lubricant viscosity with temperature. Even for one particular type of base oil, however, there will be a mixture of molecules present.

Details of the various base oil types are described in detail in reference [14]. The molecular structure of a typical base oil molecule will impact performance in two ways. Firstly, the base oil molecular structure will impact the Viscosity Index of the oil. This is a measure of how the lubricant viscosity varies with temperature. If two lubricants have the same kinematic viscosity at 100 °C, then Table 1 shows

Table 1 The effect of Viscosity Index (VI) on kinematic viscosity at various temperatures for oils with the same V_k100

	VI = 100	VI = 125	VI = 150
V_k40 (cSt)	108.00	90.44	77.66
V_k70 (cSt)	29.49	27.69	26.23
V_k100 (cSt)	12.00	12.0	12.0

the kinematic viscosity at 40 °C and 70 °C for lubricants with different Viscosity Indices. Clearly, a higher Viscosity Index results in a "flatter" viscosity temperature curve. For many car owners who only drive short distances, the engine is often not fully warmed up, and a high Viscosity Index oil can give significant fuel economy benefits under such conditions (due to the lower lubricant viscosity at these low temperatures).

Secondly, the molecular structure of the base oil molecule can impact on the high pressure viscosity of a lubricant. It has been found that viscosity increases almost exponentially with pressure for hydrocarbon-based lubricants.

$$\eta(P) = \eta(0)\exp(\alpha P) \tag{1}$$

In the above equation, $\eta(P)$ is the lubricant dynamic viscosity (Pa s) at pressure P (Pa), and α is the pressure–viscosity coefficient of the lubricant (which in general is a function of temperature). For most lubricants, α is in the range 10–25 GPa^{-1}. It has been found that the base oil molecular structure has a great impact on α, with naphthenic base oils having the highest value of α, followed by Group ɪparaffinic base oils, then Group ɪɪɪ/PAO base oils, with polyalkylene glycols (PAGs) having the lowest values. The α value of an oil is related to the limiting shear stress of the oil,[15] which directly relates to friction. Fig. 2 shows friction measurements, carried out in a PCS Instruments Mini-Traction Machine, of ISO 220 industrial gear lubricants. The friction is plotted as a function of the amount of sliding (in %). The results show that the friction increases sharply at first and then reaches a plateau value. The height of the plateau is highest for paraffinic Group ɪ base oils, is lower for polyalphaolefin base oils, and is lowest still for polyalylene glycols. We would expect, for elastohydrodynamically lubricated contacts, that the lowest friction would be achieved for PAG based lubricants, followed by PAOs, with mineral Group ɪbase oils having higher friction. Gold et al.[16] have reported useful expressions for estimating α from the kinematic viscosity of the lubricant, for a range of base oil types. Moore[17] has also reported on the relationship between molecular structure and lubricant properties.

Lubricant additives

A large number of additives are added to commercial lubricants to improve the properties of the lubricant base oil. An excellent introduction to lubricant additives and their function and chemistry is available from Mortier et al.[14] Antioxidants are used to slow down the rate of lubricant oxidation, Viscosity Index improvers are

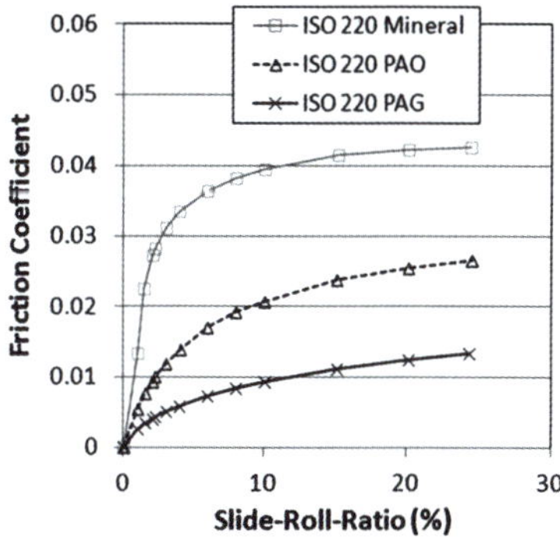

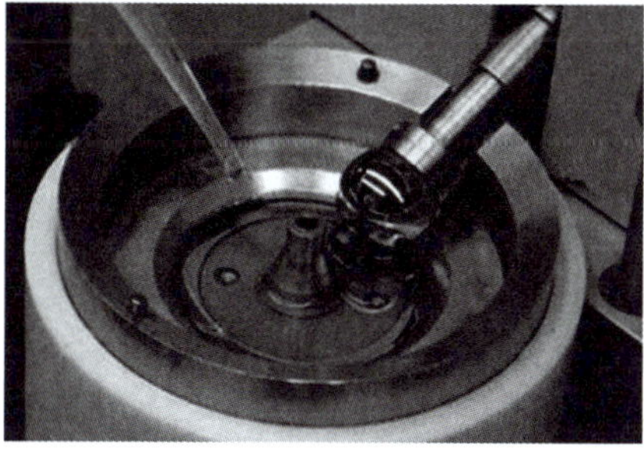

Fig. 2 Graph showing friction *versus* slide roll ratio (%), as measured in a PCS Instruments Mini Traction Machine (also shown). These results were obtained for a temperature of 100 °C, a load of 1.25 GPa, and a mean speed of 4 m s⁻¹.

added to the lubricant to increase the Viscosity Index of the lubricant. Dispersants and detergents are added to keep insoluble material in solution and to keep metal surfaces clean. Anti-wear additives are used to prevent wear when the oil film thickness separating moving components is too low to ensure hydrodynamic lubrication. Friction modifiers may also be added to reduce friction under such conditions. Other additives, such as corrosion inhibitors, anti-foam additives and pour point depressants are also used.

Of the above additives, the anti-wear additives and friction modifiers will form surface films that will greatly influence the friction coefficient under mixed/boundary lubrication conditions (in addition, certain types of other additives such as dispersants, detergents and Viscosity Index improvers may also form surface films, depending on the additive chemistry used).

The most commonly used anti-wear additive is zinc dialkyldithiophosphate (a comprehensive review of this additive has been published by Spikes[18]). This additive, often referred to as simply ZDDP, forms a complex surface film, which has been widely studied.[19] If ZDDP is added to a base oil (at a treat rate of 1%), a significant increase in friction is observed (although it may take a few minutes for this effect to be seen since the film has to first form on the surface). Fig. 3 shows typical data from a PCS Instruments Mini Traction Machine illustrating the "running-in" process during which the friction coefficient increases as the film develops. For engine oils, friction modifier (FM) additives are often added to try to reduce the friction coefficient. Friction modifiers are generally either based on molybdenum chemistry (in which a surface film of MoS_2 will form at the surface) or will be organic in nature (glycerol mono-oleate and oleylamide are commonly used organic FMs). Fig. 4 shows typical MTM data showing the friction coefficient of oils containing such additives (these MTM friction curves were measured once the "running-in" process had completed) in comparison with oils which do not contain FMs. In general, oils containing Molybdenum based friction modifiers have very low friction coefficient at the lowest MTM speeds (of the order of 0.04 or so). However, oils containing organic FMs, although having a higher friction coefficient at the lowest speeds, can have a lower friction coefficient than Molybdenum containing oils at slightly higher speeds (>200 mm s^{-1}).

Viscosity Index Improver additives have a significant effect on lubricant friction for two main reasons. Firstly, by increasing the Viscosity Index of the base oil, they cause the lubricant to have a lower viscosity at low temperatures (for oils

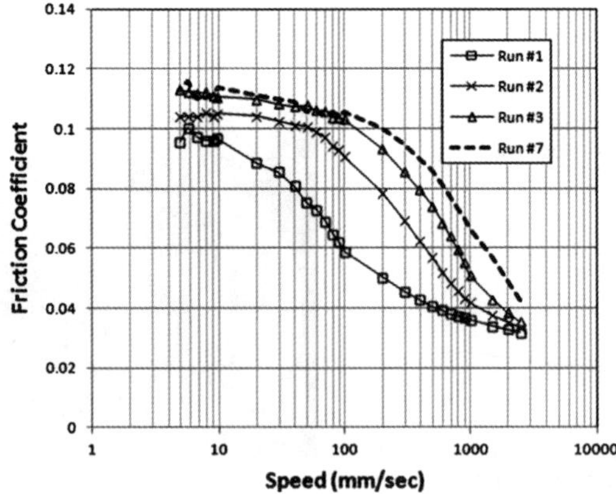

Fig. 3 Development of friction coefficient *versus* speed in MTM during "running-in". Oil used was a passenger car SAE 10W-40 motor oil, and MTM operating conditions were: oil temperature = 125 °C, load = 1.25 GPa.

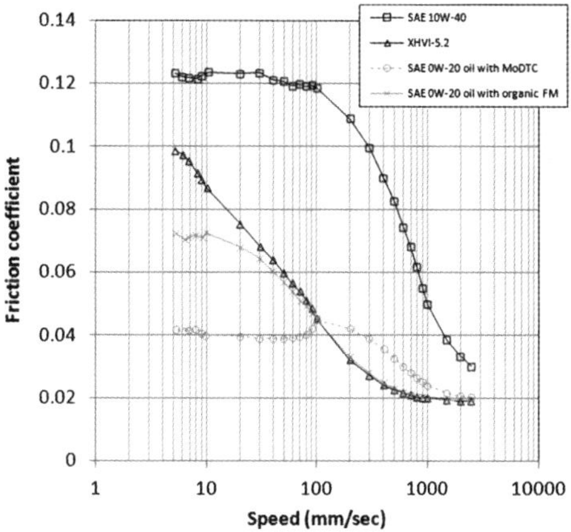

Fig. 4 MTM curve for (1) fully formulated SAE 10W-40 oil with no friction modifier, (2) XHVI™-5.2base oil, (3) fully formulated SAE 0W-20 oil containing Molybdenum based friction modifier, and (4) fully formulated SAE 0W-20 oil containing organic based friction modifier. Data above was measured after "running-in" and for operating conditions of 105 °C oil temperature, and 0.82 GPa load.

with the same V_k100), which will result in the higher VI oil giving lower friction at these lower temperatures, compared to the lower VI oil. Secondly, the Viscosity Index Improver molecules, which have a high molecular weight (>10 000) compared to the other components of a lubricant, tend to align in a shear field, causing a temporary reduction in lubricant viscosity. For engine lubricants, this is one reason why high shear viscosity measurements are carried out, in addition to standard kinematic viscosity measurements. For engine lubricants, manufacturers would typically quote V_k40 (cSt), V_k100 (cSt), HTHS (mPa s) (measured at a temperature of 150 °C and a shear rate of 10^6 s^{-1}) and the cold cranking simulator (CCS) viscosity (this is a high shear rate viscosity measurement made at sub-zero temperatures, the temperature being determined by the SAE grade of the engine lubricant). In contrast, for industrial lubricants, where Viscosity Index Improver molecules are not generally used, manufacturers would typically only quote the ISO grade (effectively the V_k40 (cSt) of the oil) and possibly also V_k100 (cSt).

Typical lubricant viscosity-shear rate curves have been previously reported by Taylor.[20]

Suggested areas for further work

It is well known that lubricants oxidise (this is the main reason why oils require changing periodically). For a hydrocarbon base oil, hydroperoxides are initially produced which then further react to form ketones, aldehydes, alcohols, and acids.[21] There has been very little study of the effect on properties such as α for used oils. When used oils are analysed, often kinematic viscosity is reported, and this can increase during an oil drain interval, and under severe conditions, the V_k100 of the oil can increase by 20–50% (this range was seen in a field trial run in Paris taxis, with oil drain intervals of 20 000 km). However, the impact of the used oil on viscosity-shear rate has not generally been studied.

Similarly, it is known that lubricant additives deplete over time. Studies[22,23] have been carried out which show that for Molybdenum friction modifiers, their lower friction only lasts as long as there is a source of sulphur available. There has been a lack of systematic study of the effect of oil aging on friction from other types of lubricant additives. In part this is likely due to there being few industry standard tests for evaluating used oil fuel economy (an exception has been the fuel economy tests from ILSAC, in which "aged" fuel economy evaluations have been used in Sequence VI-B and Sequence VI-D engine tests, and in general the "aged" fuel economy is worse than the fresh fuel economy).

3 Effect of lubricant properties on individual components

Journal bearings

It is generally accepted that plain journal bearings operate predominantly in the hydrodynamic lubrication regime,[24-26] although recent work suggests that under certain conditions, friction modifiers can influence journal bearing friction, even in the hydrodynamic lubrication regime, possibly due to modification of the "no-slip" boundary condition at the bearing surface.[27]

The short bearing theory is widely used to estimate the minimum oil film thickness and friction loss of a journal bearing. In this theory, the bearing is assumed to be short compared to its diameter, and this enables simplification of the Reynolds' equation, and for Newtonian oils, an analytical relationship can be derived relating the bearing load to the eccentricity ratio of the bearing. More recently, Taylor[28] has shown that in the high eccentricity limit (which is of greatest interest), simple expressions for the minimum oil film thickness, h_{min} (m), and friction power loss, P (Watts) can be obtained:

$$h_{min} = \sqrt{\frac{\eta \omega R L^3}{4W}}$$

(2)

$$P = \frac{2\pi \eta^{0.75} \omega^{1.75} L^{0.25} R^{2.75} W^{0.25}}{c^{0.5}}$$

(3)

where η is the lubricant dynamic viscosity (Pa s), ω is the bearing rotational speed (rad s^{-1}), R is the bearing radius (m), L is the bearing width (m), W is the load on the bearing (N), and c is the bearing radial clearance (m).

The simple theory above does not however capture dynamic effects, nor does it take account of lubricant shear thinning behaviour. A modified version of the short bearing approximation that includes "squeeze" lubrication effects and lubricant shear thinning can be developed. The basic Reynolds' equation becomes:

$$\frac{\partial}{\partial y}\left(\frac{h^3}{\eta}\frac{\partial P}{\partial y}\right) \approx 6U\frac{\partial h}{\partial x} + 12\frac{\partial h}{\partial t}$$

(4)

Where y is the coordinate across the bearing width, and x is the coordinate around the bearing circumference ($x = R\theta$, where θ is the angle around the bearing). h is the oil film thickness at position (x,y) and P is the pressure at position (x,y). U is the relative speed of the bearing surfaces ($= R\omega$).

The oil film thickness around the bearing is assumed to be independent of y:

$$h(\theta) = c(1 + \varepsilon \cos\theta)$$

(5)

Where ε is the eccentricity ratio. For a given applied load, the aim is to calculate the value of ε. Solving eqn (4) using the value for h, leads to an expression for the pressure around the bearing:

$$P(x,y) = \frac{6\eta}{h^3}\left(\frac{Uc\varepsilon}{2R}\sin\theta - c\frac{\partial \varepsilon}{\partial t}\cos\theta\right)\left(\frac{L^2}{4} - y^2\right)$$

(6)

The above equation only applies for $0 \leq \theta \leq 180°$. For angles between 180° and 360°, the pressure in the bearing is assumed to be zero (this is the cavitation region).

If lubricant shear thinning is accounted for, the lubricant viscosity will vary with x. Lubricant shear thinning is accounted for by assuming a Cross equation.[29]

$$\eta = \left[\kappa exp\left(\frac{\theta_1}{\theta_2 + T}\right) \right] \left[\frac{\eta_\infty}{\eta_o} + \frac{1 - \frac{\eta_\infty}{\eta_o}}{1 + \frac{\gamma}{\gamma_c}} \right] \tag{7}$$

Where η is the lubricant dynamic viscosity (Pa s) at temperature $T/^\circ C$ and shear rate γ (s^{-1}). κ (Pa s), θ_1 ($^\circ C$) and θ_2 ($^\circ C$) are constants that describe the variation of lubricant viscosity with temperature (the Vogel equation[30,31]). The term in the first bracket on the right side of eqn (6) is η_o, the lubricant dynamic viscosity at zero shear rate, whilst η_∞ is the lubricant dynamic viscosity at infinitely high shear rates. γ_c is the shear rate (s^{-1}) at which the lubricant dynamic viscosity is exactly half way between η_o and η_∞. γ_c is a strong function of temperature.[30–32]

Taking this into account leads to the following set of equations which require solving.

$$W_1 = \frac{\eta_\infty L^3}{2c^2} \int_0^\pi \left(\frac{U\varepsilon sin\theta - 2R\frac{\partial\varepsilon}{\partial t}cos\theta}{(1 + \varepsilon\, cos\theta)^3} \right) cos\theta\, d\theta$$

$$+ \frac{(\eta_o - \eta_\infty)L^3}{2c^2} \int_0^\pi \left(\frac{U\varepsilon sin\theta - 2R\frac{\partial\varepsilon}{\partial t}cos\theta}{(1 + \varepsilon cos\theta)^2(1 + \Delta + \varepsilon cos\theta)} \right) cos\theta\, d\theta \tag{8}$$

$$W_2 = \frac{\eta_\infty L^3}{2c^2} \int_0^\pi \left(\frac{U\varepsilon sin\theta - 2R\frac{\partial\varepsilon}{\partial t}cos\theta}{(1 + \varepsilon cos\theta)^3} \right) sin\theta\, d\theta$$

$$+ \frac{(\eta_o - \eta_\infty)L^3}{2c^2} \int_0^\pi \left(\frac{U\varepsilon sin\theta - 2R\frac{\partial\varepsilon}{\partial t}cos\theta}{(1 + \varepsilon cos\theta)^2(1 + \Delta + \varepsilon cos\theta)} \right) sin\theta\, d\theta \tag{9}$$

$$W = \sqrt{W_1^2 + W_2^2} \tag{10}$$

In the above equations, $\Delta = U/(\gamma_c c)$. To solve these equations for a time dependent load, $W(t)$, an initial guess for ε is chosen, and the above equations are solved for $\partial\varepsilon/\partial t$. In MATLAB[33] or Python(x,y)[34] a nonlinear equation solver known as **fsolve** is used. The next value of ε is then given by: $\varepsilon_{i+1} = \varepsilon_i + (\partial\varepsilon/\partial t)\Delta t$. This process is continued for two complete load cycles to ensure the eccentricity ratio *versus* crank angle has converged.

Fig. 5 shows the predicted oil film thickness and friction power loss for three different oils (an SAE 50 monograde oil, and SAE 15W-40 and SAE 0W-20 multigrade oils), for a typical con-rod bearing load (the bearing load curve is also shown in Fig. 5 along with the oil film thickness). For these simulations, the following values were used: $L = 20$ mm, $R = 25$ mm, $c = 30$ μm and $\omega = 2500$ rpm and the lubricant temperature was assumed to be 100 $^\circ C$. Viscometric properties of the oils are given in Table 2. The values for κ, θ_1, θ_2, η_∞/η_o and γ_c (at 40 $^\circ C$ and 100 $^\circ C$) are summarised in Table 3.

Simulations were also performed for a lubricant temperature of 40 $^\circ C$. Table 4 summarises the minimum oil film thickness and average friction power loss, for

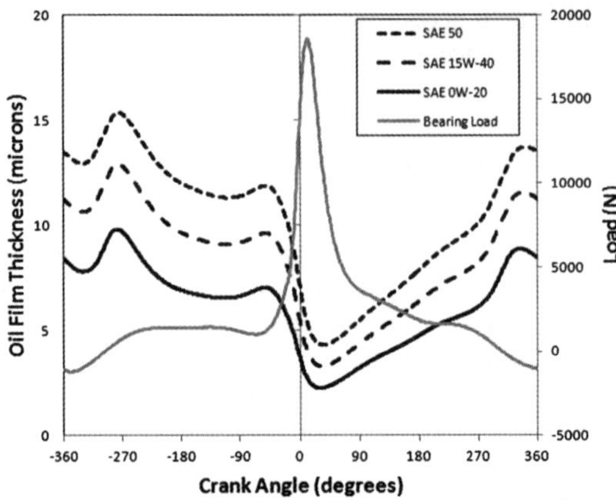

Fig. 5 Oil film thickness and friction power loss for three different lubricants ($T = 100\ °C$).

Table 2 Viscometric properties of lubricants considered in bearing simulations shown in Fig. 5

	SAE-50	SAE 15W-40	SAE 0W-20
V_k40 (cSt)	215.6	108.3	43.56
V_k100 (cSt)	19.37	14.80	8.80
HTHS (mPa s)	5.03	3.91	2.62

Table 3 Values of for κ, θ_1, θ_2, η_∞/η_0 and γ_c (at 40 °C and 100 °C) for SAE 50, SAE 15W-40 and SAE 0W-20 lubricants considered in bearing simulations. For the SAE 50 lubricant, there is no shear thinning, so no values for γ_c are given

	SAE-50	SAE 15W-40	SAE 0W-20
κ (mPa s)	0.0493	0.0292	0.0844
θ_1 (°C)	1161.84	1424.3	988.61
θ_2 (°C)	101.24	137.2	124.81
η_∞/η_0	1.0	0.79	0.70
γ_c (40 °C) (s^{-1})	N/A	3.47×10^3	2.61×10^3
γ_c (100 °C) (s^{-1})	N/A	1.25×10^5	6.17×10^4

Table 4 Minimum oil film thickness and average power losses for journal bearing of Fig. 6, for the three lubricants, SAE 50, SAE 15W-40 and SAE 0W-20, at temperatures of 40 °C and 100 °C. Values in brackets are from the "simple" model

	SAE-50	SAE 15W-40	SAE 0W-20
Minimum OFT (μm) at 40 °C	15.43 (11.41)	9.77 (7.56)	5.40 (4.52)
Average power loss (W) at 40 °C	855.89 (580.43)	356.94 (313.12)	137.82 (144.68)
Minimum OFT (μm) at 100 °C	4.32 (3.35)	3.28 (2.73)	2.25 (2.03)
Average power loss (W) at 100 °C	98.10 (92.25)	67.45 (68.14)	39.28 (43.55)

all three lubricants, at both 40 °C and 100 °C. Values estimated using the "simple" equations (eqn (1) and (2)) are also shown, in red, for comparison. (For the "simple" equations, the effect of lubricant shear thinning is not taken into account and so an "average" viscosity of ½($\eta_0 + \eta_\infty$) was used.)

  This journal is © The Royal Society of Chemistry 2012

In summary, it is expected that the main lubricant effect on bearing friction is due to viscosity. A lower viscosity lubricant should give lower bearing friction, but will also result in a lower minimum oil film thickness. It is not thought that friction modifier additives currently have a major effect on bearing friction, but as engine loads and oil temperatures increase, coupled with increasing use of stop-start systems in vehicles, friction modifier effects could become more important and more research in this area is desirable. The effect of lubricant shear thinning needs to be taken into account for accurate friction estimates. For example it is possible to formulate lubricants with the same HTHS viscosity by two different routes. One could use a low base oil viscosity and a lot of VI improver, or one could use a higher base oil viscosity with less VI improver. The first approach would usually result in lower bearing friction. (These two oils, despite having the same HTHS viscosity, can be distinguished viscometrically since the first oil would have a lower CCS viscosity).

The piston assembly

Furuhama[35] reported, in 1984, that the minimum oil film thickness for a piston ring is given by:

$$h_{min} \propto \sqrt{\frac{\eta U}{W}} \tag{11}$$

In the above equation, h_{min} is the minimum oil film thickness under the piston ring (m), η is the lubricant dynamic viscosity (Pa s), U is the speed of the piston ring relative to the piston liner (which varies approximately sinusoidally with crank angle, with a peak value of 10 m s^{-1} or greater at mid-stroke, whilst at top and bottom dead centre the speed would be zero), and W is the force acting on the back of the piston ring.

Similarly, the friction power loss of a piston ring is given by:

$$P \propto \sqrt{\eta U^3 W} \tag{12}$$

Where P is the power loss (Watts). In both eqn (10) and (11) the constant of proportionality will be sensitive to the precise ring shape presented to the liner. The piston ring profile is typically measured using a profilometer, and there can be large differences between the shape of a new piston ring compared to one that is "run-in"—the implications of this will be discussed later.

Therefore, it is expected that lower piston friction losses would result from using a lower viscosity lubricant, but this would be at the expense of lower oil film thicknesses.

Data from experiments that directly measure piston assembly friction (using a floating liner technique) broadly agree with the above conclusions,[36] with the exception that mixed/boundary lubrication is seen at top dead centre firing (which is where the simple theory would predict the thinnest oil films). The size of the friction "spike", F_m, close to top dead centre firing varies inversely with lubricant viscosity (i.e. the thickest oils give the smallest "spikes", with lower viscosity values giving larger friction at this position). Results from these experiments, which were conducted with a lubricant sump temperature of 70 °C, are summarised in Fig. 6 and in Table 5. Fig. 6 shows results just for monograde oils, whilst Table 5 includes two SAE 10W-50 multigrade oils. In Table 5, the estimated high shear viscosity of the lubricants at 70 °C is also included.

Further experiments were conducted using low viscosity SAE 5W-20 oils, with and without friction modifiers to study the effect of friction modifiers on the friction "spike" close to top dead centre firing. Typical results from this second set of experiments are shown in Fig. 7 and the full dataset obtained is summarised in Table 6. The SAE 5W-20 oils were formulated to have a V_k100 of approx 8.7 cSt, and

Table 5 Measured friction mean effective pressure (FMEP), and peak friction force (just after TDC firing) for the piston assembly

	η_∞ (70 °C) (mPa s)	Measured FMEP (kPa)	Measured F_m (N)
SAE 10W	11.39	37.9	490
SAE 10W-50A	17.65	40.8	460
SAE 10W-50B	20.14	43.4	440
SAE 30	23.95	51.0	380
SAE 50	47.12	64.5	300

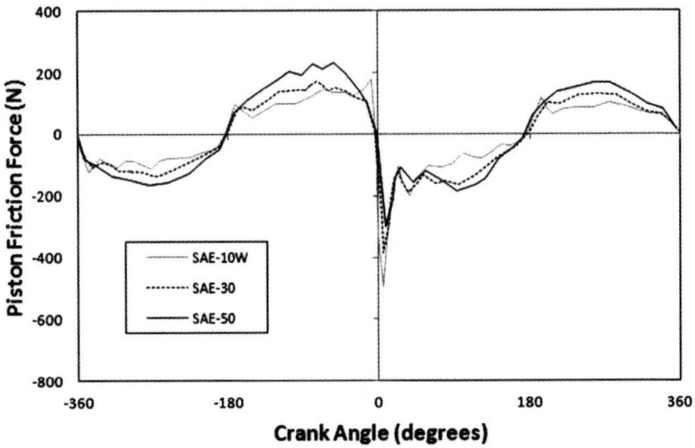

Fig. 6 Piston assembly friction *versus* crank angle for three different monograde oils (SAE 10, SAE 30 and SAE 50) determined in a floating liner piston experiment. Engine conditions were: 1000 rpm, ¼ load.

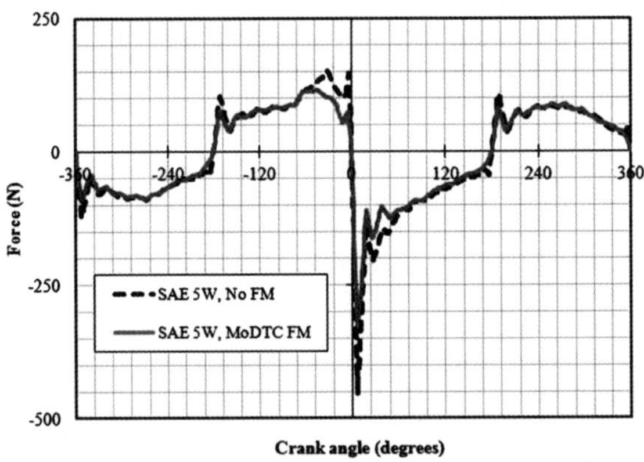

Fig. 7 Piston assembly friction *versus* crank angle for two SAE 5W oils at 800 rpm, one containing a MoDTC friction modifier, and one containing no friction modifier.

a HTHS viscosity of approximately 2.8 mPa s (the estimated high shear dynamic viscosity of the oil at 70 °C is 15.4 mPa s).

The above set of experiments showed that friction modifiers can influence the size of the friction spike just after TDC firing considerably (for the best friction modifier, MoDTC, the friction spike is only 72% of that of an oil without a friction modifier).

Table 6 Measured friction mean effective pressure (FMEP), and peak friction force (just after TDC firing) for the piston assembly, for a series of SAE 5W-20 oils containing different friction modifier additives

	Measured FMEP (kPa)	Measured F_m (N)
SAE 5W-20: no FM	40.2	456
SAE 5W-20: ester FM	39.7	422
SAE 5W-20: amide FM	39.4	398
SAE 5W-20: ester + amide FM	38.2	364
SAE 5W-20: MoDTC FM	37.7	330

On the other hand, the FMEP is relatively unaffected (decreasing by approximately 6% with the MoDTC oil compared to the non friction modified oil). Considering that these experiments were performed at only ¼ load, modern engines with much higher combustion chamber pressures are likely to have more mixed/boundary lubrication than was found in the above study.[36]

Other studies have also found evidence of mixed/boundary friction in the piston assembly.[37,38] Mufti and Priest[37] found that piston ring friction was hydrodynamic in mid-stroke positions, was mixed/boundary around top dead centre firing, and found that the piston skirt was hydrodynamic throughout. Cho *et al.*[38] found that it was the oil control ring that was predominantly in mixed/boundary lubrication.

In addition to experimental determinations of piston assembly friction, and the sensitivity thereof to lubricant properties, there have been many attempts at modelling piston assembly friction.[39–48] It is particularly important to include three effects: (1) lubricant starvation of the upper piston rings[48] (due to the scraping action of the oil control ring)–such effects are most important at mid-stroke positions, (2) "squeeze" lubrication effects,[41] which prevent the oil film thickness dropping to zero at dead centre positions, and (3) the effect of lubricant shear thinning must be included[45] (due to the high shear rates under a piston ring).

It is also important to use correct piston ring shapes in the lubrication models, since the detailed profile that the piston ring presents to the cylinder liner has a significant impact on the oil film thickness. Often, new top piston rings are quite curved, which would lead to high oil film thicknesses at mid-stroke positions, but relatively thin films at dead centre positions. However, these thin oil films lead to wear, and over time the piston ring shape changes, and generally becomes flatter. This leads to thinner oil films at mid-stroke positions, and crucially, larger oil film thicknesses at dead centre positions. Therefore, during the "running-in" process, which may last for 10 000 miles for many cars, use of a "new" piston ring profile would tend to overestimate friction and underestimate oil film thickness, compared to a model which used a "run-in" piston ring profile. More details on these issues can be found in references [49] and [50].

In summary, piston assembly friction is primarily determined by lubricant viscosity. A lower lubricant viscosity generally leads to lower average piston friction (as indicated by a lower FMEP). However, for low viscosities, low speeds, and high loads, mixed/boundary friction can occur particularly around top dead centre firing positions, and under these conditions, friction modifiers in the lubricant can be beneficial.

The valve train

There are many different types of valve train designs in use. Some discussion of the lubrication implications of these different designs is given in reference [51]. It is generally assumed that the valve train is in the elastohydrodynamic lubrication

(EHD) regime. Calculations of the oil film thickness between the valve and tappet[52–58] use elastohydrodynamic lubrication theory—predominantly using the EHD oil film thickness correlation equations of Dowson and Higginson,[59] although there are also reports where full elastohydrodynamic lubrication simulations, including "squeeze" effects, have been carried out.[60]

Fig. 8 shows the measured average friction torque data from a Mercedes Benz M111 cylinder head, as a function of lubricant temperature, for SAE 5W-20 lubricants, with high temperature high shear (HTHS) viscosities of approximately 2.9 mPa s, two of which contained friction modifiers, and one did not. The camshaft speed was 375 revs min^{-1} (equivalent to an engine speed of 750 revs min^{-1}). For temperatures greater than about 50 °C, the friction torque increases as lubricant temperature increases (in other words, friction is increasing as lubricant viscosity is decreasing, which indicates the valve train is in the mixed/boundary lubrication regime. Fig. 8 also shows that significant decreases (of the order of 13% or so at an oil temperature of 75 °C) in valve train friction can be achieved if a friction modifier is used in the oil. Similar results have been reported by other researchers.[61] For temperatures below 50 °C, friction increases as temperature decreases (*i.e.* as viscosity increases). This indicates that for temperatures below 50 °C, the valve train is in the hydrodynamic lubrication regime (probably from the camshaft bearings).

The friction losses in a valve train can be calculated with a full transient, thermo-elastohydrodynamic lubrication analysis. Usually, however, a simpler approach is adopted. In the simple approach, the oil film thickness is calculated using Dowson–Higginson correlation equations,[59] then a friction coefficient is used appropriate to that oil film thickness.[53,62] In early calculations,[62] the friction coefficient was assumed to decrease linearly from a boundary value (at zero film thickness) to zero (at an oil film thickness equal to the average surface roughness). However, more recent work has simply used measured friction coefficient *versus* oil film thickness data from a PCS Instruments Mini-Traction Machine. This data suggests that simply assuming a linearly decreasing function of friction can be quite inaccurate and unrepresentative of real lubricant behaviour.

Elastohydrodynamic contacts

There have been many studies of elastohydrodynamic (EHD) contacts[59,63–71] and although it is relatively simple to estimate the oil film thickness in an EHD contact, it has been found to be much more difficult to accurately estimate friction in an EHD contact[72–79]—unlike the case for oil film thickness, no simple formulae for accurately estimating friction are available. It is important to be able to estimate both the oil

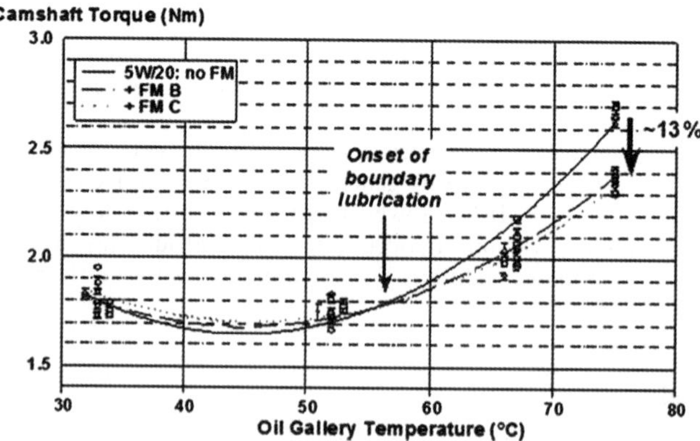

Fig. 8 Measured average valve train friction torque (Nm) *versus* oil gallery temperature /°C for a Mercedes Benz M111 valve train, operating at a camshaft speed of 375 revs min^{-1}.

film thickness and the friction in an EHD contacts, since there are many machine elements which operate in this lubrication regime (gears, valve trains, rolling element bearings, *etc.*)

The choice of lubricant has a significant influence on friction in an EHD contact[80-87]—the limiting shear stress of a lubricant is directly related to the pressure viscosity coefficient (α) of the lubricant,[14] so that lubricants based on synthetic base stocks (Group III, polyalphaolefin (PAO) or polyalkylene gycol (PAG)) will generally have less friction than lubricants containing mineral base stocks (Group I)—as shown earlier in Fig. 2.

The shear rates in an EHD contact are high enough (of the order of 10^8 s^{-1} or so[88]) that the effects of base oil shear thinning need accounting for, and in addition, the lubricant generally heats up as it passes through the contact, so thermal effects also need to be included. It is then possible to estimate friction in EHD contacts reasonably accurately, as reported by Roper and Taylor[89] for EHD line contacts. In general, such studies find that the lubricants formulated using synthetic basestocks are predicted to give lower friction losses, which is in agreement with experimental and field test data.

However there are still some significant unknowns: (1) most theoretical studies have only considered base oils—the effect of additives such as the Viscosity Index Improver, on EHD film thickness, and friction are not well known, (2) the effect of lubricant shear thinning is significant, but there is a lack of data on lubricant shear thinning properties under high pressure conditions, and (3) many simple models of lubricant rheology (such as the Eyring model[90]) do not accurately represent the rheology of realistic lubricants, and finally, (5) there is no agreement on how to accurately model grease lubricated elastohydrodynamic contacts.

4   Effect of lubricant properties on complete systems

In the earlier part of this paper, it has been demonstrated that the choice of lubricant base oil(s) and additives can significantly affect viscosity and friction in individual lubricated contacts, so it is unsurprising that different lubricants can give different friction losses in complete systems. In this section, a "snapshot" is given of some of the friction benefits that can be achieved through intelligent choice of the lubricant, in hydraulic systems (fork lift trucks), in vehicles (cars and trucks) and in gearboxes. No attempt is made here to calculate cost savings (or potential CO_2 savings) but such calculations are straightforward if energy costs are known.

Hydraulic systems

In hydraulic systems, the pump delivers a pressure sufficient to overcome all the pressure drops in the hydraulic circuit. Therefore, if the lubricant is changed, in general, the pressure drops in the circuit change, and so the pressure delivered by the pump also changes. This is why it is important to treat the complete hydraulic system as a whole when considering energy efficient hydraulic lubricants, as opposed to carrying out tests in individual components (such as pumps).

It is generally accepted that one of the most important friction losses in a hydraulic circuit is in the pipes.[91,92] If we can design a lubricant which has a lower dynamic viscosity, this will give lower friction losses in the pipes, and should result in overall energy savings.

Work has been carried out to look at fork lift trucks operating in a refrigerated ware house. The fork lift truck was stationary and a 1000 kg was lifted up and down for a set number of cycles, with the lubricant sump temperature kept constant at temperatures ranging from -20 °C to $+40$ °C (at 5 °C intervals). A selection of hydraulic lubricants were tested, with the same ISO 32 grade (in other words, all the lubricants tested had a kinematic viscosity at 40 °C of approximately 32 cSt) but different Viscosity Indices. Recall that a higher VI oil will have a "flatter" viscosity temperature curve, and so for oils with the same ISO 32 grade, the higher the VI, the lower the viscosity will be for temperatures less than 40 °C. Fig. 9 shows the average power loss for the different lubricants data from these tests. The higher the VI, the lower the energy loss as measured in these tests, and significant differences between the oils were seen at the lowest temperature of -20 °C.

A high VI hydraulic lubricant can be designed by either using (1) synthetic base stocks, and/or (2) using a Viscosity Index Improver additive. Researchers from Rohmax have published papers on the benefits of high VI hydraulic fluids (containing VI improvers) in improving the energy efficiency of hydraulic systems.[93,94]

Cars and trucks

Direct measurements of friction mean effective pressure (FMEP) on car engines show a strong response of engine friction to lubricant viscosity and additive chemistry. Fig. 10 shows the FMEP of a 1.8 litre gasoline engine, as a function of engine speed, for SAE 5W-30 and SAE 0W-20 lubricants, for sump oil temperatures of 40 °C and 100 °C. The measurements were made on a motored engine.

Fig. 10 clearly shows that the lubricant sump temperature has a significant effect on engine friction, with higher friction at lower sump oil temperatures—this is primarily due to the higher lubricant viscosity at these lower temperatures (although note that the lubricant temperature in specific engine components may well be higher than that in the sump). Fig. 10 also shows that the lower viscosity oil, the SAE 0W-20 lubricant, gives lower friction than that of the SAE 5W-30 lubricant, which indicates that engine friction is dominated by hydrodynamic lubrication. However, at a sump temperature of 100 °C, there is some indication at the lowest speeds (750 rpm) that friction is higher than that at 1000 rpm, which indicates mixed/boundary lubrication effects may start appearing at idle, with a fully warmed up engine. This could be significant in some driving cycles (such as the NEDC) where there is a high proportion of engine idling, particularly once the engine is fully warmed up. Shayler et al.[95,96] have investigated the effect of temperature on engine friction in European light duty diesel engines, down to extremely low temperatures (-20 °C or lower) and have found significantly higher FMEP at low temperatures. Shayler et al.[95,96] reported that FMEP varies with viscosity, η, as:

$$FMEP = \left(\frac{\eta}{\eta_{ref}}\right)^{n} FMEP_{ref} \tag{13}$$

Where FMEP (kPa) is the engine friction mean effective pressure when lubricated with an oil of viscosity η (Pa s), whilst FMEP$_{ref}$ (kPa) is the engine friction mean

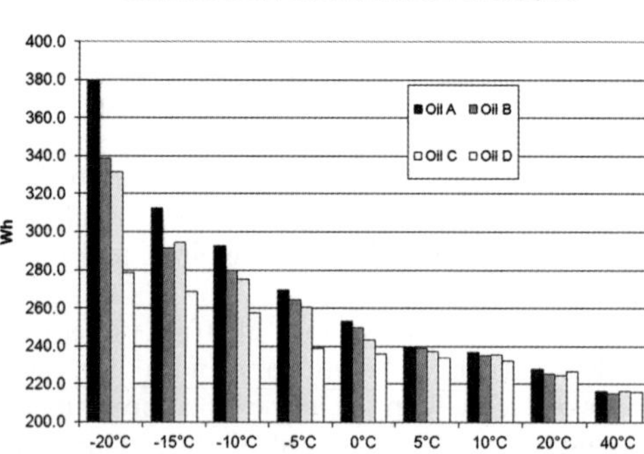

Fig. 9 Effect of lubricant Viscosity Index (VI) on energy consumption, as a function of lubricant temperature, for equivalent ISO 32 hydraulic fluids in a fork lift truck test. The Viscosity Index of the oils are: Oil A—99, Oil B—150, Oil C—162, Oil D—352.

 This journal is © The Royal Society of Chemistry 2012

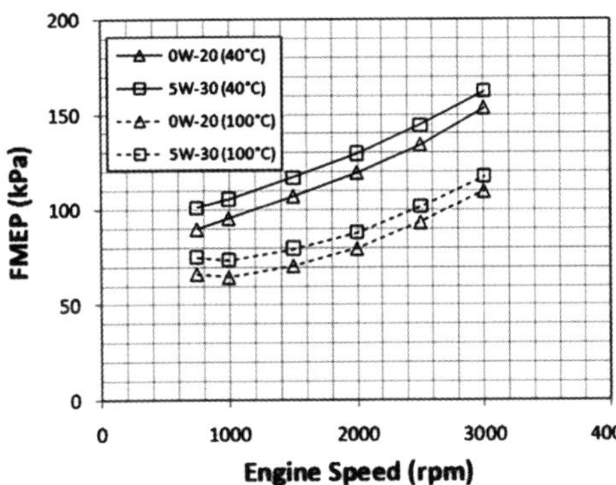

	5W-30	0W-20
V_k40 (cSt)	68.85	43.36
V_k100 (cSt)	12.01	8.04

Fig. 10 FMEP (kPa) *versus* engine speed for a motored 1.8 litre gasoline engine for two lubricants (SAE 5W-30 and SAE 0W-20 at sump oil temperatures of 40 °C and 100 °C). V_k40 and V_k100 data for oils also shown.

effective pressure when lubricated with the reference oil of viscosity η_{ref} (Pa s). n is in the range 0.19–0.30, and a value of 0.25 is typically used. If, for example, the reference lubricant is an SAE 15W-40 oil at 100 °C, a typical kinematic viscosity would be 14 cSt, then the same oil at 40 °C would typically have a kinematic viscosity of 100 cSt, and so the above equation would indicate the FMEP at 40 °C would be approximately 1.6 times that at 100 °C, which is consistent with the data of Fig. 10.

To calculate vehicle fuel consumption, it is necessary to calculate the power required from the fuel.[97–99] Power is required to overcome engine friction (FMEP) and power is also required to account for the fact that the driveline is not 100% efficient. If engine lubricants are used which give lower FMEP, and driveline lubricants (gearbox and axle lubricants) are used which increase driveline efficiency, then this will reduce the power required from the fuel, and lead to fuel consumption savings.

Standard tests are available for evaluating the engine lubricant influence on passenger car fuel consumption. In Europe, the M111 fuel consumption test is used.[100] In the USA, for ILSAC GF-5, the Sequence VI-D engine test is used.[101]

Typical results from the M111 fuel economy test have previously been reported for two SAE 0W-20 lubricants (as compared to the SAE 15W-40 reference oil) by Taylor *et al.*[102] Fig. 11 shows the range of M111 fuel economy test benefits found by Shell for a range of viscosity grades (compared to the RL-191 reference oil). Note that the oil labelled "0W-10" in Fig. 11 is not an official SAE grade.

It is useful to consider where the fuel savings come from in the European M111 engine test (this is a 2.0 litre gasoline engine). The M111 test uses a driving cycle based on the New European Driving Cycle (NEDC), and the sump oil temperature is kept constant at 20 °C, 33 °C, 75 °C and 88 °C. For the lower temperatures, two

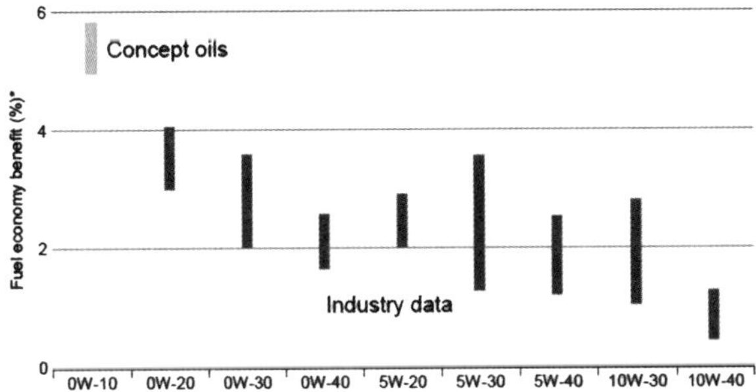

Fig. 11 Range of M111 fuel efficiency results plotted as a function of SAE viscosity grade.

ECE driving cycles are run on the engine, whilst at the higher temperature (88 °C), the higher speed EUDC portion of the driving cycle is run. For full details on how the test is conducted, see reference [100]. The candidate engine oil is compared to a reference SAE 15W-40 engine oil (RL-191). In order to pass the engine test, the candidate oil needs to give a fuel consumption benefit greater than 2.5%. Table 7 gives typical fuel savings, in grams, for each of the different stages of the test, for a candidate oil which just passes the test. Table 7 shows that approximately 60% of the fuel savings come from the colder, city type driving associated with the ECE driving cycle, and around 40% of the fuel savings come from the hotter, higher speed EUDC driving cycle.

In the driving cycle used in the M111 fuel economy engine test, the engine is idling for approximately 25% of the driving cycle, and it has been estimated that approximately 10% of the fuel burned in the M111 test is from idling conditions (this would be equivalent to around 77 grams referring to Table 7). It is worthwhile carrying out a "thought experiment" to try to estimate the importance of friction modifiers in the M111 engine test. For the idling portion of the test, if we assume the valve train is 40% of the total friction, and that under these conditions, 25% of the fuel is used to overcome friction, then the fuel used to overcome valve train friction, at idle is approximately $0.1 \times 0.25 \times 0.4 = 1\%$ (10% of fuel used at idling, of which 25% used to overcome engine friction, of which we assume 40% is from the valve train). If the friction modifier can reduce valve train friction by 20%, then the FM benefit under engine idling conditions would be 0.2%. For the remaining 90% of fuel used, assume that 15% of the fuel is used to overcome friction, and that valve train friction is only 15% of total engine friction (because of the higher speeds). Under these circumstances, the fuel used to overcome valve train friction would be $0.9 \times 0.15 \times 0.15 = 2\%$, and, if we can reduce the friction coefficient in the valve train by 15%, then the FM benefit would be 0.3%. Therefore, from the valve train alone, we may expect 0.5% fuel economy benefit from a friction modifier. Clearly there are many uncertainties in this calculation, so a better estimate may be that FM effects in this test would be in the range 0.2–0.8%. This simple analysis suggests that most of the fuel economy benefit would arise from the use of lower viscosity lubricants, rather than from additive chemistry. However this conclusion may change for different engine designs and different driving cycles, and operating temperatures. Since the size of the benefit depends on the size of friction reduction achievable, there is much research ongoing into finding optimum lubricant/materials/surface finish combinations which give the lowest possible friction—although again, most of this research is concentrated on new lubricants/new materials/new surface finish, and less work has been done on aged lubricants *etc.*

There are no industry standard fuel consumption tests for commercial vehicles. However, recent work[99] has attempted to model the fuel consumption benefits that can be achieved by changing both engine and driveline lubricants. Laboratory tests showed that lower viscosity engine oils (SAE 5W-30 synthetic *versus* SAE

Table 7 Typical fuel consumption data (in grams) from an M111 fuel economy test, for an SAE 5W-30 lubricant which just passes the test (*i.e.* gives a fuel economy benefit of 2.5% compared to the SAE 15W-40 reference oil, RL-191)

	Fuel consumption (g) RL-191	Fuel consumption (g) Candidate oil	Difference in fuel consumption (g)
ECE 20 °C	140.41	135.83	4.58
ECE 33 °C	126.64	123.36	3.28
ECE 75 °C	121.51	118.08	3.43
EUDC 88 °C	393.47	385.20	8.27
Total	782.03	762.48	19.56

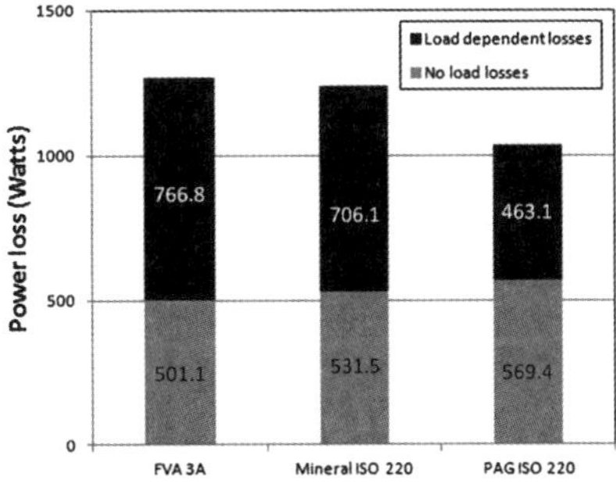

	α (GPa⁻¹) at 70°C	η (mPa.s) at 70°C	VI
FVA 3A	15.57	20.65	85
Mineral ISO 220	16.84	45.51	100
PAG ISO 220	10.52	80.82	203

Fig. 12 FZG efficiency test results on a range of ISO 220 industrial gear oils. FVA 3A is a reference mineral based oil. The sump oil temperature was 70 °C, and the gear speed was 8.3 m s⁻¹. "No load losses" losses were evaluated at Load Stage 0, and total losses were evaluated at Load Stage 7. The difference between the Load Stage 7 and Load Stage 0 results are denoted above as the "Load independent losses."

15W-40 mineral) gave lower engine friction, and that synthetic gearbox and axle lubricants gave higher efficiency compared to their mineral counterparts. These synthetic lubricants were found to give approximately 1.8% fuel consumption benefit compared to their mineral counterparts. This does not sound substantial, but could equate to a fuel saving of approximately 0.5 kg h⁻¹ for a 20 tonne truck. Approximately half the benefit was from the engine oil, with the other half coming from the driveline lubricants. For full details see references [99] and [103].

Gearboxes

In a gearbox, there are (1) churning and windage losses, (2) gear tooth losses, and (3) losses from rolling element bearings and seals.[104–107] If two gearbox lubricants are formulated, with an equivalent ISO grade, but one is formulated from mineral basestocks (Group I) and the other is formulated using synthetic basestocks (*e.g.* PAO), then the oil formulated from synthetic basestocks will have a higher Viscosity Index than the lubricant made from mineral basestocks. If the gearbox sump temperature is 70 °C, the high VI oil may have a higher dynamic viscosity under these conditions than the lower VI oil—in this case we would expect the higher VI oil to have higher churning losses. On the other hand, the high VI oil is likely to have a lower pressure-viscosity coefficient (α), which would lead to fewer gear teeth losses. Whether or not the synthetic based lubricant gives an energy efficiency benefit depends on operating conditions. For low gear loads, the higher churning losses will probably mean the mineral based oil will be more energy efficient, whereas at high loads, fewer gear teeth losses will probably mean that the synthetic based oil will be more energy efficient. However, these conclusions will be highly dependent on the gearbox hardware. However, it is generally observed that sump oil temperature increases in gearboxes are lower when synthetic based lubricants are used, supporting the theory that such lubricants give less gear teeth friction. Fig. 12 shows data generated on the FZG energy efficiency test,[108] for a range of lubricants of the same ISO grade but different Viscosity Index, which broadly speaking support the above conclusions. The PAG based lubricant, with the lowest estimated α value, and highest VI, gives substantially lower load dependent losses, but higher idle losses, compared to a mineral based lubricant (which has a higher α value, and lower VI).

5 Conclusions

The detailed base oil and additive chemistry used in a lubricant has a large effect on the frictional properties of the lubricant. Oils containing antiwear additives (such as

ZDDP) tend give relatively high friction (compared to a base oil alone) and can take some time to fully form. Accurate friction measurements should only be performed once this "running-in" process is complete. To reduce the friction of such oils, friction modifier additives can be added to the lubricant. Oils which contain Molybdenum based FMs tend to give very low friction coefficients under boundary lubrication conditions, but oils containing organic FMs can be more effective in the mixed lubrication regime. Most work that has been reported on friction properties of lubricants has been with "fresh" lubricants, and one area of research which may gain importance in the near future is looking at the friction properties of lubricants as they age.

Another lubricant additive which has a large effect on friction is the Viscosity Index Improver. These molecules affect the way that lubricant viscosity varies with temperature—in general the higher the VI of the oil, the better this will be for energy efficiency. The Viscosity Index Improvers, which are generally quite large polymers, tend to align in shear flows, so that the actual lubricant viscosity in a lubricated contact is lower than expected, which again is usually advantageous for energy efficiency.

The effect of these lubricant variables on component friction has been considered for (1) journal bearings, (2) the piston assembly, (3) the valve train, and (4) elasto-hydrodynamically lubricated contacts.

Finally, the effect of these lubricant variables have also been considered for complete systems, ranging from hydraulically operated forklift trucks, cars, trucks, to gearboxes.

Acknowledgements

The author would like to thank the following Shell colleagues for useful discussions during the preparation of this paper: Richard Dixon, Mark Draper, Simon Dunning, Alison Falender, Rafael Herrera, Bob Mainwaring, Glyn Roper, Paul Savage and Keith Selby.

References

1 Regulation (EC) No 443/2009 of the European Parliament and of the Council of 23 April 2009.
2 US Presidential Memorandum Regarding Fuel Efficiency Standards, May 21, 2010, http:// www.whitehouse.gov/the-press-office/presidential-memorandum-regarding-fuel-efficiency-standards.
3 M. Yamada, Fuel Economy Engine Oils: Present and Future, *Japanese Journal of Tribology*, 1996, **41**(8), 783–791.
4 K. Hoshino, H. Kawai and K. Akiyama, Fuel Efficiency of SAE-5W/20 Friction Modified Gasoline Engine Oil, *SAE paper 982506*, 1998.
5 H. Tanaka, T. Nagashima, T. Sato and S. Kawauchi, The Effect of 0W/20 Low Viscosity Engine Oil on Fuel Economy, *SAE paper 1999-01-3468*, 1999.
6 R. I. Taylor and R. C. Coy, Improved Fuel Efficiency by Lubricant Design: A Review, *Proc Inst. Mech. Eng., Part J*, 2000, **214**, 1–15.
7 D. A. Green, K. Selby, R. Mainwaring & R. Herrera, The Effect of Engine, Axle and Transmission Lubricant, and Operating Conditions on Heavy Duty Diesel Fuel Economy. Part 1: Measurements, JSAE 20119224.
8 R. I. Taylor, K. Selby, R. Herrera & D. A. Green, The Effect of Engine, Axle and Transmission Lubricant, and Operating Conditions on Heavy Duty Diesel Fuel Economy. Part 2: Predictions, JSAE 20119236.
9 J. Ang-Olson and W. Schroeer, Energy Efficiency Strategies for Freight Trucking: Potential Impact on Fuel Use and Greenhouse Gas Emissions, *Transportation Research Record*, 2002, **1815**, 11–18.
10 S. Korcek, R. K. Jensen, M. D. Johnson & J. Sorab, Fuel Efficient Engine Oils, Additive Interactions, Boundary Friction and Wear, Tribology Series, Volume 36, *Lubrication at the Frontier*, Elsevier, pp 13–24, 1999.

11 T. Miller, The Road to Improved Heavy Duty Fuel Economy, presentation at Directions in Energy-Efficiency and Emissions Research Conference, 2010, online at: http://www1.eere.energy.gov/vehiclesandfuels/pdfs/deer_2010/thursday/presentations/deer10_miller.pdf.

12 ASTM Standard D 7589-11, Standard Test Method for Measurement of Effects of Automotive Engine Oils on Fuel Economy of Passenger Cars and Light-Duty Trucks in Sequence VID Spark Ignition Engine.

13 CEC L-54-T-96 Fuel Economy Effects of Engine Lubricants (MB M111 E20), 1996 (Coordinating European Council for the Development of Performance Tests for Lubricants and Engine Fuels).

14 R. M. Mortier & S. T. Orszulik, Chemistry and Technology of Lubricants, 2nd Edition, Springer, 1996.

15 S. Gunsel, S. Korcek, M. Smeeth and H. A. Spikes, The Elastohydrodynamic Friction and Film Forming Properties of Lubricant Base Oils, *Tribol. Trans.*, 1999, **42**(3), 559–569.

16 P. W. Gold, A. Schmidt, H. Dicke, J. Loos and C. Assmann, Viscosity-pressure temperature behaviour of mineral and synthetic oils, *J. Synth. Lubr.*, 2001, **18**(1), 51–79.

17 A. J. Moore, The Behaviour of Lubricants in Elastohydrodynamic Contacts, *Proc Inst. Mech. Eng., Part J*, 1997, **211**, 91–106.

18 H. A. Spikes, The History and Mechanisms of ZDDP, *Tribol. Lett.*, 2004, **17**(3), 469–489.

19 S. Bec, A. Tonck, J. M. Georges, R. C. Coy, J. C. Bell and G. W. Roper, Relationship Between Mechanical Properties and Structures of Zinc Dithiophosphate Anti-Wear Films, *Proc. R. Soc. London, Ser. A*, 1999, **455**, 4181–4203.

20 R. I. Taylor, The Inclusion of Lubricant Shear Thinning in the Short Bearing Approximation, *Proc Inst. Mech. Eng., Part J*, 1999, **213**, 35–46.

21 S. K. Naidu, E. E. Klaus and J. L. Duda, Evaluation of Liquid Phase Oxidation Products of Ester and Mineral Oil Lubricants, *Ind. Eng. Chem. Prod. Res. Dev.*, 1984, **23**, 613–619.

22 J. Graham, H. Spikes and S. Korcek, The Friction Reducing Properties of Molybdenum Dialkyldithiocarbamate Additives: Part I—Factors Influencing Friction Reduction, *Tribol. Trans.*, 2001, **44**(4), 626–636.

23 J. Graham, H. Spikes and R. Jensen, The Friction Reducing Properties of Molybdenum Dialkyldithiocarbamate Additives: Part II—Durability of Friction Reducing Capability, *Tribol. Trans.*, 2001, **44**(4), 637–647.

24 G. W. Stachowiak & A. K. Batchelor, Engineering Tribology, *Tribology Series 24*, published by Elsevier, 1993.

25 B. J. Hamrock, S. R. Schmid & B. O. Jacobson, *Fundamentals of Fluid Film Lubrication*, CRC Press, 2004.

26 R. A. Mufti and M. Priest, Theoretical and Experimental Evaluation of Engine Bearing Performance, *Proc Inst. Mech. Eng., Part J*, 2009, **223**, 629–644.

27 H. J-Choo, A. K. Forrest and H. A. Spikes, Influence of Organic Friction Modifier on Liquid Slip: A New Mechanism of Organic Friction Modifier Action, *Tribol. Lett.*, 2007, **27**, 239–244.

28 R. I. Taylor, Simplifications to the Short Bearing Approximation, *Proc Inst. Mech. Eng., Part J*, 2004, **218**, 569–573.

29 M. M. Cross, Rheology of Non-Newtonian Fluids: A New Flow Equation for Pseudo Plastic Systems, *J. Colloid Sci.*, 1965, **20**, 417–437.

30 R. I. Taylor, The Inclusion of Lubricant Shear Thinning in the Short Bearing Approximation, *Proc Inst. Mech. Eng., Part J*, 1999, **213**, 35–46.

31 R. I. Taylor, The Inclsusion of Lubricant Shear Thinning in Journal Bearing Models, *Proceedings of 1998 Leeds-Lyon Symposium*, published by Elsevier 1999.

32 B. Wright, N. M. van Os & J. A. Lyons, European Activity Concerning Engine Oil Viscosity Classification—Part IV—The Effects of Shear Rate and Temperature on the Viscosity of Multigrade Oils, SAE 830027.

33 http://www.mathworks.co.uk/products/matlab/index.html.

34 http://code.google.com/p/pythonxy/.

35 S. Furuhama & S. Sasaki, Effect of Oil Properties on Piston Frictional Forces, JSAE Review, pp 68–76, November 1984.

36 R. I. Taylor, T. Kitahara, T. Saito & R. C. Coy, Piston Assembly Friction and Wear: The Influence of Lubricant Viscometry, *Proceedings of the International Tribology Conference*, Yokohama, Japan, 1995.

37 R. A. Mufti, M. Priest and R. J. Chittenden, Analysis of Piston Assembly Friction Using the Indicated Mean Effective Pressure Experimental Method to Validate Mathematical Models, *Proc. Inst. Mech. Eng., Part D*, 2008, **222**, 1441–1457. Part D: J. Automobile Engineering.

38 S. Cho, S. Choi and C. Bae, An Experimental Measurement of Lubrication Behaviour of Piston Rings in a Spark Ignition Engine, *JSME Int. J., Ser. B*, 2002, **45**(2), 373–378.

39 R. A. Castleman, A Hydrodynamic Theory of Piston Ring Lubrication, *Physics*, 1936, **7**(9), 364–367.

40 S. Eilon and O. A. Saunders, A Study of Piston Ring Lubricaton, Proc. Inst. Mech, *Eng.*, 1957, **171**(11), 427–433.

41 S. Furuhama, A Dynamic Theory of Piston-Ring Lubrication (1st Report, Calculation), *Bull. JSME*, 1959, **2**(7), 423–428.

42 G. M. Hamilton and S. L. Moore, Comparison Between Measured and Calculated Thickness of the Oil Film Lubricating Piston Rings, *ARCHIVE: Proceedings of the Institution of Mechanical Engineers 1847-1982 (vols 1-196)*, 1974, **188**, 262–268.

43 D. Dowson, P. N. Economou, B. L. Ruddy, P. J. Strachan & A. J. S. Baker, Piston Ring Lubrication—Part II. Theoretical Analysis of a Single Ring and a Complete Ring Pack, in *Energy Conservation Through Fluid Film Lubrication Technology—Frontier in Research and Design*, editors: S. M. Rohde, D. F. Wilcock and H. S. Cheng, pp 23–52, 1979.

44 Y. Wakuri, M. Soejima, T. Kitahara, S. Wada & M. Ootsubo, Studies on the Characteristics of Piston Ring Friction, *Memoirs of the Faculty of Engineering*, Kyushu University, Vol. 50, (No. 3), pp 251–275, 1990.

45 R. I. Taylor, M. A. Brown, D. M. Thompson & J. C. Bell, The Influence of Lubricant Rheology on Friction in the Piston Ring-Pack, SAE 941981.

46 Y.-R. Jeng, Theoretical Analysis of Piston-Ring Lubrication Part I—Fully Flooded Lubrication, *Tribol. Trans.*, 1992, **35**(4), 696–706.

47 Y.-R. Jeng, Theoretical Analysis of Piston-Ring Lubrication Part II—Starved Lubrication and Its Application to a Complete Ring Pack, *Tribol. Trans.*, 1992, **35**(4), 707–714.

48 S. Sanda, M. Murakami, T. Noda and T. Konomi, Analysis of Lubrication of a Piston Ring Package (Effect of Oil Starvation on Oil Film Thickness), *JSME International Journal, Series B*, 1997, **40**(3), 478–486.

49 M. Priest, The Wear and Lubrication of Piston Rings, PhD Thesis, University of Leeds, 1996.

50 M. Priest, D. Dowson and C. M. Taylor, Predictive Wear Modelling of Lubricated Piston Rings in a Diesel Engine, *Wear*, 1999, **231**, 89–101.

51 J. C. Bell, Effect of Valve Train Design Evolution on Motor Oil Anti-Wear Requirements, *CEC97–EL02, 5th CEC International Symposium on the Performance Evaluation of Automotive Fuels and Lubricants*, Gothenburg, Sweden, 1997.

52 A. Dyson, Elastohydrodynamic Lubrication and Wear of Cams Bearing Against Cylindrical Tappets, SAE 770018.

53 J. T. Staron & P. A. Willermet, An Analysis of Valve Train Friction in Terms of Lubrication Principles, SAE 830165.

54 C. M. Taylor, Valve Train—Cam and Follower: Background and Lubrication Analysis, pp 159–182 in *Engine Tribology*, Elsevier, Tribology Series 26, 1983.

55 D. Dowson, P. Harrison & C. M. Taylor, The Lubrication of Automotive Cams and Followers, Proceedings of the 1985 Leeds-Lyon Symposium on Tribology, Elsevier, pp 305–322, 1986.

56 J. C. Bell and T. A. Colgan, Critical Physical Conditions in the Lubrication of Automotive Valve Train Systems, *Tribol. Int.*, 1991, **24**(2), 77–84.

57 L. Yang, A. Ito & H. Negishi, A Valve Train Friction and Lubrication Analysis Model and Its Application in a Cam/Tappet Wear Study, SAE962030.

58 C. Bovington, Elastohydrodynamic Lubrication: A Lubricant Industry Perspective, *Proc Inst. Mech. Eng., Part J*, 1999, **213**, 417–426.

59 D. Dowson & G. R. Higginson, *Elasto-Hydrodynamic Lubrication*, Pergamon Press, 1966.

60 L. E. Scales, J. E. Rycroft, N. R. Horswill & B. P. Williamson, Simulation and Observation of Transient Effects in Elastohydrodynamic Lubrication, SAE961143.

61 D. Dowson, C. M. Taylor & G. Zhu, An Experimental Study of the Tribology of a Cam and Flat Faced Follower, *2nd International Conference on Combustion Engines—Reduction of Friction and Wear*, Instn. Mech. Engrs. Conf. Pub., London, Paper, C375/025, pp 97–108, 1989.

62 R. C. Coy, Practical Applications of Lubrication Models in Engines, *Tribol. Int.*, 1998, **31**(10), 563–571.

63 A. N. Grubin, Investigation of the Contact of Machine Componentsin *Central Scientific Research Institute for Technology and Mechanical Engineering*, Moscow, DSIR, Translation No. 337, 1949.

64 A. I. Petrusevich, Fundamental Conclusions from the Contact Hydrodynamic Theory of Lubrication, *Izvestiya Akademii Nauk SSSR (OTN)*, 1951, **3**(2), 209–223.

65 A. Cameron, Righting a 40-Year-Old Wrong: A.M. Ertel—The True Author of Grubin's EHL Solution, *Tribol. Int.*, 1985, **18**(2), 92.

66 D. Dowson and G. R. Higginson, A Numerical Solution to the Elasto-Hydrodynamic Problem, *J. Mech. Eng. Sci.*, 1959, **1**, 6–15.

67 R. Gohar, *Elastohydrodynamics*, Imperial College Press, 2001.

68 H. A. Spikes, Sixty years of EHL, *Lubr. Sci.*, 2006, **18**(4), 265–291.

69 P. M. Lugt and G. E. Morales-Espejel, A Review of Elasto-Hydrodynamic Lubrication Theory, *Tribol. Trans.*, 2011, **54**(3), 470–496.

70 S. Bair, High-Pressure Rheology for Quantitative Elastohydrodynamics, published by Elsevier, *Tribology and Interface Engineering Series 54*, 2007.

71 C. H. Venner, Multilevel Solution of the EHL Line and Point Contact Problems, PhD Thesis, University of Twente, 1991.

72 M. A. Plint, Third Paper: Traction in Elastohydrodynamic Contacts, *ARCHIVE: Proceedings of the Institution of Mechanical Engineers 1847-1982 (vols 1-196)*, 1967, **182**, 300–306.

73 A. Dyson, Frictional Traction and Lubricant Rheology in Elastohydrodynamic Lubrication, *Philos. Trans. R. Soc. London, Ser. A*, 1970, **266**(1170), 1–33.

74 W. Hirst and A. J. Moore, Non-Newtonian Behaviour in Elastohydrodynamic Lubrication, *Proc. R. Soc. London, Ser. A*, 1974, **337**(1608), 101–121.

75 K. L. Johnson and J. A. Greenwood, Thermal Analysis of an Eyring Fluid in Elastohydrodynamic Traction, *Wear*, 1980, **61**(2), 353–374.

76 C. R. Evans and K. L. Johnson, Regimes of Traction in Elastohydrodynamic Lubrication, *Proc. Instn. Mech. Engrs, Part C, Journal of Mechanical Engineering Science*, 1986, **200**(C5), 313–324.

77 A. V. Olver and H. A. Spikes, Prediction of Traction in Elastohydrodynamic Lubrication, *Proc Inst. Mech. Eng., Part J*, 1998, **212**, 321–332.

78 P. Ehret, D. Dowson and C. M. Taylor, On Lubricant Transport Conditions in Elastohydrodynamic Conjunctions, *Proc. R. Soc. London, Ser. A*, 1998, **454**, 763–786.

79 Y. Liu, Q. J. Wang and S. Bair, A Quantitative Solution for the Full Shear-Thinning EHL Point Contact Problem Including Traction, *Tribol. Lett.*, 2007, **28**, 171–181.

80 A. Dyson, Flow Properties of Mineral Oils in Elastohydrodynamic Lubrication, *Phil. Trans. R. Soc. Lond. A*, 1970, **258**(1093), 529–564.

81 E. G. Trachman & H. S. Cheng, Thermal and Non-Newtonian Effects on Traction in Elastohydrodynamic Contacts, in *Proceedings of Second Symposium on Elastohydrodynamic Lubrication*, Institution of Mechanical Engineers, London, pp 142–148, 1972.

82 S. Bair and W. O. Winer, A Rheological Model for Elastohydrodynamic Lubrication Based in Primary Laboratory Data, *J. Lubr. Technol.*, 1979, **101**(3), 258–265.

83 E. Höglund, Influence of Lubricant Properties on Elastohydrodynamic Lubrication, *Wear*, 1999, **232**, 176–184.

84 L. E. Scales, Quantifying the Rheological Basis of Traction Fluid Performance, SAE 1999-01-3610.

85 R. Larsson, P. O. Larsson, E. Eriksson, M. Sjöberg and E. Höglund, Lubricant Properties for Input to Hydrodynamic and Elastohydrodynamic Lubrication Analyses, *Proc Inst. Mech. Eng., Part J*, 2000, **214**, 17–27.

86 S. Bair and P. Kottke, Pressure-Viscosity Relationship for Elastohydrodynamics, *Tribol. Trans.*, 2003, **46**(3), 289–295.

87 P. Kumar and M. M. Khonsari, On the Role of Lubricant Rheology and Piezo-Viscous Properties in Line and Point Contact EHL, *Tribol. Int.*, 2009, **42**, 1522–1530.

88 H. A. Spikes, The Behaviour of Lubricants in Contacts: Current Understanding and Future Possibilities, *Proc Inst. Mech. Eng., Part J*, 1994, **208**, 3–15.

89 G. W. Roper & R. I. Taylor, Elastohydrodynamic Lubrication Modelling Case Studies, *Presentation given at STLE Annual Meeting*, Calgary, Canada, May 2006.

90 H. Eyring, Viscosty, Plasticity, and Diffusion as Examples of Absolute Reaction Rates, *J. Chem. Phys.*, 1936, **4**, 283–287.

91 A. B. Goodwin, Power Hydraulics, Cleaver-Hulme Press Ltd, 1963.

92 P. J. Chapple, *Principles of Hydraulic System Design*, Coxmoor Publishing Company, 2003.

93 D. G. Placek, S. N. Herzog, Reducing Energy Consumption with Multigrade Hydraulic Fluids, 9th Annual Fuels & Lubes Asia Conference and Exhibition, Singapore, 2003, http://www.mehf.com/FLasia03paperV12.pdf.

94 S. Herzog, C. Neveu and D. Placek, The Benefits of Maximum Efficiency Hydraulic Fluids, *Machinery Lubrication*, 2005, **7**.

95 P. J. Shayler, J. A. Burrows, C. R. Tindle and M. Murphy, Engine Friction Characteristics Under Cold Start Conditions, 2001 Fall Technical Conference, ASME Paper No. 2001-ICE-432, **37-3**, 2001.

96 P. J. Shayler, D. K. W. Leong & M. Murphy, Friction Teardown Data from Motored Engine Tests on Light Duty Automotive Diesel Engines at Low Temperatures and Speeds, 2003 Fall Technical Conference, ASME Paper No. ICEF 2003-745, 2003.

97 M. Ross, Fuel Efficiency and the Physics of Automobiles, *Contemp. Phys.*, 1997, **38**(6), 381–394.

98 M. Ross & F. An, The Use of Fuel by Spark Ignition Engines, SAE 930329.

99 R. I. Taylor, K. Selby, R. Herrera & D. A. Green, The Effect of Engine, Axle and Transmission Lubricant, and Operating Conditions on Heavy Duty Diesel Fuel Economy: Part 2: Predictions", JSAE 20119236.

100 CEC L-54-T-96 Fuel Economy Effects of Engine Lubricants (MB M111 E20), 1996 (Coordinating European Council for the Development of Performance Tests for Lubricants and Engine Fuels).

101 ASTM D7589—11 Standard Test Method for Measurement of Effects of Automotive Engine Oils on Fuel Economy of Passenger Cars and Light-Duty Trucks in Sequence VID Spark Ignition Engine.

102 R. I. Taylor, R. T. Dixon, F. D. Wayne & S. Gunsel, Lubricants & Energy Efficiency: Life-Cycle Analysis, Proceedings of the 2004 Leeds–Lyon Symposium on Tribology.

103 D. A. Green, K. Selby, R. Mainwaring & R. Herrera, The Effect of Engine, Axle and Transmission Lubricant, and Operating Conditions on Heavy Duty Diesel Fuel Economy: Part 1: Measurements, JSAE 20119224.

104 N. E. Anderson, S. H. Loewenthal, Spur-Gear-Efficiency at Part and Full Load, NASA Technical Paper 1622, 1980.

105 S. Wu and H. S. Cheng, A Friction Model of Partial-EHL Contacts and its Application to Power Loss in Spur Gears, *Tribol. Trans.*, 1991, **34**(3), 398–407.

106 A. Olver, Gear Lubrication—A Review, *Proc Inst. Mech. Eng., Part J*, 2002, **216**, 255–267.

107 D. G. Hargreaves and A. Planitz, Assessing the Energy Efficiency of Gear Oils *Via* the FZG Test Machine, *Tribol. Int.*, 2009, **42**, 918–925.

108 A. Doleschel, A Method to Determine the Frictional Behaviour of Gear Lubricants Using an FZG Gear Test Rig, FVA Information Sheet No.345, 2002.

Complex frictional analysis of self-lubricant W-S-C/Cr coating

Tomas Polcar,[*a] Fredrik Gustavsson,[b] Thomas Thersleff,[b] Staffan Jacobson[b] and Albano Cavaleiro[c]

Received 5th January 2012, Accepted 8th February 2012
DOI: 10.1039/c2fd00003b

Transition metal dichalcogenides belong to one of the most developed classes of materials for solid lubrication. However, one of the main drawbacks of most of the self-lubricating coatings is their low load-bearing capacity, particularly in terrestrial atmospheres. In our previous work, alloying thin films based on tungsten disulfide with non-metallic interstitial elements, such as carbon or nitrogen, has been studied in order to improve tribological performance in different environments. Excellent results were reached with the deposited coatings hardness, in some cases, more than one order of magnitude higher than single W-S films. In this work, W-S-C films were deposited with increasing Cr contents by co-sputtering chromium and composite WS_2-C and targets. Two films were prepared with approx. 7 and 13 at.% of Cr. Alloying with chromium led to dense films with amorphous microstructure; the hardness and adhesion was improved. Sliding tests were carried out in dry and humid air using a pin-on-disc tribometer with 100Cr6 steel balls as a counterpart. To analyse the sliding process, the surfaces in the contact were investigated by X-ray photoelectron spectroscopy (bonding), scanning electron microscopy (SEM), transmission electron microscopy (TEM), and Raman spectroscopy. Surface and sub-surface structural modification of the coating and composition of the transferred tribolayer are discussed in detail. High friction in humid air was attributed to the absence of a well-ordered WS_2 sliding interface. On the other hand, the existence of such an interface explained the very low friction observed in dry air.

1. Introduction

Transition metal dichalcogenides (TMDs), namely molybdenum and tungsten disulfides and diselenides, exist in two crystal forms, hexagonal and rhombohedral. Only the hexagonal structure will be discussed, since it is the most common and important for low-friction applications. The hexagonal crystal structure with six-fold symmetry exhibits a laminar structure. Each chalcogenide atom is equidistant from three metal atoms, and each metal atom is equidistant from six chalcogenide atoms. Large spacing between X–M–X (X – chalcogenide, M – transition metal) layers and weak van der Waals forces may facilitate easy inter or intra-crystalline slip.[1,2] Despite contradictory reports, it seems that there is no fundamental difference between interfacial and inter-crystalline friction of TMDs. Strong intra-planar

[a]Department of Control Engineering, Faculty of Electrical Engineering, Czech Technical University in Prague, Technická 2, Prague 6, Czech Republic. E-mail: polcar@fel.cvut.cz; Tel: +420 22435 7598
[b]Applied Materials Science, Department of Engineering Sciences, Uppsala University, Box 534, 751 21 Uppsala, Sweden
[c]SEG-CEMUC - Department of Mechanical Engineering, University of Coimbra, Rua Luís Reis Santos, P-3030 788 Coimbra, Portugal

covalent bonding helps resist asperity penetration even under extremely high contact pressures. Thanks to a layered structure, the properties of TMDs are highly anisotropic.[1]

The inter-lamellar bonding within a TMD crystal is at a minimum and the presence of contaminants thus hinders lubrication properties due to increasing interlamellar interaction. Thus, TMDs fundamentally differ from other well-known layered materials such as mica or graphite with strong ionic bonding. To decrease the friction of graphite, the bond energies must be reduced by the presence of contaminants, typically water vapor.[3] As a result, the friction of graphite in dry air or a vacuum is high, whereas TMDs exhibit higher friction in humid atmosphere.

TMDs are extensively used as solid lubricants as oil additives or thin films. The most convenient method to prepare these films is magnetron sputtering; thus, all references hereinafter deal with coatings deposited by this method. Sputtered coatings of MoS_2, the best known member of the TMD family, were thoroughly analyzed in the 80s and 90s. The first studies on the deposition of MoS_2 usually led to films with columnar morphologies with very high porosity and consequently very low values of hardness;[4] the adhesion to the steel substrates was limited and the coatings deteriorated in the presence of humid air. Thus, their tribological behavior was unsuitable whenever high loads were applied to the sliding contact or tests were carried out in moisture-containing atmospheres. Other transition metal dichalcogenides have similar properties to molybdenum disulfide, although diselenides exhibited improved resistance to water in relation to sulfides.[1,5]

Despite mentioned differences among pure TMD coatings, their common drawbacks are a very low load-bearing capacity, a low adhesion to the substrate and a detrimental effect of moisture in the air on the tribological contact. There are many different possibilities to improve the tribological behavior of these coatings. One of the most successful ways is to deposit a composite material associating high strength materials with self-lubricants, *i.e.* doping of the TMD film by other metals, titanium being the most successful.[6,7]

Voevodin *et al.*[8] and later Nossa and Cavaleiro[9] alloyed WS_2 with carbon and prepared a nanocomposite coating combining small hard WC and lubricant WS_2 nanograins embedded in an amorphous carbon matrix. The core idea behind this concept was to combine the excellent tribological properties of DLC films in humid air and the extremely low friction of the WS_2 phase in dry air or a vacuum. The coatings were hard (about 10 GPa) and exhibited excellent tribological properties in nitrogen. In humid air, the carbon matrix protected the WS_2 phase and the coating endurance was increased; however, the friction in humid air was still very high.

Recently we developed a novel class of self-lubricant coatings with oriented separated TMD platelets randomly dispersed in an amorphous carbon matrix.[10,11] This microstructure allowed structural adaptation of the coating material. We observed the formation of a thin TMD sliding interface; moreover, the coating below this interface was modified and the TMD platelets were re-oriented inside the carbon matrix. As a result, the sensitivity of the friction to air humidity was significantly decreased.[11] However, the nanostructure referred to above led to lower hardness values (approximately 5 GPa for WSC coatings), which limited the abrasion resistance and use of these coatings on rougher substrates. Alloying of a WSC coating with metals could lead to improved mechanical properties and adhesion of the films on steel substrates; moreover, it is possible to tune the coating microstructure by metal content.

The aim of this study is to analyze the effect of chromium on the microstructure, mechanical and, particularly, tribological properties of WSC-Cr coatings.

2. Experimental details

The WSC-Cr films were deposited using an r.f. magnetron sputtering chamber. Prior to the coating deposition, the substrates were cleaned by establishing the plasma close to the substrate electrode for 20 min. Two targets were used to deposit WSC-Cr coatings: a pure chromium target and a graphite target with WS_2 pellets placed on the erosion zone. The number of pellets was calculated to obtain approx. 40 at.% of carbon in the WSC film (*i.e.* the film without co-sputtered chromium). To improve the coating adhesion, a pure chromium interlayer was deposited on the substrates. The power applied to the C target was kept constant, whereas the power of Cr target varied to obtain different chromium contents in the coatings.

The chemical composition of the coatings was evaluated by electron probe micro-analysis (EPMA). Hardness values were determined by the depth-sensing indentation technique,[12] and adhesion was evaluated by progressive load scratch tests. The chemical bonding of the films was analyzed by Raman spectroscopy (DPSS laser, wavelength 532 nm, and Ar laser, wavelength 514.5 nm), Fourier-transform infrared spectroscopy (FTIR) and X-ray photoelectron spectroscopy (XPS; Mg-$K\alpha$ radiation). The structure was analyzed by X-ray diffraction (Co-$K\alpha$ radiation) and by transmission electron microscopy (TEM), and the morphology and film cross-section were investigated by scanning electron microscopy (SEM).

Two sets of tribological measurements were carried out. The first one was performed exclusively in humid air (relative humidity 34–45%) using a pin-on-disk tribometer with 100Cr6 balls with a diameter of 6 mm as static partners. Different contact loads, between 1 and 15 N, were applied; the test duration was 5000 laps. The second set used a similar pin-on-disc tribometer; however, the load was 10 N, the test duration 10000 laps, and the testing atmosphere was dry (relative humidity approx. 1%) or humid air (relative humidity approx. 55%). The friction coefficient values presented in this work are the average values for the entire test, unless noted otherwise. Wear rates of the coatings and of the balls were determined as worn volume (measured by a 3D white light profilometer) per sliding distance per load.

Special attention was paid to analyze the worn surfaces and the wear debris particles. The worn surfaces were observed by SEM coupled with energy dispersive X-ray spectroscopy (EDS) and characterized by Raman spectroscopy. Selected parts of the wear tracks and the tribofilms formed on the ball surfaces were examined by TEM; the TEM cross sections were prepared by using a FEI Strata DB235 Focused Ion Beam instrument (FIB). The samples were taken out by *in situ* lift out with an Omniprobe W needle and transferred to a Cu-grid and then thinned down to <50 nm thickness. As a final step, the samples were fine polished using low energetic ions to reduce the amount of surface damage. The samples were then analyzed in a FEI Tecnai F30 ST at 300 kV, equipped with a Gatan Imaging Filter which was used for EELS analysis to identify the chemical composition of the tribofilms.

3. Results

3.1 Coating characterization

3.1.1 Chemical composition. The deposition power ratio P_{Cr}/P_{C+WS_2} of the targets was varied between 0 and 0.13, resulting in different Cr contents in the films. The coatings consisted of an approximately 300 nm thick pure chromium interlayer and functional WSC-Cr film with a thickness in the range from 1.7 to 2.7 micrometres. The thicknesses were measured on a broken coated silicon wafer by SEM. The thicknesses were measured by SEM on the cross sections produced by breaking the coated silicon wafers. The coating cross-section (not shown) was featureless, showing no evidence of columnar structure, pores or voids. Table 1 summarizes the targets powers and corresponding chemical composition. Some depositions were repeated to obtain a large set of samples for tribological tests (identical depositions are denominated as A, B, *etc.*). EPMA analysis of the chemical composition demonstrated that the process was highly repeatable. The composition was also measured with XPS to confirm the EPMA result, since both methods have several limitations. The penetration depth of EPMA is about 2 microns and thus the

Table 1 Critical load, hardness and chemical composition measured by EPMA and XPS. The latter was measured at a depth of approximately 5 nm

Deposition	P_{C+WS_2} (W)	P_{Cr} (W)	Chemical composition (at.% – EPMA)					Chemical composition (at.% – XPS)					Hardness (GPa)	Critical load (N)
			W	S	C	Cr	O	W	S	C	Cr	O		
1	600	0	23.6	29.8	42.0	0.6	4.2	38.7	20.0	40.0	0.0	1.3	4.9 ± 0.2	12
2-A	600	50	20.3	25.5	40.4	7.0	7.2	34.0	20.5	33.4	6.8	5.3	5.5 ± 0.2	
2-B	600	50	19.1	26.6	38.1	7.1	9.1						6.2 ± 0.4	16
3-A	600	76	17.4	23.1	37.6	13.4	8.5	32.0	17.0	33.1	12.0	5.9	6.4 ± 0.3	
3-B	600	76	18.5	24.1	35.8	13.5	8.1						7.1 ± 0.3	19
3-C	600	76	18.2	22.4	38.1	13.5	7.8							23

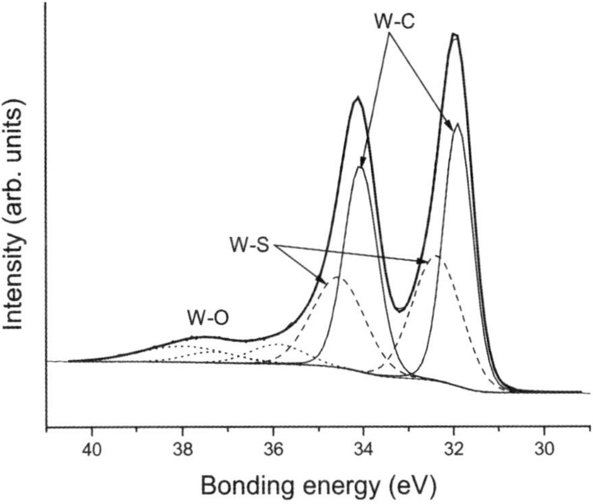

Fig. 1 W 4f XPS spectrum of the WSC-Cr13 film (approx. depth 5 nm).

detection of the interlayer could overestimate the Cr content in the film. This is clearly demonstrated in the case of the WSC film, where the chromium detected originated exclusively from the interlayer. XPS spectra were taken after etching some 5 nm of the film to reduce the effect of contamination. However, etching typically leads to preferential removal of sulfur, which results in a lower measured sulfur content.[13] The oxygen content followed the same trend for both methods, *i.e.* it increases with increasing Cr content. The lower oxygen values measured with XPS could indicate that the O concentration is lower close to the surface. It could be expected, since initial oxygen contamination of targets (note that the carbon target and WS_2 pellets are porous compared to the metallic targets) is reduced during the deposition process.

To facilitate reading, we denominate coatings as WSC-Cr0 (the film sputtered without chromium – deposition 1), WSC-Cr7 (depositions 2-A, 2-B) and WSC-Cr13 (depositions 3 A, 3 B, 3 C).

3.1.2 Chemical bonding and microstructure. XPS was acquired first on the as-deposited surfaces showing mainly tungsten and chromium oxide, and then again after 48 s of sputter cleaning, reaching a depth of approximately 5 nm. The characteristic W 4f XPS spectrum of WSC-Cr films shown in Fig. 1 is deconvoluted to display the contributions from different types of bonds. We detected the following bonds (in brackets their nominal position according to ref. 14): W–C (31.5–32.2 eV); WO_3 (35.2–36.6 eV) and WS_2 (31.6–33.2 eV) bonds. The peaks corresponding to the former bond were found to be positioned at lower binding energies than the W–S contribution, which is in good agreement with the lower electronegativity of carbon compared to sulfur.[9] In fact, a reasonable fit could be achieved even without the W–C peaks. However, such deconvolution would not satisfy the conditions suggested in that more peaks are required for a chi-squared value greater than four. The C 1s spectrum showed both C–C and W–C bonds, whereas S 2p was identified as a combination of W–S bonds and a minor peak representing S–O bonds.

The Cr 2p region of the XPS spectra showed a pair of peaks at 574.4 and ~583.7 eV, close to the position of metallic Cr (574.1 and 583.4 eV[14]). The broad elevation at approximately 590–602 eV was attributed to satellite peaks.[15] The peak separation ruled out a contribution of Cr_2O_3 with a pair of peaks at binding energies (9.3 eV for metallic Cr, 9.7 eV for Cr_2O_3) clearly indicating metallic chromium or chromium carbide. It is possible, however, that very weak peaks at the

Fig. 2 TEM images of WSC-Cr0[10] (left), WSC-Cr7 (centre) and WSC-Cr13 (right) coatings.

positions associated with Cr_2O_3 (576.6 and 586.3 eV) were present and contributed minimally to the spectra. However, the position of the Cr 2p peaks is also very close to the ones characteristic of Cr–S, Cr–C and Cr–W which does not rule out the possibility of having Cr bonded to those elements, particularly when considering the amorphous nature of the films. Nevertheless, the W 4f, C 1s and S 2p spectra of all coatings were almost identical; thus, the alloying of the WSC film with chromium did not change the bonding state of the film.

The WSC-Cr0 coating was investigated by TEM in our previous study, where it was shown to involve randomly oriented WS_2 platelets embedded in a carbon matrix.[16] TEM analysis of the Cr-doped films showed an amorphous-like microstructure (see Fig. 2). The XRD patterns were characteristic of an amorphous material and thus confirmed the TEM observations (not shown).

The analysis of FTIR spectra (not shown) was difficult due to a very noisy background. Only one region, 900 to 1300 cm^{-1}, was clearly distinguishable from the background. Two prominent peaks at approximately 980 and 1260 cm^{-1} together with a barely visible peak at approximately 1140 cm^{-1}, are similar to those for tungsten bonded to carbon.[17] However, peaks at 1079 and 983 cm^{-1}, as well as the broad band from 500 to 1000 cm^{-1}, are associated with W–O bonds and thus make it very difficult to distinguish tungsten oxides and carbides.[18] We could identify a sharp valley at 1633 cm^{-1} as WS_2, although the signal in the 1400–1800 cm^{-1} region was particularly noisy. The same reason hinders the identification of possible Cr_2O_3 peaks that should appear at 1450 and 1490 cm^{-1}[19] as well as C–C bonds at 1640 cm^{-1}.[20]

Raman spectroscopy is a very sensitive method for the chemical identification and the structural analysis of WS_2 and carbon. $2H$-WS_2 single crystals have 4 Raman active crystal vibrations at the G-point of the reciprocal unit cell: A_{1g} (421 cm^{-1}), $E_{2g}^{(1)}$ (356 cm^{-1}), E_{1g} (306 cm^{-1}), and $E_{2g}^{(2)}$ (27 cm^{-1}). Carbon-based sputtered coatings exhibit two major peaks (D and G) in the range 1100–1700 cm^{-1}. Fig. 3 shows the Raman spectra of the as deposited WSC-Cr coatings. The broad peaks close to the WS_2 position were distinct in the case of WSC-Cr0. On the other hand, only vestiges of WS_2-related peaks were observed for the Cr-containing coatings. The broadening of the WS_2 Raman modes is related to the presence of structural defects and/or stress gradients in the scattering volume.[21] Therefore, the broad WS_2-related peaks indicated low structural quality of the WS_2 phase in the WSC-Cr0 coating and an amorphous nature of the chromium-containing coatings and thus corroborated the TEM observations. Since Cr_2O_3 shows a pair of peaks at 305 and 350 cm^{-1},[22,23] $i.e.$ in similar positions to WS_2, they might overlap with WS_2 peaks. However, we do not expect a significant contribution of Cr_2O_3 due to either the low oxygen content in the film or the absence both a Cr_2O_3 Raman peak at $\sim$550 cm^{-1}[24] and a Cr–O bond detected by XPS (see above). The existence of carbon D and G bands corroborates the XPS results (C 1s peak analysis), although it is difficult to estimate the fraction of free carbon and carbides in the films. We observed an

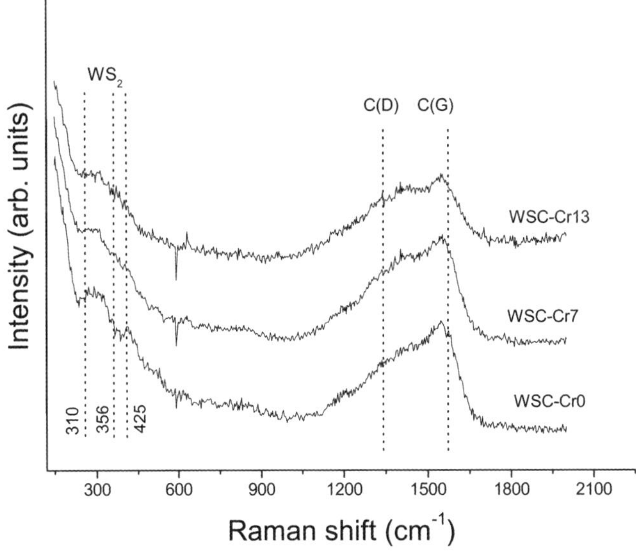

Fig. 3 Raman spectra of as-deposited coatings.

increase in the $I(D)/I(G)$ ratio when Cr was added to the films. The higher $I(D)/I(G)$ ratio is usually attributed to an increase in the number and/or size of the graphitic domains[25] and it is in accordance with results on Cr-doped DLC coatings.[26]

It should be noted that the power of the laser had to be kept very low to avoid film damage. Consequently, the spectra were of low quality hindering detailed peak analyses.

3.1.3 Adhesion and mechanical properties. The critical load and thus adhesion of the coating was increased by alloying the WSC coatings with chromium (see Table 1); a critical load around 20 N could be considered as sufficient for sliding applications. Alloying with Cr increased the coating hardness (Table 1). This trend was observed for co-sputtered WS_2 or MoS_2 films with metals and is explained by reducing the columnar morphology and consequently reducing the number of pores and voids; however, the WSC-Cr0 coating was already dense and morphologically featureless (co-deposition with carbon suppressed the columnar growth). As referred to above, WS_2 platelets observed in the WSC-Cr0 coating could decrease the hardness due to easy slip; therefore, alloying of this film with chromium eliminated the formation of WS_2 platelets and thus could justify the observed increase in hardness. In general, the presented films are softer than nanocomposite $WC/DLC/WS_2$ films;[8] on the other hand, the hardness is still significantly higher than that of sputtered WS_2 films.[10]

3.1.4 Tribological properties. Pin-on-disk sliding tests carried out using different loads (from 1 to 15 N) for 5000 cycles in humid air showed a decrease in the average friction coefficient with increasing contact load (Fig. 4). This behavior matches with similar doped TMD systems and is an indirect indication that a WS_2-rich tribolayer was formed on the coating surface and the ball.[10,11] In the very first few cycles, the friction coefficient was higher due to the polishing of asperities and removal of surface oxidation. After several hundreds of cycles the friction values decreased and a steady-state wear regime was reached. The inset of Fig. 4 shows the initial evolution of the friction. Alloying with Cr increased the friction coefficient, although it was still much lower than that of a pure WS_2 coating.[16] It should be noted that the

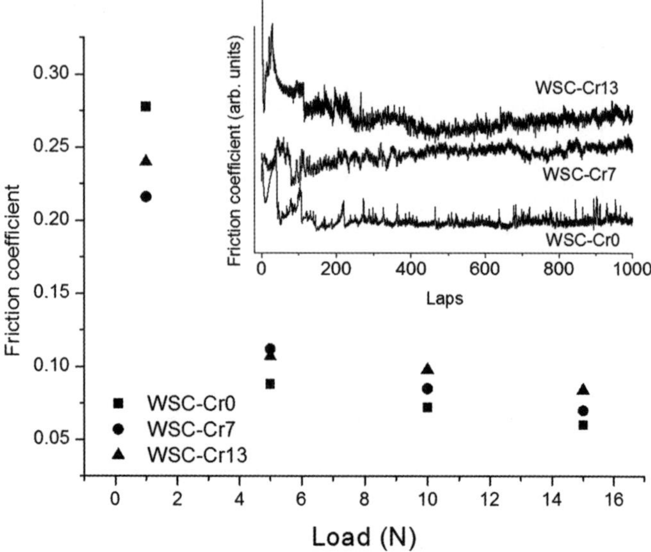

Fig. 4 Friction coefficient *vs.* applied load. The inset shows the initial evolution of the friction, load 5 N, after starting of the tests (running in).

coating with the highest Cr content exhibited an initial friction coefficient around 0.3; moreover, the wear tracks were deeper showing several scratches parallel to the sliding direction. The shapes of the wear tracks formed on the coatings of different compositions in the tests with 5 N load and 5000 cycles are illustrated in Fig. 5. The wear rates of WSC-Cr0 and WSC-Cr7 were similar and almost independent of the applied load. The wear resistance of WSC-Cr13 was the lowest with the maximum wear track depths around 1.5 micrometre, *i.e.* approx. 70% of the functional layer. The ball wear rates were very low, particularly against the WSC-Cr7 film. We also carried out longer tests to estimate evolution of the ball wear during the sliding tests. The ball wear scars had almost the same dimensions after 5000 and 50000 laps; the coating wear volume increased only about 10% compared to the 5000 laps test (thus the wear rate calculated as worn volume per load per sliding distance was significantly lower for a longer test). The wear results indicated high wear during initial contact (running-in); once a steady state was reached, the wear of the coatings and balls was minimal.

Also when sliding in dry air, the initial friction was very high and the running-in periods up towards 2000 cycles. After the running-in, μ was in the range 0.018–0.025 (Fig. 6). The main difference between the non-doped and Cr-doped films is the running-in stage. For the WSC-Cr0 film the friction rapidly dropped to the low steady state level while it took much longer for the Cr-doped films. Moreover, the Cr-doped films initially showed a relatively slowly increasing friction before reaching a maximum and falling towards the steady state level.

3.2 Analysis of the worn surfaces

3.2.1 Sliding in humid air. An example of SEM and EDS of the ball wear scar is shown in Fig. 7. The tribofilm was apparently very thin except for several strips close to the border of the wear scar where it seems thicker. On the other hand, a thick layer of adhered material accumulated in front of the ball wear scar.

Raman analysis of the ball wear scars could shed a light on the structure and composition of the adhered wear debris. The material adhered on the balls could

    This journal is © The Royal Society of Chemistry 2012

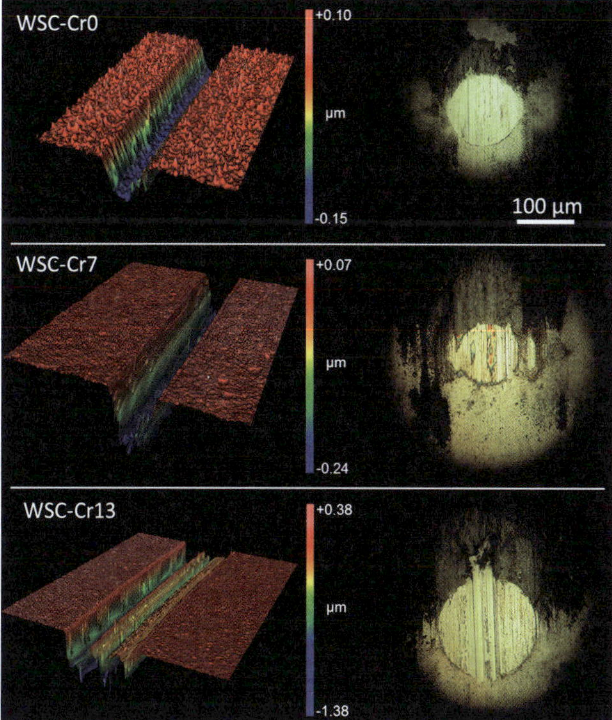

Fig. 5 Shape of the wear tracks on the coated discs (white light interference topography) and optical images of the corresponding wear scars on the balls. Sliding tests with a load of 5 N, 5000 cycles.

be divided into three groups: a) a very thin layer covering parts of the wear scar; b) wear debris attached in front of the wear scar; and c) wear debris scattered farther on both sides of the wear scar. Fig. 8 shows an example of the Raman spectra acquired from the three positions defined above in the ball wear scars after tests with the WSC-Cr0 and WSC-Cr13 coatings. The debris adhered on the sides of the wear scar (position c) was almost exclusively graphitic carbon; only vestiges of WS_2 peaks were observed. Contrastingly, the layer adhered in front of the scar (position b) consisted of graphitic carbon and WS_2. Sharp peaks at approximately 310 and 420 cm^{-1} revealed higher structural order of WS_2 phase compared to the as-deposited films (see Fig. 3). Spectra taken in positions (b) and (c) were almost identical for all three tested coatings. The tribolayer adhered directly in the ball wear scar was not homogeneous and Raman spectra taken at different spots close to the center could be split into two categories. The first one was characterized by a single large peak around 940 cm^{-1}, which was identified as iron oxide; such a spectrum was typical of the Cr-containing coatings. The second combined iron oxide, WS_2 and carbon; it was observed more often on the ball wear scar of the WSC-Cr0 coating.

A TEM cross-section sample of the tribofilm on a ball that was tested against the WSC-Cr7 coating in humid air was prepared by FIB; the position of the FIB cut is shown in Fig. 7. The tribofilm was very thin (about 20 nm) and amorphous-like, a except for some stripes of WS_2 (Fig. 9). Elemental mapping showed mainly oxygen and iron (Fig. 7), although the low thickness of the tribolayer limited more detailed chemical analysis. Nevertheless, the results are consistent with those of Raman spectroscopy.

The wear tracks on the coated samples were investigated by SEM/EDS, TEM, XPS and Raman spectroscopy. The TEM cross section micrograph of the WSC-Cr7

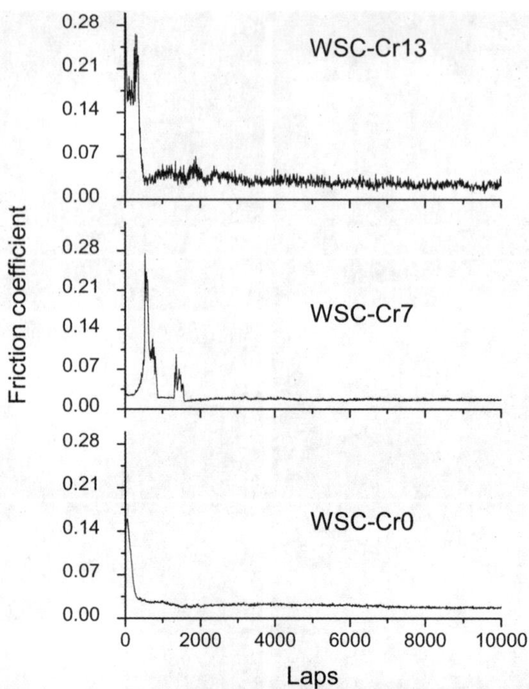

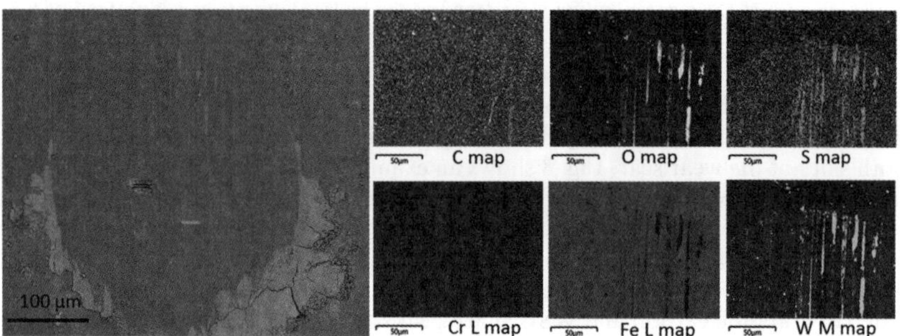

Fig. 6 Friction curves of the WSC-Cr coatings, sliding in dry air, 10 N load.

Fig. 7 SEM image of the wear scar on the ball (left) and corresponding EDS qualitative element maps (right) from the test with the WSC-Cr7 coating in humid air. Note the FIB cut of the ball tribolayer close to the center of the scar.

coating shown in Fig. 10 revealed a relatively thick tribolayer, which was significantly different from the as-deposited coating. It was mostly amorphous with only small areas showing crystalline phases, where particularly WS_2 platelets were identified. There was no indication of the WS_2 phase at the outermost surface of the tribolayer. However, a thin layer of WS_2 with basal planes parallel to the surface (002 orientation) was found on the interface between the coating and the tribolayer. The chemistry of the tribolayer was analyzed with EELS and EDS and showed a high oxygen content together with iron and tungsten (Fig. 11). The concentrations of sulfur and carbon were significantly lower in the tribolayer than in the coating below.

3.2.2 Sliding in dry air. After the sliding tests in dry air, the tribofilm formed on the ball consisted of a thick layer accumulated in front of the wear scar and a thinner

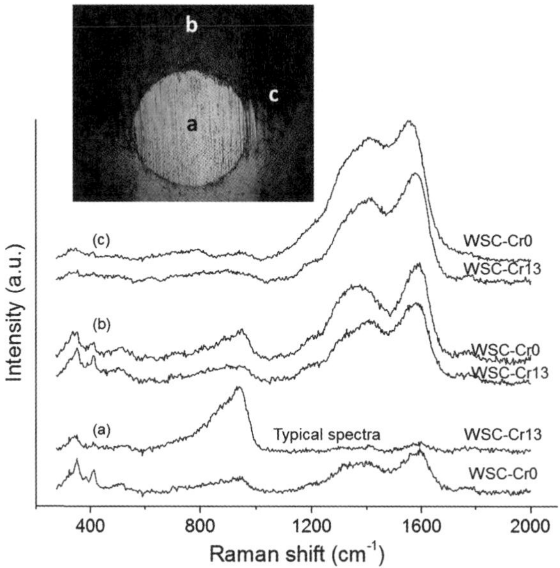

Fig. 8 Raman spectra taken from different parts of the ball (see inset and text).

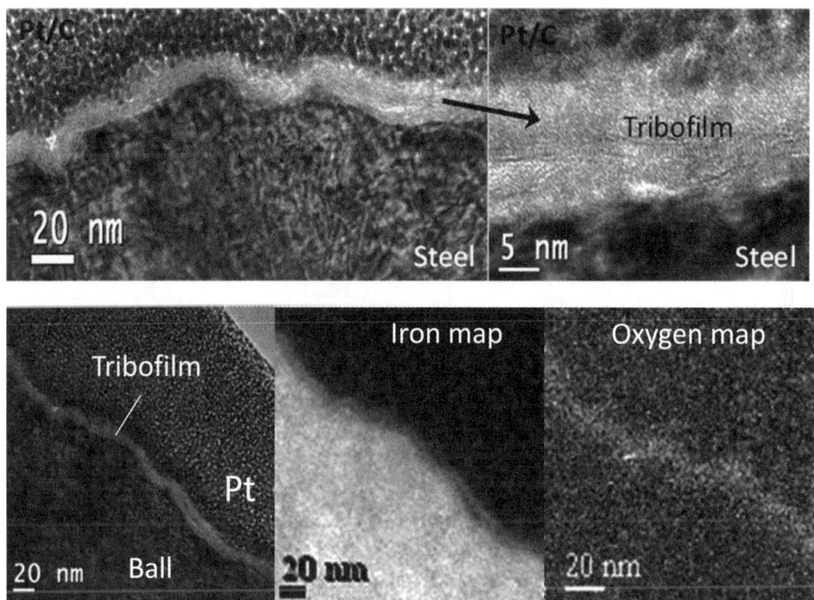

Fig. 9 TEM cross-section of the tribolayer on the worn ball surface (upper panel and lower left) and Fe and O maps of the area (lower middle and right).

layer covering major parts of the scar. Contrasting to the tests in humid air, the material adhered on the ball seems to be chemically homogeneous. No higher concentration of carbon or WS_2 (Fig. 12) was observed. One part of the scar is not covered (or only covered by a very thin layer). This part was probably not in contact with the coating and hence not participating in the sliding process.

TEM investigation of the tribofilm cross-section showed several cracks and voids (Fig. 13). However, the upper part of the tribofilm was dense and showed a distinct,

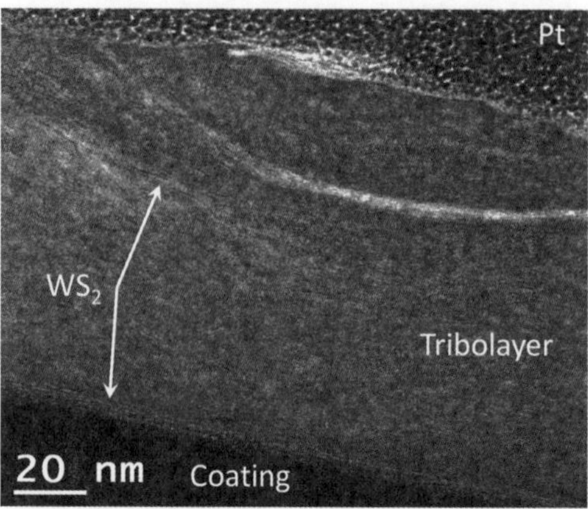

Fig. 10 TEM cross-section of the surface zone of the wear track, WSC-Cr7 coating, sliding test in humid air.

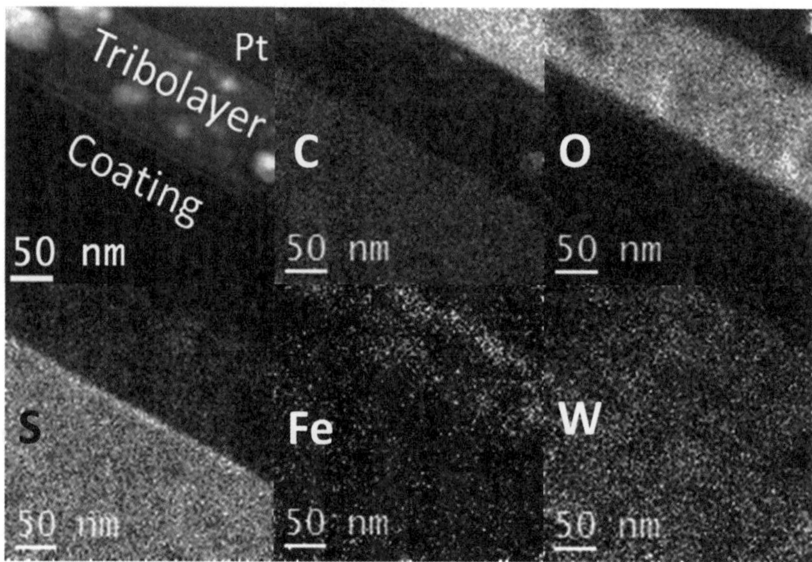

Fig. 11 EFTEM elemental mapping of the tribolayer, WSC-Cr7 coating. Note that the different maps are not quantitatively comparable.

(002) oriented WS_2 layer on top of an amorphous-like layer. The WS_2 layer was 4 to 10 molecular layers thick and seems to be covering the entire tribofilm surface (Fig. 13). Nanocrystalline tungsten oxide was observed below the WS_2 layer; however, it is probably only a measurement artifact since the amorphous tungsten oxide could be easily crystallized under the electron beam.

The tribofilm in the wear track on the coating had a thickness of approximately 40 nm and consisted of two clearly separated layers (both roughly 20 nm thick – see Fig. 14). The upper layer, closest to the interface, was identified as WS_2 with basal planes oriented parallel to the surface. The lower layer was amorphous-like and the EELS spectra indicated chromium oxides. Also, it showed a much lower carbon content in the tribofilm film than in the coating below.

Raman spectra from the wear track surface of the WSC-Cr7 coating are shown in Fig. 15. The sharp peak at 420 cm^{-1} confirmed the presence of a well-ordered and

   This journal is © The Royal Society of Chemistry 2012

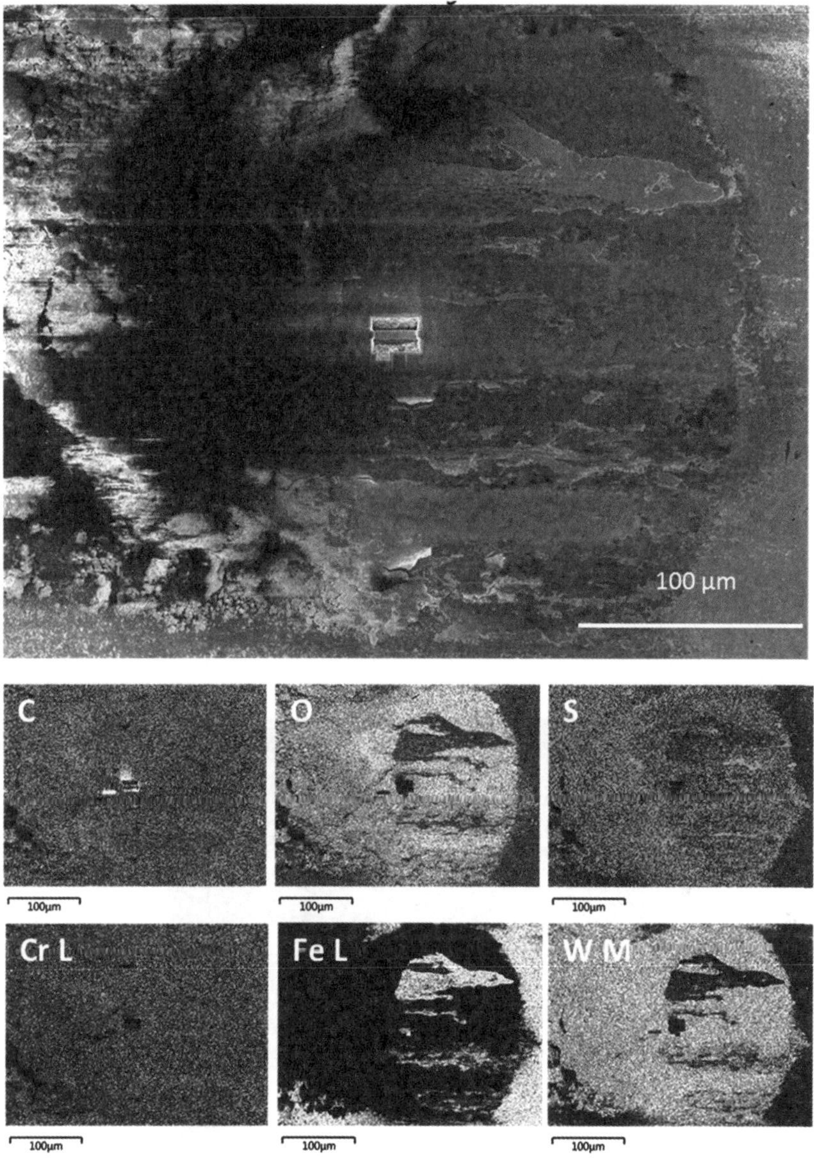

Fig. 12 SEM micrograph and EDS elemental mapping of the wear scar on the ball after a sliding test against the WSC-Cr7 coating with a 10 N load in dry air. Note the position of the FIB cut from the preparation of the TEM cross-section sample.

relatively thick WS_2 layer. It was difficult to distinguish the WS_2 E_{2g} (356 cm^{-1}) peak and Cr_2O_3 positioned at 350 cm^{-1}; however, the shape of the peak in such a position, particularly its high intensity/FWHM ratio, was typical for crystalline WS_2. The Raman spectra in the wear track thus significantly differ from those obtained after sliding in humid air (Fig. 15).

Discussion

The core objective of this study was to identify the effect of alloying a WSC coating with chromium on the structure, mechanical and tribological properties. There are

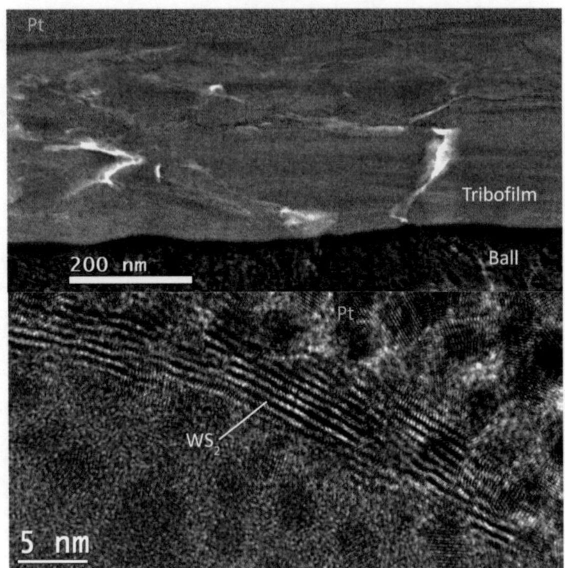

Fig. 13 TEM cross-section of the tribofilm on the ball tested against the WSC-Cr7 coating in dry air. Overview (top), and close-up (bottom), showing that the outermost 5 nm of the tribofilm has a well-ordered WS$_2$ layer.

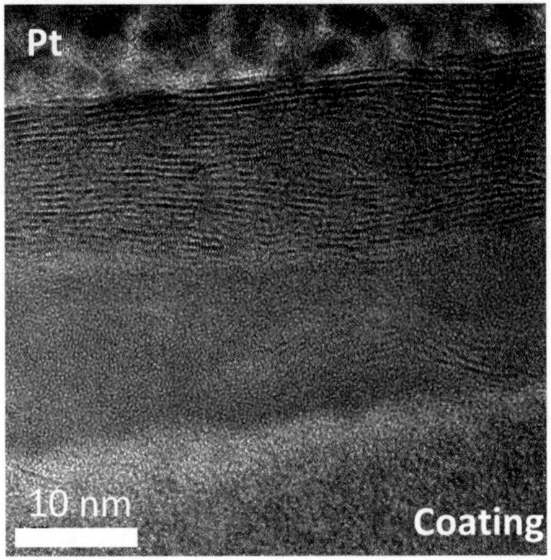

Fig. 14 TEM cross-section of the tribolayer formed in the wear track of WSC-Cr7 tested against a steel ball in a dry atmosphere, load 10 N.

several reports dealing with thin films based on TMDs alloyed with metals (such as Ti,[6,7,27] Al,[28] Au,[29,30] Pb,[31] Ni,[32,33] and Cr[34,35]); the effects of the doping metal on the coating structure, density, and mechanical properties are well studied. However, the role of the doping metal in the tribological contact remains unknown. Improved tribological properties of metal-doped TMD coatings are often attributed to reactions of the metals with residual atmosphere in the deposition chamber, particularly with oxygen. As a consequence, the composition of dichalcogenides is closer to ideal stoichiometry, which is known to be beneficial to reduce friction.[1] It has been

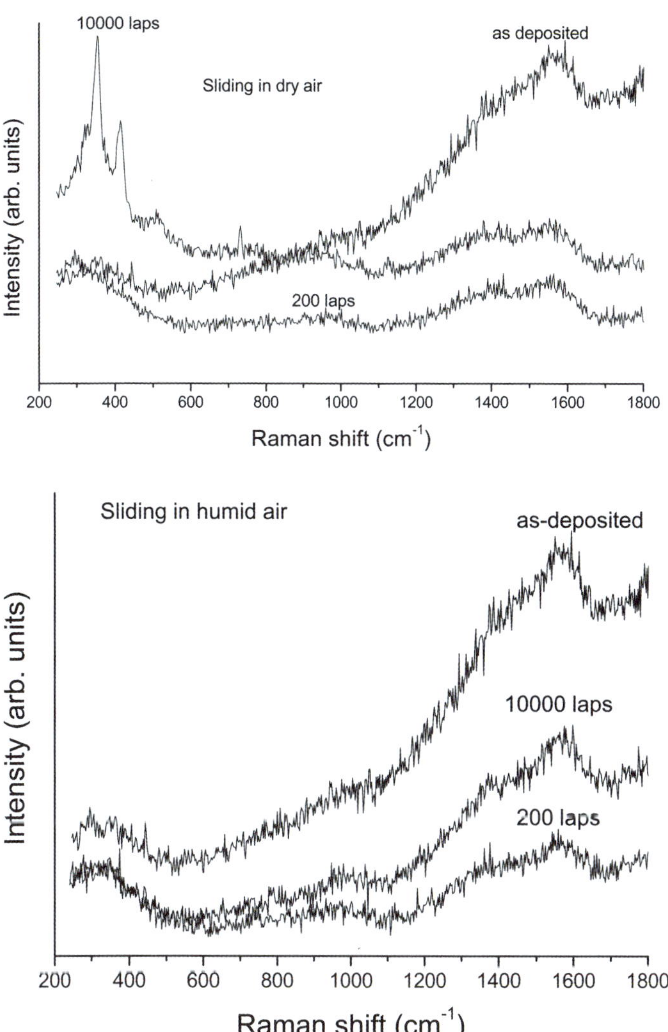

Fig. 15 Raman spectra of the as-deposited WSC-Cr7 coating and of the center of the wear tracks after 200 and 10000 cycles, sliding in dry (upper) and humid (lower) air.

speculated that the metal (namely titanium[6]) preferentially oxidizes in the contact and protects the sensitive TMD phase (oxidation and/or corrosion leads to strong bonding between basal planes). However, in a recent detailed contact analysis of a WS_2-Ti system no such behavior was found.[7]

Doping of the pure TMD typically resulted in a hardness of about one order of magnitude higher and an increase in the density of the films, which are important factors contributing to friction reduction. To distinguish the indirect effect of improved mechanical properties and the role of the metal at the sliding interface is very challenging. Wahl *et al.*[31] prepared an amorphous Pb-Mo-S film and observed a thin MoS_2 tribolayer (1–2 molecular layers) at the coating sliding interface and a relatively thick MoS_2 tribofilm adhered on the ball surface (pin-on-disc test) suggesting that Pb played only a limited role in the sliding process. Chromik *et al.* investigated complex nanocomposite $YSZ/Au/MoS_2/C$ coatings (YSZ – yttria-stabilized zirconia) showing that the low friction was related to the formation of a MoS$_2$-rich tribolayer.[36] Our recent results summarized in ref. 11 show that, in the case of TMD-C films, the TMD tribolayer is exclusively formed in the contact area, whereas carbon is immediately removed.

In this study, the chromium in the as-deposited films is not bonded to oxygen, which is preferentially bonded to tungsten (see XPS results above); thus, the gettering effect of chromium during the deposition process was limited. Alloying with chromium increased the hardness and improved the coating adhesion, although not dramatically. We have shown in our previous studies on TMD-C systems that hardness higher than 4 GPa is sufficient to support the low-friction behaviour.[11]

Nevertheless, co-sputtering with chromium significantly changes the film microstructure. In the absence of Cr (WSC-Cr0), the coating is nanostructured with separated WS$_2$ platelets embedded in a carbon matrix, while it becomes amorphous-like when the Cr content is 7 at.%. A different nanostructure could be an important factor in the formation of a tribolayer on the coating surface and material transfer to the ball surface (tribofilm). Fig. 9 and Fig. 11 indicate the presence of iron in both tribolayer and tribofilm (sliding in humid air); considering the oxygen content in the tribolayer, it is highly probable that the iron is fully oxidized. The presence of iron originating from the ball is interesting. Wear of the ball occurs mainly at the initial stage of the sliding, when the contact pressure is the highest (note high friction coefficients during running in). The size of the wear scar on the ball is almost identical after 50000 cycles and after 5000 cycles. In other words, the ball wear is very limited in the steady state regime. We expect that the ball surface becomes oxidized in the contact and that iron oxide then becomes embedded into the tribolayer on the coating surface. Such mechanical intermixing might hinder the formation of a self-lubricant WS$_2$ layer at the interface.

We have demonstrated that the wear track surface of the WSC film is covered almost exclusively by a thin WS$_2$ layer;[10] Cr-containing WSC coatings show mainly oxides at the interface and consequently exhibit higher friction coefficients.

The very low friction coefficient when sliding in dry air suggests the formation of well-ordered WS$_2$. Indeed, WS$_2$ layers were found on both sides of the contact interface, *i.e.* on the top of the wear track and the bottom of the tribofilm adhered to the ball. Interestingly, a layer consisting mostly of chromium oxide was found between the WS$_2$ top layer and the coating. The worn surfaces analyzed were sampled a long time after the friction coefficient had stabilized and thus in the steady-state regime. Chromium oxide could be formed during running in, but progressive wear (obviously there is wear during the steady-state, although very low) would eventually wear the oxide layer off, if it is not replenished. How could the chromium oxide retain its position between the unchanged (or almost unchanged) coating and the top WS$_2$ layer? And how is the top low-friction layer replenished, when it is separated from the coating by a layer of chromium/tungsten oxide?

We cannot answer these complex questions based on our experimental results; nevertheless, we can present a hypothesis based on a relatively simple model developed by Rigney and Karthikeyan.[37] They used molecular dynamics to simulate the sliding between two amorphous surfaces with different hardnesses and elastic moduli. They showed that sliding led to mechanical intermixing, which could be at least partially responsible for the development of a nanocrystalline material in the contact. They applied this model to a similar self-lubricant system, a nanocomposite WC/DLC/WS$_2$ coating,[38] and analyzed possible intermixing in the sliding interface. Both the tribolayer on the wear tracks and the tribofilm on the ball observed in our case (dry air) consisted of two well separated layers, WS$_2$ and oxide. We can expect that WS$_2$ has a lower shear resistance than the oxide layer and the latter a lower shear resistance than the ball material or unaltered coating. The sliding interface is then in the WS$_2$ layer, as expected. When the WS$_2$ top layer is worn out (*i.e.* mechanically removed from the contact area), the sliding interface moves to the softer material (in our case the oxide layer) and the oxide is mechanically mixed with the coating material. WS$_2$ is then transported to the contact and the well-

   This journal is © The Royal Society of Chemistry 2012

ordered low-friction layer is formed again on the surface. Further study will be aimed at MD simulations of such layers to investigate this hypothesis.

Finally, we will comment on the decrease of the friction coefficient with increased applied load, a typical feature of pure TMD coatings. This behaviour is often approximated by the formula integrating the shear stress of solids at high pressures and the Hertzian model for contact pressure:[39–42]

$$\mu = \tau_0 \cdot \pi \cdot \left(\frac{3R}{4E}\right)^{\frac{2}{3}} L^{-\frac{1}{3}} + \alpha, \tag{1}$$

where R is the radius of the ball, L is the normal load, τ_0 is the interfacial shear strength, α is a material constant representing the adhesive forces at zero load and E is the composite modulus of the sliding couple. Our investigation clearly demonstrates that this approximation cannot be used in the case of doped TMD films and very probably also not for pure TMD coatings. The formation of a tribofilm on the ball, together with the initial wear of both ball and coating, significantly increases the contact area and thus decreases the contact pressure; thus, the ideal Hertz contact gives unrealistically high pressures. Structural transformation in the contact leads to different elastic moduli of the materials involved; therefore, a composite modulus calculated from bulk materials cannot be used. Considering the presented results and our previous studies,[11,43] we suggest that higher contact pressure facilitates both the tribolayer formation on the coating surface and the transfer of the coating material to the ball. Moreover, well-oriented platelets of low-friction WS_2 could be formed at the interface. As a consequence, the friction will decrease with increasing load.

Conclusions

The microstructure of a WSC self-lubricant film with WS_2 platelets embedded in carbon matrix became amorphous when the film was co-sputtered with chromium. The hardness and adhesion increased linearly with chromium content from approx. 5 (WSC) to 7 GPa (13 at.% of Cr). Chromium was mostly in metallic form; chromium carbides were not observed. Compared to WSC, the friction and the wear rate of the Cr-doped films were higher. The coatings showed a very low friction in dry air attributed to the formation of a WS_2 layer at the sliding interface. Such a low-friction layer was not observed when the sliding tests were carried out in humid air. Alloying of the WSC film with chromium deteriorated the tribological properties compared to the non-doped WSC coating.

Acknowledgements

This work was supported by the Czech Science Foundation through the project 108/10/0218.

References

1 A. R. Lansdown, *Molybdenum Disulphide Lubrication*, Elsevier, 1999.
2 *Superlubricity*, ed. A. Erdemir and J.-M. Martin, Elsevier, 2007.
3 A. Erdemir and C. Donnet, *Tribology of Diamond-like Carbon Films: Fundamentals and Applications*, Springer-Verlag, New York, 2007.
4 J. Moser, F. Levy and F. Bussy, Composition and growth mode of MoS_x sputtered films, *J. Vac. Sci. Technol., A*, 1994, **12**, 494.
5 T. Kubart, T. Polcar, L. Kopecký, R. Novák and D. Nováková, *Surf. Coat. Technol.*, 2005, **193**, 230.
6 D. G. Teer, New solid lubricant coatings, *Wear*, 2001, **251**, 1068.
7 T. W. Scharf, A. Rajendran, R. Banerjee and F. Sequeda, Growth, structure and friction behavior of titanium doped tungsten disulphide (Ti-WS(2)) nanocomposite thin films, *Thin Solid Films*, 2009, **517**, 5666.

8 A. A. Voevodin, J. P. O'Neill and J. S. Zabinski, Nanocomposite tribological coatings for aerospace applications, *Surf. Coat. Technol.*, 1999, **116–119**, 36–45.

9 A. Nossa and A. Cavaleiro, Chemical and physical characterization of C(N)-doped W–S sputtered films, *J. Mater. Res.*, 2004, **19**, 2356.

10 T. Polcar, M. Evaristo and A. Cavaleiro, Self-lubricating W-S-C nanocomposite coatings, *Plasma Processes Polym.*, 2009, **6**, 417–424.

11 T. Polcar and A. Cavaleiro, Review on self-lubricant transition metal dichalcogenide nanocomposite coatings alloyed with carbon, *Surf. Coat. Technol.*, 2011, **206**, 686–695.

12 W. C. Oliver and G. M. Pharr, An improved technique for determining hardness and elastic modulus using load and displacement sensing indentation experiments, *J. Mater. Res.*, 1992, **7**, 1564.

13 L. E. Rumaner, T. Tazawa and F. S. Ohuchi, Compositional change of (0001) WS2 surfaces induced by ion beam bombardment with energies between 100 and 1500 eV, *J. Vac. Sci. Technol., A*, 1994, **12**, 2451.

14 C. D. Wagner, W. H. Riggs, C. E. David, J. F. Moulder and G. E. Muilenberg, in Handbook of X-ray photoelectron spectroscopy, Perkin-Elmer Corporation, 1979.

15 Masaoki Oku, Shigeru Suzuki, Naofumi Ohtsu, Toetsu Shishido and Kazuaki Wagatsuma, Comparison of intrinsic zero-energy loss and Shirley-type background corrected profiles of XPS spectra for quantitative surface analysis: Study of Cr, Mn and Fe oxides, *Appl. Surf. Sci.*, 2008, **254**, 5141–5148.

16 T. Polcar, M. Evaristo and A. Cavaleiro, Friction of self-lubricating W-S-C sputtered coatings sliding under increasing load, *Plasma Processes Polym.*, 2007, **4**, S541–S546.

17 P. Hoffman, H. Galindo, G. Zambrano, C. Rincón and P. Prieto, FTIR studies of tungsten carbide in bulk material and thin film samples, *Mater. Charact.*, 2003, **50**, 255–259.

18 B.-H. Xu, B.-Z. Lin, Z.-J. Chen, X.-L. Li and Q.-Q. Wang, Preparation and electrical conductivity of polypyrrole/WS2 layered nanocomposites, *J. Colloid Interface Sci.*, 2009, **330**, 220–226.

19 B. Adamczyk, O. Boese, N. Weiher, S. L. M. Schroeder and E. Kemnitz, Fluorine modified chromium oxide and its impact on heterogeneously catalyzed fluorination reactions, *J. Fluorine Chem.*, 2000, **101**, 239–246.

20 D. Adliene, J. Laurikaitiene, V. Kopustinskas, S. Meskinis and V. Sablinskas, Radiation induced changes in amorphous hydrogenated DLC films, *Mater. Sci. Eng., B*, 2008, **152**, 91–95.

21 J. Álvarez-Garsía, J. Marcos-Ruzafa, A. Pérez-Rodríguez, A. Romano-Rodríguez, J. R. Morante and R. Scheer, *Thin Solid Films*, 2000, **361–362**, 208.

22 M. Bouchard, D. C. Smith and C. Carabatos-Nédelec, An investigation of the feasibility of applying Raman microscopy for exploring stained glass, *Spectrochim. Acta, Part A*, 2007, **68**, 1101–1113.

23 J. E. Maslar, W. S. Hurst, W. J. Bowers Jr, J. H. Hendricks, M. I. Aquino and I. Levin, In situ Raman spectroscopic investigation of chromium surfaces under hydrothermal conditions, *Appl. Surf. Sci.*, 2001, **180**, 102–118.

24 P. M. Sousa, A. J. Silvestre, N. Popovici and O. Conde, Morphological and structural characterization of CrO2/Cr2O3 films grown by Laser-CVD, *Appl. Surf. Sci.*, 2005, **247**, 423–428.

25 A. C. Ferrari and J. Robertson, Interpretation of Raman spectra of disordered and amorphous carbon, *Phys. Rev. B: Condens. Matter*, 2000, **61**, 14095.

26 V. Rigato, G. Maggioni, D. Boscarino, G. Mariotto, E. Bontempi, A. H. S. Jones, D. Camino, D. Teer and C. Santini, Ion beam analysis and Raman characterisation of coatings deposited by cosputtering carbon and chromium in a closed field unbalanced magnetron sputter ion plating system, *Surf. Coat. Technol.*, 1999, **116–119**, 580.

27 A. Savan, M. C. Simmonds, Y. Huang, C. P. Constable, S. Creasey, Y. Gerbig, H. Haefke and D. B. Lewis, Effects of temperature on the chemistry and tribology of co-sputtered MoSx-Ti composite thin films, *Thin Solid Films*, 2005, **489**, 137.

28 J. D. Holbery, E. Pflueger, A. Savan, Y. Gerbig, Q. Luo, D. B. Lewis and W.-D. Munz, Alloying MoS2 with Al and Au: structure and tribological performance, *Surf. Coat. Technol.*, 2003, **169–170**, 716.

29 S. Mikhailov, A. Savan, E. Pflueger, L. Knoblauch, R. Hauert, M. Simmonds and H. Van Swygenhoven, Morphology and tribological properties of metal (oxide)–MoS2 nanostructured multilayer coatings, *Surf. Coat. Technol.*, 1998, **105**, 175.

30 J. R. Lince, Tribology of co-sputtered nanocomposite Au/MoS2 solid lubricant films over a wide contact stress range, *Tribol. Lett.*, 2004, **17**, 419.

31 K. J. Wahl, D. N. Dunn and I. L. Singer, Wear behavior of Pb–Mo–S solid lubricating coatings, *Wear*, 1999, **230**, 175.

32 J. R. Lince, M. R. Hilton and A. S. Bommannavar, Metal incororporation in sputter-deposited MoS2 films studied by EXAFS, *J. Mater. Res.*, 1995, **10**, 2091.

33 M. R. Hilton, G. Jayaram and L. D. Marks, Microstructure of cosputter-deposited metal- and oxide-MoS_2 solid lubricant thin films, *J. Mater. Res.*, 1998, **13**, 1022.
34 Y. L. Su and W. H. Kao, Tribological behaviour and wear mechanism of MoS_2–Cr coatings sliding against various counterbody, *Tribol. Int.*, 2003, **36**, 11.
35 M. C. Simmonds, A. Savan, E. Pfluger and H. Van Swygenhoven, Mechanical and tribological performance of MoS_2 co-sputtered composites, *Surf. Coat. Technol.*, 2000, **126**, 15.
36 C. C. Baker, R. R. Chromik, K. J. Wahl, J. J. Hu and A. A. Voevodin, Preparation of chameleon coatings for space and ambient environments, *Thin Solid Films*, 2007, **515**, 6737.
37 D. A. Rigney and S. Karthikeyan, The Evolution of Tribomaterial During Sliding: A Brief Introduction, *Tribol. Lett.*, 2010, **39**, 3.
38 J.-H. Wu, D. A. Rigney, M. L. Falk, J. H. Sanders, A. A. Voevodin and J. S. Zabinski, Tribological behavior of WC/DLC/WS_2 nanocomposite coatings, *Surf. Coat. Technol.*, 2004, **188–189**, 605.
39 B. J. Briscoe and A. C. Smith, The interfacial shear strengths of molybdenum disulphide and graphite films, *ASLE Trans.*, 1982, **25**, 349.
40 I. L. Singer, R. N. Bolster, J. Wegand, S. Fayeulle and B. C. Stupp, Hertzian stress contribution to low friction behavior of thin MoS2 coatings, *Appl. Phys. Lett.*, 1990, **57**, 995.
41 J. L. Grosseau-Poussard, P. Moine and M. Brendle, Shear strength measurements of parallel MoSx thin films, *Thin Solid Films*, 1997, **307**, 163.
42 T. W. Scharf, S. V. Prasad, M. T. Dugger, P. G. Kotula, R. S. Goeke and R. K. Grubbs, Growth, structure, and tribological behavior of atomic layer-deposited tungsten disulphide solid lubricant coatings with applications to MEMS, *Acta Mater.*, 2006, **54**, 4731.
43 T. Polcar, M. Evaristo, R. Colaço, C. S. Sandu and A. Cavaleiro, Nanoscale triboactivity: The response of Mo-Se-C coatings to sliding, *Acta Mater.*, 2008, **56**, 5101.

Polyelectrolyte brushes: a novel stable lubrication system in aqueous conditions

Motoyasu Kobayashi,[a] Masami Terada[a] and Atsushi Takahara[*ab]

Received 27th November 2011, Accepted 22nd December 2011
DOI: 10.1039/c2fd00123c

Surface-initiated controlled radical copolymerizations of 2-dimethylaminoethyl methacrylate (DMAEMA), 2-(methacryloyloxy)ethyl phosphorylcholine (MPC), 2-(methacryloyloxy)ethyltrimethylammonium chloride) (MTAC), and 3-sulfopropyl methacrylate potassium salt (SPMK) were carried out on a silicon wafer and glass ball to prepare polyelectrolyte brushes with excellent water wettability. The frictional coefficient of the polymer brushes was recorded on a ball-on-plate type tribometer by linear reciprocating motion of the brush specimen at a selected velocity of 1.5×10^{-3} m s^{-1} under a normal load of 0.49 N applied to the stationary glass ball ($d = 10$ mm) at 298 K. The poly(DMAEMA-co-MPC) brush partially cross-linked by bis(2-iodoethoxy)ethane maintained a relatively low friction coefficient around 0.13 under humid air (RH > 75%) even after 200 friction cycles. The poly(SPMK) brush revealed an extremely low friction coefficient around 0.01 even after 450 friction cycles. We supposed that the abrasion of the brush was prevented owing to the good affinity of the poly(SPMK) brush for water forming a water lubrication layer, and electrostatic repulsive interactions among the brushes bearing sulfonic acid groups. Furthermore, the poly(SPMK-co-MTAC) brush with a chemically cross-linked structure showed a stable low friction coefficient in water even after 1400 friction cycles under a normal load of 139 MPa, indicating that the cross-linking structure improved the wear resistance of the brush layer.

1. Introduction

Biological surfaces of synovial joints, such as the hip, knee, and shoulders show extremely low friction coefficients in the range of 0.001–0.03, supported by water lubrication.[1] However, extremely low friction in natural joint systems cannot be achieved by water alone, because the viscosity of water is too low even at high pressure to form useful boundary films.[2] Nature overcomes the disadvantage by biological lubricant additives such as glycoproteins with bottle-brush structure,[3] which are ion-containing polymers having suitable viscoelastic properties in solution[4] and which immobilize large amounts of water molecules to aid lubrication.

It has been widely reported that surface-tethered ion-containing polymers or polyelectrolytes reduce the friction coefficient under wet conditions. In particular, well-defined surface-grafted polymers with sufficiently high graft density, called polymer brushes,[5,6] have attracted much attention to the tribology field.

[a]JST ERATO Takahara Soft Interfaces Project, CE80, Kyushu University, 744 Motooka, Nishi-ku, Fukuoka, Japan. E-mail: motokoba@cstf.kyushu-u.ac.jp; Fax: +81-92-802-2544; Tel: +81-92-802-2543
[b]Institute for Materials Chemistry and Engineering, Kyushu University, 744 Motooka, Nishi-ku, Fukuoka, Japan. E-mail: takahara@cstf.kyushu-u.ac.jp; Fax: +81-92-802-2518; Tel: +81-92-802-2517

Klein *et al.* found a reduction of frictional forces between solid surfaces bearing tethered polymers using a surface force balance, and they also reported that the polyelectrolyte brushes could act as efficient lubricants between mica surfaces in an aqueous medium, even though the graft density was not so high.[7–9]

Similarly, Osada *et al.* reported that gel-terminated polyelectrolyte brushes reduce the friction force between the hydrogels and a glass plate across water.[10] Klein recently found that the poly(2-methacryloyloxyethyl phosphorylcholine) (MPC) brush surface under wet conditions showed an extremely low friction coefficient, as low as 0.0004 at pressures as high as 7.5 MPa, due to the strong hydration of the phosphorylcholine units of the polymer.[11,12]

Theoretical studies[13,14] on the frictional properties of polyelectrolyte brushes have been undertaken to understand the effect of charge density, chain length, graft density,[15–17] ionic strength[18] and solvent quality[19,20] on the structure of polyelectrolyte brushes. The direct measurement of the repulsive and attractive interactions of polyelectrolyte brushes[21,22] has been also performed by surface force apparatus[23,24] and AFM[25] because of their importance in understanding the friction. The effect of solvent quality on the lubrication of non-ionic polymer brushes was also studied by Tsujii.[26]

The macroscopic lubrication properties of a comb-like polyelectrolyte consisting of poly(L-lysine)-*graft*-poly(ethylene glycol) adsorbed onto silicon oxide and iron oxide surfaces have been studied by Spencer and coworkers using ultra-thin-film interferometry, a mini-traction machine, and pin-on-disk tribometry.[27,28] They reported that the graft polymer formed a stable lubricant layer on the tribological interface in aqueous solution and reduced the friction. Kobayashi and coworkers investigated the macroscopic frictional properties of poly(methyl methacrylate) (PMMA)[29] and poly(2,3-dihydroxypropyl methacrylate)[30] brushes prepared by a "grafting form" method using a reciprocating ball-on-plate type tribometer under a pressure of 139 MPa to found out the dependence of the solvent quality, friction velocity, and salt concentration on the friction coefficient of the polymer brush.[31] The reduction in the friction coefficient was observed in a good solvent which swells the brush. In particular, the poly(MPC) brush in water or in humid air showed a low friction coefficient.[32]

In general, polymer brushes are grown from surface radical polymerization initiators that are immobilized on friction probe surfaces or substrates through covalent bonding. As a result, the brush chains are strongly anchored and hardly detached from the substrate, even in a good solvent solution or by friction under a low normal load. However, polymer brushes are usually worn out within 50–100 cycles of macroscopic reciprocating friction by the sliding probe under a high normal load around 100 MPa, resulting in a high friction coefficient due to the exposure of the bare substrate. Thus, the wear resistance for the application of a polymer brush is not sufficient for its practical use under load bearing conditions.

In this study, we proposed that partially cross-linked ion-containing polymer brushes were effective for the improvement of wear resistance without loss of good lubrication. The polymer brushes were prepared by surface-initiated controlled radical polymerization and successive reaction using a hydrophilic cross-linker to maintain the hydrophilicity of the surface and low friction coefficient under wet conditions over a long period of reciprocating friction under a high normal pressure. The effect of cross-linking on the macroscopic tribological character of ion-containing high-density polymer brushes in aqueous solution is described.

2. Experimental

2.1. Preparation of ion-containing polymer brushes

All brush samples were prepared by surface-initiated atom transfer radical polymerization (SI-ATRP) from a silicon wafer immobilized with a surface initiator. The

     This journal is © The Royal Society of Chemistry 2012

surface initiator, (2-bromo-2-methyl)propionyloxyhexyltriethoxysilane (BHE),[33] was immobilized on a clean silicon wafer by the chemical vapor adsorption method.[34] The chemical structures of the monomers and polymer brushes are illustrated in Fig. 1 and 2. An unbound initiator as a sacrificial initiator is necessary to control the degree of polymerization and to estimate the number-average molecular weight (M_n) of the resulting polymer.[35,36] A few sheets of the BHE-immobilized silicon wafers, CuBr (0.020 mmol), 4,4′-dimethyl-2,2′-bipyridyl (Me$_2$bpy, 0.040 mmol), 4.0 mL of MPC/methanol solution (2.0 M), and 0.4 mL of DMAEMA/methanol solution (2.0 M) were charged in a well-dried glass tube with a stopcock and then degassed using a freeze-thaw process that was repeated three times. Ethyl 2-bromoisobutylate (EB) (0.020 mmol) diluted with methanol was injected into the monomer solution. The resulting reaction mixture was degassed again by repeated freeze-thaw cycles to remove the oxygen and then stirred in an oil bath at 303 K for 48 h under argon, which simultaneously generated poly(MPC-*co*-DMAEMA) brushes from the substrate and free (unbound) copolymer from EB. The reaction was stopped by opening the glass vessel to air at 293 K. The reaction mixture was poured into THF to precipitate the free polymer. The silicon wafers were washed with methanol using a Soxhlet apparatus for 12 h to remove the free polymer absorbed on their surfaces and dried under nitrogen gas pressure at room temperature. The thickness of the copolymer brush was found to be 85 nm in the dry state by ellipsometer.

One of the poly(MPC-*co*-DMAEMA) brush substrates was immersed in a bis(2-iodoethoxy)ethane/methanol solution at r.t. for 24 h to quaternize the dimethylamino group forming a cross-linking structure. The poly(MPC-*co*-DMAEMA) brush was also reacted with methyl iodide in water at r.t. for 24 h to form poly[MPC-*co*-{2-(methacryloyloxy)ethyltrimethylammonium iodide} (MTAI)] brush. The PMPC brush was synthesized in a similar manner using CuBr and Me$_2$bpy in methanol at 303 K for 12 h.[32] Surface-initiated radical copolymerization of 3-sulfopropyl methacrylate potassium salt (SPMK) and MTAC was carried out in methanol/water (5/2, v/v) (1.7 M of SPMK) without a free initiator at 298 K for 15 h using a reaction system consisting of SPMK/MTAC/CuBr/CuBr$_2$/Me$_2$bpy in the following molar ratios: 180/20/2/0.4/4.

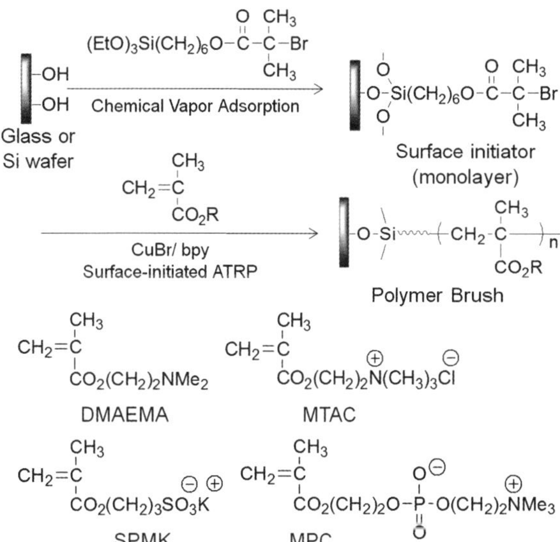

Fig. 1   Scheme of surface-initiated ATRP and chemical structures of electrolyte monomers.

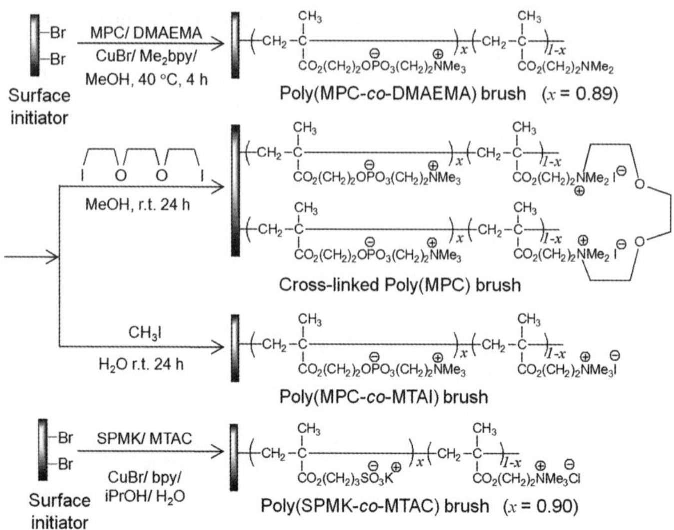

Fig. 2 Preparation of cross-linked poly(MPC), poly(MPC-*co*-MTAI), and poly(SPMK-*co*-MTAC) brushes.

2.2. Measurements

The molecular weight and molecular weight distribution of the unbound polymers were estimated by size exclusion chromatography (SEC) using a Shimadzu HPLC system equipped with a multi angle light scattering detector (MALS; Wyatt Technology DAWN -EOS, 30 mW GaAs linearly polarized laser, wavelength: $\lambda = 690$ nm) and refractive index detector (Shimadzu RID-10A, tungsten lamp (wavelength 470–950 nm)). The Rayleigh ratio at a scattering angle of 90° was based on that of pure toluene at a wavelength of 632.8 nm at 298 K. SEC of poly(MPC) was performed with three polystyrene gel columns connecting with two super AW3000 and super AW4000 (Tosoh Bioscience) using water containing 0.01 M LiBr as an eluent at a rate of 0.5 mL min⁻¹ at 313 K. The thickness of the polymer brushes immobilized on a silicon wafer in air (the relative humidity was *ca.* 45%) was determined by a spectroscopic ellipsometer MASS-102 (Five Lab Co.) with a xenon arc lamp (wavelength of 380–890 nm) at a fixed incident angle of 70°. AFM observation was performed with SPA 400 with an SPI 3800N controller (SII NanoTechnology Inc.) in air at room temperature, using a Si_3N_4 integrated tip on a commercial triangle 200 mm cantilever (Olympus Co., Ltd.) with a spring constant of 0.09 N m⁻¹.

The water contact angles on the polymer brush surfaces were recorded with a drop shape analysis system, DSA10 Mk2 (KRÜSS, Inc.), equipped with a video camera using an inclinable plane. A 2.0 μL droplet of water was placed on the surface using a micropipette to measure the static contact angle. All these evaluations were conducted in ambient air at room temperature (approximately 298 K). The relative humidity was approximately 40%.

Macroscopic friction tests on polymer brushes were carried out on a conventional ball-on-plate type reciprocating tribotester, Tribostation Type32 (Shinto Scientific Co. Ltd., Tokyo), by sliding a glass ball on the substrates at a reciprocating distance of 20 mm and a rate of 1.5×10^{-1} m s⁻¹ in a dry nitrogen atmosphere and water under a normal load of 0.49 N at room temperature. The root mean square (rms) surface roughness of the glass ball was approximately 2.4 nm in a 10×10 μm² area. The friction force was measured by a strain gauge attached to the arm of the tester and was recorded as a function of time. The friction coefficient was given by the friction force divided by the normal load. Every friction test used a virgin surface area on the brush substrate to measure the friction coefficient of the first reciprocating scan of the sliding probe. The substrate of the test piece was pinned in a stainless steel trough filled with water, which was fixed on a moving stage. In the case of a non-modified silicon wafer under a normal load of 50 g (0.49 N), the theoretical contact area between the glass probe and substrate could be estimated to be 3.51×10^{-9} m^2 by Hertz's contact mechanics theory[37] and the average pressure on the contact area was estimated to be 139 MPa.

3. Results and discussion

A typical AFM image of the poly(MPC) brush surface is displayed in Fig. 3. The rms value of the brush in air (RH = 45%) was approximately 1.6 nm in a 10×10 μm^2 area. The transformation of the dimethylamino group in the poly(MPC-*co*-DMAEMA) brush to the ammonium group was confirmed by N_{1s} peaks in the XPS spectra before and after the reaction. The conversion of quaternization of the amino group by methyl iodide was achieved at 95%, while the cross-linking reaction by bis(2-iodeethoxy)ethane was estimated to be 70%. Considering the unit ratio of MPC/DMAEMA (89/11), the cross-linking density must be only a few percent. However, several changes in the surface properties were observed as follows.

Fig. 4 shows photographs (side view) of water on the polyelectrolyte brushes in air. The poly(MPC) brush showed an extremely low contact angle below 3°, while slightly higher water contact angles were observed on the poly(MPC-*co*-DMAEMA) brush. The non-ionic amino group in the DMAEMA unit transformed to ionic ammonium salt after the cross-linking reaction or quaternization by using alkyliodides, however, the water contact angles increased up to 26°–36° probably because of the introduction of relatively hydrophobic bis(2-iodoethoxy)ethane. The poly-(SPMK-*co*-MTAC) brush showed a low water contact angle of 10°, which was slightly higher than that of the normal poly(SPMK) brush surface probably due to the hydrophobic property of the ion complex formed by SPMK and MTAC.

Fig. 5 shows the friction coefficients of poly(MPC) brushes measured by a conventional ball-on-plate type reciprocating tribotester using a glass ball probe (diameter = 10 mm) sliding on the substrates along a distance of 20 mm at a rate of 1.5×10^{-3} m s^{-1} in humid air (relative humidity RH > 75%) under a normal load of 0.49 N at 298 K. We previously reported that the poly(MPC) brush showed the lowest frictional coefficient under humid air probably due to moisture adsorption on the deliquescent poly(MPC) forming a good lubrication layer.[32] The friction coefficient of the poly(MPC) brush was about 0.08. A larger friction coefficient than 0.1 was observed in the poly(MPC-*co*-DMAEMA), cross-linked poly(MPC), and poly-(MPC-*co*-MTAI) brushes. The polymer brushes with higher water contact angle showed larger friction coefficients, indicating that the surface hydrophilicity was strongly related to the frictional property in humid air.

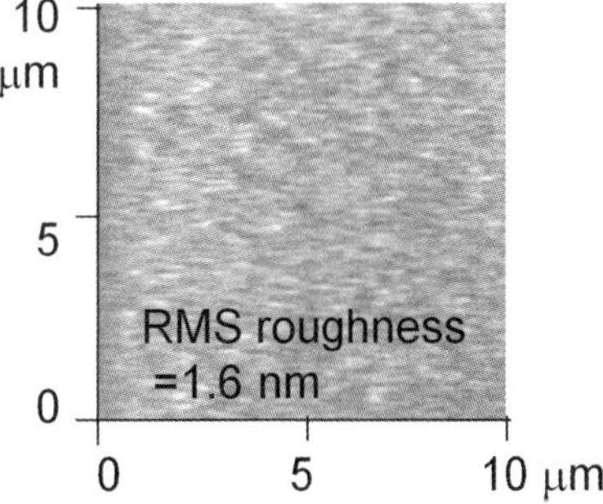

Fig. 3 Topographic AFM image of the poly(MPC) brush surface in air (humidity RH = 45%). The polymer brush was prepared on silicon wafer by surface-initiated ATRP.

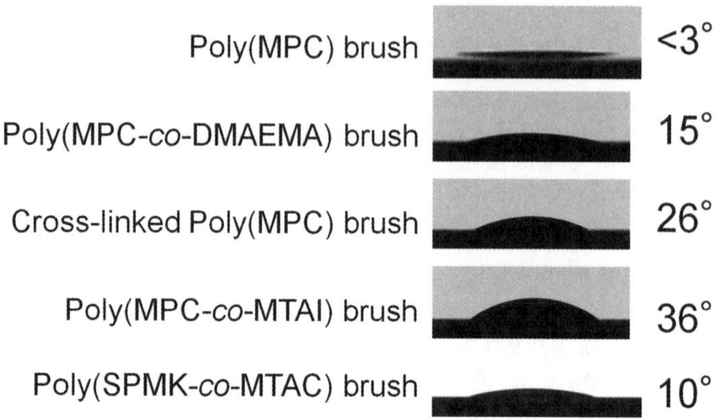

Fig. 4 Water contact angles of poly(MPC), poly(MPC-*co*-DMAEMA), cross-linked poly-(MPC), poly(MPC-*co*-MTAI), and poly(SPMK-*co*-MTAC) brushes in air.

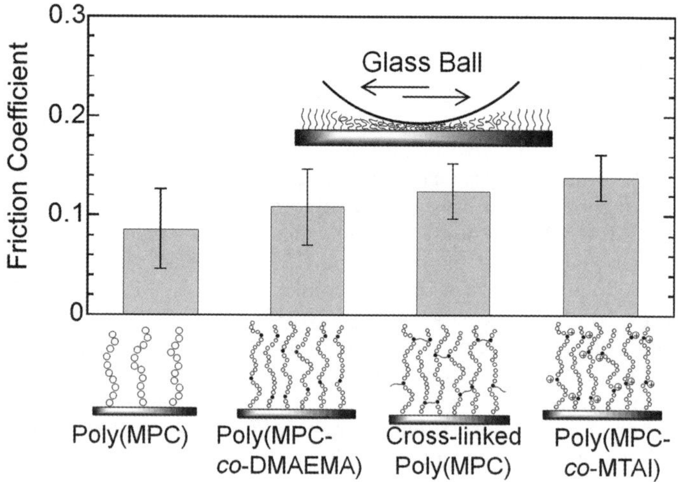

Fig. 5 Friction coefficients of poly(MPC), poly(MPC-*co*-DMAEMA) (MPC/DMAEMA = 89/11), cross-linked poly(MPC), and poly(MPC-*co*-MTAI) brushes measured by sliding a glass ball at a reciprocating distance of 20 mm and a rate of 1.5×10^{-3} m s^{-1} in a humid air atmosphere (RH > 75%) under a normal load of 0.49 N at 298 K.

The tethered polymer chain end is bound to the substrate by a covalent bond and multiple hydrogen bonds, however, the brush layers gradually wear thin at the friction track under the load of 139 MPa, and are scratched out eventually by the sliding probe. Fig. 6(a) and (b) show the evolution of the friction coefficient of poly(MPC) and the copolymer brush during the continuous reciprocating sliding of a glass ball probe along a distance of 10 mm at a rate of 1.5×10^{-3} m s^{-1} in humid air (RH > 75%) under a normal load of 0.49 N at 298 K. The friction coefficients of poly(MPC) and the poly(MPC-*co*-DMAEMA) brushes were constant at around 0.1–0.15, but increased after 50–80 friction cycles due to the wearing out of the brush. A similar result was obtained for the quaternized poly(MPC) brushes.

In contrast, the cross-linked poly(MPC) showed a stable friction coefficient of 0.13 even after 200 friction cycles, as shown in Fig. 6(c). This result indicated that the cross-linked structure effectively improved the wear resistance of the brush because the shear stress under friction distributed to the polymer network.

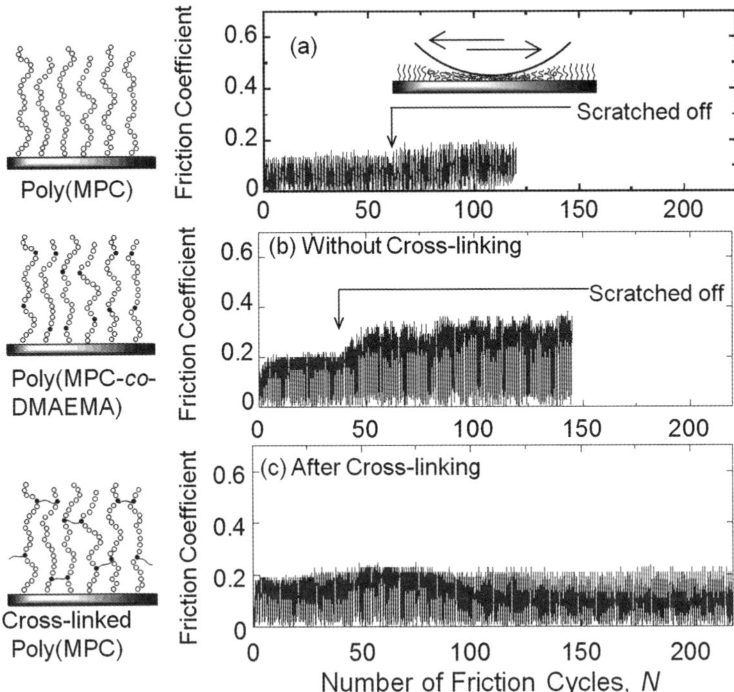

Fig. 6 Evolution of the friction coefficient *vs.* the number of friction cycles *N* for the surface of (a) poly(MPC), (b) poly(MPC-*co*-DMAEMA), and (c) cross-linked poly(MPC) by sliding a glass ball at a reciprocating distance of 20 mm and a rate of 1.5×10^{-3} m s^{-1} under a load of 0.49 N in a humid air atmosphere (RH $>$ 75%) at 298 K.

Fig. 7 shows the friction coefficients of the poly(MTAC), poly(SPMK), and poly-(MPC) brushes in air, water, and in humid air measured by sliding a glass ball immobilized with the corresponding polyelectrolyte brushes. Compared with the nonmodified glass ball sliding probe, a much lower friction coefficient was observed by the brush-grafted glass probe. The opposing swollen brushes in water would form a thicker boundary layer to restrict the direct contact of the glass probe with the silicon substrate. Interestingly, the friction coefficient of the poly(MPC) brush under the highly humidified air condition was significantly reduced to 0.02, which is lower than that in water, while the friction coefficients of the poly(MTAC) and poly-(SPMK) brushes in water were lower than those in humid air. Although the mechanism for the unique frictional property of the poly(MPC) brush under the humid air condition is still unclear, it is supposed that water molecules in the humid air adsorbed in/on the poly(MPC) brush and acted as a sufficient lubricant to reduce the friction force.

The lowest friction coefficient in water was observed for the poly(SPMK) brush in Fig. 7. Therefore, less wear was expected for the poly(SPMK) brush than the poly-(MPC) brush.

Fig. 8(a) shows the evolution of the friction coefficient of the poly(SPMK) brush during the continuous reciprocating sliding of a brush-immobilized glass ball probe in water. The friction test of the poly(SPMK) brush under a load of 0.49 N in water showed an extremely low friction coefficient of around 0.018 continuously even after 450 friction cycles. Although a wear track formed on the brush surface by the friction test, the components of the brush remained in the wear track, which was confirmed by XPS. The abrasion of the brush was supposed to be prevented owing to the good affinity of the poly(SPMK) brush for water and the electrostatic

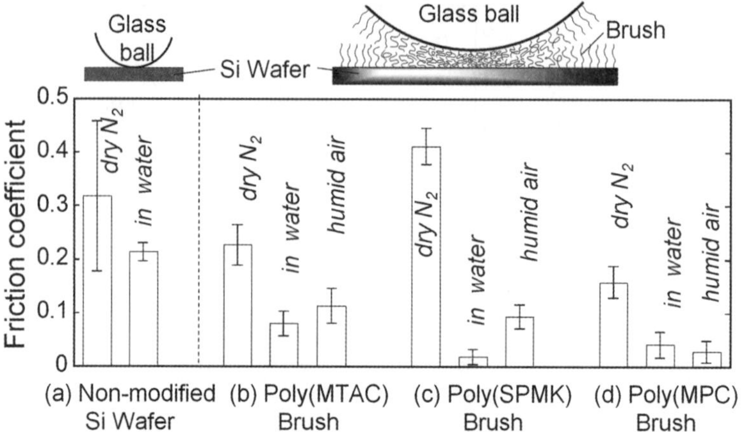

Fig. 7 Friction coefficient of (a) non-modified silicon wafer by sliding non-modified glass ball in dry N_2 atmosphere and water, (b) poly(MTAC), (c) poly(SPMK), and (d) poly(MPC) brushes in dry N_2 atmosphere, water, and in humid air (RH > 75%) by sliding a glass ball immobilized with the corresponding polyelectrolyte brushes at a reciprocating distance of 20 mm and a rate of 1.5×10^{-3} m s^{-1} under a normal load of 0.49 N at 298 K.

repulsive interactions among opposing swollen brushes bearing sulfonic acid groups to form a water lubrication layer preventing the direct contact of the glass probe with the silicon substrate.

Interestingly, further improvement in the low friction and wear resistance were observed for the poly(SPMK-*co*-MTAC) brush in water, as shown in Fig. 8(b). The unit ratio of SPMK and MTAC in the copolymer was 90/10. This ionic copolymer showed an extremely low friction coefficient around 0.015 continuously in water after 1400 friction cycles even under a load of 0.49 N. The poly(SPMK-*co*-MTAC) brush can be regarded as a partially cross-linked polymer brush because

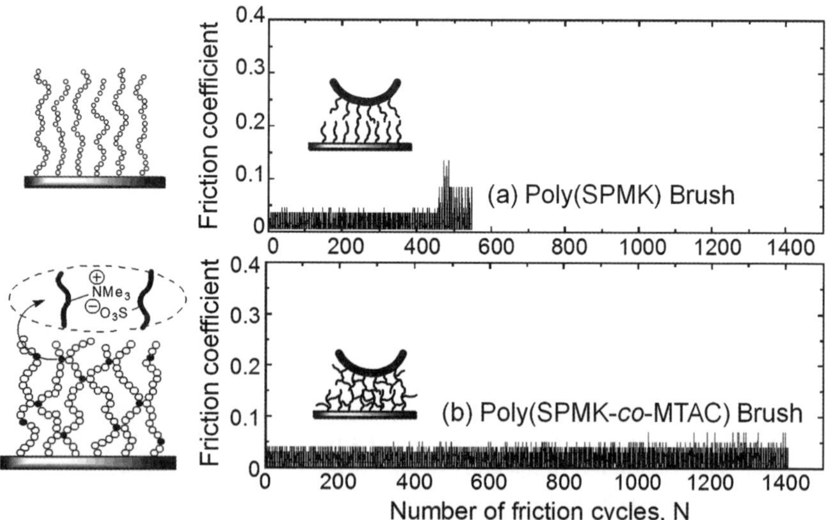

Fig. 8 Evolution of the friction coefficient *vs.* the number of friction cycles N for the surface of (a) poly(SPMK) and (b) poly(SPMK-*co*-MTAC) (SPMK/MTAC = 90/10) brushes by sliding a glass ball immobilized with the corresponding polymer brushes at a reciprocating distance of 10 mm and a rate of 1.5×10^{-3} m s^{-1} under a load of 0.49 N in water at 298 K.

the electrostatic attractive interactions between the sulfonate group in the SPMK unit and the ammonium group in the MTAC unit would form a cross-linking point binding the neighboring brush chains. We supposed that the cross-linked structure improved the shear strength of the polymer brush preventing wear of the brush and maintaining water in the brush layer. As a result, low friction based on water lubrication was achieved for a long period of over 1000 friction cycles even under severe normal pressure.

4. Conclusions

The abrasion of polyelectrolyte brushes under wet conditions and high normal loads was moderated by forming a cross-linked structure in the brushes. Poly(MPC) showed a low friction coefficient under humid air (RH > 75%), however, the brush layer was scratched by sliding a glass probe within 50 reciprocating friction cycles. In contrast, partially cross-linked poly(MPC) maintained a relatively low friction coefficient around 0.13 in humid air even after 200 friction cycles. The poly(SPMK) brush revealed an extremely low friction coefficient of around 0.01 even after 450 friction cycles because of a good affinity of poly(SPMK) for water forming a water lubrication layer, and electrostatic repulsive interactions among the brushes bearing sulfonic acid groups. Furthermore, the poly(SPMK-*co*-MTAC) brush with electro-statically cross-linked structure showed an extremely low friction coefficient in water, even after 1400 friction cycles under a pressure of 139 MPa, because the cross-linking structure improved the shear strength of the polymer brush thin films preventing wear of the brush, and maintaining hydrophilicity to assist water lubrication. The cross-linked polyelectrolyte brushes can be expected to contribute to applications in bio- or medical devices, which require low friction under wet conditions.

Notes and references

1 C. W. McCutchen, *Wear*, 1962, **5**, 1–17.
2 M. Scherge and S. N. Gorb, *Biological Micro- and Nano-tribology*, Springer, Berlin, 2001, pp. 79–127.
3 L. Han, D. Dean, C. Ortiz and A. J. Grodzinsky, *Biophys. J.*, 2007, **92**, 1384.
4 J. Celli, B. Gregor, B. Turner, N. H. Afdhal, R. Bansil and S. Erramilli, *Biomacromolecules*, 2005, **6**, 1329.
5 A. M. Granville and W. J. Brittain, in *Polymer Brushes: Synthesis, Characterization, Applications*, ed. R. C. Advincula, W. J. Brittain, K. C. Caster and J. Rühe, Wiley-VCH, Weinheim, Germany, 2004, pp. 35–50.
6 Y. Tsujii, K. Ohno, S. Yamamoto, A. Goto and T. Fukuda, *Adv. Polym. Sci.*, 2006, **197**, 1.
7 J. Klein, E. Kumacheva, D. Mahalu, D. Perahia and L. J. Fetters, *Nature*, 1994, **370**, 634.
8 N. Kampf, J. F. Gohy, R. Jerome and J. Klein, *J. Polym. Sci., Part B: Polym. Phys.*, 2005, **43**, 193.
9 U. Raviv, S. Giasson, N. Kamph, J. F. Gohy, R. Jérôme and J. Klein, *Nature*, 2003, **425**, 163.
10 Y. Ohsedo, R. Takashina, J. P. Gong and Y. Osada, *Langmuir*, 2004, **20**, 6549.
11 M. Chen, W. H. Briscoe, S. P. Armes and J. Klein, *Science*, 2009, **323**, 1698.
12 M. Chen, W. H. Briscoe, S. P. Armes, H. Cohen and J. Klein, *Eur. Polym. J.*, 2011, **47**, 511.
13 J. Ruhe, M. Ballauff, M. Biesalski, P. Dziezok, F. Gröhn, D. Johannsmann, N. Houbenov, N. Hugenberg, R. Konradi, S. Minko, M. Motornov, R. R. Netz, M. Schmidt, C. Seidel, M. Stamm, T. Stephan, D. Usov and H. Zhang, *Adv. Polym. Sci.*, 165–166, Springer, New-York, 2004, pp. 79–150.
14 I. Luzinov, S. Minko and V. V. Tsukruk, *Prog. Polym. Sci.*, 2004, **29**, 635.
15 R. Israels, F. A. M. Leermakers, G. J. Fleer and E. B. Zhulina, *Macromolecules*, 1994, **27**, 3249.
16 Y. V. Lyatskaya, F. A. M. Leermakers, G. J. Fleer, E. B. Zhulina and T. M. Birshtein, *Macromolecules*, 1995, **28**, 3562.
17 E. B. Zhulina, J. K. Wolterink and O. V. Borisov, *Macromolecules*, 2000, **33**, 4945.
18 P. Pincus, *Macromolecules*, 1991, **24**, 2912.
19 R. S. Ross and P. Pincus, *Macromolecules*, 1992, **25**, 2177.

20 V. A. Pryamitsyn, F. A. M. Leermakers, G. J. Fleer and E. B. Zhulina, *Macromolecules*, 1996, **29**, 8260.
21 H. J. Taunton, C. Toprakcioglu, L. J. Fetters and J. Klein, *Nature*, 1988, **332**, 712.
22 E. Eiser, J. Klein, T. A. Witten and L. J. Fetters, *Phys. Rev. Lett.*, 1999, **82**, 5076.
23 S. Hayashi, T. Abe, N. Higashi, M. Niwa and K. Kurihara, *Langmuir*, 2002, **18**, 3932.
24 N. Kampf, D. Ben-Yaakov, D. Andelman, S. A. Safran and J. Klein, *Phys. Rev. Lett.*, 2009, **103**, 118304.
25 T. W. Kelley, P. A. Shorr, D. J. Kristin, M. Tirrell and C. D. Frisbie, *Macromolecules*, 1998, **31**, 4297.
26 A. Nomura, K. Okayasu, K. Ohono, T. Fukuda and Y. Tsujii, *Macromolecules*, 2011, **44**, 5013.
27 S. Lee, M. Müller, M. Ratoi-Salagean, J. Vörös, S. Pasche, S. M. De Paul, H. A. Spikes, M. Textor and N. D. Spencer, *Tribol. Lett.*, 2003, **15**, 231.
28 M. Müller, S. Lee, H. A. Spikes and N. D. Spencer, *Tribol. Lett.*, 2003, **15**, 395.
29 H. Sakata, M. Kobayashi, H. Otsuka and A. Takahara, *Polym. J.*, 2005, **37**, 767.
30 M. Kobayashi and A. Takahara, *Chem. Lett.*, 2005, **34**, 1582.
31 M. Kobayashi and A. Takahara, *Chem. Rec.*, 2010, **10**, 208.
32 M. Kobayashi, Y. Terayama, N. Hosaka, M. Kaido, A. Suzuki, N. Yamada, N. Torikai, K. Ishihara and A. Takahara, *Soft Matter*, 2007, **3**, 740.
33 K. Ohno, T. Morinaga, K. Koh, Y. Tsujii and T. Fukuda, *Macromolecules*, 2005, **38**, 2137.
34 H. Tada and H. Nagatama, *Langmuir*, 1994, **10**, 1472.
35 M. Kobayashi, M. Terada, Y. Terayama, M. Kikuchi and A. Takahara, *Macromolecules*, 2010, **43**, 8409.
36 Y. Terayama, M. Kikuchi, M. Kobayashi and A. Takahara, *Macromolecules*, 2011, **44**, 104.
37 If a circle with radius a (m) is regarded as the contact area between a stainless steel ball and substrate under a normal load P (0.49 N), Hertz's theory affords the following relationship using Young's modulus of a glass and silicon wafer, E_A (7.16 × 10^{10} Pa), E_B (1.30 × 10^{11} Pa), and Poisson's ratio v_A (0.23), v_B (0.28), respectively:

$$\frac{1}{E} = \frac{1 - v_A^2}{E_A} + \frac{1 - v_B^2}{E_B}$$

$$a = \left(\frac{3PR_A}{4E}\right)^{1/3}$$

where R_A is the curvature radius (5.00 × 10^{-3} m) of the glass ball. The contact area can be calculated by πa^2.

General discussion

Professor Dr Vernes opened the discussion of the paper by Professor Martin: Commonly, chemical reactions in nanotribological systems cannot be accessed by classical MD simulations. Was only the mechanical dissociation of iron oxide particles investigated here?

Professor Martin responded: Yes, this is correct. We made additional simulations by TB-QCMD in the case of the iron oxide/zinc phosphate system (not in our paper here). These simulations gave similar results and confirm that MD simulation is sufficient to describe the situation with a good accuracy.

Professor Dr Vernes commented: You concluded that the driving force of the tribochemical reaction in the case of ZDDP is the increase of the entropy during sliding. How difficult is it to estimate this by using your MD data?

Professor Martin replied: Entropy is the result of statistics. We have a small number of atoms in the cell and it is not possible to calculate accurately the entropy change by MD. The entropy of mixing can be calculated theoretically if we know the atomic fraction of oxide in the phosphate and the temperature. Then the Gibbs free energy of mixing can also be calculated. In our case, mixing is not a spontaneous process because the component are not ideal materials. In our case $T\Delta S(\text{mix}) = 810.6$ J mol^{-1} with 10% of oxide dissolved in the phosphate at 300 K. This has to be compared with $\Delta H(\text{mix})$. More work is necessary to confirm all these results. Also the relation between entropy increase and the coefficient of friction is an interesting topic.

Professor Dr Vernes remarked: You studied the flow behaviour of the polyphosphate glass during sliding by visualising the atomic trajectories and observed that this is fluid-like. What can be said about the collective motion of the particles?

Professor Martin said: It is very difficult to visualize the collective motion of atoms in the simulation. A possibility is to calculate the radial distribution function of each atom and to see how it changes with time. But the RDF is short distance information. Another possibility is to calculate the vibrational spectrum (IR or Raman) and to observe changes in the collective motion of the atoms. This is currently under consideration. However, due to the small number of atoms in the cell, these data are not very accurate.

Mr Eder addressed Professor Martin and Professor Dr Kubo: In addition to the systems you discussed in the paper, you showed a system in your presentation which had an iron substrate underneath a layer of hematite. Which class of potential did you use to realistically model the interactions between these two materials?

Professor Martin replied: For the interaction between Fe and Fe$_2$O$_3$, we use the Lennard-Jones potential. The different types of force-field that we used were BMH for the Zn(PS$_{0.5}$O$_{2.5}$)$_2$ layer, Fe$_2$O$_3$ layer and Zn(PS$_{0.5}$O$_{2.5}$)$_2$ layer–Fe$_2$O$_3$ layer, and LJ for the Zn(PS$_{0.5}$O$_{2.5}$)$_2$ layer–Fe substrate and Fe$_2$O$_3$ layer–Fe substrate.

Professor Dr Kubo responded: For the iron substrate, the conventional Lennard-Jones potential is employed. For hematite and Zn(PS$_{0.5}$O$_{2.5}$)$_2$, the Born–Mayer–Huggins potential including coulomb and exchange repulsion terms is employed.

For interactions between these two materials, the conventional Lennard-Jones potential is employed.

Mr Eder addressed Professor Dr Kubo: If your iron–hematite interaction is assumed purely coulombic, which charges do you assume for the iron, and do you have to modify the charges within the hematite? Which possibilities are there to validate your assumptions for the mixed potential?

Professor Dr Kubo answered: I am very sorry that my previous answer is not enough for the explanation of the potential for the interactions of the two materials' interface. The hematite–$Zn(PS_{0.5}O_{2.5})_2$ interaction is expressed by the Born–Mayer–Huggins potential and then the coulombic energy is dominant. The potential parameters including atomic charges are determined so as to reproduce the structures, lattice constants, and other physical properties of hematite and $Zn(PS_{0.5}O_{2.5})_2$. On the other hand, the iron–hematite interaction is expressed by the conventional Lennard-Jones potential.

Mr Eder addressed Professor Martin and Professor Dr Kubo: What made you prefer the thermostatting *via* rescaling of velocities over common thermostats which are in accordance with some thermodynamical ensemble? Is the entire system thermostatted or only the substrate? If the entire system is thermostatted by "hard-resetting" the velocities of the atoms every 100 time steps, might this significantly alter the physico-chemical properties of the lubricant?

Professor Martin replied: Actually, we tried both temperature control systems. We obtained similar results. Also we decreased the sliding speed to a low value (0.1 m s^{-1}) to decrease any temperature and we also decreased the contact pressure down to 1 MPa. We observed that digestion occurs in all cases, but at different kinetics.

When using the thermostat, we only controlled a part of the iron substrate to simulate thermal conductivity. The lubricant is not present at the interface. Only the tribofilm formed enters the contacting zone. Of course this is a simulation but we could not measure (or calculate) any significant temperature increase in practical lubricated tests under the same tribological conditions. So we believe that our simulations conditions are valid and that it is entropy which increases and not temperature.

Professor Dr Kubo said: We compared the effect of the thermostat methods on the calculation results of the SiO_2 system previously and the difference in the calculation results are not significant. Compared to the other thermostat methods, the velocity scaling method is faster and so we employed the velocity scaling method. We would like to perform calculations as large and long as possible, so a faster calculation method is preferable. The thermostat is only applied to the iron substrate.

Dr Oesterle asked: You mentioned the importance of metal sulfides for the tribofilm functionality but such species did not appear, either in your TEM-micrographs, or in your simulation. Why? Are the sulfides eventually digested more quickly than the oxides?

Professor Martin answered: Metal sulfides are formed in the extreme-pressure conditions when nascent iron is exposed to remaining organic sulphur species. However, in the anti-wear regime, (which is actually simulated here), sulphur is present both as thiophosphate and as ZnS. Both forms are amorphous and cannot be recognized in the zinc phosphate glass.

The chemical hardness model implies that metal oxides react with phosphates (to form ionic species) and metallic iron prefers to react with sulphides (to form covalent species). So metal sulfides do not react with zinc phosphate. On the other hand metal sulfides are not mechanically hard and they cannot scratch the metal surface.

Professor Bain commented: You have presented a thermodynamic model for the digestion of iron oxide nanoparticles in the zinc polyphosphate glass and have argued that the digestion is entropy-driven. In calculating the free energy, the entropy is multiplied by temperature and temperature does not appear explicitly in your model. If entropy is the driving force then you should find that at low temperatures digestion is thermodynamically unfavourable, though you may not be able to test this hypothesis if the kinetics are too slow. But this thought raises a more general question: given that your simulations are not equilibrated, how can you distinguish thermodynamically driven digestion of nanoparticles from kinetic effects *e.g.* mechanical break-up by shear?

Professor Martin replied: First of all, this is the first time that an MD-derived entropy-driven mechanism is explicitly proposed for tribochemical reactions with anti-wear additives. That is to say that it certainly needs further study to be confirmed. In the practical case, both temperature and entropy increases can co-exist, and this promotes the reaction. However, in the MD calculation, we fixed the temperature to 300 K. So only the entropy can increase and could be calculated by the entropy mixing model (for ideal materials). Because we use a very small number of atoms in the simulation, it is not easy to distinguish the effect of molecular shearing (between two atoms) and thermodynamic effects that are statistical in nature. For example, we observed by TB-QCMD the shearing of the Fe–O bond (not in this paper) but it is not possible to calculate from MD the entropy change because of the small number of atoms. The model needs to be refined in the future, definitely.

Dr Mischler said: You propose that the anti-wear action of ZDDP consists essentially of the formation of a glassy zinc phosphate able to dissolve abrasive iron oxide nanoparticles. You clearly show that the activation of this mechanism at relatively low temperatures requires a combination of pressure and shear. You interpret this in terms of thermodynamics suggesting that the increase in entropy is the driving force. I am wondering if kinetics considerations may be more appropriate. Essentially the digestion of iron oxide particles consists of solid-state diffusion of iron ions into phosphate. Thus the description in terms of diffusion laws (Fick's laws) and diffusion coefficients seems appropriate. In this way the need for mechanical activation can be easily explained by the introduction of additional structural defects into the phosphate, speeding up diffusion and thus iron oxide digestion. This phenomenon is well known in the field of high temperature wear where sliding may enhance metal oxidation by several orders of magnitude (see papers by T. F. J. Quinn). Can you comment on the suitability of kinetics *versus* thermodynamical approaches?

Professor Martin answered: Yes indeed, as you pointed out, the digestion of iron oxide particles consists of solid-state diffusion (or migration) of iron ions into zinc phosphate but also the migration of individual oxygen atoms (from the oxide) into the phosphate chain. This is at the origin of shortening the polyphosphate chain length (the so-called depolymerization process) evidenced many times by XANES investigations. The description in terms of diffusion laws needs the presence of structural defects in the phosphate material. However, the zinc thiophosphate thermal film is always amorphous in nature (by HRTEM and electron diffraction) and it is difficult to say if defects are present or not in the structure. Moreover, amorphous ZnS (as seen by EXAFS) is usually mixed with the (thio)phosphate. On the other hand, temperature calculation failed to find a temperature-driven kinetic process under BL conditions. To conclude, we think that the thermodynamical approach is more appropriate in these particular cases (compared with high temperature oxidational wear prevailing in Quinn's theory).

Dr Oesterle remarked: According to my experience, small oxide particles will not abrade the tribofilm but rather will be mixed with the amorphous constituent of the film, as shown by your TEM micrographs.

Professor Martin responded: Yes, nanometer scale iron oxide particles are not abrasive at all, but even lubricious (maghemite in particular; never hematite at this scale). However, we used 1 nm diameter particles because of the cell size in the simulator. In practical cases, the tribofilm thickness is several tens of nanometers and possible iron oxides particles much bigger than the nanoscale. In this case, the oxide is hematite and is strongly abrasive.

Dr Mischler enquired: You attribute abrasive properties to iron oxide nanoparticles. Usually, nanoparticles have rather a more or less pronounced beneficial anti-wear effect.[1] Possibly the digestion of iron oxide nanoparticles rather prevents them from agglomerating and forming larger micrometre sized particles that indeed are usually considered as abrasive. Can you comment on this?

1 A. Hernández Battez, R. González, D. Felgueroso, J. E. Fernández, Ma. del Rocío Fernández, M. A. García and I. Peñuelas, Wear prevention behaviour of nanoparticle suspension under extreme pressure conditions, *Wear*, 2007, **263**, 1568.

Professor Martin answered: This is an interesting comment. Nanometer-scale iron oxide particles consist of magnetite or maghemite γ-Fe_2O_3 oxide forms. Hematite (α-Fe_2O_3) is not stable at the nanometer scale. Indeed, hematite can form from the agglomeration (and growing) of magnetite and maghemite particles. As you pointed out, nanometer scale magnetite and maghemite can form an anti-wear tribofilm and are not abrasive (depicted as lubricious oxides in the literature). However, hematite sub-micron scale grains are highly abrasive. In our MD simulations, we are forced to use a nanoparticle of oxide because of the cell size in the tribo-simulator. But this particle does not cause abrasive wear before being digested. Either the nanoparticle originates from the native iron oxide film or it is produced by milling of bigger grains coming from the induction period (where oxide grains are much bigger and contain hematite). To conclude, the digestion certainly prevents nanograins from further agglomeration and merging, resulting in a more abrasive situation.

Professor Dr Bhushan opened the discussion of the paper by Professor Leggett: We have performed some experiments on SAMs with linear molecular chains and cross-linked molecular chains.[1] We reported that SAMs with linear molecular chains exhibited lower friction than those with cross-linked molecular chains. We proposed that linear molecular chains behave like linear springs and facilitate sliding. Have you performed or modeled cross-linked systems and have any comments?

1 B. Bhushan and H. Liu, *Phys. Rev. B*, 2001, **63**, 245412.

Professor Leggett responded: We have not measured the behaviour of cross-linked monolayer systems. However, we recently published data from a study of films of polystyrene and poly(methyl methacrylate) as a function of their molecular weight.[1] For those materials we observed that the coefficient of friction increased with polymer molecular weight, until the critical molecular weight for entanglement was reached, at which point the friction varied little as the molecular weight was changed. Entanglement introduces cross-links into the polymer film. Probably, the effect on the frictional behaviour is similar to that observed for monolayers, although the densities of cross-links may be different.

1 T. J. Whittle and G. J. Leggett, *Langmuir*, 2009, **25**, 2217.

Dr Koutsos commented: This is very interesting work. Have you investigated the effect of speed on friction in the system you described?

Professor Leggett replied: We published a study of the correlation between the friction force and the scan rate for monolayers a few years ago.[1] For systems consisting of a weakly interacting probe and sample (methyl–methyl or dissimilar functional groups), the friction force increased logarithmically with the scan rate. For hydrogen bonding systems, the friction force increased logarithmically with speed at first but then reached a limiting value. We explained this in terms of the disruption of lateral hydrogen bonding interactions in the SAMs. Such explanations may go some way to explaining why many published studies report larger coefficients of friction for hydrogen bond-forming SAMs—in fact, the energy dissipation is not in tip–sample adhesion but in the disruption of lateral interactions. This requires further investigation. Such effects may well be rate-dependent, and so studies of velocity-dependence may help us to unpick things.

1 N. J. Brewer, B. D. Beake and G. J. Leggett, *Langmuir*, 2001, **17**, 1970.

Dr Koutsos said: Could you envisage a situation where the two friction terms depend on each other, and the model is more complex? Are they separable in all situations?

Professor Leggett answered: This is an interesting question. I hesitate to be too dogmatic, given that we have not studied very many systems. However, my understanding is that the two terms in the equation come from very different phenomena. The area-dependent term comes from energy dissipated in the shearing of adhesive interactions (*i.e.* non-covalent interactions across the interface) while the load-dependent term comes from energy dissipation in deformations of the alkyl chains of molecules under the probe. If this is a correct way to picture things, then it is not unreasonable to expect that the two terms will, in general, remain separable.

Professor Spencer enquired: Concerning the speed dependence of the adhesion forces, would it be of use to use deuterated carboxylic acids and/or solvents, in order to see if this affects the friction as a function of speed? The H-bonding time constant should be affected by D-substitution.

Professor Leggett responded: This is a very interesting question. I think that there is a great deal to be learned from studying the velocity-dependence of both friction and adhesion forces in molecular contacts. I cannot predict or speculate at this time what the outcome would be but, as you suggest, one might expect that there would be a characteristic time constant associated with the hydrogen bonding interaction and depending on the tip velocity (very much larger velocities are, of course, accessible nowadays in "high-speed" AFM systems) one might be able to learn from the velocity-dependence. As you say, deuteration may affect this, and the experiment you have suggested is a very interesting one.

Professor Spencer commented: Beautiful work, Graham. This is a very important study. I have a question concerning your first figure, where you show that there are large changes in pull-off force for small changes in dielectric constant, and then very small changes for a wide range of dielectric constant. I think that this is understandable in terms of the Lifshitz theory, in that the second term, which involves the refractive index, n, (related to the dielectric constant *via* a $\sqrt{}$ term), contains differences of squared n values, again squared. This means that the Hamaker constant (and therefore the van der Waals interaction) is indeed very sensitive to n over a small range. In other words, while the effects that you describe are undoubtedly dominant for polar solvents, the Lifshitz effect is important when the polar effects are absent.

Professor Leggett replied: Thank you for your comments. I would agree that one might expect the behaviour to be different when strong dipole interactions are absent. Indeed, Nikos Nikogeorgos has recently examined this effect, and finds that for non-polar SAMs, pull-off forces measured using the AFM for similar monolayer systems in liquid media are indeed consistent with the predictions of Lifshitz theory. In Chris Hunter's model, the interaction free energies are predicted using eqn (2) and (3) in our paper. The contribution of the dispersion interaction is given as 6 kJ mol^{-1}. This is an acceptable approximation when the predominant interactions are strong dipole forces, but in the absence of hydrogen bonds, the subtle effects of the dispersion forces become very important, consistent with the results in your own very elegant paper[1] which was a significant part of the motivation for starting our study of liquid mixtures.

1 K. Feldman, T. Tervoort, P. Smith and N. D. Spencer, *Langmuir*, 1998, **14**, 372.

Professor Klein asked: Are the friction *vs.* load plots in your study, *e.g.* Fig. 4 or 9, reversible? That is, as the load decreases following its maximal value, would the friction forces be similar to those on increasing the load? I ask because one might expect the sharp tip to cause some damage on initial loading and sliding.

Professor Leggett answered: This is a good question. The answer is that the friction–load plots are indeed reversible, and we routinely check this because, as you say, permanent damage to either the sample or the probe would lead to a change in the slope of the friction–load plot. Repeated measurements are made at different locations using the same probe, and good agreement is observed. So we feel confident that the probe is not damaging the sample. Indeed, we can go further. It is possible to deliberately remove material from the monolayer using an AFM probe, and we have used this "nanoshaving" technique as a nanolithography tool. We have acquired a good knowledge of the conditions under which plastic deformation of the monolayer occurs (*ca.* 100 nN), and are confident that the range of loads used in our paper lies comfortably below this limit. Plastic deformation leads to visible modification (roughening) of the sample topography, when it is imaged by the AFM in topographical mode; if one scans a larger area, a damaged region is readily visible. At loads below 100 nN we did not observe such modification.

Professor Klein queried: In your presentation you showed the AFM tip as a smooth curved object. In practice AFM tips may be quite 'jagged' over the final few angstroms as atoms stick out. Do you feel this might be important on the sub-nanometre scale over which the tip penetrates the layer, and might it change some of your contact-mechanics interpretation?

Professor Leggett responded: You are quite correct to point out that cartoons can be dangerously misleading. The AFM probe is certainly not a smooth sphere. However, we are content that the roughness is not great on molecular length scales. We have characterised representative probes by electron microscopy (although not every probe is imaged). We find that the radius of curvature of the probe is not greatly increased by the deposition of a gold film (confirmed by modelling the radius as the probe slides over a well-defined wedge-shaped test specimen), and the electron micrographs show that the tip surface is typically covered with a small number of grains of gold that are similar in size (a few tens of nm) to the grain size of the gold films that are used as a substrate for SAM formation on planar surfaces. Hence within the resolution limit of our SEM (*ca.* 1 nm) we see no evidence for the existence of sharp protrusions at the tip surface. Of course, gold is a rather unusual metal, and tends to flow and self-smooth itself at interfaces; this may help us.

Professor Klein commented: In connection with friction measurements on polymer brushes, I wonder whether the penetration and ploughing of the AFM tip in the brush might not result in effects that are difficult to interpret. Thus you say that for pMPC brushes in pure water you observe a non-linear friction–load relation; we have found, as in Chen *et al.*[1] or in Fig. 9 in our paper in the current Faraday Discussion,[2] where we measure using a surface force balance, quite a linear relation between the friction and the load for pMPC brushes solvated by pure water. I suspect that FFM may not be the ideal approach for measuring friction coefficients of soft surfaces such as solvated-brush-coated surfaces, or other relatively soft coatings, precisely because of the penetration/ploughing effect.

1 M. Chen, W. H. Briscoe, S. P. Armes and J. Klein, *Science*, 2009, **323**, 1698–1701.
2 A. Gaisinskaya, L. Ma, G. Silbert, R. Sorkin, O. Tairy, R. Goldberg, N. Kampf and J. Klein, *Faraday Discuss.*, 2012, **156**, DOI: 10.1039/C2FD00127F.

Professor Leggett replied: Ploughing does appear to occur, for solvated brushes. Whether this represents "non-ideality" or simply different behaviour is, I would suggest, moot. Undoubtedly the contact area is different in the SFA, and the pressure is lower because the load is applied through a larger region. One must thus be careful when comparing contact mechanics for two instruments so similar and yet so subtly different as the AFM and SFA! I would suggest that a proper understanding of the mechanics of the tip–sample interaction in FFM will yield insights into the mechanics of brush layers that may rely upon similar molecular mechanisms to those invoked in studies by SFA (*e.g.* explanations in terms of solvation) even though the data on which they are based are phenomenologically different (for example the friction–load relationship may be linear in one and not the other). We have found that your own work on brush layers has been enormously helpful in understanding data acquired by FFM, even though the phenomenology may be subtly different. One needs just to bear in mind the differences in the experimental set-up and the mechanics of interaction in the SFA and AFM.

Professor Dr Vernes asked: Starting from the two-term friction law in eqn (5), the substitution of the DMT contact area as given by eqn (6) cannot result in the three-term friction law from eqn (7). Why was μF_a *ad hoc* added to the load-controlled term in the latter equation?

Professor Leggett answered: Our equation contains two terms, a load-dependent term and an area-dependent term. Fitting of the friction–load plots that exhibit non-linearity indicates that DMT mechanics are obeyed; hence the area may be determined from the DMT model. The DMT model is a modification of the Hertz model that takes account of adhesion; the adhesion force F_a is added to the load F_n. If one takes the view that the load is the sum of the normal force and the adhesion force in the area-dependent term, it seems to me that consistency demands that the load must be the same sum in the other term of the equation, *i.e.* the first term is not $\mu \times F_n$, but $\mu \times (F_n + F_a)$, because otherwise one is claiming that, simultaneously, the load is and is not corrected by adding F_a to F_n. To view this another way, we made the assumption that F_a should not appear in the first term, the load-dependent term, and then fitted the data again. We found that the "coefficient of friction" that resulted varied strongly with F_a, which is plainly a contradictory result. The inclusion of F_a in the load-dependent first term of our equation is thus far from arbitrary, I would argue, but is, in fact necessary both for the internal consistency of the equation and also to avoid a logical contradiction.

Professor Dr Vernes queried: Introducing F_0 as μF_a in eqn (7), the so-resulting three-term friction law becomes identical with that proposed in our paper[1] based on classical MD simulations. Why can this Derjaguin-offset F_0 not be seen as the strength of adhesion you are looking for and directly measured in AFM experiments?

1 A. Vernes, S. Eder, G. Vorlaufer and G. Betz, *Faraday Discuss.*, 2012, **156**, DOI: 10.1039/C2FD00120A.

Professor Leggett replied: Yes, from a mathematical perspective this is true. My personal feeling is that I prefer not to talk about a Derjaguin offset because of some historical inaccuracies in the literature. In the early days of FFM, "offsets", *i.e.* non-zero intercepts with the friction axis, were often reported in friction–load plots. In many cases people fitted straight lines to these graphs, and invoked Derjaguin's modification of Amontons' law. However, while this non-zero intercept was often equated with the adhesion force, I am skeptical about this. We have taken a great deal of care about all sorts of things (we keep adding things to our list of what must be controlled during an experiment!). One thing we check carefully is that the lateral deflection of the cantilever is zero at zero load. [Scott Perry made some very interesting remarks about this in a talk a few years ago, which set us to work trying to tie that variable down better.] If this really is zeroed properly, we find that the only significant non-zero intercepts with the friction axis are observed when the friction–load relationship is non-linear; linear friction–load plots are generally accompanied by zero or near-zero intercepts (in the latter case, the intercept is within the bounds of experimental uncertainty in the value of zero lateral deflection). So in view of this, with my background making measurements in the area, you may understand why I feel uncomfortable talking about offsets. However, you are right that there is mathematical equivalence, provided the strength of adhesion is allowed to vary with the medium.

Dr Zekonyte asked: In the experimental part it was mentioned that AFM tips were contaminated with PDMS, and that the presence of it influences adhesion measurements even if tips were later functionalized. How much (in % if possible) could be attributed to PDMS from the whole adhesion curve?

Professor Leggett responded: The importance of PDMS cannot be stressed too strongly. For a series of liquids, we found that contaminated probes yielded either negligible differences in adhesion forces, or even trends that were the opposite to those observed for clean probes. Even after gold coating (involving significant radiative heating) and immersion for 18 h in a solution of thiol in ethanol, imaging SIMS showed that probes remained completely covered in PDMS unless they were first cleaned in piranha solution, prior to gold deposition. Under these circumstances the interaction between the probe and the surface will be dominated by the properties of the PDMS covering the probe; hydrogen bonding will be greatly weakened or non-existent. After cleaning in piranha solution, probes were not found to be significantly blunted, and PDMS was not detectable by imaging SIMS. Force curves yielded much smaller errors and much larger changes in the adhesion force as the medium was changed. As noted in the paper, this problem was first reported a decade ago. There is generally very little surface spectroscopy done in the AFM community and one suspects that much of the literature is influenced by PDMS contamination—anybody who uses a probe packed in a gel pack will probably have the same problems that we reported.

Dr Limbert opened the discussion of the paper by Professor Dr Larsson: Have you measured the strains experienced by the contacting asperities? If strains are large the correct intended mechanical behaviour cannot be captured by the proposed model.

Professor Dr Larsson answered: We have not monitored the strain directly. The deformations have been on roughness level or smaller, meaning that the small strain approximation, and likewise the small angle approximation, can be seen as a valid approximate assumption. A more correct analysis would require a full solution of the stress and strain fields in the contact surfaces. This would also require much greater computational effort. By using the present method it is expected that the error in deformation (elastic and plastic) is relatively small for contacts with nominally flat rough surfaces but bigger for cases where the sub-surface stress field dominates the deformation. This will be investigated in future studies.

Dr Limbert enquired: Could you elaborate on how the plastic deformations are calculated in your model?

Professor Dr Larsson replied: The elastic deformation is calculated up to an elastic limit on the contact pressure, above which the contact material floats with constant load carrying capacity. Deformations above this elastic limit are plastic. A detailed description is given in ref. 1 and 2 below.

1 F. Sahlin, R. Larsson, A. Almqvist, P. M. Lugt and P. Marklund, A mixed lubrication model incorporating measured surface topography. Part 1: Theory of flow factors, *Proc. Inst. Mech. Eng. Part J: J. Eng. Tribol.*, 2010, **224**(4), 335–351.
2 F. Sahlin, R. Larsson, P. Marklund, A. Almqvist and P. M. Lugt, A mixed lubrication model incorporating measured surface topography. Part 2: Roughness treatment, model validation, and simulation, *Proc. Inst. Mech. Eng. Part J: J. Eng. Tribol.*, 2010, **224**(4), 353–365.

Professor Dr Vernes asked: Why is the term related to a possible non-vanishing tangential force neglected in eqn (1)?

Professor Dr Larsson responded: The tangential force will have some influence on the deformation in the normal direction. Its effect on the deformation in the normal direction is, however, much smaller than the effect of the contact pressure. In this study, it is assumed that the friction coefficient is relatively low (in the range 0.1 to 0.2), meaning that the effect of the tangential force is only a few percent in comparison to the effect of contact pressure. In order to keep the computational time as low as possible it was decided to neglect the effect of tangential force.

Professor Dr Vernes commented: The calculated load-dependent contact area could be introduced into the Arrhenius equation and Archard's wear law. Would this make the formation of tribofilms in your approach more realistic?

Professor Dr Larsson replied: This is already in the model. There is a strong coupling between contact area, wear and tribofilm growth. Wear and tribofilm formation occurs only in the contact spots, as a direct function of contact pressure, friction force and velocity.

Dr Taylor noted: This is a very nice piece of work. It has been observed that for some tribofilms (such as ZDDP) the measured friction coefficient increases with the film thickness. Since, in your calculation you use the friction power loss, which incorporates the friction coefficient, I was wondering if you could allow for such tribofilms by making the friction coefficient a function of the tribofilm thickness?

Professor Dr Larsson answered: Thank you. Yes, this can be easily achieved by directly altering the friction coefficient as a function of tribofilm height. The reason it has not been done in this study is to keep the model as simple as possible, mainly for a clearer analysis of the results. One should also think about the reason why the friction increases with increasing thickness of the tribofilm. One reason could be the roughening of the surface due to the growth of the film, mainly at the summits. If the friction test is carried out under mixed lubrication conditions this would lead to a greater degree of boundary lubrication and higher friction.

Professor Klein continued the discussion of the paper by Professor Leggett: Since the AFM tip is not smooth on a subnanometer level, do you feel that treating local deformations and pressures at these length scales in the language of DMT or JKR is correct? I think I have in mind quite sharp AFM tips, while the tip radii in your study—*ca.* 60 nm—are quite large compared with the extent of penetration into the surfactant layers.

Professor Leggett responded: As I mentioned earlier, we have characterised our probes by electron microscopy and found that within the limits of resolution of our instrument (*ca.* 1 nm), the probes are not excessively rough. Grains can be observed on the tip surface, but typically our data suggest that the assumption of a hemispherical apex is not unreasonable. It is possible that the self-smoothing characteristics of gold are an advantage here. So, given that we are not looking at atomic contacts, because our probes are, as you state, somewhat larger, I am not surprised that a continuum model applies. The fit to DMT mechanics appears to be very good for systems with strong hydrogen bonding interactions, so the simplest explanation (applying Ockham's razor) is that DMT mechanics do describe the contact.

Professor Klein remarked: As a corollary to my last question concerning the applicability of contact mechanics to the AFM-tip/substrate contact, if this is done, what would be the mean pressure across the contact region at the highest loads? How does this compare with the elastic moduli of surfactant films and of polymer brush layers?

Professor Leggett replied: Estimating the contact area accurately is complicated by the fact that the modulus of a SAM is not easy to measure. Estimates suggest that the modulus may be *ca.* 1 GPa in size. Depending on the assumptions made in the calculation, a simple analysis of the tip–sample contact using DMT theory suggests that the contact area may be in the range 1–10 nm in diameter. For the range of loads used here, this suggests a pressure in the range 100s of MPa to a few GPa. This plainly underlines the fact that one needs to take great care (as we have done) to ensure that no plastic deformation is occurring during the measurement. However, the experimental tests for such permanent modification of the samples are straightforward and unambiguous and we are thus happy that there us not a problem in this regard. It is harder to say what the situation will be for brush layers; we expect these to be mechanically softer (they are probably much less close-packed than the SAMs) but also, in the right solvent, much more lubricious (based on your data). So I think that there are a few unanswered (but very interesting) questions.

Professor Klein asked: Did you examine the surfaces before and after FFM measurements? Was there any indication—at the resolution of the AFM—of damage to the surfactant layers following friction measurements at the highest loads?

Professor Leggett answered: This is an important question. As I already noted previously, there are a number of things that one can look for (variability in data, non-reversibility of friction–load plots, changes in the sample topography). We have looked carefully and systematically at the effect on the surface of increasing the load. Around 100 nN we see the onset of plastic deformation, but at the modest loads used here (no greater than 30 nN) we see no evidence at all of damage to either the sample or the probe.

Professor Bain commented: When applying Chris Hunter's model to the solvation of surface functional groups, you propose that a solvation layer is retained on each surface if the interaction with the solvent is sufficiently strong. This residual solvent layer at the interface should be detectable by techniques such as the surface force apparatus (SFA), where the minimum separation at contact will be larger if the solvating layers are not displaced. Do you know of SFA measurements on surfaces similar to those you have studied? We have looked for solvent layers by *in situ* Raman spectroscopy[1] but only for non-polar surfaces and non-polar solvents. As your model predicts, we did not detect residual solvent layers. One limitation is that the gold substrates that you use for alkanethiol SAMs are not ideal for either the SFA or *in situ* spectroscopic measurements, but it might be possible to design other monolayer systems to test your predictions directly.

1 D. A. Beattie, S. A. Winget and C. D. Bain, *Tribol. Lett.*, 2007, **27**, 159.

Professor Leggett responded: This is a very interesting suggestion. Measurements using the SFA would be extremely helpful here as a means to test the adhesion data we have obtained by AFM. I am not aware of any such studies to date on these kinds of systems, but I think that they are feasible. Although, as you suggest, gold is not an ideal substrate in this regard, we have recently carried out measurements in which a silane is the hydrogen bond acceptor (DPTS), and silanes can of course form monolayers on mica. One would need to find a silane to act as the hydrogen bond donor. This is less trivial than it might seem at first, because the molecular structure needs to be carefully selected to enable accurate comparison with the modelling data and, because the preparation of films of silanes terminating in an H-bond donor, this is fiddly. However, I think the problems are not insuperable. Thus one can indeed envisage the possibility of carrying out analogous experiments using the SFA, and the results would be of significant interest to us.

Professor Klein said: I would like to make a small comment concerning surface force balance studies of surfactant layers in aqueous media, which may have some bearing on this question. In our group (ref. 17 in our paper) we measured the interactions between two uniform monolayers of a polar surfactant, $(C_{11}H_{12})_2N^+(CH_3)$ $2Br^-$, attached to the mica surface by the charged N^+ headgroup. These surfactant monolayers were not thiol-attached but rather self-assembled spontaneously on the mica from solution, then rinsed and thoroughly dried. On adding water to the system, a clear swelling of each layer to the extent of some 2.5 Å was observed. Since the monolayers, each exposing the alkyl tails of the surfactants, were hydrophobic, the swelling was the result of water penetrating the head-group/mica interface and hydrating the charged N^+ group. This hydration and swelling occurred even when the two surfaces were held in strong adhesive contact in air during the addition of water to the system. I should also mention, since you refer to it, that it is possible to create large area gold surfaces smooth to ± 2 Å over their cm^2 area, suitable for use in the surface force balance,[1] which could then be coated with alkanethiol SAMs.

1 L. Chai and J. Klein, *Langmuir*, 2007, **23**, 7777–7783.

Dr Oesterle continued the discussion of the paper by Professor Martin: Since our MCA-model simulates the sliding of oxide films mixed with soft particles (most likely metal sulfides in your case) the release of oxide nanoparticles into the amorphous film can be understood readily, whereas the sliding behaviour and digestion of the oxide particles is explained very well by the MD-model. Therefore, I would conclude that boundary lubrication by ZDDP consists at least of two processes: i) tribooxidation and mixing with metal sulfide on the nanometre scale and ii) amorphous film formation and digestion of oxide nanoparticles on the atomic scale.

Professor Martin answered: I agree with your comment. In practical situations, due to sudden increases of contact pressure, both HSAB reactions take place successively, the first one releasing zinc and iron poly (thio)phosphate and ZnS, the second iron sulfides. After a certain time, all these compounds mix together in the tribofilm composition. However, only iron oxides and iron sulfides are crystallized and can be visualized by TEM.

Mr Niste enquired: What is the depth of the film at which you start to see Fe in the Auger spectra?

Professor Martin replied: It is difficult to know accurately the etching rate with the argon ion gun used for profiling. However it can be estimated from the disappearance of the 4–5 nm thick native ion oxide layer (outside the wear scar). Using this reference, the iron-free zinc thiophosphate top layer is about 10 nm thick.

Mr Niste remarked: As opposed to many opinions expressed in the literature, which suggest that it is the sulfur in ZDDP that is mainly responsible for the anti-wear properties of the additive, your proposed mechanism and model make no use of sulfur atoms, implying they are not important in this aspect. Sulfur does however show a small shift in the Auger spectra and the complex structure of ZDDP has not been abandoned in favor of simpler and cleaner sulfurless additives. In your view, what is responsible for the sulfur shift in the Auger spectra and what is the role of sulfur in ZDDP?

Professor Martin responded: I do not think that sulphur is often said to be responsible for anti-wear properties in the literature. It is more involved in extreme-pressure efficiency because it quickly reacts with metal ions exposed in severe friction conditions. It has been published that zinc phosphate (ZP) additive has better anti-wear properties that ZDDP. However, the molecule loses its anti-oxidant and EP capabilities. There is a strong depletion of sulphur in the tribofilm compared to the ZDDP molecule. In mild wear conditions, our simulations show that the presence of sulphur in the zinc phosphate increases the digestion rate. Sulphur in the tribofilm is both in thiophosphate and ZnS forms. Both are amorphous (by EXAFS) and it is very difficult to distinguish these two forms by TEM, XPS and Auger. The ZDDP complex structure is definitely abandoned in the tribofilm. This has been extensively studied by XANES by Kasrai in Canada. To conclude, the role of sulphur is to slightly improve the anti-wear properties and to bring EP and anti-oxidant performances.

Professor Williams opened the discussion of the paper by Dr Taylor: As your data illustrate, one of the simplest ways to improve mechanical engine efficiency is to reduce bulk lubricant viscosity and so bring down parasitic losses—but at the cost of reducing the hydrodynamically generated film thicknesses in the plain bearings. Are we now reaching the limit of that philosophy when minimum clearances are becoming limited by manufacturing tolerances or the capacity to filter out particulate contaminants from the oil? Do you think this might lead to the adoption of rather more radical development in engine design—such as dry sumps or electrically actuated valve gear?

Dr Taylor answered: Ideally, the best lubricant would be one with constant viscosity, which operated over a wide temperature range (from -50 to 300 °C). The constant viscosity would be the lowest that could still guarantee engine durability. Essentially the move to synthetic lubricants with higher and higher Viscosity Index is going that way. It would also be possible to get better energy efficiency if you had separate oils for the valve train system and the rest of the engine.

Dry sumps are already used in applications such as Formula One. Superfinishing of components would enable thinner oil films to be maintained. I think, in future, to get the optimum in fuel economy, engine and lubricant designers should collaborate to "co-engineer" the optimum solution.

Professor Dowson said: Ian, you showed and discussed viscosity–shear rate traces for two different lubricants. How were the measurements made over such a wide range of shear rates?

Dr Taylor replied: The viscosity *versus* shear rate curves shown were "schematic" and were intended to show that at 150 °C, you can formulate lubricants in different ways to meet the same High Temperature High Shear (HTHS) viscosity (this is the viscosity at 150 °C and a shear rate of 10^6 s^{-1}). You could choose a low base oil viscosity and put in a higher proportion of Viscosity Index Improver, or you could choose a higher base oil viscosity and a lower proportion of Viscosity Index Improver. In general, using a low base oil viscosity will give better fuel economy figures. Such curves can be measured from 10^6 to about 10^7 s^{-1} (using a PCS Instruments Ultra Shear Viscometer) and below 10^4 s^{-1}. However it is not straightforward to measure the complete viscosity–shear rate curve over the full range of shear rates.

Professor Bain remarked: The viscosity under pressure and shear is a key parameter in determining the behaviour of a lubricant in the EHD regime. Conventional viscometers measure the steady-state shear viscosity, usually in the linear regime. Rheometers for measuring very high shear rates (such as a piezo-axial vibrator) may also apply very small strains. In an EHD contact, however, the strain rate is highly time-dependent, the strain is large and may not be in the linear regime, and there is an extensional as well as shear component to the deformation of the fluid. How much is known about the rheology of oils and the performance of VI improvers under such conditions?

Dr Taylor answered: It is difficult to measure viscosity *versus* shear under high pressures, and it is also difficult to accurately measure fluid visco-elastic properties under high temperature/high pressure conditions. Some work has been reported, mainly in the 1990s, on the potential benefit of visco-elastic lubricants (acting through a "normal force") to give a higher than expected load bearing capacity for a given oil film thickness in a journal bearing. I am not aware of work that has been carried out to look at the extensional properties of commercial lubricants.

Dr Ratoi asked: With the trend of decreasing viscosity of oils to achieve fuel efficiency and considering the new range of multifunctional coatings and polyelectrolyte brush additives, should the lubrication specialists revisit the option of using water as a base fluid for engine lubrication? Published experimental research has shown that despite having a pressure viscosity coefficient of zero, water builds an EHD film which follows the Hooke equation for elastic-isoviscous contacts.

Dr Taylor replied: Water can be a good lubricant under certain circumstances, in the temperature range 0–100 °C. Water has the advantage that over this temperature range, the viscosity is more or less constant. If we could find a hydrocarbon based lubricant which had constant viscosity (of the order of 3 mPa s or so) then this would give substantial energy efficiency benefits (since most car drivers do a lot of short journeys where the engine is not fully warmed up). The advantage of hydrocarbon lubricants, compared to water, is that they are fluid over a much wider temperature range. If you are restricted to temperatures in the range 0–100 °C, then water, or a water/oil emulsion, is potentially an interesting option to explore further.

Dr Pauschitz noted: Besides relevant operation conditions other than temperature, contact to air and materials there are further influencing factors becoming more and more important, *e.g.* fuels or fuel additives from natural sources or more and more "bio"-additives in lubricants, which could result in tremendous oil stress. Interestingly, these impacts are widely neglected in bench tests or laboratory based tests.

Did you carry out tests with new oils only? At AC^2T, an application-oriented artificial alteration method (3 litre aged oil in approximately 80 to 100 h), representing the oil life-time in an engine, was developed to run tribo-tests with more relevant oil behaviour. We found that sometimes the aged oil has better friction and wear behaviour than the new oil. Do you have similar experience? How do the fuel saving factors you mentioned change with the use of application-oriented aged oils?

Dr Taylor responded: In general, most lubricant tests, either in tribology rigs, or in industry standard tests, use fresh lubricant. In our group, some limited work has been done with aged oils, and it has been found that under certain conditions, there is depletion of the additives (anti-oxidants, anti-wear additives, friction modifiers *etc.*). Work has also been carried out with lubricants contaminated with bio components from the fuel (either ethanol or biodiesel). Certainly lubricants contaminated with certain types of biodiesel can be greatly affected—in particular their oxidation performance. When oils are aged, it is often found that friction and wear can improve initially, although if the oil is left in the machine for too long, ultimately friction and wear will get worse. Some of the oxidation products of the base oil (esters, alcohols, ketones, acids) could be better for friction. In addition, as the anti-wear additive depletes and forms thinner films, this would usually give lower friction. Very few fuel economy engine tests have been performed using aged oil, as far as I am aware, and I think looking at the impact of aged oil on tribological and fuel economy performance would be a very useful area of research in the coming decade.

Professor Spencer commented: I have the impression that the car companies and therefore the oil companies are bending over backwards to meet the government CO_2 and fuel economy standards, since the auto makers will incur heavy fines if they do not. Since this is based on a given drive cycle, does that mean that approaches that would improve fuel economy but have negligible effect on behavior in the standard cycle are being de-emphasized as research targets?

Dr Taylor replied: In certain regions, such as Europe, there is the potential for fines to be imposed if the fleet average CO_2 emissions are above a certain level (130 g km^{-1} by 2015). These emissions are measured on a specific driving cycle, the New European Driving Cycle (NEDC), and fuel consumption, and its response to the lubricant used, could well be different on other driving cycles. In fact many OEMs do indeed have their own fuel consumption tests, but it is true that a great deal of focus is placed on regulatory tests demanded by the Government. In terms of the NEDC, it is a cold start cycle, with a high proportion of idling, so is quite representative of cold start city type driving, but not as representative of fully warmed up engines driving on the motorway. In fact, if we compare trends in passenger car motor oils (where there are many 0W-x and 5W-x viscosity grades) with those of heavy duty truck oils (which operate primarily with fully warmed up engines), there are far fewer 0W-x and 5W-x heavy duty engine oils, and most operators still use 15W-x or 10W-x, as there is less focus on cold starts. I think there is a sufficient range of driving cycles in use worldwide that the scenario you suggest would not arise in practice, although it is worth keeping in mind.

Professor Klein remarked: I found your survey of the relation between lubricant molecular properties and machine friction most interesting. You did not discuss at

 This journal is © The Royal Society of Chemistry 2012

length the possibility of polymeric additives, but in different contexts—for example, tertiary oil recuperation—'smart' polymers have been developed that can undergo either shear thinning or shear thickening, and at controllable shear rates. Is this— *i.e.* incorporation of smart polymers into machine lubricants—an area of current development?

Dr Taylor said: Polymers are already added to lubricants, and the temporary shear thinning that these polymers undergo helps reduce friction. By judicious choice of the type of polymer (known as a Viscosity Index Improver, or alternatively a Viscosity Modifier) and the amount used, the variation of viscosity *versus* shear rate can to a certain extent be controlled. However, in most lubricant applications, shear thickening polymers are not currently used, although this could be an interesting option for the future where we are trying to increase the oil film thickness in heavily loaded contacts, whilst trying to decrease the oil film thickness under more lightly loaded conditions.

Dr Mischler opened the discussion of the paper by Dr Polcar: The tribofilms you observe consist mainly of iron oxide, tungsten disulphide and carbon with chromium oxide in only a few cases. This is rather surprising (and interesting) since the formation of chromium oxide and tungsten oxides is thermodynamically more favourable than of iron oxide. Also, one would expect sulphur to react with moisture and oxygen. Have you any evidence excluding the occurrence of these reactions? Is it possible that such reactions occur but the products form as loose or volatile debris and are therefore not detected? How would such reactions interfere with the coating performance?

Dr Polcar responded: We observed iron oxide on the ball wear scar forming a thin (about 20 nm) tribolayer. However, the tribolayer adhered on the coating (*i.e.* observed in the coating wear track) was much thicker (about 100 nm) containing iron and tungsten oxides together with few isolated WS_2 platelets. Considering the hardness of the coating and high contact pressure, we suppose that the conditions are favourable to form all referred metallic oxides simultaneously. The sliding process then could separate different oxides forming a predominant iron oxide tribolayer. Sulphur is indeed expected to react with moisture/oxygen forming volatile products. In fact, the absence of sulphur in the contact is indirect evidence of such reactions. As a consequence, the coating loses its self-lubricant properties. However, a well ordered WS_2 tribolayer with basal planes parallel to the surface has good resistant to oxidation, which occurs mainly at the reactive edges of the WS_2 crystal. The formation of a WS_2 interlayer was observed in case of the W-S-C films; it is apparent that alloying of the W-S-C coating with chromium hinders the ability to form a WS_2 tribolayer in humid air.

Dr Oesterle enquired: Do you observe fluctuations of the friction force, and might these be related to changes of the layer structure?

Dr Polcar replied: We did not observe any fluctuations which could be related to any possible change of the tribolayer structure (*i.e.* complex tribolayer formed in dry air consisting of exclusive WS_2 and chromium oxide layers, see Fig. 14). We suppose that the wear takes place in small localized areas of the contact, where the top WS_2 layer is worn out and then replenished. Although a localized increase of the friction during re-building of the tribolayer is expected, its contribution to global friction measured by pin-on-disc is negligible.

Dr Oesterle commented: Your Fig. 4 implies that a certain amount of load is needed to produce a crystalline layer which provides antifriction properties.

Dr Polcar responded: I agree. We observed in our previous studies (ref. 10 and 16 in our paper) that the low-friction WS_2 tribolayer was thicker and more compact under higher contact pressures. Moreover, the sliding distance required to reach the steady state increases when the contact pressure is lower.

Dr Wahl queried: What role do you think carbon is playing in the sliding process, particularly in light of the observation that it is found primarily at the sides of the ball transfer film? That observation suggests to me that higher friction materials are preferentially ejected from the contact in favor of forming the most easily sheared interface. Do you think this is likely? We have seen such behavior in one composite system, boric acid on a B_4C substrate.[1] In that case, once boric acid was depleted from the contact, an intermediate friction coefficient and higher carbon content was found in the contact before high friction (failure) once that was depleted.

1 S. D. Dvorak, K. J. Wahl and I. L. Singer, Friction Behavior of Boric Acid and Annealed Boron Carbide Coatings Studied by In Situ Raman Tribometry, *Tribol. Trans.*, 2002, **45**, 354–362.

Dr Polcar replied: The exact effect of carbon on the tribological properties is still not clear. It was always found only on the sides of the wear track, typically as graphitic carbon (Raman analysis). The friction of carbon/graphite is significantly higher in dry air than that of WS_2; thus, carbon is probably preferentially removed from the contact. It should be pointed out that the wear rate of some of our films is extremely low—more than 1000 cycles on a tribometer (pin-on-disc or reciprocal) was required to remove approximately 1 nm of the film in the steady-state regime. Since we have never found carbon in the contact area in the present or previous studies (we carried out surface sensitive analyses as AES, Raman, or TEM, see ref. 11 and 43), we suppose that the release of carbon from the contact is a quick process. As a consequence, the effect of carbon on the friction is considered negligible.

Dr Wahl remarked: Your paper discusses the application of the Hertzian contact model and shear stress of a solid to explain load dependent friction of solid lubricating thin films, eqn (1). This equation couples Bowden and Tabor's model of lubrication by a soft, thin film[1] with a pressure-dependent shear term, providing an analytical expression linking friction to pressure. While I confess that I am somewhat agnostic about this expression, in my experience in macroscopic sliding contacts, we have never observed a thin film solid lubricant system where the expression did not hold and provide some informative value. Of course, the assumption of Hertzian contact mechanics means that neither the ball nor coating can wear substantially. That appears to be the case in the present work. Also interesting is the question of the role of the thin film mechanics. If the solid lubricant film, of thickness t, is much thinner than the contact diameter, $2a$, (e.g. $t \ll 2a$), the mechanics of the substrate plays the greatest role in determining the contact size, and hence coating mechanical properties (assuming a dense, elastic layer) do not impact the measurement. Thus, as the size of the contact is reduced, say in micro-scale contacts, the application of this model and processes of lubrication by a thin solid film may be impacted by the coating mechanics much more strongly.

1 F. P. Bowden and D. Tabor, *The Friction and Lubrication of Solids*, Part 1, Clarendon Press, Oxford, 1950, ch. V.

Dr Polcar answered: The equation in question predicts macroscopic contact well; however, we have doubts about its use in microscopic contacts. Firstly, the ideal Hertzian contact pressure is typically higher than the real pressure due to wear and material transfer on the ball. Secondly, the elastic modulus measured of the as-deposited sample differs significantly from that of real material in the contact.

It is extremely difficult to measure elastic moduli of very thin tribolayers and/or modified coating structure, particularly due to surface roughness in the wear track. Lastly, the zero-load friction is not a clearly defined parameter. All our self-lubricant coatings based on transition metal dichalcogenides exhibited deviations from eqn (1) (see ref. 11, 16, and 43 in the paper). We suggested a simple power law fit, *i.e.* friction coefficient $\approx Lb$, where L is the load and b is a constant dependent on material and contact conditions. We believe the decrease of friction with increased pressure is mostly related to optimized formation of a well-ordered transition metal dichalcogenide tribolayer. On the other hand, we agree that most of the low-friction coating systems based on MoS_2 or WS_2 fit eqn (1) well, although it is not clear why.

Professor Klein opened the discussion of the paper by Dr Kobayashi: I have two questions in connection with the efficient brush lubrication that you report. At the pressure you apply, 139 MPa, one might expect much if not all of the water to be squeezed out of the brush layers, although this process may require time. Given that you are sliding at 0.15 m s^{-1}, I presume that some water remains trapped in the brush layers—especially in your most efficient system, p(SPMK-*co*-MTAC)— as the slider moves across them. One would then expect friction to increase significantly at lower sliding velocities, as more water would have time to squeeze out of the layers. Did you find evidence of this?

My second question relates to the high efficiency of the p(SPMK-*co*-MTAC) brushes, which I would expect to be due to their strong hydration. Have you some direct measure of this—other than the contact angle measurements, which are also revealing—for example spectroscopic or other indications?

Dr Kobayashi replied: In answer to your first question, the friction coefficient of polyelectrolyte brushes in aqueous media strongly depends on the sliding velocity. Fig. 1 here shows the sliding velocity dependence of the friction coefficient of poly(MTAC), poly(SPMK), and poly(MPC) brushes in water under a load of 0.49 N (= 139 MPa) at 298 K. The friction coefficients of these brushes were 0.1–0.2 at slower friction velocities of 10^{-5}–10^{-3} m s^{-1}, whereas the

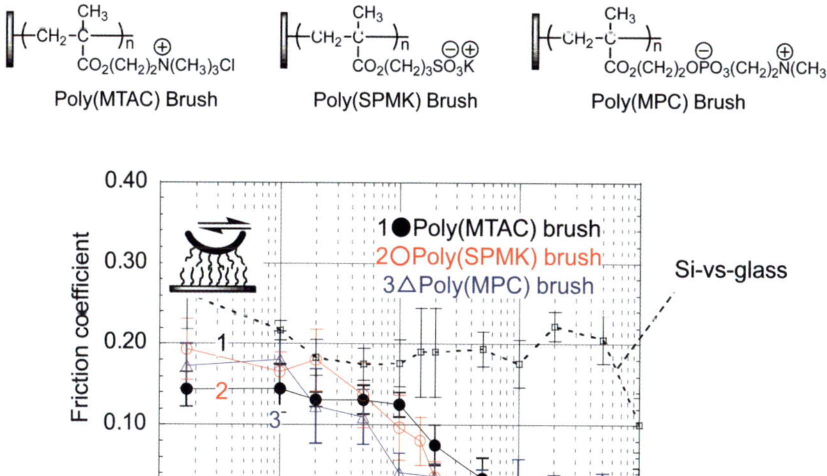

Fig. 1 Sliding velocity dependence of the friction coefficient of poly(MTAC), poly(SPMK), and poly(MPC) brushes in water under a load of 0.49 N (= 139 MPa) at 298 K.

friction coefficient dropped to 0.01–0.03 at higher sliding velocities over the range 10^{-3}–10^{-1} m s^{-1}. As you point out, we suppose that the water would be squeezed out of the brush layers at a lower sliding velocity under a pressure of 139 MPa to increase the friction. In contrast, a lower friction coefficient at higher sliding velocity would be caused by trapped water in the brush layer because not all the water of the brush layer could have enough time to be squeezed out when the friction probe was sliding at much higher velocity. At a high sliding velocity, we suppose that hydrodynamic lubrication partially occurs at the interface between the oppositely sliding swollen brushes, to reduce the friction.

Unfortunately, we do not have any evidence for the water remaining at the sliding interface at present. We are trying to measure the thickness of the sliding brush layer under wet conditions by ultra-thin film interferometry. In addition, we are going to measure the *in situ* Raman spectra combined with optical microscopy of the brush layer during the sliding to see if the water is squeezed out or not.

In answer to your second question, actually, polyelectrolyte brushes with higher hydrophilicity revealed a low friction coefficient under wet conditions. However, we do not have any experimental evidence for the degree of hydration or hydrophilicity of the polyelectrolyte brush, except for the contact angles, at this moment. Prof. Kitano *et al.* at Toyama University investigated the structure and hydrogen-bonded network of water in the vicinity of a polyelectrolyte, such as carboxybetaine polymer[1] and poly(MPC),[2] by analysis of their aqueous solutions and thin films with contours of O–H stretching of the Raman and ATR-IR spectra. The number of hydrogen bonds collapsed by the presence of ionic functional groups of the polymers might be related to the hydration state of the polyelectrolyte.

1 H. Kitano, S. Tada, T. Mori, K. Takaha, M. Gemmei-Ide, M. Tanaka, M. Fukuda and Y. Yokoyama, *Langmuir*, 2005, **21**, 11932.
2 H. Kitano, M. Imai, T. Mori, M. Gemmei-Ide, Y. Yokoyama and K. Ishihara, *Langmuir*, 2003, **19**, 10260.

Professor Klein asked: In your very nice study, did you also examine the effect of added salt? We have found that salt can act in two different modes: either to reduce the screening between charged polymer segments, and thus the brush swelling, or to compete with the charged/zwitterionic monomers for water of hydration, which can affect the hydration lubrication mechanism.

Dr Kobayashi answered: We have reported the friction coefficient of polyelectrolyte brushes in aqueous NaCl solution in a previous paper.[1] Typically, the friction coefficient of polyelectrolyte brushes in aqueous solution increase with the concentration of added salt. However, the effect of added salt on the hydration lubrication depends on the type of polyelectrolyte. In the case of positively or negatively charged polymers, such as the poly(MTAC) and poly(SPMK) brushes, the friction coefficient increases with the salt concentration (see Fig. 2 here) because the added salt ions reduce the electrostatic repulsive interaction among the polymer segments leading to a reduction in the swollen thickness of the brushes, and thus their collapse. This result might be caused by the competition of hydration and salting-out of the charged monomers by the added salt ions.

The friction coefficient of zwitterionic poly(MPC) brushes is also increased in 1–5 M aqueous NaCl solution (see Fig. 3 here). However, the hydration state of poly(MPC) seems to be different from that of the other polyelectrolytes. The dimension and hydrodynamic radius of poly(MPC) in aqueous solution are hardly changed by the added salt concentration, which was confirmed by light scattering[2] and SAXS.[3] Neutron reflectivity measurements at the interface of the poly(MPC) brushes/D$_2$O solution showed independency of the swollen thickness from the added salt concentration.[4] The reason why poly(MPC) behaves like a neutral polymer even in an aqueous salt solution is still unclear. We suppose that it might be related to the

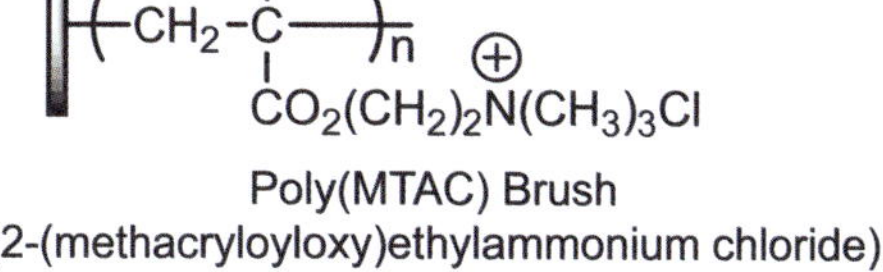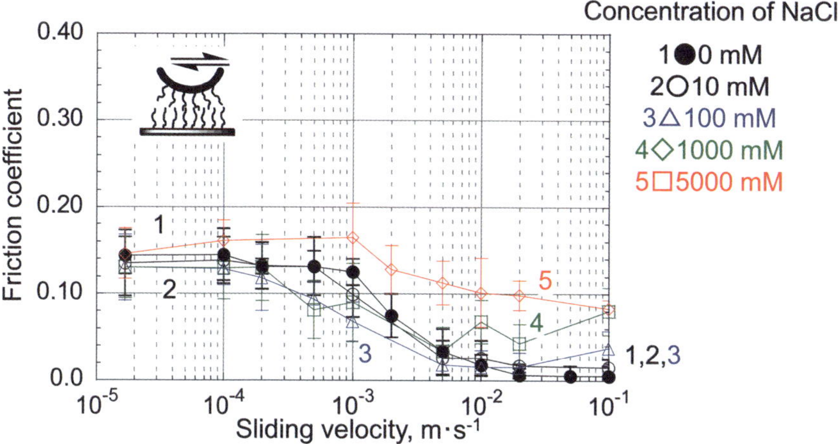

Fig. 2 Sliding velocity dependence of the friction coefficient of poly(MTAC) brushes in NaCl aqueous solution under a load of 0.49 N (= 139 MPa) at 298 K. With an increase in NaCl concentration, larger friction coefficients were observed.

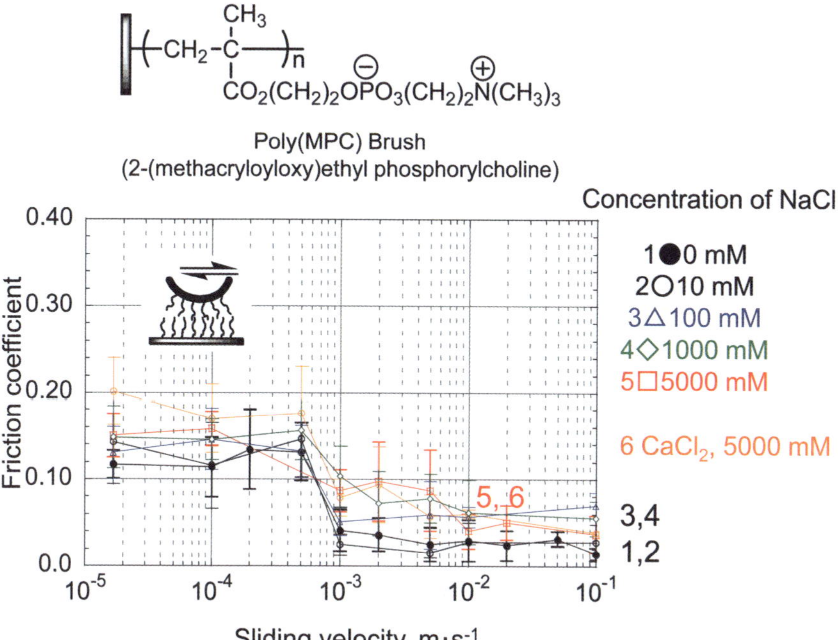

Fig. 3 Sliding velocity dependence of the friction coefficient of poly(MPC) brushes in NaCl aqueous solution under a load of 0.49 N (= 139 MPa) at 298 K.

hydration structure of the MPC units. Prof. Kitano at Toyama University, Japan, reported that the structure and hydrogen bonding of water surrounding poly(MPC) was different from that of conventional polyelectrolytes by the analysis of Raman and ATR-IR spectroscopy.[5] Poly[3-(*N*-2-methacryloyloxyethyl-*N,N*-dimethyl) ammonatopropanesulfonate] (poly(MAPS)) is also one of the polyzwitterions, however, poly(MAPS) is insoluble in deionized water at room temperature because of the strong attractive dipole–dipole interaction between the sulfobetaine units. Poly(MAPS) is soluble in the aqueous salt solution due to a reduction in the interaction between the sulfobetaine units by the hydrated added ions. Although we have not examine the friction tests of poly(MAPS) brushes in aqueous solution yet, a large dependence of the frictional properties on the salt concentration in aqueous solution must be observed.

1 M. Kobayashi and A. Takahara, *Chem. Rec.*, 2010, **10**, 208.
2 Y. Matsuda, M. Kobayashi, M. Annaka, K. Ishihara and A. Takahara, *Langmuir*, 2008, **24**, 8772.
3 M. Kikuchi, Y. Terayama, T. Ishikawa, T. Hoshino, M. Kobayashi, H. Ogawa, H. Masunaga, J. Koike, M. Horigome, K. Ishihara and A. Takahara, *Polym. J.*, 2012, **44**, 121.
4 M. Kobayashi, K. Mitamura, M. Terada, N. L. Yamada and A. Takahara, *J. Phys. Conf. Ser.*, 2011, **272**, 012019.
5 H. Kitano, M. Imai, T. Mori, M. Gemmei-Ide, Y. Yokoyama and K. Ishihara, *Langmuir*, 2003, **19**, 10260.

Mr Snow enquired: In the data presented in Fig. 6 in your paper, there appears to be an emergent trend as highlighted here in Fig. 4. For the cross-linked poly(MPC) polymer it would appear that the trend indicates a general reduction in the friction co-efficient over the running of the experiment. Is this a demonstration of the polymer brushes showing 'wearing in' behaviour as is seen in other lubrication systems; furthermore is this trend seen in other polymer brush systems?

1 M. Kobayashi, M. Terada and A. Takahara, *Faraday Discuss.*, 2012, **156**, DOI: 10.1039/C2FD00123C.

Dr Kobayashi responded: When two solid bodies contact each other, in general, the friction force increases from zero to some maximum value at the beginning of the friction due to the surface roughness (preliminary displacement), and then reduces or levels off due to the deformation of the protuberances or elongation of

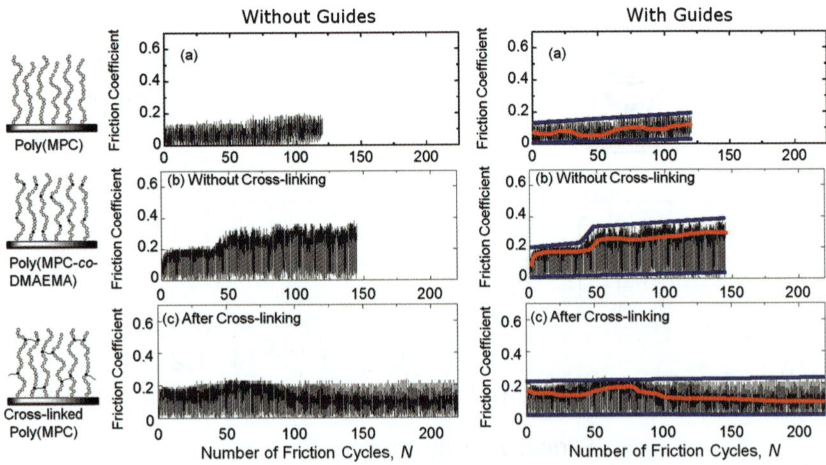

Fig. 4 Adapted from Fig. 6 of Kobayashi *et al.*[1] The blue line is illustrating the average noise, the orange line appears to indicate a general trend in the data presented.

the contact point in the direction of sliding motion, called wearing-in of a friction pair. As you pointed out, the evolution of the friction coefficient in Fig. 6(c) showed a similar trend with the wearing-in behavior. In this experiment, the wear track formed on the polymer brush surface after sliding under a pressure of 139 MPa, indicating the deformation of the brush layer or wear during the sliding. However, we do not have experimental evidence for the wearing-in behavior of the brush layer at the moment. Further analysis of the wear track surface would be required. At least, the period for the preliminary displacement should be terminated within 5–10 cycles of the sliding in the case of Fig. 6(b) and 6(c).

Typically, the friction coefficient of the polymer brushes (without cross-linking) under a pressure of 139 MPa maintains a relatively stable value for a while, but increases at a certain number of sliding cycles due to wear, as shown in Fig. 6(a) and 6(b).[1,2]

1 M. Kobayashi, Y. Terayama, N. Hosaka, M. Kaido, A. Suzuki, N. Yamada, N. Torikai, K. Ishihara and A. Takahara, *Soft Matter*, 2007, **3**, 740.
2 M. Kobayashi and A. Takahara, *Chem. Rec.*, 2010, **10**, 208.

Dr Wang queried: Why is the friction recorded so noisy and has this anything to do with interactions between the brush layers on both surfaces? Is this stick–slip?

Dr Kobayashi answered: This was electric noise due to the reciprocating tribo-tester. Even if the moving stage is stopping, the strain gauge shows a friction coefficient width of ± 0.02 at the center of zero. In addition, a reduction in the friction coefficient takes place at the moment of the change in sliding direction during the reciprocating motion. In the case of Fig. 6(b), for example, while a glass ball was sliding on the surface, the friction coefficient was 0.18, however, the friction coefficient became zero at the moment of switching back the sliding direction. Therefore, the evolution of the friction coefficient looks like a noisy pattern. This is not stick–slip.

Dr Wang said: Please explain how the wear was measured to quantify the wear resistance of both surfaces.

Dr Kobayashi responded: In this study, we compared the wear resistance of the polymer brushes by the number of friction cycles when the friction coefficient significantly increased due to the complete abrasion of the brush thin films. The wear track was analyzed by XPS after the friction test in order to confirm whether the brush components remained in the wear track or not. However, we did not quantitatively measure the amount of wear and wear debris on both surfaces after the friction test.

Dr Wang asked: Could you please comment on the materials you tested in your study and how they are linked to medical/bio applications in your mind? Would the molecules react the same way to materials other than silicon or do you need to find other brush molecules for real applications?

Dr Kobayashi replied: PMPC is one of the most useful materials for medical applications. The PMPC brush tethered surface shows excellent blood and biocompatibilities due to the zwitterionic phosphorylcholine groups. In general, polymer brushes can be fabricated on the surface of various materials, such as polypropylene, poly (vinylidene fluoride-*co*-trifluoroethylene), stainless steel, aluminum, silica, and titanium oxide, by surface initiated polymerization. Various molecules and substrate materials are available for the preparation of polymer brushes. Of course, we should use biocompatible and low toxicity materials for real medical/bio applications

Professor Bain commented: ATRP is a very general approach that can be used to generate polyelectrolyte brushes on a wide range of substrates. My colleague at Durham, Prof. Jas Pal Badyal, has shown that pulsed plasma polymerisation can be used to deposit a thin precursor polymer layer containing an initiator group on almost any solid substrate and that ATRP and other polymerisation techniques can then be used to grow brushes from the surface. See, for example, GB patent 2437476 B.

Dr Kobayashi said: Thank you very much for your information. The immobilization of alkyl halides by pulsed plasma must be widely useful for the fabrication of polymer brushes on the surface of various materials.

                    www.rsc.org/faraday_d | Faraday Discussions

Tribology

Nicholas D. Spencer

Received 16th April 2012, Accepted 18th April 2012
DOI: 10.1039/c2fd20075a

The 156th Faraday Discussion covered the field of tribology, focussing on the subtopics of biotribology, predictive modelling, smart surfaces, and future lubricated systems. The papers themselves covered topics that drew on the fields of biology, medicine, chemistry, physics, materials science and mechanical engineering, providing a challenging and fascinating insight into the current state of the field of tribology.

1   Introduction

This was the first time in the history of the Faraday Discussions that tribology had been the focus of attention. This is quite surprising, given the preponderance of chemists in the field, particularly in lubrication. The consequence was that, for many of those present, the Faraday format was a novelty, but it rapidly became clear that most of the attendees were very enthusiastic about the possibilities for in-depth discussions that it enabled.

Rather than regurgitating a dry sentence on each presentation, I have focussed on a few lectures in which I felt the authors have taken particularly significant steps forward.

2   Biotribology

Prof. Duncan Dowson, of the University of Leeds, set the tone of the meeting with his authoritative and fascinating tour of the various facets of biotribology. The field has broadened significantly beyond its original focus on hip and knee joints and their replacements, to become a respectable and important component of industrial research in the contact-lens and personal-care industries. Furthermore, studies of molecular motors (such as those that power flagellae in bacteria) and animal locomotion (lubricated or unlubricated, as exemplified by snails and geckos, respectively) are now widespread, also driving forwards the fields of biomimetics and bioinspired systems.

Prof. Dowson also touched upon the tendency of certain researchers to cling on to concepts of lubrication that work well for oil-lubricated steel machines and to apply these doggedly to biological systems. He made the point that naturally lubricated systems, such as the hip joint, probably transition between different lubrication modes, depending on the conditions. This point was further emphasized in the following talk by Prof. Greg Sawyer,[1] of the University of Florida, who reported his findings in the area of the tribology of eyes. His work on the frictional behavior of corneal cells, both *in vitro* and *in vivo*, has shown that the lubricant system is extremely complex, involving the presence of rheological gradients on the eye, and that lubrication regimes are probably quite different, depending on whether the eye is moving (*i.e.* panning) or the lid is moving (*i.e.* blinking). Prof. Sawyer also mentioned that the measured friction coefficients on the eye are consistent with

Laboratory for Surface Science and Technology, Wolfgang-Pauli-Strasse 10, ETH Zurich, 8093 Zurich, Switzerland. E-mail: nspencer@ethz.ch; Fax: +41 44 633 1027; Tel: +41 44 632 5850

a very low shear stress, implying that a brush-type lubrication mechanism[2,3] may be at work. The most impressive aspect of Sawyer's results is the extraordinary experimental developments in his lab, which have now opened up the field of eye tribology. While Sawyer could already identify the sliding conditions leading to cell death, and could observe recovery of the cornea within a short time, *in vivo*, he is now in an excellent position to study the intricacies of the relationship between eye mechanosensing and corneal cell signalling.

3 Predictive modelling

Prof. Pwt Evans,[4] of the University of Cardiff, described his groundbreaking work on the prediction of fatigue failure in lubricated contacts. This work is of particular relevance to power-generation systems, such as wind turbines, where significant problems with gears are leading to far less favourable economics than expected. Micropitting is a frequent early indication of such problems, and it can proceed to crack branching and ultimately tooth breakage. The research has involved, in the first instance, investigating a mixed-lubrication regime by constraining elastohydrodynamic calculations with contact mechanics, using actual, measured surface roughness profiles. In this way, the likelihood of fatigue on different areas of the measured system can be predicted. In a further extension, the consequences of stresses resulting from plastic deformation have also been taken into account. Since boundary lubrication is key to the operation of such systems involving transient contact conditions, the authors expressed the hope that a greater understanding of additive chemistry and mechanisms would enable them to make the model even more comprehensive, and ultimately turn it into a valuable predictive tool.

Brakes are an excellent example of systems necessitating low wear and high friction. Brake pads consist of extremely complex mixtures of materials that have been developed over decades in a highly empirical manner. Understanding the roles of the different components and the processes taking place in operating brakes could greatly assist in the design of improved braking systems. Dr Werner Österle[5] of the Federal Institute for Materials Research and Testing, in Berlin, described an approach to understanding how materials mix and forces are generated during braking. The technique involved Movable Cellular Autonoma—a method that has also been used for geological modelling. Of particular interest in this study was the role of so-called *ultra-mild wear* and its associated nanocrystalline surface-film formation and mechanically mixed layers, in operating brakes. Slowly building up from simple systems to complex mixtures with compositions close to those of real brakes, Österle and his team were able to show that while iron oxides alone led to cracking and stick-slip motion, the incorporation of soft components, such as graphite, copper, or a mixture of both, led to a nanocrystalline, mechanically mixed layer and smooth sliding. Further incorporation of a hard component, such as SiC, did not affect the layer or the sliding mode, but did lead to higher friction. Interestingly, although the size scales of the techniques are entirely different, results are strikingly reminiscent of results from the group of David Rigney,[6] who applied molecular dynamics to dry-sliding problems.

4 Smart surfaces

Professor Jacob Klein,[7] of the Weizmann Institute of Science, presented his exploration of the new concept of *hydration lubrication*. This phenomenon, which involves lubrication at close quarters by highly fluid hydration shells around charges in water, can be observed between mica surfaces in a surface forces balance, even in systems as simple as 0.1 M NaCl. At mica–mica separations of around 1 Å, friction coefficients as low as 2×10^{-4} could be measured. The experimental challenges involved in such measurements are enormous, and the authors were even able to distinguish between different batches of high-purity salts, presumably due to a small number of impurity atoms jamming the system. The hydration-lubrication mechanism appears to be widespread, and Klein was able to show its applicability in tribosystems including surfactants on surfaces, polyzwitterionic brushes, and gel-phase, surface-attached liposomes.

Despite the fact that scientists from Leonardo da Vinci onwards have been investigating friction, the way in which energy is dissipated during sliding remains an important research topic in tribology. The elegant experimental approach adopted by Prof. Liliane Léger,[8] of the Université Paris-Sud, involved microfabricating an array of silicone pillars, each of which was several micrometers in diameter, and measuring sliding friction against smooth silicone lenses. The approach enabled the real and apparent contact areas to be measured at all times, and related to the measured friction. A very interesting, and quite counterintuitive observation was that the real-contact-area-normalised friction against the pillars was higher than that against a smooth silicone surface. The authors explain this effect by suggesting that the dissipation mechanism involves the elastic energy stored in the pillars and the underlying substrate being released after the sliding contact has passed. Consistent with this hypothesis, the dissipation was found to scale inversely with the diameter of the pillars.

5 Future lubricated systems

Prof. Graham Leggett,[9] of the University of Sheffield, presented a study of the effects of surface solvation on nanoscale adhesion and friction measurements. Key to this novel line of investigation is the hydrogen-bonding interaction of solvents such as acetone with surfaces, and the way in which this can drastically change the interaction of tip and surface. By systematically examining a series of liquid mixtures that lead to increasing degrees of H-bonding-mediated surface solvation, Leggett was able to show that a major change in nanoscopic adhesion coincided with a sharp transition in the calculated degree of surface solvation. In the case of liquid mixtures with little H-bonding ability, non-linear friction-load curves were obtained that corresponded to DMT mechanics, while highly solvated surfaces yielded linear friction–load curves. By assuming that the friction force is composed of a load-dependent (*i.e.* Amontons) and a shear (*i.e.* adhesion-dependent) term,

Fig. 1 The behaviour of polymer brushes in a good solvent, mimed by Faraday Discussion participants (left to right): Prof. Graham Leggett, Prof. Colin Bain, Prof. Jacob Klein, Dr Kathy Wahl, Prof. Greg Sawyer, Dr Connor Myant and Dr Motoyasu Kobayashi. (Photo: Ian Taylor).

Leggett could use tribological and adhesion measurements to predict thermodynamic properties of the interacting functional groups. He was also able to show that while the shear term certainly depended on surface functionality, the friction coefficient did not, which suggests that a number of published nanotribological studies of self-assembled monolayers are in urgent need of re-evaluation.

Dr Motoyasu Kobayashi,[10] of Japan Science and Technology agency ERATO Takahara Soft Interfaces Project, showed tribological results measured under humid conditions, obtained with a number of polyelectrolyte brushes that had been grafted from surfaces. Two aspects of this work stood out particularly: firstly, the low friction coefficients measured on the brushes, despite the fact that only a thin, condensed layer of water was present, and secondly, the fact that crosslinking, either covalent or electrostatic, seemed to influence the abrasion rate of the brushes. There is clearly a very promising future in intelligent tuning of the charge distribution within polymer brushes, as well as the degree and type of interchain crosslinking.

The behavior of polymer brushes under solvents of varying quality was later ably demonstrated by a number of conference participants (Fig. 1).

Acknowledgements

All the participants are greatly indebted to Professor Robert Wood, of the University of Southampton, who spearheaded this meeting, and, in collaboration with his Scientific Committee (Professors Colin Bain, Phil Bartlett, Stefano Mischler, Anne Neville, John Williams and Dr Kathryn Wahl), wisely chose the subject areas and speakers. We are also grateful for the administrative skills of Rebecca Quine, of RSC Events. The meeting was a resounding success, and greatly benefited from the Faraday format. It is to be hoped that there will be many more tribology-based Faraday Discussions in the future.

References

1 T. E. Angelini, A. C. Dunn, J. M. Uruena, D. J. Dickrell, D. L. Burris and W. G. Sawyer, *Faraday Discuss.*, 2012, **156**, DOI: 10.1039/c2fd00130f.
2 R. Tadmore, J. Janik and J. Klein, *Phys. Rev. Lett.*, 2003, **91**, 115503.
3 S. Lee and N. D. Spencer, *Science*, 2008, **319**, 575.
4 H. P. Evans, R. W. Snidle, K. J. Sharif and M. J. Bryant, *Faraday Discuss.*, 2012, **156**, DOI: 10.1039/c2fd00116k.
5 W. Österle, A. I. Dmitriev and H. Kloß, *Faraday Discuss.*, 2012, **156**, DOI: 10.1039/c2fd00117a.
6 H. J. Kim, W. K. Kim, M. L. Falk and D. A. Rigney, *Tribol. Lett.*, 2007, **28**, 299–306.
7 A. Gaisinskaya, L. Ma, G. Silbert, R. Sorkin, O. Tairy, R. Goldberg, N. Kampf and J. Klein, *Faraday Discuss.*, 2012, **156**, DOI: 10.1039/c2fd00127f.
8 E. Degrandi-Contraires, C. Poulard, F. Restagno and L. Léger, *Faraday Discuss.*, 2012, **156**, DOI: 10.1039/c2fd00121g.
9 K. Busuttil, N. Nikogeorgos, Z. Zhang, M. Geoghegan, C. A. Hunter and G. J. Leggett, *Faraday Discuss.*, 2012, **156**, DOI: 10.1039/c2fd00133k.
10 M. Kobayashi, M. Terada and A. Takahara, *Faraday Discuss.*, 2012, **156**, DOI: 10.1039/c2fd00123c.

Poster titles

Interactions between thermo-responsive polymer brushes, **T. Snow**, *University of Bristol, UK*

Structural transitions in a model hydrophobic boundary layer under water, **N. N. Gosvami, M. L. Berkowitz, B. W. Hoogenboom and S. Perkin**, *University College London, UK*

Understanding the fundamentals of tyre friction on snow, **S. Ella, J. R. Blackford, V. Koutsos and J.-B. Fourrel De Frettes**, *University of Edinburgh, UK*

White structure flaking (WSF) in wind turbine gearbox bearings: effects of lubrication, additives and hydrogen, **M. Evans, L. Wang, T. J. Harvey and R. J. K. Wood**, *University of Southampton, UK*

Molecular dynamics simulations of the adsorption of long-chain alkyl amides on metal oxide surfaces under shear conditions, **M. Doig and P. J. Camp**, *University of Edinburgh, UK*

New test rig "CaTri" for tribological characterization of materials, coatings and lubricants in UHV, **M. Conte, E. Berriozabal, A. Igartua and R. Nevshupa**, *Teknika, Spain*

Amontonian frictional behaviour of nanostructured surfaces, **G. A. Pilkington, W. H. Briscoe, P. Claesson, E. Thormann, M. Ashfold, G. Fuge, O. Fox, D. Mattia and H. Leese**, *University of Bristol, UK*

Ionic liquids as lubricants and additives: structure and friction of molecularly confined films, **A. M. Smith, K. R. J. Lovelock, N. N. Gosvami, P. Licence and S. Perkin**, *University College London, UK*

Friction on ice: what's happening at the interface? **T. Parkanyi, J. R. Blackford and V. Koutsos**, *University of Edinburgh, UK*

Controlling friction and wetting with reconfigurable surface roughness, **N. J. Morris, K. A. Sierros and D. R. Cairns**, *West Virginia University, USA*

Using neutron reflection to understand the structural origin of liquid crystal lubrication, **L. L. E. Mears, T. Cosgrove, G. Magro, S. W. Prescott, R. M. Richardson, M. W. A. Skoda, W. M. de Vos and H. Zimmerman**, *University of Bristol, UK*

Wear behaviour of ultra-fine grained titanium processed by high-pressure torsion and subsequent TiN coating, **C. T. Wang, N. Gao, M. G. Gee, R. J. K. Wood and T. G. Langdon**, *University of Southampton, UK*

Superior friction reduction and wear resistance of nanocrystalline Co-Ni-P coatings, **C. Ma, S. C. Wang, L. P. Wang and F. C. Walsh**, *University of Southampton, UK*

Tailored friction properties and enhanced run-in behaviour by geometrical interlocking of laser interference structured surfaces on a mesoscopic scale, **A. Rosenkranz, C. Gachot, L. Reinert and F. Mücklich**, *Saarland University, Germany*

Exploring wear and abrasive protection of light alloys *via* ionic liquid pretreatment, **A. E. Jiménez, J. Sanes, T. Espinosa, G. Martínez-Nicolás and M. D. Bermúdez**, *Universidad Politécnica de Cartagena, Spain*

Friction force microscopy of polymer brushes, **Z. Zhang, M. Moxey, A. J. Morse, S. P. Armes, A. L. Lewis, M. Geoghegan and G. J. Leggett**, *University of Sheffield, UK*

Stick–slip friction of articular joints and effect of selective digestion, **D. W. Lee, X. Banquy and J. N. Israelachvili**, *University of California, Santa Barbara, USA*

Enhanced tribological and corrosion resistance of pulsed electron beam surface melting of Ti6Al4V for biomedical applications, **J. C. Walker, R. B. Cook, M. Nie, J. Murray and A. T. Clare**, *University of Southampton, UK*

Self-assembled monolayer protective films for hybrid contacts, **L. Wang, M. Y. Nie, J. Rumbol and B. Craig**, *University of Southampton, UK*

An investigation into the differences in deformation behaviour on Si(100) in nano-indentation, nano-scratch and nano-fretting tests, **B. D. Beake, T. W. Liskiewicz and J. F. Smith**, *Micro Materials Ltd, UK*

Interfacial spectroscopy: *in situ* approaches to understand barnacle adhesion, **D. E. Barlow, D. K. Burden, R. K. Everett, C. M. Spillmann and K. J. Wahl**, *U.S. Naval Research Laboratory, USA*

Understanding the wear behaviour and transfer film formation of diamond-like carbon films in distilled water, **D. Sutton, R. J. K. Wood, G. Limbert and B. Burdett**, *University of Southampton, UK*

Smart DLC top coating for reduction of counter surface wear in fuel contact, **F. Gustavsson, V. Renman, P. Forsberg, A. Hieke and S. Jacobson**, *Uppsala University, Sweden*

Tribocorrosion: building a unique high temperature and high pressure wear rig, **M. A. Craig, T. W. Rose, R. G. Wellman and J. R. Nicholls**, *Cranfield University, UK*

The Skinner Prize for the best poster was awarded to Mr Alexander M. Smith of University College London, UK, for his poster on Ionic liquids as lubricants and additives: structure and friction of molecularly confined films.

List of participants

Mr S. Alexander, *Procter & Gamble, United Kingdom*
Mr J. Andersson, *Luleå University of Technology, Sweden*
Professor M. Ashfold, *University of Bristol, United Kingdom*
Professor C. Bain, *Durham University, United Kingdom*
Professor P. Bartlett, *University of Southampton, United Kingdom*
Professor B. Beake, *Micro Materials Ltd, United Kingdom*
Ms E. Berriozabal, *Tekniker, Spain*
Professor Dr B. Bhushan, *Ohio State University, USA*
Dr J. Blackford, *University of Edinburgh, United Kingdom*
Mr K. Bruen, *Whitford Ltd, United Kingdom*
Professor A. Cavaleiro, *University of Coimbra, Portugal*
Ms J. Choe, *University of Warwick, United Kingdom*
Mr W. Chong, *Loughborough University, United Kingdom*
Dr R. Cook, *University of Southampton, United Kingdom*
Dr M. Craig, *Cranfield University, United Kingdom*
Professor Z. Dai, *Nanjing University of Aeronautics and Astronautics, China*
Dr S. Dennington, *National Centre for Advanced Tribology nCATS, United Kingdom*
Mr M. Doig, *University of Edinburgh, United Kingdom*
Professor D. Dowson, *University of Leeds, United Kingdom*
Miss K. Dryden-Holt, *Royal Society of Chemistry, United Kingdom*
Mr S. Eder, *AC2T research GmbH, Austria*
Miss S. Ella, *University of Edinburgh, United Kingdom*
Mrs A. Ennis, *Royal Society of Chemistry, United Kingdom*
Professor H. P. Evans, *Cardiff School of Engineering, United Kingdom*
Mr M. Evans, *University of Southampton, United Kingdom*
Professor J. Fisher, *University of Leeds, United Kingdom*
Professor Dr F. Franek, *AC2T research GmbH, Austria*
Mr C. Gachot, *Saarland University, Germany*
Professor M. Gee, *National Physical Laboratory, United Kingdom*
Dr N. N. Gosvami, *University College London, United Kingdom*
Mr F. Gustavsson, *Uppsala University, Sweden*
Dr T. Harvey, *University of Southampton, United Kingdom*
Dr M. Ingram, *PCS Instruments, United Kingdom*
Dr A.-E. Jimenez-Ballesta, *Universidad Politecnica de Cartagena, Spain*
Dr R. Jones, *Agilent Technologies, United Kingdom*
Professor J. Klein, *Weizmann Institute of Science, Israel*
Dr M. Kobayashi, *JST ERATO, Japan*
Dr V. Koutsos, *University of Edinburgh, United Kingdom*
Professor Dr M. Kubo, *Tohoku University, Japan*
Professor Dr R. Larsson, *Luleå University of Technology, Sweden*
Dr T. Lawless, *M.O.D., United Kingdom*
Mr D. W. Lee, *UC Santa Barbara, U.S.A.*
Professor Dr L. Léger, *CNRS & Université Paris-Sud 11, France*
Professor G. Leggett, *University of Sheffield, United Kingdom*
Dr G. Limbert, *University of Southampton, United Kingdom*
Professor Dr W. Liu, *Lanzhou Institute of Chemical Physics, CAS, China*
Mr B. Lloyd, *University of Southampton, United Kingdom*
Mr C. Love, *University of Southampton, United Kingdom*
Miss C. Ma, *University of Southampton, United Kingdom*
Dr G. Marinov, *Unilever, United Kingdom*

Professor J. M. Martin, *Ecole Centrale De Lyon, France*
Miss L. Mears, *University of Bristol, United Kingdom*
Dr S. Mischler, *EPFL, Switzerland*
Mr N. Morris, *West Virginia University, U.S.A.*
Dr D. Murray, *Bruker, United Kingdom*
Dr C. Myant, *Imperial College London, United Kingdom*
Dr M. Nie, *University of Southampton, United Kingdom*
Mr V. Niste, *University of Southampton, United Kingdom*
Dr P. Norris, *Afton Chemical Limited, United Kingdom*
Dr W. Österle, *BAM Federal Institute for Materials Research and Testing, Germany*
Dr S. Papanicolaou, *Bruker, United Kingdom*
Mr T. Parkanyi, *University of Edinburgh, United Kingdom*
Dr A. Pauschitz, *AC2T research GmbH, Austria*
Dr T. Phillips, *Royal Society of Chemistry, United Kingdom*
Dr T. Polcar, *Czech Technical University in Prague, Czech Republic*
Mr M. Possiwan, *Durham University, United Kingdom*
Mr B. Proudlove, *Merrow Scientific Ltd, United Kingdom*
Mr B. Quignon, *University of Bristol, United Kingdom*
Miss R. Quine, *Royal Society of Chemistry, United Kingdom*
Professor Dr H. Rahnejat, *Loughborough University, United Kingdom*
Professor M. Rainforth, *University of Sheffield, United Kingdom*
Dr M. Ratoi, *University of Southampton, United Kingdom*
Mr A. Rosenkranz, *Saarland University, Germany*
Professor Dr W. G. Sawyer, *University of Florida, USA*
Mr A. Smith, *UCL, United Kingdom*
Dr M. Smith, *Royal Society of Chemistry, United Kingdom*
Professor R. Snidle, *Cardiff University, United Kingdom*
Mr T. Snow, *University of Bristol, United Kingdom*
Professor N. Spencer, *ETH-Zurich, Switzerland*
Mr M. Stolz, *University of Southampton, United Kingdom*
Dr P. Stoodley, *University of Southampton, United Kingdom*
Dr B. Su, *University of Bristol, United Kingdom*
Mr D. Sutton, *University of Southampton, United Kingdom*
Dr R. I. Taylor, *Shell Research Limited, United Kingdom*
Professor Dr A. Vernes, *AC2T research GmbH, Austria*
Dr K. Wahl, *Naval Research Laboratory, USA*
Dr J. Walker, *University of Southampton, United Kingdom*
Mr C. T. Wang, *University of Southampton, United Kingdom*
Dr L. Wang, *University of Southampton, United Kingdom*
Dr S. Wang, *University of Southampton, United Kingdom*
Dr H. Washizu, *Toyota Central R&D Labs, Inc., Japan*
Dr J. Wharton, *University of Southampton, United Kingdom*
Professor J. A. Williams, *Cambridge University, United Kingdom*
Dr E. Wise, *Royal Society of Chemistry, United Kingdom*
Professor R. Wood, *University of Southampton, United Kingdom*
Dr J. Zekonyte, *National Centre for Advanced Tribology nCATS, United Kingdom*
Dr Z. Zhang, *University of Sheffield, United Kingdom*

Index of contributors*

---

* The page numbers in **bold** type indicate papers submitted for discussions.